BERLITZ TRAVEL GUIDES

Africa
○ Algeria
Kenya
Morocco
South Africa
Tunisia

Asia, Middle East
○ China
Hong Kong
○ India
○ Indonesia*
○ Japan
Nepal
Singapore
Sri Lanka
Thailand
Egypt
Jerusalem/Holy Land
Saudi Arabia

Australasia
○ Australia
New Zealand

Austria/Switzerland
Tyrol
Vienna
○ Switzerland

British Isles
Channel Islands
Ireland
London
Oxford and Stratford
Scotland

Belgium/Netherlands
Brussels
Amsterdam

France
Brittany
○ France
French Riviera
Loire Valley
Normandy
Paris

Germany
Berlin
Munich
The Rhine Valley

Greece, Cyprus and Turkey
Athens
Corfu
Crete
Greek Islands Aegean
Peloponnese
Rhodes
Salonica/N. Greece
Cyprus
Istanbul/Aegean Coast
○ Turkey

Italy and Malta
Florence
Italian Adriatic
Italian Riviera
○ Italy
Naples/Amalfi Coast*
Rome
Sicily
Venice
Malta

Scandinavia
Copenhagen
Helsinki
Oslo/Bergen
Stockholm

Spain
Barcelona
Canary Islands
Costa Blanca
Costa Brava
Costa del Sol/Andalusia
Costa Dorada/Barcelona
Ibiza and Formentera
Madrid
Majorca and Minorca
Seville

Portugal
Algarve
Lisbon
Madeira

Eastern Europe
Budapest
Dubrovnik/S. Dalmatia
○ Hungary
Istria and Croatian Coast
Moscow and Leningrad
The Hermitage, Leningrad*
Prague
Split and Dalmatia
○ Yugoslavia

North America
○ U.S.A.
California
Florida
Hawaii
Miami
New York
Washington
○ Canada
Montreal
Toronto

Caribbean, Lat. Ar
Bahamas
Bermuda
French West Indies
Jamaica
Puerto Rico
Southern Caribbean
Virgin Islands
Brazil (Highlights of)
○ Mexico*
Mexico City
Rio de Janeiro

Address Books
London/New York
Paris/Rome

Blueprint Guides
Europe A-Z/France
Germany/Britain
Greece/Hungary
Italy/Spain/USSR*

More for the $
France/Italy

Cruise Guides
Alaska
Caribbean
Handbook to Cruising

Ski Guides
Austria/France
Italy/Switzerland
Skiing the Alps

Europe
Business Travel Guide
Train Travel
Pocket Guide-Europe
Cities of Europe

* in preparation/○ country guides 192 or 256 p.

S0-BZT-353

Berlitz Dictionaries

Dansk	Engelsk, Fransk, Italiensk, Spansk, Tysk
Deutsch	Dänisch, Englisch, Finnisch, Französisch, Italienisch, Niederländisch, Norwegisch, Portugiesisch, Schwedisch, Spanisch
English	Danish, Dutch, Finnish, French, German, Italian, Norwegian, Portuguese, Spanish, Swedish, Turkish
Español	Alemán, Danés, Finlandés, Francés, Holandés, Inglés, Noruego, Sueco
Français	Allemand, Anglais, Danois, Espagnol, Finnois, Italien, Néerlandais, Norvégien, Portugais, Suédois
Italiano	Danese, Finlandese, Francese, Inglese, Norvegese, Olandese, Svedese, Tedesco
Nederlands	Duits, Engels, Frans, Italiaans, Portugees, Spaans
Norsk	Engelsk, Fransk, Italiensk, Spansk, Tysk
Português	Alemão, Francês, Holandês, Inglês, Sueco
Suomi	Englanti, Espanja, Italia, Ranska, Ruotsi, Saksa
Svenska	Engelska, Finska, Franska, Italienska, Portugisiska, Spanska, Tyska
Türkçe	İngilizce

BERLITZ®

turkish-english english-turkish dictionary

sözlük türkçe-ingilizce ingilizce-türkçe

By the Staff of Berlitz Guides

Copyright © 1991, 1988 by Berlitz Publishing S.A.,
Avenue d'Ouchy 61, 1000 Lausanne 6, Switzerland

All rights reserved. No part of this book may be reproduced
or transmitted in any form or by any means, electronic or mechanical,
including photocopying, recording or by any information storage
and retrieval system, without permission in writing from the publisher.

Berlitz Trademark Reg. U.S. Patent Office and other countries—
Marca Registrada.

1st printing
Printed in Switzerland

Contents

İçindekiler

Preface

In selecting the 12,500 word-concepts in each language for this dictionary, the editors have had the traveller's needs foremost in mind. This book will prove invaluable to all the millions of travellers, tourists and business people who appreciate the reassurance a small and practical dictionary can provide. It offers them—as it does beginners and students—all the basic vocabulary they are going to encounter and to have to use, giving the key words and expressions to allow them to cope in everyday situations.

This dictionary—created with the help of a computer data bank—is designed to slip into pocket or purse and be your handy companion at all times. Besides just about everything you normally find in dictionaries, there are these Berlitz bonuses:

- a simple system indicating which syllable is stressed, helping you to pronounce words whose spelling may look forbidding
- a unique, practical glossary to simplify reading a foreign restaurant menu and to take the mystery out of complicated dishes and indecipherable names on bills of fare
- useful information on how to tell the time and how to count, commonly seen abbreviations and converting to the metric system, in addition to basic phrases.

While no dictionary of this size can pretend to completeness, we expect the user of this book will feel well armed to tackle foreign travel with confidence. We should, however, be very pleased to receive comments, criticism and suggestions that you think may be of help in preparing future editions.

Önsöz

Bu sözlüğün her bir bölümünde yer alan 12500 kelime ve kavramın seçiminde, seyahat edenin bütün ihtiyaçları göz önüne alınmıştır. Bu çalışma aynı zamanda, küçük ve kullanışlı bir sözlüğün sağlayacağı yarara değer veren milyonlarca turist, işadamı için de vazgeçilmez bir kaynak niteliğindedir. Berlitz sözlüğünü kullananlar, onda günlük yaşamın çesitli durumlarında karşılarına çıkacak tüm temel kelime, deyim ve deyişleri bulacaklardır.

Bu sözlük bilgisayar yardımı ile hazırlanmış olup cepte veya çantada kolaylıkla taşınılması düşünülerek, her zaman ayrılmaz bir parçanız olacaktır.

Sözlüklerde genellikle bulunan bilgilerin yanı sıra, Berlitz sözlüğü size aşağıdaki üstünlükleri de sunmaktadır:

- Her kelimenin basitleştirilmiş okunuşu. Böylece yazılışları karmaşık ve ürkütücü görünen kelimeleri bile kolaylıkla telaffuz edebileceksiniz.
- Yabancı restoranlarda karşılaşacağınız yemek listelerini okumanızı kolaylaştıracak, karmaşık yemeklerin şifresini çözüp sırlarını ortaya koyacak açıklamalı bir bölüm.
- Günlük konuşmalarda kullanılan temel ifadelerin yanı sıra, saati söyleme, sayı sayma, düzensiz fiillerin çekimi, yaygın kısaltmalar ve ölçüleri metrik sisteme çevirmeye ilişkin yararlı bilgiler.

Bu çaptaki hiçbir sözlüğün eksiksiz olduğu iddia edilemezse de, elinizdeki çalışmanın dil eğitiminiz ve yurtdışı yolculuklarınız sırasında gerek duyacağınız bilgileri sağlayacağına inanıyoruz. Bununla birlikte, gelecekteki baskıların hazırlanmasında çalışmalarımıza ışık tutabileceğini düşündüğünüz öneri ve eleştirilerinizi duymak bizleri mutlu kılacaktır.

turkish-english

türkçe-ingilizce

Introduction

The dictionary has been designed to take account of your practical needs. Unnecessary linguistic information has been avoided. The entries are listed in alphabetical order, regardless of whether the entry word is printed in a single word or in two or more separate words. As the only exception to this rule, a few idiomatic expressions are listed alphabetically as main entries, according to the most significant word of the expression. When an entry is followed by sub-entries such as expressions and locutions, these, too, have been listed in alphabetical order.

Each Turkish main-entry word is followed by a special stress pattern (see Guide to Pronunciation). Following the stress pattern is the part of speech of the entry word whenever applicable. When an entry word may be used as more than one part of speech, the translations are grouped together after the respective part of speech.

Whenever an entry word is repeated in sub-entries, a tilde (~) is used to represent the full entry word.

An asterisk (*) in front of an English verb indicates that the verb is irregular. All Turkish verbs are conjugated regularly.

Abbreviations

adj	adjective
adj Am	adjective (American)
adj Br	adjective (British)
Am	American
art	article
Br	British
conj	conjunction
n	noun
nAm	noun (American)
nBr	noun (British)
num	numeral
p	past tense
pl	plural
plAm	plural (American)
plBr	plural (British)
pp	past participle
pr	present tense
pref	prefix
prep	preposition
pron	pronoun
v	verb
vAm	verb (American)
vBr	verb (British)

Guide to Pronunciation

Turkish is quite simple to read because in most cases each letter represents one sound (always the same). Note, however, that Turkish has some diacritical letters—letters with special markings—which we don't have in English.

With the information provided below, you should find it fairly easy to pronounce the Turkish words in this dictionary.

Consonants

b, d, f, l, m, n, p, t, z	as in English, but when pronouncing **d, n** and **t,** the front of the tongue touches the upper teeth, not the gums behind them
c	like **j** in **j**am
ç	like **ch** in **ch**ip
g	1) before or after **a, ı, o, u,** as in go 2) before or after **e, i, ö, ü,** it is followed by a **y**-sound as in angular
ğ	1) when preceded and followed by **e, i, ö, ü,** usually a **y**-sound as in lawyer 2) otherwise indicates that the preceding vowel is lengthened
h	always pronounced as in **h**it
j	like s in pleasure
k	1) before or after **a, ı, o, u,** like **c** in **c**ool 2) before or after **e, i, ö, ü,** it is followed by a **y**-sound, like **c** in **c**ure
r	with the tip of the tongue touching the gums just behind the teeth; at the end of a word, it often sounds almost like **sh** in **sh**ell
s	always as in so, never as in is.
ş	like **sh** in **sh**ell
v	often pronounced so weakly that it sounds more like a **w**
y	1) when at the beginning of a word or after a consonant, like **y** in **y**es 2) when **y** comes between **e, i, ö** or **ü** and a consonant, the vowel is lengthened 3) after a vowel, it becomes part of a diphthong

Doubled consonants

These represent not two separate sounds, but a single, long one, like, for example, the **pp** in a rapid pronunciation of lam**pp**ost.

Vowels

In Turkish, vowels are generally short but can be lengthened by **ğ** or **y**; or when used in some words borrowed from Persian or Arabic.

a 1) generally like a short version of the **a** in c**a**r, i.e. a sound between **a** in c**a**t and **u** in c**u**t
2) when long, as in c**a**r

e 1) usually as in m**e**t
2) sometimes (especially when long) like **a** in l**a**te, but a pure vowel, not a diphthong

i as in mach**i**ne

ı a sound between **i** as in b**i**g and **u** as in b**u**g; with your lips spread as if to say **ee**, try to pronounce **u** as in p**u**t

o 1) as in t**o**ne, but a pure vowel, not a diphthong; sometimes as in h**o**t
2) when long, like **aw** in s**aw**

ö like **u** in f**u**r, but shorter and with the lips a little rounded

u as in p**u**ll

ü pronounce **ee** as in s**ee**, but round your lips, without moving your tongue

1) A circumflex accent (ˆ) over a vowel indicates that the preceding **g, k** or **l** is followed by a short **y**-sound, e.g. **zekâ.**
2) Elsewhere the circumflex indicates that a vowel is long.

Diphthongs

ay like **igh** in s**igh**t

ey like **ay** in s**ay**

oy like **oy** in c**oy**

Stress

The stress pattern is indicated in our dictionary by means of a simple system. After each main entry, the stress pattern is shown between diagonal lines, where a dot (·) stands for a short syllable and a dash (–) for a long syllable. A stressed syllable has a small stress mark (ˈ) placed slightly before the dot or dash that represents that syllable. Thus the word **sadık,** with the first syllable long and the second one short and stressed, is represented as /–ˈ·/, and **araba,** a word containing three short syllables, the third of which is stressed, is represented as /··ˈ·/.

A

aba /·ˈ·/ *n* coarse woolen cloth; cloak
abajur /··ˈ·/ *n* lampshade
abanmak /··ˈ·/ *v* *lean over; push with the body
abanoz /··ˈ·/ *n* ebony
abartmak /··ˈ·/ *v* exaggerate
abes /·ˈ·/ *adj* useless; absurd, nonsensical; *n* absurdity, nonsense
abide /–·ˈ·/ *n* monument, memorial
abla /ˈ··/ *n* elder sister
ablak /·ˈ·/ *adj* round, chubby
abluka /·ˈ··/ *n* blockade; ~ **etmek** blockade; **ablukayı yarmak** *run the blockade
abone /··ˈ·/ *n* subscriber; subscription; ~ **olmak** subscribe
abonman /··ˈ·/ *n* subscription; season ticket
acaba /ˈ··–/ *adv* I wonder if
acayip /·–ˈ·/ *adj* strange, queer
acele /··ˈ·/ *n* hurry, haste; *adj* urgent; hasty, hurried; ~ **etmek** hurry; *be in a hurry
acemi /··ˈ·/ *adj* inexperienced
acemilik /···ˈ·/ *n* awkwardness; inexperience
acente /·ˈ··/ *n* agent, representative; agency
acı /·ˈ·/ *adj* bitter; sharp; hot; pungent; *n* pain, ache; sorrow; ~ **çekmek** *feel pain, suffer
acıklı /··ˈ·/ *adj* sad, touching, tragic
acıkmak /··ˈ·/ *v* *feel hungry
acımak /··ˈ·/ *v* *hurt, *feel sore; pity; turn rancid
acındırmak /···ˈ·/ *v* arouse compassion
acıtmak /··ˈ·/ *v* cause pain; *hurt
acil /–ˈ·/ *adj* immediate, urgent
aciz /–ˈ·/ *adj* incapable, impotent; ~ **kalmak** *be incapable
aç *adj* hungry; greedy; ~ **kalmak** *go without food
açgözlü /ˈ···/ *adj* greedy; insatiable
açı /·ˈ·/ *n* angle
açık /·ˈ·/ *adj* open; uncovered; clear, cloudless; *n* deficit; ~ **artırma** auction; ~ **fikirli** open-minded; ~ **sözlü** frank, outspoken
açıkça /·ˈ··/ *adv* frankly; clearly; openly
açıkgöz /··ˈ·/ *adj* clever, sharp; shrewd
açıklamak /···ˈ·/ *v* reveal; explain; announce
açılış /··ˈ·/ *n* opening
açış /·ˈ·/ *n* opening; inauguration
açlık /·ˈ·/ *n* hunger; starvation,

famine
açmak /·ˈ·/ *v* open; open up
ad *n* name; fame, reputation; **adına** in the name of
ada /·ˈ·/ *n* island; city block
adak /·ˈ·/ *n* vow, promise; ~ **adamak** vow
adale /··ˈ·/ *n* muscle
adaleli /···ˈ·/ *adj* muscular
adalet /·–ˈ·/ *n* justice; equity; courts
adaletli /·–ˈ·/ *adj* just; equitable
adaletsiz /·–ˈ·/ *adj* unjust; inequitable
adam /·ˈ·/ *n* man; human being; person; ~ **başına** per person
adamak /··ˈ·/ *v* vow, *give to; dedicate
adamakıllı /·ˈ····/ *adv* thoroughly
aday /·ˈ·/ *n* candidate
adaylık /··ˈ·/ *n* candidacy; **adaylığını koymak** announce one's candidacy
addetmek /ˈ···/ *v* count, deem
adet /·ˈ·/ *n* number; unit
âdet /–ˈ·/ *n* custom, habit; menses; ~ **edinmek** form a habit; ~ **görmek** menstruate
adeta /ˈ–·–/ *adv* almost; in fact; simply
adım /·ˈ·/ *n* step, pace; ~ ~ step by step; ~ **atmak** *take a step; ~ **başında** at every step
adi /–ˈ–/ *adj* customary, usual; common; vulgar
adil /–ˈ·/ *adj* just, fair
adilik /––ˈ·/ *n* vulgarity; commonness
adlandırmak /···ˈ·/ *v* name
adli /·ˈ–/ *adj* juridical, judicial
adliye /··ˈ·/ *n* administration of justice; courthouse
adres /·ˈ·/ *n* address
af *n* forgiveness, pardon; exemption; dismissal; ~ **dilemek** apologize, beg pardon
afallamak /···ˈ·/ *v* *be bewildered
aferin /ˈ–··/ bravo!, well done!, good for you!
afet /–ˈ·/ *n* calamity, disaster; woman of bewitching beauty
affetmek /ˈ···/ *v* *forgive; excuse; **affedersiniz!** I beg your pardon!, please excuse me!
afiş /·ˈ·/ *n* poster, placard, bill
afiyet /–·ˈ·/ *n* health
Afrika /·ˈ··/ Africa
Afrikalı /·ˈ···/ *n, adj* African
afyon /·ˈ·/ *n* opium
ağ *n* net; network; ~ **atmak** *cast a net
ağa /·ˈ·/ *n* local big landowner, agha
ağabey /·ˈ··/ *n* elder brother
ağaç /·ˈ·/ *n* tree; wood; *adj* wooden; ~ **kabuğu** bark
ağaçkakan /···ˈ·/ *n* woodpecker
ağaçlandırma /····ˈ·/ *n* afforestation
ağaçlandırmak /····ˈ·/ *v* afforest
ağarmak /··ˈ·/ *v* turn gray or white
ağı /·ˈ·/ *n* poison, venom
ağır /·ˈ·/ *adj* heavy; serious; severe; slow; ~ **basmak** weigh heavily; *have a strong influence; ~ **işitmek** *be partly deaf; ~ **konuşmak** use hard words; ~ **yaralı** seriously wounded
ağırbaşlı /·ˈ···/ *adj* serious-minded, dignified
ağırkanlı /·ˈ···/ *adj* lazy, indolent
ağırlamak /···ˈ·/ *v* entertain with honor and respect
ağırlaşmak /···ˈ·/ *v* *get heavy; *get more serious
ağırlık /··ˈ·/ *n* weight, heaviness; ~ **basmak** *get sleepy
ağız /·ˈ·/ *n* mouth; opening;

entrance; rim
ağızlık /··ˈ·/ *n* cigarette holder
ağlamak /··ˈ·/ *v* *weep, cry
ağrı /·ˈ·/ *n* ache, pain
ağrımak /··ˈ·/ *v* ache, *hurt
ağustos /··ˈ·/ August
ağustosböceği /··ˈ····/ *n* cicada
ah ah!, oh!, alas!; ~ **almak** *be cursed for causing unhappiness; ~ **çekmek** sigh
ahbap /·ˈ·/ *n* acquaintance; friend; ~ **olmak** *become friends
ahçı /·ˈ·/ *n* cook
ahır /·ˈ·/ *n* stable, barn
ahize /–·ˈ·/ *n* receiver
ahlak /·ˈ·/ *n* morals, morality; character
ahlakçı /··ˈ·/ *n* moralist
ahlaki /·–ˈ–/ *adj* moral, ethical
ahlaklı /··ˈ·/ *adj* of good conduct, decent
ahlaksız /··ˈ·/ *adj* immoral, dissolute
ahmak /·ˈ·/ *adj* stupid, foolish; *n* fool, idiot
ahret /·ˈ·/ *n* the next world
ahşap /·ˈ·/ *adj* wooden, made of timber
ahtapot /··ˈ·/ *n* octopus
ahududu /–ˈ–··/ *n* raspberry
aidat /–·ˈ·/ *n* subscription, dues
aile /–·ˈ·/ *n* family; ~ **reisi** head of the family
ailevi /–··ˈ–/ *adj* regarding the family; domestic
ait /–ˈ·/ *adj* relating to; belonging to
ajan /·ˈ·/ *n* agent; spy
ajanda /·ˈ··/ *n* engagement calendar, agenda
ajans /·ˈ·/ *n* agency; news agency
ak *adj* white; clean
akarsu /·ˈ··/ *n* river, stream
akaryakıt /·ˈ···/ *n* fuel oil
akasya /·ˈ··/ *n* acacia
akbaba /ˈ···/ *n* vulture
akciğer /ˈ···/ *n* lungs
akçaağaç /·ˈ···/ *n* maple
Akdeniz /ˈ···/ Mediterranean
akıbet /–·ˈ·/ *n* consequence, outcome
akıcı /··ˈ·/ *adj* fluid, liquid; fluent
akıl /·ˈ·/ *n* intelligence, wisdom; mind; ~ **almaz** unbelievable, inconceivable; ~ **danışmak** *get advice, consult
akıllanmak /···ˈ·/ *v* *become wiser by bitter experience
akıllı /··ˈ·/ *adj* wise, intelligent
akıllıca /··ˈ··/ *adv* intelligently, wisely
akılsız /··ˈ·/ *adj* foolish, unreasonable
akım /·ˈ·/ *n* current, trend; electrical current; **dalgalı** ~ alternating current; **doğru** ~ direct current
akın /·ˈ·/ *n* rush; raid; ~ **etmek** rush together, attack
akıntı /··ˈ·/ *n* current, flow
akış /·ˈ·/ *n* flow, course
akıtmak /··ˈ·/ *v* cause to flow, pour; *shed
aklamak /··ˈ·/ *v* clear one's honor
akmak /·ˈ·/ *v* flow; *run
akort /·ˈ·/ *n* being in tune; **akordu bozuk** out of tune; ~ **etmek** tune
akraba /··ˈ–/ *n* relative, relatives
akran /·ˈ·/ *n* equal, peer, match
akreditif /···ˈ·/ *n* letter of credit
akrep /·ˈ·/ *n* scorpion; hour hand of clock
aksak /·ˈ·/ *adj* limping, lame
aksamak /··ˈ·/ *v* limp; *be delayed
aksan /·ˈ·/ *n* accent, stress
aksatmak /··ˈ·/ *v* hinder; delay
aksesuar /···ˈ·/ *n* accessory; stage prop

aksetmek /ˈ···/ *v* *be reflected; echo
aksırık /··ˈ·/ *n* sneeze
aksırmak /··ˈ·/ *v* sneeze
aksi /·ˈ·/ *adj* opposite, contrary; unlucky; cross; ~ **gitmek** *go wrong
aksileşmek /···ˈ·/ *v* *have a fit of temper
aksilik /··ˈ·/ *n* misfortune; obstinacy
akşam /·ˈ·/ *n* evening; ~ **yemeği** dinner, supper
akşamleyin /·ˈ···/ *adv* in the evening
aktarma /··ˈ·/ *n* transfer; transshipment; ~ **bileti** transfer ticket; ~ **yapmak** change trains, buses, etc.
aktarmak /··ˈ·/ *v* transfer; quote
aktris /·ˈ·/ *n* actress
aktüalite /···ˈ··/ *n* current events
aktüel /··ˈ·/ *adj* modern, contemporary
akü /·ˈ·/, **akümülatör** /····ˈ·/ *n* storage battery
akvaryum /·ˈ··/ *n* aquarium
al *adj* scarlet, red
ala /·ˈ·/ *adj* spotted, speckled
âlâ /–ˈ–/ *adj* very good, excellent
alabalık /·ˈ···/ *n* speckled trout
alabildiğine /ˈ······/ *adv* to the utmost
alabora olmak /··ˈ·· ··/ capsize, turn over
alacak /··ˈ·/ *n* credit, receivable
alacaklı /···ˈ·/ *n* creditor
alacalı /···ˈ·/ *adj* speckled; ~ **bulacalı** of mixed colors, gaudy
alaka /·–ˈ·/ *n* connection; interest; ~ **duymak** *be interested
alakadar /·–·ˈ·/ *adj* concerned; interested
alan /·ˈ·/ *n* open space, clearing; square; zone; field
alaşağı etmek /ˈ···· ··/ *tear down; *overthrow, depose
alaturka /··ˈ··/ *adj* Turkish style
alay[1] /·ˈ·/ *n* regiment; parade
alay[2] /·ˈ·/ *n* mockery, ridicule; ~ **etmek** *make fun of; **alaya almak** tease
alaycı /··ˈ·/ *adj* mocking
albay /·ˈ·/ *n* colonel; navy captain
albeni /··ˈ·/ *n* charm, attractiveness, allure
alçak /·ˈ·/ *adj* low; vile, mean; short
alçaklık /··ˈ·/ *n* lowness; vileness
alçalmak /··ˈ·/ *v* *become low; stoop; degrade oneself
alçı /·ˈ·/ *n* plaster of Paris
aldanmak /··ˈ·/ *v* *be deceived; *be wrong
aldatmak /··ˈ·/ *v* cheat, deceive, dupe
aldırmak /··ˈ·/ *v* *send someone to get; mind; *pay attention
aldırmaz /··ˈ·/ *adj* indifferent
aldırmazlık /···ˈ·/ *n* indifference
alelacele /·ˈ····/ *adv* hastily, hurriedly
alelade /ˈ···–·/ *adj* ordinary, usual
âlem /–ˈ·/ *n* world, universe; people
alerji /··ˈ·/ *n* allergy
alerjik /··ˈ·/ *adj* allergic
alet /–ˈ·/ *n* tool, instrument; apparatus
alev /·ˈ·/ *n* flame; ~ **almak** *catch fire
alevlenmek /···ˈ·/ *v* blaze; *become excited; flare up
alevli /··ˈ·/ *adj* flaming, blazing
aleyhte /··ˈ·/ *adv* in opposition
algı /·ˈ·/ *n* perception
algılamak /···ˈ·/ *v* perceive

alıcı /··ˈ·/ *n* customer; receiver
alık /·ˈ·/ *adj* stupid, silly
alıkoymak /·ˈ···/ *v* *keep, detain; stop
alım /·ˈ·/ *n* attraction, charm; taking; buying; ~ **satım** business, trade
alımlı /··ˈ·/ *adj* attractive, charming
alın /·ˈ·/ *n* forehead, brow; ~ **yazısı** destiny; **alnı açık** blameless, innocent
alındı /··ˈ·/ *n* receipt
alıngan /··ˈ·/ *adj* touchy, easily offended
alınganlık /···ˈ·/ *n* touchiness
alınmak /··ˈ·/ *v* *take offense, *be hurt
alışık, alışkın /··ˈ·/ *adj* used to, accustomed to
alışmak /··ˈ·/ *v* *get accustomed; *become familiar; *become addicted
alıştırma /···ˈ·/ *n* exercise; training
alıştırmak /···ˈ·/ *v* accustom, familiarize; addict; tame
alışveriş /···ˈ·/ *n* buying and selling, trade; shopping; ~ **etmek** shop
âlim /–ˈ·/ *n* scholar
alkış /·ˈ·/ *n* applause
alkışlamak /···ˈ·/ *v* acclaim, applaud
alkol /·ˈ·/ *n* alcohol
alkolik /··ˈ·/ *adj, n* alcoholic
alkollü /··ˈ·/ *adj* containing alcohol
Allah /·ˈ·/ *n* God
allahaısmarladık /··ˈ····/ good-by
allahsız /··ˈ·/ *adj* atheist
allahtan /··ˈ·/ *adv* luckily, fortunately
almak /·ˈ·/ *v* *take, *get; *buy; receive; accept
Alman /·ˈ·/ *n, adj* German
Almanca /·ˈ··/ *n* German language
Almanya /·ˈ··/ Germany
alt *n* bottom; lower part; base; *adj* lower, inferior; ~ **geçit** underpass; **altını çizmek** underline
altı /·ˈ·/ *num* six
altın /·ˈ·/ *n* gold; gold coin; *adj* golden
altıncı /··ˈ·/ *num* sixth
altmış /·ˈ·/ *num* sixty
altüst /·ˈ·/ *adv* upside down, in utter confusion; ~ **etmek** *upset, mess up; ~ **olmak** *be in a mess
altyapı /ˈ···/ *n* substructure; infrastructure
altyazı /ˈ···/ *n* subtitle
alyans /·ˈ·/ *n* wedding ring
ama /ˈ··/ *conj* but, yet, still
âmâ /–ˈ-/ *adj* blind
amaç /·ˈ·/ *n* aim, goal
amaçlamak /···ˈ·/ *v* intend, aim
aman /·ˈ·/ *n* pardon; please!; for goodness-sake!; mercy!
amansız /··ˈ·/ *adj* merciless
ambalaj /··ˈ·/ *n* packing, package; ~ **yapmak** pack, wrap up
ambar /·ˈ·/ *n* warehouse, storehouse
amca /ˈ··/ *n* (paternal) uncle
amcazade /·–ˈ·/ *n* (paternal) cousin
amele /··ˈ·/ *n* worker, workman
ameliyat /···ˈ·/ *n* surgical operation; ~ **etmek** operate; ~ **olmak** *have an operation
ameliyathane /····–ˈ·/ *n* operation room, surgery
Amerika /··ˈ··/ America; ~ **Birleşik Devletleri** United States of America
Amerikalı /··ˈ···/ *n* American
Amerikan /···ˈ·/ *adj* American
amir /–ˈ·/ *n* superior, chief, person in charge
amiral /··ˈ·/ *n* admiral

amorti /··'·/ *n* redemption; ~ **etmek** *pay off, amortize
ampul /·'·/ *n* electric bulb
amyant /·'·/ *n* asbestos
an *n* moment, instant
ana /·'·/ *n* mother; *adj* principal; main
anadili /·'···/ *n* mother tongue
Anadolu /···'·/ Anatolia
anafikir /·'···/ *n* central theme
anafor /··'·/ *n* eddy
anahtar /··'·/ *n* key; wrench; electric switch; ~ **deliği** keyhole
anahtarlık /···'·/ *n* key ring, key holder
analık /··'·/ *n* maternity, motherhood; stepmother
ananas /··'·/ *n* pineapple
anane /··'·/ *n* tradition
anaokulu /·'····/ *n* kindergarten
anapara /·'···/ *n* capital
anarşi /··'·/ *n* anarchy
anavatan /·'···/ *n* motherland
anayasa /·'···/ *n* constitution
anayol /·'··/ *n* main road
anayurt /·'··/ *n* motherland
ancak /'··/ *adv* only; just; hardly; *conj* but; however
andırmak /··'·/ *v* *bear a resemblance
angarya /·'··/ *n* forced labor; unpaid job
anı /·'·/ *n* memory, remembrance
anıt /·'·/ *n* monument
anıtkabir /·'···/ *n* mausoleum; **Anıtkabir** Atatürk's tomb
anıtsal /··'·/ *adj* monumental
ani /–'–/ *adj* sudden
aniden /'––·/ *adv* suddenly
anjin /·'·/ *n* angina
anket /·'·/ *n* inquiry, questionnaire
anlam /·'·/ *n* meaning, sense
anlamak /··'·/ *v* *understand; *know about; appreciate
anlamdaş /··'·/ *adj* synonymous
anlamlı /··'·/ *adj* meaningful
anlamsız /··'·/ *adj* meaningless
anlaşma /··'·/ *n* agreement, treaty; **anlaşmaya varmak** *come to an agreement
anlaşmak /··'·/ *v* *understand each other; *come to an agreement
anlaşmazlık /···'·/ *n* disagreement; incompatibility
anlatım /··'·/ *n* narration
anlatmak /··'·/ *v* explain; *tell; describe
anlayış /··'·/ *n* understanding; intelligence
anlayışlı /···'·/ *adj* understanding; intelligent
anlayışsız /···'·/ *adj* intolerant, inconsiderate
anma /·'·/ *n* remembrance; commemoration; ~ **günü** memorial day
anmak /·'·/ *v* call to mind; remember; mention
anne /'··/ *n* mother
anneanne /·'···/ *n* (maternal) grandmother
anormal /··'·/ *adj* abnormal
ansızın /'···/ *adv* suddenly
ant *n* oath; ~ **içmek** *swear, *take an oath
antepfıstığı /'·····/ *n* pistachio
antika /·'··/ *n* antique; *adj* antique; queer, eccentric
antikacı /·'···/ *n* antique dealer
antipati /···'·/ *n* antipathy
antlaşma /··'·/ *n* solemn agreement, pact
antlaşmak /··'·/ *v* *swear an oath with one another
antre /·'·/ *n* entrance, doorway
antrenman /··'·/ *n* exercise, training
antrenör /··'·/ *n* trainer, coach

apansız /'···/ *adv* unexpectedly, without warning
apartman /··'·/ *n* apartment house; ~ **dairesi** apartment *nAm;* flat *nBr*
apayrı /'···/ *adj* completely different
apse /·'·/ *n* abscess
aptal /·'·/ *n* simpleton, fool; *adj* stupid, dumb
aptalca /·'··/ *adv* stupidly
aptallaşmak /···'·/ *v* *become stupid
aptallık /··'·/ *n* stupidity, foolishness; ~ **etmek** act like a fool
aptes /·'·/ *n* ritual ablution; bowel movement; ~ **almak** perform an ablution
ar[1] *n* shame; shyness; modesty
ar[2] *n* are, a hundred square meters
ara /·'·/ *n* distance; interval; *adj* intermediate; middle; ~ **kapı** connecting door; ~ **vermek** pause, *make a break; stop for a while
araba /··'·/ *n* car, automobile; carriage; ~ **kullanmak** *drive a car; ~ **vapuru** car ferry
arabacı /···'·/ *n* coachman, cabman
Arabistan /···'·/ Arabia
arabozucu /·'····/ *n* telltale, troublemaker
arabulucu /·'····/ *n* mediator, go-between
aracı /··'·/ *n* mediator, go-between; broker
araç /·'·/ *n* means, medium; tool
arada /··'·/ *adv* in between; sometimes; ~ **sırada** from time to time
aralamak /···'·/ *v* separate; space; half-open
aralık[1] /··'·/ *n* space; opening; interval
aralık[2] /··'·/ December
arama /··'·/ *n* search; ~ **tarama** police search
aramak /··'·/ *v* *seek, look for; search
Arap /·'·/ *n* Arab
araştırıcı /····'·/ *adj* searching
araştırma /···'·/ *n* investigation; research
araştırmacı /····'·/ *n* researcher
arazi /·–'–/ *n* land; territory; estates; ~ **arabası** jeep, land-rover
ardiye /··'·/ *n* warehouse
argo /'··/ *n* slang
arı[1] /·'·/ *n* bee; ~ **kovanı** beehive
arı[2] /·'·/ *adj* clean, pure
arınmak /··'·/ *v* *become clean, *be purified
arıtmak /··'·/ *v* cleanse, purify
arıza /–·'·/ *n* defect, failure, breakdown
arızalanmak /–···'·/ *v* *break down
arızalı /–··'·/ *adj* out of order; uneven, rugged
ark *n* irrigation trench, canal
arka /·'·/ *n* back; *adj* rear, reverse
arkadaş /··'·/ *n* friend, companion; ~ **olmak** *become friends
arkadaşça /··'··/ *adj* friendly; *adv* in a friendly way
arkadaşlık /···'·/ *n* friendship
armağan /··'·/ *n* gift, present
armatör /··'·/ *n* shipowner
armut /·'·/ *n* pear
arpa /·'·/ *n* barley
arsa /·'·/ *n* building lot
arsız /·'·/ *adj* insolent, shameless
arşiv /·'·/ *n* archives
art *n* back, rear; the space behind; ~ **arda** one after another; ~ **düşünce** hidden intent
artakalmak /·'···/ *v* *be left over

artezyen /··'·/ *n* artesian well, drilled well
artı /·'·/ *n* plus sign; *adj* positive
artık[1] /·'·/ *adj* remaining, left; *n* remnant, residue
artık[2] /'··/ *adv* now, well then; any more, any longer
artırım /··'·/ *n* economy, thrift
artırma /··'·/ *n* act of increasing; auction
artırmak /··'·/ *v* increase; save, economize
artış /·'·/ *n* increase
artist /·'·/ *n* actor, actress
artmak /·'·/ *v* increase; *be left over
arz[1] *n* the earth
arz[2] *n* presentation, demonstration; ~ **etmek** present; offer; submit
arzu /·'·/ *n* wish; request; desire, longing; ~ **etmek** wish, desire
arzulamak /···'·/ *v* desire, long for
asabi /··'–/ *adj* nervous, irritable
asabiye /···'·/ *n* nervous diseases; neurology
asabiyeci /····'·/ *n* nerve specialist, neurologist
asal /·'·/ *adj* basic, fundamental; ~ **sayı** prime number
asalak /··'·/ *n* parasite
asalet /–'·/ *n* nobility, nobleness
asansör /··'·/ *n* elevator *nAm;* lift *nBr*
asap /–'·/ *n* nerves; **asabı bozulmak** *get nervous, *be upset
asayiş /––'·/ *n* public order, public security
asgari /··'–/ *adj* minimum, least
asık /·'·/ *adj* sulky
asıl[1] /·'·/ *n* origin, essence
asıl[2] /'··/ *adj* essential; real; true
asılı /··'·/ *adj* hanging, suspended
asılmak /··'·/ *v* *be hanged; *cling to; *hang on
asılsız /··'·/ *adj* unfounded; insubstantial
asır /·'·/ *n* century; age; time
asi /–'–/ *adj* rebellious, refractory; *n* rebel
asil /·'·/ *adj* noble; fully appointed
asilzade /··–'·/ *n* aristocrat, nobleman
asistan /··'·/ *n* assistant
asistanlık /···'·/ *n* assistantship
asit /·'·/ *n* acid
asker /·'·/ *n* soldier
askeri /··'–/ *adj* military; ~ **mıntıka** military zone
askerlik /··'·/ *n* military service
askı /·'·/ *n* hanger; suspenders; coat rack; **askıda bırakmak** *leave in doubt
asla /'·–/ *adv* never, by no means
aslan /·'·/ *n* lion; brave man; ~ **payı** the lion's share
aslen /'··/ *adv* originally, essentially
aslında /··'·/ *adv* fundamentally, originally
asli /·'–/ fundamental, essential
asma[1] /·'·/ *n* grapevine, vine
asma[2] /·'·/ *adj* suspended, pendulous; ~ **kilit** padlock; ~ **köprü** suspension bridge
asmak /·'·/ *v* *hang; suspend; **okulu** ~ play truant
aspiratör /···'·/ *n* suction mechanism, aspirator
asri /·'–/ *adj* modern, up-to-date
assubay /'···/ *n* noncommissioned officer
astar /·'·/ *n* lining
astarlamak /···'·/ *v* line
asteğmen /'···/ *n* second lieutenant
astım /·'·/ *n* asthma
astımlı /··'·/ *adj* asthmatic
Asya /'··/ Asia
Asyalı /'···/ *n, adj* Asian

aş *n* cooked food
aşağı /··'·/ *adv* below; down; *adj* lower, inferior; *n* lower part; ~ **görmek** despise; ~ **yukarı** approximately, more or less
aşağıda /···'·/ *adv* below; downstairs
aşağılamak /····'·/ *v* degrade; treat as inferior
aşağılık /···'·/ *n* vulgarity; *adj* vulgar, mean; ~ **duygusu** inferiority complex
aşağıya /···'·/ *adv* downwards, down
aşçı /·'·/ *n* cook
aşermek /··'·/ *v* *have capricious desires during pregnancy
aşı /·'·/ *n* vaccination; inoculation
aşık /–'·/ *n* lover; *adj* in love; ~ **olmak** *fall in love
aşılamak /···'·/ *v* inoculate, vaccinate
aşınma /··'·/ *n* wear and tear; erosion
aşınmak /··'·/ *v* *wear away; *be eroded
aşırı /··'·/ *adj* excessive, extreme; *adv* over, beyond; ~ **derecede** excessively; ~ **gitmek** *go beyond bounds
aşırılık /···'·/ *n* excess
aşırmak /··'·/ *v* pass over; swipe, *steal
aşikâr /–·'·/ *adj* obvious, evident, clear
aşina /–·'–/ *adj* familiar
aşinalık /–·–'·/ *n* acquaintance, intimacy
aşiret /·–'·/ *n* tribe
aşk *n* love, passion
aşkın /·'·/ *prep* more than; over, beyond
aşmak /·'·/ *v* pass over, *go beyond; surpass
at *n* horse; ~ **meydanı** hippodrome; ~ **yarışı** horse race; **ata binmek** mount a horse; *ride a horse
ata /·'·/ *n* ancestor
atak /·'·/ *n* rash, audacious, reckless
atamak /··'·/ *v* appoint
atanmak /··'·/ *v* *be appointed
atardamar /·'···/ *n* artery
atasözü /·'···/ *n* proverb
ateş /·'·/ *n* fire, heat; fever; vivacity, ardor; ~ **açmak** open fire; ~ **almak** *catch fire; ~ **etmek** fire; ~ **pahası** very expensive; ~ **püskürmek** *spit fire; *be very angry; **ateşe vermek** *set on fire
ateşböceği /·'····/ *n* firefly
ateşçi /··'·/ *n* fireman
ateşkes /··'·/ *n* cease-fire
ateşleme /···'·/ *n* ignition; ~ **bobini** ignition coil
ateşlemek /···'·/ *v* *set fire, ignite
ateşlenmek /···'·/ *v* *get a fever; *catch fire
ateşli /··'·/ *adj* fiery, fervent; feverish
atılgan /··'·/ *adj* dashing, bold, reckless
atılım /··'·/ *n* advance; dash
atılmak /··'·/ *v* *be thrown ; *be dismissed; rush
atışmak /··'·/ *v* quarrel, squabble
atıştırmak /···'·/ *v* bolt (food); *begin to rain *or* snow slowly
atkestanesi /'··–··/ *n* horse chestnut
atkı /·'·/ *n* shawl, stole
atlama /··'·/ *n* jump
atlamak /··'·/ *v* jump, *leap; skip, omit
Atlantik Okyanusu /··'· ····/ Atlantic Ocean
atlas /·'·/ *n* satin
atlatmak /·''·/ *v* *overcome; *put off; *get rid (of a person)

atlet /·ˈ·/ *n* athlete; undershirt
atletizm /··ˈ·/ *n* athletics
atlı /·ˈ·/ *n* horseman, rider
atlıkarınca /·ˈ····/ *n* merry-go-round
atmaca /··ˈ·/ *n* hawk
atmak /·ˈ·/ *v* *throw
atmosfer /··ˈ·/ *n* atmosphere
atom /·ˈ·/ *n* atom; ~ **bombası** atomic bomb
atölye /·ˈ··/ *n* workshop
atsineği /ˈ····/ *n* horsefly
av *n* hunting; game; chase; ~ **köpeği** hunting dog; **ava çıkmak** *go hunting
avans /·ˈ·/ *n* advance; ~ **almak** *get an advance
avare /––ˈ·/ *adj* idle; wandering; vagabond
avcı /·ˈ·/ *n* hunter
avcılık /··ˈ·/ *n* hunting, shooting
avlamak /··ˈ·/ *v* hunt, *shoot
avlu /·ˈ·/ *n* court, courtyard
Avrupa /·ˈ··/ Europe
Avrupalı /·ˈ···/ *n, adj* European
avuç /·ˈ·/ *n* palm; handful; ~ **dolusu** handful
avuçlamak /···ˈ·/ *v* grasp, grip
avukat /··ˈ·/ *n* lawyer; solicitor
avunmak /··ˈ·/ *v* *be consoled; *be distracted
avuntu /··ˈ·/ *n* consolation; distraction
Avustralya /··ˈ··/ Australia
Avustralyalı /··ˈ···/ *adj, n* Australian
Avusturya /··ˈ··/ Austria
Avusturyalı /··ˈ···/ *adj, n* Austrian
avutmak /··ˈ·/ *v* console; divert
ay *n* moon; month; ~ **ışığı** moonlight
ayak /·ˈ·/ *n* foot; ~ **bileği** ankle; ~ **izi** foot print; ~ **parmağı** toe; ~ **sesi** footstep; **ayakta durmak** remain standing
ayakkabı /·ˈ···/ *n* shoe, boot; footwear; ~ **bağı** shoelace; ~ **boyası** shoe polish
ayakkabıcı /·ˈ····/ *n* shoemaker; shoeseller
ayaklanmak /···ˈ·/ *v* revolt; rebel
ayaktakımı /·ˈ····/ *n* rabble; mob
ayar /·ˈ·/ *n* adjustment, accuracy; standard; carat; ~ **etmek** adjust, regulate; **ayarı bozuk** out of order
ayarlamak /···ˈ·/ *v* adjust, regulate; fix, arrange
ayarlı /··ˈ·/ *adj* adjusted
ayartıcı /···ˈ·/ *adj* seductive, corrupting
ayartmak /··ˈ·/ *v* seduce; entice
ayaz /·ˈ·/ *n* dry cold; frost
aybaşı /ˈ···/ *n* first days of a month; menstruation
ayçiçeği /ˈ····/ *n* sunflower
aydın /·ˈ·/ *adj* educated, enlightened; bright; *n* intellectual
aydınlatıcı /····ˈ·/ *adj* illuminating; enlightening; informative
aydınlatmak /···ˈ·/ *v* illuminate; *light up; clarify
aydınlık /··ˈ·/ *n* light; clearness; *adj* clear, bright
aygıt /·ˈ·/ *n* tool; instrument; apparatus
ayı /·ˈ·/ *n* bear
ayıbalığı /·ˈ····/ *n* seal
ayık /·ˈ·/ *adj* sober
ayıklamak /···ˈ·/ *v* pick; sort out; shell
ayıp /·ˈ·/ *n* shame; defect, fault; *adj* shameful, disgraceful; ~ **etmek** behave shamefully
ayıplamak /···ˈ·/ *v* *find fault with;

censure
ayırmak /··'·/ *v* part, separate
ayırt etmek /·'· ··/ distinguish, discriminate
ayin /–'·/ *n* rite; ceremony
aykırı /··'·/ *adj* contrary; perverse
aylak /·'·/ *adj* idle, unemployed
aylık /·'·/ *adj* monthly; *n* monthly salary; ~ **dergi** monthly magazine
ayna /'··/ *n* mirror, looking glass
aynen /'··/ *adv* exactly, without change
aynı /'··/ *adj* same, identical
ayran /·'·/ *n* drink made of yoghurt and water; buttermilk
ayrı /·'·/ *adj* separate; different, distinct
ayrıca /'···/ *adv* in addition, further
ayrılık /··'·/ *n* separation; difference
ayrılmak /··'·/ *v* separate from one another; *leave; *be divorced
ayrım /·'·/ *n* distinction; difference; point of separation
ayrıntı /··'·/ *n* detail
ayrıntılı /···'·/ *adj* detailed
ayva /·'·/ *n* quince
ayyaş /·'·/ *n* drunkard
az *adj* few, little; ~ **çok** more or less
aza /–'–/ *n* member; limbs
azalmak /··'·/ *v* *become less, *be reduced
azaltmak /··'·/ *v* lessen, decrease
azami /–·'–/ *adj* utmost, maximum
azap /·'·/ *n* pain, torture, torment
azar /·'·/ *n* scolding, reproach; ~ **işitmek** *be scolded
azar azar /·'· ··/ *adv* little by little
azarlamak /···'·/ *v* scold, reproach
azdırmak /··'·/ *v* irritate; *make worse
azgelişmiş /'····/ *adj* under-developed
azgın /·'·/ *adj* furious; mad, wild
azılı /··'·/ *adj* wild, violent, dangerous
azımsamak /···'·/ *v* consider something too little
azim /·'·/ *n* resolution, determination
aziz /·'·/ *adj* dear, beloved; *n* saint
azletmek /'···/ *v* dismiss, fire
azmak /·'·/ *v* *get wild; *become unmanageable
azmetmek /'···/ *v* resolve upon; decide firmly
azot /·'·/ *n* nitrogen

B

baba /·'·/ *n* father
babaanne /·'···/ *n* (paternal) grandmother
babacan /··'·/ *adj* good-natured, fatherly
babalık /··'·/ *n* fatherhood; stepfather
babayiğit /·'···/ *n* heroic man; *adj* brave
baca /·'·/ *n* chimney
bacak /·'·/ *n* leg
bacanak /··'·/ *n* husband of one's wife's sister, brother-in-law
badana /·'··/ *n* whitewash
badem /–'·/ *n* almond
bademcik /–·'·/ *n* tonsil; ~ **iltihabı** tonsilitis
bagaj /·'·/ *n* luggage, baggage
bağ[1] *n* tie, string; relationship
bağ[2] *n* vineyard
bağdaş kurmak /·'· ··/ *sit crosslegged
bağdaşmak /··'·/ *v* fit together,

harmonize, agree
bağımlı /··ˈ·/ *adj* dependent
bağımlılık /···ˈ·/ *n* dependence
bağımsız /··ˈ·/ *adj* independent
bağımsızlık /···ˈ·/ *n* independence
bağır /·ˈ·/ *n* breast, bosom
bağırmak /··ˈ·/ *v* shout, cry out
bağırsak /··ˈ·/ *n* intestine, bowels
bağış /·ˈ·/ *n* grant, donation
bağışık /··ˈ·/ *adj* immune
bağışıklık /···ˈ·/ *n* immunity; ~ **kazandırmak** immunize
bağışlamak /···ˈ·/ *v* donate; *forgive, pardon
bağlaç /·ˈ·/ *n* conjunction
bağlama /··ˈ·/ *n* folk instrument with three double strings
bağlamak /··ˈ·/ *v* tie, fasten; connect
bağlantı /··ˈ·/ *n* connection, tie
bağlı /·ˈ·/ *adj* bound; attached; dependent on
bağlılık /··ˈ·/ *n* devotion, loyalty, attachment
bahane /–ˈ·/ *n* excuse, pretext
bahar /·ˈ·/ *n* spring; springtime
baharat /·–ˈ·/ *n* spices
baharatlı /·–ˈ·/ *adj* spiced, spicy
bahçe /·ˈ·/ *n* garden
bahçıvan /··ˈ·/ *n* gardener
bahis /·ˈ·/ *n* subject, topic; wager, bet; **bahse girmek** *bet
bahsetmek /ˈ···/ *v* *speak of, discuss; mention
bahşiş /·ˈ·/ *n* tip; ~ **vermek** tip
baht *n* fortune, luck
bahtsız /·ˈ·/ *adj* unlucky
bakan /·ˈ·/ *n* minister
bakanlık /··ˈ·/ *n* ministry
bakıcı /··ˈ·/ *n* attendant, nurse
bakım /·ˈ·/ *n* care, attention
bakımlı /··ˈ·/ *adj* well-cared for
bakımsız /··ˈ·/ *adj* unkempt, neglected
bakınmak /··ˈ·/ *v* look around
bakır /·ˈ·/ *n* copper
bakırcı /··ˈ·/ *n* coppersmith
bakış /·ˈ·/ *n* glance, look; view
bakışmak /··ˈ·/ *v* look at one another
bakire /–ˈ·/ *n* virgin, maiden
bakkal /·ˈ·/ *n* grocer
bakla /·ˈ·/ *n* broad bean
bakmak /·ˈ·/ *v* look; look at; care for, look after
bakraç /·ˈ·/ *n* copper bucket
bal *n* honey
balarısı /ˈ····/ *n* honeybee
balayı /ˈ···/ *n* honeymoon
baldız /·ˈ·/ *n* sister-in-law, wife's sister
balık /·ˈ·/ *n* fish; ~ **ağı** fishing net; ~ **avlamak** fish; ~ **kılçığı** fishbone
balıkadam /·ˈ···/ *n* skin diver
balıkçı /··ˈ·/ *n* fisherman
balina /·ˈ··/ *n* whale
balkabağı /ˈ····/ *n* sweet yellow gourd, pumpkin
balmumu /ˈ···/ *n* wax, beeswax
balta /·ˈ·/ *n* axe
baltalamak /···ˈ·/ *v* sabotage, block
bamya /ˈ··/ *n* okra, gumbo
bana /·ˈ·/ *pron* to me
bando /ˈ··/ *n* band of musicians
banka /ˈ··/ *n* bank; ~ **cüzdanı** bankbook; ~ **hesabı** bank account
banliyö /ˈ···/ *n* suburb; ~ **treni** commuter train
bant *n* band; tape; **banda almak** record on tape
banyo /ˈ··/ *n* bath; bathroom; ~ **havlusu** bath towel; ~ **yapmak** *have a bath
baraj /·ˈ·/ *n* dam
baraka /·ˈ··/ *n* shed, hut
barbar /·ˈ·/ *adj* barbaric,

barbarous; *n* barbarian
barbunya /·ˈ··/ *n* red mullet; a kind of bean
bardak /·ˈ·/ *n* glass, cup
barınak /··ˈ·/ *n* shelter
barındırmak /···ˈ·/ *v* *give shelter
barınmak /··ˈ·/ *v* *take shelter
barış /·ˈ·/ *n* peace
barışçı /··ˈ·/ *adj* peace-loving
barışmak /··ˈ·/ *v* *make peace, *be reconciled
barıştırmak /···ˈ·/ *v* reconcile
bari /ˈ–·/ *adv* at least, for once
barmen /·ˈ·/ *n* barman, bartender
baro /ˈ··/ *n* the body of lawyers, bar
barok /·ˈ·/ *adj* baroque
barut /·ˈ·/ *n* gunpowder
basamak /··ˈ·/ *n* step, stair
basık /·ˈ·/ *adj* low, squat; pressed down
basımevi /·ˈ···/ *n* printing house
basın /·ˈ·/ *n* press, newspapers; ~ **toplantısı** press conference
basınç /·ˈ·/ *n* pressure; **atmosfer basıncı** atmospheric pressure
basit /·ˈ·/ *adj* simple, easy; ordinary
baskı /·ˈ·/ *n* oppression; press; edition; circulation; ~ **altında** under pressure; ~ **yapmak** *put pressure on
baskın /·ˈ·/ *n* sudden attack, raid; *adj* more powerful; superior; ~ **çıkmak** surpass; ~ **yapmak** attack by surprise; **baskına uğramak** *be raided
baskıncı /··ˈ·/ *n* raider
baskül /·ˈ·/ *n* weighing machine
basma /·ˈ·/ *n* printed cloth; calico
basmak /·ˈ·/ *v* *tread on; *stand on; print
bastırmak /··ˈ·/ *v* suppress
baston /·ˈ·/ *n* walking stick, cane
basur /–ˈ·/ *n* hemorrhoids, piles
baş *n* head; chief, leader; beginning; *adj* main, chief, principal; **başı dönmek** *feel dizzy
başarı /··ˈ·/ *n* success
başarılı /···ˈ·/ *adj* successful
başarmak /··ˈ·/ *v* *succeed, accomplish, achieve
başbakan /ˈ···/ *n* prime minister, premier
başhekim /ˈ···/ *n* head doctor
başıboş /··ˈ·/ *adj* untethered; free
başka /·ˈ·/ *adj* other, another; different, separate
başkalık /··ˈ·/ *n* difference, change
başkan /·ˈ·/ *n* president; chairman; chief
başkanlık /··ˈ·/ *n* presidency; chairmanship
başkası /··ˈ·/ *pron* someone else, another
başkent /ˈ··/ *n* capital
başkonsolos /ˈ····/ *n* consul general
başlamak /··ˈ·/ *v* *begin, start
başlangıç /··ˈ·/ *n* beginning, start
başlı başına /·ˈ· ···/ *adv* independently, by oneself
başlıca /ˈ···/ *adj* principal, main
başlık /·ˈ·/ *n* cap, headgear; heading; headline
başöğretmen /ˈ····/ *n* school principal
başörtüsü /ˈ····/ *n* scarf
başparmak /ˈ···/ *n* thumb; big toe
başsavcı /ˈ···/ *n* attorney general
başşehir /ˈ···/ *n* capital
baştan başa /·ˈ· ··/ *adv* completely, thoroughly
başvurmak /ˈ···/ *v* *have recourse to, apply for
başyazar /ˈ···/ *n* editor-in-chief

başyazı /'···/ *n* editorial, leader
bataklık /··'·/ *n* bog, marsh, swamp
batı /·'·/ *n* west
batık /·'·/ *adj* sunken, submerged
batıl /–'·/ *adj* superstitious; ~ **itikat** superstition
batılı /··'·/ *adj* western; *n* westerner
batırmak /··'·/ *v* *sink; submerge; dip; ruin; prick
batmak /·'·/ *v* *sink
battaniye /·–·'·/ *n* blanket
bavul /·'·/ *n* suitcase
bay Mr.; gentleman; sir
bayağı[1] /··'·/ *adj* ordinary, common; mean, vulgar
bayağı[2] /'···/ *adv* simply; thoroughly
bayan /·'·/ Miss, Mrs. Ms.; lady; ma'am
bayat /·'·/ *adj* stale, not fresh
bayatlamak /···'·/ *v* *get stale
baygın /·'·/ *adj* faint; unconscious
bayılmak /··'·/ *v* faint; *feel faint; *be thrilled with, like a lot
bayındır /··'·/ *adj* prosperous; developed
bayır /·'·/ *n* slope; slight rise; hill
baykuş /·'·/ *n* owl
bayrak /·'·/ *n* flag
bayram /·'·/ *n* religious festival; national holiday, Bairam
bayramlaşmak /···'·/ *v* exchange Bairam greetings
bayramlık /··'·/ *adj* fit for a festival; *n* one's best dress; Sunday best
baytar /·'·/ *n* veterinary surgeon
bazen /'–·/ *adv* sometimes
bazı /'–·/ *adj* some, certain
bebek /·'·/ *n* baby; doll
beceri /··'·/ *n* skill
becerikli /···'·/ *adj* skillful
beceriksiz /···'·/ *adj* clumsy
becermek /··'·/ *v* carry out skillfully, manage
bedava /·–'·/ *adj* free, without charge
bedavacı /·–·'·/ *n* sponger
bedbaht /·'·/ *adj* miserable; unhappy
beddua /··'–/ *n* curse
bedel /·'·/ *n* equivalent; price, value
beden /·'·/ *n* body; trunk; size
bedesten /··'·/ *n* covered bazaar
beğenmek /··'·/ *v* like; *choose
bekâr /·'·/ *adj* single, unmarried; *n* bachelor
bekçi /·'·/ *n* watchman; guard
beklemek /··'·/ *v* wait for; expect; guard
beklenmedik /·'···/ *adj* unexpected
beklenti /··'·/ *n* expectation
bel *n* waist; loins
bela /·'–/ *n* trouble; calamity; misfortune
Belçika /·'··/ Belgium
Belçikalı /·'···/ *n, adj* Belgian
belediye /···'·/ *n* municipality; ~ **başkanı** mayor
belge /·'·/ *n* document; certificate
belgesel /··'·/ *n, adj* documentary
belirgin /··'·/ *adj* clear, evident
belirlemek /···'·/ *v* determine, fix
belirli /··'·/ *adj* determined, specific
belirmek /··'·/ *v* appear; *become evident
belirsiz /··'·/ *adj* indefinite, uncertain
belirti /··'·/ *n* sign; symptom
belirtmek /··'·/ *v* state; *make clear; specify; determine
belki /'··/ *adv* perhaps, maybe; ~ **de** or maybe
bellemek /··'·/ *v* learn by heart, memorize
belli /·'·/ *adj* evident, obvious;

definite; ~ **başlı** main, chief; ~ **etmek** *show, *make clear
ben[1] *pron* I
ben[2] mole, beauty spot
bencil /·ˈ·/ *adj* selfish, egoistic
benek /·ˈ·/ *n* speckle, small spot
beni /·ˈ·/ *pron* me
benim /·ˈ·/ *adj* my
benimki /··ˈ·/ *pron* mine
benimsemek /···ˈ·/ *v* adopt as one's own; consider one's own
benlik /·ˈ·/ *n* personality; ego
benzemek /··ˈ·/ *v* resemble, look like
benzerlik /··ˈ·/ *n* similarity, resemblance
benzetmek /··ˈ·/ *v* liken, compare; *mistake for
benzin /·ˈ·/ *n* gas *nAm;* gasoline *nAm;* petrol *nBr;* ~ **istasyonu** gas station *Am;* petrol station *Br;* filling station *Br*
beraat /··ˈ·/ *n* acquittal; ~ **etmek** *be acquitted
beraber /·–ˈ·/ *adv* together; **bununla** ~ nevertheless
berbat /·ˈ·/ *adj* very bad, disgusting; soiled, filthy
berber /·ˈ·/ *n* barber, hairdresser
bere /·ˈ·/ *n* bruise; beret
bereket /··ˈ·/ *n* abundance, plenty
berelemek /···ˈ·/ *v* bruise
bereli /··ˈ·/ *adj* bruised
beri /·ˈ·/ *n* the near side, this side; *adv* here, hither
berrak /·ˈ·/ *adj* clear
berraklaşmak /···ˈ·/ *v* *get clear
berraklık /··ˈ·/ *n* clearness
besbelli /ˈ···/ *adj* obvious, quite evident; *adv* evidently
besleme /··ˈ·/ *n* feeding, nourishing
beslemek /··ˈ·/ *v* *feed, nourish; rear; support
besleyici /···ˈ·/ *adj* nutritious, nourishing
beste /·ˈ·/ *n* tune, composition; ~ **yapmak** compose
besteci /··ˈ·/ *n* composer
beş *num* five
beşik /·ˈ·/ *n* cradle
beşinci /··ˈ·/ *num* fifth
beton /·ˈ·/ *n* concrete
bey *n* gentleman, Sir; Mr.
beyan /·ˈ·/ *n* declaration, expression; ~ **etmek** express, declare
beyanname /···ˈ·/ *n* manifesto, declaration
beyaz /·ˈ·/ *adj* white
beyazlaşmak /···ˈ·/ *v* turn white
beyazlatmak /···ˈ·/ *v* whiten, bleach
beyazperde /·ˈ···/ *n* motion picture screen
beyazpeynir /·ˈ···/ *n* white cheese
beyefendi /ˈ····/ *n* sir; Mr.
beygir /·ˈ·/ *n* horse, pack horse
beyhude /·–ˈ·/ *adj* useless; *adv* in vain; unsuccessfully
beyin /·ˈ·/ *n* brain; mind, brains, intelligence
beyinsiz /··ˈ·/ *adj* stupid
beyit /·ˈ·/ *n* couplet
beynelmilel /ˈ····/ *adj* international
beysbol /ˈ··/ *n* baseball
bez *n* cloth; piece of cloth; gland
bezdirmek /··ˈ·/ *v* sicken, disgust, weary
beze /·ˈ·/ *n* gland; inflamed gland
bezelye /·ˈ··/ *n* pea
bezemek /··ˈ·/ *v* adorn, decorate
bezenmek /··ˈ·/ *v* decorate oneself; *be ornamented *or* decorated
bezgin /·ˈ·/ *adj* wearied; depressed
bezginlik /··ˈ·/ *n* weariness
bezmek /·ˈ·/ *v* *get tired of
bıçak /·ˈ·/ *n* knife
bıkkın /·ˈ·/ *adj* disgusted, bored,

fed up

bıkkınlık /··ˈ·/ *n* boredom, disgust

bıkmak /·ˈ·/ *v* *grow tired, *be fed up

bıldırcın /··ˈ·/ *n* quail

bırakmak /··ˈ·/ *v* *leave; *set down; *let go; drop

bıyık /·ˈ·/ *n* mustache

biber /·ˈ·/ *n* pepper

biçim /·ˈ·/ *n* form, shape; manner

biçimli /··ˈ·/ *adj* well-shaped

biçimsiz /··ˈ·/ *adj* ill-shaped, ugly

biçmek /·ˈ·/ *v* *cut out; reap, mow

bidon /·ˈ·/ *n* metal barrel

biftek /·ˈ·/ *n* beefsteak, steak

bigudi /·ˈ··/ *n* hair curler

bilardo /·ˈ··/ *n* billiards

bildiri /··ˈ·/ *n* announcement, notice, proclamation

bildirmek /··ˈ·/ *v* *tell, inform

bile /·ˈ·/ *adv* even; actually; ~ ~ on purpose

bilek /·ˈ·/ *n* wrist

bilemek /··ˈ·/ *v* sharpen, whet, *grind

bilet /·ˈ·/ *n* ticket

biletçi /··ˈ·/ *n* ticket collector

bilezik /··ˈ·/ *n* bracelet

bilge /·ˈ·/ *n* wise man, sage

bilgi /·ˈ·/ *n* knowledge; information; ~ **vermek** inform

bilgiişlem /···ˈ·/ *n* data processing

bilgili /··ˈ·/ *adj* well-informed

bilgin /·ˈ·/ *n* scholar, scientist

bilgisayar /···ˈ·/ *n* computer

bilgisiz /··ˈ·/ *adj* ignorant, uninformed

bilhassa /ˈ···/ *adv* especially, particularly

bilim /·ˈ·/ *n* science

bilimsel /··ˈ·/ *adj* scientific

bilinç /·ˈ·/ *n* the conscious

bilinçaltı /·ˈ···/ *n* the subconscious

bilinçlenmek /···ˈ·/ *v* *become conscious

bilinçli /··ˈ·/ *adj* conscious

bilirkişi /·ˈ···/ *n* expert

billur /·ˈ·/ *n* crystal

bilmece /··ˈ·/ *n* puzzle, riddle

bilmeden /ˈ···/ *adv* unintentionally

bilmek /·ˈ·/ *v* *know

bilmezlik /··ˈ·/ *n* ignorance; **bilmezlikten gelmek** pretend not to know, act innocent

bin *num* thousand; **binde bir** scarcely, very rarely

bina /·ˈ–/ *n* building

binbaşı /ˈ···/ *n* major

bindirmek /··ˈ·/ *v* collide with, *run into

binek /·ˈ·/ *n* mount; riding; ~ **atı** saddle horse

binici /··ˈ·/ *n* rider, horseman

binmek /·ˈ·/ *v* *get on, mount, *ride

bir *num* one; *art* a, an; *adj* unique; same

bira /ˈ··/ *n* beer; ~ **fabrikası** brewery; ~ **mayası** yeast

birader /–ˈ·/ *n* brother

biraz /ˈ··/ *adj* a little, some; *adv* somewhat

birazdan /ˈ···/ *adv* a little later

birbiri /··ˈ·/ *pron* each other

birçok /ˈ··/ *adj* many, a lot

birden /ˈ··/ *adv* all at once, suddenly

birdenbire /·ˈ···/ *adv* suddenly

birer /·ˈ·/ *adv* one each, one apiece; ~ ~ singly, one by one

birey /·ˈ·/ *n* individual

biri /·ˈ·/, **birisi** /··ˈ·/ *pron* someone; one of them

biricik /ˈ···/ *adj* unique, the only

birikim /··ˈ·/ *n* accumulation

birikinti /···ˈ·/ *n* accumulation, heap

birikmek /··ˈ·/ *v* *come together, assemble; accumulate

biriktirmek /···ˈ·/ *v* gather, save up, collect
birim /·ˈ·/ *n* unit
birincilik /···ˈ·/ *n* first rank, championship
birkaç /·ˈ·/ *adj* a few, some, several
birleşik /··ˈ·/ *adj* united, joint
birleşmek /··ˈ·/ *v* unite; combine
Birleşmiş Milletler /··ˈ· ···/ United Nations
birleştirmek /···ˈ·/ *v* *put together, unite, connect
birlik /·ˈ·/ *n* unity; association
birlikte /··ˈ·/ *adv* together
birtakım /ˈ···/ *adj* some, a certain number of
bisküvi /··ˈ·/ *n* biscuit
bit *n* louse
bitap /–ˈ·/ *adj* exhausted; ~ **düşmek** *be exhausted
bitirmek /··ˈ·/ *v* finish, complete; exhaust, use up
bitişik /··ˈ·/ *adj* adjacent; next door
bitki /·ˈ·/ *n* plant
bitkin /·ˈ·/ *adj* exhausted, very tired
bitkisel /··ˈ·/ *adj* vegetal, vegetable
bitmek /·ˈ·/ *v* *be used up; finish, end
bitpazarı /ˈ····/ *n* flea market
biz *pron* we
bize /·ˈ·/ *pron* (to) us
bizi /·ˈ·/ *pron* us
bizim /·ˈ·/ *adj* our
bizimki /··ˈ·/ *pron* ours
bizzat /ˈ··/ *adv* personally, in person
blok *n* block
blucin /·ˈ·/ *n* jeans, blue jeans
bluz *n* blouse
bocalamak /···ˈ·/ *v* falter
bodrum /·ˈ·/ *n* cellar, basement
bodur /·ˈ·/ *adj* short, squat
boğa /·ˈ·/ *n* bull; ~ **güreşi** bullfight
boğaz /·ˈ·/ *n* throat; ~ **ağrısı** sore throat
boğazlamak /···ˈ·/ *v* strangle
boğmaca /··ˈ·/ *n* whooping cough
boğmak /·ˈ·/ *v* choke, strangle; suffocate; drown
boğucu /··ˈ·/ *adj* suffocating
boğuk /·ˈ·/ *adj* hoarse; muffled
boğulmak /··ˈ·/ *v* *be drowned, drown
boğum /·ˈ·/ *n* node, joint
boğuşmak /··ˈ·/ *v* *be at each other's throat, *fight
bohça /·ˈ·/ *n* bundle, package
bohçalamak /···ˈ·/ *v* wrap up in a bundle
bol *adj* wide and loose-fitting; abundant, ample; ~ ~ abundantly, generously
bollaşmak /··ˈ·/ *v* *become loose; *become plentiful
bolluk /·ˈ·/ *n* wideness, looseness; abundance
bomba /ˈ··/ *n* bomb
bombalamak /···ˈ·/ *v* bomb
bomboş /ˈ··/ *adj* altogether empty
boncuk /·ˈ·/ *n* bead
bone /·ˈ·/ *n* bonnet
bonfile /ˈ···/ *n* sirloin steak
bono /ˈ··/ *n* promissory note; bond, bill
bonservis /··ˈ·/ *n* letter of recommendation
borazan /··ˈ·/ *n* trumpet
borç *n* debt, loan; ~ **almak** borrow (money); ~ **para** loan; ~ **vermek** *lend money
borçlanmak /··ˈ·/ *v* *get into debt
borçlu /·ˈ·/ *n* debtor; *adj* indebted
bordo /ˈ··/ *adj* claret red
bordro /ˈ··/ *n* payroll
bornoz /·ˈ·/ *n* bathrobe
borsa /ˈ··/ *n* stock exchange
boru /·ˈ·/ *n* pipe, tube;

~ **hattı** pipeline
bostan /·ˈ·/ *n* vegetable garden
boş *adj* empty; hollow; blank; vacant; useless; idle
boşalım /··ˈ·/ *n* discharge
boşalmak /··ˈ·/ *v* *be emptied, *be discharged
boşaltmak /··ˈ·/ *v* empty; evacuate; pour out; unload
boşanma /··ˈ·/ *n* divorce
boşanmak /··ˈ·/ *v* *be divorced
boşluk /·ˈ·/ *n* blank; cavity; vacuum
boşuna /ˈ···/ *adv* in vain
bot *n* boat; boot
boy *n* height; stature; length; size
boya /·ˈ·/ *n* paint; dye
boyacı /··ˈ·/ *n* dyer; bootblack
boyamak /··ˈ·/ *v* paint; dye; color
boylam /·ˈ·/ *n* longitude
boylu /·ˈ·/ *adj* tall
boynuz /·ˈ·/ *n* horn, antler
boyun /·ˈ·/ *n* neck
boyuna[1] /··ˈ·/ *adv* lengthwise
boyuna[2] /ˈ···/ *adv* continually
boyunbağı /·ˈ···/ *n* necktie
boyunduruk /···ˈ·/ *n* yoke
boyut /·ˈ·/ *n* dimension
boz *adj* gray
bozdurmak /··ˈ·/ *v* change; cash
bozgun /·ˈ·/ *n* rout, defeat; **bozguna uğramak** *be defeated; **bozguna uğratmak** defeat
bozmak /·ˈ·/ *v* *undo; *spoil; ruin
bozuk /·ˈ·/ *adj* spoilt; broken; out of order; ~ **para** small change
bozukluk /··ˈ·/ *n* defect; corruption, disorder; small change
bozulmak /··ˈ·/ *v* *be spoilt; *break down; *go bad
böbrek /·ˈ·/ *n* kidney
böbürlenmek /···ˈ·/ *v* boast
böcek /·ˈ·/ *n* bug; insect
böğürtlen /··ˈ·/ *n* blackberry
bölge /·ˈ·/ *n* region, zone
bölgesel /···/ *adj* regional
bölme /·ˈ·/ *n* division; compartment; dividing wall
bölmek /·ˈ·/ *v* separate; divide
bölük /·ˈ·/ *n* squadron
bölüm /·ˈ·/ *n* section, part, division
bölünme /··ˈ·/ *n* division
bölünmek /··ˈ·/ *v* *be divided; *be separated
bölünmez /··ˈ·/ *adj* indivisible
bölüşmek /··ˈ·/ *v* divide up; share out
börek /·ˈ·/ *n* flaky pastry
böyle /ˈ··/ *adv* thus, so, in this way
böylece /ˈ···/ *conj* then, so
böylelikle /··ˈ··/ *conj* in this way, thus
branda /ˈ··/ *n* sailor's hammock; ~ **bezi** canvas
bravo /ˈ–·/ bravo! well done!
briç *n* bridge (card game)
bronşit /·ˈ·/ *n* bronchitis
bronz *n* bronze
broşür /·ˈ·/ *n* brochure
bröve /·ˈ·/ *n* pilot's license; certificate, license
brüt *adj* gross
bu *adj, pron* this; ~ **arada** meanwhile; among other things; ~ **bakımdan** in this respect; ~ **defa** this time; ~ **kadar** this much, so many; ~ **yüzden** for this reason, so; **bundan böyle** henceforth; **bundan dolayı** therefore
buçuk /·ˈ·/ *n* half (after numerals)
budala /··ˈ·/ *adj* foolish, imbecile
budalalık /···ˈ·/ *n* foolishness; stupidity
bugün /ˈ··/ *adv* today
bugünkü /ˈ···/ *adj* of today, today's
bugünlerde /ˈ····/ *adv* nowadays
bugünlük /ˈ···/ *adv* for today

buğday /·'·/ *n* wheat
buğu /·'·/ *n* mist, vapor
buhar /·'·/ *n* steam; vapor
buharlaşmak /···'·/ *v* evaporate
buharlı /··'·/ *adj* steamy; with steam power; ~ **gemi** steamer
buhran /·'·/ *n* crisis
buji /'··/ *n* spark plug
buket /·'·/ *n* bunch of flowers, bouquet
bukle /·'·/ *n* curl of hair, lock
bulandırmak /···'·/ *v* *make muddy; cloud
bulanık /··'·/ *adj* turbid, cloudy; dim
bulantı /··'·/ *n* nausea
bulaşıcı /···'·/ *adj* contagious
bulaşık /··'·/ *n* dirty dishes; ~ **yıkamak** *do the dishes
Bulgar /·'·/ *n, adj* Bulgarian
Bulgarca /·'··/ *n* Bulgarian language
Bulgaristan /···'·/ Bulgaria
bulgu /·'·/ *n* finding, discovery
bulgur /·'·/ *n* boiled and pounded wheat
bulmaca /··'·/ *n* puzzle, crossword puzzle
bulmak /·'·/ *v* *find; discover; invent
buluğ /·'·/ *n* puberty
bulundurmak /···'·/ *v* *have ready, *keep in stock
bulunmak /··'·/ *v* *be present; exist; *be available
buluş /·'·/ *n* invention; discovery; original thought
buluşma /··'·/ *n* *meeting
buluşmak /··'·/ *v* *come together, *meet
bulut /·'·/ *n* cloud
bulutlu /··'·/ *adj* cloudy, overcast
bunalım /··'·/ *n* depression; crisis
bunalmak /··'·/ *v* *be bored; *be depressed
bunaltıcı /···'·/ *adj* boring; depressing
bunca /'··/ *adj* this much, so much; ~ **zaman** for such a long time
burada /'···/ *adv* here
burası /'···/ *n* this place
burç *n* tower; sign of the zodiac
burkmak /·'·/ *v* sprain
burkulmak /··'·/ *v* *be sprained
burmak /·'·/ *v* twist; *wring
burs *n* scholarship
buruk /·'·/ *adj* acrid, sour
burun /·'·/ *n* nose; tip; headland
buruşmak /··'·/ *v* *be wrinkled *or* creased
buruşturmak /···'·/ *v* wrinkle, crease
buruşuk /··'·/ *adj* wrinkled, creased
buyruk /·'·/ *n* command, decree
buyurmak /··'·/ *v* command
buz *n* ice; ~ **kesesi** ice bag; ~ **tutmak** ice up, *freeze
buzağı /··'·/ *n* calf
buzdağı /'···/ *n* iceberg
buzdolabı /'····/ *n* refrigerator
buzlu /·'·/ *adj* icy, covered with ice
büfe /'··/ *n* buffet
bükmek /·'·/ *v* *bend; twist, curl
bükük /·'·/ *adj* bent; twisted; curled
bülbül /·'·/ *n* nightingale
bünye /·'·/ *n* structure
büro /'··/ *n* office
bürokrasi /···'·/ *n* bureaucracy
bürünmek /··'·/ *v* wrap oneself up
büsbütün /'···/ *adv* altogether, wholly, completely
bütçe /'··/ *n* budget
bütün /·'·/ *n* the whole; *adj* entire, complete; undivided
büyü /·'·/ *n* spell, charm; sorcery;

~ **yapmak** practice sorcery, *cast a spell
büyücü /··ˈ·/ *n* sorcerer, witch
büyücülük /···ˈ·/ *n* sorcery, witchcraft
büyük /·ˈ·/ *adj* great; big; important; major; **Büyük Britanya** Great Britain; **Büyük Okyanus** Pacific Ocean
büyükanne /·ˈ···/ *n* grandmother
büyükbaba /·ˈ···/ *n* grandfather
büyükbaş /·ˈ··/ *n* cattle
büyükelçi /·ˈ···/ *n* ambassador
büyükelçilik /·ˈ····/ *n* embassy
büyüklük /··ˈ·/ *n* greatness; seniority; importance; size; ~ **göstermek** *show generosity
büyülemek /···ˈ·/ *v* bewitch; charm, fascinate
büyümek /··ˈ·/ *v* *grow; increase in size *or* importance
büyüteç /··ˈ·/ *n* magnifying glass
büyütme /··ˈ·/ *n* enlargement, blowup
büyütmek /··ˈ·/ *v* enlarge; exaggerate; *bring up, rear

C

cadde /·ˈ·/ *n* main road, street
cadı /·ˈ·/ *n* witch, hag
cadılık /··ˈ·/ *n* witchcraft
cahil /–ˈ·/ *adj* ignorant; uneducated
cahillik /–·ˈ·/ *n* ignorance
cam *n* glass; window pane
cambaz /·ˈ·/ *n* acrobat
camekân /··ˈ·/ *n* shop window; showcase
camgöbeği /ˈ····/ *adj* turquoise, glass-green
cami /–ˈ·/ *n* mosque
can *n* soul; life; vitality
canavar /··ˈ·/ *n* wild beast; brute; ~ **düdüğü** siren
candan /·ˈ·/ *adj* cordial; sincere
canım /·ˈ·/ *adj* beloved; *n* my dear, darling
canavarlık /···ˈ·/ *n* savagery
cani /–ˈ–/ *n* murderer
cankurtaran /···ˈ·/ *adj* lifesaving; ~ **arabası** ambulance; ~ **kemeri** safety belt; ~ **yeleği** life vest
canlandırıcı /····ˈ·/ *adj* enlivening, refreshing
canlandırmak /···ˈ·/ *v* refresh; vitalize
canlanmak /··ˈ·/ *v* *come to life; *become active
canlı /·ˈ·/ *n* living being; *adj* lively, active; ~ **yayın** live broadcast
cansız /·ˈ·/ *adj* lifeless; dull
cari /–ˈ–/ *adj* current, in force; valid
cariye /–·ˈ·/ *n* female slave
casus /–ˈ·/ *n* spy
caydırmak /··ˈ·/ *v* dissuade; deter
caymak /·ˈ·/ *v* deviate from one's purpose, *give up
cazibe /–·ˈ·/ *n* charm, attractiveness
cazip /–ˈ·/ *adj* attractive, charming
cefa /·ˈ–/ *n* cruelty, unkindness; suffering; ~ **çekmek** suffer
cefakâr /·–ˈ·/ *adj* long-suffering
cehalet /·–ˈ·/ *n* ignorance
cehennem /··ˈ·/ *n* hell
ceket /·ˈ·/ *n* jacket
cellat /·ˈ·/ *n* executioner
celse /·ˈ·/ *n* session; hearing
cemaat /··ˈ·/ *n* community; group; congregation
cemiyet /··ˈ·/ *n* society; gathering, assembly
cenaze /·–ˈ·/ *n* corpse; funeral

cennet /·ˈ·/ *n* paradise, heaven
cep *n* pocket; ~ **saati** pocket watch
cephane /–ˈ·/ *n* ammunition
cephe /·ˈ·/ *n* front; ~ **almak** *take sides against
cepkitabı /ˈ····/ *n* pocketbook
cerahat /··ˈ·/ *n* pus
cereyan /··ˈ·/ *n* current; draft; ~ **etmek** happen
cerrah /·ˈ·/ *n* surgeon
cerrahlık /··ˈ·/ *n* surgery
cesaret /–ˈ·/ *n* courage; ~ **etmek** dare; **cesaretini kırmak** discourage
cesaretlenmek /–··ˈ·/ *v* *take courage
cesaretli /·–ˈ·/ *adj* courageous
ceset /·ˈ·/ *n* corpse
cesur /·ˈ·/ *adj* brave, bold, courageous
cet *n* forefather; grandfather
cetvel /·ˈ·/ *n* list, schedule; ruler
cevap /·ˈ·/ *n* answer, reply; ~ **vermek** answer, reply
cevaplandırmak /····ˈ·/ *v* answer
cevher /·ˈ·/ *n* ore; essence; ability
ceviz /·ˈ·/ *n* walnut
ceylan /·ˈ·/ *n* gazelle, antelope
ceza /·ˈ–/ *n* punishment; penalty; fine
cezaevi /·ˈ–··/ *n* prison, jail
cezalandırmak /·–··ˈ·/ *v* punish
cezve /·ˈ·/ *n* Turkish coffee pot
cılız /·ˈ·/ *adj* thin, undersized
cımbız /·ˈ·/ *n* tweezers
cırcırböceği /·ˈ····/ *n* cricket
cıva /ˈ··/ *n* mercury
cıvata /·ˈ··/ *n* bolt; ~ **anahtarı** wrench; ~ **somunu** screw nut
cıvık /·ˈ·/ *adj* wet, sticky
cıvıldamak /···ˈ·/ *v* chirp, twitter
cızırdamak /···ˈ·/ *v* sizzle
cibinlik /··ˈ·/ *n* mosquito net
ciddi /·ˈ–/ *adj* serious, earnest; **ciddiye almak** *take seriously
ciddileşmek /–·ˈ·/ *v* *get serious
ciddiyet /··ˈ·/ *n* seriousness
ciğer /·ˈ·/ *n* liver; lungs
cihan /·ˈ·/ *n* world; universe
cihaz /·ˈ·/ *n* apparatus
cila /·ˈ–/ *n* polish; varnish
cilalamak /·–·ˈ·/ *v* polish
cilalı /·–ˈ·/ *adj* polished, glossy
cilt *n* skin; binding; volume
ciltçi /·ˈ·/ *n* bookbinder
ciltlemek /··ˈ·/ *v* *bind
ciltli /·ˈ·/ *adj* bound
cilveli /··ˈ·/ *adj* coquettish
cimri /·ˈ·/ *adj* mean
cimrilik /··ˈ·/ *n* stinginess
cin *n* genie; spirit
cinayet /·–ˈ·/ *n* murder
cingöz /·ˈ·/ *adj* shrewd
cinnet /·ˈ·/ *n* madness, insanity; ~ **getirmek** *go mad
cins *n* kind, sort; class; sex; race; ~ ~ of various kinds
cinsel /·ˈ·/ *adj* sexual
cinsiyet /··ˈ·/ *n* sex; sexuality
ciro /ˈ··/ *n* endorsement; turnover; ~ **etmek** endorse
cisim /·ˈ·/ *n* body; substance; material thing
civar /·ˈ·/ *n* neighborhood, environs
civciv /·ˈ·/ *n* chick
cop *n* nightstick, truncheon
coşku /·ˈ·/ *n* enthusiasm
coşkun /·ˈ·/ *adj* enthusiastic; overflowing
coşmak /·ˈ·/ *v* overflow; *be enthusiastic
cömert /·ˈ·/ *adj* generous
cuma /·ˈ–/ Friday
cumartesi /·ˈ···/ Saturday
cumhurbaşkanı /·ˈ····/ *n* president of the republic

cumhuriyet /-–ˈ·/ *n* republic
cüce /·ˈ·/ *adj, n* dwarf
cümbüş /·ˈ·/ *n* merrymaking; a mandolin with a metal body
cümle /·ˈ·/ *n* sentence
cüppe /·ˈ·/ *n* robe with full sleeves and long skirts; academic gown
cüret /·ˈ·/ *n* boldness, daring; ~ **etmek** dare
cüretkâr /··ˈ·/ *adj* bold, daring
cüzam /·ˈ·/ *n* leprosy
cüzdan /·ˈ·/ *n* wallet

Ç

çaba /·ˈ·/ *n* effort
çabalamak /···ˈ·/ *v* struggle, *strive
çabuk /·ˈ·/ *adj* quick; *adv* quickly, in a hurry; ~ **ol!** hurry up!, be quick!
çabukluk /··ˈ·/ *n* quickness
çadır /·ˈ·/ *n* tent
çağ *n* time; age, period
çağdaş /·ˈ·/ *adj* contemporary
çağırmak /··ˈ·/ *v* call; invite
çağlayan /··ˈ·/ *n* waterfall
çağrı /·ˈ·/ *n* call; invitation
çağrılmak /··ˈ·/ *v* *be invited
çakı /·ˈ·/ *n* pocketknife
çakıl /·ˈ·/ *n* pebble
çakılı /··ˈ·/ *adj* fixed, nailed
çakır /·ˈ·/ *adj* grayish blue
çakışmak /··ˈ·/ *v* fit into one another; collide
çakmak[1] /·ˈ·/ *v* *drive in by blows; *strike
çakmak[2] /·ˈ·/ *n* lighter
çakmaktaşı /·ˈ···/ *n* flint
çalar saat /·ˈ· ··/ alarm clock
çalgı /·ˈ·/ *n* musical instrument; ~ **çalmak** play music
çalgıcı /··ˈ·/ *n* musician
çalı /·ˈ·/ *n* bush
çalılık /··ˈ·/ *n* thicket, bushes
çalım /·ˈ·/ *n* swagger, affected dignity
çalışkan /··ˈ·/ *adj* hard-working, industrious, diligent
çalışkanlık /···ˈ·/ *n* diligence
çalışmak /··ˈ·/ *v* work; study; try, *strive
çalkalamak /···ˈ·/ *v* *shake; toss around; rinse
çalmak /·ˈ·/ *v* *steal; play an instrument
çam *n* pine
çamaşır /··ˈ·/ *n* underclothing; laundry; ~ **ipi** clothes line; ~ **makinesi** washing machine; ~ **yıkamak** *do the laundry
çamaşırcı /···ˈ·/ *n* washerwoman; laundryman
çamaşırhane /···–ˈ·/ *n* laundry room
çamfıstığı /ˈ····/ *n* pine nut
çamsakızı /ˈ····/ *n* resin
çamur /·ˈ·/ *n* mud
çamurlanmak /···ˈ·/ *v* *get muddy
çamurlu /··ˈ·/ *adj* muddy
çamurluk /··ˈ·/ *n* fender, mudguard
çan *n* bell; ~ **çalmak** *ring the bell; ~ **kulesi** belfry
çanak /·ˈ·/ *n* earthenware pot; ~ **çömlek** pots and pans, crockery
çanta /ˈ··/ *n* bag, handbag; **evrak çantası** briefcase
çap *n* diameter; bore; caliber
çapa /ˈ··/ *n* anchor
çapkın /·ˈ·/ *n* woman-chaser, vagabond
çapraşık /··ˈ·/ *adj* involved, tangled
çapraz /·ˈ·/ *adj* crossing, crosswise; diagonal
çapulculuk /···ˈ·/ *n* pillage, looting
çarçabuk /ˈ···/ *adv* very quickly, speedily

çare /–'·/ *n* remedy, means; ~ **bulmak** *find a remedy
çaresiz /–'·/ *adj* helpless; irreparable
çaresizlik /–··'·/ *n* helplessness
çarık /·'·/ *n* rawhide sandal
çarmıh /·'·/ *n* cross for crucifying; **çarmıha germek** crucify
çarpık /·'·/ *adj* crooked, bent; warped
çarpıntı /··'·/ *n* palpitation
çarpışma /··'·/ *n* clash; collision
çarpışmak /··'·/ *v* collide; *fight
çarpıtmak /··'·/ *v* *make crooked; distort
çarpmak /·'·/ *v* bump, *hit, *strike; multiply
çarşaf /·'·/ *n* bed sheet; dress with veil
çarşamba /··'·/ Wednesday
çarşı /·'·/ *n* bazaar, shopping district; **çarşıya çıkmak** *go shopping
çatal /·'·/ *n* fork
çatallanmak /···'·/ *v* fork, *become forked
çatı /·'·/ *n* roof; framework; ~ **arası,** ~ **katı** attic
çatık /·'·/ *adj* frowning; ~ **kaşlı** frowning, beetle-browed
çatırdamak /···'·/ *v* *make a crackling noise
çatırtı /··'·/ *n* crackling noise
çatışma /··'·/ *n* conflict; combat
çatışmak /··'·/ *v* clash; *be in conflict
çatlak /·'·/ *n* crack; *adj* split; cracked
çatlamak /··'·/ *v* crack
çavdar /·'·/ *n* rye
çavuş /·'·/ *n* sergeant
çay *n* tea; brook, stream; ~ **bahçesi** tea garden
çaydanlık /··'·/ *n* teapot
çayevi /'···/ *n* teahouse, tearoom
çayır /·'·/ *n* meadow; pasture
çehre /·'·/ *n* face; appearance
çek *n* check; ~ **defteri** checkbook
çekecek /··'·/ *n* shoehorn
çekememek /·'···/ *v* *be jealous
çekememezlik /·'····/ *n* envy, jealousy
çekici /··'·/ *adj* attractive; pulling, dragging
çekiç /·'·/ *n* hammer
çekidüzen /···'·/ *n* tidiness, orderliness; ~ **vermek** *put in order, tidy up
çekilmek /··'·/ *v* *withdraw; retire
çekilmez /··'·/ *adj* unbearable, intolerable
çekingen /··'·/ *adj* shy
çekingenlik /···'·/ *n* shyness
çekinmek /··'·/ *v* beware; refrain from
çekirdek /··'·/ *n* pip, seed, stone of fruit; nucleus
çekirdeksiz /···'·/ *adj* seedless
çekirge /·'··/ *n* grasshopper; locust
çekişmek /··'·/ *v* quarrel, argue
çekmece /··'·/ *n* drawer
çekme /·'·/ *n* pull; hauling
çekmek /·'·/ *v* pull, *draw; suffer, *bear; *shrink
çelenk /·'·/ *n* wreath; garland
çelik /·'·/ *n* steel
çelimsiz /··'·/ *adj* frail, thin
çelişik /··'·/ *adj* contradictory
çelişmek /··'·/ *v* *be in contradiction
çelişki /··'·/ *n* contradiction
çember /·'·/ *n* hoop; ring; circle
çene /·'·/ *n* jaw; chin
çenebaz /··'·/ *adj* talkative
çengel /·'·/ *n* hook
çengelli /··'·/ *adj* hooked; ~ **iğne** safety pin
çentik /·'·/ *n* notch, dent

çentmek /·ˈ·/ *v* notch, nick; chop up
çerçeve /··ˈ·/ *n* frame
çerçevelemek /····ˈ·/ *v* frame
çerez /·ˈ·/ *n* snack; appetizer
çeşit /·ˈ·/ *n* kind, variety
çeşitli /··ˈ·/ *adj* assorted, various
çeşitlilik /···ˈ·/ *n* assortment, variety
çeşme /·ˈ·/ *n* fountain
çete /ˈ··/ *n* band, gang
çeteci /ˈ···/ *n* raider
çetin /·ˈ·/ *adj* hard, difficult
çevik /·ˈ·/ *adj* quick, agile, swift
çeviri /··ˈ·/ *n* translation
çevirmek /··ˈ·/ *v* turn, turn round; encircle; change; translate
çevirmen /··ˈ·/ *n* translator
çevre /·ˈ·/ *n* surroundings, environment; circumference
çevrelemek /···ˈ·/ *v* surround, encircle
çevresel /··ˈ·/ *adj* peripheral; environmental
çeyrek /·ˈ·/ *n* quarter; ~ **saat** quarter of an hour
çıban /·ˈ·/ *n* boil
çığ *n* avalanche
çığlık /·ˈ·/ *n* scream; ~ **atmak** scream
çıkar /·ˈ·/ *n* benefit, interest; ~ **yol** way out
çıkarcı /··ˈ·/ *n* opportunist
çıkartmak /··ˈ·/ *v* *take out; *remove; subtract
çıkık /·ˈ·/ *adj* dislocated; projecting
çıkıntı /··ˈ·/ *n* projection
çıkış /·ˈ·/ *n* exit
çıkmak /·ˈ·/ *v* *go out; start off; *get out
çıkmaz /·ˈ·/ *adj* dead-end; *n* dilemma, impasse
çıldırmak /··ˈ·/ *go mad
çılgın /·ˈ·/ *adj* mad, insane
çılgınca /·ˈ··/ *adv* madly
çılgınlık /··ˈ·/ *n* madness, frenzy
çınar /·ˈ·/ *n* plane tree
çıngırak /··ˈ·/ *n* small bell
çıngırdamak /···ˈ·/ *v* jingle
çınlamak /··ˈ·/ *v* *give out a ringing sound
çıplak /·ˈ·/ *adj* naked, nude; bare
çırak /·ˈ·/ *n* apprentice
çıraklık /··ˈ·/ *n* apprenticeship
çırılçıplak /·ˈ···/ *adj* stark naked
çırpınmak /··ˈ·/ *v* flutter; struggle
çırpmak /·ˈ·/ *v* *strike lightly and repeatedly; *beat, whip; flutter
çıta /·ˈ·/ *n* lath
çıtçıt /·ˈ·/ *n* snap fastener
çıtırdamak /···ˈ·/ *v* crackle
çiçek[1] /·ˈ·/ *n* flower; ~ **açmak** bloom
çiçek[2] /·ˈ·/ *n* smallpox; ~ **aşısı** vaccination
çiçeklenmek /···ˈ·/ *v* flower, blossom
çift *n* couple, pair; *adj* even; double; ~ **hatlı** double-track; ~ **sayı** even number
çiftçi /·ˈ·/ *n* farmer
çiftçilik /··ˈ·/ *n* agriculture, farming
çiftleşme /··ˈ·/ *n* mating
çiftleşmek /··ˈ·/ *v* *become a pair; mate
çiftlik /·ˈ·/ *n* farm
çiğ *adj* raw; unripe
çiğnemek /··ˈ·/ *v* chew; trample down
çiklet /·ˈ·/ *n* chewing gum
çil *n* spot, freckle
çile /·ˈ·/ *n* sufferance, trial
çilek /·ˈ·/ *n* strawberry
çilingir /··ˈ·/ *n* locksmith
çim *n* garden grass, lawn
çimdik /·ˈ·/ *n* pinch
çimdiklemek /···ˈ·/ *v* pinch

çimen /·ˈ·/ *n* meadow, lawn
çimenlik /··ˈ·/ *n* meadow land
çimento /·ˈ··/ *n* cement
çimentolamak /·ˈ····/ *v* cover with cement
çimlenmek /··ˈ·/ *v* sprout; *be covered with grass
Çin China
Çince /ˈ··/ *n* Chinese language
Çingene /··ˈ·/ *n* Gypsy
çini /·ˈ·/ *n* colored tile; porcelain
çinko /ˈ··/ *n* zinc
Çinli /·ˈ·/ *n, adj* Chinese
çirkin /·ˈ·/ *adj* ugly; unseemly
çirkinlik /··ˈ·/ *n* ugliness
çiselemek /···ˈ·/ *v* drizzle
çit *n* hedge; fence
çivi /·ˈ·/ *n* nail; pin
çivilemek /···ˈ·/ *v* nail
çiy *n* dew
çizelge /··ˈ·/ *n* table, chart
çizgi /·ˈ·/ *n* line; stripe
çizgili /··ˈ·/ *adj* lined; striped
çizik /·ˈ·/ *n* scratch
çizme /·ˈ·/ *n* topboot
çizmek /·ˈ·/ *v* *draw; sketch
çoban /·ˈ·/ *n* shepherd
çocuk /·ˈ·/ *n* child; infant; ~ **aldırmak** *have an abortion ~ **arabası** baby carriage *Am;* pram *nBr;* ~ **bahçesi** children's park; ~ **bakımı** child care; ~ **bezi** diaper *nAm;* nappy *nBr;* ~ **düşürmek** *have a miscarriage; ~ **yuvası** nursery school; **çoluk** ~ all the family
çocukça /·ˈ··/ *adj* childish
çocukluk /··ˈ·/ *n* childhood
çocuksu /··ˈ·/ *adj* childish
çoğalmak /··ˈ·/ *v* increase; multiply
çoğaltmak /··ˈ·/ *v* *make more, increase
çoğu /ˈ··/ *pron* the greater part; *adj* most
çoğul /·ˈ·/ *adj* plural
çoğunluk /··ˈ·/ *n* majority
çok *adj* much; many; too much; very; ~ **fazla** too much; ~ **geçmeden** soon, before long
çokluk /·ˈ·/ *n* abundance
çolak /·ˈ·/ *adj* crippled in one hand *or* arm
çorak /·ˈ·/ *adj* arid, barren
çorap /·ˈ·/ *n* stocking, sock, hose
çorba /·ˈ·/ *n* soup; ~ **kaşığı** tablespoon
çökmek /·ˈ·/ *n* collapse, *fall in; cave in; settle, *sink
çökük /·ˈ·/ *adj* collapsed
çöküntü /··ˈ·/ *n* debris; sediment
çöl *n* desert
çömelmek /··ˈ·/ *v* squat down on one's heels
çömlek /·ˈ·/ *n* earthen pot
çöp *n* rubbish, garbage; ~ **kutusu** garbage can *Am,* trash can *Am;* dustbin *nBr*
çöpçatan /··ˈ·/ *n* go-between, matchmaker
çöpçü /·ˈ·/ *n* street sweeper; garbage collector *Am;* dustman *nBr*
çöplük /·ˈ·/ *n* rubbish dump
çörek /·ˈ·/ *n* bun
çözmek /·ˈ·/ *v* unfasten; solve; dissolve
çözük /·ˈ·/ *adj* loose, untied
çözülmek /··ˈ·/ *v* *be solved; *be unfastened; decompose
çözüm /·ˈ·/ *n* solution
çözümleme /···ˈ·/ *n* analysis
çözümlemek /···ˈ·/ *v* analyze
çubuk /·ˈ·/ *n* shoot, twig; stick
çukur /·ˈ·/ *n* hole, ditch; cavity; *adj* sunken
çuval /·ˈ·/ *n* sack
çünkü /ˈ··/ *conj* because
çürük /·ˈ·/ *adj* rotten, decayed;

bruised; unsound; *n* bruise
çürümek /..ˈ./ *v* *be bruised; rot, decay

D

da, de *adv* too, also; and
dadı /.ˈ./ *n* child's nurse
dağ *n* mountain; ~ **geçidi** mountain pass; ~ **silsilesi** mountain range
dağcı /.ˈ./ *n* mountaineer
dağılmak /..ˈ./ *v* scatter; *spread; *fall to pieces; *get untidy
dağınık /..ˈ./ *adj* scattered; untidy; disorganized
dağınıklık /...ˈ./ *n* untidiness
dağıtmak /..ˈ./ *v* scatter; distribute; mess up, disarrange
dağlamak /..ˈ./ *v* brand; *burn; cauterize
dağlık /.ˈ./ *adj* mountainous
daha /.ˈ./ *adj* more; further; *adv* not yet; **bir** ~ once more
dâhi /–ˈ–/ *n* genius
dahil /–ˈ./ *adv* inclusive, included; *n* interior; ~ **etmek** insert, include; ~ **olmak** *be included in
dahili /–ˈ–/ *adj* internal, inner
dahiliye /–..ˈ./ *n* interior; internal diseases; ~ **mütehassısı** internist
daima /ˈ––/ *adv* always, perpetually
daimi /–ˈ–/ *adj* constant, permanent
dair /–ˈ./ *prep* about, concerning, related to
daire /–ˈ./ *n* circle; department; office; flat *nBr;* apartment *nAm*
dakik /.ˈ./ *adj* punctual
dakika /.–ˈ./ *n* minute
daktilo /.ˈ../ *n* typewriter; ~ **etmek** type

dal *n* branch; subdivision
dalak /.ˈ./ *n* spleen
dalaşmak /..ˈ./ *v* *fight savagely; quarrel violently
dalavere /..ˈ../ *n* trick, intrigue; ~ **çevirmek** plot
dalga /.ˈ./ *n* wave; undulation
dalgakıran /...ˈ./ *n* breakwater
dalgalanmak /...ˈ./ *v* undulate, wave
dalgalı /..ˈ./ *adj* wavy; rough; ~ **akım** alternating current
dalgıç /.ˈ./ *n* diver
dalgın /.ˈ./ *adj* absentminded
dalgınlık /..ˈ./ *n* absentmindedness
dallanmak /..ˈ./ *v* branch out, ramify; *spread
dalmak /.ˈ./ *v* plunge, dive; *be absorbed
dam *n* roof; lady partner
dama /.ˈ./ *n* checkers *nAm;* draughts *nBr*
damak /.ˈ./ *n* palate
damar /.ˈ./ *n* blood vessel, vein
damat /–ˈ./ *n* son-in-law; bridegroom
damga /.ˈ./ *n* stamp, rubber stamp; mark; ~ **pulu** revenue stamp; ~ **resmi** stamp duty; ~ **vurmak** stamp
damgalamak /...ˈ./ *v* mark with a stamp; brand
damgalı /..ˈ./ *adj* stamped, marked
damla /.ˈ./ *n* drop
damlalık /..ˈ./ *n* medicine dropper
damlamak /..ˈ./ *v* drip
damlatmak /..ˈ./ *v* pour out drop by drop
dana /.ˈ./ *n* calf; ~ **eti** veal
danışma /..ˈ./ *n* information; inquiry
danışmak /..ˈ./ *v* consult; ask; confer
danışman /..ˈ./ *n* counselor,

advisor
dansöz /·ˈ·/ *n* woman dancer
dantel /·ˈ·/ *n* lace, lacework
dar *adj* narrow; tight; ~ **kafalı** narrow-minded
darağacı /ˈ····/ *n* gallows
daralmak /··ˈ·/ *v* *become narrow; *shrink
daraltmak /··ˈ·/ *v* *make narrow, restrict
darbe /·ˈ·/ *n* blow, stroke; coup
darbuka /·ˈ··/ *n* clay drum
dargın /·ˈ·/ *adj* cross, irritated
darı /·ˈ·/ *n* millet
darılmak /··ˈ·/ *v* *get cross, *be offended; scold
darlaşmak /··ˈ·/ *v* *become narrow; *become tight
darlık /·ˈ·/ *n* poverty, need
darmadağın /ˈ····/ *adj* in utter confusion; all over the place
darülaceze /ˈ–····/ *n* poorhouse
dava /-ˈ-/ *n* lawsuit; trial; ~ **açmak** *bring a suit against
davacı /––ˈ·/ *n* plaintiff; claimant
davalı /––ˈ·/ *n* defendant
davar /·ˈ·/ *n* sheep *or* goat
davet /–ˈ·/ *n* invitation; ~ **etmek** call, invite; summon
davetiye /–··ˈ·/ *n* invitation card
davetli /–·ˈ·/ *n* invited guest
davranış /··ˈ·/ *n* behavior, attitude
davranmak /··ˈ·/ *v* behave; *take action
davul /·ˈ·/ *n* drum
dayak /·ˈ·/ *n* beating; ~ **atmak** *give a beating
dayamak /··ˈ·/ *v* prop up; *lean against
dayanak /··ˈ·/ *n* support, base
dayanıklı /···ˈ·/ *adj* lasting, enduring
dayanıksız /···ˈ·/ *adj* weak, not lasting
dayanılmaz /···ˈ·/ *adj* irresistible; unbearable
dayanışma /···ˈ·/ *n* solidarity
dayanışmak /···ˈ·/ *v* act with solidarity
dayanmak /··ˈ·/ *v* *lean on, push, press; *be based on
dayatmak /··ˈ·/ *v* insist
dayı /·ˈ·/ *n* (maternal) uncle
dazlak /·ˈ·/ *adj* bald
debdebe /··ˈ·/ *n* pomp, display
debriyaj /··ˈ·/ *n* clutch pedal
dede /·ˈ·/ *n* grandfather; old man
dedikodu /···ˈ·/ *n* rumor, gossip
defa /·ˈ–/ *n* time, turn; **birkaç** ~ on several occasions; **çok** ~ often
defetmek /ˈ···/ *v* repel, rebuff
defile /··ˈ·/ *n* fashion show
defin /·ˈ·/ *n* burial, internment
define /·–ˈ·/ *n* buried treasure, treasure
defnetmek /ˈ···/ *v* bury
defolmak /ˈ···/ *v* *go away; clear out
defter /·ˈ·/ *n* notebook; list; register
değer /·ˈ·/ *n* value; worth; price
değerlendirmek /····ˈ·/ *v* appraise, evaluate
değil /·ˈ·/ *adv* not; not only, let alone
değin /·ˈ·/ *prep* until
değinmek /··ˈ·/ *v* touch (on a subject)
değirmen /··ˈ·/ *n* mill
değiş /·ˈ·/ *n* exchange; ~ **tokuş** exchange, barter
değişik /··ˈ·/ *adj* changed; varied; different
değişiklik /···ˈ·/ *n* adjustment, alteration
değişim /··ˈ·/ *n* exchange; variation
değişken /··ˈ·/ *adj* changeable;

variable
değişmek /··ˈ·/ *v* change, alter, vary; substitute; exchange
değişmez /··ˈ·/ *adj* unchangeable, constant, immutable
değiştirmek /···ˈ·/ *v* change; exchange; alter
değmek /·ˈ·/ *v* touch; *hit, reach; *be worthwhile
değnek /·ˈ·/ *n* stick, rod, cane; **koltuk değneği** crutch
dehşet /·ˈ·/ *n* terror, horror, awe
dehşetli /··ˈ·/ *adj* terrible, horrible
dek *prep* until, as far as
dekor /·ˈ·/ *n* stage scenery, setting
delege /··ˈ·/ *n* delegate, representative
delgi /·ˈ·/ *n* drill, gimlet
deli /·ˈ·/ *adj* insane, crazy, mad
delik /·ˈ·/ *n* hole, opening; ~ **deşik** full of holes
delikanlı /·ˈ···/ *n* youth; young man
delikli /··ˈ·/ *adj* having holes
deliksiz /··ˈ·/ *adj* without a hole; ~ **uyku** sound sleep
delil /·ˈ·/ *n* evidence, proof
delilik /··ˈ·/ *n* insanity, mania; madness
delirmek /··ˈ·/ *v* *go mad
delmek /·ˈ·/ *v* *make a hole (in), pierce
demeç /·ˈ·/ *n* speech; statement
demek[1] /·ˈ·/ *v* *say; *tell; *mean
demek[2] /·ˈ·/ *adv* so, thus, therefore
demet /·ˈ·/ *n* bunch, bundle; sheaf
demin /ˈ··/ *adv* just now; a second ago
demir /·ˈ·/ *n* iron; anchor
demirci /··ˈ·/ *n* blacksmith
demirhane /·–ˈ·/ *n* ironworks
demirlemek /···ˈ·/ *v* anchor; bolt and bar; ~ **almak** raise anchor; ~ **atmak** *cast anchor
demiryolu /·ˈ···/ *n* railway
demode /··ˈ·/ *adj* old-fashioned, out-of-date
deneme /··ˈ·/ *n* essay; trial
denemek /··ˈ·/ *v* test, try, experiment; attempt
denetlemek /···ˈ·/ *v* check, control
deney /·ˈ·/ *n* experiment
deneyim /··ˈ·/ *n* experimentation, experience
deneysel /··ˈ·/ *adj* experimental
denge /·ˈ·/ *n* equilibrium
dengelemek /···ˈ·/ *v* balance
deniz /·ˈ·/ *n* sea; ~ **kazası** shipwreck
denizaltı /·ˈ···/ *n* submarine
denizanası /·ˈ····/ *n* jellyfish
denizaşırı /·ˈ····/ *adj* overseas
denizci /··ˈ·/ *n* sailor
denizcilik /···ˈ·/ *n* navigation
denizkızı /·ˈ···/ *n* mermaid, siren
denk *n* bale; *adj* equal; equivalent
denklem /·ˈ·/ *n* equation
denkleştirmek /···ˈ·/ *v* *bring into balance
depo /ˈ··/ *n* depot; warehouse, store
depozit /··ˈ·/ *n* deposit, advance payment
deprem /·ˈ·/ *n* earthquake
derbeder /··ˈ·/ *adj* vagrant; disorderly
dere /·ˈ·/ *n* stream
derece /··ˈ·/ *n* degree; rank; thermometer
dergi /·ˈ·/ *n* magazine, periodical
derhal /ˈ··/ *adv* at once, immediately
deri /·ˈ·/ *n* skin, hide; leather
derin /·ˈ·/ *adj* deep; profound
derinleşmek /···ˈ·/ *v* *get deep; specialize
derinlik /··ˈ·/ *n* depth; profundity
derleme /··ˈ·/ *n* collection
derlemek /··ˈ·/ *v* gather together;

collect
derli toplu /·ˈ· ··/ *adj* tidy; well coordinated; organized
derman /·ˈ·/ *n* cure; strength, energy
dermansız /··ˈ·/ *adj* exhausted, feeble
dernek /·ˈ·/ *n* association, society, club
ders *n* lesson, class, lecture; moral; ~ **çalışmak** study
dershane /·–ˈ·/ *n* classroom; specialized school
dert *n* pain, suffering; grief, trouble
dertleşmek /··ˈ·/ *v* *have a heart-to-heart talk
dertli /·ˈ·/ *adj* sorrowful, pained
derya /·ˈ–/ *n* sea, ocean
desen /·ˈ·/ *n* design; drawing
destan /·ˈ·/ *n* epic
deste /·ˈ·/ *n* bunch, bouquet; packet
destek /·ˈ·/ *n* prop, support
desteklemek /···ˈ·/ *v* support, prop up
detay /·ˈ·/ *n* detail
detaylı /··ˈ·/ *adj* detailed
dev *n* giant, ogre
deva /·ˈ–/ *n* remedy, medicine, cure
devam /·ˈ·/ *n* continuation; attendance; duration; ~ **etmek** continue, *go on; attend
devamlı /··ˈ·/ *adj* continuous, lasting; regular
devamsızlık /···ˈ·/ *n* absenteeism, lack of continuity
deve /·ˈ·/ *n* camel
devekuşu /·ˈ···/ *n* ostrich
devir /·ˈ·/ *n* period, epoch; cycle; rotation, transfer
devirli /··ˈ·/ *adj* periodic
devirmek /··ˈ·/ *v* knock down; overturn; *overthrow
devlet /·ˈ·/ *n* state, government; ~ **adamı** statesman; ~ **başkanı** president, head of state
devletlerarası /··ˈ····/ *adj* international
devletleştirmek /····ˈ·/ *v* nationalize
devralmak /ˈ···/ *v* *take over
devretmek /ˈ···/ *v* transfer, turn over
devrim /·ˈ·/ *n* reform, revolution
devrimci /··ˈ·/ *adj, n* revolutionary
devriye /··ˈ·/ *n* patrol, police round; ~ **gezmek** patrol
deyim /·ˈ·/ *n* idiom, phrase, expression
deyiş /·ˈ·/ *n* style of speech
dezenfektan /···ˈ·/ *n* disinfectant
dezenfekte /···ˈ·/ *adj* disinfected; ~ **etmek** disinfect
dış *n* outside, exterior; *adj* external; outer; foreign
dışadönük /·ˈ···/ *adj* extrovert
dışarı /··ˈ·/ *n* outside; exterior; ~ **gitmek** *go out, *go abroad; ~ **vurmak** *show; manifest
dışarıda /···ˈ·/ *adv* outside; abroad
dışarıya /···ˈ·/ *adv* out, outside; abroad
dışlamak /··ˈ·/ *v* exclude
Dicle /ˈ··/ Tigris River
diğer /ˈ··/ *adj* other; another
dik *adj* perpendicular; upright; vertical; steep; ~ **başlı** pig-headed, obstinate
dikdörtgen /··ˈ·/ *n* rectangle
diken /·ˈ·/ *n* thorn
dikenli /··ˈ·/ *adj* thorny; prickly
dikey /·ˈ·/ *adj* vertical, perpendicular
dikilitaş /··ˈ··/ *n* obelisk
dikilmek /··ˈ·/ *v* *be planted; *be erected

dikine /··ˈ·/ *adv* vertically
dikiş /·ˈ·/ *n* seam; stitch; sewing; ~ **makinesi** sewing machine; ~ **dikmek** sew
dikiz aynası /·ˈ· ···/ rear view mirror
dikkat /·ˈ·/ *n* attention; ~ **etmek** *pay attention, *be careful; **dikkate almak** *take into consideration
dikkatle /·ˈ··/ *adv* carefully
dikkatli /··ˈ·/ *adj* careful
dikkatsiz /··ˈ·/ *adj* careless
dikkatsizlik /···ˈ·/ *n* carelessness
dikmek /·ˈ·/ *v* *sew; stitch; plant; erect
diktafon /··ˈ·/ *n* dictaphone
diktatör /··ˈ·/ *n* dictator
dikte /·ˈ·/ *n* dictation; ~ **etmek** dictate
dil *n* tongue; language
dilek /·ˈ·/ *n* wish; desire; request; ~ **dilemek** *make a wish
dilekçe /··ˈ·/ *n* petition
dilemek /··ˈ·/ *v* wish, desire; request
dilenci /··ˈ·/ *n* beggar
dilenmek /··ˈ·/ *v* beg
dilim /·ˈ·/ *n* slice
dilimlemek /···ˈ·/ *v* slice
dillenmek /··ˈ·/ *v* *begin to talk; *become talkative
dilli /·ˈ·/ *adj* talkative
dilsiz /·ˈ·/ *adj* dumb, mute
dimağ /·ˈ·/ *n* brain, mind
din *n* religion; ~ **değiştirmek** convert
dinamo /·ˈ··/ *n* dynamo
dinç *adj* robust, vigorous
dindar /·ˈ·/ *adj* religious, pious
dini /–ˈ–/ *adj* religious
dinlemek /··ˈ·/ *v* listen to; obey
dinlenmek /··ˈ·/ *v* rest, relax; *be listened to
dinleyici /···ˈ·/ *n* listener
dinleyiciler /····ˈ·/ *pl* audience
dinmek /·ˈ·/ *v* stop, cease; calm down
dinsel /·ˈ·/ *adj* religious
dinsiz /·ˈ·/ *adj* atheistic, irreligious
dip *n* bottom; lowest part
diploma /ˈ···/ *n* diploma, certificate
dipnot /ˈ··/ *n* footnote
dipsiz /·ˈ·/ *adj* bottomless
direk /·ˈ·/ *n* pole, post
direksiyon /···ˈ·/ *n* steering wheel
direktif /··ˈ·/ *n* instruction, order
direnç /·ˈ·/ *n* resistance
direniş /··ˈ·/ *n* active opposition, resistance
direnmek /··ˈ·/ *v* insist, *hold out; resist
diretmek /··ˈ·/ *v* *be insistent
diri /·ˈ·/ *adj* alive; fresh; undercooked
diriliş /··ˈ·/ *n* revival
dirilmek /··ˈ·/ *v* return to life; *be revived
diriltmek /··ˈ·/ *v* *bring to life, revive
dirlik /·ˈ·/ *n* peace, affluence; ~ **düzenlik** peace and harmony
dirsek /·ˈ·/ *n* elbow; bend
diş *n* tooth; ~ **ağrısı** toothache; ~ **fırçası** toothbrush; ~ **macunu** toothpaste; ~ **tozu** tooth powder; ~ **çekmek** pull out a tooth
dişçi /·ˈ·/ *n* dentist
dişi /·ˈ·/ *adj, n* female
dişli /·ˈ·/ *n* cogwheel, gear
diyanet /·–ˈ·/ *n* piety; religion
diyar /·ˈ·/ *n* country, land
diyare /··ˈ·/ *n* diarrhea
diye /·ˈ·/ *adv* saying; thinking that, hoping that
diyet /·ˈ·/ *n* diet
diz *n* knee; ~ **çökmek** *kneel
dizgi /·ˈ·/ *n* composition,

typesetting
dizi /·ˈ·/ *n* line, row; series
dizin /·ˈ·/ *n* index
dizkapağı /ˈ····/ *n* kneecap
dizmek /·ˈ·/ *v* arrange in a row
doçent /·ˈ·/ *n* associate professor
doğa /·ˈ·/ *n* nature; **~ ötesi** metaphysical; **~ üstü** supernatural
doğal /·ˈ·/ *adj* natural; **~ olarak** naturally
doğan /·ˈ·/ *n* falcon, hawk
doğma /·ˈ·/ *adj* born; **~ büyüme** native, born and bred
doğmak /·ˈ·/ *v* *be born; *rise, *arise
doğrama /··ˈ·/ *n* woodwork
doğramacı /···ˈ·/ *n* carpenter
doğramak /··ˈ·/ *v* *cut into pieces; chop to bits
doğru /·ˈ·/ *adj* right, true; straight; honest; *adv* straight; correctly
doğruca /ˈ···/ *adv* directly
doğruluk /··ˈ·/ *n* honesty; straightness
doğu /·ˈ·/ *n* east; *adj* eastern
doğum /·ˈ·/ *n* birth; **~ günü** birthday; **~ sancısı** labor pains; **~ yapmak** *give birth
doğumevi /·ˈ···/ *n* maternity hospital
doğurgan /··ˈ·/ *adj* prolific, fecund
doğurmak /··ˈ·/ *v* *give birth to; *give rise to
doğuştan /··ˈ·/ *adj* innate; from birth
doksan /·ˈ·/ *num* ninety
doktor /·ˈ·/ *n* doctor; physician
doku /·ˈ·/ *n* tissue; texture
dokuma /··ˈ·/ *n* weaving; woven cloth
dokumacı /···ˈ·/ *n* weaver
dokumacılık /····ˈ·/ *n* textile industry
dokumak /··ˈ·/ *v* *weave
dokunaklı /···ˈ·/ *adj* touching, moving
dokunma /··ˈ·/ *n* sense of touch
dokunmak /··ˈ·/ *v* touch, *feel; affect; harm
dokunulmazlık /····ˈ·/ *v* immunity
dokuz /·ˈ·/ *num* nine
dokuzuncu /···ˈ·/ *num* ninth
doküman /··ˈ·/ *n* document
dolamak /··ˈ·/ *v* twist, *wind round
dolambaçlı /···ˈ·/ *adj* not straight-forward, circuitous
dolandırıcı /····ˈ·/ *n* crook, swindler
dolandırıcılık /·····ˈ·/ *n* fraud
dolandırmak /···ˈ·/ *v* cheat, swindle, nick
dolanmak /··ˈ·/ *v* *wind around; circulate; wander around
dolap /·ˈ·/ *n* cupboard; wardrobe; cabinet
dolaşık /··ˈ·/ *adj* intricate, confused, tangled
dolaşım /··ˈ·/ *n* circulation
dolaşmak /··ˈ·/ *v* *go around, wander
dolay /·ˈ·/ *n* surroundings; environment
dolayı /··ˈ·/ *adv* because of
dolayısıyla /···ˈ··/ *adv* consequently; on account of
dolaylı /··ˈ·/ *adj* indirect
dolaysız /··ˈ·/ *adj* direct
doldurmak /··ˈ·/ *v* fill; stuff; complete, fill in
dolgu /·ˈ·/ *v* filling; **~ yaptırmak** *have a tooth filled
dolgun /·ˈ·/ *adj* full; plump
dolmak /·ˈ·/ *v* *become full
dolmakalem /·ˈ···/ *n* fountain pen
dolmuş /·ˈ·/ *n* shared taxi
dolu[1] /·ˈ·/ *adj* full; charged; loaded
dolu[2] /·ˈ·/ *n* hail; **~ yağmak** hail
doludizgin /·ˈ···/ *adv* at full speed

dolunay /·'··/ *n* full moon
domuz /·'·/ *n* pig, swine; ~ **eti** pork; ~ **gibi** obstinate, pigheaded
don *n* frost; underpants
donakalmak /·'···/ *v* *be petrified with horror; *freeze
donanım /··'·/ *n* hardware
donanma /··'·/ *n* fleet, navy
donanmak /··'·/ *v* *be decked out; *be equipped
donatım /··'·/ *n* equipment
donatmak /··'·/ *v* deck out, ornament; equip
dondurma /··'·/ *n* ice cream
dondurmak /··'·/ *v* *freeze
donmak /·'·/ *v* *freeze; solidify
donuk /·'·/ *adj* dull; frozen
donuklaşmak /···'·/ *v* *become dull
doruk /·'·/ *n* summit
dosdoğru /'···/ *adv* straight ahead; absolutely right
dost *n* friend; lover, mistress; ~ **olmak** *become friends; ~ **edinmek** *make friends
dostça /'··/ *adj* friendly; *adv* in a friendly way
dostluk /·'·/ *n* friendship
dosya /'··/ *n* file, dossier
dosyalamak /'····/ *v* file
doyasıya /·'···/ *adv* as much as one can
doygun /·'·/ *adj* satiated, saturated
doygunluk /··'·/ *n* satiation
doyma /·'·/ *n* satiety; saturation
doymak /·'·/ *v* *be full up, *be satisfied
doymaz /·'·/ *adj* insatiable, greedy
doyum /·'·/ *n* satiety, satisfaction
doyurmak /··'·/ *v* fill, satisfy
doz *n* dose; **dozunu kaçırmak** *overdo
dökme /·'·/ *adj* cast; ~ **demir** cast iron
dökmek /·'·/ *v* pour, *spill; *cast
dökülmek /··'·/ *v* *be poured; *fall out
döküm/·'·/ *n* casting; breakdown
dökümhane /··–'·/ *n* foundry
döküntü /··'·/ *n* remains, remnants, debris
döl *n* seed, sperm; offspring
dölyatağı /'····/ *n* womb, uterus
döndürmek /··'·/ *v* turn round, *spin, rotate
dönek /·'·/ *adj* fickle, untrustworthy; renegade
dönem /·'·/ *n* period of time; term
dönemeç /··'·/ *n* bend, curve
dönemeçli /···'·/ *adj* winding
döner /·'·/ *adj* turning, revolving; ~ **kapı** revolving door; ~ **sermaye** working capital
dönme /·'·/ *n* rotation
dönmek /·'·/ *v* revolve, turn; return
dönüm /·'·/ *n* 1.000 square meters; turn, revolution; ~ **noktası** turning point
dönüş /·'·/ *n* return
dönüşmek /··'·/ *v* change; *be transformed
dönüşüm /··'·/ *n* transformation
dönüştürmek /···'·/ *v* transform
döpiyes /··'·/ *n* two-piece suit
dördüncü /··'·/ *num* fourth
dördüz /·'·/ *n* quadruplet
dört *num* four; **dörtte bir** a quarter
dörtnala /'···/ *adv* galloping; ~ **gitmek** *go at a gallop
dörtyol /'··/ *n* crossroads
döşek /·'·/ *n* mattress, bed
döşeme /··'·/ *n* floor; upholstery; furniture
döşemeci /···'·/ *n* upholsterer
döşemek /··'·/ *v* furnish; *lay down, *spread
döviz /·'·/ *n* foreign exchange;

placard; ~ **kuru** exchange rate
dövme /·ˈ·/ *n* tattoo; beating
dövmek /·ˈ·/ *v* *beat; hammer
dövünmek /··ˈ·/ *v* lament
dövüş /·ˈ·/ *n* fight
dövüşçü /··ˈ·/ *n* fighter
dövüşken /··ˈ·/ *adj* combative
dövüşmek /··ˈ·/ *v* *fight
dua /·ˈ–/ *n* prayer; ~ **etmek** pray
dudak /·ˈ·/ *n* lip; ~ **boyası** lipstick
dul *n* widow, widower; ~ **kalmak** *be widowed
duman /·ˈ·/ *n* smoke
durak /·ˈ·/ *n* stop; stopping place; pause
duraklamak /···ˈ·/ *v* pause
duraksamak /···ˈ·/ *v* hesitate
durdurmak /··ˈ·/ *v* stop
durgun /·ˈ·/ *adj* calm, stagnant
durgunlaşmak /···ˈ·/ *v* *get calm; *be dull
durgunluk /··ˈ·/ *n* calmness; stagnation
durmadan /ˈ···/ *adv* continually
durmak /·ˈ·/ *v* stop, cease
duru /·ˈ·/ *adj* clear, limpid
durulamak /···ˈ·/ *v* rinse
durulmak /··ˈ·/ *v* calm down; *become clear
durum /·ˈ·/ *n* condition, state; case; situation
duruş /·ˈ·/ *n* position, posture
duş *n* shower; ~ **yapmak** *take a shower
dut *n* mulberry
duvak /·ˈ·/ *n* bride's veil
duvar /·ˈ·/ *n* wall; ~ **kâğıdı** wallpaper
duyarlı /··ˈ·/ *adj* sensitive
duyarlılık /···ˈ·/ *n* sensitivity
duygu /·ˈ·/ *n* sense, sensation; feeling
duygulanmak /···ˈ·/ *v* *be affected; *be touched
duygusal /··ˈ·/ *adj* emotional, sentimental
duygusuz /··ˈ·/ *adj* insensitive
duymak /·ˈ·/ *v* *hear; *feel, sense
duyurmak /··ˈ·/ *v* announce
duyuru /··ˈ·/ *n* announcement
düdük /·ˈ·/ *n* whistle, pipe
düdüklü tencere /··ˈ· ···/ pressure cooker
düğme /·ˈ·/ *n* button; switch
düğmelemek /···ˈ·/ *v* button up
düğüm /·ˈ·/ *n* knot
düğümlemek /···ˈ·/ *v* knot
düğün /·ˈ·/ *n* wedding
dükkân /·ˈ·/ *n* shop, store
dümbelek /··ˈ·/ *n* small drum
dümdüz /ˈ··/ *adj* perfectly smooth; *adv* straight ahead
dümen /·ˈ·/ *n* rudder, helm
dümenci /··ˈ·/ *n* steersman, helmsman
dün *adv* yesterday
dünya /·ˈ–/ *n* world, earth; **dünyaca ünlü** world-famous; **dünyaya gelmek** *be born; ~ **çapında** worldwide; ~ **savaşı** world war
düpedüz /ˈ···/ *adv* openly, completely
dürbün /·ˈ·/ *n* binoculars; field glasses
dürmek /·ˈ·/ *v* roll up, fold
dürtmek /·ˈ·/ *v* prod, goad; stimulate; incite
dürtü /·ˈ·/ *n* drive, motive
dürüst /·ˈ·/ *adj* honest, straight
dürüstlük /··ˈ·/ *n* honesty, uprightness
düstur /·ˈ·/ *n* principle; norm, rule
düş *n* dream; ~ **görmek** *have a dream; ~ **kırıklığı** disappointment; ~ **kurmak** *daydream
düşkün /·ˈ·/ *adj* fallen, disgraced;

addicted to; devoted to
düşkünlük /··ˈ·/ *n* decay; excessive fondness *or* addiction
düşman /·ˈ·/ *n* enemy
düşmanca /·ˈ··/ *adv* in a hostile manner
düşmanlık /··ˈ·/ *n* enmity, hostility
düşmek /·ˈ·/ *v* *fall; decrease; *fall on hard times
düşük /·ˈ·/ *adj* fallen; drooping; low; *n* miscarriage
düşünce /··ˈ·/ *n* thought, idea
düşünceli /···ˈ·/ *adj* thoughtful; worried
düşüncesiz /···ˈ·/ *adj* careless, inconsiderate
düşündürücü /····ˈ·/ *adj* thought-provoking
düşünmek /··ˈ·/ *v* *think, consider
düşünür /··ˈ·/ *n* thinker
düşünüş /··ˈ·/ *n* way of thinking
düşürmek /··ˈ·/ *v* drop, *let fall; reduce
düşüş /·ˈ·/ *n* fall; decrease
düz *adj* smooth, flat; straight
düzelmek /··ˈ·/ *v* improve, *get better
düzeltme /··ˈ·/ *n* correction
düzeltmek /··ˈ·/ *v* improve; correct; straighten
düzen /·ˈ·/ *n* order; regularity
düzenbaz /··ˈ·/ *adj* tricky; *n* cheat
düzenlemek /···ˈ·/ *v* *put in order; organize; arrange
düzenli /··ˈ·/ *adj* in order, tidy; regular
düzensiz /··ˈ·/ *adj* irregular, untidy
düzey /·ˈ·/ *n* level
düzgün /·ˈ·/ *adj* smooth; level; tidy
düzine /·ˈ··/ *n* dozen
düzlem /·ˈ·/ *n* plane
düzlük /·ˈ·/ *n* plain
düzme /·ˈ·/ *adj* made-up, false, fake, sham
düzmek /·ˈ·/ *v* arrange, gather; compose; *make up; invent; prepare
düzyazı /ˈ···/ *n* prose

E

ebe /·ˈ·/ *n* midwife
ebedi /··ˈ–/ *adj* eternal
ebeveyn /··ˈ·/ *n* parents
ecel /·ˈ·/ *n* time of death; death
ecza /·ˈ–/ *n* drugs, chemicals
eczacı /·–ˈ·/ *n* pharmacist
eczane /·–ˈ·/ *n* pharmacy; drugstore *nAm;* chemist's *nBr*
edat /·ˈ·/ *n* particle; preposition; postposition
edebi /··ˈ–/ *adj* literary
ebebiyat /···ˈ·/ *n* literature
edep /·ˈ·/ *n* breeding, manners
edepli /··ˈ·/ *adj* well-behaved, polite
edepsiz /··ˈ·/ *adj* ill-mannered, rude
edepsizlik /···ˈ·/ *n* rudeness, shamelessness; ~ **etmek** misbehave
edilgen /··ˈ·/ *adj* passive
edinmek /··ˈ·/ *v* acquire, *get, obtain
editör /··ˈ·/ *n* editor
efendi /·ˈ··/*n* gentleman; master; *adj* polite; gentlemanly
eflatun /·–ˈ·/ *adj* lilac-colored
efsane /·–ˈ·/ *n* myth, legend
efsanevi /·–ˈ–/ *adj* mythical, legendary
Ege Denizi/ˈ·· ···/ Aegean Sea
egemen /··ˈ·/ *adj* sovereign, dominant
egemenlik /···ˈ·/ *n* domination
egoist /··ˈ·/ *adj* selfish

egzoz /·ˈ·/ *n* exhaust
eğe /·ˈ·/ *n* file
eğelemek /···ˈ·/ *v* file
eğer /ˈ··/ *adv* if
eğik /·ˈ·/ *adj* bent down; inclined
eğilim /··ˈ·/ *n* tendency; inclination
eğilmek /··ˈ·/ *v* *bend; bow; incline, *lean
eğim /·ˈ·/ *n* slope, declivity
eğirmek /··ˈ·/ *v* *spin
eğitici /···ˈ·/ *n* pedagogue; *adj* educational, instructive
eğitmek /··ˈ·/ *v* educate, train
eğitmen /··ˈ·/ *n* instructor, teacher
eğlence /··ˈ·/ *n* amusement, entertainment
eğlenceli /···ˈ·/ *adj* amusing, entertaining
eğlenmek /··ˈ·/ *v* *have a good time, enjoy oneself; mock
eğlenti /··ˈ·/ *n* party, feast
eğmek /·ˈ·/ *v* *bend, curve
eğri /·ˈ·/ *adj* crooked, bent
eğrilmek /··ˈ·/ *v* *become bent; incline
ehil /·ˈ·/ *n* qualified person; expert
ehli /·ˈ–/ *adj* domestic, tame
ehlileştirmek /–··ˈ·/ *v* domesticate, tame
ehliyet /··ˈ·/ *n* efficiency, capacity; driving license
ehliyetli /···ˈ·/ *adj* qualified
ehliyetsiz /···ˈ·/ *adj* incapable
ejder /·ˈ·/, **ejderha** /··ˈ–/ *n* dragon
ek *n* addition; appendix; sequel; supplement; extra; *adj* supplementary
ekim[1] /·ˈ·/ *n* planting, sowing
ekim[2] /·ˈ·/ October
ekin /·ˈ·/ *n* crop; growing grain; ~ **biçmek** reap, harvest
ekip /·ˈ·/ *n* team, crew, group
eklem /·ˈ·/ *n* joint
eklemek /··ˈ·/ *v* add; join together
ekmek /·ˈ·/ *n* bread; *v* sow
ekonomi /···ˈ·/ *n* economy; economics
ekonomik /···ˈ·/ *adj* economic; economical
ekran /·ˈ·/ *n* screen
eksen /·ˈ·/ *n* axis
ekseri /ˈ··–/ *adj* most
ekseriya /ˈ···–/ *adv* usually
eksi /·ˈ·/ *prep* minus; *adj* negative
eksik /·ˈ·/ *adj* lacking, missing; incomplete; *n* deficiency
eksiklik /··ˈ·/ *n* lack, deficiency
eksiksiz /··ˈ·/ *adj* complete; perfect
eksilmek /··ˈ·/ *v* decrease, *grow less
eksiltmek /··ˈ·/ *v* reduce, decrease
ekşi /·ˈ·/ *adj* sour, acid
ekşilik /··ˈ·/ *n* acidity
ekşimek /··ˈ·/ *v* turn sour; ferment
ekvator /··ˈ·/ *n* equator
Ekvator /··ˈ·/ Ecuador
el *n* hand; ~ **âlem** everybody; ~ **bileği** wrist; ~ **çantası** handbag; ~ **feneri** flashlight; ~ **freni** handbrake; **elden düşme** secondhand
ela /·ˈ–/ *adj* light brown (eyes)
elbette /ˈ···/ *adv* of course, certainly
elbirliği /ˈ····/ *n* cooperation
elbise /·–ˈ·/ *n* clothes, dress, suit; ~ **fırçası** clothes brush
elçi /·ˈ·/ *n* ambassador; envoy
elçilik /··ˈ·/ *n* embassy
eldiven /··ˈ·/ *n* glove
elek /·ˈ·/ *n* sieve
elektrik /··ˈ·/ *n* electricity; ~ **düğmesi** switch; ~ **kablosu** electric cord; ~ **kontağı** short circuit; ~ **santralı** power plant; ~ **süpürgesi** vacuum cleaner; ~ **tablosu** switchboard

elektrikli /···ˈ·/ *adj* electric; ~ **tıraş makinesi** electric razor
elem /·ˈ·/ *n* pain, sorrow
eleman /··ˈ·/ *n* staff, member, employee; element
eleme /··ˈ·/ *n* screening, sifting; elimination
elemek /··ˈ·/ *v* sieve, sift; eliminate
eleştiri /···ˈ·/ *n* criticism
eleştirici /····ˈ·/ *n* critic
eleştirmek /···ˈ·/ *v* criticize
eleştirmen /···ˈ·/ *n* critic
elkitabı /ˈ····/ *n* handbook
ellemek /··ˈ·/ *v* handle, *feel with the hand
elli /·ˈ·/ *num* fifty
elma /·ˈ·/ *n* apple
elmacık kemiği /··ˈ· ···/ cheekbone
elmas /·ˈ·/ *n* diamond
elti /·ˈ·/ *n* sister-in-law
elveda /··ˈ–/ farewell, good-by
elverişli /···ˈ·/ *adj* suitable; convenient
elverişsiz /···ˈ·/ *adj* inconvenient
elzem /·ˈ·/ *adj* most necessary; indispensable
emanet /·–ˈ·/ *n* anything entrusted to someone; deposit; ~ **bürosu** baggage deposit office *Am;* left luggage office *Br;* ~ **etmek** entrust, commit to another
emanetçi /·–ˈ·/ *n* depository
emaneten /·ˈ–··/ *adv* on deposit
emaye /··ˈ·/ *adj* enamelled; glazed
emek /·ˈ·/ *n* labor, work ; ~ **vermek** labor, work hard
emekçi /··ˈ·/ *n* worker
emeklemek /···ˈ·/ *v* *creep; crawl
emekli /··ˈ·/ *adj, n* retired
emel /·ˈ·/ *n* desire, wish; goal
emin /·ˈ·/ *adj* safe, secure; confident, sure; trustworthy; ~ **olmak** *be sure
emir /·ˈ·/ *n* order; command
emlak /·ˈ·/ *n* real estate; property
emmek /·ˈ·/ *v* suck; absorb
emniyet /··ˈ·/ *n* safety, security; confidence; ~ **kemeri** safety belt; ~ **etmek** trust
emniyetli /···ˈ·/ *adj* safe, secure; reliable
emniyetsiz /···ˈ·/ *adj* unsafe
emretmek /ˈ···/ *v* command, order
emsal /·ˈ·/ *n* equals, peers
emsalsiz /··ˈ·/ *adj* matchless, peerless
emzik /·ˈ·/ *n* nipple; pacifier; spout
emzirmek /··ˈ·/ *v* *breast-feed, nurse, suckle
en[1] *adv* most; ~ **aşağı,** ~ **az** at least, minimum; ~ **başından** from the very beginning; ~ **önce** first of all; ~ **son** final; ~ **sonra** last of all
en[2] *n* width, breadth; **enine** in width; **enine boyuna** fully; **eninde sonunda** eventually, in the end
ender /·ˈ·/ *adj* very rare; *adv* rarely
endişe /·–ˈ·/ *n* anxiety, worry
endişelenmek /·–··ˈ·/ *v* *be worried
endişeli /·–ˈ·/ *adj* anxious, troubled
endişesiz /·–ˈ·/ *adj* carefree, unworried
endüstri /··ˈ·/ *n* industry
endüstriyel /···ˈ·/ *adj* industrial
enerji /··ˈ·/ *n* energy, power
enerjik /··ˈ·/ *adj* energetic, forceful
enfes /·ˈ·/ *adj* delicious, delightful
engebe /··ˈ·/ *n* unevenness, rough country
engel /·ˈ·/ *n* obstacle, barrier
engellemek /···ˈ·/ *v* hinder, block; prevent
engin /·ˈ·/ *adj* open, vast,

boundless
enginar /··ˈ·/ *n* artichoke
enişte /·ˈ··/ *n* sister's *or* aunt's husband
enkaz /·ˈ·/ *n* ruins; wreckage; debris
enlem /·ˈ·/ *n* latitude
enli /·ˈ·/ *adj* wide, broad
ense /·ˈ·/ *n* nape, back of the neck
ensiz /·ˈ·/ *adj* narrow
entari /·–ˈ·/ *n* loose robe
entrika /·ˈ··/ *n* trick; intrigue; ~ **çevirmek** intrigue, plot
epey /ˈ··/, **epeyce** /ˈ···/ *adv* pretty well; fairly, considerably
er *n* male; brave man; private, soldier
erat /·ˈ·/ *n* privates, recruits
erdem /·ˈ·/ *n* virtue
erdemli /··ˈ·/ *adj* virtuous
er geç /ˈ·ˌ·/ *adv* sooner or later
ergen /·ˈ·/ *n* adolescent; youth of marriageable age
ergenlik /··ˈ·/ *n* youthful acne; adolescence
erginlik /··ˈ·/ *n* maturity
erik /·ˈ·/ *n* plum
eril /·ˈ·/ *adj* masculine
erimek /··ˈ·/ *v* melt; dissolve; thaw
erimez /··ˈ·/ *adj* insoluble
erir /·ˈ·/ *adj* soluble
erişkin /··ˈ·/ *adj* adult, mature
erişmek /··ˈ·/ *v* reach; attain
eritmek /··ˈ·/ *v* melt, dissolve
erkek /·ˈ·/ *n* man; *adj* male, manly; **erkekler tuvaleti** men's room
erken /·ˈ·/ *adv* early
ermek /·ˈ·/ *v* reach, attain
Ermeni /··ˈ·/ *n, adj* Armenian
ertelemek /···ˈ·/ *v* postpone, *put off
ertesi /··ˈ·/ *adj* next, following; ~ **gün** the following day
erzak /·ˈ·/ *n* provisions, stored food
esans /·ˈ·/ *n* perfume
esaret /·–ˈ·/ *n* slavery, captivity
esas /·ˈ·/ *n* foundation, base; principle; *adj* principal, basic; ~ **itibarıyla** in principle
esasen /·ˈ–·/ *adv* essentially; anyhow
esaslı /··ˈ·/ *adj* sound, solid; fundamental
esef /·ˈ·/ *n* regret; ~ **etmek** *be sorry
esefle /·ˈ··/ *adv* regretfully
esen /·ˈ·/ *adj* healthy, sound
esenlik /··ˈ·/ *n* health, soundness
eser /·ˈ·/ *n* work of art, written work
esin /·ˈ·/ *n* inspiration
esinlenmek /···ˈ·/ *v* *be inspired
esinti /··ˈ·/ *n* breeze
esir /·ˈ·/ *n* slave; captive; ~ **düşmek** *be taken prisoner
esirgemek /···ˈ·/ *v* spare, protect
eski /·ˈ·/ *adj* old, ancient; secondhand; worn out; former; ~ **moda** old-fashioned; ~ **zaman** antiquity
eskici /··ˈ·/ *n* secondhand dealer
eskiçağ /·ˈ··/ *n* prehistoric period
eskiden /··ˈ·/ *adv* formerly
eskimek /··ˈ·/ *v* *wear out, *get old in service
eskitmek /··ˈ·/ *v* *wear out; cause to grow old
eskrim /·ˈ·/ *n* fencing; ~ **yapmak** fence
esmek /·ˈ·/ *v* *blow
esmer /·ˈ·/ *adj* dark; *n* brunette
esnaf /·ˈ·/ *n* tradesman
esnek /·ˈ·/ *adj* flexible
esneklik /··ˈ·/ *n* elasticity
esnemek /··ˈ·/ *v* yawn; stretch; *bend

espri /·ˈ·/ *n* wit, joke
esprili /··ˈ·/ *adj* witty
esrar[1] /·ˈ·/ *n* mystery
esrar[2] /·ˈ·/ *n* hashish
esrarengiz /·–ˈ·/ *adj* mysterious
esrarlı /··ˈ·/ *adj* mysterious
eş *n* one of a pair; mate; husband, wife
eşanlamlı /ˈ····/ *adj* synonymous
eşantiyon /···ˈ·/ *n* sample
eşarp /·ˈ·/ *n* scarf
eşcinsel /ˈ···/ *n* homosexual
eşdeğerli /ˈ····/ *adj* equivalent
eşek /·ˈ·/ *n* donkey
eşekarısı /·ˈ····/ *n* wasp, hornet
eşik /·ˈ·/ *n* threshold
eşit /·ˈ·/ *adj* equal
eşitlemek /···ˈ·/ *v* equalize
eşitlik /··ˈ·/ *n* equality
eşkıya /··ˈ–/ *n* bandit, brigand
eşlik /·ˈ·/ *n* accompaniment; ~ **etmek** accompany, escort
eşmek /·ˈ·/ *v* *dig up, scratch
eşofman /··ˈ·/ *n* tracksuit
eşsiz /·ˈ·/ *adj* matchless, unique
eşya /·ˈ–/ *n* furniture; belongings; goods; objects
et *n* meat; flesh
etajer /··ˈ·/ *n* dresser
etek /·ˈ·/ *n* skirt
eteklik /··ˈ·/ *n* skirt
Eti /ˈ··/ *adj, n* Hittite
etiket /··ˈ·/ *n* label, ticket, sticker
etken /·ˈ·/ *n* agent, factor; *adj* active, effective
etki /·ˈ·/ *n* effect, influence
etkilemek /···ˈ·/ *v* effect, influence
etkili /··ˈ·/ *adj* effective
etkin /·ˈ·/ *adj* active, effective
etkinlik /··ˈ·/ *n* activity, effectiveness
etkisiz /··ˈ·/ *adj* ineffective
etmek /·ˈ·/ *v* *do; *make; *be worth
etmen /·ˈ·/ *n* factor
etraf /·ˈ·/ *n* sides; surroundings
etrafında /·–ˈ·/ *prep* around; round
etraflı /··ˈ·/ *adj* detailed
etüt /·ˈ·/ *n* study, research; ~ **etmek** study
ev *n* house; home, household; ~ **halkı** household; ~ **idaresi** housekeeping; ~ **işi** housework; ~ **kadını** housewife
evcil /·ˈ·/ *adj* domesticated, tame
evcilleştirmek /····ˈ·/ *v* domesticate
evcimen /··ˈ·/ *adj* domestic
evet /ˈ··/ yes
evham /·ˈ·/ *n* apprehensions, doubts
evhamlı /··ˈ·/ *adj* hypochondriac
evlat /·ˈ·/ *n* child; ~ **edinmek** adopt a child
evlatlık /··ˈ·/ *n* adopted child
evlenme /··ˈ·/ *n* marriage
evlenmek /··ˈ·/ *v* *get married, marry
evli /·ˈ·/ *adj* married
evliya /··ˈ–/ *n* Muslim saint
evrak /·ˈ·/ *n* documents, papers
evren /·ˈ·/ *n* universe; cosmos
evrensel /··ˈ·/ *adj* universal
evrim /·ˈ·/ *n* evolution
evrimsel /··ˈ·/ *adj* evolutionary
evvel /·ˈ·/ *adv* first; before, ago, earlier
evvela /ˈ··–/ *adv* firstly; to begin with
evvelce /·ˈ··/ *adv* previously
evvelden /··ˈ·/ *adv* beforehand
evvelki /··ˈ·/ *adj* former; previous
eyalet /·–ˈ·/ *n* province; State *nAm*
eyer /·ˈ·/ *n* saddle
eylem /·ˈ·/ *n* action; operation
eylemek /··ˈ·/ *v* *make, *do
eylül /·ˈ·/ September

ezberlemek /···'·/ *v* memorize
ezel /·'·/ *n* past eternity
ezeli /··'–/ *adj* eternal
ezgi /·'·/ *n* tune, melody
ezici /··'·/ *adj* crushing
ezik /·'·/ *adj* crushed; bruised; squashed
ezilmek /··'·/ *v* *be crushed
eziyet /··'·/ *n* torture, torment, suffering
ezmek /·'·/ *v* crush; mash; suppress

F

faal /·'·/ *adj* active
faaliyet /·–'·/ *n* activity
fabrika /·'··/ *n* factory, plant
fabrikatör /···'·/ *n* factory owner
facia /–'·/ *n* calamity; tragedy
fahişe /–'·/ *n* prostitute, whore
faiz /–'·/ *n* interest; ~ **oranı** rate of interest
fakat /'··/ *conj* but, however
fakir /·'·/ *adj* poor; *n* poor fellow
fakirleşmek /···'·/ *v* *become poor
fakirlik /··'·/ *n* poverty
fakülte /·'··/ *n* faculty
fal *n* fortunetelling, soothsaying; ~ **bakmak** *tell fortunes
falan /·'·/ *adv* so-and-so; and such; and such like
falcı /·'·/ *n* fortuneteller
falcılık /··'·/ *n* fortunetelling
fanatik /··'·/ *adj* fanatical
fanila /·'··/ *n* flannel
far *n* headlight
faraza /'·–/ *adv* supposing, let us suppose
fare /–'·/ *n* mouse
fark *n* difference; discrimination; ~ **etmek** distinguish; notice
farklı /·'·/ *adj* different
farklılık /··'·/ *n* difference
farksız /·'·/ *adj* same
farz *n* obligatory act; hypothesis; ~ **etmek** suppose
Fas Morocco
fasıl /·'·/ *n* chapter, section
fasıla /–'·/ *n* interval; interruption
Faslı /·'·/ *adj, n* Moroccan
fasulye /·'··/ *n* bean
faşist /·'·/ *n* fascist
faşizm /·'·/ *n* fascism
fatih /–'·/ *n* conqueror
fatura /·'··/ *n* invoice, bill
favori /··'·/ *n* sideburns, whiskers; *adj* favorite
fayans /·'·/ *n* wall tiling, faience
fayda /·'·/ *n* profit; use; advantage
faydalanmak /···'·/ *v* *make use of
faydalı /··'·/ *adj* useful
faydasız /··'·/ *adj* useless
fazilet /·–'·/ *n* virtue; merit
faziletli /·–'·/ *adj* virtuous
fazla /·'·/ *adj* extra; more; *adv* too much; ~ **gelmek** *be too much; ~ **mesai** overtime
fazlalaşmak /···'·/ *v* increase
fazlalık /··'·/ *n* excess; superfluity
fazlasıyla /··'··/ *adv* amply
feci /·'–/ *adj* terrible
feda /·'–/ *n* sacrifice; ~ **etmek** sacrifice
fedakâr /·–'·/ *adj* self-sacrificing
fedakârlık /·–'·/ *n* sacrifice, devotion
felaket /·–'·/ *n* disaster, calamity
felç *n* paralysis; **felce uğramak** *be paralyzed
felçli /·'·/ *adj* paralyzed
fen *n* science
fena /·'–/ *adj* bad; ill; ~ **halde** badly; ~ **olmak** *feel bad
fenalaşmak /·–'·/ *v* *grow worse
fenalık /·–'·/ *n* mischief; harm; ~ **etmek** harm; ~ **gelmek** faint

fener /·ˈ·/ *n* lantern; lighthouse
fenni /·ˈ–/ *adj* scientific
ferah /·ˈ·/ *adj* spacious, roomy
ferahlamak /···ˈ·/ *v* *feel relieved; *become spacious
ferahlık /··ˈ·/ *n* relief; roominess
fermuar /··ˈ·/ *n* zipper
fert *n* person, individual; member
fesat /·ˈ·/ *n* malice, mischief
feshetmek /ˈ···/ *v* abolish, cancel
fethetmek /ˈ···/ *v* conquer
fetih /·ˈ·/ *n* conquest
fevkalade /ˈ··–·/ *adj* extraordinary; excellent
fevkaladelik /ˈ··–··/ *n* singularity; peculiarity
fıçı /·ˈ·/ *n* barrel; tub
fıkra /·ˈ·/ *n* anecdote; newspaper article
fındık /·ˈ·/ *n* hazelnut
Fırat /ˈ··/ Euphrates River
fırça /·ˈ·/ *n* brush
fırçalamak /···ˈ·/ *v* brush
fırın /·ˈ·/ *n* oven; furnace
fırıncı /··ˈ·/ *n* baker
fırlamak /··ˈ·/ *v* *fly out; *leap up; rush
fırlatmak /··ˈ·/ *v* launch; hurl
fırsat /·ˈ·/ *n* opportunity
fırtına /·ˈ··/ *n* storm, tempest
fırtınalı /·ˈ···/ *adj* stormy
fısıldamak /···ˈ·/ *v* whisper
fısıltı /··ˈ·/ *n* whisper
fıskıye /··ˈ·/ *n* jet, fountain
fıstık /·ˈ·/ *n* peanut, pistachio nut
fışkırmak /··ˈ·/ *v* gush out; *burst forth
fıtık /·ˈ·/ *n* hernia, rupture
fidan /·ˈ·/ *n* sapling, shoot
fide /ˈ··/ *n* seedling
fidye /·ˈ·/ *n* ransom
figüran /··ˈ·/ *n* walk-on; extra
fihrist /·ˈ·/ *n* index
fiil /·ˈ·/ *n* act, action; verb
fikir /·ˈ·/ *n* thought; idea; opinion
fil *n* elephant
fildişi /ˈ···/ *n* ivory
file /·ˈ·/ *n* net
Filipin /·ˈ··/ *adj* Philippine
Filipinler /·ˈ···/ Philippines
Filipinli /·ˈ···/ *n* Filipino
Filistin /·ˈ··/ Palestine
Filistinli /·ˈ···/ *n, adj* Palestinian
filiz /·ˈ·/ *n* young shoot; bud
film *n* film; movie; ~ **çekmek** film; X-ray; ~ **çevirmek** *make a movie; ~ **makinesi** movie camera
filo /ˈ··/ *n* fleet
filozof /··ˈ·/ *n* philosopher
filtre /ˈ··/ *n* filter
Fin *n* Finn
finans /·ˈ·/ *n* finance
finansal /··ˈ·/ *adj* financial
fincan /·ˈ·/ *n* cup
Fince /ˈ··/ *n* Finnish language
Finlandiya /·ˈ···/ Finland
firkete /·ˈ··/ *n* hairpin
firma /ˈ··/ *n* firm
fiş *n* plug; card, slip; counter, chip
fişek /·ˈ·/ *n* cartridge; rocket
fişlemek /··ˈ·/ *v* *make a card index
fitil /·ˈ·/ *n* wick; fuse; suppository
fiyasko /·ˈ··/ *n* failure, fiasco
fiyat /·ˈ·/ *n* price
fiyonk /·ˈ·/ *n* bowknot
fizik /·ˈ·/ *n* physics
fizikçi /··ˈ·/ *n* physicist
fiziksel /··ˈ·/ *adj* physical
fizyoloji /···ˈ·/ *n* physiology
flört *n* flirt; ~ **etmek** flirt
flüt *n* flute
fok *n* seal
fokurdamak /···ˈ·/ *v* boil up, bubble noisily
fon *n* fund, asset; background
fonetik /··ˈ·/ *adj* phonetic

fonksiyon /..'./ *n* function
forma /'../ *n* uniform; colors; form
formalite /..'../ *n* formality
formül /.'./ *n* formula; form
fosfor /.'./ *n* phosphorus
fotoğraf /..'./ *n* photograph; ~ **çekmek** *take a photograph
fotoğrafçı /...'./ *n* photographer
fotoğrafçılık /....'./ *n* photography
fötr *n* felt
francala /'.../ *n* fine white bread
frank *n* Franc
Fransa /'../ France
Fransız /'../ *adj* French; *n* Frenchman
Fransızca /.'../ *n* French language
frekans /.'./ *n* frequency
fren *n* brake; ~ **yapmak** brake
Frenk *adj* European
frenlemek /...'./ *v* brake; *hold back; restrain
fresk *n* fresco; wall-painting
fuar /.'./ *n* fair
fukara /..'–/ *adj* poor
fukaralık /..–'./ *n* poverty
fulya /'../ *n* jonguil
funda /.'./ *n* heath
fundalık /...'./ *n* shrubbery
futbol /'../ *n* football, soccer; ~ **sahası** football field; ~ **takımı** football team
fuzuli /–'–/ *adj* unneccessary
füze /'../ *n* rocket, missile

G

gaddar /.'./ *adj* cruel, pitiless
gaddarlık /..'./ *n* cruelty
gaf *n* blunder, gaffe; ~ **yapmak** blunder
gafil /–'./ *adj* unaware, inattentive; ~ **avlamak** *catch unawares
gaflet /.'./ *n* inattention, heedlessness
gaga /.'./ *n* beak, bill
galeri /..'./ *n* art gallery; gallery
galeta /.'../ *n* dried bread stick
galiba /'––/ *adv* probably, presumably
galibiyet /–...'./ *n* victory
galip /–'./ *n* victor, winner; *adj* victorious; ~ **gelmek** *win; *be victorious
gam *n* grief, care, worry
gamlı /.'./ *adj* worried, sorrowful
gamze /.'./ *n* dimple
gar *n* station
garaj /.'./ *n* garage
garanti /..'./ *n* guarantee; ~ **etmek** guarantee
garantilemek /....'./ *v* guarantee
garantili /...'./ *adj* guaranteed
garantör /..'./ *n* guarantor
gardırop /..'./ *n* wardrobe
gardiyan /..'./ *n* prison guard
garez /.'./ *n* rancor, grudge
gargara /.'../ *n* gargling; gargle; ~ **yapmak** gargle
garip /.'./ *adj* queer, strange; poor; lonely
garipsemek /...'./ *v* *find strange
garson /.'./ *n* waiter
gasp /.'./ *n* extortion; usurpation
gaspetmek /'.../ *v* usurp; extort
gaye /–'./ *n* aim, goal, object
gayet /'–./ *adv* very, extremely, quite
gayret /.'./ *n* effort, energy; ~ **etmek** try hard, *do one's best
gayretli /..'./ *adj* persevering, zealous
gayrı /'../ *adv* henceforth; finally, other than
gayri /'../ *negative particle* ~ **meşru** illegitimate; ~ **resmi** unofficial; ~ **sâfi** gross
gaz *n* kerosene; gas; ~ **lambası**

kerosene lamp; ~ **ocağı** gas cooker; ~ **pedalı** accelerator; ~ **sobası** gas stove
gazap /·ˈ·/ *n* wrath, fury
gazete /·ˈ··/ *n* newspaper
gazeteci /·ˈ···/ *n* journalist
gazetecilik /·ˈ····/ *n* journalism
gazi /–ˈ–/ *n* war veteran
gazino /·ˈ··/ *n* large coffeehouse, restaurant; nightclub
gazlı /·ˈ·/ *adj* gaseous
gazoz /·ˈ·/ *n* soda, fizzy lemonade
gazyağı /ˈ···/ *n* kerosene
gebe /·ˈ·/ *adj* pregnant
gece /·ˈ·/ *n* night; **bu** ~ tonight; ~ **kremi** night cream; ~ **kulübü** nightclub; ~ **tarifesi** night rate; ~ **treni** night train; ~ **uçuşu** night flight; ~ **yarısı** midnight
gecelemek /···ˈ·/ *v* *spend the night
geceleyin /·ˈ···/ *adv* by night
gecelik /··ˈ·/ *n* nightdress, nightgown
gecikme /··ˈ·/ *n* delay
gecikmek /··ˈ·/ *v* *be late; *be delayed
geciktirmek /···ˈ·/ *v* delay, postpone
geç *adj* late; ~ **kalmak** *be late
geçen /·ˈ·/ *adj* past; last; ~ **gün** the other day; ~ **sefer** last time
geçenlerde /···ˈ·/ *adv* lately, recently
geçer /·ˈ·/ *adj* current; valid
geçerli /··ˈ·/ *adj* current; valid
geçersiz /··ˈ·/ *adj* invalid, null
geçici /··ˈ·/ *adj* passing, temporary
geçim /·ˈ·/ *n* living, livelihood
geçimsiz /··ˈ·/ *adj* difficult, quarrelsome
geçindirmek /···ˈ·/ *v* support, sustain
geçirmek /··ˈ·/ *v* *make pass, *let pass; *go through; *get over
geçiş /·ˈ·/ *n* transition; passing
geçit /·ˈ·/ *n* passage; mountain pass; ~ **töreni** parade
geçkin /·ˈ·/ *adj* elderly; overripe
geçmek /·ˈ·/ *v* pass; exceed
gedik /·ˈ·/ *n* breach, gap
gelecek /··ˈ·/ *adj* coming, next; *n* future
gelenek /··ˈ·/ *n* tradition
geleneksel /···ˈ·/ *adj* traditional
gelgit /·ˈ·/ *n* tide
gelin /·ˈ·/ *n* bride; daughter-in-law
gelincik /··ˈ·/ *n* poppy
gelinlik /··ˈ·/ *n* wedding dress
gelir /·ˈ·/ *n* income, revenue; ~ **vergisi** income tax
geliş /·ˈ·/ *n* arrival
gelişigüzel /····ˈ·/ *adv* by chance, at random; casually
gelişim /··ˈ·/ *n* development, progress
gelişmek /··ˈ·/ *v* *grow up; mature; develop
geliştirmek /···ˈ·/ *v* improve, develop
gelmek /·ˈ·/ *v* *come; arrive
gemi /·ˈ·/ *n* ship, vessel, boat
gemici /··ˈ·/ *n* sailor
gemicilik /···ˈ·/ *n* navigation; seamanship
genç *adj* young, youthful; *n* young man
gençleşmek /··ˈ·/ *v* *become youthful; *be rejuvenated
gençleştirmek /···ˈ·/ *v* rejuvenate
gene /ˈ··/ *adv* again
genel /·ˈ·/ *adj* general; ~ **olarak** in general
genelev /·ˈ··/ *n* brothel
genelge /··ˈ·/ *n* circular, notice
genellikle /··ˈ··/ *adv* generally, in general
general /··ˈ·/ *n* general
geniş /·ˈ·/ *adj* broad, wide;

extensive; vast; ~ **fikirli** broad-minded; ~ **ölçüde** on a large scale
genişlemek /···ˈ·/ *v* widen, expand; broaden
genişlik /··ˈ·/ *n* wideness, width; extensiveness
geometri /··ˈ··/ *n* geometry
gerçek /·ˈ·/ *adj* real, true; *n* reality, truth, fact
gerçekçi /··ˈ·/ *adj* realistic
gerçekçilik /···ˈ·/ *n* realism
gerçekdışı /·ˈ···/ *adj* unreal
gerçekleşmek /···ˈ·/ *v* *become true; *be realized
gerçekleştirmek /····ˈ·/ *v* realize
gerçekten /ˈ···/ *adv* in fact, indeed
gerçi /ˈ··/ *conj* though, although
gerdan /·ˈ·/ *n* neck, throat; double chin
gerdanlık /··ˈ·/ *n* necklace
gereç /·ˈ·/ *n* materials; equipment
gereğince /··ˈ··/ *adv* in accordance with, as required
gerek[1] /·ˈ·/ *conj* whether . . . or . . . ; both . . . and . . .
gerek[2] /·ˈ·/ *adj* necessary; *n* necessity
gerekli /··ˈ·/ *adj* required, necessary
gerekmek /··ˈ·/ *v* *be necessary
gereksinim /···ˈ·/ *n* need
gereksinmek /···ˈ·/ *v* consider necessary
gereksiz /··ˈ·/ *adj* unnecessary
gergedan /··ˈ·/ *n* rhinoceros
gergin /·ˈ·/ *adj* stretched, tight; tense
gerginleşmek /···ˈ·/ *v* *become tense
gerginlik /··ˈ·/ *n* tightness, tension, strain
geri /·ˈ·/ *n* the back; remainder; *adv* backward; *adj* back; backward; rear; ~ **dönmek** *come back, return; ~ **getirmek** *bring back; ~ **göndermek** *send back; ~ **vermek** *give back
gerilemek /···ˈ·/ *v* *draw back, recede
gerilim /··ˈ·/ *n* tension
gerinmek /··ˈ·/ *v* stretch oneself
germek /·ˈ·/ *v* stretch, tighten
getirmek /··ˈ·/ *v* *bring
getirtmek /··ˈ·/ *v* *send for; order
geveze /··ˈ·/ *adj* talkative, chattering; *n* chatterbox
gevezelik /···ˈ·/ *n* chattering; gossip; ~ **etmek** babble, chatter
gevrek /·ˈ·/ *adj* crisp
gevşek /·ˈ·/ *adj* loose, slack
gevşeklik /··ˈ·/ *n* slackness
gevşemek /··ˈ·/ *v* *become loose; slacken; relax
gevşetmek /··ˈ·/ *v* loosen
geyik /·ˈ·/ *n* deer
gezdirmek /··ˈ·/ *v* *take someone for a walk, *show around
gezegen /··ˈ·/ *n* planet
gezgin /·ˈ·/ *n* tourist, traveler
gezi /·ˈ·/ *n* excursion, trip
gezici /··ˈ·/ *adj* itinerant
gezinmek /··ˈ·/ *v* wander about
gezinti /··ˈ·/ *n* walk, stroll
gezmek /·ˈ·/ *v* *go about, walk about; *go places; travel
gıcırdamak /···ˈ·/ *v* creak
gıda /·ˈ–/ *n* food, nourishment
gıdıklamak /···ˈ·/ *v* tickle
gıpta /·ˈ·/ *n* envy without malice; ~ **etmek** envy
gırtlak /·ˈ·/ *n* throat
gibi /·ˈ·/ *adv* such as, like; almost, nearly
gider /·ˈ·/ *n* expense, expenditure
giderek /·ˈ··/ *adv* gradually
gidermek /··ˈ·/ *v* remove, eliminate

gidiş /·ˈ·/ *n* departure; going; ~ **dönüş** round trip
gidişat /·–ˈ·/ *n* goings-on; situation
girdap /·ˈ·/ *n* whirlpool
girdi /·ˈ·/ *n* input
giriş /·ˈ·/ *n* entry, entrance; introduction; ~ **ücreti** entrance fee
girişim /··ˈ·/ *n* enterprise
girişimci /···ˈ·/ *n* entrepreneur
girişken /··ˈ·/ *adj* enterprising
girişmek /··ˈ·/ *v* attempt; *undertake
girmek /·ˈ·/ *v* *come in, enter; **girilmez** no entry
gişe /ˈ··/ *n* box-office
gitgide /ˈ···/ *adv* as time goes on
gitmek /·ˈ·/ *v* *go; *go away
giydirmek /··ˈ·/ *v* dress, clothe
giyecek /··ˈ·/ *n* clothes, dress
giyim /·ˈ·/ *n* clothing, dress
giyimli /··ˈ·/ *adj* dressed
giyinmek /··ˈ·/ *v* dress oneself
giymek /·ˈ·/ *v* *put on, *wear
giysi /·ˈ·/ *n* clothing, garment
gizlemek /··ˈ·/ *v* *hide, conceal
gizli /·ˈ·/ *adj* hidden, secret, confidential; ~ **kapaklı** clandestine; ~ **tutmak** *hide, *keep secret
gizlice /·ˈ··/ *adv* secretly
gizlilik /··ˈ·/ *n* secrecy
gol *n* goal; ~ **atmak** score a goal
golf *n* golf
gonca /·ˈ·/ *n* bud
gondol /·ˈ·/ *n* gondola
göbek /·ˈ·/ *n* navel; belly; center; generation; ~ **atmak** dance the belly dance
göç *n* migration, immigration; ~ **etmek** migrate, immigrate
göçebe /·ˈ··/ *n* nomad; *adj* nomadic
göçebelik /·ˈ···/ *n* nomadism
göçmek /·ˈ·/ *v* immigrate, migrate; *fall down, cave in
göçmen /·ˈ·/ *n* immigrant, settler
göğüs /·ˈ·/ *n* chest, breast; bosom; ~ **germek** face; **göğsü kabarmak** *swell with pride
gök *n* sky; ~ **gürültüsü** thunder; ~ **mavisi** sky blue; **göklere çıkarmak** exalt, extol
gökdelen /··ˈ·/ *n* skyscraper
gökkuşağı /ˈ····/ *n* rainbow
göktaşı /ˈ···/ *n* meteor
gökyüzü /ˈ···/ *n* sky
göl *n* lake
gölet /·ˈ·/ *n* pool, puddle
gölge /·ˈ·/ *n* shadow, shade; **gölgede kalmak** *keep in the background
gölgelemek /···ˈ·/ *v* overshadow
gölgeli /··ˈ·/ *adj* shadowy
gölgelik /··ˈ·/ *n* shady spot
gömlek /·ˈ·/ *n* shirt
gömlekçi /··ˈ·/ *n* shirt maker *or* seller
gömme /·ˈ·/ *n* burial; *adj* embedded; inlaid
gömmek /·ˈ·/ *v* bury
gömülmek /··ˈ·/ *v* *be buried; *sink deeply
gömülü /··ˈ·/ *adj* buried; sunk
gönderme /··ˈ·/ *n* sending; reference
göndermek /··ˈ·/ *v* *send, dispatch; refer
gönül /·ˈ·/ *n* heart, feelings; inclination, desire; ~ **kırmak** *hurt the feelings; ~ **vermek** *give one's heart, *fall in love; **gönlünü almak** placate; please
gönüllü /··ˈ·/ *n* volunteer; *adj* willing
gönülsüz /··ˈ·/ *adj* unwilling
göre /·ˈ·/ *adv* according to
görenek /··ˈ·/ *n* custom; usage

görev /·'·/ *n* duty; function
görevlendirmek /····'·/ *v* *give work to someone
görevli /··'·/ *adj* in charge; *n* employee, official
görgü /·'·/ *n* experience, good manners; ~ **kuralları** rules of good manners; ~ **tanığı** eyewitness
görgülü /··'·/ *adj* having good manners
görgüsüz /··'·/ *adj* ill-bred
görkem /·'·/ *n* splendor, magnificence
görkemli /··'·/ *adj* majestic, splendid, magnificent
görme /·'·/ *n* sight, vision
görmek /·'·/ *v* *see; notice; consider; *understand; **görmüş geçirmiş** experienced
görmez /·'·/ *adj* blind, unseeing; **görmezlikten gelmek** pretend not to see
görsel /·'·/ *adj* visual
görücü /··'·/ *n* woman sent to find a prospective bride
görümce /·'··/ *n* husband's sister
görünmek /··'·/ *v* *show oneself, *be visible; appear, seem
görünmez /··'·/ *adj* invisible
görüntü /··'·/ *n* phantom; image
görünüm /··'·/ *n* appearance
görünüş /··'·/ *n* appearance, sight; external view; aspect
görüş /·'·/ *n* sight, view; opinion; ~ **açısı** point of view
görüşme /··'·/ *n* interview; negotiation; meeting; conversation
görüşmek /··'·/ *v* *meet; converse; confer with; *have an interview
gösterge /··'·/ *n* indicator; gauge
göstermek /··'·/ *v* *show, display; indicate
gösteri /··'·/ *n* show; demonstration; ~ **yapmak** demonstrate
götürmek /··'·/ *v* *take away; *lead; carry off; accompany
gövde /·'·/ *n* body, trunk
göz *n* eye; drawer; cell; ~ **doktoru** oculist; ~ **kamaştırmak** dazzle; ~ **kırpmak** blink, wink; ~ **korkutma** threat
gözaltı /'···/ *n* custody
gözbebeği /'····/ *n* pupil of the eye; apple of the eye
gözcü /·'·/ *n* watchman
gözdağı /'···/ *n* intimidation; ~ **vermek** intimidate
gözde /·'·/ *adj* favorite
gözenek /··'·/ *n* pore
gözetim /··'·/ *n* supervision; watch, care
gözetleme /···'·/ *n* watching, observation
gözetlemek /···'·/ *v* observe secretly, peep
gözetme /··'·/ *n* protection
gözetmek /··'·/ *v* *take care, protect
gözkapağı /'····/ *n* eyelid
gözlem /·'·/ *n* observation
gözlemek /··'·/ *v* watch for; wait for
gözlemevi /·'···/ *n* observatory
gözleyici /···'·/ *n* observer
gözlük /·'·/ *n* spectacles, glasses
gözlükçü /··'·/ *n* optician
gözükmek /··'·/ *v* *be seen; *show oneself
gözyaşı /'···/ *n* tear
grafik /·'·/ *n* graph, diagram; graphics
grafiker /··'·/ *n* (graphic) artist
gramer /·'·/ *n* grammar
granit /·'·/ *n* granite
gravür /·'·/ *n* engraving
gravürcü /···'·/ *n* engraver

grev *n* strike; ~ **yapmak** *go on strike
grevci /·ˈ·/ *n* striker
greyfurt /ˈ··/ *n* grapefruit
gri *n* gray
grip *n* influenza, flu
grup *n* group
guguk /·ˈ·/ *n* cuckoo
gurbet /·ˈ·/ *n* absence from one's home; foreign land
guruldamak /···ˈ·/ *v* rumble
gurultu /··ˈ·/ *n* rumbling noise
gurup /·ˈ·/ *n* sunset, sundown
gurur /·ˈ·/ *n* pride, vanity
gururlanmak /···ˈ·/ *v* *feel proud, *be proud
gübre /·ˈ·/ *n* dung, manure, fertilizer
gübrelemek /···ˈ·/ *v* manure
gücendirmek /···ˈ·/ *v* offend, *hurt, anger
gücenik /··ˈ·/ *adj* offended, vexed
gücenmek /··ˈ·/ *v* *be offended, *be hurt
güç *n* strength, force; power; **gücüne gitmek** *be offended; **gücü yetmek** afford; *be able to
güçlü /·ˈ·/ *adj* strong, powerful
güçlük /·ˈ·/ *n* difficulty, trouble; ~ **çekmek** *have difficulty; ~ **çıkarmak** *make difficulties
güçlükle /·ˈ··/ *adv* with great difficulty, hardly
güçsüz /·ˈ·/ *adj* weak, feeble
güfte /·ˈ·/ *n* text for music
gül *n* rose
güldürmek /··ˈ·/ *v* *make laugh
güldürü /··ˈ·/ *n* comedy
güle güle /·ˈ···/ good-bye
güleryüzlü /·ˈ···/ *adj* cheerful, friendly
gülme /·ˈ·/ *n* laughing, laughter
gülmek /·ˈ·/ *v* laugh
gülümseme /···ˈ·/ *n* smile
gülümsemek /···ˈ·/ *v* smile
gülünç /·ˈ·/ *adj* ridiculous, laughable
gülüşmek /··ˈ·/ *v* laugh together
gümbürdemek /···ˈ·/ *v* boom, thunder, roar
gümbürtü /··ˈ·/ *n* booming noise
gümrük /·ˈ·/ *n* customs; ~ **almak** collect duty; ~ **dairesi** customs house; ~ **kaçakçısı** smuggler; **gümrüğe tabi** dutiable; **gümrükten geçirmek** clear through the customs
gümrüksüz /··ˈ·/ *adj* duty-free
gümüş /·ˈ·/ *n* silver; ~ **ayarı** silver carat; ~ **kaplama** silver-plated
gün *n* day; daytime; period; ~ **ağarması** daybreak
günah /·ˈ·/ *n* sin; ~ **çıkartmak** confess; **günaha sokmak** tempt
günahkâr /··ˈ·/ *n* sinner
günahsız /··ˈ·/ *adj* innocent
günaşırı /ˈ····/ *adv* every other day
günaydın /··ˈ·/ good morning!
günbatımı /ˈ····/ *n* sunset
gündelik /··ˈ·/ *adj* daily; *n* daily wage, daily fee
gündelikçi /···ˈ·/ *n* day laborer; ~ **kadın** hired woman
gündoğusu /ˈ····/ *n* easterly wind
gündüz /·ˈ·/ *n* daytime; daylight
gündüzün /·ˈ··/ *adv* during the day, by day
güneş /·ˈ·/ *n* sun; sunshine; ~ **açmak** *become sunny; ~ **banyosu** sun bath; ~ **batmak** *set, *go down (sun); ~ **çarpması** sunstroke; ~ **doğmak** *rise (sun); ~ **gözlüğü** sunglasses; ~ **sistemi** solar system
güneşlenmek /···ˈ·/ *v* sunbathe
güneşli /··ˈ·/ *adj* sunny

güneşlik /··'·/ *n* sunshade
güney /·'·/ *n* south; *adj* southern
günlerce /·'··/ *adv* for days, day after day
günlük /·'·/ *adj* daily; *n* diary; ~ **güneşlik** sunny
günübirlik /·'···/ *adj* confined to the day; **günübirliğine gitmek** *make a day visit
güpegündüz /·'···/ *adv* in broad daylight
gür *adj* abundant, dense, thick
gürbüz /·'·/ *adj* robust, sturdy
gürbüzlük /··'·/ *n* sturdiness
güreş /·'·/ *n* wrestling
güreşçi /··'·/ *n* wrestler
güreşmek /··'·/ *v* wrestle
gürgen /·'·/ *n* hornbeam, horn beech
gürlemek /··'·/ *v* thunder, roar
gürüldemek /···'·/ *v* thunder
gürül gürül /·'· ··/ *adj* bubbling, gurgling
gürültü /··'·/ *n* noise; trouble, confusion; ~ **çıkarmak** kick up a row; ~ **patırtı** noise, trouble; ~ **yapmak** *make a noise
gürültücü /···'·/ *adj* noisy, troublesome
gürültülü /···'·/ *adj* noisy, tumultuous, clamorous
gütmek /·'·/ *v* *drive, pursue
güve /·'·/ *n* clothes moth
güveç /·'·/ *n* casserole; stew
güven /·'·/ *n* trust, confidence, reliance; **güveni olmak** *have confidence
güvence /··'·/ *n* guarantee
güvenilir /···'·/ *adj* reliable
güvenli /··'·/ *adj* safe
güvenmek /··'·/ *v* trust; rely on
güvensiz /··'·/ *adj* distrustful
güvercin /··'·/ *n* pigeon
güverte /·'··/ *n* deck
güya /'– –/ *conj* as though, as if
güz *n* autumn, fall
güzel /·'·/ *adj* beautiful, pretty; good, nice; *n* a beauty; ~ **sanatlar** fine arts
güzelleşmek /···'·/ *v* *become beautiful
güzelleştirmek /····'·/ *v* beautify
güzellik /··'·/ *n* beauty
güzellikle /··'··/ *adv* gently, softly
güzergâh /··'·/ *n* route, itinerary
güzide /–'·/ *adj* distinguished, select, choice

H

haber /·'·/ *n* news, information, message; ~ **almak** receive information; ~ **göndermek** *send news; **haberi olmak** *be informed
haberci /··'·/ *n* messenger
haberleşme /···'·/ *n* communication
haberleşmek /···'·/ *v* communicate
habersiz /··'·/ *adj* uninformed
habis /·'·/ *adj* malignant
hac *n* pilgrimage to Mecca; **hacca gitmek** *go on a pilgrimage to Mecca
hacı /·'·/ *n* pilgrim, hadji
hacim /·'·/ *n* volume, size
haciz /·'·/ *n* sequestration, seizure; ~ **koymak** sequestrate
haç *n* the cross
had *n* limit, boundary; degree; **haddini bilmek** *know one's place
hademe /··'·/ *n* servant in public buildings
hadım /·'·/ *n* eunuch; ~ **etmek** castrate
hadise /–'·/ *n* event, incident; ~ **çıkarmak** *make a scene
hafif /·'·/ *adj* light in weight; slight

hafifçe /·ˈ··/ *adv* lightly
hafta /·ˈ·/ *n* week; ~ **arasında** during the week; ~ **sonu** weekend
haftalık /··ˈ·/ *adj* weekly; *n* weekly wages
hain /–ˈ·/ *n* traitor
hainlik /–ˈ·/ *n* treachery
hak *n* justice; law; a right; ~ **etmek** deserve
hakaret /·–ˈ·/ *n* insult; ~ **etmek** insult; **hakarete uğramak** *be insulted
hakem /·ˈ·/ *n* referee; umpire
hakikat /·–ˈ·/ *n* truth, reality; sincerity
hakikaten /·ˈ–··/ *adv* really, actually
hakikatli /·–ˈ·/ *adj* faithful
hakiki /·–ˈ–/ *adj* true, real; genuine; sincere
hâkim /–ˈ·/ *n* judge
hâkimiyet /–··ˈ·/ *n* sovereignty; domination; rule
hakir /·ˈ·/ *adj* despicable, mean; ~ **görmek** despise, *hold in contempt
hakkında /··ˈ·/ *prep* about, concerning, regarding
hakkıyla /·ˈ··/ *adv* properly, rightfully; thoroughly
haklı /·ˈ·/ *adj* right
haksız /·ˈ·/ *adj* unjust; wrong
haksızlık /··ˈ·/ *n* injustice, unfairness; ~ **etmek** act unjustly
hal *n* condition, state, circumstance
hala /ˈ··/ *n* (paternal) aunt; father's sister
hâlâ /ˈ––/ *adv* still, yet
halat /·ˈ·/ *n* rope, hawser
halbuki /·ˈ··/ *conj* whereas; however, nevertheless
halef /·ˈ·/ *n* successor
halel /·ˈ·/ *n* injury, harm; ~ **gelmek** *be injured
halen /ˈ–·/ *adv* now, at the present time
halı /·ˈ·/ *n* carpet
Haliç /ˈ··/ the Golden Horn
halife /·–ˈ·/ *n* caliph
halis /–ˈ·/ *adj* pure; genuine
haliyle /–ˈ··/ *adv* as a matter of course; consequently
halk *n* people; crowd
halka /·ˈ·/ *n* ring; circle; ~ **olmak** form a circle
halletmek /ˈ···/ solve; settle; explain; analyze; dissolve
halter /·ˈ·/ *n* dumbbell, barbell
ham *adj* crude, raw; unripe, green
hamak /·ˈ·/ *n* hammock
hamal /·ˈ·/ *n* porter, carrier
hamam /·ˈ·/ *n* Turkish bath; public bath
hamamböceği /·ˈ····/ *n* cockroach
hamarat /··ˈ·/ *adj* hardworking, diligent
hamile /–·ˈ·/ *adj* pregnant; ~ **kalmak** *become pregnant
hamilelik /–··ˈ·/ *n* pregnancy
hamsi /·ˈ·/ *n* anchovy
hamur /·ˈ·/ *n* dough, paste; *adj* half-baked; ~ **açmak** roll out dough; ~ **işi** pastry
han *n* inn; large commercial building
hancı /·ˈ·/ *n* innkeeper
hançer /·ˈ·/ *n* dagger
hane /–ˈ·/ *n* house, building
hanedan /–·ˈ·/ *n* dynasty; noble family
hanedanlık /–··ˈ·/ *n* nobility
hangi /ˈ··/ *adj* which; whichever
hanım /·ˈ·/ *n* lady, woman; Mrs., Miss; wife
hanımböceği /·ˈ····/ *n* ladybug
hanımeli /·ˈ···/ *n* honeysuckle
hani /ˈ··/ *adv* where? where is it?; well?; well, what about it?; after

all
hantal /·ˈ·/ *adj* clumsy, awkward
hap *n* pill; **hapı yutmak** *be in trouble
hapis /·ˈ·/ *n* prison, imprisonment; ~ **yatmak** *be in prison; **hapse atmak** imprison
hapishane /··–ˈ·/ *n* prison, jail
hapsetmek /ˈ···/ *v* *put in prison
hapşırmak /··ˈ·/ *v* sneeze
harabe /·–ˈ·/ *n* ruin
haram /·ˈ·/ *adj* forbidden by religion, unlawful
harap /·ˈ·/ *adj* ruined; ~ **etmek** destroy, ruin; ~ **olmak** *fall into ruin
hararet /·–ˈ·/ *n* heat, warmth; thirst
hararetlenmek /·–··ˈ·/ *v* *become warm; *become feverish; *get thirsty
hararetli /·–ˈ·/ *adj* ardent; feverish; vehement
harcama /··ˈ·/ *n* expenditure
harcamak /··ˈ·/ *v* *spend; expend, use up
harcırah /··ˈ·/ *n* travel allowance
harç[1] *n* expenditure; fees
harç[2] *n* mortar
harçlık /·ˈ·/ *n* allowance; pocket money
hardal /·ˈ·/ *n* mustard
hareket /··ˈ·/ *n* movement; action; behavior; departure; excitement; ~ **etmek** move; behave; depart; **harekete geçmek** start action
hareketlenmek /····ˈ·/ *v* *get into motion *or* action
hareketli /···ˈ·/ *adj* active; mobile
hareketsiz /···ˈ·/ *adj* motionless
harf *n* letter of the alphabet
harici /–·ˈ–/ *adj* external, exterior; foreign
hariç /–ˈ·/ *adv* except; *n* exterior, outside; foreign country
harika /–·ˈ·/ *adj* marvelous, wonderful; *n* wonder, miracle
harikulade /ˈ–··–/ *adj* extraordinary, unusual, wonderful
haris /·ˈ·/ *adj* ambitious, greedy, avaricious
harita /·ˈ··/ *n* map
harman /·ˈ·/ *n* harvest; blend; threshing
harp[1] *n* war; battle, fight
harp[2] *n* harp
has *adj* special, peculiar to; pure
hasar /·ˈ·/ *n* damage; **hasara uğramak** suffer damage
hasat /·ˈ·/ *n* harvest; ~ **etmek** reap
hâsıl /–ˈ·/ *adj* resulting; produced, growing; ~ **olmak** result; *be produced, *be obtained
hâsılat /–·ˈ·/ *n* return, revenue, products
hasım /·ˈ·/ *n* adversary; enemy
hasır /·ˈ·/ *n* rush mat, matting
hasis /·ˈ·/ *adj* mean; stingy
hasislik /··ˈ·/ *n* stinginess, meanness
hasret /·ˈ·/ *n* longing, homesickness, nostalgia
hasretmek /ˈ···/ *v* confine; devote, dedicate
hassas /·ˈ·/ *adj* sensitive; touchy
hassasiyet /·–ˈ·/ *n* sensitivity
hasta /·ˈ·/ *adj* sick, ill; *n* patient; ~ **düşmek** *fall sick; ~ **etmek** *make ill; ~ **olmak** *become ill
hastabakıcı /·ˈ····/ *n* nurse
hastalık /··ˈ·/ *n* disease; sickness
hastane /·–ˈ·/ *n* hospital; **hastaneye yatırmak** hospitalize
haşarı /··ˈ·/ *adj* naughty, mischievous
haşere /··ˈ·/ *n* insect

haşhaş /·ˈ·/ *n* poppy
haşlama /··ˈ·/ *adj* boiled; *n* boiled meat
haşlamak /··ˈ·/ *v* boil; scold, reprimand
hat *n* line; route
hata /·ˈ–/ *n* mistake; fault, error; wrong action; ~ **etmek** *make a mistake; ~ **işlemek** *do wrong
hatalı /·–ˈ·/ *adj* erroneous, faulty, wrong
hatır /·ˈ·/ *n* memory; feelings; consideration; influence; **hatıra gelmek** occur, *come to mind; **hatırda kalmak** *be remembered; **hatırım için** for my sake
hatıra /–·ˈ·/ *n* memory; souvenir
hatırlamak /···ˈ·/ *v* remember
hatırlatmak /···ˈ·/ *v* remind
hatip /·ˈ·/ *n* public speaker, orator
hatta /ˈ·–/ *adv* even; so much so that; besides
hava /·ˈ·/ *n* air; weather; climate; ~ **almak** *get fresh air; *be left empty-handed; ~ **atmak** *show off; ~ **kirliliği** air pollution; **havaya uçurmak** *blow up
havaalanı /·ˈ····/ *n* airfield; airport
havacı /··ˈ·/ *n* pilot, aviator
havacılık /···ˈ·/ *n* aviation
havadar /··ˈ·/ *adj* airy
havagazı /·ˈ···/ *n* coal gas
havalanmak /···ˈ·/ *v* *be aired; *be airborne; *take off
havale /·–ˈ·/ *n* transfer; money order; ~ **etmek** transfer, assign, refer; ~ **göndermek** *send a money order
havalimanı /·ˈ····/ *n* airport
havasız /··ˈ·/ *adj* airless, stuffy
havayolu /·ˈ···/ *n* airline
havlamak /··ˈ·/ *v* bark, bay
havlu /·ˈ·/ *n* towel
havra /ˈ··/ *n* synagogue
havuç /·ˈ·/ *n* carrot
havuz /·ˈ·/ *n* pond, pool
havyar /·ˈ·/ *n* caviar
hayal /·ˈ·/ *n* image; imagination; illusion; ~ **etmek** imagine; dream; ~ **kırıklığı** disappoinment
hayali /–ˈ–/ *adj* imaginary
hayalperest /···ˈ·/ *n* dreamer
hayat /·ˈ·/ *n* life; existence; ~ **pahalılığı** high cost of living
haydi /ˈ··/ hurry up!; come on!; ~ **bakalım** come on then!
haydut /·ˈ·/ *n* bandit, robber
haydutluk /··ˈ·/ *n* brigandage; mischief
hayır[1] /ˈ–·/ no; on the contrary
hayır[2] /·ˈ·/ *n* goodness; charity
hayırlı /··ˈ·/ *adj* good, auspicious, blessed; **hayırlı olsun!** good luck!, congratulations!; **hayırlı yolculuklar!** have a good trip!
hayırsız /··ˈ·/ *adj* useless, good for nothing
haykırmak /··ˈ·/ *v* cry out, shout, scream
haylaz /·ˈ·/ *adj* lazy, idle
haylazlık /··ˈ·/ *n* idleness
hayli /ˈ··/ *adv* many, much, very
hayran /·ˈ·/ *n* admirer, lover, fan; *adj* bewildered; ~ **olmak** *be impressed; admire
hayranlık /··ˈ·/ *n* admiration
hayret /·ˈ·/ *n* astonishment, amazement; ~ **etmek** *be astonished; marvel; **hayrette bırakmak** astound
haysiyet /··ˈ·/ *n* dignity, honor
haysiyetli /···ˈ·/ *adj* dignified, honorable
haysiyetsiz /···ˈ·/ *adj* dishonorable
hayvan /·ˈ·/ *n* animal, beast
hayvanat bahçesi /··ˈ· ···/ zoo
hayvancılık /···ˈ·/ *n* cattle-breeding

haz *n* pleasure, delight, enjoyment; ~ **duymak** *be delighted; enjoy
hazım /·'·/ *n* digestion
hazır /·'·/ *adj* ready; ready-made; present; ~ **bulunmak** *be present; *be ready
hazırcevap /···'·/ *adj* quick-witted, witty
hazırlama /···'·/ *n* preparation
hazırlamak /···'·/ *v* prepare, *make ready
hazırlık /··'·/ *n* readiness; preparation
hazin /·'–/ *adj* sad; pathetic
hazine /·–'·/ *n* treasure; treasury
haziran /·–'·/ June
hazmetmek /'···/ *v* digest
hece /·'·/ *n* syllable
hecelemek /···'·/ *v* spell out by syllables
hedef /·'·/ *n* target; object; aim
hediye /··'·/ *n* gift, present; ~ **etmek** *give as a gift
hediyelik /···'·/ *adj* fit for a present
hekim /·'·/ *n* physician, doctor
hekimlik /··'·/ *n* medicine
hela /·'–/ *n* toilet, water closet
helal /·'·/ *adj* lawful, legitimate
hele /'··/ *adv* especially, above all
hem *adv* and also, in fact; ~ . . . ~ . . . both . . . and . . . ; **hem de** moreover
hemen /'··/ *adv* at once, immediately; right now; ~ ~ nearly, almost
hemfikir /··'·/ *adj* like-minded
hemşeri /··'·/ *n* fellow townsman
hemşire /·–'·/ *n* sister; nurse
hendek /·'·/ *n* ditch, trench
henüz /'··/ *adv* just now; yet
hep *adv* all; wholly, entirely; always; ~ **beraber** all together
hepsi /'··/ *pron* all of it; all of them
her *adj* every, each; ~ **an** any moment; ~ **biri** each one; ~ **gün** every day; ~ **kim** whoever; ~ **nasılsa** somehow or other; ~ **şey** everything; ~ **yerde** everywhere; ~ **zaman** always
herhalde /'···/ *adv* in any case
hesap /·'·/ *n* calculation; arithmetic; account; bill; plan; ~ **açmak** open an account; ~ **etmek** plan; calculate; ~ **vermek** account for
hesaplaşmak /···'·/ *v* settle accounts mutually
hesaplı /··'·/ *adj* economical; well-considered
hesapsız /··'·/ *adj* countless; unplanned; uneconomical
heves /·'·/ *n* desire; inclination; zeal
hevesli /··'·/ *adj* eager
heybe /·'·/ *n* saddlebag
heybet /·'·/ *n* majesty; grandeur
heybetli /··'·/ *adj* majestic, grand
heyecan /··'·/ *n* excitement, enthusiasm, emotion
heyecanlanmak /····'·/ *v* *get excited
heyecanlı /···'·/ *adj* exciting; excited
heyecansız /···'·/ *adj* unexciting; unexcited
heyelan /··'·/ *n* landslide
heyet /·'·/ *n* committee, board
heykel /·'·/ *n* statue
heykeltıraş /···'·/ *n* sculptor
heykeltıraşlık /····'·/ *n* sculpture
hıçkırık /··'·/ *n* hiccup; sob
hıçkırmak /··'·/ *v* sob
hınç *n* rancor, hatred; revenge **hıncını almak** revenge
hırçın /·'·/ *adj* ill-tempered, peevish

hırçınlaşmak /···ˈ·/ *v* *become cross *or* obstinate
hırçınlık /··ˈ·/ *n* bad temper, peevishness
hırdavat /··ˈ·/ *n* hardware
Hıristiyan /···ˈ·/ *adj, n* Christian
hırka /·ˈ·/ *n* woolen jacket, cardigan
hırlaşmak /··ˈ·/ *v* snarl at each other; squabble
hırpalamak /···ˈ·/ *v* ill-treat; misuse
hırs *n* greed, ambition; anger; passion
hırsız /·ˈ·/ *n* thief, burglar
hırsızlık /··ˈ·/ *n* theft, burglary; ~ **etmek** *steal, burgle
hırslanmak /··ˈ·/ *v* *get angry
hırslı /·ˈ·/ *adj* ambitious; angry, furious
hısım /·ˈ·/ *n* relative, kin
hısımlık /··ˈ·/ *n* relationship, kinship
hışım /·ˈ·/ *n* anger, fury
hışırdamak /···ˈ·/ *v* *make a continuous rustling noise
hıyanet /·–ˈ·/ *n* treachery, treason; perfidy
hız *n* speed; rate; ~ **almak** *speed up
hızlandırmak /···ˈ·/ *v* accelerate
hızlı /·ˈ·/ *adj* swift, quick
hibe /–ˈ·/ *n* donation; gift; ~ **etmek** donate
hiç *n* nothing; *adj* no; *adv* not at all; ever; never; ~ **kimse** no one, nobody; ~ **olmazsa** at least
hiddet /·ˈ·/ *n* anger, rage
hiddetlenmek /···ˈ·/ *v* *become angry
hiddetli /··ˈ·/ *adj* angry; passionate
hikâye /·–ˈ·/ *n* story, tale
hikmet /·ˈ·/ *n* wisdom; hidden cause, motive
hilal /·ˈ·/ *n* crescent
hile /–ˈ·/ *n* trick, ruse, cheating; ~ **yapmak** swindle, cheat
hilekâr /–·ˈ·/ *n* trickster; cheat
hileli /–·ˈ·/ *adj* dishonest; tricky, false; impure
hilesiz /–·ˈ·/ *adj* honest, true, genuine
himaye /·–ˈ·/ *n* protection; ~ **etmek** protect, defend
hindi /·ˈ·/ *n* turkey
Hindistan /··ˈ·/ India
hindistancevizi /··ˈ····/ *n* coconut
Hintli /·ˈ·/ *n* Indian
his *n* sense; feeling, sensation
hisar /·ˈ·/ *n* castle, fortress
hisli /·ˈ·/ *adj* sensitive; sentimental
hisse /·ˈ·/ *n* share; part; ~ **senedi** share, stock
hissedar /··ˈ·/ *n* shareholder
hissetmek /ˈ···/ *v* *feel; notice
hissi /·ˈ–/ *adj* sentimental; sensory
hitabe /·–ˈ·/ *n* speech, address
hitap /·ˈ·/ *n* address, addressing ~ **etmek** address; *make a speech
hiza /·ˈ–/ *n* level, line
hizmetçi /··ˈ·/ *n* servant
hizmetkâr /··ˈ·/ *n* servant
hoca /ˈ··/ *n* teacher; hodja, Muslim teacher
hokkabaz /··ˈ·/ *n* juggler, conjurer
hokkabazlık /···ˈ·/ *n* trickery, jugglery
hol *n* entrance, hall, corridor
holding /ˈ··/ *n* holding company
Hollanda /·ˈ··/ Holland
Hollandaca /·ˈ···/ *n* Dutch language
Hollandalı /·ˈ···/ *adj* Dutch; *n* Dutchman
homurdanmak /···ˈ·/ *v* grumble
homurtu /··ˈ·/ *n* muttering, grumbling
hoparlör /··ˈ·/ *n* loudspeaker

hoplamak /··ˈ·/ *v* *leap, hop
hor *adj* contemptible; ~ **görmek** look down upon; ~ **kullanmak** misuse
horlamak /··ˈ·/ *v* snore
hormon /·ˈ·/ *n* hormone
horoz /·ˈ·/ *n* cock, rooster
hortlak /·ˈ·/ *n* ghost, specter
hortum /·ˈ·/ *n* hose; waterspout; trunk
horultu /··ˈ·/ *n* snore, snoring
hostes /·ˈ·/ *n* air hostess, stewardess
hoş *adj* pleasant, nice; charming; **hoş geldiniz** welcome; ~ **görmek** tolerate, allow; ~ **tutmak** treat well; **hoşuna gitmek** please
hoşaf /·ˈ·/ *n* compote
hoşça /·ˈ·/ *adv* pleasantly, agreeably; ~ **kal** good-bye
hoşlanmak /··ˈ·/ *v* like, *be pleased with
hoşnut /·ˈ·/ *adj* satisfied, pleased
hoşnutluk /··ˈ·/ *n* contentment
hoyrat /·ˈ·/ *adj* rough, coarse, boorish
hörgüç /·ˈ·/ *n* camel's hump
höyük /·ˈ·/ *n* mound, tumulus
hububat /·–ˈ·/ *n* cereals, grain
hudut /·ˈ·/ *n* frontier, border; limit
hukuk /·ˈ·/ *n* law
hukukçu /··ˈ·/ *n* jurist
hukuki /·–ˈ–/ *adj* legal
hurafe /·–ˈ·/ *n* superstition
hurda /·ˈ·/ *n* old iron, scrap metal; junk
huri /–ˈ·/ *n* houri; ~ **gibi** very beautiful
hurma /·ˈ·/ *n* date
husus /·ˈ·/ *n* matter, case; subject
hususi /·–ˈ–/ *adj* special, private, personal
huy *n* habit, temper; temperament; ~ **edinmek** acquire a habit
huylanmak /··ˈ·/ *v* *be irritated; *feel suspicious
huysuz /·ˈ·/ *adj* bad-tempered
huysuzluk /··ˈ·/ *n* bad temper, obstinacy
huzur /·ˈ·/ *n* peace of mind; comfort
huzurlu /··ˈ·/ *adj* at ease
huzursuz /··ˈ·/ *adj* uneasy, troubled
huzursuzluk /···ˈ·/ *n* unrest
hücre /·ˈ·/ *n* cell, room, chamber
hücum /·ˈ·/ *n* attack, assault; charge; ~ **etmek** attack, assault; **hücuma uğramak** *be attacked
hüküm /·ˈ·/ *n* rule, command; sentence, judgment; ~ **sürmek** reign, rule
hükümdar /··ˈ·/ *n* ruler, monarch
hükümdarlık /···ˈ·/ *n* monarchy
hükümet /·–ˈ·/ *n* government; ~ **darbesi** coup d'état
hükümlü /··ˈ·/ *adj* sentenced, condemned; *n* convict
hükümsüz /··ˈ·/ *adj* null, invalid, abolished
hüner /·ˈ·/ *n* skill; ability; talent
hünerli /··ˈ·/ *adj* skillful, talented
hünersiz /··ˈ·/ *adj* unskilled
hür *n* free, independent
hürmet /·ˈ·/ *n* respect; regard; ~ **etmek** respect
hürmetkâr /··ˈ·/ *adj* respectful
hürriyet /··ˈ·/ *n* freedom, liberty; independence
hüsran /·ˈ·/ *n* disappointment; frustration
hüviyet /··ˈ·/ *n* identity; ~ **cüzdanı** identity card
hüzün /·ˈ·/ *n* sadness, grief; melancholy
hüzünlenmek /···ˈ·/ *v* *feel sad
hüzünlü /··ˈ·/ *adj* sad, gloomy

I

ıhlamur /··ˈ·/ *n* lime tree, linden tree; linden-flower tea
ılıca /·ˈ··/ *n* hot spring, spa, health resort
ılık /·ˈ·/ *adj* lukewarm
ılıklaşmak /···ˈ·/ *v* *become lukewarm
ılıman /··ˈ·/ *adj* mild
ılımlı /··ˈ·/ *adj* moderate
ılımlılık /···ˈ·/ *n* moderation
ılınmak /··ˈ·/ *n* *grow lukewarm
ılıştırmak /···ˈ·/ *v* *make tepid *or* lukewarm
ırak /·ˈ·/ *adj* distant, far
Irak /ˈ··/ Iraq
Iraklı /ˈ···/ *adj, n* Iraqi
ırk *n* race
ırkçı /·ˈ·/ *n, adj* racist
ırkçılık /··ˈ·/ *n* racism
ırmak /·ˈ·/ *n* river
ırz *n* chastity; purity, honor; **ırzına geçmek** violate, rape
ısı /·ˈ·/ *n* heat
ısınma /··ˈ·/ *n* heating, warming up
ısınmak /··ˈ·/ *v* *grow warm; *grow to like
ısırgan /··ˈ·/ *n* stinging nettle
ısırık /··ˈ·/ *n* bite; sting
ısırmak /··ˈ·/ *v* *bite
ısıtmak /···ˈ·/ *v* warm, heat
ıskonto /·ˈ··/ *n* discount
ıslah /·ˈ·/ *n* improvement, reformation, correction; **~ etmek** improve, correct; **~ olmak** improve one's conduct
ıslahat /··ˈ·/ *n* reform, improvement; **~ yapmak** *make reforms
ıslahevi /·ˈ···/ *n* reformatory
ıslak /·ˈ·/ *adj* wet
ıslaklık /··ˈ·/ *n* wetness
ıslatmak /··ˈ·/ *v* wet; soak
ıslık /·ˈ·/ *n* whistle; **~ çalmak** whistle
ısmarlama /···ˈ·/ *adj* made to order
ısmarlamak /···ˈ·/ *v* order
ıspanak /··ˈ·/ *n* spinach
ısrar /·ˈ·/ *n* insistence, persistence; **~ etmek** insist on, persist in
ısrarla /·ˈ··/ *adv* insistently, persistently
ısrarlı /··ˈ·/ *adj* insistent
ıssız /·ˈ·/ *adj* lonely, desolate, deserted
ıssızlık /··ˈ·/ *n* loneliness, desolation
ıstakoz /··ˈ·/ *n* lobster
ıstırap /··ˈ·/ *n* suffering, pain; **~ çekmek** suffer
ışık /·ˈ·/ *n* light; **~ saçmak** emit light, *shine
ışıklandırmak /····ˈ·/ *v* illuminate; *light up
ışıklı /··ˈ·/ *adj* lighted, illuminated
ışıldak /··ˈ·/ *n* searchlight; projector
ışıldamak /···ˈ·/ *v* sparkle, *shine, twinkle
ışıltı /··ˈ·/ *n* twinkle, brightness, flash, glitter
ışıma /··ˈ·/ *n* radiation
ışımak /··ˈ·/ *v* glow, radiate
ışın /·ˈ·/ *n* ray
ızgara /·ˈ··/ *n* grill; grate; *adj* grilled; **~ yapmak** grill

İ

iade /–ˈ·/ *n* giving back; return; rejection; **~ etmek** *give back, return
iadeli /·–ˈ·/ *adj* returnable; *adv*

on a return basis; ~ **taahhütlü mektup** registered letter with record of delivery returned to sender
ibadet /–ˈ·/ *n* worship; ~ **etmek** worship
ibadethane /·––ˈ·/ *n* house of God
ibik /·ˈ·/ *n* comb, crest
iblis /·ˈ·/ *n* satan, devil
ibret /·ˈ·/ *n* lesson; example; warning; admonition; ~ **almak** *draw a lesson; ~ **olmak** *be a lesson
icap /–ˈ·/ *n* necessity, requirement; demand; ~ **etmek** *be required; **icabına bakmak** *see to
icat /–ˈ·/ *n* invention; ~ **etmek** invent; create
icra /·ˈ–/ *n* execution, performance; ~ **etmek** execute, perform
icraat /·–ˈ·/ *n* activities, performances
iç *n* interior, inside; *adj* inner; ~ **açıcı** pleasant, cheering; ~ **çamaşırı** underwear; ~ **çekmek** sigh; ~ **savaş** civil war
içecek /··ˈ·/ *n* drink, beverage
içedönük /·ˈ··/ *adj* introvert
içeri /··ˈ·/ *n* inside, interior; *adv* in; to the inside; ~ **girmek** *go in, enter
içerik /··ˈ·/ *n* content
içerlemek /···ˈ·/ *v* resent
içermek /··ˈ·/ *v* contain, include, comprise
içgüdü /··ˈ·/ *n* instinct
için /·ˈ·/ *prep* for; *conj* in order to; so that
içirmek /··ˈ·/ *v* cause to drink
içki /·ˈ·/ *n* drink
içkici /··ˈ·/ *n* heavy drinker
içkili /··ˈ·/ *adj* drunk
içlidışlı /·ˈ··/ *adj* familiar, intimate
içmek /·ˈ·/ *v* *drink
içmeler /··ˈ·/ *n* mineral springs
içten /·ˈ·/ *adj* sincere, friendly
idam /–ˈ·/ *n* execution, capital punishment
idare /·–ˈ·/ *n* management, administration; thrift; ~ **etmek** manage, administer, govern; economize
idareci /·–·ˈ·/ *n* manager, organizer, administrator
idareli /·–·ˈ·/ *adj* economical; ~ **kullanmak** use economically
idari /·–ˈ–/ *adj* administrative
iddia /··ˈ–/ *n* claim; bet; obstinacy; ~ **etmek** claim; contend; **iddiaya tutuşmak** *bet
iddiacı /··–ˈ·/ *n* persistent; arrogant; assertive
iddialı /··–ˈ·/ *adj* pretentious, arrogant
iddiasız /··–ˈ·/ *adj* unpretentious
ideal /··ˈ·/ *adj* ideal
idman /·ˈ·/ *n* gymnastics, workout, training
idrak /·ˈ·/ *n* comprehension, perception; ~ **etmek** perceive
idrar /·ˈ·/ *n* urine
ifa /–ˈ–/ *n* performance, fulfillment; ~ **etmek** fulfill, perform
ifade /·–ˈ·/ *n* explanation; expression; statement; **ifadesini almak** question, interrogate; ~ **etmek** express; ~ **vermek** *make a declaration before a judge *or* other recognized authoritiy
iffet /·ˈ·/ *n* chastity; honesty; uprightness
iflas /·ˈ·/ *n* bankruptcy; ~ **etmek** *go bankrupt
ifşa /·ˈ–/ *n* disclosure, revelation;

~ **etmek** disclose, reveal
ifşaat /·–'·/ *n* revelations
iftar /·'·/ *n* breaking of one's fast; ~ **etmek** *break one's fast
iftihar /··'·/ *n* pride; ~ **etmek** *be proud of
iftira /··'–/ *n* slander; ~ **etmek** slander
iftiracı /·–'·/ *n* slanderer
iğfal /·'·/ *n* rape; ~ **etmek** rape
iğne /·'·/ *n* needle, pin; injection; ~ **yapmak** *give an injection
iğnelemek /···'·/ *v* pin; prick; *hurt with words
iğneli /··'·/ *adj* having pins; biting; ~ **söz** biting word
iğrenç /·'·/ *adj* disgusting; loathsome; abhorrent
iğrendirmek /···'·/ *v* disgust
iğrenmek /··'·/ *v* loathe, abhor, *feel disgust
ihale /·–'·/ *n* tender, bid; ~ **etmek** award a contract
ihanet /·–'·/ *n* treachery, betrayal; ~ **etmek** betray
ihbar /·'·/ *n* notice, warning ~ **etmek** inform, report
ihbarname /··–'·/ *n* notice, warning, notification
ihlal /·'·/ *n* disobeying; infringement; ~ **etmek** *break, violate; infringe
ihmal /·'·/ *n* neglect; ~ **etmek** neglect
ihmalci /··'·/ *adj* negligent, careless
ihracat /·–'·/ *n* exports; exportation
ihracatçı /·–·'·/ *n* exporter
ihraç /·'·/ *n* exportation; ~ **etmek** export
ihtar /·'·/ *n* warning; ~ **etmek** warn
ihtilaf /··'·/ *n* conflict; dispute; disagreement
ihtilaflı /···'·/ *adj* controversial
ihtimal /··'·/ *n* probability; *adv* probably; ~ **vermek** deem likely
ihtiras /··'·/ *n* passion, ambition, greed
ihtiraslı /···'·/ *adj* passionate; ambitious
ihtisas /··'·/ *n* specialization; expert knowledge; ~ **yapmak** specialize
ihtiyaç /··'·/ *n* necessity, need; **ihtiyacı olmak** *be in need of
ihtiyar /··'·/ *adj* aged, old
ihtiyari /·–'–/ *n* optional
ihtiyarlamak /····'·/ *v* *grow old
ihtiyarlık /···'·/ *n* old age
ihtiyat /··'·/ *n* precaution; reserves
ihtiyatlı /···'·/ *adj* prudent, cautious
ihtiyatsız /···'·/ *adj* imprudent
ikametgâh /·–·'·/ *n* residence; house
ikaz /–'·/ *n* warning; ~ **etmek** caution, warn
iken /·'·/ *conj* while, when, during
iki /·'·/ *num* two; **ikide bir** every now and then; all the time; ~ **günde bir** every other day; ~ **kat** double; twice
ikili /··'·/ *adj* double, dual; bilateral
ikilik /··'·/ *n* disagreement; duality
ikinci /··'·/ *num* second
ikindi /··'·/ *n* afternoon
ikiyüzlü /·'···/ *adj* two-faced, hypocritical
ikiyüzlülük /·'····/ *n* hypocrisy
ikiz /·'·/ *n* twins
iklim /·'·/ *n* climate
ikmal /·'·/ *n* completion; make-up examination; reinforcement; **ikmale kalmak** *have to take a make-up; ~ **etmek** complete, finish
ikram /·'·/ *n* honoring, kindness; ~ **etmek** *show honor to; offer

ikramiye /·–·ˈ·/ *n* bonus; prize in a lottery; ~ **kazanmak** *win a prize
iktidar /··ˈ·/ *n* power; the ruling party; **iktidara gelmek** *come to power
iktidarsız /···ˈ·/ *adj* impotent
iktisat /··ˈ·/ *n* economy; frugality; economics
il *n* administrative province
ilaç /·ˈ·/ *n* medicine; drug
ilaçlamak /···ˈ·/ *v* medicate; disinfect
ilaçlı /··ˈ·/ *adj* medicated
ilah /·ˈ·/ *n* god
ilahe /·–ˈ·/ *n* goddess
ilahi /·–ˈ·/ *n* hymn, psalm
ilahiyat /·–·ˈ·/ *n* theology
ilan /–ˈ·/ *n* announcement, declaration; advertisement; ~ **etmek** declare; advertise; announce
ilave /·–ˈ·/ *n* addition; appendix; sequel; supplement; extra; *adj* additional; ~ **etmek** add to
ilçe /·ˈ·/ *n* administrative district
ile /·ˈ·/ *conj* with; by; and; by means of, through
ilelebet /·ˈ···/ *adv* forever
ileri /··ˈ·/ *adv* further, forward, ahead; *adj* advanced; ~ **gitmek** *go forward; *go too far; ~ **sürmek** *put forward; ~ **geri** forwards and backwards; ~ **görüşlü** farsighted
ilerlemek /···ˈ·/ *v* advance, *go forward; progress; improve
iletişim /···ˈ·/ *n* communication
iletmek /··ˈ·/ *v* *send; carry; transmit; conduct, convey
ilgi /·ˈ·/ *n* interest; relation, connection; ~ **göstermek** *show interest
ilgilendirmek /····ˈ·/ *v* concern
ilgilenmek /···ˈ·/ *v* *be interested
ilgili /··ˈ·/ *adj* interested, connected with
ilginç /·ˈ·/ *adj* interesting
ilgisiz /··ˈ·/ *adj* indifferent, irrelevant
ilgisizlik /···ˈ·/ *n* indifference
ilik[1] /·ˈ·/ *n* marrow
ilik[2] /·ˈ·/ *n* buttonhole
iliklemek /···ˈ·/ *v* button, fasten
ilim /·ˈ·/ *n* science
ilişik /··ˈ·/ *adj* attached; enclosed herewith; connected, related
ilişki /··ˈ·/ *n* contact, connection, relationship
ilişkin /··ˈ·/ *adj* concerning, regarding; related to
ilişmek /··ˈ·/ *v* touch lightly; *sit lightly
iliştirmek /···ˈ·/ *v* attach, fasten
ilk *adj* first; initial; primary; original; ~ **defa** for the first time; ~ **fırsatta** at the first opportunity; ~ **önce** first of all
ilkbahar /ˈ···/ *n* spring, springtime
ilkçağ /ˈ··/ *n* antiquity
ilke /·ˈ·/ *n* principle, basis
ilkel /·ˈ·/ *adj* primitive; elementary
ilkokul /ˈ···/ *n* primary school
ilkyardım /ˈ···/ *n* first aid
iltihap /··ˈ·/ *n* infection, inflammation
iltihaplanmak /····ˈ·/ *v* *become inflamed
iltimas /··ˈ·/ *n* favoritism, preferential treatment; ~ **etmek** favor, protect
ima /–ˈ–/ *n* allusion, hint; ~ **etmek** hint at
imal /–ˈ·/ *n* manufacture; ~ **etmek** manufacture, produce, *make
imalat /––ˈ·/ *n* products, manufactured goods; production

imalathane /–––'·/ *n* workshop, factory
iman /–'·/ *n* faith, belief; ~ **etmek** *have faith in God
imanlı /–·'·/ *adj* having faith, religious
imansız /–·'·/ *adj* unbelieving; cruel
imar /–'·/ *n* public works; ~ **etmek** develop, improve
imdat /·'·/ *n* help, aid
imha /·'–/ *n* destruction; ~ **etmek** destroy
imkân /·'·/ *n* possibility; opportunity
imkânsız /··'·/ *adj* impossible
imla /·'–/ *n* orthography; spelling
imparator /···'·/ *n* emperor
imparatoriçe /····'··/ *n* empress
imparatorluk /····'·/ *n* empire
imrenmek /··'·/ *v* envy; crave; covet
imtihan /··'·/ *n* examination, exam, test; ~ **etmek** examine; ~ **olmak** *take an examination
imza /·'–/ *n* signature; ~ **atmak** sign; ~ **sahibi** signatory
in *n* lair; cave
inadına /'····/ *adv* out of obstinacy
inanç /·'·/ *n* belief
inandırıcı /····'·/ *adj* convincing; persuasive
inandırmak /···'·/ *v* convince, persuade
inanılır /···'·/ *adj* believable
inanış /··'·/ *n* belief; faith
inanmak /··'·/ *v* believe
inat /·'·/ *n* obstinacy; ~ **etmek** *be obstinate
inatçı /··'·/ *adj* obstinate, stubborn
inatçılık /···'·/ *n* obstinacy; stubbornness
ince /·'·/ *adj* slender, thin; refined
inceleme /···'·/ *n* study, survey
incelemek /···'·/ *v* examine carefully
incelik /··'·/ *n* slenderness; fineness
incelmek /··'·/ *v* *become thin
inci /·'·/ *n* pearl
İncil /·'·/ *n* the Gospel, the New Testament
incinmek /··'·/ *v* *be hurt; *be offended
incir /·'·/ *n* fig
incitmek /··'·/ *v* *hurt; offend
indirim /··'·/ *n* discount
indirimli /···'·/ *adj* reduced
indirmek /··'·/ *v* lower; *take down; *bring down; reduce
inek /·'·/ *n* cow
infilak /··'·/ *n* explosion, blowup
İngiliz /'···/ *adj* English; *n* Englishman
İngilizce /··'··/ *n* English language
İngiltere /··'··/ England
iniş /·'·/ *n* downward slope; descent
inkâr /·'·/ *n* denial, refusal; ~ **etmek** deny, refuse
inlemek /··'·/ *v* moan, groan
inme /·'·/ *n* stroke, apoplexy, paralysis; ~ **inmek** *have a stroke
inmek /·'·/ *v* descend; dismount; land; *fall down; decrease
insaf /·'·/ *n* justice, fairness; **insafa gelmek** *come to reason; *become fair
insaflı /··'·/ *adj* just; fair
insafsız /··'·/ *adj* unfair; cruel
insan /·'·/ *n* human being; mankind; one; *adj* human; humane
insanlık /··'·/ *n* humanity; humaneness; human nature
inşa /·'–/ *n* construction, building; ~ **etmek** *build, construct

inşaat /·–ˈ·/ *n* buildings, construction
inşallah /ˈ···/ God willing; if God wills; I hope so
intiba /··ˈ–/ *n* impression
intibak /··ˈ·/ *n* adjustment; adaptation; ~ **etmek** *be adjusted
intihar /··ˈ·/ *n* suicide; ~ **etmek** commit suicide
intikam /··ˈ·/ *n* revenge; ~ **almak** *take revenge
ip *n* rope, string
ipek /·ˈ·/ *n* silk
ipekböceği /·ˈ····/ *n* silkworm
ipekli /··ˈ·/ *adj* silken
iplik /·ˈ·/ *n* thread; sewing cotton
ipotek /··ˈ·/ *n* mortgage
iptal /·ˈ·/ *n* annulment, cancellation; ~ **etmek** annul; cancel
ipucu /ˈ···/ *n* clue, hint; ~ **vermek** *give a clue
irade /·–ˈ·/ *n* will, willpower; command
iradeli /·–ˈ·/ *adj* strong-willed
İran /ˈ–·/ Iran
İranlı /ˈ–··/ *adj, n* Iranian, Persian
iri /·ˈ·/ *adj* large, huge, big
iriyarı /·ˈ···/ *adj* huge, burly
İrlanda /·ˈ··/ Ireland
İrlandalı /·ˈ···/ *adj* Irish; *n* Irishman
irsi /·ˈ–/ *adj* hereditary; inherited
irsiyet /··ˈ·/ *n* heredity
irtibat /··ˈ·/ *n* connection; tie; communication
irtica /··ˈ–/ *n* political reaction; a going back
irticalen /··ˈ–·/ *adv* extemporarily, off the cuff
irtifa /··ˈ–/ *n* altitude
is *n* soot
İsa /–ˈ–/ Jesus
isabet /·–ˈ·/ *n* hitting; ~ **etmek** *hit; act appropriately
isabetsiz /·–ˈ·/ *adj* inexact, improper
ise /·ˈ·/ *conj* although; however; as for; if; ~ **de** although
ishal /·ˈ·/ *n* diarrhea
isim /·ˈ·/ *n* name, title; noun
iskambil /··ˈ·/ *n* card game; ~ **kâğıdı** playing card; ~ **oynamak** play cards
İskandinav /···ˈ·/ *adj, n* Scandinavian
İskandinavya /···ˈ··/ Scandinavia
iskele /·ˈ··/ *n* jetty, pier, wharf; scaffolding; ~ **kurmak** erect scaffolding
iskelet /··ˈ·/ *n* skeleton; framework
iskemle /·ˈ··/ *n* chair
İskoç /·ˈ·/ *adj* Scottish, Scotch
İskoçya /·ˈ··/ Scotland
İskoçyalı /·ˈ···/ *n* Scotsman
İslam /·ˈ·/ *n* Islam; *adj* Muslim
İspanya /·ˈ··/ Spain
İspanyol /··ˈ·/ *adj* Spanish; *n* Spaniard
İspanyolca /··ˈ··/ *n* Spanish language
ispat /·ˈ·/ *n* proof, evidence; ~ **etmek** prove; affirm
ispatlamak /···ˈ·/ *v* prove
ispirto /·ˈ··/ *n* alcohol; spirits
israf /·ˈ·/ *n* squandering, waste; ~ **etmek** squander, waste
İsrail /·ˈ–·/ Israel
İsrailli /·ˈ–··/ *adj, n* Israeli
İstanbul Boğazı /·ˈ·· ···/ the Bosphorus, Bosporus
istasyon /··ˈ·/ *n* station
istatistik /···ˈ·/ *n* statistics
istavrit /··ˈ·/ *n* horse mackerel
istavroz /··ˈ·/ *n* cross, crucifix; ~ **çıkarmak** *make the sign of the cross

istek /·'·/ *n* wish, desire
isteklendirmek /····'·/ *v* motivate
istekli /··'·/ *adj* desirous, willing; keen
isteksiz /··'·/ *adj* disinclined; reluctant
isteksizlik /···'·/ *n* reluctance, unwillingness
istemek /··'·/ *v* want; require; need; ask for; wish; **ister istemez** willy-nilly
istifa /··'–/ *n* resignation; ~ **etmek** resign
istifade /··–'·/ *n* profit, benefit, advantage; ~ **etmek** benefit; *take advantage
istifadeli /··–'·/ *adj* profitable
istikamet /··–'·/ *n* direction
istikbal /··'·/ *n* future
istiklal /··'·/ *n* independence
istikrar /··'·/ *n* stability, stabilization
istila /·–'–/ *n* invasion; ~ **etmek** invade
istimlak /··'·/ *n* legal expropriation; ~ **etmek** expropriate
istirahat /···'·/ *n* rest, repose; ~ **etmek** rest, repose
istiridye /··'··/ *n* oyster
istismar /··'–/ *n* exploitation; ~ **etmek** exploit
istisna /··'–/ *n* exception
istisnai /··–'–/ *adj* exceptional
İsveç /'··/ Sweden
İsveççe /·'··/ *n* Swedish language
İsveçli /'···/ *n* Swede; *adj* Swedish
İsviçre /·'··/ Switzerland
İsviçreli /·'···/ *adj, n* Swiss
isyan /·'·/ *n* rebellion, revolt, mutiny; ~ **etmek** rebel
isyancı /··'·/ *n* rebel
isyankâr /··'·/ *adj* rebellious
iş *n* work, job; occupation; business; affair; ~ **başında** at work; ~ **görmek** perform a service
işadamı /'····/ *n* businessman
işaret /·–'·/ *n* sign, mark; signal; ~ **etmek** *make a sign; mark; indicate; ~ **parmağı** index finger
işaretlemek /·–·'·/ *v* mark
işbirliği /'····/ *n* cooperation
işbirlikçi /'····/ *n* cooperator
işbölümü /'····/ *n* division of labor
işçi /·'·/ *n* workman, worker
işçilik /··'·/ *n* workmanship
işemek /··'·/ *v* urinate
işgal /·'·/ *n* occupation; ~ **altında** under occupation; ~ **etmek** occupy
işgücü /'···/ *n* workforce, manpower
işgünü /'···/ *n* workday
işitme /··'·/ *n* hearing
işitmek /··'·/ *v* *hear
işkembe /·'··/ *n* tripe
işkence /·'··/ *n* torture, torment; ~ **etmek** torture, torment
işlek /·'·/ *adj* busy, much used
işlem /·'·/ *n* procedure; operation; process
işleme /··'·/ *n* handwork, embroidery
işlenmemiş /·'···/ *adj* raw, unprocessed
işlenmiş /··'·/ *adj* processed
işletme /··'·/ *n* administration; management; enterprise
işletmeci /···'·/ *n* manager; administrator
işletmecilik /····'·/ *n* business administration
işletmek /··'·/ *v* *run, operate, work; exploit;
işlev /·'·/ *n* function
işporta /·'··/ *n* peddler pushcart; ~ **malı** shoddy goods
işportacı /·'···/ *n* street vendor

işsiz /·ˈ·/ *adj* jobless, unoccupied, unemployed; ~ **güçsüz** idle
iştah /·ˈ·/ *n* appetite; desire; ~ **açıcı** appetizing; ~ **açmak** whet the appetite
iştahlı /··ˈ·/ *adj* having an appetite
işte /·ˈ·/ *adv* look; here; there; like that; ~ **böyle** such is the matter
iştirak /··ˈ·/ *n* participation; ~ **etmek** participate in
işveren /··ˈ·/ *n* employer
işyeri /ˈ···/ *n* place of employment
itaat /·–ˈ·/ *n* obedience; ~ **etmek** obey
itaatli /·–ˈ·/ *adj* obedient
itaatsiz /·–ˈ·/ *adj* disobedient
itaatsizlik /·–··ˈ·/ *n* disobedience
İtalya /·ˈ··/ Italy
İtalyan /··ˈ·/ *adj, n* Italian
İtalyanca /··ˈ··/ *n* Italian language
itfaiye /·–ˈ·/ *n* fire brigade
itfaiyeci /·–··ˈ·/ *n* fireman
ithaf /·ˈ·/ *n* dedication; ~ **etmek** dedicate
ithal /·ˈ·/ *n* importation; ~ **etmek** import
ithalat /·–ˈ·/ *n* imports; importation
ithalatçı /·–·ˈ·/ *n* importer
itham /·ˈ·/ *n* accusation; charge; ~ **etmek** accuse
itibar /–·ˈ·/ *n* esteem, prestige, regard; ~ **etmek** esteem; ~ **görmek** *be respected
itibaren /–·ˈ–·/ *adv* from, dating from, as from
itikat /–·ˈ·/ *n* belief; creed
itimat /–·ˈ·/ *n* confidence, trust; ~ **etmek** *have confidence in; trust; rely upon
itina /–·ˈ–/ *n* care; ~ **etmek** *take great care
itiraf /–·ˈ·/ *n* confession; ~ **etmek** confess, admit
itiraz /–·ˈ·/ *n* objection; disapproval; protest; ~ **etmek** object, raise an objection
itişmek /··ˈ·/ *v* push one another; **itişip kakışmak** push and shove one another
itiyat /–·ˈ·/ *n* habit, custom
itmek /·ˈ·/ *v* push
ittifak /··ˈ·/ *n* agreement, alliance
ittifakla /··ˈ··/ *adv* unanimously
iyi /·ˈ·/ *adj* good; well; kind; beneficial; ~ **etmek** cure; ~ **gelmek** *do good; ~ **gitmek** *go well; ~ **kalpli** kind-hearted; ~ **ki** luckily, fortunately
iyice /·ˈ··/ *adv* pretty well, thoroughly
iyileşmek /···ˈ·/ *v* *get better; recover
iyilik /··ˈ·/ *n* goodness, kindness; ~ **etmek** *do kindness
iyiliksever /····ˈ·/ *adj* benevolent
iyimser /··ˈ·/ *adj* optimistic
iyimserlik /···ˈ·/ *n* optimism
iz *n* footmark, footprint; trail, trace
izah /–ˈ·/ *n* explanation; ~ **etmek** explain
izahat /––ˈ·/ *n* explanation
izci /·ˈ·/ *n* scout, boy scout
izdiham /··ˈ·/ *n* crowd, crowding
izin /·ˈ·/ *n* permission; permit; license; ~ **almak** *get permission
izinli /··ˈ·/ *adj* on leave, on vacation
izinsiz /··ˈ·/ *adj* without permission
izlemek /··ˈ·/ *v* follow; trace; watch
izleyici /···ˈ·/ *n* spectator
izmarit /··ˈ·/ *n* sea bream; cigarette butt
izolebant /···ˈ·/ *n* insulating tape
izzetinefis /····ˈ·/ *n* self-respect

J

jaluzi /··ˈ·/ *n* Venetian blind
jambon /·ˈ·/ *n* ham
jandarma /·ˈ··/ *n* gendarme
jant *n* rim
Japon /·ˈ·/ *n, adj* Japanese
Japonca /·ˈ··/ *n* Japanese language
Japonya /·ˈ··/ Japan
jarse /ˈ··/ *n* jersey
jartiyer /··ˈ·/ *n* garter
jelatin /··ˈ·/ *n* gelatine
jeneratör /···ˈ·/ *n* generator
jeoloji /···ˈ·/ *n* geology
jest *n* gesture
jet *n* jet
jeton /·ˈ·/ *n* token
jilet /·ˈ·/ *n* razor blade
jimnastik /··ˈ·/ *n* gymnastics
jinekolog /···ˈ·/ *n* gynecologist
jöle /ˈ··/ *n* jelly
judo /ˈ··/ *n* judo
jurnal /·ˈ·/ *n* report of informer
jüri /ˈ··/ *n* jury

K

kaba /·ˈ·/ *adj* rough; vulgar; ~ **et** buttocks; ~ **saba** coarse; vulgar, common
kabaca /·ˈ··/ *adv* grossly, roughly
kabadayı /·ˈ···/ *n* bully, tough guy
kabadayılık /·ˈ····/ *n* bravado; ~ **etmek** swagger
kabahat /··ˈ·/ *n* fault, offense
kabahatli /···ˈ·/ *adj* faulty, guilty
kabak /·ˈ·/ *n* squash, pumpkin; *adj* bare; unripe; ~ **kafalı** bald-headed
kabakulak /···ˈ·/ *n* mumps
kabalaşmak /···ˈ·/ *v* *become impolite
kabalık /··ˈ·/ *n* roughness, vulgarity; ~ **etmek** act rudely
kabarcık /··ˈ·/ *n* small bubble; blister
kabare /··ˈ·/ *n* cabaret
kabarık /··ˈ·/ *adj* swollen, puffy
kabarıklık /···ˈ·/ *n* bulge, swelling, puffiness
kabarma /··ˈ·/ *n* high tide; swelling
kabarmak /··ˈ·/ *v* *swell, *rise; increase
kabartma /··ˈ·/ *n* relief; *adj* in relief
Kâbe /–ˈ·/ Kaaba at Mecca
kabız /·ˈ·/ *n* constipation; *adj* constipated; ~ **olmak** *be constipated
kabile /·–ˈ·/ *n* tribe, clan
kabiliyet /–··ˈ·/ *n* ability; capability, capacity
kabiliyetli /–···ˈ·/ *adj* talented, able
kabine /·ˈ··/ *n* cabinet; small room
kabir /·ˈ·/ *n* grave, tomb
kablo /ˈ··/ *n* cable
kabristan /··ˈ·/ *n* cemetery, graveyard
kabuk /·ˈ·/ *n* outer covering; skin; shell; bark; scab
kabuklanmak /···ˈ·/ *v* *grow bark, form rind; form a skin
kabuklu /··ˈ·/ *adj* having a shell, barky
kabuksuz /··ˈ·/ *adj* without bark; shelled, peeled
kabul /·ˈ·/ *n* acceptance; reception; ~ **etmek** accept; admit; receive
kaburga /·ˈ··/ *n* rib
kâbus /–ˈ·/ *n* nightmare
kabza /·ˈ·/ *n* handle, butt
kabzımal /··ˈ·/ *n* middleman in fruit and vegetables
kaç *adj* how many, how much;

kaça what is the price?; ~ **defa** how many times?; ~ **tane** how many?; ~ **yaşında** how old is he?
kaçak /·ˈ·/ *n* fugitive, escapee; leakage; *adj* smuggled
kaçakçı /··ˈ·/ *n* smuggler
kaçakçılık /···ˈ·/ *n* smuggling; ~ **yapmak** smuggle
kaçamak /··ˈ·/ *n* subterfuge; evasion; escape
kaçık /·ˈ·/ *adj* crazy, mad
kaçınılmaz /···ˈ·/ *adj* inevitable, inescapable
kaçınmak /··ˈ·/ *v* abstain, avoid, evade, refrain
kaçırmak /··ˈ·/ *v* kidnap; abduct; hijack; miss
kaçışmak /··ˈ·/ *v* *flee in confusion; disperse
kaçkın /·ˈ·/ *n* fugitive, runaway
kaçmak /·ˈ·/ *v* *flee; *run away
kadar /·ˈ·/ *prep* until, till; up to
kadeh /·ˈ·/ *n* drinking glass, cup
kademe /··ˈ·/ *n* grade, degree; echelon
kader /·ˈ·/ *n* destiny, fate; **kaderin cilvesi** irony of fate
kadercilik /···ˈ·/ *n* fatalism
kadın /·ˈ·/ *n* woman, lady; female; ~ **avcısı** womanizer; ~ **doktoru** gynecologist
kadınlık /··ˈ·/ *n* womanhood
kadınsı /··ˈ·/ *adj* feminine; effeminate
kadife /··ˈ·/ *n* velvet
kadir[1] /–ˈ·/ *adj* mighty, powerful, strong
kadir[2] /·ˈ·/ *n* value, worth; dignity; magnitude
kadirşinas /···ˈ·/ *adj* grateful, appreciative
kadran /·ˈ·/ *n* face, dial
kadro /ˈ··/ *n* staff; workforce
kafa /·ˈ·/ *n* head; mind, brain; mentality; ~ **dengi** like-minded
kafadar /··ˈ·/ *n* intimate friend, buddy
kafalı /··ˈ·/ *adj* intelligent
kafasız /··ˈ·/ *adj* stupid
kafatası /·ˈ···/ *n* skull
kafes /·ˈ·/ *n* cage
kâfi /–ˈ–/ *adj* sufficient, enough
kafile /–·ˈ·/ *n* caravan; convoy; group
kâfir /–ˈ·/ *n* unbeliever
kâfirlik /–ˈ·/ *n* unbelief, irreligion
kafiye /–ˈ·/ *n* rhyme
Kafkasya /·ˈ··/ Caucasia
Kafkasyalı /·ˈ···/ *n, adj* Caucasian
kaftan /·ˈ·/ *n* robe of honor, caftan
kâgir /–ˈ·/ *adj* built of bricks *or* stone
kâğıt /·ˈ·/ *n* paper; playing card; document; ~ **oynamak** play cards; ~ **para** paper money
kağnı /·ˈ·/ *n* ox-cart with two solid wooden wheels
kahır /·ˈ·/ *n* grief, deep sorrow; distress, anxiety
kahırlanmak /···ˈ·/ *v* *be grieved, *be distressed
kâhin /–ˈ·/ *n* soothsayer
Kahire /ˈ–··/ Cairo
kahkaha /··ˈ·/ *n* loud laughter, chuckle; ~ **atmak** *burst out laughing
kahraman /··ˈ·/ *n* hero
kahramanca /··ˈ··/ *adv* heroically
kahramanlık /···ˈ·/ *n* heroism; ~ **göstermek** *show courage; behave as a hero
kahrolmak /ˈ···/ *v* *be depressed; *feel greatly annoyed
kahvaltı /··ˈ·/ *n* breakfast; ~ **etmek** *have breakfast
kahve /·ˈ·/ *n* coffee; coffeehouse; ~ **değirmeni** coffee mill

kahveci /··ˈ·/ *n* keeper of a coffee shop
kahvehane /·–ˈ·/ *n* coffee shop
kahverengi /·ˈ··/ *adj* brown
kâhya /·ˈ·/ *n* steward; caretaker in a parking lot
kaide /–ˈ·/ *n* rule; base
kâinat /–ˈ·/ *n* universe, cosmos, all creation
kâkül /–ˈ·/ *n* lock of hair, side lock
kalabalık /···ˈ·/ *n* crowd; *adj* crowded; overpopulated
kalakalmak /·ˈ··/ *v* *stand petrified with fear *or* surprise
kalan /·ˈ·/ *adj* remaining; *n* remainder
kalas /·ˈ·/ *n* beam, plank
kalay /·ˈ·/ *n* tin; tinfoil
kalaycı /··ˈ·/ *n* tinner, tinsmith
kalben /ˈ··/ *adv* cordially, heartily
kalbur /·ˈ·/ *n* sieve, riddle
kalça /·ˈ·/ *n* hip
kaldıraç /··ˈ·/ *n* crank, lever
kaldırım /··ˈ·/ *n* pavement; sidewalk; ~ **taşı** paving stone; ~ **kenarı** curb
kaldırmak /··ˈ·/ *v* lift, raise; *bear, endure
kale /·ˈ·/ *n* fortress, castle; goal
kaleci /··ˈ·/ *n* goalkeeper
kalem /·ˈ·/ *n* pencil, pen; ~ **açmak** sharpen a pencil; **kaleme almak** *write out, *draw up
kalemtıraş /···ˈ·/ *n* pencil sharpener
kalender /··ˈ·/ *adj* easygoing, unconventional, unpretentious
kalfa /·ˈ·/ *n* assistant master; qualified workman
kalıcı /··ˈ·/ *adj* permanent, lasting
kalın /·ˈ·/ *adj* thick; coarse; ~ **kafalı** thickheaded, stupid; ~ **ses** deep voice
kalınlaşmak /···ˈ·/ *v* thicken
kalınlık /··ˈ·/ *n* thickness
kalıntı /··ˈ·/ *n* remnant; remainder; leftover
kalıp /·ˈ·/ *n* mold, pattern; shape, form
kalıt /·ˈ·/ *n* inheritance
kalıtım /··ˈ·/ *n* heredity
kalıtsal /··ˈ·/ *adj* hereditary; inherited
kalite /·ˈ··/ *n* quality
kalkan /·ˈ·/ *n* shield, buckler; ~ **balığı** turbot
kalker /·ˈ·/ *n* limestone; chalky stone
kalkık /·ˈ·/ *adj* raised, erect
kalkınma /··ˈ·/ *n* progress, development, improvement
kalkınmak /··ˈ·/ *v* develop; *make progress
kalkış /·ˈ·/ *n* rising; departure
kalkışmak /··ˈ·/ *v* attempt, try, dare
kalkmak /·ˈ·/ *v* *get up; *stand up, *rise; *leave, depart
kalleş /·ˈ·/ *adj* untrustworthy, unreliable, deceitful
kalleşlik /··ˈ·/ *n* deceit, treachery, dirty trick; ~ **etmek** play a dirty trick on someone
kalmak /·ˈ·/ *v* remain, *be left; stay
kalorifer /···ˈ·/ *n* central heating
kalp[1] *n* heart; center; feeling; ~ **ağrısı** heartache; ~ **çarpıntısı** palpitation; ~ **krizi** heart attack
kalp[2] *adj* false, forged; ~ **para** false money, counterfeit coin
kalpazan /··ˈ·/ *n* counterfeiter
kalpsiz /·ˈ·/ *adj* heartless, cruel
kalsiyum /ˈ···/ *n* calcium
kama /·ˈ·/ *n* dagger; wedge
kamara /·ˈ··/ *n* cabin
kamarot /··ˈ·/ *n* ship's steward
kambiyo /ˈ···/ *n* foreign exchange
kambur /·ˈ·/ *n* hump, hunch; *adj* humpbacked, hunchbacked

kamburlaşmak /···ˈ·/ *v* *become hunchbacked
kamçı /·ˈ·/ *n* whip
kamçılamak /···ˈ·/ *v* whip, lash; stimulate
kamış /·ˈ·/ *n* reed
kâmil /–ˈ·/ *adj* perfect; complete; mature; well-conducted
kamp *n* camp; ~ **kurmak** pitch camp; ~ **yeri** campsite
kampçı /·ˈ·/ *n* camper
kamping /·ˈ·/ *n* camping place
kamyon /·ˈ·/ *n* truck *nAm;* lorry *nBr*
kamyonculuk /···ˈ·/ *n* trucking
kamyonet /··ˈ·/ *n* small truck
kan *n* blood; ~ **ağlamak** *be in deep distress; ~ **akıtmak** *shed blood; ~ **basıncı** blood pressure; ~ **vermek** donate blood
kanaat /··ˈ·/ *n* opinion, conviction; contentment, satisfaction; ~ **etmek** *be satisfied, *be contented
kanaatkâr /···ˈ·/ *adj* satisfied with little, unassuming, contented
Kanada /·ˈ··/ Canada
Kanadalı /·ˈ···/ *adj, n* Canadian
kanal /·ˈ·/ *n* channel; canal, waterway
kanalizasyon /····ˈ·/ *n* drainage, sewerage
kanama /··ˈ·/ *n* bleeding
kanamak /··ˈ·/ *v* *bleed
kanarya /·ˈ··/ *n* canary; **Kanarya Adaları** Canary Islands
kanat /·ˈ·/ *n* wing
kanatlı /··ˈ·/ *adj* winged
kanatsız /··ˈ·/ *adj* wingless
kanca /·ˈ·/ *n* hook
kancalı /··ˈ·/ *adj* hooked; ~ **iğne** safety pin
kandırıcı /···ˈ·/ *adj* convincing; deceiving
kandırmak /··ˈ·/ *v* deceive, cheat; seduce, *mislead; convince
kandil /·ˈ·/ *n* old-fashioned oil lamp; religious night feast in Islam
kanepe[1] /·ˈ··/ *n* sofa, couch
kanepe[2] /·ˈ··/ *n* canapé
kanı /·ˈ·/ *n* conviction, opinion
kanıksamak /···ˈ·/ *v* *become indifferent, *be satiated
kanıt /·ˈ·/ *n* evidence, proof
kanıtlamak /···ˈ·/ *v* prove
kani /–ˈ·/ *adj* convinced; ~ **olmak** *be convinced, *be satisfied
kanlı /·ˈ·/ *adj* bloody
kanmak /·ˈ·/ *v* *be deceived, *be cheated; *be seduced; *be convinced
kansız /·ˈ·/ *adj* bloodless; anemic
kansızlık /··ˈ·/ *n* anemia
kanun /–ˈ·/ *n* law; rule; **kanuna aykırı** illegal, lawless
kanunen /–ˈ–·/ *adv* by law, according to law; legally
kanuni /––ˈ–/ *adj* lawful, legal
kanunsuz /–·ˈ·/ *adj* illegal, lawless
kanyak /·ˈ·/ *n* cognac, brandy
kap *n* vessel, container; ~ **kacak** pots and pans
kapak /·ˈ·/ *n* cover, lid
kapaklanmak /···ˈ·/ *v* *fall flat on one's face
kapalı /··ˈ·/ *adj* closed, covered up, shut
kapamak /··ˈ·/ *v* *shut, close; turn off, switch off
kapan /·ˈ·/ *n* trap; ~ **kurmak** *set a trap; **kapana kısılmak** *be caught in a trap
kapanık /··ˈ·/ *adj* cloudy; shy, unsociable
kapanış /··ˈ·/ *n* closing
kapanmak /··ˈ·/ *v* *be shut,

*be closed
kaparo /·ˈ··/ *n* deposit, earnest money
kapatmak /··ˈ·/ *v* close, *shut
kapı /·ˈ·/ *n* door, gate; ~ **komşu** next door neighbor
kapıcı /··ˈ·/ *n* doorkeeper, janitor
kapışılmak /···ˈ·/ *v* *be sold like hot cakes
kapışmak /··ˈ·/ *v* *buy eagerly; *get to grips with somebody
kapitalist /···ˈ·/ *n* capitalist
kapitalizm /···ˈ·/ *n* capitalism
kaplama /··ˈ·/ *n* coating, plate; crown of a tooth; *adj* covered, coated
kaplamak /··ˈ·/ *v* cover over; cover; plate, coat
kaplan /·ˈ·/ *n* tiger
kaplı /·ˈ·/ *adj* covered, coated, plated
kaplıca /·ˈ··/ *n* hot spring
kaplumbağa /·ˈ···/ *n* tortoise, turtle
kapmak /·ˈ·/ *v* snatch, seize, carry off; *learn quickly
kapris /·ˈ·/ *n* caprice, fancy
kaprisli /··ˈ·/ *adj* capricious
kapsamak /··ˈ·/ *n* comprise, include, involve
kapsamlı /··ˈ·/ *adj* comprehensive, overall
kaptan /·ˈ·/ *n* captain
kaput /·ˈ·/ *n* military cloak
kaputbezi /·ˈ···/ *n* coarse calico
kar *n* snow, snowfall; **kardan adam** snowman; ~ **yağmak** snow; ~ **tanesi** snowflake
kâr *n* profit, gain; ~ **bırakmak** yield a profit; ~ **etmek** *make a profit; ~ **haddi** profit limit; ~ **ve zarar** profit and loss
kara[1] /·ˈ·/ *adj* black; bad; unlucky; dark
kara[2] /·ˈ·/ *n* land, shore; ground; *adj* territorial; ~ **kuvvetleri** land forces; **karaya ayak basmak** land, disembark
karabiber /·ˈ···/ *n* black pepper
karaborsa /·ˈ···/ *n* black market
karaca /·ˈ··/ *n* roe deer
karaciğer /·ˈ···/ *n* liver; ~ **iltihabı** hepatitis
Karadeniz /·ˈ···/ Black Sea
karafatma /·ˈ···/ *n* black beetle
karagöz /··ˈ·/ *n* Turkish shadow show; ~ **balığı** sea bream
karakış /·ˈ··/ *n* severe winter
karakol /··ˈ·/ *n* police station; patrol
karakter /··ˈ·/ *n* character
karalamak /···ˈ·/ *v* blacken; scribble; *write hastily; slander
karaltı /··ˈ·/ *n* indistinct figure; blackness
karamela /··ˈ··/ *n* caramel, toffee
karamsar /··ˈ·/ *adj* pessimistic
karanfil /··ˈ·/ *n* carnation; clove
karanlık /··ˈ·/ *n* darkness; *adj* dark; obscure
karantina /··ˈ··/ *n* quarantine
karar /·ˈ·/ *n* decision, resolution, determination; judgment; ~ **almak,** ~ **vermek** decide; *make a decision; **karara varmak** *come to a decision
karargâh /··ˈ·/ *n* headquarters
kararlaştırmak /····ˈ·/ *v* decide, agree on, arrange, settle
kararlı /··ˈ·/ *adj* decided, determined; fixed
kararmak /··ˈ·/ *v* *become black, dark *or* obscure; darken
kararsız /··ˈ·/ *adj* irresolute, undecided; unstable
kararsızlık /···ˈ·/ *n* indecision, hesitation, wavering; instability
karartma /··ˈ·/ *n* blackout
karartmak /··ˈ·/ *v* *make dark *or*

obscure; shade, *make shadows
karasevda /·ˈ···/ *n* melancholy
karasinek /·ˈ··/ *n* housefly
karatahta /·ˈ··/ *n* blackboard
karavan /··ˈ·/ *n* caravan
karayel /·ˈ··/ *n* northwest wind
karayolu /·ˈ···/ *n* highway, road
kardeş /·ˈ·/ *n* brother *or* sister; ~ **payı** equal share
kardeşçe /·ˈ··/ *adv* sisterly, brotherly
kardeşlik /··ˈ·/ *n* brotherhood, sisterhood, fraternity
kare /·ˈ·/ *n* square
karga /·ˈ·/ *n* crow
kargaşa /··ˈ·/ *n* confusion, disorder; dispute, quarrel
kargı /·ˈ·/ *n* pike; javelin; lance
karı /·ˈ·/ *n* woman; wife
karıkoca /···ˈ·/ *n* wife and husband, married couple
karın /·ˈ·/ *n* abdomen; stomach, belly; womb; ~ **ağrısı** stomach-ache
karınca /·ˈ··/ *n* ant
karıncalanmak /·ˈ····/ *v* *feel pins and needles
karış /·ˈ·/ *n* span; ~ **karış** inch by inch
karışık /··ˈ·/ *adj* mixed, not pure; complicated; confused; miscellaneous, assorted
karışıklık /···ˈ·/ *n* disorder, confusion; agitation
karışım /··ˈ·/ *n* mixture
karışlamak /···ˈ·/ *v* measure by the span
karışmak /··ˈ·/ *v* mix, mingle; *become confused; interfere; *be involved
karıştırmak /···ˈ·/ *v* mix, blend, stir; confuse
karides /·ˈ··/ *n* shrimp, prawn
karikatür /···ˈ·/ *n* cartoon; caricature
karikatürcü /····ˈ·/ *n* cartoonist
karlı /·ˈ·/ *adj* snowy
kârlı /·ˈ·/ *adj* profitable, fruitful
karma /·ˈ·/ *adj* mixed; ~ **öğretim** coeducation; ~ **takım** mixed team
karmak /·ˈ·/ *v* mix, blend; shuffle
karmakarışık /ˈ·····/ *adj* in utter disorder, in a mess
karmaşık /··ˈ·/ *adj* complex
karnabahar /···ˈ·/ *n* cauliflower
karnaval /··ˈ·/ *n* carnival
karne /·ˈ·/ *n* school report
karpuz /·ˈ·/ *n* watermelon
karşı /·ˈ·/ *adj* opposite; *prep* against; toward; in return for; ~ **çıkmak** oppose; disagree; ~ **gelmek** disobey; ~ **koymak** resist; ~ **olmak** *be against
karşılama /···ˈ·/ *n* meeting, greeting, reception, welcome
karşılamak /···ˈ·/ *v* *go to meet, welcome; receive; cover
karşılaşma /···ˈ·/ *n* game, match; meeting
karşılaşmak /···ˈ·/ *v* *meet face to face
karşılaştırma /····ˈ·/ *n* comparison
karşılaştırmak /····ˈ·/ *v* compare
karşılaştırmalı /·····ˈ·/ *adj* comparative
karşılık /··ˈ·/ *n* return, response; equivalent; answer; recompense; ~ **olarak** in return; in reply; ~ **vermek** answer back
karşılıklı /···ˈ·/ *adj* mutual; ~ **olarak** mutually
karşın /·ˈ·/ *prep* in spite of
karşıt /·ˈ·/ *adj* opposite, contrary
karşıtlık /··ˈ·/ *n* contrast
kart[1] *adj* tough, hard; old
kart[2] *n* card; postcard; visiting card

kartal /·'·/ *n* eagle
kartlaşmak /··'·/ *v* *become tough *or* old
karton /·'·/ *n* cardboard; cartoon
kartopu /'···/ *n* snowball
kartvizit /··'·/ *n* visiting card
karyola /·'··/ *n* bed, bedstead
kas *n* muscle
kasa /'··/ *n* cash box, safe; till; cashier's office; ~ **açığı** cash deficit
kasaba /·'··/ *n* small town; ~ **halkı** townsfolk, townspeople
kasabalı /·'···/ *n* townsman
kasap /·'·/ *n* butcher; butcher's shop
kâse /–'·/ *n* bowl
kasık /·'·/ *n* groin
kasılmak /··'·/ *v* contract, *be stretched tight; swagger
kasım /·'·/ November
kasımpatı /·'···/ *n* chrysanthemum
kasırga /·'··/ *n* whirlwind, cyclone
kasıt /·'·/ *n* intention, purpose, aim
kasıtlı /··'·/ *adj* deliberate, intentional, purposeful
kasket /·'·/ *n* cap
kasmak /·'·/ *v* stretch tight; curtail
kasten /'··/ *adv* intentionally, deliberately
kastetmek /'···/ *v* purpose; *have a design against; *mean
kasvet /·'·/ *n* depression, gloom; ~ **basmak** *become depressed; ~ **vermek** depress
kasvetli /··'·/ *adj* sad, gloomy, depressing
kaş *n* eyebrow; ~ **çatmak** frown; **kaşla göz arasında** in the twinkling of an eye
kaşık /·'·/ *n* spoon; ~ ~ by spoonfuls
kaşıklamak /···'·/ *v* spoon up
kaşımak /··'·/ *v* scratch with the nails
kaşıntı /··'·/ *n* itching
kâşif /–'·/ *n* discoverer, explorer
kaşkol /·'·/ *n* scarf
kat *n* story; floor; fold; layer; multiple; ~ ~ in layers
katar /·'·/ *n* railway train
katetmek /'···/ *v* travel over
katı /·'·/ *adj* hard, solid, rigid; ~ **yürekli** heartless, hard-hearted
katık /·'·/ *n* anything eaten with bread
katılaşma /···'·/ *n* solidification
katılaşmak /···'·/ *v* *become hard, dry, solid *or* stiff; harden
katılık /··'·/ *n* hardness, stiffness; solidity; rigidness
katılmak /··'·/ *v* join, participate; *be added, *be mixed
katır /·'·/ *n* mule
kati /·'–/ *adj* decisive, definite, final; absolute
katil /–'·/ *n* murderer, killer, assassin
kâtip /–'·/ *n* clerk; secretary
katiyen /·'–·/ *adv* definitely, absolutely
katiyet /·–'·/ *n* definiteness, irrevocability
katkı /·'·/ *n* contribution, addition; **katkıda bulunmak** contribute
katlamak /··'·/ *v* fold, pleat
katlanmak /··'·/ *v* *be folded; *bear, tolerate, endure
katletmek /'···/ *v* kill, murder
katliam /··'·/ *n* massacre
katma /·'·/ *n* addition; *adj* additional, supplementary; ~ **bütçe** supplementary budget; ~ **değer vergisi, KDV** value added tax, VAT
katmak /·'·/ *v* add, mix
katran /·'·/ *n* tar

katsayı /'···/ *n* coefficient
kauçuk /··'·/ *n* rubber, India rubber
kavak /·'·/ *n* poplar
kaval /·'·/ *n* shepherd's pipe
kavalye /·'··/ *n* a lady's escort
kavanoz /··'·/ *n* jar, pot
kavga /·'·/ *n* quarrel, brawl, fight; **~ etmek** quarrel, *fight
kavgacı /··'·/ *adj* quarrelsome
kavis /·'·/ *n* bend, curve
kavram /·'·/ *n* concept, notion
kavrama /··'·/ *n* comprehension; clutch
kavramak /··'·/ *v* comprehend, conceive; seize, grasp, clutch
kavrayış /··'·/ *n* comprehension, conception
kavrulmak /··'·/ *v* *be roasted, *be scorched
kavrulmuş /··'·/ *adj* roasted
kavşak /·'·/ *n* junction, crossroads
kavun /·'·/ *n* melon, muskmelon
kavuniçi /·'···/ *adj* pinkish yellow
kavurma /··'·/ *n* fried meat
kavurmak /··'·/ *v* fry; roast; dry
kavuşmak /··'·/ *v* *meet, *meet again after a long absence; reach, attain
kavuşturmak /···'·/ *v* *bring together, unite
kaya /·'·/ *n* rock
kayak /·'·/ *n* skiing; **~ yapmak** ski
kayalık /··'·/ *adj* rocky; *n* rocky place, cliff
kaybetmek /'···/ *v* *lose
kaybolmak /'···/ *v* *be lost; disappear
kaydetmek /'···/ *v* enroll; register; note down
kaydırak /··'·/ *n* hopscotch
kaygan /·'·/ *adj* slippery
kaygı /·'·/ *n* anxiety, grief; care
kaygılandırmak /····'·/ *v* worry, *make anxious
kaygılanmak /···'·/ *v* worry, *feel anxious
kaygılı /··'·/ *adj* worried, anxious
kaygısız /··'·/ *adj* carefree
kayık /·'·/ *n* boat, rowboat
kayıkçı /··'·/ *n* boatman
kayın /·'·/ *n* beech
kayınbirader /·'··–·/ *n* brother-in-law
kayınpeder /·'···/ *n* father-in-law
kayınvalide /·'–··/ *n* mother-in-law
kayıp /·'·/ *n* loss; casualties; *adj* lost; **~ eşya** lost property
kayırmak /··'·/ *v* protect, favor, back; look after
kayısı /··'·/ *n* apricot
kayış /·'·/ *n* strap, belt
kayıt /·'·/ *n* registration, record, enrollment; **kayda değer** noteworthy
kayıtlı /··'·/ *adj* registered, recorded; inscribed
kayıtsız /··'·/ *adj* unregistered; unconcerned; **~ şartsız** unconditional; without any condition
kayıtsızlık /···'·/ *n* indifference
kaymak[1] /·'·/ *v* slip, *slide, skate
kaymak[2] /·'·/ *n* cream, clotted cream
kaymakam /··'·/ *n* head official of a district
kaymaklı /··'·/ *adj* creamy; made *or* served with cream
kaynak /·'·/ *n* spring, fountain; source; welding; **~ yapmak** weld; patch
kaynakçı /··'·/ *n* welder
kaynamak /··'·/ *v* boil; *be hot; gush forth
kaynar /·'·/ *adj* boiling, bubbling
kaynaşmak /··'·/ *v* unite; * be

welded; *become good friends
kaynata /·ˈ··/ *n* father-in-law
kaynatmak /··ˈ·/ *v* boil
kaypak /·ˈ·/ *adj* slippery; shifty; unreliable
kaytarmak /··ˈ·/ *v* *get out of doing; shirk; dodge
kaz *n* goose
kaza[1] /·ˈ–/ *n* accident, mishap, crash; ~ **ile** by accident; **kazaya uğramak** *have an accident
kaza[2] /·ˈ–/ *n* administrative district
kazak /·ˈ·/ *n* pullover; jersey *nBr*
kazan /·ˈ·/ *n* cauldron, boiler
kazanç /·ˈ·/ *n* profit, earnings; benefit, gain, advantage
kazançlı /··ˈ·/ *adj* gainful, lucrative; advantageous; profitable
kazanmak /··ˈ·/ *v* *win; gain, acquire, earn
kazara /·ˈ––/ *adv* by accident, by chance
kazazede /·–ˈ·/ *n* accident victim; *adj* ruined; shipwrecked
kazı /·ˈ·/ *n* excavation
kazık /·ˈ·/ *n* stake, pale; deceit, trick; *adj* very expensive
kazımak /··ˈ·/ *v* scrape off; scratch; shave off
kazma /·ˈ·/ *n* pickax, mattock
kazmak /·ˈ·/ *v* *dig, excavate
kebap /·ˈ·/ *n* roast, broiled meat; *adj* roasted
keçi /·ˈ·/ *n* goat
keder /·ˈ·/ *n* grief, sorrow
kederlenmek /···ˈ·/ *v* *become sorrowful
kederli /··ˈ·/ *adj* sorrowful, grieved
kedi /·ˈ·/ *n* cat;
kefal /·ˈ·/ *n* gray mullet
kefalet /·–ˈ·/ *n* bail; guarantee
kefen /·ˈ·/ *n* shroud
kefil /·ˈ·/ *n* guarantor, sponsor; ~ **olmak** act as guarantor
kefillik /··ˈ·/ *n* guarantee, security
kehanet /·–ˈ·/ *n* soothsaying; **kehanette bulunmak** predict, prophesy
kek *n* cake
kekelemek /···ˈ·/ *v* stutter, stammer
kekik /·ˈ·/ *n* garden thyme
keklik /·ˈ·/ *n* partridge
kel *adj* bald; scabby
kelebek /··ˈ·/ *n* butterfly; moth
kelepçe /·ˈ··/ *v* handcuff
kelime /··ˈ·/ *n* word; ~ ~ word by word; ~ **oyunu** pun, quibble
kelle /·ˈ·/ *n* head
keloğlan /ˈ···/ a popular hero of Turkish folk tales
kemal /·ˈ·/ *n* perfection, maturity
keman /·ˈ·/ *n* violin
kemençe /··ˈ·/ *n* small violin
kemer /·ˈ·/ *n* belt; waist of a garment; arch
kemik /·ˈ·/ *n* bone
kemikleşmek /···ˈ·/ *v* ossify
kemikli /··ˈ·/ *adj* having bones; large boned
kemiksiz /··ˈ·/ *adj* boneless
kenar /·ˈ·/ *n* edge, border, margin; ~ **mahalle** slums, outskirts; **kenara çekilmek** step aside
kendi /·ˈ·/ *pron* oneself; self; *adj* own; ~ **başına** on one's own; ~ **halinde** quiet, harmless; ~ **kendime** by myself; **kendim** myself; **kendini beğenmiş** conceited, arrogant
kendir /·ˈ·/ *n* hemp
kenetlemek /···ˈ·/ *v* clamp together
kenevir /··ˈ·/ *n* hemp
kent *n* city, town
kentleşme /··ˈ·/ *n* urbanization
kepçe /·ˈ·/ *n* ladle, scoop; butterfly net
kepek /·ˈ·/ *n* bran; dandruff
kepekli /··ˈ·/ *adj* branny; scurfy

kepenk /·ˈ·/ *n* large pull-down shutter; wooden cover
keramet /–ˈ·/ *n* miracle
kere /·ˈ·/ *adv* time, times; **bir ~** once; just; for one thing
kereste /·ˈ··/ *n* timber, lumber
kereviz /··ˈ·/ *n* celery
kerpeten /··ˈ·/ *n* pincers
kerpiç /·ˈ·/ *n* sun-dried brick, adobe
kertenkele /·ˈ···/ *n* lizard
kervan /·ˈ·/ *n* caravan
kervansaray /·ˈ···/ *n* caravansary
kese /·ˈ·/ *n* purse; pouch; coarse bath glove
kesekâğıdı /·ˈ····/ *n* paper bag
keselemek /···ˈ·/ *v* rub the body with a bath glove
kesif /·ˈ·/ *adj* dense; thick
kesik /·ˈ·/ *adj* cut; broken; interrupted; curdled; *n* a cut; **~ ~** intermittently
kesiksiz /··ˈ·/ *adj* continued; continuous
kesilmek /··ˈ·/ *v* *be cut; *be interrupted; cease, stop; *get tired
kesim /·ˈ·/ *n* cutting, slaughtering; cut, make; zone, sector
kesin /·ˈ·/ *adj* definite, certain; **~ olarak** certainly
kesinleşmek /···ˈ·/ *v* *become definite
kesinti /··ˈ·/ *n* deduction; interruption
kesintili /···ˈ·/ *adj* interrupted, discontinuous
kesintisiz /···ˈ·/ *adj* without deduction, net; continuous
kesişmek /··ˈ·/ *v* *cut each other, intersect
keskin /·ˈ·/ *adj* sharp, acute; pungent; **~ nişancı** sharpshooter; **~ viraj** sharp bend; **~ zekâlı** sharp-witted
keskinleştirmek /····ˈ·/ *v* sharpen
keskinlik /··ˈ·/ *n* sharpness
kesme /·ˈ·/ *adj* cut; **~ işareti** apostrophe
kesmek /·ˈ·/ *v* *cut; slaughter; interrupt, *break off; *give up, abandon
kesmeşeker /·ˈ···/ *n* lump sugar
kestane /·–ˈ·/ *n* chestnut
kestirme /··ˈ·/ *n* estimate; short-cut; **~ cevap** decisive *or* short answer
kestirmek /··ˈ·/ *v* cause to cut; guess; estimate; discern, *understand clearly; *take a nap, doze
keşfetmek /ˈ···/ *v* discover
keşif /·ˈ·/ *n* discovery, exploration
keşişleme /···ˈ·/ *n* southeast wind
keşke /ˈ··/ I wish, if only
keşmekeş /··ˈ·/ *n* great confusion, disorder
keten /·ˈ·/ *n* flax; linen
ketenhelvası /·ˈ····/ *n* cotton candy
keyfi /·ˈ–/ *adj* arbitrary, despotic
keyif /·ˈ·/ *n* pleasure, enjoyment, joy; disposition, inclination; **~ çatmak** enjoy oneself; **~ sürmek** *lead a life of pleasure
keyifli /··ˈ·/ *adj* in high spirits, merry
keyifsiz /··ˈ·/ *adj* in bad humor; unwell
keyifsizlik /···ˈ·/ *n* indisposition, ailment
kez *n* time; **bu ~** this time
keza /ˈ·–/ *adv* also, likewise
kezzap /·ˈ·/ *n* nitric acid
kıble /·ˈ·/ *n* direction of Mecca
Kıbrıs /ˈ··/ Cyprus
Kıbrıslı /ˈ···/ *adj, n* Cypriot
kıç *n* buttocks, bottom, butt; stern, poop

kıdem /·ˈ·/ *n* seniority, priority
kıdemli /··ˈ·/ *adj* senior
kıdemsiz /··ˈ·/ *adj* junior
kıkırdamak /···ˈ·/ *v* giggle; chuckle
kıl *n* hair; bristle; ~ **payı kurtulmak** escape by a hair's breadth; **kılına dokunmamak** not *lay a finger on somebody
kılavuz /··ˈ·/ *n* guide; leader
kılçık /·ˈ·/ *n* fishbone
kılıbık /··ˈ·/ *adj* henpecked
kılıç /·ˈ·/ *n* sword
kılıçbalığı /·ˈ···/ *n* swordfish
kılıf /·ˈ·/ *n* case, cover
kılık /·ˈ·/ *n* dress, costume; ~ **kıyafet** external appearance; dress
kılıksız /··ˈ·/ *adj* shabby, untidy, unkempt
kıllı /·ˈ·/ *adj* hairy, bristly
kılmak /·ˈ·/ *v* *make, render; **mümkün** ~ *make possible
kımıldamak /···ˈ·/ *v* move slightly, stir, bulge
kınamak /··ˈ·/ *v* blame, reproach
kıpırdamak /···ˈ·/ *v* quiver, move, budge
kır[1] *n* countryside
kır[2] *adj* gray; ~ **düşmek** turn gray
kıraathane /···–ˈ·/ *n* coffeehouse
kırağı /··ˈ·/ *n* hoarfrost
kırbaç /·ˈ·/ *n* whip, scourge
kırbaçlamak /···ˈ·/ *v* whip, flog
kırgın /·ˈ·/ *adj* disappointed; hurt
kırgınlık /··ˈ·/ *n* disappointment; resentment
kırıcı /··ˈ·/ *adj* offensive
kırık /·ˈ·/ *adj* broken; *n* break, fracture; failing grade; ~ **dökük** in pieces; broken
kırıkçı /··ˈ·/ *n* bonesetter
kırıklık /··ˈ·/ *n* indisposition, infirmity
kırılgan /··ˈ·/ *adj* brittle, fragile
kırılma /··ˈ·/ *n* break; refraction
kırılmak /··ˈ·/ *v* *be broken; *be hurt, *be offended
kırım /·ˈ·/ *n* slaughter, massacre
Kırım /ˈ··/ Crimea
Kırımlı /ˈ···/ *adj, n* Crimean
kırıntı /··ˈ·/ *n* fragment; crumb
kırışık /··ˈ·/ *adj* wrinkled
kırışmak /··ˈ·/ *v* *become wrinkled
kırk *num* forty
kırkayak /··ˈ·/ *n* centipede
kırkmak /·ˈ·/ *v* shear
kırlangıç /··ˈ·/ *n* swallow; ~ **balığı** red gurnard
kırmak /·ˈ·/ *v* *break; offend, *hurt; **kırıp dökmek** destroy; **kırıp geçirmek** tyrannize; rage
kırmızı /··ˈ·/ *adj* red
kırmızıbiber /··ˈ···/ *n* red pepper, cayenne pepper
kırmızıturp /··ˈ··/ *n* radish
kırpıntı /··ˈ·/ *n* clippings
kırpmak /·ˈ·/ *v* clip, shear
kırsal /·ˈ·/ *adj* rural
kırtasiye /·–·ˈ·/ *n* stationery
kırtasiyeci /·–··ˈ·/ *n* stationer
kırtasiyecilik /·–···ˈ·/ *n* bureaucracy, red tape; stationery business
kısa /·ˈ·/ *adj* short; brief; concise; ~ **devre** short circuit; ~ **kesmek** *cut short; ~ **sürmek** *take a short time
kısaca /·ˈ··/ *adv* shortly
kısacası /·ˈ···/ *adv* in a word, briefly
kısacık /ˈ···/ *adj* very short
kısalık /··ˈ·/ *n* *shortness
kısalmak /··ˈ·/ *v* *become short
kısaltma /··ˈ·/ *n* abbreviation
kısaltmak /··ˈ·/ *v* shorten; abbreviate
kısık /·ˈ·/ *adj* hoarse, choked; turned down; ~ **sesli** hoarse

voiced
kısım /·ˈ·/ *n* part, piece; section, division; kind, sort
kısıntı /··ˈ·/ *n* restriction; cut
kısır /·ˈ·/ *adj* sterile, barren
kısırlaşmak /···ˈ·/ *v* *become sterile
kısırlaştırmak /····ˈ·/ *v* *make sterile
kısırlık /··ˈ·/ *n* barrenness, sterility
kısıtlamak /···ˈ·/ *v* restrict; limit
kıskaç /·ˈ·/ *n* pincers; forceps; claw
kıskanç /·ˈ·/ *adj* jealous, envious
kıskançlık /··ˈ·/ *n* jealousy
kıskandırmak /···ˈ·/ *v* arouse someone's jealousy
kıskanmak /··ˈ·/ *v* *be jealous, envy
kıskıvrak /ˈ···/ *adv* tightly
kısmak /·ˈ·/ *v* reduce, *cut down; turn down, lower
kısmen /ˈ··/ *adv* partly, partially
kısmet /·ˈ·/ *n* destiny; chance, luck
kısmetli /··ˈ·/ *adj* fortunate, lucky
kısmetsiz /··ˈ·/ *adj* unlucky
kısmi /·ˈ–/ *adj* partial
kısrak /·ˈ·/ *n* mare
kıstırmak /··ˈ·/ *v* pinch, corner; squeeze
kış *n* winter; ~ **kıyamet** severe winter; ~ **uykusu** hibernation; **kışın** in the winter; during winter
kışkırtıcı /···ˈ·/ *adj* provocative; *n* instigator, agitator
kışkırtmak /··ˈ·/ *v* incite, provoke
kışla /ˈ··/ *n* barracks
kışlık /·ˈ·/ *adj* suitable for the winter, wintery
kıt *adj* scarce, scanty; ~ **kanaat** scarcely
kıta /·ˈ·/ *n* continent; stanza
kıtlaşmak /··ˈ·/ *v* *become scarce
kıtlık /·ˈ·/ *n* famine; lack, scarcity
kıvam /·ˈ·/ *n* thickness, density; proper degree of consistency *or* density
kıvanç /·ˈ·/ *n* pleasure, joy; proper pride
kıvılcım /··ˈ·/ *n* spark
kıvılcımlanmak /····ˈ·/ *v* spark
kıvırcık /··ˈ·/ *adj* curly
kıvır kıvır /·ˈ· ··/ *adj* curly
kıvırmak /··ˈ·/ *v* curl, frizz; twist, *bend
kıvrak /·ˈ·/ *adj* brisk, alert, agile
kıvranmak /··ˈ·/ *v* writhe; suffer greatly
kıvrık /·ˈ·/ *adj* curled, twisted; hemmed, folded
kıvrılmak /··ˈ·/ *v* curl up; coil up
kıvrım /·ˈ·/ *n* curl, twist; winding; undulation
kıvrıntı /··ˈ·/ *n* winding, turn, twist, coil
kıyafet /·–ˈ·/ *n* dress, costume, clothes; ~ **balosu** fancy dress ball
kıyamet /·–ˈ·/ *n* doomsday; tumult, uproar; ~ **günü** doomsday; **kıyameti koparmak** raise hell
kıyas /·ˈ·/ *n* comparison
kıyasıya /·ˈ···/ *adv* mercilessly; ruthlessly
kıyaslamak /···ˈ·/ *v* compare; conclude by analogy
kıyı /·ˈ·/ *n* shore; edge; border; **kıyıda köşede** in out-of-the-way places
kıyma /·ˈ·/ *n* ground meat
kıymak /·ˈ·/ *v* chop up finely; not spare; *spend, sacrifice
kıymet /·ˈ·/ *n* value, worth; ~ **biçmek** evaluate, assess; ~ **vermek** esteem; **kıymetini bilmek** appreciate
kıymetlenmek /···ˈ·/ *v* increase in value
kıymetli /··ˈ·/ *adj* valuable
kıymetsiz /··ˈ·/ *adj* valueless
kıymık /·ˈ·/ *n* splinter

kız *n* girl; daughter; virgin
kızak /·ˈ·/ *n* sledge
kızamık /··ˈ·/ *n* measles
kızamıkçık /···ˈ·/ *n* German measles
kızarmak /··ˈ·/ *v* turn red, blush; *be roasted
kızarmış ekmek /··ˈ· ··/ toast
kızartma /··ˈ·/ *adj* roasted; fried; *n* roast meat, etc.
kızartmak /··ˈ·/ *v* fry
kızdırmak /··ˈ·/ *v* *make angry, irritate; heat, *make hot
kızgın /·ˈ·/ *adj* hot; angry
kızgınlık /··ˈ·/ *n* hotness; anger
kızıl /·ˈ·/ *adj* red, scarlet; *n* scarlet fever
Kızılay /·ˈ··/ Red Crescent
kızılcık /··ˈ·/ *n* cornelian cherry
kızılderili /·ˈ····/ *n* American Indian
Kızılhaç /·ˈ··/ Red Cross
kızılötesi /·ˈ····/ *adj* infrared
kızışmak /··ˈ·/ *v* *get angry *or* excited; *become heated; *get hot
kızkardeş /ˈ···/ *n* sister
kızlık /·ˈ·/ *n* girlhood; virginity
kızmak /·ˈ·/ *v* *get angry; *get hot
ki *adv* who, which, that; so that
kibar /·ˈ·/ *adj* polite, refined; well-bred
kibarca /·ˈ··/ *adv* in a refined manner, politely, civilly
kibir /·ˈ·/ *n* pride, conceit, haughtiness
kibirli /··ˈ·/ *adj* haughty, proud, conceited
kibrit /·ˈ·/ *n* match; ~ **çakmak** *strike a match; ~ **çöpü** match stick; ~ **kutusu** match box
kil *n* clay, argil
kiler /·ˈ·/ *n* pantry, storeroom, larder
kilim /·ˈ·/ *n* rug, woven matting
kilise /·ˈ··/ *n* church
kilit /·ˈ·/ *n* lock, latch, padlock
kilitlemek /···ˈ·/ *v* lock
kilitli /··ˈ·/ *n* locked
kilo /ˈ··/ *n* kilo, kilogram; ~ **almak** *put on weight; ~ **vermek** *lose weight, *grow thin
kim *pron* who, whoever; **kimi** some (of them); **kim bilir?** who knows?; **kim o?** who is it?; **kimi zaman** sometimes; **kimin** whose
kimlik /·ˈ·/ *n* identity; ~ **belgesi** identity card
kimse /·ˈ·/ *pron* someone, somebody, anyone, anybody; (with negative) nobody, no one; **kimsesi yok** he has no one
kimsesiz /··ˈ·/ *adj* without relations, friends
kimsesizlik /···ˈ·/ *n* destitution
kimya /·ˈ–/ *n* chemistry
kimyacı /·–ˈ·/ *n* chemist
kimyager /·–ˈ·/ *n* chemist
kimyevi /··ˈ–/ *adj* chemical; ~ **maddeler** chemicals
kin *n* grudge, hatred, rancor; ~ **beslemek** *bear a grudge
kinaye /·–ˈ·/ *n* allusion
kinayeli /·–·ˈ·/ *adj* allusive
kinci /·ˈ·/ *adj* vindictive
kir *n* dirt
kira /·ˈ–/ *n* hire, rent; **kiralık ev** house to let; ~ **ile** on hire, on lease; ~ **kontratı** rental contract; **kiraya vermek** *let out on hire; *let, rent
kiracı /·–ˈ·/ *n* tenant, leaseholder
kiralamak /·–ˈ·/ *v* hire, rent
kiraz /·ˈ·/ *n* cherry
kireç /·ˈ·/ *n* lime, chalk; ~ **kuyusu** lime pit; ~ **suyu** lime water
kireçli /··ˈ·/ *adj* chalky; mixed with lime
kirlenmek /··ˈ·/ *v* *become dirty *or* soiled
kirletmek /··ˈ·/ *v* *make dirty,

pollute
kirpi /·'·/ *n* hedgehog
kirpik /·'·/ *n* eyelash
kişi /·'·/ *n* person, individual, human being; one
kişilik /··'·/ *n* personality; individuality; ~ **özelliği** personality trait
kişilikli /···'·/ *adj* having a strong personality
kişisel /··'·/ *adj* personal
kişnemek /··'·/ *v* neigh, whinny
kitabe /·–'·/ *n* inscription, epitaph
kitabevi /·'···/ *n* bookshop, bookstore
kitap /·'·/ *n* book
kitapçı /··'·/ *n* bookseller
kitaplık /··'·/ *n* library; bookcase
kitle /·'·/ *n* mass; heap; ~ **iletişim araçları** mass media
klakson /·'·/ *n* horn
klasman /·'·/ *n* classification
klasör /·'·/ *n* file
klavye /·'·/ *n* keyboard
klinik /·'·/ *n* clinic
klor *n* chlorine
koalisyon /···'·/ *n* coalition
kobay /·'·/ *n* guinea pig
koca[1] /·'·/ *n* husband
koca[2] /·'·/ *adj* old, aged, ancient; large, great
kocakarı /·'···/ *n* hag, witch
kocamak /··'·/ *v* *grow old
kocaman /'···/ *adj* large, huge, enormous
koç *n* ram
koçan /·'·/ *n* corn cob; stump
kof *adj* hollow
kofana /·'··/ *n* large bluefish
kofluk /·'·/ *n* hollowness
koğuş /·'·/ *n* dormitory, ward
kok *n* coke; ~ **kömürü** coke
kokarca /·'··/ *n* polecat
koklamak /··'·/ *v* *smell; sniff
koklaşmak /··'·/ *v* *smell one another; caress and kiss one another
kokmak /·'·/ *v* *smell
kokmuş /·'·/ *adj* smelly, stinking
kokteyl /'··/ *n* cocktail
koku /·'·/ *n* smell, scent; perfume
kokulu /··'·/ *adj* odorous, fragrant, perfumed
kokusuz /··'·/ *adj* scentless
kokuşmak /··'·/ *v* *go bad, *be spoiled, putrefy
kol *n* arm; sleeve; handle; subdivision; ~ **düğmesi** cufflink; ~ **saati** wristwatch
kolaçan etmek /··'·/ look around, rummage about
kolay /·'·/ *adj* easy; simple; **kolayını bulmak** *find an easy way
kolayca /·'··/ *adv* easily
kolaylık /··'·/ *n* easiness; ~ **göstermek** help, *make things easy
kolaylıkla /··'··/ *adv* easily
kolej /·'·/ *n* private high school
koleksiyon /···'·/ *n* collection
koleksiyoncu /····'·/ *n* collector
kolera /·'··/ *n* cholera
kollamak /··'·/ *v* look after; protect; watch for
kolonya /·'··/ *n* eau-de-Cologne
kolordu /'···/ *n* army corps
koltuk /·'·/ *n* armchair; armpit; ~ **altı** armpit; ~ **değneği** crutch
kolye /·'·/ *n* necklace
kombinezon /···'·/ *n* slip
komedi /·'··/ *n* comedy
komedyen /··'·/ *n* comedian
komi /·'·/ *n* bellboy
komik /·'·/ *adj* comical, funny
komiser /··'·/ *n* superintendent of police

komisyon /··'·/ *n* commission; committee
komisyoncu /···'·/ *n* commission agent, broker
komite /·'··/ *n* committee
komodin /··'·/ *n* commode; chest of drawers
komple /'··/ *adj* full, complete
kompliman /··'·/ *n* compliment
komplo /'··/ *n* conspiracy
komposto /·'··/ *n* stewed fruit, compote
kompozisyon /···'·/ *n* composition
komprime /··'·/ *n* tablet
komşu /·'·/ *n* neighbor
komut /·'·/ *n* command, order
komutan /··'·/ *n* commander
komutanlık /···'·/ *n* commandership
komünist /··'·/ *n* communist
komünizm /··'·/ *n* communism
konak /·'·/ *n* mansion; halting place; inn
konaklamak /···'·/ *v* stay for the night
konca /·'·/ *n* bud
kondüktör /··'·/ *n* conductor
konfeksiyon /···'·/ *n* ready-made clothes
konferans /··'·/ *n* lecture; ~ **vermek** *give a lecture
konferansçı /···'·/ *n* lecturer
konfor /·'·/ *n* comfort; modern conveniences
kongre /'··/ *n* congress
koni /·'·/ *n* cone
konmak /·'·/ *v* settle on, alight, perch; *be added to
konser /·'·/ *n* concert
konservatuar /····'·/ *n* school of music *or* theater
konserve /·'··/ *n* canned food
konsey /·'·/ *n* council
konsol /·'·/ *n* chest of drawers
konsolos /··'·/ *n* consul
konsolosluk /···'·/ *n* consulate
konşimento /··'··/ *n* bill of lading
kont *n* count, earl
kontak /·'·/ *n* short circuit; ignition; ~ **açmak** turn on the engine; ~ **anahtarı** car key
kontenjan /··'·/ *n* quota
kontes /·'·/ *n* countess
kontrat /·'·/ *n* contract, lease
kontrol /·'·/ *n* checking; ~ **etmek** inspect, check, control
kontrplak /·'·/ *n* plywood
konu /·'·/ *n* subject matter, topic
konuk /·'·/ *n* guest, visitor
konukevi /·'···/ *n* guesthouse
konuksever /···'·/ *adj* hospitable
konukseverlik /····'·/ *n* hospitality
konum /·'·/ *n* position, location
konuşkan /··'·/ *adj* talkative
konuşkanlık /···'·/ *n* talkativeness
konuşma /··'·/ *n* speech; conversation
konuşmak /··'·/ *v* talk; *speak together
konuşturmak /···'·/ *v* *make talk; initiate conversation
konut /·'·/ *n* house, residence
konyak /·'·/ *n* brandy, cognac
kooperatif /····'·/ *n* cooperative organization
koparmak /··'·/ *v* pluck, pick; *break off; *take by force
kopmak /·'·/ *v* *break in two, *break off; snap
kopuk /·'·/ *adj* broken off
kopya /'··/ *n* copy; ~ **etmek** copy; ~ **kâğıdı** carbon paper
kopyacı /'···/ *n* copyist; cribber
kor *n* ember
kordiplomatik /····'·/ *n* diplomatic corps
kordon /·'·/ *n* cord; ribbon; cable
koridor /··'·/ *n* corridor; passage
korkak /·'·/ *n* coward; *adj*

cowardly
korkaklık /··ˈ·/ *n* timidity; cowardice
korkmak /·ˈ·/ *v* *be afraid, *be scared
korku /·ˈ·/ *n* fear, fright, dread; alarm; anxiety
korkulu /··ˈ·/ *adj* frightening, dreadful
korkuluk /··ˈ·/ *n* scarecrow; banister
korkunç /·ˈ·/ *adj* terrible, dreadful, awful
korkusuz /··ˈ·/ *adj* fearless, undaunted
korkusuzca /··ˈ··/ *adv* fearlessly
korkusuzluk /···ˈ·/ *n* fearlessness
korkutmak /··ˈ·/ *v* frighten, scare, daunt; threaten
korna /ˈ··/ *n* car horn
korno /ˈ··/ *n* horn
koro /ˈ··/ *n* chorus
korsan /·ˈ·/ *n* pirate; corsair
korsanlık /··ˈ·/ *n* piracy
korse /·ˈ·/ *n* corset
koru /·ˈ·/ *n* grove, small wood
korucu /··ˈ·/ *n* forest watchman
koruma /··ˈ·/ *n* protection, defense
korumak /··ˈ·/ *v* protect; defend
korunma /··ˈ·/ *n* defense
korunmak /··ˈ·/ *v* defend oneself, *take shelter; avoid
koruyucu /···ˈ·/ *n* defender; *adj* protective
koskoca /ˈ···/ *adj* enormous; huge
kostüm /·ˈ·/ *n* suit, costume
koşmak /·ˈ·/ *v* *run
koşturmak /··ˈ·/ *v* cause to run; buzz about, scurry; dispatch
koşu /·ˈ·/ *n* race; running; ~ **alanı** hippodrome
koşucu /··ˈ·/ *n* runner
koşul /·ˈ·/ *n* condition
koşullandırmak /····ˈ·/ *v* condition
koşullu /··ˈ·/ *adj* conditional
koşulsuz /··ˈ·/ *adj* unconditional
koşum /·ˈ·/ *n* harness
koşuşmak /··ˈ·/ *v* *run together; *run in all directions
kotra /ˈ··/ *n* cutter, small racing yacht
kova /·ˈ·/ *n* bucket
kovalama /···ˈ·/ *n* chase, hunt
kovalamak /···ˈ·/ *v* *run after, chase; endeavor to obtain
kovan /·ˈ·/ *n* hive; cartridge case
kovboy /·ˈ·/ *n* cowboy
kovmak /·ˈ·/ *v* *drive away, expel, discharge; *send away
kovuk /·ˈ·/ *n* hollow, cavity
kovuşturma /···ˈ·/ *n* prosecution
kovuşturmak /···ˈ·/ *v* prosecute
koy *n* bay, inlet
koymak /·ˈ·/ *v* *put, place, *set
koyu /·ˈ·/ *adj* thick, dense; dark; extreme, fanatic
koyulaşmak /···ˈ·/ *v* *become dense; *become dark
koyuluk /··ˈ·/ *n* thickness, density; intensity
koyun /·ˈ·/ *n* sheep; bosom, breast
koza /ˈ··/ *n* silk cocoon
kozalak /··ˈ·/ *n* pine cone, cone
köfte /·ˈ·/ *n* meat ball
köhne /·ˈ·/ *adj* old; worn out
kök *n* root; origin; ~ **salmak** *take root; **kökünden sökmek** uproot; **kökünü kazımak** extirpate, eradicate
köken /·ˈ·/ *n* origin, source
köklenmek /··ˈ·/ *v* *take root
köklü /·ˈ·/ *adj* rooted
köknar /·ˈ·/ *n* fir
köksüz /·ˈ·/ *adj* rootless
köle /·ˈ·/ *n* slave
köleleştirmek /····ˈ·/ *v* reduce to slavery
kölelik /··ˈ·/ *n* slavery

kömür /·'·/ *n* charcoal; coal; **~ ocağı** coal mine
kömürcü /··'·/ *n* coal dealer
kömürlük /··'·/ *n* coal hole
köpek /·'·/ *n* dog
köpekbalığı /·'····/ *n* shark, dogfish
köpekdişi /·'···/ *n* canine tooth
köprü /·'·/ *n* bridge; **~ kurmak** *build a bridge
köprücük kemiği /··'· ···/ collarbone
köpük /·'·/ *n* foam; froth; scum; lather
köpüklü /··'·/ *adj* frothy; foamy; foaming
köpürmek /··'·/ *v* froth; foam; lather; *become furious
köpürtmek /··'·/ *v* froth up
kör *adj* blind; blunt; dim; **~ olası** damned; **~ talih** bad luck
körbağırsak /'····/ *n* cecum, blind gut
kördüğüm /'···/ *n* gordian knot
körebe /·'··/ *n* blindman's buff
körelmek /··'·/ *v* *become blunt; atrophy; *become extinct
körfez /·'·/ *n* gulf; bay; inlet
körlük /·'·/ *n* blindness; bluntness
körpe /·'·/ *adj* young, tender, fresh
körük /·'·/ *n* bellows; folding roof
körüklemek /···'·/ *v* fan with bellows; incite, encourage
köse /·'·/ *adj* beardless, who is not able to grow hair on his face
kösele /·'··/ *n* stout leather
köstebek /··'·/ *n* mole
kösteklemek /···'·/ *v* *fetter; hobble; tie up; hinder
köşe /·'·/ *n* corner; angle; nook; **~ bucak** every hole and corner
köşebent /··'·/ *n* angle iron
köşk *n* villa, summerhouse
kötü /·'·/ *adj* bad; evil; **~ günler** hard days
kötülemek /···'·/ *v* *speak ill of; *become a wreck
kötüleşmek /···'·/ *v* *become bad, *become worse
kötülük /··'·/ *n* badness; bad act, harm; **~ etmek** *do someone harm
kötümser /··'·/ *adj* pessimistic
kötümserlik /···'·/ *n* pessimism
kötürüm /··'·/ *n* paralyzed; crippled; **~ olmak** *be paralyzed
köy *n* village
köylü /·'·/ *n* villager, peasant
köz *n* embers
közlemek /··'·/ *v* grill on embers
kral *n* king
kraliçe /·'··/ *n* queen
krallık /·'·/ *n* kingdom, royalty
kravat /·'·/ *n* necktie
kredi /'··/ *n* credit
krem *n* cream, cosmetic preparation for the skin
krema /'··/ *n* cream
kreş *n* public nursery for infants, crèche
kriko /'··/ *n* jack
kristal /·'·/ *n* crystal
kritik /·'·/ *adj* critical
kriz *n* crisis
kroki /'··/ *n* sketch; draft
krom *n* chromium
kronometre /··'··/ *n* chronometer
kruvazör /··'·/ *n* cruiser
kuaför /··'·/ *n* hairdresser
kubbe /·'·/ *n* dome, cupola
kucak /·'·/ *n* lap; embrace; armful; **kucakta** in arms; **~ açmak** receive with open arms
kucaklamak /···'·/ *v* *take in one's arms; embrace
kucaklaşmak /···'·/ *v* hug each other
kudret /·'·/ *n* power, strength
kudretli /··'·/ *adj* powerful
kudretsiz /··'·/ *adj* powerless

kudurmak /··ˈ·/ *v* *go mad; *be enraged; *be attacked by rabies
kudurmuş /··ˈ·/ *adj* mad; rabid
kuduz /·ˈ·/ *n* rabies
kuğu /·ˈ·/ *n* swan
kukla /ˈ··/ *n* puppet
kul *n* slave; human being; man
kulaç /·ˈ·/ *n* fathom
kulaçlamak /···ˈ·/ *v* measure in fathoms
kulak /·ˈ·/ *n* ear; ~ **asmamak** ignore; ~ **kesilmek** *be all ears
kulaklık /··ˈ·/ *n* earphone; headphone
kulakzarı /·ˈ···/ *n* eardrum
kule /·ˈ·/ *n* tower
kulis /·ˈ·/ *n* backstage; ~ **yapmak** lobby
kullanılmış /···ˈ·/ *adj* secondhand, used
kullanış /··ˈ·/ *n* use
kullanışlı /···ˈ·/ *adj* handy, practical
kullanışsız /···ˈ·/ *adj* unhandy
kullanmak /··ˈ·/ *v* use, employ; handle; *drive
kulp *n* handle
kuluçka /·ˈ··/ *n* broody hen; ~ **dönemi** incubation period; **kuluçkaya yatmak** brood
kulübe /··ˈ·/ *n* hut, shed
kulüp /·ˈ·/ *n* club
kum *n* sand; ~ **saati** hourglass
kuma /·ˈ·/ *n* fellow wife
kumanda /·ˈ··/ *n* command; ~ **etmek** command
kumandan /··ˈ·/ *n* military commander
kumandanlık /···ˈ·/ *n* commandership
kumanya /·ˈ··/ *n* portable rations
kumar /·ˈ·/ *n* gambling, gamble; ~ **oynamak** gamble
kumarbaz /··ˈ·/ *n* gambler
kumarhane /··–ˈ·/ *n* gambling den
kumaş /·ˈ·/ *n* cloth; fabric, material
kumbara /ˈ···/ *n* moneybox
kumlu /·ˈ·/ *adj* sandy; speckled with small spots
kumpanya /·ˈ··/ *n* company; troupe
kumral /·ˈ·/ *adj* light brown
kumru /·ˈ·/ *n* turtledove
kumsal /·ˈ·/ *n* sandy beach; *adj* sandy
kundak /·ˈ·/ *n* swaddling clothes
kundakçı /··ˈ·/ *n* incendiary; arsonist
kundakçılık /···ˈ·/ *n* arson
kundaklamak /···ˈ·/ *v* swaddle; *set fire to
kundura /ˈ···/ *n* shoe
kunduz /·ˈ·/ *n* beaver
kupa /ˈ··/ *n* cup
kupkuru /ˈ···/ *adj* bone-dry
kur *n* course; rate of exchange; flirtation; ~ **yapmak** court, flirt
kura /·ˈ–/ *n* lot; ~ **çekmek** *draw lots
kurabiye /·–ˈ·/ *n* cookie
kurak /·ˈ·/ *adj* dry, arid
kuraklık /··ˈ·/ *n* drought
kural /·ˈ·/ *n* rule
kuraldışı /·ˈ···/ *adj* exceptional
kurallı /··ˈ·/ *adj* regular
kuralsız /··ˈ·/ *adj* irregular
kuram /·ˈ·/ *n* theory
kuramsal /··ˈ·/ *n* theoretical
Kuran /·ˈ·/ *n* Koran
kurbağa /··ˈ·/ *n* frog
kurbağalama /····ˈ·/ *n* breast stroke
kurban /·ˈ·/ *n* sacrifice; victim; offering; **Kurban Bayramı** Moslem Festival of Sacrifices; ~ **kesmek** kill as a sacrifice; ~ **olmak** *be a victim; ~ **vermek** *lose as casualties
kurbanlık /··ˈ·/ *n* sacrificial
kurcalamak /···ˈ·/ *v* meddle with,

tamper with; scratch, rub, irritate
kurdele /'···/ *n* ribbon
kurgu /·'·/ *n* montage, editing; winder
kurgubilim /·'···/ *n* science fiction
kurmak /·'·/ *v* *set up, establish; organize; found; form
kurmay /·'·/ *n* staff
kurna /·'·/ *n* basin of a bath *or* fountain
kurnaz /·'·/ *adj* sly, cunning, foxy
kurnazlık /··'·/ *n* slyness, cunning, foxiness
kuron /·'·/ *n* crown
kurs *n* course, lesson
kurşun /·'·/ *n* lead; bullet; **kurşuna dizmek** execute by shooting
kurşuni /·–'–/ *adj* dark gray
kurşunkalem /·'···/ *n* pencil
kurşunlamak /···'·/ *v* *shoot
kurt *n* wolf; worm; ~ **gibi aç** ravenous
kurtarıcı /···'·/ *n* savior, deliverer
kurtarma /··'·/ *n* rescue, recovery
kurtarmak /··'·/ *v* *save, rescue; recover
kurtlanmak /··'·/ *v* *become maggoty; fidget
kurtlu /·'·/ *adj* maggoty, wormy; fidgety
kurtulmak /··'·/ *v* escape, *get free; *be saved; *get rid of
kurtuluş /··'·/ *n* escape; salvation; release; **Kurtuluş Savaşı** War of Independence
kuru /·'·/ *adj* dry; dried; ~ **fasulye** haricot bean; ~ **temizleme** dry cleaning; ~ **üzüm** raisin
kurucu /··'·/ *n* founder; ~ **meclis** constituent assembly
kurukafa /·'···/ *n* skull
kurukahve /·'···/ *n* roasted coffee beans
kurul /·'·/ *n* committee, council
kurulamak /···'·/ *v* wipe dry; dry
kurulmak /··'·/ *v* *be founded, *be established; pose, swagger
kurultay /··'·/ *n* council, assembly
kurulu /··'·/ *adj* established; set up; wound up
kuruluk /··'·/ *n* dryness
kuruluş /··'·/ *n* organization; foundation; establishment
kurum[1] /·'·/ *n* soot
kurum[2] /·'·/ *n* institution, association, foundation
kurumak /··'·/ *v* dry; *get dry
kuruntu /··'·/ *n* groundless fear, worry *or* apprehension
kuruş /·'·/ *n* Turkish piaster, kurush
kurutmak /··'·/ *v* dry; drain
kurutma kâğıdı /··'· ···/ blotting paper
kurutucu /···'·/ *n* drier
kuruyemiş /·'···/ *n* dried fruit and nuts
kusmak /·'·/ *v* vomit
kusur /·'·/ *n* defect, fault; imperfection, flaw
kusurlu /··'·/ *adj* faulty, defective
kusursuz /··'·/ *adj* perfect, faultless
kuş *n* bird, fowl; ~ **beyinli** stupid, bird-brained
kuşak /·'·/ *n* sash, girdle; generation; zone
kuşatmak /··'·/ *v* gird; surround; besiege
kuşbakışı /'····/ *adj* bird's-eye view
kuşet /·'·/ *n* berth, bunk
kuşkonmaz /··'·/ *n* asparagus
kuşku /·'·/ *n* suspicion, doubt; ~ **duymak** *feel suspicious
kuşkulanmak /···'·/ *v* suspect
kuşkulu /··'·/ *adj* suspicious
kuşkusuz /··'·/ *adv* certainly,

undoubtedly
kuşluk /·'·/ *n* midmorning
kuşpalazı /'····/ *n* diphtheria
kuşyemi /'···/ *n* birdseed
kutlamak /··'·/ *v* congratulate; celebrate
kutlu /·'·/ *adj* sacred, holy
kutsama /··'·/ *n* sanctification
kutsamak /··'·/ *v* sanctify
kutu /·'·/ *n* box, case; ~ **gibi** small and cosy
kutup /·'·/ *n* pole
kutuplaşmak /···'·/ *v* polarize
Kutupyıldızı /·'····/ *n* North Star, Polaris
kuvvet /·'·/ *n* strength, power, force; vigor; potency
kuvvetle /·'··/ *adv* strongly
kuvvetlendirmek /····'·/ *v* strengthen
kuvvetlenmek /···'·/ *v* *become strong
kuvvetli /··'·/ *adj* powerful, strong
kuvvetsiz /··'·/ *adj* weak
kuyruk /·'·/ *n* tail; queue; line; ~ **olmak** queue up
kuyruklu /··'·/ *adj* tailed; ~ **piano** grand piano; ~ **yalan** whopper; big lie
kuyruksuz /··'·/ *adj* tailless
kuytu /·'·/ *adj* out-of-the-way, cosy, sheltered
kuyu /·'·/ *n* well; ~ **açmak** *dig a well; **kuyusunu kazmak** *lay a trap for someone
kuyumcu /··'·/ *n* jeweler
kuzen /·'·/ *n* male cousin
kuzey /·'·/ *n* north; *adj* northern
kuzgun /·'·/ *n* raven
kuzin /·'·/ *n* female cousin
kuzu /·'·/ *n* lamb
küçük /·'·/ *adj* small, little; young; insignificant; *n* youngster; ~ **düşmek** *feel small, *lose face; ~ **düşürmek** humiliate, abase; ~ **görmek** belittle
küçükbaş /·'··/ *n* sheep, goats, etc.
küçüklük /··'·/ *n* smallness; childhood; pettiness
küçülmek /··'·/ *v* *become small; *be reduced; *be humiliated
küçültmek /··'·/ *v* *make smaller; diminish; belittle; humiliate
küçültücü /···'·/ *adj* humiliating
küçümsemek /···'·/ *v* belittle; despise
küf *n* mold
küfe /·'·/ *n* large deep basket
küflenmek /··'·/ *v* *become moldy
küflü /·'·/ *adj* moldy
küfretmek /'···/ *v* *swear, curse
küfürbaz /··'·/ *adj* foul-mouthed; swearing
küheylan /··'·/ *n* pure-bred Arab horse
kükremek /··'·/ *v* roar
kükürt /·'·/ *n* sulfur
kükürtlü /··'·/ *adj* sulfurous
kül *n* ashes; ~ **etmek** ruin; ~ **olmak** *be reduced to ashes; ~ **tablası** ashtray
külah /·'·/ *n* conical hat; cone
külçe /·'·/ *n* ingot
külfet /·'·/ *n* trouble, burden, inconvenience
külfetli /··'·/ *adj* troublesome
külfetsiz /··'·/ *adj* easy, painless
külhanbeyi /·'···/ *n* bully, rough guy
külot /·'·/ *n* underpants, briefs, panties
kültür /·'·/ *n* culture
kültürel /··'·/ *adj* cultural
kültürlü /··'·/ *adj* cultured
kültürsüz /··'·/ *adj* uncultured
kümbet /·'·/ *n* cupola, dome
küme /·'·/ *n* heap, pile; group
kümelenmek /···'·/ *v* *come

together in heaps *or* groups
kümes /·ˈ·/ *n* coop; poultry house; ~ **hayvanları** poultry
künye /·ˈ·/ *n* personal data; identification bracelet
küp[1] *n* cube
küp[2] *n* large earthenware jar
küpe /·ˈ·/ *n* earring
kür *n* health cure
kürdan /·ˈ·/ *n* toothpick
küre /·ˈ·/ *n* globe, sphere, ball
kürek /·ˈ·/ *n* shovel; oar; ~ **çekmek** row
küremek /··ˈ·/ *v* shovel up
küresel /··ˈ·/ *adj* global; spherical
kürk *n* fur; fur coat
kürkçü /·ˈ·/ *n* furrier
kürsü /·ˈ·/ *n* pulpit; desk; professorship
Kürt *n* Kurd
kürtaj /·ˈ·/ *n* abortion, curetting
küskün /·ˈ·/ *adj* offended, sore, sulky
küskünlük /··ˈ·/ *n* sulkiness
küsmek /·ˈ·/ *v* *be offended; sulk
küstah /·ˈ·/ *adj* insolent, impertinent
küstahça /·ˈ··/ *adv* insolently
küstahlaşmak /···ˈ·/ *v* start behaving insolently
küstahlık /··ˈ·/ *n* insolence; arrogance
küt *adj* blunt
kütle /·ˈ·/ *n* heap; mass
kütük /·ˈ·/ *n* tree trunk; stump; ledger, register; ~ **gibi** greatly swollen; dead drunk; **kütüğe kaydetmek** enroll in the register
kütüphane /·–ˈ·/ *n* library
küvet /·ˈ·/ *n* bathtub

L

labirent /··ˈ·/ *n* labyrinth, maze
laboratuvar /····ˈ·/ *n* laboratory
lacivert /–·ˈ·/ *adj* dark blue, navy blue
laçka /ˈ··/ *adj* slack; ~ **olmak** *get slack
lades /–ˈ·/ *n* bet with a wishbone; ~ **kemiği** wishbone; ~ **tutuşmak** *make a bet by pulling a wishbone
laf *n* word; talk; chat; empty words; ~ **anlamaz** thick-headed, obstinate; ~ **aramızda** between us; ~ **etmek** talk; gossip
lafebesi /ˈ····/ *n* chatterbox
lağım /·ˈ·/ *n* sewer, drain
lahit /·ˈ·/ *n* tomb
lakap /·ˈ·/ *n* nickname
lakırdı /··ˈ·/ *n* word; talk
lakin /ˈ–·/ *conj* but; still; yet; however
lale /–ˈ·/ *n* tulip
lamba /ˈ··/ *n* lamp
lanet /–ˈ·/ *n* curse, damnation; ~ **etmek** damn
lanetli /–·ˈ·/ *adj* cursed
lapa /·ˈ·/ *n* watery boiled rice; ~ **gibi** soft, mushy; ~ ~ in large flakes
lastik /·ˈ·/ *n* rubber; tire
latif /·ˈ·/ *adj* fine; pleasant; charming; gracious
latife /·–ˈ·/ *n* joke
laubali /·–ˈ·/ *adj* saucy, pert, free and easy
lavabo /·ˈ··/ *n* washbowl, sink
lavanta /·ˈ··/ *n* lavender water; ~ **çiçeği** lavender

layık /–ˈ·/ *adj* worthy, deserving
layıkıyla /–ˈ··/ *adv* properly, as it should be
lazım /–ˈ·/ *adj* necessary; essential
leblebi /··ˈ·/ *n* roasted chickpeas
leğen /·ˈ·/ *n* basin
leh *n* in favor of; **lehimde** in my favor; **lehine** in one's favor; **lehte ve aleyhte** for and against
Leh *n* Pole; *adj* Polish
Lehçe /ˈ··/ *n* Polish language
lehçe /·ˈ·/ *n* dialect
lehim /·ˈ·/ *n* solder
lehimlemek /···ˈ·/ *v* solder
lehimli /··ˈ·/ *adj* soldered
leke /·ˈ·/ *n* stain; spot of dirt; blot; shame; ~ **çıkarmak** remove a stain; ~ **sürmek** besmirch
lekelemek /···ˈ·/ *v* stain; soil; blemish
lekeli /··ˈ·/ *adj* stained, spotted; blemished
lekesiz /··ˈ·/ *adj* spotless, stainless
lenf *n* lymph
lens *n* lens
leş *n* carcass
levazım /·–ˈ·/ *n* supplies, provisions
levha /·ˈ·/ *n* signboard
levrek /·ˈ·/ *n* sea bass
leylak /·ˈ·/ *n* lilac
leylek /·ˈ·/ *n* stork
leziz /·ˈ·/ *adj* delicious; tasty
lezzet /·ˈ·/ *n* taste; flavor
lezzetli /··ˈ·/ *adj* tasty, delicious
libre /·ˈ·/ *n* pound
lider /–ˈ·/ *n* leader
lif *n* fiber
lifli /·ˈ·/ *adj* fibrous
lig *n* league
likör /·ˈ·/ *n* liqueur
liman /·ˈ·/ *n* harbor; seaport
limanlamak /···ˈ·/ *v* anchor in a harbor
limon /·ˈ·/ *n* lemon
limonata /··ˈ··/ *n* lemonade
limonluk /··ˈ·/ *n* greenhouse; lemon squeezer
linç *n* lynching; ~ **etmek** lynch
linyit /·ˈ·/ *n* lignite
lir *n* lyre
lira /·ˈ·/ *n* Turkish pound, lira
liret /·ˈ·/ *n* Italian lira
lirik /·ˈ·/ *adj* lyrical
lisan /·ˈ·/ *n* language
lisans /·ˈ·/ *n* bachelor's degree; license
lise /ˈ··/ *n* high school
liseli /ˈ···/ *n* high school student
liste /ˈ··/ *n* list
litre /ˈ··/ *n* liter
liyakat /·–ˈ·/ *n* merit, capacity; suitability
lodos /·ˈ·/ *n* southwest wind
loğusa /·ˈ··/ *n* woman after child-birth
lokal /·ˈ·/ *n* clubroom; *adj* local
lokanta /·ˈ··/ *n* restaurant
lokavt /·ˈ·/ *n* lockout
lokma /·ˈ·/ *n* morsel
lokomotif /···ˈ·/ *n* railway engine, locomotive
lokum /·ˈ·/ *n* Turkish delight
Londra /ˈ··/ London
lop *adj* round and soft; ~ **yumurta** hard-boiled egg
losyon /·ˈ·/ *n* lotion
loş *adj* dim, murky, dark, gloomy
Lübnan /ˈ··/ Lebanon
Lübnanlı /ˈ···/ *adj, n* Lebanese
lüfer /·ˈ·/ *n* bluefish
lügat /·ˈ·/ *n* dictionary
lüks *n* luxury; ~ **lambası** pressurized kerosene lamp with an incandescent mantle; ~ **mevki** deluxe class
lüle /·ˈ·/ *n* curl, ringlet, fold; spout

lületaşı /·ˈ···/ *n* meerschaum
lütfen /ˈ··/ please; kindly
lütuf /·ˈ·/ *n* kindness, favor
lütufkâr /··ˈ·/ *adj* gracious, kind
lüzum /·ˈ·/ *n* necessity;
~ **görmek** deem necessary
lüzumlu /··ˈ·/ *adj* necessary
lüzumsuz /··ˈ·/ *adj* unnecessary

M

maada /–ˈ–/ *adv* besides, except; in addition to
maalesef /·ˈ···/ *adv* unfortunately
maaş /·ˈ·/ *n* salary
maaşlı /··ˈ·/ *adj* salaried
mabet /–ˈ·/ *n* temple
Macar /·ˈ·/ *adj, n* Hungarian
Macarca /·ˈ··/ *n* Hungarian language
Macaristan /···ˈ·/ Hungary
macera /–·ˈ–/ *n* adventure
maceracı /–·–ˈ·/ *n* adventurer
maceralı /–·–ˈ·/ *adj* adventurous
maceraperest /–·–·ˈ·/ *n* adventurer
macun /–ˈ·/ *n* paste; putty
maç *n* game, match
madalya /·ˈ··/ *n* medal
madalyon /··ˈ·/ *n* medallion
madde /·ˈ·/ *n* matter, substance; material; clause, article
maddeci /··ˈ·/ *n* materialist
maddesel /··ˈ·/ *adj* material
maddeten /ˈ···/ *adv* materially
maddi /·ˈ–/ *adj* material; physical
maddiyat /··ˈ·/ *n* material things
madem /ˈ–·/ *conj* since, as, now that
maden /–ˈ·/ *n* mine; mineral; metal; ~ **damarı** vein; ~ **işçisi** miner; ~ **ocağı** mine, pit; ~ **yatağı** ore, bed
madenkömürü /–ˈ····/ coal
madensel /–·ˈ·/ *adj* mineral
madensuyu /–ˈ···/ *n* mineral water
madrabaz /··ˈ·/ *n* cheat; middleman
mafsal /·ˈ·/ *n* joint, articulation
mağara /·ˈ··/ *n* cave
mağaza /·ˈ··/ *n* large store, shop
mağdur /·ˈ·/ *adj* wronged; *n* victim, sufferer
mağlubiyet /·–·ˈ·/ *n* defeat
mağlup /·ˈ·/ *adj* defeated, overcome; ~ **etmek** defeat, *overcome; ~ **olmak** *be defeated
mağrur /·ˈ·/ *adj* proud, conceited
mağrurluk /··ˈ·/ *n* conceit
mahal /·ˈ·/ *n* place, locality, spot; ~ **vermemek** not give occasion for
mahalle /··ˈ·/ *n* quarter, district; ward
mahalli /··ˈ–/ *adj* local
maharet /·–ˈ·/ *n* skill, ability, proficiency
maharetli /·–·ˈ·/ *adj* skillful
mahcubiyet /·–·ˈ·/ *n* shyness; bashfulness; modesty
mahcup /·ˈ·/ *adj* shy; ashamed; ~ **etmek** *put to shame, abash, mortify; ~ **olmak** *be ashamed, *be mortified
mahdut /·ˈ·/ *adj* limited; restricted; few
mahir /–ˈ·/ *adj* expert, skillful
mahiyet /–·ˈ·/ *n* nature, character
mahkeme /··ˈ·/ *n* law court; ~ **kararı** sentence, verdict
mahkûm /·ˈ·/ *adj* sentenced, condemned; *n* convict; ~ **etmek** condemn, sentence; ~ **olmak** *be condemned
mahkûmiyet /·–·ˈ·/ *n* condemnation
mahluk /·ˈ·/ *n* creature

mahmur /·ˈ·/ *adj* sleepy, drowsy
mahmurluk /··ˈ·/ *n* sleepiness
mahpus /·ˈ·/ *adj* imprisoned; *n* prisoner
mahrem /·ˈ·/ *adj* confidential, secret, private
mahremiyet /···ˈ·/ *n* privacy, intimacy, secrecy
mahrum /·ˈ·/ *adj* deprived; ~ **etmek** deprive of
mahrumiyet /·–ˈ·/ *n* deprivation; ~ **bölgesi** underdeveloped area
mahsul /·ˈ·/ *n* product; crop, produce; result
mahsur /·ˈ·/ *adj* confined, cut off; stuck; ~ **kalmak** *be stuck, *be cut off
mahsus[1] /·ˈ·/ *adj* special, peculiar to; reserved for
mahsus[2] /ˈ··/ *adv* especially, on purpose; deliberately
mahşer /·ˈ·/ *n* the last judgment; great crowd
mahvetmek /ˈ···/ *v* destroy
mahvolmak /ˈ···/ *v* *be destroyed; *be ruined
mahzun /·ˈ·/ *adj* sad, grieved
mahzur /·ˈ·/ *n* drawback; objection
mahzurlu /··ˈ·/ *adj* inconvenient; objectionable
makale /·–ˈ·/ *n* article
makam /·ˈ·/ *n* position, office; tune
makara /·ˈ··/ *n* bobbin; pulley; reel, spool
makas /·ˈ·/ *n* scissors, shears
makaslamak /···ˈ·/ *v* *cut with scissors
makbul /·ˈ·/ *adj* acceptable, welcome; esteemed
maket /·ˈ·/ *n* model
makine /·ˈ··/ *n* machine; engine; ~ **dairesi** engine room; ~ **mühendisi** mechanical engineer
makineci /·ˈ···/ *n* mechanic
makinist /··ˈ·/ *n* engine driver
maksat /·ˈ·/ *n* intention, purpose, aim, object
maksatlı /··ˈ·/ *adj* purposeful
makul /–ˈ·/ *adj* reasonable; conceivable; sensible
makyaj /·ˈ·/ *n* make-up
mal *n* goods, merchandise; property; wealth; ~ **mülk** goods, property
mali /–ˈ–/ *adj* financial; fiscal; ~ **yıl** fiscal year
malik /–ˈ·/ *adj* owning, possessing; *n* owner, possessor; ~ **olmak** *have, own, possess
malikâne /–·–ˈ·/ *n* large estate, stately home, mansion
maliye /–·ˈ·/ *n* finance
maliyeci /–··ˈ·/ *n* financier
maliyet /–·ˈ·/ *n* cost
malul /–ˈ·/ *adj* invalid, disabled; diseased
maluliyet /–··ˈ·/ *n* disability
malum /–ˈ·/ *adj* known; ~ **olmak** *become known; *be sensed
malumat /––ˈ·/ *n* information; **malumatı olmak** *know about; ~ **vermek** inform; supply information
malzeme /··ˈ·/ *n* materials, necessaries; stuff; supplies
mama /·ˈ·/ *n* baby's food
mamafih /ˈ–––/ *conj* nevertheless, however, yet
manastır /·ˈ··/ *n* monastery
manav /·ˈ·/ *n* greengrocer, fruitseller; vegetable man
manda /·ˈ·/ *n* water buffalo
mandal /·ˈ·/ *n* clothespin
mandalina /··ˈ··/ *n* mandarin, tangerine

mandallamak /···ˈ·/ *v* peg up; pin up; latch
mandıra /ˈ···/ *n* dairy farm
manen /ˈ–·/ *adv* morally, virtually
manevi /–·ˈ–/ *adj* moral, spiritual; ~ **evlat** adopted child
maneviyat /–··ˈ·/ *n* morale; **maneviyatı bozulmak** *lose morale; *be discouraged
mâni /–ˈ–/ *n* obstacle, impediment, hindrance; ~ **olmak** prevent, hinder, obstruct
mânia /–ˈ·/ *n* obstacle, difficulty; barrier
manidar /––ˈ·/ *adj* significant; expressive; full of meaning
manifatura /··ˈ···/ *n* drapery; textiles
manivela /··ˈ··/ *n* lever, crank
mankafa /··ˈ·/ *adj* dull, stupid; thick-headed
manken /·ˈ·/ *n* mannequin
manolya /·ˈ··/ *n* magnolia
Manş Denizi /ˈ····/ the English Channel
manşet /·ˈ·/ *n* headline; cuff
mantar /·ˈ·/ *n* mushroom; fungus; cork
mantık /·ˈ·/ *n* logic; **mantığa aykırı** illogical
mantıklı /··ˈ·/ *adj* logical; reasonable
mantıksız /··ˈ·/ *adj* illogical, unreasonable
manto /ˈ··/ *n* woman's coat
manyak /·ˈ·/ *n* maniac, stupid fool
manzara /··ˈ·/ *n* view, sight, landscape, panorama
manzaralı /···ˈ·/ *adj* having a pleasant view
marangoz /··ˈ·/ *n* carpenter, joiner
margarin /··ˈ·/ *n* margarine
marifet /–·ˈ·/ *n* skill, talent
marifetli /–··ˈ·/ *adj* skilled; skillful
marka /ˈ··/ *n* mark, brand; trademark
markalı /··ˈ·/ *adj* marked; stamped
marmelat /··ˈ·/ *n* marmalade
Marsilya /·ˈ··/ Marseilles
marş *n* starter; march; **marşa basmak** press the starter; **marş marş!** run! get going!
marşandiz /··ˈ·/ *n* goods train
mart March
martı /·ˈ·/ *n* sea gull
marul /–ˈ·/ *n* romaine lettuce
maruz /–ˈ·/ *adj* exposed to; ~ **kalmak** *be exposed to
masa /ˈ··/ *n* table; office desk; ~ **tenisi** table tennis, ping-pong ~ **örtüsü** tablecloth
masaj /·ˈ·/ *n* massage
masal /·ˈ·/ *n* story, tale; ~ **anlatmak** *tell a tale
masalcı /··ˈ·/ *n* story teller
maskara /··ˈ·/ *n* buffoon, clown; *adj* ridiculuos
maskaralık /···ˈ·/ *n* buffoonery; making oneself ridiculous; shame
maske /·ˈ·/ *n* mask
maskelemek /···ˈ·/ *v* mask, hide; camouflage
maskeli /··ˈ·/ *adj* masked; ~ **balo** fancy ball
mason /·ˈ·/ *n* Freemason, Mason
masonluk /··ˈ·/ *n* Freemasonry
masraf /·ˈ·/ *n* expense, expenditure; outlay; ~ **etmek** *spend money; **masrafı çekmek** *bear the expense; **masrafını çıkarmak** *pay for itself; **masrafları kısmak** *cut down expenses
masraflı /··ˈ·/ *adj* expensive, costly
masrafsız /··ˈ·/ *adj* without expense
mastar /·ˈ·/ *n* infinitive
masum /–ˈ·/ *adj* innocent; guiltless

maşa /·'·/ *n* tongs; pincers
maşallah /'–··/ wonderful! magnificient! praise be!
maşrapa /··'·/ *n* mug
mat[1] *n* checkmate; ~ **etmek** checkmate; ~ **olmak** *be checkmated
mat[2] *adj* mat, dull
matara /·'··/ *n* canteen, water bottle
matbaa /··'·/ *n* printing house
matbaacı /···'·/ *n* printer
matbaacılık /····'·/ *n* printing
matbu /·'–/ *adj* printed
matbua /–'·/ *n* printed matter
matem /–'·/ *n* mourning; ~ **tutmak** mourn
matemli /–'·/ *adj* mournful
matine /·'··/ *n* matinée
matkap /·'·/ *n* drill
mavi /–'·/ *adj* blue
mavilik /–'·/ *n* blueness
mavimsi /–'·/ *adj* bluish
maya /·'·/ *n* ferment; yeast; leaven; essence
mayalamak /···'·/ *v* ferment, leaven
maydanoz /··'·/ *n* parsley
mayhoş /·'·/ *adj* sourish, tart
mayıs /·'·/ May
maymun /·'·/ *n* monkey
maymuncuk /··'·/ *n* skeleton key
mayo /'··/ *n* swimsuit *nAm*; bathing suit *Br*
maytap /·'·/ *n* fireworks
mazlum /·'·/ *adj* wronged, oppressed
mazot /·'·/ *n* diesel oil; fuel oil
mazur /–'·/ *adj* excused, excusable; ~ **görmek** excuse, pardon
meblağ /·'·/ *n* amount; sum of money
mebus /·'·/ *n* deputy, Member of Parliament
mecbur /·'·/ *adj* compelled, forced, bound; ~ **olmak** *be compelled
mecburen /·'–·/ *adv* by force, compulsorily
mecburi /·–'–/ *adj* compulsory, obligatory, forced; ~ **istikamet** one-way traffic
mecburiyet /·–·'·/ *n* compulsion, obligation
meclis /·'·/ *n* assembly, council
meçhul /·'·/ *adj* unknown
medeni /··'–/ *adj* civilized, civil; ~ **cesaret** moral courage; ~ **kanun** civil law; ~ **hal** marital status
medenileşmek /··–·'·/ *v* *become civilized
medenileştirmek /··–··'·/ *v* civilize
medeniyet /···'·/ *n* civilization
medrese /·'··/ *n* Moslem theological school
medyum /·'·/ *n* medium
mefruşat /·–'·/ *n* furnishings; fabrics
meğer /'··/ *conj* but, however, and yet; only; ~ **ki** provided that; only; **meğerse** and all the while
mehtap /·'·/ *n* moonlight
mehter /·'·/ *n* band of musicians
mekân /·'·/ *n* place; residence; abode; space
mekanik /··'·/ *adj* mechanics; *n* mechanical
mekanizma /··'··/ *n* mechanism
mekik /·'·/ *n* shuttle; ~ **dokumak** shuttle back and forth
Meksika /·'··/ Mexico
Meksikalı /·'···/ *adj, n* Mexican
mektep /·'·/ *n* school
mektup /·'·/ *n* letter
mektuplaşmak /···'·/ *v* *be in correspondence
melek /·'·/ *n* angel

meleke /··ˈ·/ *n* aptitude; readiness, skill
melemek /–ˈ·/ *v* bleat
melez /·ˈ·/ *adj* crossbred, hybrid
melodi /··ˈ·/ *n* melody
meltem /·ˈ·/ *n* breeze
melun /·ˈ·/ *adj* damned, cursed
memba /·ˈ–/ *n* spring, fountain; source
meme /·ˈ·/ *n* breast; nipple; ~ **vermek** suckle
memleket /··ˈ·/ *n* country; native land
memnun /·ˈ·/ *adj* pleased, glad, happy; ~ **etmek** please, satisfy; ~ **olmak** *be pleased
memnuniyetle /·–ˈ··/ *adv* with pleasure, gladly
memnunluk /··ˈ·/ *n* gladness, pleasure
memur /–ˈ·/ *n* official; employee
memuriyet /––ˈ·/ *n* office; government job, charge
mendil /·ˈ·/ *n* handkerchief
menekşe /·ˈ··/ *n* violet
menenjit /··ˈ·/ *n* meningitis
menetmek /ˈ···/ *v* *forbid
menfaat /··ˈ·/ *n* advantage; profit, benefit; interest
menfaatçi /···ˈ·/ *adj* self-seeking
menkul /·ˈ·/ *adj* movable
mensucat /·–ˈ·/ *n* textiles
mensup /·ˈ·/ *adj* belonging to; related to
menteşe /··ˈ·/ *n* hinge
merak /·ˈ·/ *n* curiosity; worry, anxiety; great interest, hobby; ~ **etmek** *be curious about something; worry
meraklı /··ˈ·/ *adj* curious, inquisitive; fond of; *n* devotee
meraksız /··ˈ·/ *adj* indifferent, uninterested
meram /·ˈ·/ *n* intention, aim; desire; **meramını anlatmak** explain oneself
mercan /·ˈ·/ *n* coral
mercek /·ˈ·/ *n* lens
merci /·ˈ–/ *n* reference, recourse; competent authority
mercimek /··ˈ·/ *n* lentil
merdane /·–ˈ·/ *n* cylinder; roller
merdiven /··ˈ·/ *n* ladder; stairs; staircase
merhaba /ˈ···/ hello! good day! hi!
merhabalaşmak /····ˈ·/ *v* greet one another
merhamet /··ˈ·/ *n* pity, mercy; ~ **etmek** pity
merhametli /···ˈ·/ *adj* merciful, tenderhearted
merhametsiz /···ˈ·/ *adj* merciless, pitiless, cruel
merhem /·ˈ·/ *n* ointment, salve
merhum /·ˈ·/ *adj* deceased, the late
meridyen /··ˈ·/ *n* meridian
merkep /·ˈ·/ *n* donkey, ass
merkez /·ˈ·/ *n* center; headquarters; central office; police station; ~ **komutanı** garrison commander
merkezi /··ˈ–/ *adj* central; main; ~ **ısıtma** central heating
merkezileşmek /··–ˈ·/ *v* *be centralized
mermer /·ˈ·/ *n* marble
mermi /·ˈ·/ *n* bullet, projectile
mersi /ˈ··/ thank you
mert *adj* brave, manly; fine in character; decent
mertçe /ˈ··/ *adv* straightforwardly
mertebe /··ˈ·/ *n* rank, grade; position
mertlik /·ˈ·/ *n* bravery; manliness
mesafe /·–ˈ·/ *n* distance
mesai /·–ˈ·/ *n* efforts, work; ~ **saatleri** work hours; **mesaiye kalmak** work overtime

mesaj /·ˈ·/ *n* message, notice
mesane /·–ˈ·/ *n* bladder
mescit /·ˈ·/ *n* small mosque
mesela /ˈ··–/ for example, for instance
mesele /··ˈ·/ *n* problem, matter; ~ **çıkarmak** *make a fuss
mesken /·ˈ·/ *n* dwelling, house, residence
meskûn /·ˈ·/ *adj* inhabited
meslek /·ˈ·/ *n* profession, career
mesleki /··ˈ–/ *adj* professional
meslektaş /··ˈ·/ *n* colleague
mesul /·ˈ·/ *adj* responsible
mesuliyet /·–·ˈ·/ *n* responsibility
mesuliyetli /·–··ˈ·/ *adj* involving responsibility
mesut /·ˈ·/ *adj* happy
meşale /··ˈ·/ *n* torch
meşe /·ˈ·/ *n* oak
meşgale /··ˈ·/ *n* occupation, business; preoccupation
meşgul /·ˈ·/ *adj* busy, occupied; ~ **etmek** *keep busy; ~ **olmak** *be busy
meşguliyet /·–·ˈ·/ *n* occupation, activity
meşhur /·ˈ·/ *adj* famous; ~ **olmak** *become famous
meşin /·ˈ·/ *n* leather
meşru /·ˈ–/ *adj* lawful, legal, legitimate
meşrubat /·–ˈ·/ *n* soft drinks
meşrutiyet /·–·ˈ·/ *n* constitutional government
metanet /·–ˈ·/ *n* firmness, fortitude; courage
metanetli /·–·ˈ·/ *adj* firm, steady
methetmek /ˈ···/ *v* praise, extol
methiye /··ˈ·/ *n* eulogy
metin[1] /·ˈ·/ *n* text
metin[2] /·ˈ–/ *adj* firm, solid; trustworthy
metot /·ˈ·/ *n* method, system
metre /ˈ··/ *n* meter
metrekare /ˈ····/ *n* square meter
metreküp /ˈ···/ *n* cubic meter
metres /·ˈ·/ *n* mistress, kept woman
metro /ˈ··/ *n* subway *nAm;* underground *nBr*
mevcudiyet /·–·ˈ·/ *n* existence; presence
mevcut /·ˈ·/ *adj* existent, existing; *n* the number present; stock; ~ **olmak** exist, *be present
mevduat /·–ˈ·/ *n* deposits; ~ **hesabı** deposit account
mevki /·ˈ–/ *n* class; place; situation; case; post
mevsim /·ˈ·/ *n* season; proper time, period
mevsimlik /··ˈ·/ *adj* seasonal
mevsimsiz /··ˈ·/ *adj* unseasonable, untimely
mevzu /·ˈ–/ *n* subject, topic
meydan /·ˈ·/ *n* open space, square; arena; **meydana çıkarmak** *bring out; *bring to light; **meydana gelmek** happen, occur; ~ **okumak** challenge
meyhane /·–ˈ·/ *n* bar, saloon, pub
meyhaneci /·–·ˈ·/ *n* tavern keeper
meyil /·ˈ·/ *n* inclination; tendency; slope
meyletmek /ˈ···/ *v* incline
meyve /·ˈ·/ *n* fruit; ~ **suyu** fruit juice
meyveli /··ˈ·/ *adj* having fruit, containing fruit
meyvesiz /··ˈ·/ *adj* fruitless
mezar /·ˈ·/ *n* tomb, grave
mezarlık /··ˈ·/ *n* graveyard, cemetery
mezat /·ˈ·/ *n* auction
mezbaha /··ˈ·/ *n* slaughterhouse
meze /ˈ··/ *n* appetizer, snack
mezhep /·ˈ·/ *n* religious sect

meziyet /··'·/ *n* virtue, merit
meziyetli /···'·/ *adj* virtuous, meritorious
mezun /–'·/ *adj* graduated from; *n* graduate
mezuniyet /–––'·/ *n* graduation
mezura /·'··/ *n* tape measure
mıknatıs /··'·/ *n* magnet
mıknatıslı /···'·/ *adj* magnetic
mırıldanmak /···'·/ *v* mutter, murmur
mırıltı /··'·/ *n* murmur, mutter, grumble
mısır /·'·/ *n* corn
Mısır /'··/ Eygpt
Mısırlı /'···/ *adj, n* Egyptian
mısra /·'–/ *n* line of poetry
mıymıntı /··'·/ *adj* lazy, slow, passive, sluggish
mızıka /·'··/ *n* harmonica
mızmız /·'·/ *adj* fussy, querulous, particular; hesitant
mızrak /·'·/ *n* spear, lance
mide /–'·/ *n* stomach; ~ **bozukluğu** indigestion; ~ **bulantısı** nausea; ~ **kanaması** gastric bleeding
midye /'··/ *n* mussel
migren /·'·/ *n* migraine
miğfer /·'·/ *n* helmet
mihrap /·'·/ *n* niche in a mosque indicating the direction of Mecca
mikrop /·'·/ *n* microbe; germ
miktar /·'·/ *n* quantity, amount
mikyas /·'·/ *n* scale; measure
miladi /––'–/ *adj* of the Christian era; ~ **takvim** the Gregorian calendar
milat /–'·/ *n* birth of Christ; **milattan önce, M.Ö.** before Christ, B.C.; **milattan sonra, M.S.** after Christ, A.D.
militan /··'·/ *n* activist, militant
millet /·'·/ *n* nation, people; **Millet Meclisi** National Assembly
milletlerarası /··'····/ *adj* international
milletvekili /·'····/ *n* deputy, member of the national assembly
milli /·'–/ *adj* national; ~ **marş** national anthem
milliyet /··'·/ *n* nationality
milliyetçilik /····'·/ *n* nationalism
milyar /·'·/ *n* a thousand million
milyarder /··'·/ *n* billionaire
milyon /·'·/ *n* million
milyoner /··'·/ *n* millionaire
mimar /–'·/ *n* architect
mimarlık /–·'·/ *n* architecture
minare /·–'·/ *n* minaret
minber /·'·/ *n* pulpit in a mosque
minder /·'·/ *n* mattress, cushion; wrestling mat
mine /'··/ *n* enamel
minibüs /·'··/ *n* minibus
minik /·'·/ *adj* dear, small and sweet
minnacık /'·–·/ *adj* very tiny
minnet /·'·/ *n* gratitude, indebtedness; ~ **etmek** ask a favor; plead
minnettar /··'·/ *adj* grateful
minnettarlık /···'·/ *n* gratitude
miras /–'·/ *n* inheritance; heritage; **mirasa konmak** inherit
mirasçı /–·'·/ *n* heir, inheritor
mirasyedi /–··'·/ *adj* spendthrift, prodigal
misafir /·–'·/ *n* guest, visitor
misafirlik /·–·'·/ *n* visit
misafirperver /·–··'·/ *adj* hospitable
misal /·'·/ *n* example
misilleme /···'·/ *n* retaliation; ~ **olarak** as a reprisal; ~ **yapmak** retaliate
misina /·'··/ *n* fishline
miskin /·'·/ *adj* idle, lazy
miskinlik /··'·/ *n* indolence, laziness

mistik /·'·/ *adj* mystic, mystical
misyoner /··'·/ *n* missionary
miting /·'·/ *n* public meeting, demonstration; ~ **yapmak** *hold a public demonstration
miyop /·'·/ *adj* shortsighted, myopic
mizaç /·'·/ *n* temperament, nature; humor, mood
mizah /·'·/ *n* joke, humor
mizahçı /··'·/ *n* humorist
mizahi /·–'–/ *adj* humorous
mobilya /·'··/ *n* furniture
mobilyalı /·'···/ *adj* furnished
moda /'··/ *n* fashion, style; ~ **olmak** *be in fashion; **modası geçmek** *be out of fashion; **modaya uygun** fashionable
modacı /'···/ *n* fashion designer
model /·'·/ *n* model
modellik /··'·/ *n* modeling
modern /·'·/ *adj* modern
mola /'··/ *n* rest, pause, break; ~ **vermek** *take a break
monoton /··'·/ *adj* monotonous
montaj /·'·/ *n* mounting, assembly
montajcı /··'·/ *n* assembler
mor *adj* violet, purple
moral /·'·/ *n* morale; **morali bozulmak** *become low-spirited; ~ **vermek** cheer someone up, reassure
morarmak /··'·/ *v* *become purple; *become bruised
morfin /·'·/ *n* morphine
morina /·'··/ *n* white sturgeon
Moskova /'···/ Moscow
motor /·'·/ *n* motor, engine
motorlu /··'·/ *adj* motorized; ~ **tren** dieşel train
motosiklet /···'·/ *n* motorcycle
muadil /·–'·/ *adj* equivalent
muaf /·'·/ *adj* exempt; immune; ~ **tutmak** exempt
muafiyet /·–'·/ *n* exemption, immunity
muallak /··'·/ *adj* suspended; **muallakta kalmak** remain in suspense
muamele /·–'·/ *n* treatment; formality; transaction; ~ **etmek** treat
muamma /··'–/ *n* mystery; puzzle, enigma
muavin /·–'·/ *n* assistant, helper
muayene /·–'·/ *n* examination; ~ **etmek** inspect; examine
muayenehane /·–··–'·/ *n* doctor's consulting room; surgery *nBr*
muayyen /··'·/ *adj* definite; determined, certain
muazzam /··'·/ *adj* great, enormous, tremendous
mucize /–·'·/ *n* miracle
muhabbet /··'·/ *n* affection, love; ~ **etmek** *have a friendly chat
muhabbetkuşu /··'···/ *n* lovebird
muhabere /·–'·/ *n* correspondence, communication
muhabir /·–'·/ *n* correspondent
muhacir /·–'·/ *n* emigrant, refugee
muhafaza /·–·'·/ *n* protection; preservation; ~ **etmek** guard, protect; *keep, preserve
muhafazakâr /·–··'·/ *adj* conservative
muhafız /·–'·/ *n* guard; warden
muhakeme /·–'·/ *n* trial; judgment; ~ **etmek** *hear a case; judge, reason
muhakkak /·'··/ *adj* certain, sure; *adv* certainly
muhalefet /·–·'·/ *n* opposition; ~ **etmek** oppose
muhalif /·–'·/ *adj* opposing, opposed; *n* opponent
muharebe /·–·'·/ *n* war; battle

muhasebe /·–'·/ *n* accountancy, bookkeeping
muhasebeci /·–·'·/ *n* accountant
muhit /·'·/ *n* surroundings; environment
muhtaç /·'·/ *adj* needy
muhtar /·'·/ *n* headman, elder of a quarter *or* village
muhtelif /··'·/ *adj* various
muhtemel /··'·/ *adj* probable, likely
muhtemelen /·'···/ *adv* probably
muhterem /··'·/ *adj* honored, respected
muhteşem /··'·/ *adj* magnificent, splendid
mukaddes /··'·/ *adj* sacred, holy
mukavele /·–'·/ *n* contract, agreement
mukavemet /·–'·/ *n* endurance, resistance
mukavva /·'··/ *n* cardboard
mukayese /·–'·/ *n* comparison; **~ etmek** compare
muktedir /··'·/ *adj* capable; **~ olmak** *be able to
mum *n* candle; wax
mumlu /·'·/ *adj* waxy; waxed; **~ kâğıt** stencil
mumya /'··/ *n* mummy
muntazam /··'·/ *adj* regular, tidy
muntazaman /·'···/ *adv* regularly
Musevi /–'–/ *adj* Jewish; *n* Jew
musibet /·–'·/ *n* calamity, disaster
musiki /–'–/ *n* music
muska /·'·/ *n* amulet, charm
musluk /·'·/ *n* faucet *nAm;* tap *nBr*
muşamba /·'··/ *n* oilcloth, oilskin
muşmula /'···/ *n* medlar
mutfak /·'·/ *n* kitchen
mutlak /·'·/ *adj* absolute
mutlaka /'··–/ *adv* absolutely
mutlakiyet /···'·/ *n* absolutism
mutlu /·'·/ *adj* happy
mutluluk /··'·/ *n* happiness
muz *n* banana
muzaffer /··'·/ *adj* victorious
muzır /·'·/ *adj* harmful; mischievous
muzırlık /··'·/ *n* harmfulness; mischievousness
muzip /–'·/ *adj* teasing
muziplik /–·'·/ *n* teasing; mischievous behavior
mübalağa /·–'·/ *n* exaggeration; **~ etmek** exaggerate
mübarek /·–'·/ *adj* blessed, holy
mücadele /·–'·/ *n* struggle, fight; **~ etmek** struggle
mücahit /·–'·/ *n* combatant, fighter
mücevher /··'·/ *n* jewel
müdafaa /·–'·/ *n* defense; **~ etmek** defend
müdahale /·–'·/ *n* interference; intervention; **~ etmek** interfere; intervene
müddet /·'·/ *n* period, duration
müdür /·'·/ *n* director, manager; headmaster
müdürlük /··'·/, **müdüriyet** /·–'·/ *n* directorate; management
müebbet /··'·/ *adj* lifelong, eternal; **~ hapis** life sentence
müessese /···'·/ *n* establishment, institution, foundation
müezzin /··'·/ *n* one who calls Muslims to prayer, muezzin
müfettiş /··'·/ *n* inspector, supervisor
müfredat /··'·/ *n* curriculum
mühendis /··'·/ *n* engineer
mühendislik /···'·/ *n* engineering
mühim /·'·/ *adj* important
mühlet /·'·/ *n* delay, respite, term
mühür /·'·/ *n* seal; **~ basmak** seal
mühürlü /··'·/ *adj* sealed
mühürsüz /··'·/ *adj* unsealed
müjde /·'·/ *n* good news

müjdelemek /···ˈ·/ *v* *give a piece of good news
mükâfat /·–ˈ·/ *n* reward
mükâfatlandırmak /·–···ˈ·/ *v* reward
mükemmel /··ˈ·/ *adj* perfect, excellent
mülk *n* property; real estate
mülkiyet /··ˈ·/ *n* possession, ownership
mülteci /··ˈ–/ *n* refugee
mümin /–ˈ·/ *n* believer, believer in Islam
mümkün /·ˈ·/ *adj* possible
münakaşa /·–ˈ·/ *n* dispute, argument; ~ **etmek** argue, dispute
münasebet /·–ˈ·/ *n* relation, connection; **münasebetiyle** on the occasion of
münasebetsiz /·–··ˈ·/ *adj* absurd, improper, unseemly
münasip /·–ˈ·/ *adj* suitable, proper; ~ **görmek** *see fit, approve
müracaat /·–ˈ·/ *n* application, reference; ~ **etmek** refer to, apply to
mürekkep /··ˈ·/ *n* ink
mürekkepbalığı /··ˈ····/ *n* cuttlefish
mürettebat /···ˈ·/ *n* crew
müsaade /·–ˈ·/ *n* permission, permit; ~ **etmek** *give permission to
müsabaka /·–ˈ·/ *n* competition, contest
müsait /·–ˈ·/ *adj* suitable, convenient
müsamere /·–ˈ·/ *n* school show
müshil /·ˈ·/ *n* purgative, laxative
Müslüman /··ˈ·/ *adj, n* Moslem, Muslim
Müslümanlık /···ˈ·/ *n* Islam
müspet /·ˈ·/ *adj* positive
müsrif /·ˈ·/ *adj* spendthrift, prodigal
müstahdem /··ˈ·/ *n* employee
müstakbel /··ˈ·/ *adj* future, prospective
müstakil /··ˈ·/ *adj* independent; separate
müstehcen /··ˈ·/ *adj* obscene, pornographic
müsterih /··ˈ·/ *adj* at ease; ~ **olmak** *be at ease; *be relieved
müstesna /··ˈ–/ *adj* except; exceptional
müsteşar /··ˈ·/ *n* undersecretary
müsvedde /··ˈ·/ *n* rough copy, draft
müşavir /··ˈ·/ *n* consultant, adviser
müşfik /·ˈ·/ *adj* kind, tender, compassionate
müşkülpesent /···ˈ·/ *adj* particular, fastidious, exacting
müşterek /··ˈ·/ *adj* common, collective, joint; cooperative
müşteri /··ˈ·/ *n* customer, buyer, client
mütareke /·–ˈ·/ *n* truce, armistice
müteahhit /···ˈ·/ *n* contractor
mütehassıs /···ˈ·/ *n* specialist, expert
mütemadiyen /··ˈ–··/ *adv* continuously
mütevazı /··–ˈ·/ *adj* humble, modest
müthiş /·ˈ·/ *adj* terrible, awful; amazing, super, terrific
müttefik /··ˈ·/ *adj* allied; *n* ally
müzakere /·–ˈ·/ *n* discussion, consultation; oral exam; ~ **etmek** discuss, debate, talk over
müzayede /·–ˈ·/ *n* auction
müze /ˈ··/ *n* museum
müzelik /··ˈ·/ *adj* worthy of a museum; ancient

müzik /·ˈ·/ *n* music
müzisyen /··ˈ·/ *n* musician
müzmin /·ˈ·/ *adj* chronic
müzminleşmek /···ˈ·/ *v* *become chronic

N

nabız /·ˈ·/ *n* pulse
nadide /––ˈ·/ *adj* rare, curious, precious
nadir /–ˈ·/ *adj* rare
nadiren /ˈ–··/ *adv* rarely, seldom
nafaka /··ˈ·/ *n* alimony; livelihood
nafile /–·ˈ·/ *adj* useless; *adv* in vain
nağme /·ˈ·/ *n* tune, melody
nahoş /–ˈ·/ *adj* unpleasant
nakış /·ˈ·/ *n* embroidery; ~ **işlemek** embroider
nakil /·ˈ·/ *n* transport, transfer
nakit /·ˈ·/ *n* ready money, cash
naklen /ˈ··/ *adv* by transfer; ~ **yayın** live broadcast
nakletmek /ˈ···/ *v* transfer, transport
nakliyat /··ˈ·/ *n* transport, shipping
nal *n* horseshoe
nalbant /·ˈ·/ *n* blacksmith
nalbur /·ˈ·/ *n* hardware dealer
nalın /·ˈ·/ *n* clogs
nam *n* name; fame, reputation; ~ **kazanmak** *become famous **namına** on behalf of; **namında** called, named; **namıyla** under the name of
namaz /·ˈ·/ *n* ritual worship; prayer
namert /–ˈ·/ *adj* cowardly, despicable
namlı /·ˈ·/ *adj* famous
namlu /·ˈ·/ *n* gun barrel
namus /–ˈ·/ *n* honor
namuslu /–·ˈ·/ *adj* honorable, honest; chaste
namussuz /–·ˈ·/ *adj* dishonest, dishonorable
namussuzca /–·ˈ··/ *adv* dishonestly
namussuzluk /–··ˈ·/ *n* dishonesty
namzet /·ˈ·/ *n* candidate; applicant
nane /–ˈ·/ *n* mint, peppermint
naneşekeri /–ˈ····/ *n* peppermint drop
nankör /·ˈ·/ *adj* ungrateful, unthankful
nankörlük /··ˈ·/ *n* unthankfulness ~ **etmek** *show ingratitude
Napoli /·ˈ··/ Naples
nar *n* pomegranate
nara /–ˈ·/ *n* loud cry, shout; ~ **atmak** yell
narenciye /–··ˈ·/ *n* citrus fruits
nargile /··ˈ·/ *n* water pipe, hubble-bubble
narin /–ˈ·/ *adj* slender, slim, delicate
narkoz /·ˈ·/ *n* anesthesia
nasıl /ˈ··/ *adv* how, what sort; **nasılsa** in any case
nasır /·ˈ·/ *n* corn, callus; ~ **bağlamak** *become calloused
nasırlaşmak /···ˈ·/ *v* *become calloused
nasırlı /··ˈ·/ *adj* calloused
nasihat /·–ˈ·/ *n* advice; ~ **etmek** advise; **nasihatını tutmak** follow someone's advice
nasip /·ˈ·/ *n* lot, share, portion; ~ **olmak** *fall to one's lot; **nasibini almak** enjoy; *get one's share
navlun /·ˈ·/ *n* freight
naz *n* coquetry, whims; coyness; ~ **etmek** feign reluctance
nazar /·ˈ·/ *n* look, glance; evil eye; ~ **değmek** *be affected by the evil eye; ~ **boncuğu** bead worn

against the evil eye
nazaran /·ˈ··/ *adv* in comparison to, according to
nazım /·ˈ·/ *n* verse
nazik /–ˈ·/ *adj* polite, kind; delicate
nazikleşmek /–··ˈ·/ *v* *become polite *or* delicate
naziklik /–·ˈ·/ *n* politeness
ne *adv* what; whatever; how; ~ . . . ~ . . . neither. . . nor. . . ; ~ **biçim** what kind of; ~ **de olsa** after all; ~ **olursa olsun** come what may
neden /·ˈ·/ *adv* why, what for, for what reason; *n* cause; **nedense** for some reason or other
nedensiz /··ˈ·/ *adj* without a reason; causeless
nefes /·ˈ·/ *n* breath; ~ **aldırmamak** *give no rest; ~ **almak** breathe; ~ **darlığı** asthma; ~ **kesici** breathtaking; ~ **nefese kalmak** *get out of breath; **nefesi kesilmek** *be out of breath
nefis[1] /·ˈ·/ *n* self, essence; one's desire; **nefsini körletmek** *take the edge off one's desire
nefis[2] /·ˈ–/ *adj* excellent, delicious, beautiful
nefret /·ˈ·/ *n* hatred, abhorrence, hate; ~ **etmek** hate; abhor, loathe
nefretle /·ˈ··/ *adv* with hatred
nehir /·ˈ·/ *n* river
nemlenmek /··ˈ·/ *v* *become damp
nemli /·ˈ·/ *adj* moist, damp
nerede /ˈ···/ *adv* where, wherever; ~ **ise** before long; almost; **nereden** from where; **nereye** to what place
nesil /·ˈ·/ *n* generation
nesir /·ˈ·/ *n* prose
nesne /·ˈ·/ *n* thing; object
neşe /·ˈ·/ *n* joy
neşelendirmek /····ˈ·/ *v* render cheerful
neşelenmek /···ˈ·/ *v* *be joyful, *grow merry
neşeli /··ˈ·/ *adj* cheerful, merry
neşesiz /··ˈ·/ *adj* joyless, in low spirits
net *adj* clear, net
netice /·–ˈ·/ *n* result, consequence
neticelendirmek /·–···ˈ·/ *v* *bring to an end
neticelenmek /·–··ˈ·/ *v* result in; *come to a conclusion
neticesiz /·–·ˈ·/ *adj* fruitless, useless
nezaket /·–ˈ·/ *n* delicacy, politeness
nezaketsiz /·–·ˈ·/ *adj* impolite
nezaret /·–ˈ·/ *n* surveillance, inspection; ~ **altına almak** *take under surveillance; ~ **etmek** superintend
nezih /·ˈ·/ *adj* upright, pure, clean
nezle /·ˈ·/ *n* head cold; ~ **olmak** *catch a cold
nice /ˈ··/ *adv* how many, many a . . .
nicelik /··ˈ·/ *n* quantity
niçin /ˈ··/ *adv* why, what for
nihayet[1] /·–ˈ·/ *n* end
nihayet[2] /ˈ···/ *adv* at last
nihayetsiz /·–·ˈ·/ *adj* endless, infinite
nikâh /·ˈ·/ *n* marriage, civil wedding; ~ **kıymak** perform a civil wedding
nikâhlanmak /···ˈ·/ *v* *get married
nilüfer /··ˈ·/ *n* water lily
nimet /–ˈ·/ *n* blessing, food, bread
nine /ˈ··/ *n* grandmother
ninni /·ˈ·/ *n* lullaby
nisan /–ˈ·/ April

nispet /·ˈ·/ *n* proportion, ratio
nispetçi /··ˈ·/ *n* spiteful
nispeten /ˈ···/ *adv* relatively, in proportion
nişan /·ˈ·/ *n* mark, sign; engagement; ~ **almak** *take aim; **nişanı bozmak** *break off an engagement; ~ **yapmak** arrange an engagement; ~ **yüzüğü** engagement ring
nişanlanmak /···ˈ·/ *v* *get engaged
nişasta /·ˈ··/ *n* starch
nitekim /ˈ···/ *adv* besides, just as; as a matter of fact
nitelemek /···ˈ·/ *v* qualify
nitelik /··ˈ·/ *n* quality
niye /·ˈ·/ *adv* why, what for
niyet /·ˈ·/ *n* intention, purpose; ~ **etmek** intend; **niyetiyle** with the intention of
niyetli /··ˈ·/ *adj* who has an intention; fasting
nizam /·ˈ·/ *n* order, regularity; law
nizami /·–ˈ–/ *adj* regular; legal
nizamlı /··ˈ·/ *adj* regular
nizamname /·–ˈ·/ *n* regulation
nizamsız /··ˈ·/ *adj* irregular; illegal
Noel /ˈ··/ Christmas; ~ **Baba** Santa Claus
nohut /·ˈ·/ *n* chick-pea
noksan /·ˈ·/ *n* deficiency, want, defect; *adj* deficient, lacking
noksansız /··ˈ·/ *adj* complete, perfect
nokta /·ˈ·/ *n* point, dot; spot; speck; full stop, period
noktalamak /···ˈ·/ *v* punctuate
noktalı /··ˈ·/ *adj* punctuated; dotted; ~ **virgül** semicolon
noktasız /··ˈ·/ *adj* undotted
Norveç /ˈ··/ Norway
Norveççe /·ˈ··/ *n* Norwegian language
Norveçli /ˈ···/ *adj, n* Norwegian
not *n* note; grade, mark; ~ **tutmak** *take notes; ~ **vermek** *give marks; size up
nota /ˈ··/ *n* musical note; diplomatic note
noter /·ˈ·/ *n* notary public
nöbet /·ˈ·/ *n* turn of duty; guard, watch; fit, attack
nöbetçi /··ˈ·/ *adj* on guard, on duty; *n* watchman
nöbetleşe /···ˈ·/ *adv* by turns
numara /·ˈ··/ *n* number; size; trick
numaracı /·ˈ···/ *n* faker, phony
numaralı /·ˈ···/ *adj* numbered
numarasız /·ˈ···/ *adj* unnumbered
numune /·–ˈ·/ *n* sample; model
nur *n* light, brilliance
nurlu /·ˈ·/ *adj* shining, bright
nutuk /·ˈ·/ *n* speech, oration; ~ **çekmek** sermonize; ~ **vermek** *make a speech
nüfus /·ˈ·/ *n* population; inhabitants; ~ **kâğıdı** identity card; ~ **kütüğü** state register of persons; ~ **patlaması** population explosion; ~ **planlaması** family planning; ~ **sayımı** census; ~ **yoğunluğu** population density
nükte /·ˈ·/ *n* witticism; ~ **yapmak** *make witty remarks
nükteci /··ˈ·/ *adj* witty
nükteli /··ˈ·/ *adj* witty
nüsha /·ˈ·/ *n* copy, issue, number

O

o *pron* he, she, it; *adj* that, those
oba /·ˈ·/ *n* large nomad tent
objektif /··ˈ·/ *n* lens, objective
obur /·ˈ·/ *adj* gluttonous, greedy
ocak[1] /·ˈ·/ January
ocak[2] /·ˈ·/ *n* furnace, kiln, hearth,

fireplace; cooker, oven
oda /·'·/ *n* room; office
odak /·'·/ *n* focus
odun /·'·/ *n* firewood, log
oduncu /··'·/ *n* wood-cutter; seller of firewood
oğlak /·'·/ *n* kid
oğlan /·'·/ *n* boy
ok *n* arrow; ~ **atmak** *shoot arrows
okçu /·'·/ *n* bowman, archer
oklava /··'·/ *n* long, thin rolling pin
okşamak /··'·/ *v* caress, pat
okul /·'·/ *n* school; ~ **kaçağı** truant
okuma /··'·/ *n* reading; ~ **yazma** literacy, reading and writing
okumak /··'·/ *v* *read; study, *learn
okumamış /·'···/ *adj* uneducated
okumuş /··'·/ *adj* educated
okunaklı /···'·/ *adj* readable, legible
okunaksız /···'·/ *adj* illegible
okur /·'·/ *n* reader
okutmak /··'·/ *v* *teach, instruct
okutman /··'·/ *n* lecturer
okuyucu /···'·/ *n* reader; singer
okyanus /··'·/ *n* ocean
olabilir /···'·/ *adj* possible
olabilirlik /····'·/ *n* possibility
olağan /··'·/ *adj* usual, ordinary, common
olağandışı /··'···/ *adj* unusual, abnormal
olağanüstü /··'···/ *adj* extraordinary, unusual
olanak /··'·/ *n* possibility; facility; ~ **vermek** enable
olanaklı /···'·/ *adj* possible
olanaksız /···'·/ *adj* impossible
olanca /·'··/ *adv* utmost, to the full
olası /··'·/ *adj* probable
olasılık /···'·/ *n* probability
olay /·'·/ *n* event; ~ **çıkarmak** provoke an incident
olaylı /··'·/ *adj* eventful
olaysız /··'·/ *adj* eventless
oldukça /·'··/ *adv* rather, fairly
olgu /·'·/ *n* fact, phenomenon
olgun /·'·/ *adj* ripe; mature
olgunlaşmak /···'·/ *v* *become ripe; mature
olgunlaştırmak /····'·/ *v* ripen; mature
olgunluk /··'·/ *n* ripeness; maturity
olmadık /'···/ *adj* unusual, unprecedented
olmak /·'·/ *v* *be; *become; *get; exist; occur
olmamış /'···/ *adj* unripe
olmayacak /'····/ *adj* unseemly, unsuitable; unlikely; impossible
olmuş /·'·/ *adj* ripe, mature
olta /·'·/ *n* fishline; ~ **iğnesi** fishhook
oluk /·'·/ *n* gutter, pipe; groove
oluklu /··'·/ *adj* grooved
olumlu /··'·/ *adj* positive, affirmative
olumsuz /··'·/ *adj* negative
oluş /·'·/ *n* existence, being
oluşmak /··'·/ *v* *take form; *come into existence
oluşum /··'·/ *n* formation
omur /·'·/ *n* vertebra
omurga /·'··/ *n* backbone, spine
omurilik /·'···/ *n* spinal cord
omuz /·'·/ *n* shoulder; ~ **silkmek** shrug
omuzlamak /···'·/ *v* shoulder
on *num* ten; **onar onar** ten by ten
ona /·'·/ *pron* to him, to her, to it
onamak /··'·/ *v* approve
onarım /··'·/ *n* repair
onarmak /··'·/ *v* repair; mend; restore
onay /·'·/ *n* approval
onaylamak /···'·/ *v* approve
onaylı /··'·/ *adj* approved

onbaşı /'···/ *n* corporal
ondalık /··'·/ *n* a tenth part; decimal; ~ **kesir** decimal fraction; ~ **sayı** decimal number
ondüle /··'·/ *adj* curled, curly
onlar /·'·/ *pron* those, they
ons *n* ounce
onu /·'·/ *pron* him, her, it
onun /·'·/ *adj* his, her, its
onunki /··'·/ *pron* his, hers, its
onur /·'·/ *n* honor, self-respect, dignity; **onuruna** in honor of; **onuruna dokunmak** *hurt someone's pride
onurlandırmak /····'·/ *v* honor
onurlu /··'·/ *adj* self-respecting, proud
onursuz /··'·/ *adj* dishonorable
operatör /···'·/ *n* surgeon; operator
optik /·'·/ *n* optics; *adj* optical
ora /'··/ *n* that place; **orada** there; **oraları** those places; **orası** that place; **oraya** there
oramiral /'····/ *n* admiral
oran /·'·/ *n* proportion; ratio, rate
oranlamak /···'·/ *v* measure, compare
oranlı /··'·/ *adj* proportional
oransız /··'·/ *adj* badly proportioned
orantı /··'·/ *n* ratio
orantılı /···'·/ *adj* proportional
ordinaryüs /··'··/ *n* senior professor holding a chair in a university
ordu /·'·/ *n* army
orduevi /·'···/ *n* officers' club
ordugâh /··'·/ *n* military camp
org *n* organ
organ /·'·/ *n* organ; ~ **nakli** transplantation
orgeneral /'····/ *n* full general
orijinal /···'·/ *adj* original; unusual
orkide /·'··/ *n* orchid
orkinos /··'·/ *n* tuna fish
orman /·'·/ *n* forest, wood
ormancı /··'·/ *n* forester
ormancılık /···'·/ *n* forestry
ormanlık /··'·/ *adj* thickly wooded; *n* woodland
orta /·'·/ *n* middle; center; **Orta Doğu** Middle East; ~ **halli** neither poor nor rich; ~ **yaşlı** middle-aged; **ortada** in the middle; **ortadan kaybolmak** disappear; **ortaya atmak** suggest; **ortaya çıkmak** emerge
ortaçağ /·'··/ *n* Middle Ages
ortak /·'·/ *n* partner, associate; *adj* common, shared; joint; ~ **olmak** *become a partner
ortaklaşa /···'·/ *adv* collectively, in common
ortaklık /··'·/ *n* partnership, company, firm
ortalama /···'·/ *n* average; ~ **olarak** on an average
ortalık /··'·/ *n* surroundings, the world around; **ortalığı süpürmek** *sweep up; **ortalığı toplamak** tidy up; **ortalığı birbirine katmak** turn the place upside down
ortam /·'·/ *n* environment, surroundings, atmosphere; circumstances
ortaokul /·'···/ *n* secondary school, middle school
ortaoyunu /·'····/ *n* Turkish folk theatre with set plots
ortaparmak /·'···/ *n* middle finger
oruç /·'·/ *n* fasting, fast; ~ **bozmak** *break the fast; ~ **tutmak** fast
oruçlu /··'·/ *adj* fasting
Osmanlı /··'·/ *adj, n* Ottoman; ~ **İmparatorluğu** the Ottoman Empire
Osmanlıca /··'··/ *n* Ottoman Turkish language

ot *n* grass, herb
otel /·ˈ·/ *n* hotel
otlak /·ˈ·/ *n* pasture, grassland
otlamak /··ˈ·/ *v* graze, *be out to pasture
otlatmak /··ˈ·/ *v* pasture cattle
otobüs /··ˈ·/ *n* bus
otogar /··ˈ·/ *n* intercity bus station
otomobil /···ˈ·/ *n* car, automobile
otopark /··ˈ·/ *n* parking lot
otopsi /··ˈ·/ *n* autopsy
otorite /···ˈ·/ *n* authority
otoriter /···ˈ·/ *adj* authoritarian
otostop /··ˈ·/ *n* hitchhiking; ~ **yapmak** hitchhike
otostopçu /···ˈ·/ *n* hitchhiker
oturak /··ˈ·/ *n* seat; chamber pot
oturaklı /···ˈ·/ *adj* well settled, dignified, sober
oturma /··ˈ·/ *n* sitting, staying; ~ **odası** living room
oturmak /··ˈ·/ *v* *sit, *sit down; live, settle; fit well
oturtmak /··ˈ·/ *v* seat, place
oturum /··ˈ·/ *n* session, sitting
otuz /·ˈ·/ *num* thirty
otuzuncu /···ˈ·/ *num* thirtieth
ova /·ˈ·/ *n* plain
ovalamak /···ˈ·/ *v* rub; *break up small, crumble
ovalık /··ˈ·/ *adj* having plains; *n* grassland
ovmak /·ˈ·/ *v* rub with hand, massage; polish
ovuşturmak /···ˈ·/ *v* rub, massage
oy *n* vote; ~ **sandığı** ballot box; **oya koymak** *put to the vote; ~ **vermek** vote
oya /·ˈ·/ *n* pinking, embroidery
oyalamak /···ˈ·/ *v* *put someone off, stall; amuse, divert
oyalanmak /···ˈ·/ *v* loiter, dally, linger
oyalı /··ˈ·/ *adj* pinked
oybirliği /ˈ····/ *n* unanimity
oylama /··ˈ·/ *n* voting
oylamak /··ˈ·/ *v* *put to the vote
oyma /·ˈ·/ *n* carving, engraving; *adj* carved, engraved
oymabaskı /·ˈ···/ *n* engraving
oymacı /··ˈ·/ *n* engraver; carver
oymak[1] /·ˈ·/ *v* carve, engrave
oymak[2] /·ˈ·/ *n* tribe, clan; troop of boy-scouts
oymalı /··ˈ·/ *adj* engraved; carved
oynak /·ˈ·/ *adj* playful, frisky; unstable; fickle
oynamak /··ˈ·/ *v* play; dance; fiddle with; move; perform; risk; amuse oneself
oynanmak /··ˈ·/ *v* *be played
oynatmak /··ˈ·/ *v* cause to play; cause to dance; move, stir; *go mad
oysa /ˈ··/ *conj* whereas, however, yet, but
oyuk /·ˈ·/ *adj* hollowed out; *n* hollow; cavity
oyun /·ˈ·/ *n* game; dance; play; performance; trick; gamble; ~ **oynamak** play a trick on; ~ **yazarı** playwright; **oyuna gelmek** *be deceived
oyunbaz /··ˈ·/ *adj* frisky, playful; *n* swindler
oyunbozan /···ˈ·/ *n* spoilsport, killjoy
oyuncak /··ˈ·/ *n* toy; plaything
oyuncu /··ˈ·/ *n* player, actor; dancer; actress
oyunlaştırmak /····ˈ·/ *v* dramatize
ozan /·ˈ·/ *n* poet

Ö

öbek /·'·/ *n* heap, pile; ~ ~ in groups
öbür /·'·/ *adj* the other; **öbürü** the other one; ~ **dünya** the next world; ~ **gün** the day after tomorrow
öç *n* revenge; ~ **almak** *take revenge
öd *n* gall, bile
ödeme /··'·/ *n* payment
ödemek /··'·/ *v* *pay
ödemeli /···'·/ *adj* cash on delivery
ödenek /··'·/ *n* appropriation; allowance
ödenti /··'·/ *n* subscription; dues
ödeşmek /··'·/ *v* settle accounts with each other
ödev /·'·/ *n* duty; obligation; homework
ödkesesi /'····/ *n* gallbladder
ödlek /·'·/ *adj* timid, cowardly
ödleklik /··'·/ *n* cowardice
ödül /·'·/ *n* prize, award; reward; ~ **kazanmak** *win a prize
ödüllendirmek /····'·/ *v* reward
ödün /·'·/ *n* compensation, concession; ~ **vermek** *make concessions
ödünç /·'·/ *adj* loaned, borrowed; ~ **almak** borrow; ~ **vermek** *lend
öfke /·'·/ *n* anger, fury, rage
öfkelendirmek /····'·/ *v* *make angry, anger
öfkelenmek /···'·/ *v* *get angry
öfkeli /··'·/ *adj* angry; hotheaded
öğe /·'·/ *n* element
öğle /·'·/ *n* noon, midday; ~ **yemeği** lunch; **öğleden önce** before noon; **öğleden sonra** in the afternoon; **öğleyin** at noon
öğrenci /··'·/ *n* student, pupil
öğrenim /··'·/ *n* education; ~ **görmek** *be educated
öğrenmek /··'·/ *v* *learn
öğreti /··'·/ *n* doctrine
öğretici /···'·/ *adj* instructive, didactic
öğretim /··'·/ *n* instruction, education; ~ **üyesi** faculty member; ~ **yılı** school year
öğretmek /··'·/ *v* *teach, instruct
öğretmen /··'·/ *n* teacher; ~ **okulu** teacher's training school
öğretmenlik /···'·/ *n* teaching
öğün /·'·/ *n* meal
öğüt /·'·/ *n* advice; ~ **vermek** *give advice
öğütmek /··'·/ *v* *grind, mill
ökçe /·'·/ *n* heel
ökçeli /··'·/ *adj* heeled
ökçesiz /··'·/ *adj* heelless
öksürmek /··'·/ *v* cough
öksürük /··'·/ *n* cough, coughing
öksüz /·'·/ *n* orphan, motherless child; ~ **kalmak** *be orphaned
öküz /·'·/ *n* ox
ölçek /·'·/ *n* measure, scale
ölçmek /·'·/ *v* measure; weigh; **ölçüp biçmek** consider carefully
ölçü /·'·/ *n* measure; measurement; moderation
ölçülü /··'·/ *adj* measured; well-balanced, temperate
ölçüm /·'·/ *n* measure, measurement
ölçüsüz /··'·/ *adj* immeasurable; immoderate, inordinate
ölçüt /·'·/ *n* criterion
öldüresiye /··'···/ *adv* to death, ruthlessly
öldürmek /··'·/ *v* kill, murder
öldürücü /···'·/ *adj* killing, deadly

ölesiye /·ˈ··/ *adv* excessively, to the death
ölmek /·ˈ·/ *v* die
ölmüş /·ˈ·/ *adj* dead, lifeless
ölü /·ˈ·/ *adj* dead; *n* dead body, corpse
ölüm /·ˈ·/ *n* death; ~ **cezası** capital punishment; ~ **kalım meselesi** matter of life or death
ölümcül /··ˈ·/ *adj* deathly, mortal
ölümlü /··ˈ·/ *adj* mortal
ölümsüz /··ˈ·/ *adj* immortal
ölümsüzlük /···ˈ·/ *n* immortality
ömür /·ˈ·/ *n* life, existence; **ömründe** in all his life, never
ömürlü /··ˈ·/ *adj* long-lived
ömürsüz /··ˈ·/ *adj* short-lived
ön *n* front, foreground; *adj* front; foremost; preliminary; ~ **ayak olmak** pioneer; *lead; **önde** ahead; **önde gelmek** *be in the most important place; **öne sürmek** *bring forward; **önünde** in front of; **önüne gelen** anyone, everybody
önce /ˈ·/ *adv* first, at first; before; ago; prior to; **önceden** beforehand, at first, in advance; **önceki** the former, the previous; **önceleri** at first, previously, formerly
öncelik /··ˈ·/ *n* priority
öncelikle /··ˈ··/ *adv* first
öncü /·ˈ·/ *n* vanguard
öncülük /··ˈ·/ *n* pioneering; ~ **etmek** pioneer
önder /·ˈ·/ *n* leader, chief
önderlik /··ˈ·/ *n*. leadership
önek /ˈ··/ *n* prefix
önem /·ˈ·/ *n* importance; ~ **vermek** attach importance
önemli /··ˈ·/ *adj* important
önemsemek /···ˈ·/ *v* consider important
önemsiz /··ˈ·/ *adj* unimportant
önerge /··ˈ·/ *n* motion, proposal
öneri /··ˈ·/ *n* proposal, offer, suggestion; **öneride bulunmak** propose
önermek /··ˈ·/ *v* propose, suggest, offer
öngörmek /ˈ···/ *v* *foresee, anticipate
önlem /·ˈ·/ *n* precaution, measure; ~ **almak** *take measures
önlemek /··ˈ·/ *v* prevent
önleyici /···ˈ·/ *adj* preventive
önlük /·ˈ·/ *n* apron
önseçim /ˈ···/ *n* primary election
önsezi /ˈ···/ *n* presentiment, intuition
önsöz /ˈ··/ *n* foreword, preface
önyargı /ˈ···/ *n* prejudice
önyargılı /ˈ····/ *adj* prejudiced
öpmek /·ˈ·/ *v* kiss
öpücük /··ˈ·/ *n* kiss
öpüş /·ˈ·/ *n* kissing
öpüşmek /··ˈ·/ *v* kiss one another
ördek /·ˈ·/ *n* duck
örgü /·ˈ·/ *n* knitting; plait, braid
örgüt /·ˈ·/ *n* organization
örgütlemek /···ˈ·/ *v* organize
örme /·ˈ·/ *adj* knitted; plaited; woven; *n* knitting; plaiting
örmek /·ˈ·/ *v* *knit; plait
örneğin /ˈ···/ for example, for instance
örnek /·ˈ·/ *n* example; sample; pattern, model; ~ **almak** copy, adopt; ~ **olmak** *be a model
örs *n* anvil
örtbas /·ˈ·/ *n* hushing up; ~ **etmek** suppress, hush up, cover up
örtmek /·ˈ·/ *v* cover; conceal; close
örtü /·ˈ·/ *n* cover, wrap
örtülü /··ˈ·/ *adj* covered; shut;

wrapped
örtünmek /··'·/ *v* cover oneself
örücü /··'·/ *n* mender, darner
örümcek /··'·/ *n* spider; ~ **ağı** cobweb; ~ **kafalı** old-fashioned
öte /·'·/ *adj* further; farther; *n* the other side; ~ **yandan** on the other hand; **ötede** over there; **ötedenberi** from of old; heretofore
öteberi /···'·/ *n* this and that, various things
öteki /··'·/ *adj* the other; *pron* the other one
ötmek /·'·/ *v* (for birds) *sing
öttürmek /··'·/ *v* *blow, sound
ötürü /··'·/ *adv* because of
övgü /·'·/ *n* praise; **övgüye değer** praiseworthy
övmek /·'·/ *v* praise, extol
övünç /·'·/ *n* pride
övüngen /··'·/ *adj* boastful
övünmek /··'·/ *v* boast; *feel proud of; brag
öykü /·'·/ *n* story
öykücü /··'·/ *n* story writer; story teller
öyle /'··/ *adv* such, like that, so; ~ **mi?** is that so?; ~ **ya!** of course!; **öylece** like that, that way; **öylelikle** thus; **öylesine . . . ki** so . . . that; **öyleyse** in that case, if so
öz *n* self; essence; *adj* own; real; pure; ~ **anne** one's own mother; ~ **Türkçe** pure Turkish
özbeöz /'···/ *adj* real, true, genuine
özdeş /·'·/ *adj* identical
özdeşleşmek /···'·/ *v* identify oneself with
özdeyiş /'···/ *n* maxim; saying, aphorism
özdirenç /'···/ *n* resistivity
özel /·'·/ *adj* private; personal; special
özellik /··'·/ *n* peculiarity, characteristic; property
özellikle /··'··/ *adv* especially, particularly
özen /·'·/ *n* care, pains; ~ **göstermek** *take pains; **özene bezene** painstakingly
özenli /··'·/ *adj* careful, painstaking
özensiz /··'·/ *adj* careless
özenti /··'·/ *n* affectation, emulation
özentili /···'·/ *adj* affected
özentisiz /···'·/ *adj* genuine
özerk /·'·/ *adj* autonomous
özerklik /··'·/ *n* autonomy
özet /·'·/ *n* summary
özetlemek /···'·/ *v* summarize
özgeçmiş /'···/ *n* curriculum vitae, résumé
özgü /·'·/ *adj* peculiar, special
özgül /·'·/ *adj* specific; ~ **ağırlık** specific weight
özgün /·'·/ *adj* original
özgür /·'·/ *adj* free
özgürce /·'··/ *adv* freely
özgürlük /··'·/ *n* freedom
özlem /·'·/ *n* longing; aspiration
özlemek /··'·/ *v* miss, long for, wish for
özleştirmek /···'·/ *v* purify
özlü /·'·/ *adj* pithy, meaty; concise
özne /·'·/ *n* subject
öznel /·'·/ *adj* subjective
öznellik /··'·/ *n* subjectiveness
özsu /'··/ *n* sap
özümleme /···'·/ *n* assimilation
özümlemek /···'·/ *v* assimilate
özür /·'·/ *n* excuse, apology; defect; impediment; ~ **dilemek** ask pardon, apologize
özürlü /··'·/ *adj* having an excuse; defective
özürsüz /··'·/ *adj* without excuse; nondefective

özveri /'···/ *n* self-denial, self-sacrifice
özverili /'····/ *adj* self-denying, unselfish
özyaşam öyküsü /··'· ···/ autobiography

P

pabuç /·'·/ *n* shoe
paça /·'·/ *n* lower part of trousers; trotters
paçavra /·'··/ *n* rag
padişah /–·'·/ *n* sultan, ruler
padişahlık /–··'·/ *n* sultanate, sovereignty
paha /·'·/ *n* price, value; ~ **biçilmez** priceless; ~ **biçmek** estimate a price;
pahalı /··'·/ *adj* expensive, dear
pahalılaşmak /····'·/ *v* *become more expensive
pahalılık /···'·/ *n* expensiveness
pak *adj* clean
paket /·'·/ *n* package, parcel
paketlemek /···'·/ *v* parcel up, package, wrap up
Pakistan /–·'·/ Pakistan
Pakistanlı /–··'·/ *adj, n* Pakistani
pala /·'·/ *n* scimitar
palabıyık /·'···/ *n* handlebar mustache
palamut (balığı) /··'·/ *n* bonito
palavra /·'··/ *n* idle talk; boast, bragging
palavracı /·'···/ *n* braggart, boaster
palaz /·'·/ *n* duckling, goosling
palazlanmak /···'·/ *v* *grow up; *grow fat
palmiye /'···/ *n* palm tree
palto /'··/ *n* coat, overcoat
palyaço /·'··/ *n* clown
pamuk /·'·/ *n* cotton
pamuklu /··'·/ *adj* made of cotton; *n* cotton cloth
panayır /··'·/ *n* fair, market; ~ **yeri** fairground
pancar /·'·/ *n* beet; ~ **şekeri** beet sugar
pandispanya /··'··/ *n* sponge cake
panik /·'·/ *n* panic; ~ **yaratmak** cause a panic; **paniğe kapılmak** *be seized with panic
panjur /·'·/ *n* shutter
pankart /·'·/ *n* banner, placard
pano /'··/ *n* panel, notice-board
panorama /··'··/ *n* panorama
pansiyon /··'·/ *n* boardinghouse
pansiyoner /···'·/ *n* boarder, lodger
pansuman /··'·/ *n* dressing for a wound
panter /·'·/ *n* panther
pantolon /··'·/ *n* trousers, pants
panzehir /··'·/ *n* antidote
papa /'··/ *n* Pope
papağan /··'·/ *n* parrot
papalık /··'·/ *n* Papacy
papatya /·'··/ *n* daisy
papaz /·'·/ *n* priest
papyon /·'·/ *n* bow tie
para /·'·/ *n* money, coin; ~ **biriktirmek** save money; ~ **bozdurmak** change money; ~ **darlığı** deflation; ~ **harcamak** *spend money; ~ **kazanmak** earn money; **paranın üstü** change
paralamak /···'·/ *v* *tear into pieces
paralanmak /···'·/ *v* *be broken to pieces; *wear oneself out
paramparça /·'···/ *adj* all in pieces; ~ **etmek** *break into pieces; ~ **olmak** *be broken into pieces
parantez /··'·/ *n* parenthesis
paraşüt /··'·/ *n* parachute
paraşütçü /···'·/ *n* parachutist
parazit /··'·/ *n* parasite;

interference
parça /·ˈ·/ *n* piece; bit; ~ **başına** per piece; ~ ~ in pieces; ~ ~ **etmek** *break into pieces
parçalamak /···ˈ·/ *v* *break into pieces
parçalı /··ˈ·/ *adj* in parts
pardon /ˈ··/ pardon me, excuse me
pardösü /··ˈ·/ *n* light overcoat
parfüm /·ˈ·/ *n* perfume
parıldamak /···ˈ·/ *v* gleam, glitter, twinkle
parıltı /··ˈ·/ *n* gleam, glitter
park *n* park; parking lot; ~ **etmek** park
parlak /·ˈ·/ *adj* bright, *shining, brilliant; influential, successful
parlaklık /··ˈ·/ *n* brilliance
parlamak /··ˈ·/ *v* *shine; flare up; gain distinction; acquire influence
parlamenter /···ˈ·/ *n* Member of Parliament
parlamento /··ˈ··/ *n* parliament
parlatmak /··ˈ·/ *v* polish, burnish
parmak /·ˈ·/ *n* finger; toe; ~ **izi** fingerprint; **parmakla göstermek** point at
parmaklık /··ˈ·/ *n* railing, balustrade, banister
parola /·ˈ··/ *n* password, watchword
pars *n* leopard
parsel /·ˈ·/ *n* plot of land
parsellemek /···ˈ·/ *v* divide into plots
parti /·ˈ·/ *n* party; political party; consignment
pas[1] *n* rust; tarnish
pas[2] *n* pass
pasaj /·ˈ·/ *n* passage; arcade
pasaklı /··ˈ·/ *adj* dirty; filthy; slovenly
pasaport /··ˈ·/ *n* passport
Pasifik Okyanusu /··ˈ· ····/ Pacific Ocean
paskalya /·ˈ··/ *n* Easter
paslanmak /··ˈ·/ *v* *become rusty
paslanmaz /··ˈ·/ *adj* rustproof
paslı /·ˈ·/ *adj* rusty
paso /ˈ··/ *n* pass
paspas /·ˈ·/ *n* doormat
pasta /ˈ··/ *n* cake; pastry, tart
pastane /·–ˈ·/ *n* pastry shop
pastırma /··ˈ·/ *n* pastrami; ~ **yazı** Indian summer
pastil /·ˈ·/ *n* pastille
pastörize /··ˈ··/ *adj* pasteurized
paşa /·ˈ·/ *n* general
patates /·ˈ··/ *n* potato
patavatsız /···ˈ·/ *adj* tactless
paten /·ˈ·/ *n* skate, roller skate
patent /·ˈ·/ *n* patent, license
patırtı /··ˈ·/ *n* noise, tumult
patik /·ˈ·/ *n* baby's shoe, bootee
patika /·ˈ··/ *n* path, track
patinaj /··ˈ·/ *n* skating; skidding; ~ **yapmak** skid; skate
patlak /·ˈ·/ *adj* burst; punctured, torn open; ~ **gözlü** popeyed; ~ **vermek** *break out, *be divulged
patlama /··ˈ·/ *n* explosion
patlamak /··ˈ·/ *v* *burst, explode
patlatmak /··ˈ·/ *v* *blow up, *burst
patlayıcı /···ˈ·/ *n* explosive
patlıcan /··ˈ·/ *n* eggplant, aubergine
patrik /·ˈ·/ *n* patriarch
patron /·ˈ·/ *n* employer; boss
pavyon /·ˈ·/ *n* nightclub; pavilion
pay *n* share, lot, portion; ~ **etmek** divide, share out
paydos /·ˈ·/ *n* break, rest, end of a work period; ~ **etmek** knock off; stop working
paylamak /··ˈ·/ *v* scold
paylaşmak /··ˈ·/ *v* share
pazar[1] /·ˈ·/ *n* market, bazaar
pazar[2] /·ˈ·/ Sunday

pazarlama /···ˈ·/ *n* marketing
pazarlamacı /····ˈ·/ *n* marketing expert
pazarlamak /···ˈ·/ *v* market
pazarlık /··ˈ·/ *n* bargaining; ~ **etmek** bargain
pazartesi /·ˈ···/ Monday
pazaryeri /·ˈ···/ *n* marketplace
peçe /·ˈ·/ *n* veil
peçeli /··ˈ·/ *adj* veiled
peçete /·ˈ··/ *n* napkin
peder /·ˈ·/ *n* father
pedikür /··ˈ·/ *n* pedicure
pehlivan /··ˈ·/ *n* wrestler
pejmürde /··ˈ·/ *adj* shabby, raggy
pek *adv* very; extremely; ~ **çok** very much
pekâlâ /ˈ·––/ very good; all right! okay!
peki /ˈ··/ all right! okay!
pekişmek /··ˈ·/ *v* *become hard, *get firm
pekiştirmek /···ˈ·/ *v* stiffen, strengthen
pekiyi /ˈ···/ very good, excellent
pekmez /·ˈ·/ *n* grape molasses
peksimet /··ˈ·/ *n* hard biscuit
pelerin /··ˈ·/ *n* cape, cloak
pelte /·ˈ·/ *n* jelly
peltek /·ˈ·/ *adj* lisping; ~ **konuşmak** lisp
pelteklik /··ˈ·/ *n* lisp
pembe /·ˈ·/ *adj* pink
pencere /ˈ···/ *n* window
pençe /·ˈ·/ *n* paw, claw
pençelemek /···ˈ·/ *v* claw, paw
pençeleşmek /···ˈ·/ *v* struggle, *come to grips
penguen /··ˈ·/ *n* penguin
pens *n* pliers, pincers
pepe /·ˈ·/ *adj* stammering
pepelemek /···ˈ·/ *v* stammer, stutter
perakende /·–ˈ·/ *adj* retail
perçem /·ˈ·/ *n* tuft of hair
perçin /·ˈ·/ *n* rivet; clenching a nail
perçinlemek /···ˈ·/ *v* rivet, clench; strengthen
perdah /·ˈ·/ *n* polish, sheen
perdahlı /··ˈ·/ *adj* polished
perdahsız /··ˈ·/ *adj* unpolished
perde /·ˈ·/ *n* curtain; screen; act; cataract; **perdeyi kapamak** *draw the curtain
perdelemek /···ˈ·/ *v* curtain, veil, conceal
perdeli /··ˈ·/ *adj* curtained, veiled
perende /·ˈ··/ *n* somersault; ~ **atmak** turn a somersault
pergel /·ˈ·/ *n* pair of compasses
perhiz /·ˈ·/ *n* diet; ~ **yapmak** diet
peri /·ˈ·/ *n* fairy
peribacası /·ˈ····/ *n* earth pillar, chimney rock
perişan /·–ˈ·/ *adj* bewildered; ruined; miserable
pestil /·ˈ·/ *n* dried fruit pulp
peş *n* back, behind; ~ **peşe** one after the other; **peşi sıra** behind him, following him; **peşinde** in pursuit of; **peşinden gitmek** *go after; **peşini bırakmak** stop following
peşin /·ˈ·/ *adj* paid in advance, ready; *adv* in advance; ~ **almak** *buy for cash; ~ **para** cash; ~ **söylemek** *tell in advance; ~ **yargı** prejudice
peştamal /··ˈ·/ *n* large bath towel
petek /·ˈ·/ *n* honeycomb
petrol /·ˈ·/ *n* petroleum, oil
peygamber /··ˈ·/ *n* prophet
peynir /·ˈ·/ *n* cheese
pıhtı /·ˈ·/ *n* clot
pıhtılaşmak /···ˈ·/ *v* coagulate, clot
pınar /·ˈ·/ *n* spring, source

pırasa /·'··/ *n* leek
pırıldamak /···'·/ *v* gleam, glitter
pırıltı /··'·/ *n* gleam, flash
pırlanta /·'··/ *n* brilliant
pıtırtı /··'·/ *n* tapping, cracking sound
piç *n* bastard
pide /·'·/ *n* a kind of flat bread
pijama /·'··/ *n* pyjamas
pikap /·'·/ *n* phonograph; small truck
pike /·'·/ *n* piqué, quilting; diving
pil *n* electric battery
piliç /·'·/ *n* chick
pilot /·'·/ *n* pilot
pineklemek /···'·/ *v* slumber, doze
pingpong /·'·/ *n* ping-pong
pinti /·'·/ *adj* stingy
pipo /'··/ *n* tobacco pipe
piramit /··'·/ *n* pyramide
pire /·'·/ *n* flea
pirelenmek /···'·/ *v* *become infested with fleas; *become uneasy
pirinç /·'·/ *n* rice; brass
pirzola /'···/ *n* cutlet
pis *adj* dirty; foul; obscene
pisboğaz /··'·/ *adj* gluttonous, greedy
piskopos /··'·/ *n* bishop
pislenmek /··'·/ *v* *become dirty
pisletmek /··'·/ *v* *make dirty, soil
pislik /·'·/ *n* dirtiness; dirt, mess
pist *n* runway
pişirmek /··'·/ *v* cook, bake
pişkin /·'·/ *adj* well-cooked, well-baked; self-assured
pişman /·'·/ *adj* sorry for, regretful of
pişmanlık /··'·/ *n* regret; penitence
pişmek /·'·/ *v* *be cooked, *be baked
piyade /·–'·/ *n* foot-soldier, infantry
piyango /·'··/ *n* lottery
piyano /·'··/ *n* piano;
~ **çalmak** play the piyano
piyasa /·'··/ *n* market, market price
piyes /·'·/ *n* drama, play
plaj *n* beach
plak *n* phonograph record
plaka /'··/ *n* number plate of a car
plan *n* plan
planör /·'·/ *n* glider
platin /·'·/ *n* platinum
poliçe /·'··/ *n* bill of exchange; insurance policy
polis /·'·/ *n* police; policeman
politika /··'··/ *n* politics; policy
politikacı /··'···/ *n* politician
Polonya /·'··/ Poland
Polonyalı /·'···/ *adj* Polish; *n* Pole
pompa /'··/ *n* pump
porselen /··'·/ *n* porcelain
porsiyon /··'·/ *n* portion, plate, helping
porsuk /·'·/ *n* badger
portakal /··'·/ *n* orange
portatif /··'·/ *adj* portable
Portekiz /'···/ Portugal
Portekizce /··'··/ *n* Portuguese language
Portekizli /'····/ *n, adj* Portuguese
portmanto /·'··/ *n* coatstand, coathanger
portre /'··/ *n* portrait
posa /'··/ *n* sediment, dregs
post *n* skin, hide
posta /'··/ *n* post, postal service;
~ **kutusu** mailbox *nAm;* post box *Br;* ~ **pulu** postage stamp
postacı /'···/ *n* mailman *nAm;* postman *nBr*
postane /·–'·/ *n* post office
potin /·'·/ *n* boot
poyraz /·'·/ *n* northeast wind
poz *n* pose
pörsük /·'·/ *adj* shrivelled up;

withered
pratik /·ˈ·/ *adj* practical; *n* practice
prens *n* prince
prenses /·ˈ·/ *n* princess
prensip /·ˈ·/ *n* principle
prim *n* premium
profesör /··ˈ·/ *n* professor
profesyonel /···ˈ·/ *adj* professional
program /·ˈ·/ *n* program
proje /ˈ··/ *n* project
projeksiyon /···ˈ·/ *n* projection
projektör /··ˈ·/ *n* searchlight
protestan /··ˈ·/ *n, adj* Protestant
protesto /·ˈ··/ *n* protest; ~ **etmek** protest against
prova /ˈ··/ *n* trial, test; rehearsal
psikanalist /···ˈ·/ *n* psychoanalyst
psikanaliz /···ˈ·/ *n* psychoanalysis
psikiyatr /··ˈ·/ *n* psychiatrist
psikolog /··ˈ·/ *n* psychologist
psikoloji /···ˈ·/ *n* psychology
psikolojik /···ˈ·/ *adj* psychological
pudra /ˈ··/ *n* powder; ~ **şekeri** powdered sugar
pudralı /ˈ···/ *adj* powdered
pudriyer /··ˈ·/ *n* powder compact
pul *n* stamp; scale
pulcu /·ˈ·/ *n* philatelist
pullamak /··ˈ·/ *v* stamp; ornament with spangles
pullu /·ˈ·/ *adj* stamped; scaly
pulsuz /·ˈ·/ *adj* unstamped
punto /ˈ··/ *n* point; size of type
puro /ˈ··/ *n* cigar
pus *n* mist, haze
puset /·ˈ·/ *n* baby carriage
puslanmak /··ˈ·/ *v* *become misty, *get cloudy
puslu /·ˈ·/ *adj* hazy, misty
pusu /·ˈ·/ *n* ambush; ~ **kurmak** *lay an ambush; **pusuya düşürmek** trap; **pusuya yatmak** *lie in wait
pusula /·ˈ··/ *n* compass; **pusulayı şaşırmak** *lose one's bearings; *be bewildered
put *n* idol; cross; ~ **gibi** as still as a statue; ~ **kesilmek** *be petrified
putlaştırmak /···ˈ·/ *v* idolize
putperest /··ˈ·/ *n* idolater
püre /·ˈ·/ *n* mashed food
pürüz /·ˈ·/ *n* roughness; difficulty
pürüzlü /··ˈ·/ *adj* uneven, knotty; difficult
pürüzsüz /··ˈ·/ *adj* smooth, even; without a hitch
püskürtmek /··ˈ·/ *v* spray; repulse

R

Rab *n* God
radar /·ˈ·/ *n* radar
radyo /ˈ··/ *n* radio
radyoevi /ˈ····/ *n* broadcasting studio
raf *n* shelf
rafadan /··ˈ·/ *adj* soft-boiled
rafineri /···ˈ·/ *n* refinery
rağbet /·ˈ·/ *n* inclination, desire; demand; ~ **görmek** *be in demand
rağmen /ˈ··/ *prep* in spite of
rahat /·ˈ·/ *n* ease, rest; comfort, tranquillity; quiet; *adj* at ease, comfortable; tranquil; easy; *adv* comfortably, quietly; ~ **etmek** *be at ease; *make oneself comfortable; rest
rahatlamak /···ˈ·/ *v* *become comfortable; *feel relieved
rahatsız /··ˈ·/ *adj* uncomfortable; sick, ill; ~ **etmek** bother, annoy, disturb
rahibe /–·ˈ·/ *n* nun
rahim /·ˈ·/ *n* uterus, womb

rahip /–'·/ *n* priest
rahmet /·'·/ *n* God's mercy and grace; rain
rahmetli /··'·/ *adj* the deceased, the late
rakam /·'·/ *n* figure, numeral; number
rakı /·'·/ *n* raki, arrack
rakip /·'·/ *n* competitor; rival
ramazan /··'·/ *n* Ramadan
rampa /'··/ *n* ramp, loading platform
randevu /··'·/ *n* appointment
randevuevi /··'···/ *n* brothel
randıman /··'·/ *n* yield
randımanlı /···'·/ *adj* profitable, productive
ranza /'··/ *n* bunk, berth
rapor /·'·/ *n* report; doctor's report
raporlu /··'·/ *adj* on medical leave
raptiye /··'·/ *n* drawing pin, thumbtack
rasathane /··–'·/ *n* observatory, meteorological station
rasgele /'···/ *adv* by chance; haphazardly; *adj* random, chance
rast gelmek /'· ··/ *meet, encounter, *come across
rastlamak /··'·/ *v* *meet by chance; coincide
rastlantı /··'·/ *n* chance, coincidence
ray *n* rail
rayiç /–'·/ *n* market price, current value
razı /–'·/ *adj* satisfied, contented; willing
reaksiyon /···'·/ *n* reaction
reçel /·'·/ *n* jam, fruit preserve
reçete /·'··/ *n* prescription; recipe
reçine /·'··/ *n* resin
reddetmek /'···/ *v* reject, refuse
refah /·'·/ *n* comfort, luxury, affluence
refakat /·–'·/ *n* companionship; accompaniment; ~ **etmek** accompany
rehber /·'·/ *n* guide; guidebook; directory; ~ **öğretmen** guidance counselor
rehberlik /··'·/ *n* guidance
rehin /·'·/ *n* pawn, pledge, security; hostage
rehine /·–'·/ *n* hostage
reis /·'·/ *n* head, chief, president
rejim /·'·/ *n* regime, system of government; diet; ~ **yapmak** diet
rejisör /··'·/ *n* director
rekabet /·–'·/ *n* rivalry, competition
reklam /·'·/ *n* advertisement
reklamcılık /···'·/ *n* advertising
rekor /·'·/ *n* record; ~ **kırmak** *break the record
rekortmen /··'·/ *n* record holder
rektör /·'·/ *n* president of a university, rector
rende /·'·/ *n* carpenter's plane; grater
rengârenk /'·–·/ *adj* multicolored
renk *n* color; **rengi atmak** *grow pale
renklendirmek /···'·/ *v* enliven, *give color
renkli /·'·/ *adj* colored; colorful
renksiz /·'·/ *adj* colorless; dull
resim /·'·/ *n* picture, photograph; drawing; illustration; painting; ~ **çekmek** *take a photograph ~ **yapmak** *draw, paint
resimlemek /···'·/ *v* illustrate
resimli /··'·/ *adj* illustrated
resmen /'··/ *adv* officially
resmi /·'–/ *adj* official, formal
resmiyet /··'·/ *n* formality
ressam /·'·/ *n* painter; designer,

draftsman
rest çekmek /'· ··/ *give an ultimatum
restoran /··'·/ *n* restaurant
ret *n* rejection, refusal
revaç /·'·/ *n* being in demand
reverans /··'·/ *n* bow, curtsy
revir /·'·/ *n* infirmary
reyon /·'·/ *n* section of a store, counter
rezalet /·–'·/ *n* scandal, scandalous behavior, disgrace
rezervasyon /···'·/ *n* reservation
rezil /·'·/ *adj* vile, disreputable, disgraced; ~ **etmek** disgrace; ~ **olmak** *be put to shame
rezillik /··'·/ *n* infamy; scandal
rıhtım /·'·/ *n* quay, wharf
rıza /·'–/ *n* consent, approval; ~ **göstermek** consent
rızk *n* one's daily food, sustenance
rica /·'–/ *n* request; ~ **etmek** request, ask for
rimel /·'·/ *n* mascara
risk *n* risk
ritim /·'·/ *n* rhythm
rivayet /·–'·/ *n* rumor
riya /·'–/ *n* hypocrisy
riyakâr /·'–·/ *adj* hypocrite, hypocritical
riziko /·'··/ *n* risk
roket /·'·/ *n* rocket
rol *n* role, part
roman /·'·/ *n* novel
romantik /··'·/ *adj* romantic
Romanya /·'··/ Rumania
romatizma /··'··/ *n* rheumatism
Romen /·'·/ *adj, n* Rumanian
Romence /·'··/ *n* Rumanian language
rosto /'··/ *n* roast meat
rota /'··/ *n* course of a ship
rozet /·'·/ *n* badge; rosette
römork /·'·/ *n* trailer
römorkör /··'·/ *n* tugboat; tractor
röntgen /·'·/ *n* X-ray
röportaj /··'·/ *n* feature article, feature story
rötar /·'·/ *n* delay
rötuş /·'·/ *n* retouching
rövanş /·'·/ *n* return match
rugan /·'·/ *n* patent leather
ruh *n* soul, spirit; essence; vitality; ghost
ruhbilim /'···/ *n* psychology
ruhi /–'–/ *adj* psychic; psyhological, mental
ruhsat /·'·/ *n* permission, permit, license
ruhsatname /··–'·/ *n* permit, license
ruj *n* lipstick
rulet /·'·/ *n* roulette
rulo /'··/ *n* roll (of paper)
Rum *n* Greek of Turkish citizenship
Rumeli /'···/ *n* European Turkey
rumuz /·'·/ *n* symbol; abbreviation
Rus *adj, n* Russian
Rusça /'··/ *n* Russian language
Rusya /'··/ Russia
rutubet /·–'·/ *n* dampness, humidity
rüküş /·'·/ *adj* comically dressed
rüşt *n* majority, coming of age
rüşvet /·'·/ *n* bribe
rütbe /·'·/ *n* degree; grade; rank
rüya /–'–/ *n* dream, vision; ~ **görmek** *have a dream
rüzgâr /·'·/ *n* wind, breeze

S

saadet /·–'·/ *n* happiness
saat /·'·/ *n* hour; watch, clock; **kalkış saati** time of departure; **varış saati** time of arrival

saatçi /··'·/ *n* watch seller; watchmaker
sabah /·'·/ *n* morning; ~ **akşam** all the time
sabahlamak /···'·/ *v* *sit up all night
sabahleyin /·'···/ *adv* in the morning
sabahlık /··'·/ *n* dressing gown
saban /·'·/ *n* plow
sabık /–'·/ *adj* former, previous
sabıka /–·'·/ *n* previous conviction
sabıkalı /–··'·/ *adj* previously convicted
sabır /·'·/ *n* patience; endurance; **sabrını taşırmak** exasperate
sabırla /·'··/ *adv* patiently
sabırlı /··'·/ *adj* patient
sabırsız /··'·/ *adj* impatient
sabırsızlıkla /···'··/ *adv* impatiently
sabit /–'·/ *adj* fixed, stationary, definite; ~ **fikir** fixed idea; ~ **olmak** *be fixed; *be confirmed
sabitleştirmek /–···'·/ *v* fix
sabotaj /··'·/ *n* sabotage
sabretmek /'···/ *v* *be patient
sabun /·'·/ *n* soap
sabunlamak /···'·/ *v* soap
saç *n* hair; ~ **fırçası** hairbrush; ~ **kesimi** haircut; ~ **kurutucusu** hair dryer
saçak /·'·/ *n* eaves; fringe
saçma /·'·/ *n* nonsense; absurdity; *adj* nonsensical; ~ **sapan konuşmak** talk nonsense
saçmak /·'·/ *v* scatter; **saçıp savurmak** squander
saçmalamak /···'·/ *v* talk *or* act nonsense
sadaka /··'·/ *n* alms, charity
sadakat /·–'·/ *n* faithfulness; loyalty
sade /–'·/ *adj* simple, plain; pure
sadece /'–··/ *adv* simply, merely
sadeleşmek /–··'·/ *v* *become simple
sadeleştirmek /–···'·/ *v* simplify
sadelik /–·'·/ *n* plainness, simplicity
sadık /–'·/ *adj* loyal, faithful; true, honest
saf[1] *adj* pure, unmixed; gullible, naive
saf[2] *n* row, line; rank; ~ ~ in rows
safha /·'·/ *n* phase
saflık /·'·/ *n* purity; ingenuousness
safra /·'·/ *n* ballast; bile
safsata /··'·/ *n* sophistry; nonsense
sağ[1] *adj* alive; safe; ~ **kalanlar** the survivors; ~ **kalmak** remain alive, survive; ~ **ol!** thank you!; ~ **salim** safe and sound
sağ[2] *adj* right; *n* right-hand side; **sağa** to the right; **sağda** on the right; **sağlı sollu** on both sides
sağanak /··'·/ *n* downpour
sağdıç /·'·/ *n* bridegroom's best man
sağduyu /'···/ *n* common sense
sağır /·'·/ *adj* deaf
sağırlaşmak /···'·/ *v* *grow deaf
sağırlık /··'·/ *n* deafness
sağlam /·'·/ *adj* sound; healthy; trustworthy; strong; **sağlama bağlamak** *make sure
sağlamak /··'·/ *v* supply, obtain
sağlamlaşmak /···'·/ *v* *become sound
sağlamlaştırmak /····'·/ *v* strengthen, consolidate
sağlamlık /··'·/ *n* soundness; safety
sağlık /·'·/ *n* health; ~ **olsun!** never mind!; ~ **sigortası** health insurance
sağlıklı /··'·/ *adj* healthy
sağlıksız /··'·/ *adj* unhealthy

sağmak /·ˈ·/ *v* milk
saha /–ˈ·/ *n* area, field, region
sahi /ˈ–·/ *adv* really, truly
sahici /–ˈ·/ *adj* genuine, real
sahiden /ˈ–··/ *adv* indeed, truly, really
sahil /–ˈ·/ *n* shore, coast
sahip /–ˈ·/ *n* owner, master; ~ **çıkmak** claim
sahipsiz /–·ˈ·/ *adj* ownerless; unprotected; abandoned
sahne /·ˈ·/ *n* scene, stage; **sahneye koymak** stage
sahra /·ˈ–/ *n* desert, wilderness
sahte /·ˈ·/ *adj* false, counterfeit; artificial
sahtekâr /··ˈ·/ *n* forger; crook; counterfeiter
sahtekârlık /···ˈ·/ *n* forgery, counterfeiting
sahur /·ˈ·/ *n* meal before dawn during the Ramadan fast
sakal /·ˈ·/ *n* beard
sakallı /··ˈ·/ *adj* bearded
sakar /·ˈ·/ *adj* awkward, clumsy
sakat /·ˈ·/ *adj* disabled, invalid, crippled; defective
sakatlamak /···ˈ·/ *v* damage, injure; cripple
sakın /·ˈ·/ mind!, beware!, take care!, don't!
sakınca /··ˈ·/ *n* drawback, objection
sakıncalı /···ˈ·/ *adj* objectionable
sakınma /··ˈ·/ *n* caution
sakınmak /··ˈ·/ *v* avoid; *be cautious
sakız /·ˈ·/ *n* chewing gum
sakin /–ˈ·/ *adj* calm; quiet; *n* inhabitant
sakinleşmek /–··ˈ·/ *v* *get quiet, calm down
saklamak /··ˈ·/ *v* *hide, conceal; save
saklambaç /··ˈ·/ *n* hide-and-seek
saklı /·ˈ·/ *adj* hidden, concealed
saksağan /··ˈ·/ *n* magpie
saksı /·ˈ·/ *n* flowerpot
sal *n* raft
salak /·ˈ·/ *adj* silly, foolish
salam /·ˈ·/ *n* salami
salamura /··ˈ··/ *n* brine, pickle; *adj* pickled
salata /·ˈ··/ *n* salad; lettuce
salatalık /·ˈ···/ *n* cucumber
salça /·ˈ·/ *n* tomato paste
saldırgan /··ˈ·/ *adj* aggressive; *n* attacker
saldırı /··ˈ·/ *n* aggression, attack
saldırmak /··ˈ·/ *v* attack
saldırmazlık /···ˈ·/ *n* nonaggression
salgı /·ˈ·/ *n* secretion
salgılamak /···ˈ·/ *v* secrete
salgın /·ˈ·/ *n* epidemic
salı /·ˈ·/ Tuesday
salıncak /··ˈ·/ *n* swing; hammock
salınmak /··ˈ·/ *v* sway; oscillate
salıvermek /·ˈ···/ *v* *let go; release, *set free
salimen /ˈ–··/ *adv* safely, safe and sound
salkım /·ˈ·/ *n* bunch, cluster; ~ **saçak** untidy
sallamak /··ˈ·/ *v* *swing; rock; *shake
sallanmak /··ˈ·/ *v* *swing, sway; linger; loiter
sallantı /··ˈ·/ *n* swinging, rocking
salmak /·ˈ·/ *v* *set free, loosen
salon /·ˈ·/ *n* parlor, hall, lounge
salt *adj* mere; *adv* merely, solely; ~ **çoğunluk** absolute majority
saltanat /··ˈ·/ *n* sovereignty, reign; ~ **sürmek** reign
salya /ˈ··/ *n* saliva
salyangoz /··ˈ·/ *n* snail
saman /·ˈ·/ *n* straw
samanyolu /·ˈ···/ *n* Milky Way

samimi /–ˈ–/ *adj* sincere
samimiyet /––ˈ·/ *n* sincerity
samimiyetle /––ˈ··/ *adv* sincerely
samur /·ˈ·/ *n* sable
sana /·ˈ·/ *pron* to you, for you
sanat /·ˈ·/ *n* art; craft; trade
sanatçı, sanatkâr /··ˈ·/ *n* artisan, craftsman; actor; artist
sanayi /·–ˈ·/ *n* industry
sanayileşmek /·–––ˈ·/ *v* *become industrialized
sancak /·ˈ·/ *n* flag; starboard side
sancı /·ˈ·/ *n* pain, stitch, ache
sancılanmak /···ˈ·/ *v* *have a pain
sancımak /··ˈ·/ *v* ache
sandal /·ˈ·/ *n* sandal (shoe); rowboat
sandalye /·ˈ··/ *n* chair
sandık /·ˈ·/ *n* chest, box, coffer; ~ **odası** storeroom
sandviç /·ˈ·/ *n* sandwich
sanık /·ˈ·/ *adj* suspected; accused; *n* suspect
saniye /–ˈ·/ *n* second
sanki /ˈ··/ *adv* as if, as though
sanmak /·ˈ·/ *v* *think, suppose, imagine
sansür /·ˈ·/ *n* censorship
sansürlemek /···ˈ·/ *v* censor
santral /·ˈ·/ *n* telephone exchange; switchboard
sap *n* handle; stem, stalk
sapa /·ˈ·/ *adj* out-of-the-way; secluded; ~ **yol** byroad, side street
sapak /·ˈ·/ *n* turn
sapan /·ˈ·/ *n* sling; catapult
sapasağlam /·ˈ···/ *adj* well and sound, very strong
sapık /·ˈ·/ *adj* perverted; *n* pervert
sapıklık /··ˈ·/ *n* perversion
sapıtmak /··ˈ·/ *v* *go off one's head; talk nonsense; *go astray
sapkın /·ˈ·/ *adj* perverse, abnormal
saplamak /··ˈ·/ *v* *thrust into, pierce
saplantı /··ˈ·/ *n* fixed idea
sapma /·ˈ·/ *n* deviation
sapmak /·ˈ·/ *v* deviate; *go astray; *fall into sin
saptamak /··ˈ·/ *v* fix; ascertain, determine
sara /·ˈ·/ *n* epilepsy; **sarası tutmak** *have an epileptic fit
saralı /··ˈ·/ *adj* epileptic
sararmak /··ˈ·/ *v* turn yellow; *grow pale
saray /·ˈ·/ *n* palace; government house
sardalye /·ˈ··/ *n* sardine
sardunya /·ˈ··/ *n* geranium
sarf *n* expenditure; consumption; ~ **etmek** *spend, expend; use
sarfiyat /··ˈ·/ *n* consumption; expenditure
sargı /·ˈ·/ *n* bandage
sarhoş /·ˈ·/ *adj* drunk; *n* drunkard; ~ **etmek** *make drunk; ~ **olmak** *get drunk
sarı /·ˈ·/ *adj* yellow
sarık /·ˈ·/ *n* turban
sarılık /··ˈ·/ *n* yellowness; jaundice
sarılmak /··ˈ·/ *v* embrace, hug; *be surrounded
sarımtırak /···ˈ·/ *adj* yellowish
sarınmak /··ˈ·/ *v* wrap oneself in
sarışın /··ˈ·/ *adj, n* blond
sari /–ˈ·/ *adj* contagious, epidemic
sarkık /·ˈ·/ *adj* hanging loosely; flabby; drooping
sarkıntılık /···ˈ·/ *n* molestation; ~ **etmek** molest
sarkmak /·ˈ·/ *v* *hang down, dangle, droop
sarmal /·ˈ·/ *adj* spiral
sarmaşık /··ˈ·/ *n* common ivy
sarmısak /··ˈ·/ *n* garlic

sarnıç /·ˈ·/ *n* cistern
sarp *adj* very steep; difficult
sarplaşmak /··ˈ·/ *v* *become steep
sarraf /·ˈ·/ *n* money changer
sarsıntı /··ˈ·/ *n* shake, jolt; concussion; earthquake
sarsmak /·ˈ·/ *v* *shake; shock; agitate; *upset
sataşmak /··ˈ·/ *v* tease, annoy; molest
saten /·ˈ·/ *n* satin
satıcı /··ˈ·/ *n* salesman, *seller
satılık /··ˈ·/ *adj* for sale; on sale
satın almak /·ˈ· ··/ *buy
satır /·ˈ·/ *n* line; chopper, cleaver
satırbaşı /·ˈ···/ *n* paragraph indentation
satış /·ˈ·/ *n* sale
satmak /·ˈ·/ *v* *sell
satranç /·ˈ·/ *n* chess
savaş /·ˈ·/ *n* war, battle; struggle
savaşçı /··ˈ·/ *n* combatant, fighter, warrior
savaşmak /··ˈ·/ *v* *fight, struggle, combat
savcı /·ˈ·/ *n* public prosecutor
savmak /·ˈ·/ *v* *send away, turn away; dismiss
savruk /·ˈ·/ *adj* untidy
savsaklamak /···ˈ·/ *v* *put off doing something
savulmak /··ˈ·/ *v* *stand aside, *get out of the way
savunma /··ˈ·/ *n* defense
savunmak /··ˈ·/ *v* defend
savurmak /··ˈ·/ *v* toss about; *blow about; *spend extravagantly
savuşmak /··ˈ·/ *v* slip away, sneak off
saydam /·ˈ·/ *adj* transparent
saydamlık /··ˈ·/ *n* transparency
sayfa /·ˈ·/ *n* page
sayfiye /··ˈ·/ *n* summer house
saygı /·ˈ·/ *n* respect, regard, esteem; ~ **göstermek** *show respect
saygıdeğer /···ˈ·/ *adj* estimable
saygılı /··ˈ·/ *adj* respectful; well-mannered
saygın /·ˈ·/ *adj* respected, esteemed, honorable
saygınlık /··ˈ·/ *n* prestige; esteem
saygısız /··ˈ·/ *adj* disrespectful
saygısızca /··ˈ··/ *adv* disrespectfully
sayı /·ˈ·/ *n* number
sayıklamak /···ˈ·/ *v* talk in one's sleep; rave
sayım /·ˈ·/ *n* enumeration; census
sayın /·ˈ·/ *adj* esteemed, honorable
sayısız /··ˈ·/ *adj* unnumbered; innumerable
saymak /·ˈ·/ *v* count; respect; consider
saz *n* musical instrument; ~ **şairi** minstrel, bard
sazan /·ˈ·/ *n* carp
sebat /·ˈ·/ *n* perseverance; ~ **etmek** persevere
sebatkâr /··ˈ·/ *adj* persevering
sebatsız /··ˈ·/ *adj* fickle, unstable
sebep /·ˈ·/ *n* cause, reason; ~ **olmak** cause; **sebebiyle** because of
sebepsiz /··ˈ·/ *adj* without any reason
sebze /·ˈ·/ *n* vegetable
sebzeci /··ˈ·/ *n* greengrocer
seccade /·–ˈ·/ *n* prayer rug
seçenek /··ˈ·/ *n* alternative
seçim /·ˈ·/ *n* election
seçkin /·ˈ·/ *adj* distinguished, select, choice
seçmek /·ˈ·/ *v* *choose, select; elect; distinguish
seçmen /·ˈ·/ *n* voter, elector
sedef /·ˈ·/ *n* mother-of-pearl
sedir /·ˈ·/ *n* divan, sofa
sedye /ˈ··/ *n* stretcher

sefalet /–ˈ·/ *n* misery, poverty; ~ **çekmek** suffer privation
sefaret /–ˈ·/ *n* embassy
sefer /·ˈ·/ *n* expedition, journey; time; state of war
seferberlik /···ˈ·/ *n* mobilization
sefertası /·ˈ···/ *n* portable food box
sefil /·ˈ·/ *adj* miserable
seher /·ˈ·/ *n* daybreak
sehpa /·ˈ–/ *n* coffee table
sekiz /·ˈ·/ *num* eight
sekizinci /···ˈ·/ *num* eighth
sekmek /·ˈ·/ *v* hop; ricochet, skip
sekreter /··ˈ·/ *n* secretary
seksek /·ˈ·/ *n* hopscotch
seksen /·ˈ·/ *num* eighty
sekte /·ˈ·/ *n* stoppage, interruption; pause
sel *n* torrent, flood
selam /·ˈ·/ *n* greeting, salutation; ~ **söylemek** *give one's kind regards; ~ **vermek** salute, greet
selamlamak /···ˈ·/ *v* greet, salute
selamlaşmak /···ˈ·/ *v* greet, salute each other
sembol /·ˈ·/ *n* symbol
semer /·ˈ·/ *n* packsaddle
seminer /··ˈ·/ *n* seminar
semiz /·ˈ·/ *adj* fat, sleek
sempatik /··ˈ·/ *adj* likeable, congenial
semt *n* region, neighborhood, quarter
sen *pron* you
senaryo /·ˈ··/ *n* scenario
senato /·ˈ··/ *n* senate
sendelemek /···ˈ·/ *v* totter, stumble, stagger
sendika /·ˈ··/ *n* trade union, labor union
sendikacı /·ˈ···/ *n* unionist
sene /·ˈ·/ *n* year
senelik /··ˈ·/ *adj* yearly, annual
senet /·ˈ·/ *n* promissory note
seni /·ˈ·/ *pron* you
senin /·ˈ·/ *adj* your
seninki /··ˈ·/ *pron* yours
senlibenli /·ˈ···/ *adj* free-and-easy, familiar
sepet /·ˈ·/ *n* basket
serap /·ˈ·/ *n* mirage
serbest /·ˈ·/ *adj* free; ~ **bırakmak** *set free; ~ **bölge** free zone; ~ **vuruş** free kick
serbestçe /·ˈ··/ *adv* freely; with ease
serbestlik /··ˈ·/ *n* freedom; independence
serçe /·ˈ·/ *n* sparrow
serçeparmak /·ˈ···/ *n* little finger
sere serpe /·ˈ· ··/ *adv* free and unrestrained; ~ **yatmak** sprawl out
sergi /·ˈ·/ *n* exhibition, show; display
sergilemek /···ˈ·/ *v* exhibit
seri[1] /·ˈ·/ *n* series; ~ **imalat** mass production
seri[2] /·ˈ–/ *adj* swift, rapid
serin /·ˈ·/ *adj* cool, chilly
serinkanlı /·ˈ···/ *adj* cool, calm
serinlemek /···ˈ·/ *v* *become cool
serinlik /··ˈ·/ *n* coolness; chilliness
serkeş /·ˈ·/ *adj* rebellious; unruly
sermaye /·–ˈ·/ *n* capital, stock
sermek /·ˈ·/ *v* *spread out, *lay out
serpinti /··ˈ·/ *n* drizzle, sprinkle
serpiştirmek /···ˈ·/ *v* sprinkle; scatter; drizzle
serpmek /·ˈ·/ *v* sprinkle, scatter
sersem /·ˈ·/ *adj* stupid, silly; stunned, bewildered
sersemlemek /···ˈ·/ *v* *be stunned; *become absentminded
sersemlik /··ˈ·/ *n* stupefaction; stupidity
serseri /··ˈ·/ *n* vagabond, tramp
serserilik /···ˈ·/ *n* vagabondage, vagrancy

sert *adj* hard, tough; sharp, severe; strong; potent
sertifika /···ˈ·/ *n* certificate
sertlik /·ˈ·/ *n* hardness; violence; potency
serüven /··ˈ·/ *n* adventure
serüvenci /···ˈ·/ *adj* adventurous
servet /·ˈ·/ *n* riches, wealth
servi /·ˈ·/ *n* cypress
servis /·ˈ·/ *n* service; department; ~ **yapmak** serve food
ses *n* sound, voice; noise
sesli /·ˈ·/ *adj* voiced
sessiz /·ˈ·/ *adj* quiet; soundless, voiceless
sessizlik /··ˈ·/ *n* silence
set *n* barrier, dam; set; ~ **çekmek** hinder; dike
sevap /·ˈ·/ *n* good deed
sevda /·ˈ–/ *n* love, passion; ~ **çekmek** *be passionately in love
sevdalanmak /·–ˈ·/ *v* *fall in love
sevdalı /·–ˈ·/ *adj* in love
sevecen /··ˈ·/ *adj* affectionate, kind
sevgi /·ˈ·/ *n* love, affection
sevgili /··ˈ·/ *adj* beloved, dear; *n* lover, darling
sevimli /··ˈ·/ *adj* sweet, lovable, charming
sevinç /·ˈ·/ *n* joy, delight
sevinçli /··ˈ·/ *adj* joyful
sevindirmek /···ˈ·/ *v* please, delight
sevinmek /··ˈ·/ *v* *be happy, *be glad, *be pleased
sevişmek /··ˈ·/ *v* *make love; love one another
sevmek /·ˈ·/ *v* love; like
seyahat /··ˈ·/ *n* journey, trip, voyage; ~ **çeki** traveler's check; ~ **etmek** travel
seyir /·ˈ·/ *n* course, progress ; watching; ~ **defteri** logbook
seyirci /··ˈ·/ *n* spectator, onlooker; ~ **kalmak** *be an onlooker, not participate; **seyirciler** audience
seyrek /·ˈ·/ *adj* sparse, thin; rare, infrequent; *adv* rarely
seyretmek /ˈ···/ *v* watch; move; sail
seyyah /·ˈ·/ *n* traveler
sezgi /·ˈ·/ *n* intuition
sezgili /··ˈ·/ *adj* intuitive
sezinlemek /···ˈ·/ *v* *become aware of; sense, *feel
sezmek /·ˈ·/ *v* perceive, sense, discern
sıcacık /ˈ···/ *adj* warm, pleasantly hot
sıcak /·ˈ·/ *adj* hot, warm; ~ **tutmak** *keep warm
sıcakkanlı /·ˈ···/ *adj* warm-blooded, friendly, lovable
sıçan /·ˈ·/ *n* rat, mouse
sıçramak /··ˈ·/ *v* jump, *leap, *spring
sıfat /·ˈ·/ *n* capacity, position; adjective; **sıfatıyla** in the capacity of
sıfır /ˈ··/ *n* zero, naught, nothing, nil; **sıfırdan başlamak** start from zero
sığ *adj* shallow
sığdırmak /··ˈ·/ *v* fit in, jam in
sığınak /··ˈ·/ *n* shelter
sığınmak /··ˈ·/ *v* *take shelter
sığır /·ˈ·/ *n* cattle; ~ **eti** beef
sığırcık /··ˈ·/ *n* starling
sığırtmaç /··ˈ·/ *n* herdsman, drover
sığışmak /··ˈ·/ *v* squeeze into
sığlık /·ˈ·/ *n* shallowness, sandbank
sığmak /·ˈ·/ *v* fit into
sıhhat /·ˈ·/ *n* health; **sıhhatinize!** to your health!
sıhhatli /··ˈ·/ *adj* healthy
sıhhi /·ˈ–/ *adj* hygienic
sık *adj* dense, thick; frequent; tight; ~ **sık** frequently, often

sıkı /·ˈ·/ *adj* tight; firmly driven *or* wedged in; strict
sıkıca /·ˈ··/ *adv* tightly, firmly
sıkıcı /·ˈ·/ *adj* boring, tiresome
sıkılgan /··ˈ·/ *adj* bashful, shy
sıkılganlık /···ˈ·/ *n* shyness
sıkılmak /··ˈ·/ *v* *be bored; *be annoyed; *be ashamed
sıkıntı /··ˈ·/ *n* boredom; bother; hardship, trouble, distress; ~ **çekmek** *have troubles; **sıkıntıda olmak** *be in difficulties
sıkıntılı /···ˈ·/ *adj* troublesome; uneasy
sıkışık /··ˈ·/ *adj* tight, close; crowded; ~ **durumda olmak** *be hard pressed
sıkışmak /··ˈ·/ *v* *be jammed in, squeeze into; *be in trouble
sıkıştırmak /···ˈ·/ *v* squeeze; press
sıkıyönetim /·ˈ····/ *n* martial law
sıklaşmak /··ˈ·/ *v* *become frequent; *become dense
sıklet /·ˈ·/ *n* heaviness, weight
sıklık /·ˈ·/ *n* frequency; density
sıkmak /·ˈ·/ *v* press, squeeze; tighten; annoy, bother; *put pressure on
sınamak /··ˈ·/ *v* try, test; examine
sınav /·ˈ·/ *n* examination, exam
sınıf /·ˈ·/ *n* class; category; classroom; **sınıfta kalmak** fail
sınıflandırmak /····ˈ·/ *v* classify
sınır /·ˈ·/ *n* frontier, border; boundary, limit
sınırlamak /···ˈ·/ *v* border; limit
sınırlı /··ˈ·/ *adj* limited
sıpa /·ˈ·/ *n* donkey foal
sır *n* secret, mystery; glaze, silvering; ~ **vermek** betray a secret; ~ **saklamak** *keep a secret
sıra /·ˈ·/ *n* desk; row; line; turn; series; ~ **beklemek** wait one's turn; ~ ~ in rows; **sıraya girmek** line up; **sıraya koymak** *put in order
sıradağ /·ˈ··/ *n* mountain range
sıralamak /···ˈ·/ *v* *set up in order; range; enumerate
sıralı /··ˈ·/ *adj* in due order
sırasız /··ˈ·/ *adj* untimely; out of order
sırça /·ˈ·/ *n* glass
sırdaş /·ˈ·/ *n* confidant, intimate
sırf *adj* pure, mere, sheer
sırık /·ˈ·/ *n* pole; stick
sırıtmak /··ˈ·/ *v* grin
sırlamak /··ˈ·/ *v* glaze; silver
sırlı /·ˈ·/ *adj* glazed
sırma /·ˈ·/ *n* silver thread
sırnaşık /··ˈ·/ *adj* tiresome, pestering, saucy
sırt *n* back; ridge; ~ **çevirmek** turn one's back on; ~ **sırta** back to back; **sırtını yere getirmek** *overcome
sırtlamak /··ˈ·/ *v* *take on one's back, shoulder; support
sırtlan /·ˈ·/ *n* hyena
sıska /·ˈ·/ *adj* thin and weak
sıtma /·ˈ·/ *n* malaria
sıva /·ˈ·/ *n* plaster
sıvamak /··ˈ·/ *v* plaster; roll up
sıvazlamak /···ˈ·/ *v* stroke, caress
sıvı /·ˈ·/ *n* liquid, fluid
sıvışmak /··ˈ·/ *v* slip away, disappear, sneak away
sıyırmak /··ˈ·/ *v* skin, graze, scrape; polish off
sıyrık /·ˈ·/ *n* scrape, scratch; *adj* scraped, grazed
sıyrılmak /··ˈ·/ *v* *be skinned; *be scraped, *be barked; slip off
sızdırmak /··ˈ·/ *v* leak; cause to ooze out
sızı /·ˈ·/ *n* ache, pain
sızıntı /··ˈ·/ *n* leakage, oozings

sızlanmak /··ˈ·/ *v* complain, moan with pain; groan
sızmak /·ˈ·/ *v* ooze; leak; trickle
sicil /·ˈ·/ *n* register
sicilli /··ˈ·/ *adj* previously convicted
sicim /·ˈ·/ *n* string
sidik /·ˈ·/ *n* urine
sifon /·ˈ·/ *n* siphon; flush tank
siftah /·ˈ·/ *n* first sale of the day; ~ **etmek** *make the first sale of the day
sigara /·ˈ··/ *n* cigarette; ~ **içmek** smoke; ~ **içilmez** no smoking
sigorta /·ˈ··/ *n* insurance; fuse
sihir /·ˈ·/ *n* magic, sorcery; spell
sihirbaz /··ˈ·/ *n* magician, sorcerer
sihirli /··ˈ·/ *adj* bewitched; enchanting
silah /·ˈ·/ *n* weapon, arm
silahlanma /···ˈ·/ *n* armament
silahlanmak /···ˈ·/ *v* *take up arms
silahlı /··ˈ·/ *adj* armed
silahsızlandırmak /·····ˈ·/ *v* disarm
silahsızlanma /····ˈ·/ *n* disarmament
silahşor /··ˈ·/ *n* warrior, musketeer
silecek /··ˈ·/ *n* windscreen wiper
silgi /·ˈ·/ *n* duster; rubber, eraser
silik /·ˈ·/ *adj* rubbed out, indistinct; insignificant
silindir /··ˈ·/ *n* cylinder; roller; ~ **şapka** top hat
silkelemek /···ˈ·/ *v* *shake off
silkinmek /··ˈ·/ *v* *shake oneself; *shake off the effects of something
silkmek /·ˈ·/ *v* *shake; *shake off
sille /·ˈ·/ *n* slap
silmek /·ˈ·/ *v* rub off, erase; wash and scrub; wipe
simge /·ˈ·/ *n* symbol
simgelemek /···ˈ·/ *v* symbolize
simit /·ˈ·/ *n* ring-shaped roll of bread covered with sesame seeds; life buoy
simsar /·ˈ·/ *n* broker, middleman
simsarlık /··ˈ·/ *n* brokerage
sincap /·ˈ·/ *n* squirrel
sindirim /··ˈ·/ *n* digestion
sindirmek /··ˈ·/ *v* digest
sinek /·ˈ·/ *n* fly
sineklik /··ˈ·/ *n* fly whisk
sinema /·ˈ··/ *n* cinema *nBr;* movies *nAm*
sinir /·ˈ·/ *n* nerve
sinirlenmek /···ˈ·/ *v* *get nervous, *be irritated
sinirli /··ˈ·/ *adj* nervous, quick-tempered
sinirsel /··ˈ·/ *adv* neural; nervous
sinmek /·ˈ·/ *v* crouch down, cower; *sink into, penetrate
sinsi /·ˈ·/ *adj* stealthy, sneaky
sinsice /·ˈ··/ *adv* stealthily
sinsilik /··ˈ·/ *n* stealthiness
sipariş /–ˈ·/ *n* order; ~ **almak** receive an order ~ **vermek** *give an order
siper /·ˈ·/ *n* shelter; shield; protection; guard
sirk *n* circus
sirke /·ˈ·/ *n* vinegar
siroz /·ˈ·/ *n* cirrhosis
sis *n* fog, mist
sisli /·ˈ·/ *adj* foggy, misty
sistem /·ˈ·/ *n* system
sistematik /···ˈ·/ *adj* systematic
site /ˈ··/ *n* housing estate
sitem /·ˈ·/ *n* reproach, rebuke; ~ **etmek** reproach
sivil /·ˈ·/ *n* civilian; *adj* civil
sivilce /·ˈ··/ *n* pimple
sivri /·ˈ·/ *adj* sharp, pointed; ~ **akıllı** eccentric
sivrilmek /··ˈ·/ *v* *become pointed; *become prominent; *make rapid progress in one's career
sivriltmek /··ˈ·/ *v* sharpen, *make pointed
sivrisinek /·ˈ···/ *n* mosquito

siyah /·'·/ *adj* black; dark
Siyam /'··/ Siam, Thailand
Siyamlı /'···/ *adj, n* Siamese, Thai
siyaset /·–'·/ *n* politics; policy; diplomacy
siyasi /·–'–/ *adj* political
siz *pron* you
size /·'·/ *pron* to you, for you
sizi /·'·/ *pron* you
sizin /·'·/ *adj* your
sizinki /··'·/ *pron* yours
smokin /·'·/ *n* dinner jacket, tuxedo
soba /'··/ *n* stove
sofa /'··/ *n* hall, anteroom
sofra /·'·/ *n* dining table; meal
sofu /·'·/ *adj* religious
soğan /·'·/ *n* onion; bulb
soğuk /·'·/ *adj* cold; frigid, unfriendly; *n* cold weather; ~ **algınlığı** a cold
soğukkanlı /·'···/ *adj* calm, cool
soğukluk /··'·/ *n* coldness; antipathy; cold sweet
soğumak /··'·/ *v* *become cold, cool; *lose love *or* enthusiasm
soğutmak /··'·/ *v* cool, chill; alienate
soğutucu /···'·/ *n* refrigerator
sohbet /·'·/ *n* conversation, chat; ~ **etmek** *have a chat
sokak /·'·/ *n* road, street; ~ **kadını** streetwalker
sokmak /·'·/ *v* introduce, *put in, insert, *let in, admit; *sting, *bite
sokulgan /··'·/ *adj* sociable, friendly
sokulmak /··'·/ *v* *be inserted in; cultivate friendly relations with
sokuşturmak /···'·/ *v* squeeze into
sol *adj* left; *n* left-hand side; **solda** on the left; **solda sıfır** a mere nothing
solak /·'·/ *adj* left-handed
solgun /·'·/ *adj* pale; faded
solist /·'·/ *n* soloist
sollamak /··'·/ *v* *overtake
solmak /·'·/ *v* fade; wither; *become pale
solucan /··'·/ *n* earthworm
soluk[1] /·'·/ *adj* pale; faded
soluk[2] /·'·/ *n* breath; ~ **almak** breathe; ~ **kesici** breathtaking; ~ **soluğa** out of breath
solumak /··'·/ *v* pant, breathe heavily
solungaç /··'·/ *n* gill
solunum /··'·/ *n* respiration
somun /·'·/ *n* loaf of bread; nut
somurtkan /··'·/ *adj* sulky, sullen
somurtmak /··'·/ *v* pout, sulk
somut /·'·/ *adj* concrete
somutlaşmak /···'·/ *v* *take a material form; *become concrete
somya /'··/ *n* spring mattress
son *n* end; result; *adj* last, final; ~ **vermek** *put an end; **sonunda** in the end, finally
sonbahar /'···/ *n* autumn, fall
sonek /'··/ *n* suffix
sonra /'··/ *adv* after; then, later, afterwards
sonraki /'···/ *adj* subsequent, following
sonsuz /·'·/ *adj* endless, eternal, infinite
sonsuzluk /··'·/ *n* infinity, eternity
sonuç /·'·/ *n* result, end, outcome, consequence; ~ **çıkarmak** *draw a conclusion
sonuçlanmak /···'·/ *v* *come to a conclusion
sonuçsuz /··'·/ *adj* fruitless, vain
sopa /·'·/ *n* stick; beating; ~ **atmak** *give a beating; ~ **yemek** *get a beating
sorgu /·'·/ *n* interrogation, inquiry; **sorguya çekmek** interrogate

sorgulamak /···ˈ·/ *v* interrogate
sormak /ˈ·/ *v* ask, inquire
soru /·ˈ·/ *n* question, interrogation; ~ **işareti** question mark
sorumlu /··ˈ·/ *adj* responsible
sorumsuz /··ˈ·/ *adj* irresponsible
sorumsuzluk /···ˈ·/ *n* irresponsibility
sorun /·ˈ·/ *n* problem
soruşturma /···ˈ·/ *n* investigation, inquiry
soruşturmak /···ˈ·/ *v* investigate, inquire about
sos *n* sauce
sosis /·ˈ·/ *n* sausage
sosyal /·ˈ·/ *adj* social
sosyete /·ˈ··/ *n* the upper classes; high society
sosyoloji /···ˈ·/ *n* sociology
Sovyetler Birliği /··ˈ· ···/ Soviet Union
soy *n* lineage, descent, family; ancestors; ~ **sop** family and relations
soyaçekim /·ˈ···/ *n* heredity
soyadı /ˈ···/ *n* surname
soyağacı /ˈ····/ *n* family tree
soydaş /·ˈ·/ *adj* of the same race
soygun /·ˈ·/ *n* robbery
soyguncu /··ˈ·/ *n* robber
soylu /·ˈ·/ *adj* noble
soyluluk /··ˈ·/ *n* nobility
soymak /·ˈ·/ *v* peel, shell; strip, undress; rob
soysuzlaşmak /···ˈ·/ *v* degenerate
soytarı /··ˈ·/ *n* clown, buffoon
soyulmak /··ˈ·/ *v* *be peeled; *be robbed
soyunmak /··ˈ·/ *v* undress oneself
soyut /·ˈ·/ *adj* abstract
soyutlama /···ˈ·/ *n* abstraction
soyutlamak /···ˈ·/ *v* abstract, isolate
söğüş /·ˈ·/ *n* boiled meat; cold meat
söğüt /·ˈ·/ *n* willow
sökmek /·ˈ·/ *v* pull up; *tear down; rip open; *break through
sökük /·ˈ·/ *adj* unraveled; unstitched; *n* rent, tear
sökülmek /··ˈ·/ *v* *be unraveled, *be unstitched
sömürge /·ˈ··/ *n* colony
sömürgeci /·ˈ···/ *n* colonist
sömürmek /··ˈ·/ *v* exploit
sömürü /··ˈ·/ *n* exploitation
sömürücü /···ˈ·/ *n* exploiter
söndürmek /··ˈ·/ *v* *put out, extinguish; turn off, switch off; deflate
söndürücü /···ˈ·/ *n* fire extinguisher
sönmek /·ˈ·/ *v* *be extinguished
sönük /·ˈ·/ *adj* extinguished; deflated; dim, dull
sövgü /·ˈ·/ *n* swear word, profanity
sövmek /·ˈ·/ *v* curse
söylemek /··ˈ·/ *v* *say, *tell
söyleniş /··ˈ·/ *n* pronunciation
söylenmek /··ˈ·/ *v* *be said; grumble, mutter
söylenti /··ˈ·/ *n* rumor
söyleşi /··ˈ·/ *n* conversation, chat
söyleşmek /··ˈ·/ *v* talk over, chat, converse, discuss
söylev /·ˈ·/ *n* speech
söz *n* word, remark; rumor, gossip; promise; ~ **almak** *begin to speak; obtain a promise; ~ **aramızda** between you and me; ~ **vermek** promise; **söze karışmak** interrupt by speaking; **sözünde durmak** *keep one's word
sözbirliği /ˈ····/ *n* unanimity, agreement; ~ **etmek** agree to say *or* do the same thing
sözcü /·ˈ·/ *n* spokesman
sözcük /·ˈ·/ *n* word
sözde /·ˈ·/ *adv* as if, as though;

adj so-called, alleged, would-be
sözgelişi /'····/ *adv* for example, supposing that
sözleşme /··'·/ *n* agreement, contract
sözleşmek /··'·/ *v* agree mutually; *make an appointment
sözlü /·'·/ *adj* verbal, oral; engaged to be married
sözlük /·'·/ *n* dictionary
spiker /·'·/ *n* announcer
spor *n* sports
sporcu /·'·/ *n* athlete, sportsman
sportmen /·'·/ *n* athlete
stad, stadyum /'··/ *n* stadium
staj *n* apprenticeship; training; ~ **görmek** *be under training
stajyer /·'·/ *n* trainee
steno /'··/ *n* shorthand
step *n* steppe
sterlin /·'·/ *n* pound sterling
stok *n* stock, inventory
stüdyo /'··/ *n* studio
su *n* water; broth; juice
sual /·'·/ *n* question
sualtı /'···/ *adj* underwater
suare /··'·/ *n* evening performance
suaygırı /'····/ *n* hippopotamus
subay /·'·/ *n* officer
sucu /·'·/ *n* water seller
sucuk /·'·/ *n* garlic-flavored sausage
suç *n* fault; offense; crime; ~ **ortağı** accomplice
suçiçeği /'····/ *n* chicken pox
suçlamak /··'·/ *v* accuse, blame
suçlu /·'·/ *adj* guilty
suçsuz /·'·/ *adj* innocent
suçüstü /'···/ *adj* red-handed, in the act
suikast /··'·/ *n* assassination plot, conspiracy
sukabağı /'····/ *n* gourd
sukemeri /'····/ *n* aqueduct
sulak /·'·/ *adj* watery, wet
sulamak /··'·/ *v* water, irrigate
sulh *n* peace; reconciliation
sultan /·'·/ *n* sultan; ruler
suluboya /·'···/ *n* watercolor
sulusepken /·'···/ *n* sleet
sundurma /··'·/ *n* penthouse
suni /·'–/ *adj* artificial, false
sunmak /·'·/ *v* offer, *put forward; present
sur *n* city wall
surat /·'·/ *n* face; ~ **asmak** *make a sour face
suratsız /··'·/ *adj* sulky; ugly
sure /–'·/ *n* sura, section of the Koran
suret /–'·/ *n* copy; form, shape; manner, way
Suriye /'–··/ Syria
Suriyeli /'–···/ *adj, n* Syrian
susam /·'·/ *n* sesame
susamak /··'·/ *v* *be thirsty; long for
susamış /·'·/ *adj* thirsty
suskun /·'·/ *adj* taciturn
susmak /·'·/ *v* *be silent; stop talking
sustalı /··'·/ *n* switchblade
susturmak /··'·/ *v* silence, hush; *shut up
susturucu /···'·/ *n* silencer
susuz /·'·/ *adj* waterless, dry; thirsty
susuzluk /··'·/ *n* thirst; aridity
sutyen /·'·/ *n* brassiere
suyolu /'···/ *n* water conduit, waterline
sükse /·'·/ *n* ostentation; success
sükûnet /–'·/ *n* rest, calm, quiet
sükût /·'·/ *n* silence
sülale /–'·/ *n* family line, lineage
sülük /·'·/ *n* leech
sülün /·'·/ *n* pheasant
sümbül /·'·/ *n* hyacinth

sümkürmek /··ˈ·/ *v* *blow one's nose
sümük /·ˈ·/ *n* mucus
sümüklüböcek /··ˈ···/ *n* snail
sünepe /··ˈ·/ *adj* slovenly, sluggish
sünger /·ˈ·/ *n* sponge
süngü /·ˈ·/ *n* bayonet
sünnet /·ˈ·/ *n* circumcision
süprüntü /··ˈ·/ *n* sweepings, rubbish
süpürge /··ˈ·/ *n* broom
süpürmek /··ˈ·/ *v* *sweep
sürahi /–ˈ·/ *n* pitcher, jug
sürat /·ˈ·/ *n* speed
süratle /·ˈ··/ *adv* speedily
süratli /··ˈ·/ *adj* quick, rapid
sürçmek /·ˈ·/ *v* stumble, slip; *make a mistake
süre /·ˈ·/ *n* period
süreç /·ˈ·/ *n* process
sürekli /··ˈ·/ *adj* continuous
süreksiz /··ˈ·/ *adj* transitory
süreli /··ˈ·/ *adj* periodic
sürgü /·ˈ·/ *n* bolt
sürgülemek /···ˈ·/ *v* bolt
sürgülü /··ˈ·/ *adj* bolted
sürgün /·ˈ·/ *n* exile; shoot; diarrhea; ~ **etmek** banish, exile
sürme /·ˈ·/ *n* bolt; drawer
sürmek /·ˈ·/ *v* *drive; exile; *spread; last
sürmelemek /···ˈ·/ *v* bolt
sürpriz /·ˈ·/ *n* surprise
sürtmek /·ˈ·/ *v* rub against
sürtünmek /··ˈ·/ *v* rub oneself against
sürü /·ˈ·/ *n* herd, flock
sürücü /··ˈ·/ *n* driver
sürüklemek /···ˈ·/ *v* drag, trail
sürükleyici /····ˈ·/ *adj* fascinating, attractive
sürümek /··ˈ·/ *v* drag along the ground
sürünceme /···ˈ·/ *n* delay; a matter's dragging on; **sürüncemede kalmak** drag on
sürüngen /··ˈ·/ *n* reptile
sürünmek /··ˈ·/ *v* *creep, crawl; *lead a dog's life
süs *n* ornament, decoration
süslemek /··ˈ·/ *v* adorn, embellish, decorate
süslenmek /··ˈ·/ *v* adorn oneself, deck oneself out
süslü /·ˈ·/ *adj* ornamented
süssüz /·ˈ·/ *adj* plain, unadorned
süt *n* milk; ~ **tozu** milk powder
sütanne /ˈ···/ *n* wet nurse; foster mother
sütçü /·ˈ·/ *n* milkman, dairyman
sütdişi /ˈ···/ *n* milk tooth
sütkardeş /ˈ···/ *n* foster brother *or* sister
sütun /·ˈ·/ *n* column
süvari /–ˈ·/ *n* rider, cavalryman
süveter /··ˈ·/ *n* sweater
Süveyş Kanalı /ˈ·· ···/ Suez Canal
süzgeç /·ˈ·/ *n* strainer, filter
süzgün /·ˈ·/ *adj* languid; grown thin
süzmek /·ˈ·/ *v* strain, filter

Ş

şadırvan /··ˈ·/ *n* fountain for ablutions
şafak /·ˈ·/ *n* dawn; ~ **sökmesi** break of dawn
şah *n* shah
şahane /––ˈ·/ *adj* magnificent, wonderful
şahıs /·ˈ·/ *n* person, individual
şahin /–ˈ·/ *n* falcon
şahit /–ˈ·/ *n* witness; ~ **olmak** witness
şahlanmak /··ˈ·/ *v* rear; *fly into a passion

şahsen /'··/ *adv* personally
şahsi /·'–/ *adj* personal, private
şahsiyet /··'·/ *n* personality
şahsiyetli /···'·/ *adj* having a strong personality
şahsiyetsiz /···'·/ *adj* insignificant, having a weak personality
şair /–'·/ *n* poet
şairane /–·–'·/ *adj* poetical
şaka /·'·/ *n* joke, fun, jest; ~ **etmek** joke
şakadan /'···/ *adv* as a joke
şakak /·'·/ *n* temple
şakalaşmak /···'·/ *v* joke with one another
şakımak /··'·/ *v* *sing loudly
şakırdamak /···'·/ *v* jingle; rattle
şaklaban /··'·/ *n* buffoon, jester; flatterer
şakrak /·'·/ *adj* noisy; lively; mirthful; chatty
şal *n* shawl
şalgam /·'·/ *n* turnip
şalter /·'·/ *n* power switch
şalvar /·'·/ *n* baggy trousers
Şam Damascus
şamandıra /·'···/ *n* buoy, float
şamar /·'·/ *n* slap, box on the ear; ~ **atmak** slap; ~ **oğlanı** scapegoat
şamata /·'··/ *n* commotion, hubbub, uproar
şamdan /·'·/ *n* candlestick
şamfıstığı /'····/ *n* pistachio nut
şampanya /·'··/ *n* champagne
şampiyon /··'·/ *n* champion
şampuan /··'·/ *n* shampoo
şan *n* reputation, glory, fame; **şanına yakışmak** befit one's dignity
şangırdamak /···'·/ *v* rattle; crash
şangırtı /··'·/ *n* noise of breaking glass; crash
şanjman /·'·/ *n* gearbox
şanlı /·'·/ *adj* glorious
şans *n* luck, chance; **şansı olmak** *have a chance; **şansını denemek** *take one's chance
şanslı /·'·/ *adj* lucky
şanssız /·'·/ *adj* unlucky
şantaj /·'·/ *n* blackmail
şantajcı /··'·/ *n* blackmailer
şantiye /··'·/ *n* shipyard; building site
şantöz /·'·/ *n* female singer
şapka /'··/ *n* hat
şarampol /··'·/ *n* roadside ditch
şarap /·'·/ *n* wine
şarapnel /··'·/ *n* shrapnel
şarıltı /··'·/ *n* gurgling, splashing noise
şarjör /·'·/ *n* battery charger
şarkı /·'·/ *n* song; ~ **söylemek** *sing
şarkıcı /··'·/ *n* singer
şarküteri /···'·/ *n* delicatessen
şarlatan /··'·/ *n* charlatan; quack
şart *n* condition, stipulation; **şartıyla** on condition that; ~ **koşmak** stipulate
şartlı /·'·/ *adj* conditional; conditioned
şartname /·–'·/ *n* list of conditions; specifications
şasi /·'·/ *n* chassis
şaşalamak /···'·/ *v* *be taken aback, *be bewildered
şaşı /·'·/ *adj* cross-eyed
şaşırmak /··'·/ *v* *be surprised, *be confused; **şaşırıp kalmak** *be at a loss
şaşırtıcı /···'·/ *adj* amazing, surprising
şaşkın /·'·/ *adj* bewildered; stupid, silly
şaşmak /·'·/ *v* *be surprised; deviate; miss its object
şatafat /··'·/ *n* ostentation; luxury

şatafatlı /···'·/ *adj* showy, pretentious
şato /'··/ *n* castle, chateau
şayet /'–·/ *conj* if
şayia /–·'·/ *n* rumor
şebek /·'·/ *n* a long-tailed monkey
şebeke /·'··/ *n* network; student's pass
şecere /··'·/ *n* genealogical tree
şef *n* chief, leader
şeffaf /·'·/ *adj* transparent
şefkat /·'·/ *n* compassion, affection; pity
şeftali /·–'·/ *n* peach
şehir /·'·/ *n* city, town
şehirlerarası /··'····/ *adj* intercity; long-distance
şehirli /··'·/ *n* townsman; citizen
şehit /·'·/ *n* martyr
şehvet /·'·/ *n* lust, sexual desire
şehzade /·–'·/ *n* a sultan's son
şeker /·'·/ *n* sugar; sweet *nBr;* candy *nAm;* **Şeker Bayramı** the Lesser Bairam; feast following Ramadan; ~ **hastası** diabetic
şekerci /··'·/ *n* confectioner
şekerkamışı /·'····/ *n* sugar cane
şekerleme /···'·/ *n* candy; nap
şekerlemek /···'·/ *v* sugar, sweeten
şekerlik /··'·/ *n* sugar bowl
şekerpancarı /·'····/ *n* sugar beet
şekil /·'·/ *n* form, shape; figure; illustration; ~ **almak** *take shape; ~ **vermek** *give a form
şelale /·–'·/ *n* waterfall
şema /'··/ *n* plan, diagram
şempanze /··'·/ *n* chimpanzee
şemsiye /··'·/ *n* umbrella, parasol
şen *adj* cheerful, joyful, merry
şenlik /·'·/ *n* cheerfulness, merriment; public celebration; festival
şerbet /·'·/ *n* sweet drink
şeref /·'·/ *n* honor, glory; ~ **vermek** honor; grace; **şerefe!** cheerio! cheers!; **şerefine** in honor of
şereflendirmek /····'·/ *v* honor
şerefli /··'·/ *adj* honored
şerefsiz /··'·/ *adj* dishonest; dishonorable
şerefsizlik /···'·/ *n* dishonor
şeriat /·–'·/ *n* Islamic law, canonical law
şerit /·'·/ *n* ribbon, tape; tapeworm
şevk *n* eagerness, ardor, enthusiasm; **şevke gelmek;** *become eager
şevkle /'··/ *adv* eagerly
şey *n* thing
şeyh *n* sheikh
şeytan /·'·/ *n* satan, devil; ~ **gibi** as cunning as a fox; **şeytana uymak** yield to temptation
şeytanca /·'··/ *adj* devilish; *adv* devilishly
şeytani /·–'–/ *adj* devilish
şeytanlık /··'·/ *n* devilry; mischief, trick
şezlong /·'·/ *n* chaise longue
şık *adj* smart, elegant
şıkırtı /··'·/ *n* jingling, clinking
şıklık /·'·/ *n* elegance, smartness
şımarık /··'·/ *adj* spoilt; impertinent
şımarmak /·'·/ *v* *get spoilt
şımartmak /·'·/ *v* *spoil, pamper, indulge
şıpırtı /··'·/ *n* splash
şıpsevdi /··'·/ *adj* susceptible; quick to fall in love
şıra /'··/ *n* slightly fermented grape juice
şırıldamak /···'·/ *v* splash, babble
şırıltı /··'·/ *n* splashing, gurgling
şırınga /·'··/ *n* syringe
şiddet /·'·/ *n* violence; intensity,

strength
şiddetlenmek /···'·/ *v* *become violent; *become intensified
şiddetli /··'·/ *adj* severe, violent; strong
şifa /·'–/ *n* restoring to health; cure; ~ **bulmak** recover health; ~ **vermek** restore to health
şifalı /·–'·/ *adj* healing, curative
şifré /·'·/ *n* cipher; code
şiir /·'·/ *n* poetry, poem, verse
şikâyet /–'·/ *n* complaint; ~ **etmek** complain
şikâyetçi /–'·/ *n* complainant
şike /·'·/ *n* rigging
şilep /·'·/ *n* cargo ship
Şili /'··/ Chile
Şilili /'···/ *adj, n* Chilean
şilin /·'·/ *n* shilling
şilte /·'·/ *n* thin mattress
şimdi /'··/ *adv* now, at present; **şimdiki** present; **şimdilik** for the present, for the time being; **şimdiye kadar** until now, up to now
şimşek /·'·/ *n* lightning; ~ **çakmak** flash; ~ **gibi** like lightning
şirin /·'·/ *adj* sweet; charming, affable
şirket /·'·/ *n* company, firm
şirret /·'·/ *adj* bad-tempered, quarrelsome; malicious
şiş[1] *n* spit, skewer; knitting-needle
şiş[2] *adj* swollen; *n* swelling
şişe /·'·/ *n* bottle
şişirmek /··'·/ *v* *blow up, inflate; exaggerate
şişman /·'·/ *adj* fat, obese
şişmanlamak /···'·/ *v* *grow fat
şişmanlık /··'·/ *n* fatness, obesity
şişmek /·'·/ *v* *swell; *be inflated
şive /–'·/ *n* accent
şizofreni /···'·/ *n* schizophrenia
şofben /·'·/ *n* water heater
şoför /·'·/ *n* driver
şok *n* shock
şort *n* shorts
şose /'··/ *n* paved road
şöhret /·'·/ *n* fame, reputation, renown
şöhretli /··'·/ *adj* famous
şölen /·'·/ *n* feast, banquet
şömine /·'··/ *n* fireplace
şövalye /·'··/ *n* knight
şöyle /'··/ *adv* in this way, like this, like that, thus; *adj* of that sort, such; ~ **böyle** so so; ~ **dursun** let alone; **şöylece** in this way; thus; ~ **ki** in such a way; as follows
şu *adj, pron* this, that; ~ **günlerde** in these days; ~ **halde** in that case
şubat /·'·/ February
şube /–'·/ *n* branch, department, section
şuh *adj* coquettish, pert
şuhluk /·'·/ *n* coquettishness, pertness
şunlar /·'·/ *pron* those
şurada /'···/ *adv* there; ~ **burada** here and there
şurası /'···/ *n* this place; this fact
şurup /·'·/ *n* syrup; sweet medicine
şuur /·'·/ *n* the conscious (mind); consciousness
şuuraltı /·'···/ *n* subconscious
şuurlu /··'·/ *adj* conscious; sensible
şuursuz /··'·/ *adj* unconscious
şükran /·'·/ *n* thanksgiving, thanks
şükretmek /'···/ *v* thank; *be thankful for
şükür /·'·/ *n* gratitude
şüphe /·'·/ *n* doubt; suspicion; uncertainty; ~ **etmek** doubt, suspect

şüpheci /··ˈ·/ *n* sceptic, suspicious person
şüphelenmek /···ˈ·/ *get suspicious; doubt
şüpheli /··ˈ·/ *adj* doubtful, uncertain; suspicious

T

ta /–/ *adv* even; until; even as far as; ~ **ki** so that, in order that
taahhüt /··ˈ·/ *n* undertaking, commitment, obligation
taahhütlü /···ˈ·/ *adj* registered (letter)
taarruz /··ˈ·/ *n* attack; ~ **etmek** attack
tabak /·ˈ·/ *n* plate, dish
tabaka /·ˈ··/ *n* layer, stratum; sheet; tobacco box
taban /·ˈ·/ *n* sole; base; floor; plateau; ~ **fiyat** the lowest price; ~ **tabana zıt** diametrically opposite
tabanca /·ˈ··/ *n* pistol, gun; ~ **çekmek** *draw one's gun
tabela /·ˈ··/ *n* sign, signboard
tabetmek /ˈ···/ *v* print
tabi /–ˈ–/ *adj* dependent, subject
tabiat /··ˈ·/ *n* nature; character; habit
tabiatıyla /···ˈ··/ *adv* naturally
tabii[1] /ˈ·––/ of course, naturally
tabii[2] /··ˈ·/ *adj* natural
tabiiyet /–·–ˈ·/ *n* nationality, citizenship
tabir /–ˈ·/ *n* expression, idiom, phrase
tabla /ˈ··/ *n* ashtray
tabldot /·ˈ·/ *n* table d'hôte
tablo /ˈ··/ *n* picture, painting
tabu /·ˈ·/ *n* taboo
tabur /·ˈ·/ *n* battalion
taburcu /··ˈ·/ *adj* discharged from a hospital
tabure /·ˈ··/ *n* footstool
tabut /·ˈ·/ *n* coffin
taciz –ˈ·/ *n* a disturbing; ~ **etmek** annoy, bother, harass
taç *n* crown; ~ **giymek** *be crowned
taçlı /·ˈ·/ *adj* crowned
tadımlık /··ˈ·/ *adj* just enough to taste
tadilat /––ˈ·/ *n* alteration, restoration, modification
tafsilat /·–ˈ·/ *n* details
tafsilatlı /·–ˈ·/ *adj* detailed
tahammül /··ˈ·/ *n* endurance; patience; ~ **etmek** *put up with, endure
tahıl /·ˈ·/ *n* grain; cereal
tahin /–ˈ·/ *n* sesame oil
tahkikat /·–ˈ·/ *n* investigation, inquiries
tahlil /·ˈ·/ *n* analysis
tahliye etmek /··ˈ· ··/ *set free
tahmin /·ˈ·/ *n* estimate, guess, conjecture; ~ **etmek** estimate
tahrik /·ˈ·/ *n* provocation, incitement; excitation; ~ **etmek** provoke, incite
tahrip /·ˈ·/ *n* destruction, devastation, ruining; ~ **etmek** destroy, ruin, devastate
tahriş /·ˈ·/ *n* irritation; ~ **etmek** irritate
tahsil /·ˈ·/ *n* study, education; ~ **görmek** receive an education
tahsildar /··ˈ·/ *n* tax collector
taht *n* throne; **tahta çıkmak** ascend the throne; **tahttan indirmek** dethrone
tahta /·ˈ·/ *n* board, plank, wood; *adj* wooden
tahtakurusu /·ˈ····/ *n* bedbug
tahterevalli /···ˈ··/ *n* seesaw

tahvil /·ˈ·/ *n* transforming, converting; conversion; bond
tak *n* arch; vault
taka /·ˈ·/ *n* small sailboat
takas /·ˈ·/ *n* exchange; clearing; barter; ~ **etmek** clear, exchange; barter
takat /–ˈ·/ *n* strength; potency
takatsız /–ˈ·/ *adj* exhausted, weak
takdim /·ˈ·/ *n* presentation; introduction; offer; ~ **etmek** present; offer; introduce
takdir /·ˈ·/ *n* appreciation; estimate; fate; ~ **etmek** appreciate; **takdirde** in the event of, if, in case
takdirname /··–ˈ·/ *n* letter of appreciation
takdis /·ˈ·/ *n* sanctification; ~ **etmek** sanctify
takı /·ˈ·/ *n* gift of jewelry as wedding present; ornament
takılmak /··ˈ·/ *v* kid; *be tangled up; annoy with ridicule; *be affixed; *get stuck on
takım /·ˈ·/ *n* team; gang, band, crew; set, squad, class; suit
takınmak /··ˈ·/ *v* *put on, *wear; assume, affect
takip /–ˈ·/ *n* pursuit, chase; ~ **etmek** follow; pursue
takla /·ˈ·/ *n* somersault; ~ **atmak** turn a somersault
taklit /·ˈ·/ *n* imitation; counterfeit; *adj* imitated; sham; ~ **etmek** imitate, counterfeit
taklitçi /··ˈ·/ *n* imitator; mimic
takma /·ˈ·/ *adj* attached; ~ **ad** nickname
takmak /·ˈ·/ *v* attach, affix; *put on
takoz /·ˈ·/ *n* wooden wedge
takriben /·ˈ–·/ *adv* about, more or less, approximately
taksi /ˈ··/ *n* taxi, cab
taksim /·ˈ·/ *n* division; ~ **etmek** divide, distribute
taksit /·ˈ·/ *n* installment
takunya /·ˈ··/ *n* clog; sabot
takvim /·ˈ·/ *n* calendar
takviye /··ˈ·/ *n* reinforcement; ~ **etmek** reinforce
talan /·ˈ·/ *n* pillage, plunder; ~ **etmek** pillage, plunder
talaş /·ˈ·/ *n* wood shavings; sawdust
talebe /··ˈ·/ *n* student, pupil
talep /·ˈ·/ *n* request, demand; ~ **etmek** demand, request
talih /–ˈ·/ *n* fortune, luck
talihli /–·ˈ·/ *adj* lucky
talihsiz /–·ˈ·/ *adj* unlucky
talim /–ˈ·/ *n* teaching, training; practice
talimat /––ˈ·/ *n* instructions; ~ **vermek** *give instructions
talip /–ˈ·/ *adj* desirous, seeking; *n* suitor; ~ **olmak** *put oneself in for, *seek, aspire
tam *adj* complete, entire, whole; exact, perfect; ~ **gelmek** fit well; ~ **vaktinde** just in time
tamam /·ˈ·/ *adj* complete; finished; ready; correct; *n* the whole; ~ **olmak** end, *be over
tamamen /·ˈ–·/ *adv* completely, fully, entirely
tamamlamak /···ˈ·/ *v* complete, finish
tamamlayıcı /····ˈ·/ *adj* complementary, supplementary
tambur /·ˈ·/ *n* classical lute
tamir /–ˈ·/ *n* repair; ~ **etmek** repair, mend
tamirci /–·ˈ·/ *n* repairman
tamirhane /–·–ˈ·/ *n* repair shop
tampon /·ˈ·/ *n* bumper; buffer; wad

tan *n* dawn
tandır /·ˈ·/ *n* oven made in a hole in the earth
tane /–ˈ·/ *n* grain, seed; pip; piece; ~ ~ piece by piece
tanı /·ˈ·/ *n* diagnosis
tanıdık /··ˈ·/ *n* acquaintance
tanık /·ˈ·/ *n* witness; ~ **olmak** witness
tanıklık /··ˈ·/ *n* testimony
tanım /·ˈ·/ *n* definition
tanımak /··ˈ·/ *v* recognize; *know; acknowledge
tanımlamak /···ˈ·/ *v* define
tanınmak /··ˈ·/ *v* *become known, gain fame
tanınmış /··ˈ·/ *adj* well-known; famous
tanışmak /··ˈ·/ v *get acquainted; *know one another
tanıştırmak /···ˈ·/ *v* introduce to one another
tanıtmak /··ˈ·/ *v* introduce, *make known; promote
Tanrı /·ˈ·/ *n* God
Tanrıbilim /·ˈ···/ *n* theology
Tanrıça /·ˈ··/ *n* goddess
Tanrılaştırmak /····ˈ·/ *v* deify
Tanrısız /··ˈ·/ *n* atheist
tansiyon /··ˈ·/ *n* blood pressure
tantana /··ˈ·/ *n* pomp, display
tantanalı /···ˈ·/ *adj* pompous
tanyeri /ˈ···/ *n* daybreak, dawn
tapınak /··ˈ·/ *n* place of worship, temple
tapınmak /··ˈ·/ *v* worship, adore
tapmak /·ˈ·/ *v* worship, adore
tapu /·ˈ·/ *n* title deed
taraf /·ˈ·/ *n* side, edge, border; place, site; party; ~ **tutmak** *take sides
taraflı /··ˈ·/ *adj* having sides; partial
tarafsız /··ˈ·/ *adj* impartial
taraftar /··ˈ·/ *n* supporter
tarak /·ˈ·/ *n* comb; harrow, rake
tarama /··ˈ·/ *n* hatching; research; soft roe; red caviar
taramak /··ˈ·/ *v* comb; harrow; rake; search thoroughly, scan
tarçın /·ˈ·/ *n* cinnamon
tarım /·ˈ·/ *n* agriculture
tarif /–ˈ·/ *n* description; definition; ~ **etmek** describe; define
tarife /–ˈ·/ *n* price list; tariff; timetable
tarih /–ˈ·/ *n* date; history; ~ **atmak** date; **tarihe karışmak** vanish, *be a thing of the past
tarihi /–ˈ–/ *adj* historic; historical
tarihli /–·ˈ·/ *adj* dated
tarihöncesi /–ˈ···· / *n* prehistoric period
tarihsel /–·ˈ·/ *adj* historic; historical
tarihsiz /–·ˈ·/ *adj* undated
tarikat /·–ˈ·/ *n* religious order, sect
tarla /ˈ··/ *n* arable field
tartaklamak /···ˈ·/ *v* manhandle, harass
tartı /·ˈ·/ *n* weight, balance; scales
tartışılmaz /···ˈ·/ *adj* indisputable
tartışma /··ˈ·/ *n* discussion; argument, dispute
tartışmak /··ˈ·/ *v* dispute, argue; discuss
tartışmalı /···ˈ·/ *adj* argumentative, controversial
tartmak /·ˈ·/ *v* weigh; consider carefully; balance
tarz *n* style, manner, way
tas *n* bowl
tasa /·ˈ·/ *n* worry, anxiety
tasalanmak /···ˈ·/ *v* worry; *be anxious
tasalı /··ˈ·/ *adj* anxious, worried
tasarı /··ˈ·/ *n* project; draft, bill
tasarım /··ˈ·/ *n* imagination; design

tasarlamak /···ˈ·/ *v* plan; draft in outline
tasarruf /··ˈ·/ *n* saving, economy; ~ **etmek** save, economize
tasarruflu /···ˈ·/ *adj* economical, thrifty
tasasız /··ˈ·/ *adj* carefree, lighthearted
tasavvuf /··ˈ·/ *n* Islamic mysticism, Sufism
tasavvur /··ˈ·/ *n* imagination; idea; ~ **etmek** imagine
tasdik /·ˈ·/ *n* confirmation; affirmation; approval; ~ **etmek** affirm, confirm
tasdikli /··ˈ·/ *adj* certified
tasdikname /··–ˈ·/ *n* certificate
tasdiksiz /··ˈ·/ *adj* uncertified
tasfiye /··ˈ·/ *n* purification; cleaning; liquidation
taslak /·ˈ·/ *n* draft, sketch; ~ **halinde** in draft
taslamak /··ˈ·/ *v* pretend to be something; *make a show of
tasma /·ˈ·/ *n* collar
tasvir /·ˈ·/ *n* description; picture; design
taş *n* stone; rock; ~ **gibi** very hard, stony; ~ **kesilmek** *be petrified; **taşa tutmak** stone
taşımak /··ˈ·/ *v* carry; transport, convey; *bear, sustain
taşınmak /··ˈ·/ *v* move; *be carried
taşıt /·ˈ·/ *n* vehicle
taşkın /·ˈ·/ *adj* overflowing, exuberant
taşkınlık /··ˈ·/ *n* rowdiness, exuberance
taşkömürü /ˈ····/ *n* coal
taşlamak /··ˈ·/ *v* stone
taşlı /·ˈ·/ *adj* stony
taşmak /·ˈ·/ *v* overflow, *run over; boil over
taşra /ˈ··/ *n* provinces
taşralı /ˈ···/ *adj* provincial
taşyürekli /ˈ····/ *adj* hardhearted, cruel
tat *n* taste; ~ **almak** taste; enjoy; ~ **vermek** flavor; **tadını kaçırmak** *spoil, *go too far
tatbik /·ˈ·/ *n* application, adaptation; ~ **etmek** *put into effect, apply
tatil /–ˈ·/ *n* holiday, vacation; ~ **etmek** close temporarily; ~ **yapmak** *take a holiday; **tatile çıkmak** *go on a holiday;
tatlı /·ˈ·/ *adj* sweet; *n* dessert; ~ **dilli** speaking in a pleasant way
tatlılık /··ˈ·/ *n* sweetness; pleasantness; kindness
tatlılıkla /··ˈ··/ *adv* kindly, gently
tatmak /·ˈ·/ *v* taste; experience
tatmin /·ˈ·/ *n* satisfaction; ~ **etmek** satisfy
tatminkâr /··ˈ·/ *adj* satisfactory
tatsız /·ˈ·/ *adj* tasteless, unpleasant
tatsızlık /··ˈ·/ *n* dullness; disagreeable behavior
tava /·ˈ·/ *n* frying pan
tavan /·ˈ·/ *n* ceiling
taverna /·ˈ··/ *n* tavern
tavır /·ˈ·/ *n* mode, manner, attitude; ~ **takınmak** assume an attitude
taviz /–ˈ·/ *n* concession; compensation; ~ **vermek** *make concessions
tavla /ˈ··/ *n* backgammon
tavsiye /··ˈ·/ *n* recommendation; advice; ~ **etmek** recommend, advise
tavşan /·ˈ·/ *n* rabbit, hare
tavuk /·ˈ·/ *n* hen, chicken
tavus /·ˈ·/ *n* peacock
tay *n* colt, foal
tayf *n* spectrum

tayfa /·ˈ·/ *n* crew
tayin /–ˈ·/ *n* appointment; ~ **etmek** appoint, designate
tayyör /·ˈ·/ *n* tailor-made costume
taze /–ˈ·/ *adj* fresh, new; young
tazelemek /–··ˈ·/ *v* freshen, renew
tazelik /–ˈ·/ *n* freshness; youth
tazı /·ˈ·/ *n* greyhound
tazminat /·–ˈ·/ *n* indemnity, compensation; reparations
tazyik /·ˈ·/ *n* pressure
tebessüm /··ˈ·/ *n* smile
tebeşir /··ˈ·/ *n* chalk
tebliğ /·ˈ·/ *n* proclamation; announcement; ~ **etmek** notify, communicate
tebrik /·ˈ·/ *n* congratulation; ~ **etmek** congratulate
tecavüz /·–ˈ·/ *n* attack, aggression; violation; ~ **etmek** attack, rape
tecil /–ˈ·/ *n* delay, postponement; ~ **etmek** postpone
tecrübe /··ˈ·/ *n* trial; experiment; experience; ~ **etmek** try, test
tecrübeli /···ˈ·/ *adj* experienced
tecrübesiz /···ˈ·/ *adj* inexperienced
tedarik /·–ˈ·/ *n* preparation; ~ **etmek** procure, provide, prepare
tedarikli /·–ˈ·/ *adj* prepared
tedariksiz /·–ˈ·/ *adj* unprepared
tedavi /·–ˈ·/ *n* medical treatment, cure; ~ **etmek** cure, treat
tedbir /·ˈ·/ *n* measure, precaution; ~ **almak** *take measures
tedbirli /··ˈ·/ *adj* cautious
tedbirsiz /··ˈ·/ *adj* improvident, incautious
tedirgin /··ˈ·/ *adj* uneasy, restless; ~ **etmek** discompose, disturb
tedirginlik /···ˈ·/ *n* uneasiness
teessüf /··ˈ·/ *n* regret; sorrow; ~ **etmek** regret
tefeci /··ˈ·/ *n* usurer
teferruat /···ˈ·/ *n* details
teferruatlı /····ˈ·/ *n* detailed
teftiş /·ˈ·/ *n* inspection; ~ **etmek** inspect
teğmen /·ˈ·/ *n* lieutenant
tehdit /·ˈ·/ *n* threat, menace; ~ **etmek** threaten, menace
tehir /–ˈ·/ *n* delay, postponement
tehlike /··ˈ·/ *n* danger, risk
tehlikeli /···ˈ·/ *adj* dangerous
tek *n* single thing; *adj* only; unique; odd; ~ **başına** alone; ~ **tük** only a few; ~ **yanlı** unilateral, one-sided
tekdüze /··ˈ·/ *adj* monotonous
tekel /ˈ··/ *n* monopoly
tekerlek /··ˈ·/ *n* wheel
tekil /·ˈ·/ *adj* singular
tekir /·ˈ·/ *n* striped goatfish; red mullet
teklif /·ˈ·/ *n* proposal; motion; offer; ~ **etmek** propose, offer
tekme /·ˈ·/ *n* kick
tekmelemek /···ˈ·/ *v* kick
tekne /·ˈ·/ *n* trough; vessel
teknik /·ˈ·/ *n* technique; *adj* technical
tekrar /·ˈ·/ *n* repetition; *adv* again; ~ **etmek** repeat; ~ ~ again and again
tekrarlamak /···ˈ·/ *v* repeat
teksir /·ˈ·/ *n* duplication
tel *n* wire; string; fiber; telegram, cable; ~ **örgü** wire fence
telaffuz /··ˈ·/ *n* pronunciation
telafi /·–ˈ·/ *n* compensation; ~ **etmek** compensate
telaş /·ˈ·/ *n* flurry, hurry; ~ **etmek** bustle, *be flustered
telaşlanmak /···ˈ·/ *v* *get flurried, *be alarmed
telaşlı /··ˈ·/ *adj* flurried, agitated
telaşsız /··ˈ·/ *adj* calm
teleferik /···ˈ·/ *n* cable car

telefon /··'·/ *n* telephone; ~ **etmek** telephone, *make a phone call
telefonlaşmak /····'·/ *v* talk over the telephone
telepati /···'·/ *n* telepathy
teleskop /··'·/ *n* telescope
televizyon /···'·/ *n* television
telgraf /·'·/ *n* telegram; ~ **çekmek** *send a telegram
telif /–'–/ *n* compilation, composition; ~ **hakkı** copyright
telsiz /·'·/ *n* wireless
telsizci /··'·/ *n* wireless operator
telve /·'·/ *n* coffee grounds
temas /·'·/ *n* contact; ~ **etmek** touch; **temasa geçmek** contact; *get in touch
tembel /·'·/ *adj* lazy
tembellik /··'·/ *n* laziness
tembih /·'·/ *n* warning; ~ **etmek** warn
temel /·'·/ *n* foundation; *adj* main, basic, fundamental; ~ **atmak** *lay a foundation
temelli[1] /'···/ *adv* permanently
temelli[2] /··'·/ *adj* well-founded
temenni /··'–/ *n* wish, desire; ~ **etmek** wish, desire
temin /–'·/ *n* assurance; ~ **etmek** assure, ensure; procure, provide
teminat /––'·/ *n* guarantee, security; deposit
temiz /·'·/ *adj* clean, pure
temizlemek /···'·/ *v* clean; clean up; *eat up
temizlik /··'·/ *n* cleanliness; cleaning
temizlikçi /···'·/ *n* cleaner
temmuz /·'·/ July
tempo /'··/ *n* tempo, time; ~ **tutmak** *keep time
temsil /·'·/ *n* representation; performance; ~ **etmek** represent
temsilci /··'·/ *n* agent, representative
temyiz etmek /·'– ··/ appeal, *take a case to a higher court
ten *n* skin, flesh; complexion
tencere /'···/ *n* saucepan
teneffüs /··'·/ *n* respiration; rest, break
teneke /·'··/ *n* tin
tenha /·'–/ *adj* uncrowded, solitary
tenkit /·'·/ *n* criticism; ~ **etmek** criticize
tentürdiyot /···'·/ *n* tincture of iodine
tenzilat /·–'·/ *n* reduction of prices, discount; **tenzilatlı satış** bargain sale
tepe /·'·/ *n* hill; peak, top; **tepeden bakmak** look down on; **tepesi atmak** *lose one's temper
tepinmek /··'·/ *v* kick and stamp
tepki /·'·/ *n* reaction; ~ **göstermek** react
tepmek /·'·/ *v* kick; *throw away
tepsi /·'·/ *n* tray
ter *n* sweat, perspiration; ~ **basmak** *break out into a sweat; ~ **boşanmak** perspire suddenly
teras /·'·/ *n* terrace; balcony
terazi /·–'·/ *n* pair of scales
terbiye /··'·/ *n* education; training; good manners; seasoning; ~ **etmek** train; educate
terbiyeli /···'·/ *adj* good-mannered, polite
terbiyesiz /···'·/ *adj* ill-mannered, rude
terbiyesizce /···'··/ *adv* rudely
tercih /·'·/ *n* preference; ~ **etmek** prefer
tercüman /··'·/ *n* interpreter; translator
tercümanlık /···'·/ *n* interpretership
tercüme /··'·/ *n* translation;

~ **etmek** translate
tere /·ˈ·/ *n* garden cress
tereddüt /··ˈ·/ *n* hesitation; ~ **etmek** hesitate
tereyağı /·ˈ···/ *n* butter
terfi /·ˈ–/ *n* promotion; ~ **etmek** *be promoted
terhis /·ˈ·/ *n* discharge, demobilization; ~ **etmek** discharge, demobilize
terk *n* abandonment; ~ **etmek** abandon, *leave
terkip /·ˈ·/ *n* composition, compound
terlemek /··ˈ·/ *v* sweat
terli /·ˈ·/ *adj* sweaty
terlik /·ˈ·/ *n* slippers
termometre /··ˈ··/ *n* thermometer
termos /·ˈ·/ *n* thermos flask
termosifon /···ˈ·/ *n* water heater
termostat /··ˈ·/ *n* thermostat
ters *adj* reverse; opposite; *adv* upside down, inside out; ~ **anlamak** *misunderstand; ~ **bakmak** look daggers at; ~ **gitmek** *go wrong
tersane /·–ˈ·/ *n* dockyard
terslemek /··ˈ·/ *v* snap at; snub; answer harshly
tertibat /·–ˈ·/ *n* arrangement, apparatus
tertip /·ˈ·/ *n* arrangement; plan; trick; composition; ~ **etmek** arrange, organize
tertiplemek /···ˈ·/ *v* organize, arrange
tertipli /··ˈ·/ *adj* well-organized; tidy
terzi /·ˈ·/ *n* dressmaker, tailor
tesadüf /·–ˈ·/ *n* coincidence, chance; ~ **etmek** *meet by chance; *come across; coincide with
tesadüfen /·ˈ–··/ *adv* by chance, by accident
tescil /·ˈ·/ *n* registration; **tescilli marka** trademark
teselli /··ˈ–/ *n* consolation, comfort; ~ **etmek** console, comfort
tesir /–ˈ·/ *n* effect, influence; ~ **etmek** affect, influence, impress
tesirli /–·ˈ·/ *adj* effective
tesirsiz /–·ˈ·/ *adj* ineffective
tesisat /––ˈ·/ *n* installation
teslim /·ˈ·/ *n* delivery; surrender, submission; ~ **almak** *take delivery of; ~ **etmek** deliver; admit; ~ **olmak** surrender, submit
tespih /·ˈ·/ *n* prayer beads
tespit etmek /·ˈ– ··/ fix; prove
testere /ˈ···/ *n* saw
testi /·ˈ·/ *n* pitcher, earthenware jug
teşebbüs /··ˈ·/ *n* attempt; enterprise; ~ **etmek** attempt
teşekkür /··ˈ·/ *n* thanks; ~ **ederim** thank you; ~ **etmek** thank
teşhir /·ˈ·/ *n* exhibition, display; ~ **etmek** exhibit, display
teşhis /·ˈ·/ *n* recognition; diagnosis; ~ **etmek** identify, diagnose
teşkilat /·–ˈ·/ *n* organization
teşvik /·ˈ·/ *n* encouragement; ~ **edici** encouraging; ~ **etmek** encourage
tetik /·ˈ·/ *n* trigger; *adj* agile, quick; **tetikte durmak** *be on the alert
tetkik /·ˈ·/ investigation; ~ **etmek** investigate
tevkif /·ˈ·/ *n* arrest, detention; ~ **etmek** arrest, detain
Tevrat /·ˈ·/ *n* Pentateuch
teyp *n* tape recorder
teyze /ˈ··/ *n* (maternal) aunt,

mother's sister
tez *adj* quick, prompt; *adv* quickly, promptly
tezat /·ˈ·/ *n* contrast, contradiction
tezgâh /·ˈ·/ *n* counter; workbench; loom
tezgâhlamak /···ˈ·/ *v* arrange *or* *make ready; *set up in business
tezgâhtar /··ˈ·/ *n* shop assistant *Br;* clerk *nAm*
tezkere /··ˈ·/ *n* note, memorandum; official certificate *or* receipt
tıbben /ˈ··/ *adv* medically
tıbbi /·ˈ–/ *adj* medical
tıbbiye /··ˈ·/ *n* medical school
tıka basa /·ˈ· ··/ *adj* crammed full
tıkaç /·ˈ·/ *n* plug, stopper
tıkamak /··ˈ·/ *v* stuff up; plug; gag
tıkanık /··ˈ·/ *adj* stopped up
tıkanıklık /···ˈ·/ *n* being stopped up; suffocation
tıkanmak /··ˈ·/ *v* *be stopped up; choke; *be suffocated
tıkırtı /··ˈ·/ *n* rattle, clatter
tıklım tıklım /·ˈ· ··/ *adj* very full, crowded
tıkmak /·ˈ·/ *v* cram, jam, squeeze into
tıknaz /·ˈ·/ *adj* plump, fat and short
tılsım /·ˈ·/ *n* talisman, charm
tılsımlı /··ˈ·/ *adj* enchanted
tımar /·ˈ·/ *n* grooming; ~ **etmek** groom
tımarhane /·–ˈ·/ *n* lunatic asylum
tıngırdamak /····/ *v* tinkle, clink
tıngırtı /··ˈ·/ *n* clang, rattle, clinking noise
tınmamak /ˈ···/ *v* *take no notice
tıp *n* medicine
tıpa /·ˈ·/ *n* stopper; cork
tıpkı /ˈ··/ *adj* exactly like; just like
tırabzan /··ˈ·/ *n* handrail, banister
tıraş /·ˈ·/ *n* shaving, haircut; ~ **olmak** shave; *have a haircut
tıraşlı /··ˈ·/ *adj* shaved
tıraşsız /··ˈ·/ *adj* unshaved
tırıs /·ˈ·/ *n* trot; ~ **gitmek** trot
tırmalamak /···ˈ·/ *v* scratch
tırmanmak /··ˈ·/ *v* climb
tırmık /·ˈ·/ *n* scratch; harrow, rake
tırmıklamak /···ˈ·/ *v* scratch, harrow, rake
tırnak /·ˈ·/ *n* fingernail; toenail; claw; hoof; ~ **işareti** quotation mark
ticaret /·–ˈ·/ *n* trade, commerce; ~ **merkezi** commercial center; **ticaret odası** chamber of commerce; ~ **yapmak** engage in commerce; ~ **yasası** commercial law
ticarethane /·––ˈ·/ *n* business, firm, company
ticari /·–ˈ–/ *adj* commercial
tifo /ˈ··/ *n* typhoid fever
tiksinmek /··ˈ·/ *n* *be disgusted; abhor, loathe
tiksinti /··ˈ·/ *n* disgust, loathing
tilki /·ˈ·/ *n* fox
timsah /·ˈ·/ *n* crocodile
tip *n* type
tipi /·ˈ·/ *n* blizzard, snowstorm
tipik /·ˈ·/ *adj* typical
tiraj /·ˈ·/ *n* circulation
tirbuşon /··ˈ·/ *n* corkscrew
tire /·ˈ·/ *n* hyphen, dash
tiryaki /·–ˈ·/ *n* addict
titiz /·ˈ·/ *adj* particular; fastidious; peevish
titizlenmek /···ˈ·/ *v* *be tiresome and hard to please
titizlik /··ˈ·/ *n* peevishness, irritability
titizlikle /··ˈ··/ *adv* fastidiously
titrek /·ˈ·/ *adj* shaky, tremulous,

trembling
titremek /··'·/ *v* shiver, tremble, quiver
titreşim /·'·/ *n* vibration
tiyatro /·'··/ *n* theater
tohum /·'·/ *n* seed, grain
tok *adj* full; filled; thick; deep; ~ **olmak** *be full
toka /'··/ *n* buckle
tokalaşmak /···'·/ *v* *shake hands
tokat /·'·/ *n* blow, slap, cuff; ~ **atmak** slap, cuff
tokatlamak /···'·/ *v* slap
tokgözlü /'···/ *adj* contented
tokmak /·'·/ *n* mallet; beetle
tokuşturmak /···'·/ *v* cause to collide
tomar /·'·/ *n* roll
tombala /'···/ *n* bingo
tombul /·'·/ *adj* plump
tomruk /·'·/ *n* heavy log
tomurcuk /··'·/ *n* bud
ton[1] *n* ton
ton[2] *n* tone; color quality *or* value
tonbalığı /'····/ *n* tunny, tuna
top *n* ball; gun, cannon
topak /·'·/ *n* lump
topal /·'·/ *adj* lame, crippled
topallamak /···'·/ *v* limp
toparlak /··'·/ *adj* round
toparlamak /···'·/ *v* gather together; collect; summarize
toparlanmak /···'·/ *v* *be collected together; pull oneself together
topçu /·'·/ *n* artilleryman
toplam /·'·/ *n* total
toplama /··'·/ *n* addition
toplamak /··'·/ *v* collect, gather; pick; sum up; tidy up; *put on weight
toplantı /··'·/ *n* meeting, assembly
toplardamar /·'···/ *n* vein
toplu /·'·/ *adj* collected; plump; tidy; collective
topluiğne /·'···/ *n* pin
topluluk /··'·/ *n* community; group
toplum /·'·/ *n* society, community
toplumbilim /·'···/ *n* sociology
toplumcu /··'·/ *n* socialist
toplumsal /··'·/ *adj* social
toprak /·'·/ *n* earth, soil; land; **toprağa vermek** bury
toptan /·'·/ *adj* wholesale; ~ **satış** wholesale trade
toptancı /··'·/ *n* wholesaler
topuk /·'·/ *n* heel
topuz /·'·/ *n* knob; knot of hair
torba /·'·/ *n* bag
torik /·'·/ *n* large bonito
tornavida /··'··/ *n* screwdriver
torpido /·'··/ *n* torpedo
torpil /·'·/ *n* torpedo
tortu /·'·/ *n* sediment; dregs
torun /·'·/ *n* grandchild
toslamak /··'·/ *v* butt, *have a slight collision
tost *n* toasted sandwich
toy *adj* inexperienced, raw
toynak /·'·/ *n* hoof
toz *n* dust; powder; ~ **almak** dust; ~ **bezi** dustcloth; ~ **bulutu** cloud of dust
tozlanmak /··'·/ *v* *get dusty
tozlu /·'·/ *adj* dusty
tozşeker /'···/ *n* granulated sugar
tökezlemek /···'·/ *v* stumble
töre /·'·/ *n* customs; rules
törel /·'·/ *adj* moral, ethical
tören /·'·/ *n* ceremony; celebration
törpü /·'·/ *n* rasp, file
törpülemek /···'·/ *v* file, rasp
tövbe /·'·/ *n* penitence, repentance; ~ **etmek** *forswear, repent
tövbekâr /··'·/ *adv* penitent, repentant
trafik /·'·/ *n* traffic
Trakya /'··/ Thrace

trampet /·ˈ·/ *n* snare drum
tramplen /·ˈ·/ *n* springboard
tramvay /·ˈ·/ *n* streetcar, trolley, tram
tren *n* train
trençkot /·ˈ·/ *n* raincoat
tribün /·ˈ·/ *n* platform; stand
triko /ˈ··/ *n* tricot, knitted wear
trilyon /·ˈ·/ *n* a million million, trillion
tropikal /··ˈ·/ *adj* tropical
tröst *n* trust
tufan /–ˈ·/ *n* flood
tugay /·ˈ·/ *n* brigade
tuhaf /·ˈ·/ *adj* strange, odd, queer
tuhafiye /–·ˈ·/ *n* small articles, clothing accessories
tulum /·ˈ·/ *n* skin made into a bag; overalls
tulumba /·ˈ··/ *n* pump
Tuna /ˈ··/ the Danube
tunç *n* bronze
Tunus /ˈ··/ Tunisia
Tunuslu /ˈ···/ *adj, n* Tunisian
tur *n* tour; round
turfanda /··ˈ·/ *adj* early (fruit, vegetables)
turist /·ˈ·/ *n* tourist
turistik /··ˈ·/ *adj* touristic
turizm /·ˈ·/ *n* tourism
turna /·ˈ·/ *n* crane
turne /·ˈ·/ *n* tour
turnike /·ˈ··/ *n* turnstile
turnuva /·ˈ··/ *n* tournament
turp *n* radish
turşu /·ˈ·/ *n* pickle
turuncu /··ˈ·/ *adj* orange colored
turunç /·ˈ·/ *n* bitter orange
tuş *n* key
tutam /·ˈ·/ *n* pinch, small handful
tutanak /··ˈ·/ *n* minutes; court record
tutar /·ˈ·/ *n* total, sum
tutarlı /··ˈ·/ *adj* coherent, consistent
tutarlılık /···ˈ·/ *n* consistency
tutarsız /··ˈ·/ *adj* incoherent, inconsistent
tutkal /·ˈ·/ *n* glue
tutkallamak /···ˈ·/ *v* glue
tutku /·ˈ·/ *n* passion
tutkun /·ˈ·/ *adj* in love with; affected by
tutmak /·ˈ·/ *v* *hold; *catch; *keep; bridle; occupy; engage; hire; rent
tutsak /·ˈ·/ *n* captive; prisoner
tutsaklık /··ˈ·/ *n* captivity
tutturmak /··ˈ·/ *v* insist; cause to hold
tutucu /··ˈ·/ *adj* conservative
tutuk /·ˈ·/ *adj* tongue-tied, hesitant; shy
tutukevi /·ˈ···/ *n* prison; jail
tutuklamak /···ˈ·/ *v* arrest
tutuklu /··ˈ·/ *n* prisoner; *adj* arrested
tutukluluk /···ˈ·/ *n* detention
tutulmak /··ˈ·/ *v* *be caught; *be held; *be eclipsed; *fall in love with
tutum /·ˈ·/ *n* conduct, manner; economy
tutumlu /··ˈ·/ *adj* wasteful
tutumsuz /··ˈ·/ *adj* extravagant, thriftless
tutunmak /··ˈ·/ *v* *hold on, *cling
tutuşmak /··ˈ·/ *v* *catch fire
tutuşturmak /···ˈ·/ *v* *set fire, ignite
tuval /·ˈ·/ *n* canvas
tuvalet /··ˈ·/ *n* toilet; woman's evening dress; ~ **kâğıdı** toilet paper
tuz *n* salt
tuzak /·ˈ·/ *n* trap;
tuzağa düşmek *fall into a trap
tuzlamak /··ˈ·/ *v* salt, pack in salt
tuzlu /·ˈ·/ *adj* salty
tuzluk /·ˈ·/ *n* saltcellar, saltshaker

tuzruhu /'···/ *n* household hydrochloric acid
tuzsuz /·'·/ *adj* unsalted
tüberküloz /···'·/ *n* tuberculosis
tüccar /·'·/ *n* merchant
tüfek /·'·/ *n* gun, rifle
tükenmek /··'·/ *v* *come to an end; *be exhausted; *run out
tükenmez kalem /··'· ··/ ball-point pen, Biro
tüketici /···'·/ *n* consumer
tüketim /··'·/ *n* consumption
tüketmek /··'·/ *v* consume, use up
tükürmek /··'·/ *v* *spit
tükürük /··'·/ *n* spittle, spit
tül *n* tulle
tülbent /·'·/ *n* gauze
tüm *adj* whole; total
tümen /·'·/ *adj* division
tümör /·'·/ *n* tumor
tümsek /·'·/ *n* small mound; protuberance
tünek /·'·/ *n* perch
tünel /·'·/ *n* tunnel
tünemek /··'·/ *v* perch
tüp *n* tube
türbe /·'·/ *n* tomb, mausoleum
türedi /··'·/ *n* parvenu, upstart
türemek /··'·/ *v* *spring up, *come into existence; appear; *be derived
türetmek /··'·/ *v* *make up, create; derive
Türk *n* Turk; *adj* Turkish
Türkçe /'··/ *n* Turkish language
Türkiye /'···/ Turkey
türkü /·'·/ *n* folk song
türlü /·'·/ *adj* sort, kind; *n* mixed vegetable stew
tütmek /·'·/ *n* smoke; fume
tütsü /·'·/ *n* incense, smoke
tütsülemek /···'·/ *v* smoke; fumigate
tüttürmek /··'·/ *v* smoke
tütün /·'·/ *n* tobacco
tüy *n* feather, down; hair; ~ **gibi** very light
tüylenmek /··'·/ *v* *grow feathers; *become hairy
tüzük /·'·/ *n* regulations, statutes

U

ucuz /·'·/ *adj* inexpensive, cheap
ucuzlamak /···'·/ *v* *get cheap, *go down in price
ucuzluk /··'·/ *n* cheapness; sale
uç *n* point, tip; end; ~ **uca** end to end; barely; **ucunu kaçırmak** *lose the thread of
uçak /·'·/ *n* airplane
uçaksavar /···'·/ *n* antiaircraft
uçan daire /·'· ···/ flying saucer
uçarı /··'·/ *adj* dissolute
uçmak /·'·/ *v* *fly; evaporate; *go with great speed
uçsuz bucaksız /·'· ···/ *adj* immense, vast
uçucu /··'·/ *adj* flying; volatile
uçuçböceği /·'····/ *n* ladybird
uçuk /·'·/ *adj* pale, faded
uçurmak /··'·/ *v* cause to fly; *fly
uçurtma /··'·/ *n* kite
uçurum /··'·/ *n* cliff, abyss, precipice
uçuş /·'·/ *n* flying; flight
uçuşmak /··'·/ *v* *fly about
ufak /·'·/ *adj* small, little; ~ **para** change; ~ **tefek** small and short; unimportant; ~ ~ in small pieces
ufalamak /···'·/ *v* crumble
ufalmak /··'·/ *v* *become smaller, shorten, *shrink
ufuk /·'·/ *n* horizon
uğrak /·'·/ *n* much frequented place

uğramak /··ˈ·/ *v* drop in; stop by; call in
uğraş /·ˈ·/ *n* struggle; occupation
uğraşmak /··ˈ·/ *v* struggle, *strive; work at
uğuldamak /···ˈ·/ *v* hum, buzz
uğultu /··ˈ·/ *n* humming, buzzing noise
uğur[1] /·ˈ·/ *n* good omen; good luck; ~ **getirmek** *bring good luck
uğur[2] /·ˈ·/ *n* purpose, aim; **uğruna** for the sake of
uğurlamak /···ˈ·/ *v* *see someone off
uğurlu /··ˈ·/ *adj* lucky, auspicious
uğursuz /··ˈ·/ *adj* inauspicious, ill-omened; unfortunate
ukala /··ˈ–/ *n* wiseacre, smart aleck, know-it-all
ulak /·ˈ·/ *n* courier, messenger
ulaşım /··ˈ·/ *n* communication; contact; transport
ulaşmak /··ˈ·/ *v* reach
ulaştırma /···ˈ·/ *n* communication
ulaştırmak /···ˈ·/ *v* convey, communicate; transport
ulu /·ˈ·/ *adj* great; exalted
uluorta /·ˈ···/ *adv* rashly, recklessly, without thinking
ulus /·ˈ·/ *n* nation, people
ulusal /··ˈ·/ *adj* national
uluslararası /··ˈ····/ *adj* international
ummak /·ˈ·/ *v* hope, hope for; expect
umum /·ˈ·/ *adj* general, all; *n* the public, people
umumi /·–ˈ–/ *adj* general, public
umursamak /···ˈ·/ *v* *be concerned about; care
umut /·ˈ·/ *n* hope, expectation; ~ **etmek** hope; ~ **vermek** *give hope; **umudunu kesmek** *give up hope of; **umuduyla** in the hope of
umutlu /··ˈ·/ *adj* hopeful
umutsuz /··ˈ·/ *adj* hopeless
un *n* flour
unlu /·ˈ·/ *adj* floury
unutkan /··ˈ·/ *adj* forgetful
unutkanlık /···ˈ·/ *n* forgetfulness
unutmak /··ˈ·/ *v* *forget
unvan /·ˈ·/ *n* title
ur *n* tumor
urgan /·ˈ·/ *n* rope
usanç /·ˈ·/ *n* boredom; ~ **vermek** bore, disgust
usandırıcı /····ˈ·/ *adj* boring, tedious
usandırmak /···ˈ·/ *v* bore, sicken
usanmak /··ˈ·/ *v* *be fed up; *be disgusted
uskumru /·ˈ··/ *n* mackerel
uslanmak /··ˈ·/ *v* *become sensible, listen to reason
uslu /·ˈ·/ *adj* well-behaved, good
usta /·ˈ·/ *n* craftsman; master workman; *adj* skilled
ustabaşı /·ˈ···/ *n* foreman
ustaca /·ˈ··/ *adv* skillfully
ustalık /··ˈ·/ *n* mastery, skill
ustura /·ˈ··/ *n* straight razor
usul /·ˈ·/ *n* method; procedure
usulca /·ˈ··/ *adv* slowly, gently
usulsüz /··ˈ·/ *adj* unmethodical; irregular; contrary to rules
uşak /·ˈ·/ *n* male servant
utanç /·ˈ·/ *n* shame
utandırmak /···ˈ·/ *v* *make ashamed
utangaç /··ˈ·/ *adj* shy, bashful, timid
utanmak /··ˈ·/ *v* *be ashamed, *feel ashamed
utanmaz /··ˈ·/ *adj* shameless, impudent
uvertür /··ˈ·/ *n* overture

uyandırmak /···'·/ *v* awaken; arouse
uyanık /··'·/ *adj* awake; wide awake, sharp
uyarı /··'·/ *n* warning
uyarıcı /···'·/ *n* stimulant
uyarmak /··'·/ *v* stimulate, excite
uydu /·'·/ *n* satellite
uydurma /··'·/ *adj* made-up, false; invented
uydurmak /··'·/ *v* invent; *make up
uyduruk /··'·/ *adj* made-up
uygar /·'·/ *adj* civilized
uygarlaşmak /···'·/ *v* *become civilized
uygarlık /··'·/ *n* civilization
uygulamak /···'·/ *v* apply
uygulamalı /····'·/ *adj* practical, applied
uygun /·'·/ *adj* appropriate, suitable; reasonable; favorable; ~ **bulmak** *see fit, *find satisfactory
uygunluk /··'·/ *n* appropriateness; conformity
uygunsuz /··'·/ *adj* unsuitable; improper; inappropriate
uyku /·'·/ *n* sleep; ~ **tutmamak** *be unable to get to sleep; **uykusu ağır** heavy sleeper; **uykusu gelmek** *feel sleepy; **uykusu kaçmak** *lose one's sleep; **uykuya dalmak** *fall asleep
uykulu /··'·/ *adj* sleepy
uykusuz /··'·/ *adj* sleepless
uykusuzluk /···'·/ *n* sleeplessness; insomnia
uyluk /·'·/ *n* thigh
uymak /·'·/ *v* suit; fit; agree with; adapt oneself; follow
uyruk /·'·/ *n* subject, citizen
uyruklu /··'·/ *adj* citizen of
uyrukluk /··'·/ *n* citizenship
uysal /·'·/ *adj* docile, easygoing
uyuklamak /···'·/ *v* doze
uyum /·'·/ *n* accord, harmony
uyumak /··'·/ *v* *sleep; *go to sleep
uyumlu /··'·/ *adj* harmonious
uyumsuz /··'·/ *adj* inharmonious
uyurgezer /···'·/ *n* sleepwalker
uyuşmak /··'·/ *v* *get along together; *be compatible; reach an agreement; *become numb
uyuşmazlık /···'·/ *n* disagreement; incompatibility
uyuşturmak /···'·/ *v* cause to come to an agreement; reconcile; anesthetize
uyuşturucu /····'·/ *n* narcotic; anesthetic; ~ **maddeler** narcotics
uyuşuk /··'·/ *adj* numbed; sluggish; insensible
uyuşum /··'·/ *n* harmony
uyutmak /··'·/ *v* *put to sleep; deceive, fool
uyuz /·'·/ *n* scab; itch; mange
uzak /·'·/ *adj* far, distant, remote
uzaklaşmak /···'·/ *v* *go away; *become alienated
uzaklaştırmak /····'·/ *v* *take away, remove
uzaklık /··'·/ *n* distance; remoteness
uzamak /··'·/ *v* extend, stretch, lengthen; drag on
uzay /·'·/ *n* space
uzaygemisi /·'····/ *n* spaceship
uzlaşma /··'·/ *n* reconciliation
uzlaşmak /··'·/ *v* *come to an agreement, *be reconciled
uzman /·'·/ *n* specialist, expert
uzmanlık /··'·/ *n* specialization
uzun /·'·/ *adj* long; tall; ~ **atlama** long jump; ~ **boylu** tall
uzunluk /··'·/ *n* length

Ü

ücra /·ˈ–/ *adj* out-of-the-way, remote
ücret /·ˈ·/ *n* wage, pay; cost, price; charge
ücretli /··ˈ·/ *adj* paid, salaried
ücretsiz /··ˈ·/ *adj* free; unpaid
üç *num* three; ~ **aşağı beş yukarı** approximately; ~ **boyutlu** three-dimensional
üçgen /·ˈ·/ *n* triangle; *adj* triangular
üçkâğıtçı /···ˈ·/ *n* crook, swindler
üçüncü /··ˈ·/ *num* third
üçüz /·ˈ·/ *adj* triplet
üflemek /··ˈ·/ *v* *blow, puff; *blow out
üfürmek /··ˈ·/ *v* *blow, puff, *blow away
ülke /·ˈ·/ *n* country; territory
ülkü /·ˈ·/ *n* ideal
ülkücü /··ˈ·/ *n* idealist
ülser /·ˈ·/ *n* ulcer
ümit /·ˈ·/ *n* hope; ~ **etmek** hope; expect
ümitlenmek /···ˈ·/ *v* *be hopeful
ümitli /··ˈ·/ *adj* hopeful
ümitsiz /··ˈ·/ *adj* hopeless
ün *n* fame, reputation; ~ **kazanmak** *become famous
üniforma /··ˈ··/ *n* uniform
ünite /·ˈ··/ *n* unit
üniversite /··ˈ···/ *n* university
ünlü /·ˈ·/ *adj* famous; *n* vowel
ünsüz /·ˈ·/ *adj* unknown; *n* consonant
Ürdün /ˈ··/ Jordan
Ürdünlü /ˈ···/ *adj, n* Jordanian
üreme /··ˈ·/ *n* reproduction
üremek /··ˈ·/ *v* reproduce; multiply, increase
üretici /···ˈ·/ *n* producer; *adj* productive
üretim /··ˈ·/ *n* production
üretmek /··ˈ·/ *v* produce; *breed, raise
ürkek /·ˈ·/ *adj* timid, fearful; ~ ~ timidly
ürkmek /·ˈ·/ *v* *be frightened; *be scared
ürkütmek /··ˈ·/ *v* frighten, scare
ürpermek /··ˈ·/ *v* shudder, shiver
ürperti /··ˈ·/ *n* shudder, shiver
ürün /·ˈ·/ *n* product, produce
üs *n* base; exponent; military installation
üslup /·ˈ·/ *n* style
üst *n* upper side, upper part; superior; *adj* upper, uppermost; ~ **baş** clothes; **üstünde** on, over; ~ **üste** one on top of the other
üstat /·ˈ·/ *n* master, expert
üsteğmen /ˈ···/ *n* first lieutenant
üstelemek /···ˈ·/ *v* dwell on, insist
üstelik /ˈ···/ *adv* furthermore, in addition
üstgeçit /ˈ···/ *n* overpass
üstlenmek /··ˈ·/ *v* *take on, *undertake
üstün /·ˈ·/ *adj* superior
üstünkörü /·ˈ···/ *adj* superficial; *adv* superficially
üstünlük /··ˈ·/ *n* superiority
üşengeç /··ˈ·/ *adj* lazy
üşenmek /··ˈ·/ *v* *be too lazy to do something
üşümek /··ˈ·/ *v* *feel cold, *be cold
üşüşmek /··ˈ·/ *v* flock together, crowd
üşütmek /··ˈ·/ *v* cause to feel cold; *catch cold
ütü /·ˈ·/ *n* iron; ironing
ütücü /··ˈ·/ *n* ironer
ütülemek /···ˈ·/ *v* iron

ütülü /··ˈ·/ *adj* ironed
üvey /·ˈ·/ *adj* step-; ~ **anne** stepmother; ~ **baba** stepfather
üye /·ˈ·/ *n* member
üyelik /··ˈ·/ *n* membership
üzere /··ˈ·/ *prep* on condition of, at the point of; just about to
üzerinde /···ˈ·/ *prep* on, over; ~ **durmak** consider; dwell on
üzerine /···ˈ·/ *prep* onto, over; about, on; ~ **almak** *undertake
üzgün /·ˈ·/ *adj* sad, anxious, sorry
üzgünlük /··ˈ·/ *n* sadness, anxiety
üzmek /·ˈ·/ *v* trouble, bother; sadden, worry
üzücü /··ˈ·/ *adj* depressing, troubling
üzülmek /··ˈ·/ *v* *be sorry, regret, *be worried
üzüm /·ˈ·/ *n* grape
üzüntü /··ˈ·/ *n* sadness; anxiety; sorrow
üzüntülü /···ˈ·/ *adj* worried, anxious; unhappy

V

vaat /·ˈ·/ *n* promise; ~ **etmek** promise
vaaz /·ˈ·/ *n* sermon
vade /–ˈ·/ *n* due date; **vadesi geçmek** *be overdue; **vadesi gelmek** *fall due
vadi /–ˈ·/ *n* valley
vaftiz /·ˈ·/ *n* baptism; ~ **etmek** baptize
vagon /·ˈ·/ *n* railway car
vah oh! alas!; ~ ~ ! what a pity!; too bad!
vahim /·ˈ·/ *adj* grave, serious
vahşet /·ˈ·/ *n* atrocity, savagery
vahşi /·ˈ–/ *adj* savage, wild; brutal
vahşice /·ˈ–·/ *adv* brutally; wildly, barbarously
vahşilik /·–ˈ·/ *n* savageness; brutality
vaiz /–ˈ·/ *n* preacher
vakfetmek /ˈ···/ *v* devote, dedicate
vakıf /·ˈ·/ *n* foundation
vakit /·ˈ·/ *n* time; hour; season; ~ **geçirmek** pass the time
vakitli /··ˈ·/ *adj* opportune, timely
vakitsiz /··ˈ·/ *adj* unseasonable, untimely
vaktiyle /·ˈ··/ *adv* in the past, once
vali /–ˈ·/ *n* governor
valide /–·ˈ·/ *n* mother
valiz /·ˈ·/ *n* suitcase
vallahi /ˈ·–·/ by God; I swear it is so
vals *n* waltz
vampir /·ˈ·/ *n* vampire
vanilya /·ˈ··/ *n* vanilla
vantilatör /···ˈ·/ *n* ventilator; fan
vantuz /·ˈ·/ *n* sucker
vapur /·ˈ·/ *n* steamship, ferry
var *adj* existent, available; *v* there is, there are; ~ **etmek** create; ~ **olmak** exist
vardiya /ˈ···/ *n* watch; shift
varış /·ˈ·/ *n* arrival
varil /·ˈ·/ *n* barrel, cask
varis /·ˈ·/ *n* varicose veins
vâris /–ˈ·/ *n* heir, inheritor
varlık /·ˈ·/ *n* existence, presence; riches, wealth; ~ **göstermek** *make one's presence felt
varlıklı /··ˈ·/ *adj* wealthy
varmak /·ˈ·/ *v* arrive at; *get to; reach; approach
varsaymak /ˈ···/ *v* suppose
vasıf /·ˈ·/ *n* quality, characteristic
vasıflı /··ˈ·/ *adj* qualified, skilled
vasıfsız /··ˈ·/ *adj* unqualified, unskilled
vasıta /–·ˈ·/ *n* means; vehicle
vasıtasıyla /–··ˈ··/ *adv* by means of
vasıtasız /–··ˈ·/ *adj* direct, without

intermediary
vasi /·ˈ–/ *n* guardian; executor
vasiyet /··ˈ·/ *n* will, testament; ~ **etmek** bequeath
vasiyetname /···–ˈ·/ *n* written will
vatan /·ˈ·/ *n* native country, motherland
vatandaş /··ˈ·/ *n* citizen, fellow countryman
vatandaşlık /···ˈ·/ *n* citizenship
vazgeçmek /ˈ···/ *v* *quit, *give up, abandon
vazife /·–ˈ·/ *n* duty, task; obligation
vazifeli /·–·ˈ·/ *adj* in charge, on duty
vaziyet /··ˈ·/ *n* position, situation; attitude
vazo /ˈ··/ *n* vase
ve *conj* and
veba /·ˈ–/ *n* plague, pestilence
vecize /·–ˈ·/ *n* saying, maxim
veda /·ˈ–/ *n* farewell; ~ **etmek** *say farewell, *say good-bye
vedalaşmak /·–ˈ·/ *v* *say good-bye to each other
vefa /·ˈ–/ *n* loyalty, faithfulness
vefalı /·–ˈ·/ *adj* faithful, loyal
vefasız /·–ˈ·/ *adj* disloyal, faithless
vefat /·ˈ·/ *n* death, decease; ~ **etmek** die, decease
vekâlet /·–ˈ·/ *n* attorneyship, procuration; ~ **etmek** represent somebody, deputize; ~ **vermek** *give the power of attorney
vekâleten /·ˈ–··/ *adv* by proxy
vekâletname /·–·–ˈ·/ *n* proxy, power of attorney
vekil /·ˈ·/ *n* agent, representative; deputy
veli /·ˈ–/ *n* guardian; protector; saint
veliaht /·–ˈ·/ *n* heir to the throne
Venezüella /···ˈ··/ Venezuela
Venezüellalı /···ˈ···/ *adj, n* Venezuelan
veraset /·–ˈ·/ *n* inheritance
verem /·ˈ·/ *n* tuberculosis
veremli /··ˈ·/ *adj* tuberculous
veresiye /···ˈ·/ *adj* on credit
vergi /·ˈ·/ *n* tax, duty; **vergiye tabi** taxable
vergilendirmek /····ˈ·/ *v* tax
veri /·ˈ·/ *n* datum, information
verici /··ˈ·/ *n* transmitter
verim /·ˈ·/ *n* output; return; efficiency
verimli /··ˈ·/ *adj* productive
verimlilik /···ˈ·/ *n* productivity
verimsiz /··ˈ·/ *adj* fruitless
veriştirmek /···ˈ·/ *v* *swear at
vermek /·ˈ·/ *v* *give, hand
vernik /·ˈ·/ *n* varnish
verniklemek /···ˈ·/ *v* varnish
vesaire, vs. /·ˈ–··/ et cetera, etc.
vesait /·–ˈ·/ *n* means; vehicles
vesile /·–ˈ·/ *n* means; cause; opportunity, occasion
vestiyer /··ˈ·/ *n* cloakroom
vesvese /··ˈ·/ *n* anxiety, misgivings; ~ **etmek** *be anxious, *have misgivings
veteriner /···ˈ·/ *n* veterinarian
veya /ˈ·– / *conj* or
veyahut /·ˈ–·/ *conj* or
vezne /·ˈ·/ *n* cashier's desk
veznedar /··ˈ·/ *n* cashier, treasurer
vınlamak /··ˈ·/ *v* buzz; complain endlessly
vızıldamak /···ˈ·/ *v* buzz
vicdan /·ˈ·/ *n* conscience; ~ **azabı** pangs of conscience
vicdanen /·ˈ–·/ *adv* in accordance with one's conscience
vicdanlı /··ˈ·/ *adj* honest, conscientious
vicdansız /··ˈ·/ *adj* remorseless, unscrupulous

vida /'··/ *n* screw
vidalamak /'····/ *v* screw down
vidalı /'···/ *adj* fastened with screws
vilayet /·–'·/ *n* province
vinç *n* crane, winch
viraj /·'·/ *n* bend, curve
virgül /·'·/ *n* comma
viski /'··/ *n* whiskey
vişne /'··/ *n* sour cherry, morello
vites /·'·/ *n* gear; ~ **değiştirmek** shift gears; ~ **kolu** gearshift; **viteste** in gear
vitrin /·'·/ *n* shop window
vize /'··/ *n* visa
vizite /·'··/ *n* medical visit; doctor's fee
vizon /·'·/ *n* mink
voleybol /·'··/ *n* volleyball
volt *n* volt
votka /'··/ *n* vodka
vurdumduymaz /···'·/ *adj* thick-skinned, insensitive
vurgu /·'·/ *n* stress, accent
vurgulamak /···'·/ *v* stress, emphasize
vurgulu /··'·/ *adj* accented, stressed
vurgun /·'·/ *adj* in love with; struck; *n* killing; good stroke of business; ~ **vurmak** *make a killing, pull a deal
vurguncu /··'·/ *n* profiteer, speculator
vurgunculuk /···'·/ *n* speculation, profiteering
vurgusuz /··'·/ *adj* unstressed
vurmak /·'·/ *v* *hit, *strike, knock
vurulmak /··'·/ *v* *be shot, *be hit; *fall in love with
vuruş /·'·/ *n* blow, hit, stroke; beat
vuruşmak /··'·/ *v* *strike one another; *have a fight, *hit each other
vücut /·'·/ *n* human body; ~ **bulmak** *come into existence; **vücuda getirmek** *bring into being, create

ya yes, yeah, uh-huh; of course; but what if; **ya . . . ya . . .** either . . . or . . .
yaban /·'·/ *n* wilderness
yabanarısı /·'····/ *n* wasp
yabancı /··'·/ *n* stranger, foreigner; *adj* foreign; ~ **dil** foreign language; **yabancısı olmak** *be a stranger to
yabancılaşma /····'·/ *n* estrangement, alienation
yabandomuzu /·'····/ *n* boar
yabanıl /··'·/ *adj* wild; primitive; undomesticated
yabani /·–'–/ *adj* untamed, wild; unmannerly
yabansı /··'·/ *adj* strange, weird
yabansımak /···'·/ *v* *find strange
yad *adj* strange; ~ **elde** in a foreign land
yâd /–/ *n* remembrance, mention; ~ **etmek** call to mind; mention
yadırgamak /···'·/ *v* *find strange
yadigâr /–·'–/ *n* souvenir
yadsımak /··'·/ *v* deny, reject
yafta /·'·/ *n* label
yağ *n* oil, fat; grease
yağış /·'·/ *n* rain, precipitation
yağışlı /··'·/ *adj* rainy, snowy
yağışsız /··'·/ *adj* dry, arid
yağız /·'·/ *adj* black; swarthy
yağlamak /··'·/ *v* oil, grease, lubricate; flatter
yağlı /·'·/ *adj* fat; greasy, oily; lucrative, profitable; ~ **müşteri** profitable customer

yağlıboya /·ˈ···/ *n* oil paint
yağma /·ˈ·/ *n* booty, loot; pillage; ~ **etmek** plunder, pillage
yağmacılık /···ˈ·/ *n* pillage, plundering
yağmak /·ˈ·/ *v* rain; *be poured out in great quantity
yağmalamak /···ˈ·/ *v* pillage, plunder
yağmur /·ˈ·/ *n* rain; ~ **boşanmak** pour heavily; ~ **yağmak** rain
yağmurlu /··ˈ·/ *adj* rainy, wet
yağmurluk /··ˈ·/ *n* raincoat
yağmursuz /··ˈ·/ *adj* dry
yağsız /·ˈ·/ *adj* without fat *or* oil; skim
yahudi /··ˈ·/ *n* Jew; *adj* Jewish
yahut /ˈ–·/ *conj* or; or else; otherwise
yaka /·ˈ·/ *n* collar; shore, side; ~ **paça** by the head and ears, by force; ~ **silkmek** *be fed up (with); **yakayı kurtarmak** escape
yakacak /··ˈ·/ *n* fuel
yakalamak /···ˈ·/ *v* *catch, seize
yakamoz /··ˈ·/ *n* phosphorescence
yakarış /··ˈ·/ *n* entreaty, begging
yakarmak /··ˈ·/ *v* entreat, implore
yakasız /··ˈ·/ *adj* collarless
yakı /·ˈ·/ *n* plaster; cautery
yakıcı /··ˈ·/ *adj* burning
yakın /·ˈ·/ *adj* near, close; *n* nearby place; *adv* closely; ~ **akraba** close relative; **yakında** soon; nearby
yakınlaşmak /···ˈ·/ *v* *be near, approach; *become friends
yakınlık /··ˈ·/ *n* closeness; ~ **göstermek** behave warmly; *be friendly
yakınmak /··ˈ·/ *v* complain
yakışık /··ˈ·/ *n* suitability
yakışıklı /···ˈ·/ *adj* handsome, comely
yakışıksız /···ˈ·/ *adj* unsuitable, unbecoming
yakışmak /··ˈ·/ *v* *be suitable *or* becoming
yakıştırmak /···ˈ·/ *v* *make something suitable; ascribe, impute
yakıt /·ˈ·/ *n* fuel
yaklaşık /··ˈ·/ *adj* approximate
yaklaşmak /··ˈ·/ *v* approach; *come near
yaklaştırmak /···ˈ·/ *v* *bring near
yakmak /·ˈ·/ *v* burn; *set on fire; *light
yakut /–ˈ·/ *n* ruby
yalak /·ˈ·/ *n* trough
yalamak /··ˈ·/ *v* lick
yalan /·ˈ·/ *n* lie; *adj* false, untrue; ~ **dolan** lies and frauds; ~ **söylemek** lie; ~ **yanlış** false; carelessly
yalancı /··ˈ·/ *n* liar; *adj* imitated; deceitful; ~ **çıkarmak** *make someone look a liar; ~ **şahit** false witness
yalancıktan /···ˈ·/ *adv* in pretense, in play; not meaning it
yalancılık /···ˈ·/ *n* lying
yalandan /··ˈ·/ *adv* not seriously, only for appearance
yalanlamak /···ˈ·/ *v* deny, contradict
yalanmak /··ˈ·/ *v* lick oneself
yalaz /·ˈ·/ *n* flame
yalçın /·ˈ·/ *adj* rugged; steep
yaldız /·ˈ·/ *n* gilding
yaldızlamak /···ˈ·/ *v* gild; *put a false finish
yaldızlı /··ˈ·/ *adj* gilt; falsely adorned
yalı /·ˈ·/ *n* shore; beach; waterside residence; ~ **boyu** shore, beach
yalın /·ˈ·/ *adj* bare, simple
yalınayak /·ˈ···/ *adj* barefoot
yalıtmak /··ˈ·/ *v* insulate
yalnız[1] /·ˈ·/ *adj* alone, lonely; *adv* only, solely; ~ **başına** alone, by oneself
yalnız[2] /ˈ··/ *conj* but, however

yalnızlık /··ˈ·/ *n* loneliness
yaltaklanmak /···ˈ·/ *v* fawn, cringe
yalvarmak /··ˈ·/ *v* beg, entreat, implore
yama /·ˈ·/ *n* patch
yamaç /·ˈ·/ *n* slope; side
yamak /·ˈ·/ *n* assistant, apprentice
yamalamak /···ˈ·/ *v* patch
yamalı /··ˈ·/ *adj* patched
yamamak /··ˈ·/ *v* patch
yaman /·ˈ·/ *adj* smart, capable; violent, strong
yamrı yumru /·ˈ· ··/ *adj* uneven and lumpy
yamuk /·ˈ·/ *adj* bent, crooked; lopsided
yamyam /·ˈ·/ *n* cannibal
yamyamlık /··ˈ·/ *n* cannibalism
yamyassı /ˈ···/ *adj* very flat
yan *n* side; direction; ~ **bakmak** look askance; ~ **çizmek** shirk, evade; ~ ~ sideways, sidelong; ~ **yana** side by side; **yanı sıra** beside; together; in addition; **yanlamasına** sideways
yanak /·ˈ·/ *n* cheek
yanardağ /·ˈ··/ *n* volcano
yanaşık /··ˈ·/ *adj* adjacent
yanaşıklık /···ˈ·/ *n* contiguity
yanaşılmaz /···ˈ·/ *adj* unapproachable, inaccesible
yanaşmak /··ˈ·/ *v* *draw near, approach; *draw up alongside
yandaş /·ˈ·/ *n* supporter
yangın /·ˈ·/ *n* fire; ~ **çıkarmak** start a fire; **yangını söndürmek** *put out the fire
yanık /·ˈ·/ *adj* burnt; *n* burn; ~ **kokmak** *smell of burning
yanılgı /··ˈ·/ *n* mistake, error
yanılmak /··ˈ·/ *v* *make a mistake, *go wrong, *be mistaken
yanılmaz /··ˈ·/ *adj* infallible
yanıltmaca /···ˈ·/ *n* riddle based on a pun; fallacy
yanıltmak /··ˈ·/ *v* *mislead
yanıt /·ˈ·/ *n* answer
yani /ˈ–/ *conj* that is, namely, in other works, in short
yankesici /···ˈ·/ *n* pickpocket
yankı /·ˈ·/ *n* echo; reaction
yanlamak /··ˈ·/ *v* move sideways
yanlı /·ˈ·/ *adj* subjective
yanlış /·ˈ·/ *n* error, mistake; *adj* incorrect, wrong; ~ **kapı çalmak** bark up the wrong tree; **yanlışını çıkarmak** *find out someone's mistake
yanlışlık /··ˈ·/ *n* mistake, error
yanlışlıkla /··ˈ··/ *adv* by mistake
yanmak /·ˈ·/ *v* *burn, *be on fire; *be scorched; *be ruined; **yanıp tutuşmak** *burn with great passion
yansılamak /···ˈ·/ *v* reflect; imitate
yansıma /··ˈ·/ *n* reflection; reflex
yansımak /··ˈ·/ *v* *be reflected
yapağı /··ˈ·/ *n* wool
yapay /·ˈ·/ *adj* artificial
yapayalnız /·ˈ···/ *adj* absolutely alone
yapı /·ˈ·/ *n* building; construction
yapılı /··ˈ·/ *adj* well-built
yapılış /··ˈ·/ *n* structure
yapım /·ˈ·/ *n* making, building; manufacture, production
yapımevi /·ˈ···/ *n* workshop, factory
yapışık /··ˈ·/ *adj* stuck on, joined together; adhering
yapışkan /··ˈ·/ *adj* sticky, adhesive; persistent, importunate
yapışkanlık /···ˈ·/ *n* stickiness; pertinacity
yapışma /··ˈ·/ *n* sticking, clinging
yapışmak /··ˈ·/ *v* *stick, adhere
yapıştırmak /···ˈ·/ *v* *stick on, glue on
yapış yapış /·ˈ· ··/ *adj* sticky
yapıt /·ˈ·/ *n* work of art *or* literature, creation

yapma /·ˈ·/ *n* doing, making; *adj* artificial
yapmacık /··ˈ·/ *adj* artificial, affected, put on; false
yapmak /·ˈ·/ *v* *do; *make; construct, *build; arrange
yaprak /·ˈ·/ *n* leaf; sheet of paper
yaptırım /··ˈ·/ *n* sanction
yâr /–/ *n* lover; ~ **olmak** assist, help
yar *n* precipice
yara /·ˈ·/ *n* wound; injury; ~ **açmak** wound; *hurt
yaradan /··ˈ·/ *n* the Creator
yaradılış /···ˈ·/ *n* creation; nature, temperament
yaralamak /···ˈ·/ *v* wound
yaralanmak /···ˈ·/ *v* *be wounded
yaralı /··ˈ·/ *adj* wounded
yaramak /··ˈ·/ *v* *be of use; *do good; benefit
yaramaz /··ˈ·/ *adj* useless; naughty
yaranma /··ˈ·/ *n* fawning; polite attention
yaranmak /··ˈ·/ *v* curry favor, *pay polite attention
yarar /·ˈ·/ *n* use; advantage; **yararı olmak** help, benefit
yararlı /··ˈ·/ *adj* useful
yararsız /··ˈ·/ *adj* useless
yarasa /·ˈ··/ *n* bat
yaraşmak /··ˈ·/ *v* *be suitable, *become; *be pleasing
yaraştırmak /···ˈ·/ *v* *make suitable; deem suitable
yaratıcı /···ˈ·/ *adj* creative; *n* creator
yaratık /··ˈ·/ *n* creature
yaratmak /··ˈ·/ *v* create; produce
yarbay /·ˈ·/ *n* lieutenant colonel
yarda /·ˈ·/ *n* yard
yardakçı /··ˈ·/ *n* accomplice
yardakçılık /···ˈ·/ *n* complicity
yardım /·ˈ·/ *n* help, aid, assistance; ~ **etmek** help, aid, assist
yardımcı /··ˈ·/ *n* helper, assistant
yardımlaşmak /···ˈ·/ *v* help one another
yardımsever /···ˈ·/ *adj* benevolent, charitable
yargı /·ˈ·/ *n* judgment
yargıç /·ˈ·/ *n* judge
yargılamak /···ˈ·/ *v* try; judge
yarı /·ˈ·/ *adj* half; **yarıda bırakmak** interrupt, discontinue; **yarıda kalmak** *be left half-finished; ~ **yolda** halfway
yarıçap /·ˈ··/ *n* radius
yarık /·ˈ·/ *adj* split; *n* crack, fissure
yarıküre /·ˈ···/ *n* hemisphere
yarılamak /···ˈ·/ *v* *be halfway through; half finish
yarım /·ˈ·/ *adj* half; incomplete; invalid; ~ **ağızla** halfheartedly; ~ **saat** half an hour; **yarımda** at half past twelve
yarımada /·ˈ···/ *n* peninsula
yarımküre /·ˈ···/ *n* hemisphere
yarın /ˈ–·/ *n* tomorrow; ~ **akşam** tomorrow night **yarınki** of tomorrow
yarış /·ˈ·/ *n* race; competition
yarışçı /··ˈ·/ *n* competitor
yarışma /··ˈ·/ *n* competition
yarışmak /··ˈ·/ *v* race; compete
yarma /·ˈ·/ *n* act of splitting; fissure; breakthrough
yarmak /·ˈ·/ *v* *split; *break through; *cut
yas *n* mourning; ~ **tutmak** *v* mourn
yasa /·ˈ·/ *n* law
yasadışı /·ˈ···/ *adj* illegal
yasak /·ˈ·/ *n* prohibition; *adj* forbidden, prohibited; ~ **etmek** *forbid
yasaklamak /···ˈ·/ *v* prohibit,

*forbid
yasal /·ˈ·/ *adj* legal
yasallaştırmak /····ˈ·/ *v* legalize
yasama /··ˈ·/ *n* legislation; ~ **dokunulmazlığı** legislative immunity; ~ **gücü** legislative power
yasemin /–·ˈ·/ *n* jasmine
yaslamak /··ˈ·/ *v* prop, *lean
yaslanmak /··ˈ·/ *v* *lean against
yaslı /·ˈ·/ *adj* in mourning
yassı /·ˈ·/ *adj* flat and wide
yastık /·ˈ·/ *n* pillow; cushion; pad; ~ **kılıfı** pillowcase
yaş[1] *adj* wet, damp, moist; *n* tear; ~ **tahtaya basmak** *be cheated
yaş[2] *n* age; ~ **günü** birthday; . . . **yaşında** in his . . .th year, . . . years old
yaşam /·ˈ·/ *n* life
yaşamak /··ˈ·/ *v* live, experience
yaşantı /··ˈ·/ *n* life style, experience
yaşarmak /··ˈ·/ *v* *fill with tears
yaşatmak /··ˈ·/ *v* cause to live; *keep alive
yaşayış /··ˈ·/ *n* manner of living; life; livelihood
yaşıt /·ˈ·/ *adj* of the same age
yaşlanmak /··ˈ·/ *v* *grow old, age
yaşlı /·ˈ·/ *adj* old; ~ **başlı** of mature years
yaşlıca /··ˈ·/ *adj* oldish
yaşlılık /··ˈ·/ *n* old age
yaşmak /·ˈ·/ *n* veil
yaşmaklı /··ˈ·/ *adj* veiled
yat *n* yacht
yatak /·ˈ·/ *n* bed; ~ **çarşafı** bed sheet; ~ **odası** bedroom; ~ **takımı** set of bedding
yatakhane /··–ˈ·/ *n* dormitory
yataklı /··ˈ·/ *adj* having beds; ~ **vagon** sleeping car
yatalak /··ˈ·/ *adj* bedridden
yatay /·ˈ·/ *adj* horizontal
yatık /·ˈ·/ *adj* leaning to one side
yatırım /··ˈ·/ *n* investment; ~ **yapmak** *make an investment
yatırmak /··ˈ·/ *v* *put to bed, *lay down; deposit; invest
yatışmak /··ˈ·/ *v* calm down, cool down
yatıştırmak /···ˈ·/ *v* calm, tranquilize
yatkın /·ˈ·/ *adj* inclined, predisposed
yatkınlık /··ˈ·/ *n* aptness, inclination; familiarity
yatmak /·ˈ·/ *v* *lie down; *go to bed; *be in bed
yavan /·ˈ·/ *adj* plain, tasteless; unpleasant
yavanlaşmak /···ˈ·/ *v* *become tasteless *or* insipid
yavaş /·ˈ·/ *adj* slow; gentle, soft; docile
yavaşça /·ˈ··/ *adv* slowly, gently
yavaşlamak /···ˈ·/ *v* *become slow *or* mild; slow down
yavaşlık /··ˈ·/ *n* slowness; gentleness
yaver /–ˈ·/ *n* helper, assistant; aide-de-camp, adjutant
yavru /·ˈ·/ *n* young; cub
yavrulamak /···ˈ·/ *v* *bring forth young
yay *n* bow; spring; arc
yaya /·ˈ·/ *n* walker, pedestrian; *adv* on foot; ~ **geçidi** pedestrian crossing; ~ **kaldırımı** sidewalk
yayan /·ˈ·/ *adv* on foot, walking; ~ **gitmek** *go on foot
yaygara /··ˈ·/ *n* clamor, uproar, outcry; ~ **koparmak** *make a great ado about nothing
yaygaracı /···ˈ·/ *adj* noisy; brawling, clamorous
yaygı /·ˈ·/ *n* something spread out

as a covering
yaygın /·ˈ·/ *adj* widespread, common
yayılmak /··ˈ·/ *v* *spread, *be spread
yayım /·ˈ·/ *n* publication; publishing
yayımcı /··ˈ·/ *n* publisher
yayımlamak /···ˈ·/ *v* publish
yayın /·ˈ·/ *n* publication; broadcast
yayıncı /··ˈ·/ *n* publisher
yayıncılık /···ˈ·/ *n* publishing
yayınevi /·ˈ···/ *n* publishing house
yayla /ˈ··/ *n* high plateau
yaylanmak /··ˈ·/ *v* *spring, bounce
yaylı /·ˈ·/ *adj* having springs; ~ **çalgılar** instruments played with a bow
yaymak /·ˈ·/ *v* *spread, scatter
yayvan /·ˈ·/ *adj* broad and shallow
yaz *n* summer; ~ **kış** all year long; **yazın** in summer
yazar /·ˈ·/ *n* writer, author
yazı /·ˈ·/ *n* writing; article; destiny; ~ **makinesi** typewriter; ~ **tura** toss-up; ~ **tahtası** blackboard
yazıcı /··ˈ·/ *n* secretary, clerk
yazıhane /·–ˈ·/ *n* office
yazık /·ˈ·/ *n* a pity, a shame; ~ **olmak** *be too bad
yazılı /··ˈ·/ *adj* written, registered; destined; *n* written examination
yazılım /··ˈ·/ *n* software
yazılış /··ˈ·/ *n* spelling; method of writing
yazılmak /··ˈ·/ *v* *be written; *be registered
yazım /·ˈ·/ *n* spelling, orthography
yazın /·ˈ·/ *n* literature
yazışma /··ˈ·/ *n* correspondence
yazışmak /··ˈ·/ *v* correspond, *write to each other
yazıt /·ˈ·/ *n* inscription
yazlık /·ˈ·/ *n* summerhouse; *adj* suitable for summer
yazma /·ˈ·/ *n* writing, manuscript, handwriting
yazmak /·ˈ·/ *v* *write; inscribe; register; enroll
yazman /·ˈ·/ *n* secretary
yedek /·ˈ·/ *n* substitute, reserve; *adj* spare, extra; ~ **parça** spare part; ~ **subay** reserve conscript officer
yedi /·ˈ·/ *num* seven
yedinci /··ˈ·/ *num* seventh
yedirmek /··ˈ·/ *v* *feed; *let absorb; mix in slowly
yedişer /··ˈ·/ *adv* seven each
yegâne /ˈ·–·/ *adj* sole, unique
yeğ *adj* better, preferable
yeğen /·ˈ·/ *n* nephew; niece
yeğlemek /··ˈ·/ *v* prefer
yeis *n* despair
yekûn /·ˈ·/ *n* total, sum
yel *n* wind; ~ **değirmeni** windmill; ~ **gibi** fast, quickly
yele /·ˈ·/ *n* mane
yelek /·ˈ·/ *n* waistcoat, vest
yelken /·ˈ·/ *n* sail; ~ **açmak** hoist sails
yelkenci /··ˈ·/ *n* sailor
yelkenli /··ˈ·/ *adj* fitted with sails; *n* sailboat
yelkovan /··ˈ·/ *n* minute hand
yelpaze /·–ˈ·/ *n* fan
yelpazelemek /·–··ˈ·/ *v* fan
yeltenmek /··ˈ·/ *v* try, attempt
yem *n* fodder, feed; bait
yemek[1] /·ˈ·/ *n* food, meal; dish, course; dinner, supper; ~ **kitabı** cookbook; ~ **listesi** menu; ~ **odası** dining room; ~ **seçmek** *be choosy in eating; ~ **vermek** *give a dinner; ~ **yemek** *eat
yemek[2] /·ˈ·/ *v* *eat; *spend;

consume; **yiyip içmek** *eat and *drink
yemekhane /···ˈ·/ *n* large dining room
yemeni /··ˈ·/ *n* colored cotton kerchief
yemin /·ˈ·/ *n* oath; ~ **etmek** *swear
yeminli /··ˈ·/ *adj* sworn, bound by an oath
yemiş /·ˈ·/ *n* fruit; ~ **vermek** *bear fruit
yenge /ˈ··/ *n* uncle's wife; brother's wife; sister-in-law
yengeç /·ˈ·/ *n* crab
yeni /·ˈ·/ *adj* new; recent; ~ **baştan** over again; ~ **yıl** New Year; **Yeni Zelanda** New Zealand
yeniçeri /·ˈ···/ *n* Janissary
Yenidünya /·ˈ··–/ *n* the New World, America
yenik /·ˈ·/ *adj* defeated; ~ **düşmek** *be defeated
yenilemek /···ˈ·/ *v* renew; renovate
yenilgi /··ˈ·/ *n* defeat
yenilik /··ˈ·/ *n* novelty, newness
yenilikçi /···ˈ·/ *n* reformist
yenilmek /··ˈ·/ *v* *be eaten; *be beaten
yenir /·ˈ·/ *adj* eatable, edible
yenmek /·ˈ·/ *v* *overcome; *be victorious; conquer; *beat
yer *n* place; space; ground; seat; the earth
yeraltı /ˈ···/ *adj* underground
yerçekimi /ˈ····/ *n* gravitation; gravity
yerel /·ˈ·/ *adj* local
yerfıstığı /ˈ····/ *n* peanut
yerküre /ˈ···/ *n* earth; globe
yerleşik /··ˈ·/ *adj* established, settled
yerleşme /··ˈ·/ *n* settlement
yerleşmek /··ˈ·/ *v* settle down; *become established
yerli /·ˈ·/ *adj* local; native; fixed; built-in; *n* native
yermek /·ˈ·/ *v* disparage; satirize; criticize
yersarsıntısı /ˈ·····/ *n* earthquake
yersiz /·ˈ·/ *adj* homeless; irrelevant, inappropriate
yeryüzü /ˈ···/ *n* world, the earth's surface
yeşermek /·ˈ·/ *v* turn green
yeşil /·ˈ·/ *adj* green; ~ **ışık** green light
yeşillenmek /···ˈ·/ *v* turn green
yeşillik /··ˈ·/ *n* greenness; green vegetables; meadow
yeşim /·ˈ·/ *n* jade
yetenek /··ˈ·/ *n* ability, capacity
yeter /·ˈ·/ *adj* sufficient; enough
yeterince /··ˈ··/ *adv* sufficiently
yeterli /··ˈ·/ *adj* adequate; sufficient
yeterlik /··ˈ·/ *n* capacity; efficiency
yeterliilik /···ˈ·/ *n* sufficiency
yetersiz /··ˈ·/ *adj* insufficient, inadequate; inefficient
yetersizlik /···ˈ·/ *n* inefficiency; inadequacy
yetim /·ˈ·/ *n* orphan
yetimhane /·–ˈ·/ *n* orphanage
yetinmek /··ˈ·/ *v* *be contented with
yetişkin /··ˈ·/ *n* adult; grown-up
yetişmek /··ˈ·/ *v* reach; *catch; *be enough; *be brought up, *grow
yetişmiş /··ˈ·/ *adj* grown-up, mature
yetiştirmek /···ˈ·/ *v* raise (plants, animals); train; *breed
yetki /·ˈ·/ *n* authority; power; ~ **vermek** authorize
yetkili /··ˈ·/ *adj* authorized, qualified, competent; *n* authority

yetmek /·ˈ·/ *v* *be enough; reach, attain
yetmiş /·ˈ·/ *num* seventy
yevmiye /··ˈ·/ *n* daily pay, day's wages; ~ **defteri** daybook
yığılmak /··ˈ·/ *v* accumulate; crowd together
yığın /·ˈ·/ *n* heap, pile; mass; **bir** ~ a great deal; **yığınla** in heaps
yığıntı /··ˈ·/ *n* accumulation, heap
yığmak /·ˈ·/ *v* pile up; accumulate
yıkamak /··ˈ·/ *v* wash
yıkanmak /··ˈ·/ *v* *be washed; *have a bath, bathe
yıkıcı /··ˈ·/ *adj* destructive
yıkık /·ˈ·/ *adj* fallen down, ruined
yıkılmak /··ˈ·/ *v* *be destroyed; collapse
yıkım /·ˈ·/ *n* ruin; disaster
yıkıntı /··ˈ·/ *n* ruins, debris
yıkmak /·ˈ·/ *v* pull down; knock down; demolish
yıl *n* year
yılan /·ˈ·/ *n* snake
yılanbalığı /·ˈ····/ *n* eel
yılbaşı /ˈ···/ *n* New Year's Day
yıldırım /··ˈ·/ *n* thunderbolt, lightning; ~ **çarpmış** struck by lightning; ~ **telgraf** urgent telegram, express telegram
yıldırmak /··ˈ·/ *v* daunt, cow
yıldız /·ˈ·/ *n* star; ~ **falı** astrology
yıldönümü /ˈ····/ *n* anniversary
yılışık /··ˈ·/ *adj* importunate, sticky
yıllanmak /··ˈ·/ *v* *grow old, age; stay for several years
yıllık /·ˈ·/ *adj* annual, yearly; . . . years old; *n* yearly salary *or* rent; yearbook
yılmak /·ˈ·/ *v* *be daunted, dread
yılmaz /·ˈ·/ *adj* undaunted, unshrinking, intrepid
yıpranmak /··ˈ·/ *v* *be worn out; *lose authority
yırtıcı /··ˈ·/ *adj* rapacious, tearing; ~ **hayvan** beast of prey
yırtık /·ˈ·/ *adj* torn, rent; ~ **pırtık** in rags
yırtılmak /··ˈ·/ *v* *be torn
yırtınmak /··ˈ·/ *v* *wear oneself out; shout at the top of one's voice; struggle hopelessly
yırtmaç /·ˈ·/ *n* slit
yırtmak /·ˈ·/ *n* *tear, *rend
yiğit /·ˈ·/ *n* young man; hero; *adj* brave
yiğitçe /·ˈ··/ *adv* bravely
yiğitlik /··ˈ·/ *n* heroism, courage
yine /ˈ··/ *adv* again, still
yinelemek /···ˈ·/ *v* repeat
yirmi /·ˈ·/ *num* twenty; ~ **yaş dişi** wisdom tooth
yirminci /··ˈ·/ *num* twentieth
yirmişer /··ˈ·/ *adv* twenty each
yitik /·ˈ·/ *adj* lost
yitirmek /··ˈ·/ *v* *lose
yitmek /·ˈ·/ *v* *be lost
yiyecek /··ˈ·/ *n* food
yobaz /·ˈ·/ *n* fanatic, bigot
yobazlık /··ˈ·/ *n* fanaticism
yoğun /·ˈ·/ *adj* dense, concentrated
yoğunlaşmak /···ˈ·/ *v* *become dense
yoğunluk /··ˈ·/ *n* density
yoğurmak /··ˈ·/ *v* knead
yoğurt /·ˈ·/ *n* yoghurt
yok *v* there is not; *adj* absent; non-existent; ~ **canım!** you don't say!; ~ **etmek** destroy utterly; ~ **olmak** disappear, cease to exist; ~ **yere** without reason; uselessly
yoklama /··ˈ·/ *n* test; quiz; roll call
yoklamak /··ˈ·/ *v* *feel, examine, search; inspect; visit
yokluk /·ˈ·/ *n* absence; non-existence; poverty
yoksa /ˈ··/ *conj* otherwise, if not,

or else
yoksul /·ˈ·/ *adj* poor, needy
yoksulluk /··ˈ·/ *n* poverty, destitution
yoksun /·ˈ·/ *adj* deprived; ~ **bırakmak** deprive of
yokuş /·ˈ·/ *n* ascent, slope; ~ **aşağı** downhill; ~ **yukarı** uphill; **yokuşa sürmek** create difficulties
yol *n* road; street; method, manner; means, medium; stripe; ~ **açmak** *make way for; cause; ~ **kesmek** *waylay; **yola çıkmak** *set out, start out; **yola getirmek** *bring to reason; **yolunda** all right, well
yolcu /·ˈ·/ *n* traveler, passenger; ~ **etmek** *see someone off
yolculuk /··ˈ·/ *n* traveling, journey, trip
yoldaş /·ˈ·/ *n* fellow traveler, companion; comrade
yollamak /··ˈ·/ *v* *send, dispatch, forward
yolmak /·ˈ·/ *v* pluck, pull out; *tear out, uproot
yolsuz /·ˈ·/ *adj* roadless; unlawful
yolsuzluk /··ˈ·/ *n* irregularity; malpractice
yonca /·ˈ·/ *n* clover
yontmak /·ˈ·/ *v* *cut, chip
yontulmak /··ˈ·/ *v* *be chipped; learn manners
yontulmamış /·ˈ···/ *adj* not chipped, uncut; unrefined, rough
yorgan /·ˈ·/ *n* quilt; ~ **yüzü** quilt cover
yorgun /·ˈ·/ *adj* tired, weary; ~ **argın** dead tired; ~ **düşmek** *be worn out
yorgunluk /··ˈ·/ *n* tiredness, fatigue
yormak /·ˈ·/ *v* tire, fatigue
yortu /·ˈ·/ *n* Christian feast
yorucu /··ˈ·/ *adj* tiring, wearisome
yorulmak /··ˈ·/ *v* *get tired
yorum /·ˈ·/ *n* interpretation; commentary; comment
yorumcu /··ˈ·/ *n* commentator
yorumlamak /···ˈ·/ *v* comment on; interpret
yosun /·ˈ·/ *n* moss
yozlaşmak /··ˈ·/ *v* degenerate
yön *n* direction; aspect, side; ~ **vermek** *set a course
yönelmek /··ˈ·/ *v* incline, tend; *go towards
yönetici /···ˈ·/ *n* administrator, director
yönetim /··ˈ·/ *n* administration, management; ~ **kurulu** board of directors
yönetmek /··ˈ·/ *v* administer; manage
yönetmelik /···ˈ·/ *n* regulations, statutes
yönetmen /··ˈ·/ *n* director
yöntem /·ˈ·/ *n* method, way
yöre /·ˈ·/ *n* environs; neighborhood
yörünge /·ˈ··/ *n* orbit
yufka /·ˈ·/ *n* thin sheet of dough
Yugoslav /··ˈ·/ *adj, n* Yugoslav
Yugoslavya /··ˈ··/ Yugoslavia
yuhalamak /···ˈ·/ *v* boo, jeer, hoot
yukarı *adj* high; upper, top; *adv* upwards; above, upstairs
yulaf /·ˈ·/ *n* oat
yular /·ˈ·/ *n* halter
yumak /·ˈ·/ *n* ball of wool, string, etc.
yummak /·ˈ·/ *v* *shut, close (eye)
yumruk /·ˈ·/ *n* fist; blow
yumruklamak /···ˈ·/ *v* *hit with fist
yumurcak /··ˈ·/ *n* child; brat
yumurta /··ˈ·/ *n* egg; ~ **akı** white of an egg; ~ **sarısı** yolk
yumurtalık /···ˈ·/ *n* ovary; egg cup

yumurtlamak /···'·/ *v* *lay eggs
yumuşak /··'·/ *adj* soft; mild, tender; ~ **başlı** docile
yumuşaklık /···'·/ *n* softness; gentleness
yumuşamak /···'·/ *v* *become soft; calm down
Yunanca /·'··/ *n* Greek language
Yunanistan /···'·/ Greece
Yunanlı /··'·/ *n, adj* Greek
yunusbalığı /·'····/ *n* dolphin
yurt *n* native land; student dormitory, youth hostel
yurtsever /··'·/ *adj* patriotic
yurtsuz /·'·/ *adj* homeless
yurttaş /·'·/ *n* fellow countryman
yurttaşlık /··'·/ *n* citizenship
yutkunmak /··'·/ *v* gulp, swallow
yutmak /·'·/ *v* swallow
yuva /·'·/ *n* nest; home; crèche; kindergarten; ~ **bozmak** *break up a home; ~ **kurmak** *set up a home
yuvarlak /··'·/ *adj* round, spherical; *n* globe, ball; ~ **hesap** round figure
yuvarlamak /···'·/ *v* roll, roll up; gulp down; roll along
yuvarlanmak /···'·/ *v* turn round; roll along; tumble
yüce /·'·/ *adj* high, exalted
yücelmek /··'·/ *v* *become high, *rise
yüceltmek /··'·/ *v* exalt
yük *n* burden, load, cargo
yüklemek /··'·/ *v* load, burden; impute, attribute
yüklenmek /··'·/ *v* *take upon oneself, *undertake
yüklü /·'·/ *adj* loaded; burdened
yüksek /·'·/ *adj* high, superior; loud (voice); ~ **atlama** high jump; **yüksekten atmak** boast, bluster

yükseklik /··'·/ *n* height, elevation, altitude
yüksekokul /·'···/ *n* university, college
yükselmek /··'·/ *v* mount, *rise
yükselti /··'·/ *n* elevation
yüksük /·'·/ *n* thimble
yüküm /·'·/ *n* obligation
yükümlü /··'·/ *adj* bound, liable, obliged
yükümlülük /···'·/ *n* liability, obligation
yün *n* wool; *adj* woolen
yünlü /·'·/ *adj* woolen; wooly; *n* woolen cloth
yürek /·'·/ *n* heart; courage, spirit
yürekli /··'·/ *adj* bold, brave
yüreksiz /··'·/ *adj* faint-hearted, cowardly
yürekten /··'·/ *adv* sincerely
yürüme /··'·/ *n* walk; pace
yürümek /··'·/ *v* walk, move, advance
yürürlük /··'·/ *n* validity; **yürürlüğe girmek** *come into force
yürütmek /··'·/ *v* cause to walk; carry out, execute; *steal
yürüyüş /··'·/ *n* march
yüz[1] *num* hundred
yüz[2] *n* face, surface; impudence, cheek; ~ **bulmak** *be spoilt, *be emboldened
yüzbaşı /'···/ *n* army captain, lieutenant
yüzde /·'·/ *n* percent, percentage
yüzdürmek /··'·/ *v* float
yüzey /·'·/ *n* surface
yüzkarası /'····/ *n* dishonor, disgrace, shame
yüzleşmek /··'·/ *v* confront one another
yüzmek /·'·/ *v* *swim; float

yüznumara /'····/ *n* toilet, WC
yüzölçümü /'····/ *n* area
yüzsüz /·'·/ *adj* cheeky, shameless, impudent
yüzücü /··'·/ *n* swimmer
yüzük /·'·/ *n* ring
yüzükoyun /·'···/ *adv* face downwards; upside down
yüzünden /··'·/ *adv* because of, on account of
yüzüstü /'···/ *adv* face downwards; ~ **bırakmak** *leave something unfinished; *leave someone in the lurch
yüzyıl /·'·/ *n* century

Z

zabıt /·'·/ *n* minutes (of a meeting), protocol, proceedings; ~ **tutmak** *take minutes
zabıta /–'·/ *n* police
zafer /·'·/ *n* triumph; victory
zafiyet /–'·/ *n* weakness, debility, thinness; tuberculosis
zahmet /·'·/ *n* trouble, difficulty, distress, fatigue; ~ **çekmek** *go to a lot of trouble, *have difficulty
zahmetli /··'·/ *adj* troublesome; difficult; fatiguing
zalim /–'·/ *adj* unjust, cruel
zam *n* increase, addition
zaman /·'·/ *n* time, period, epoch, era; present life; ~ ~ occasionally, from time to time; **zamanla** in the course of time
zambak /·'·/ *n* lily
zamir /·'·/ *n* pronoun
zamk *n* glue, paste, gum
zan *n* opinion; surmise, suspicion
zanaat /··'·/ *n* craft, handicraft
zannetmek /'···/ *v* *think, suppose
zapt *n* seizure, control; ~ **etmek** *hold firmly, seize, *take possession of; conquer
zar *n* membrane, film; thin skin; die, dice
zarafet /·–'·/ *n* elegance, grace, delicacy
zarar /·'·/ *n* damage, injury; loss; harm; ~ **etmek** *lose money; *make a loss; *have a deficit; ~ **ziyan** damages
zararlı /··'·/ *adj* harmful
zararsız /··'·/ *adj* harmless, safe
zarf *n* envelope; adverb
zarfında /··'·/ *adv* during, within
zarflamak /··'·/ *v* *put in an envelope
zarif /·'·/ *adj* graceful, elegant, delicate
zariflik /··'·/ *adj* elegance, delicacy
zaruret /·–'·/ *n* need, want, necessity; requirement
zaruri /·–'–/ *adj* necessary
zar zor /'··/ *adv* willy-nilly, barely
zat /–/ *n* person, individual, personality
zaten /–'·/ *adv* essentially, in any case, as a matter of fact
zatürree /–··'·/ *n* pneumonia
zavallı /'···/ *adj* miserable, wretched, unlucky
zayıf /·'·/ *adj* weak; thin; infirm
zayıflamak /···'·/ *v* *get thin *or* weak; *lose weight
zayıflık /··'·/ *n* weakness; debility
zayiat /–·'·/ *n* losses; ~ **vermek** suffer losses
zedelemek /···'·/ *v* damage by striking; maltreat; bruise
zehir /·'·/ *n* poison
zehirlemek /···'·/ *v* poison
zehirli /··'·/ *adj* poisonous, venomous
zekâ /·'–/ *n* quickness of mind, intelligence

zekât /·ˈ–/ *n* alms
zeki /·ˈ–/ *adj* sharp, quick-witted, intelligent, clever
zelzele /··ˈ·/ *n* earthquake
zemin /·ˈ·/ *n* ground; background
zencefil /··ˈ·/ *n* ginger
zenci /·ˈ·/ *n* negro, black
zengin /·ˈ·/ *adj* rich, wealthy
zenginleşmek /···ˈ·/ *v* *get rich
zenginlik /··ˈ·/ *n* riches, wealth
zerdali /·–ˈ·/ *n* wild apricot
zerzevat /··ˈ·/ *n* vegetables
zevk *n* taste, flavor; pleasure
zevkli /·ˈ·/ *adj* pleasant, amusing; with good taste
zevksiz /·ˈ·/ *adj* tasteless, ugly, in bad taste
zeytin /·ˈ·/ *n* olive
zeytinyağı /·ˈ···/ *n* olive oil
zımba /·ˈ·/ *n* drill, punch
zımbalamak /···ˈ·/ *v* drill; punch
zımpara /ˈ···/ *n* emery; ~ **kâğıdı** sandpaper
zıngırdamak /···ˈ·/ *v* tremble violently, rattle
zıpkın /·ˈ·/ *n* fish spear, harpoon
zıplamak /··ˈ·/ *v* jump, hop, skip
zıpzıp /·ˈ·/ *n* marble (plaything)
zırdeli /ˈ···/ *adj* raving mad
zırh *n* armor
zırhlı /·ˈ·/ *adj* armored, armor plated; *n* battleship
zırlamak /··ˈ·/ *v* *keep up a continous noise; *weep
zırva /·ˈ·/ *n* silly chatter, nonsense
zırvalamak /···ˈ·/ *v* talk nonsense
zıt *adj* contrary, opposite
zift *n* pitch, tar
ziftlemek /··ˈ·/ *v* tar
zihin /·ˈ·/ *n* mind, intelligence, intellect; memory
zihniyet /··ˈ·/ *n* mentality
zil *n* bell, electric bell; cymbals
zimmet /·ˈ·/ *n* charge, debt; **zimmetine geçirmek** embezzle
zina /·ˈ–/ *n* adultery
zincir /·ˈ·/ *n* chain; fetters; succession, series
zincirleme /···ˈ·/ *adj* in a continous series
zincirlemek /···ˈ·/ *v* chain, connect in a series *or* chain
zindan /·ˈ·/ *n* prison, dungeon
zinde /·ˈ·/ *adj* alive, active, energetic
zira /ˈ––/ *conj* because
ziraat /··ˈ·/ *n* agriculture
zirve /·ˈ·/ *n* summit, peak, apex; ~ **toplantısı** summit meeting
ziyadesiyle /–ˈ··/ *adv* very much, excessively
ziyafet /·–ˈ·/ *n* feast, banquet, dinner party; ~ **vermek** *give a banquet
ziyan /·ˈ·/ *n* loss, damage
ziyaret /·–ˈ·/ *n* visit; ~ **etmek** visit
ziyaretçi /·–ˈ·/ *n* visitor
ziynet /·ˈ·/ *n* ornament, decoration, adornment; jewelry
zor *adj* hard, difficult; *n* difficulty; *adv* with difficulty
zoraki /·–ˈ·/ *adj* forced, involuntary; *adv* under compulsion, by force
zorba /·ˈ·/ *n* rebel, bully; *adj* violent, brutal
zorlamak /··ˈ·/ *v* force, use force, coerce; exert one's strength
zorlaşmak /··ˈ·/ *v* *grow difficult, *become harder
zorlu /·ˈ·/ *adj* strong, violent; powerful, influential
zorluk /·ˈ·/ *n* difficulty, hardness
zorunlu /··ˈ·/ *adj* obligatory
zulmetmek /ˈ···/ *v* tyrannize, torture
zulüm /·ˈ·/ *n* oppression, cruelty
zurna /·ˈ·/ *n* shrill pipe
züğürt /·ˈ·/ *adj* penniless, broke
zümrüt /·ˈ·/ *n* emerald
züppe /·ˈ·/ *n* dandy; *adj* affected, snobbish
zürafa /·–ˈ··/ *n* giraffe

Menu Reader

Food

acıbadem kurabiyesi almond cookie, macaroon
ahududu raspberry
akşam yemeği dinner
alabalık trout
anason aniseed
ançüez anchovy
armut pear
arnavutciğeri fried mutton liver
aşure Noah's pudding; sweet pudding made of cereals, nuts and fruits
av eti game
ayva quince
 ~ **kompostosu** quince compote
 ~ **reçeli** quince preserves
az pişmiş rare
baba tatlısı ring-shaped cake with a center filling of custard and fruits, macerated in syrup
badem almond
 ~ **tatlısı** almond cake in syrup
 ~**ezmesi** almond paste, marzipan
 ~**şekeri** sugared almonds
baharat spices
 ~**lı** hot, spicy
bahçıvan kebabı meat with mixed vegetables
baklava sweet pastry filled with nuts *or* pistachios
bal honey
balık fish
 ~ **çorbası** fish soup
 ~ **pilakisi** stewed cold fish
 ~ **suyu** fish broth
 ~ **tavası** fried fish
balkabağı pumpkin
bamya gumbo, okra
barbunya red mullet
 ~ **fasulyesi** small, reddish kind of shelled bean
 ~ **pilakisi** stewed red beans
beğendili kebap broiled lamb with eggplant purée
beyazpeynir feta cheese, soft white cheese
beyaz salça white sauce, béchamel
beyin brain
 ~ **salatası** brain salad; boiled brains with olive oil and lemon
 ~ **tavası** fried brains
Beykoz usulü paça lamb knuckles Beykoz style
bezelye green peas
 ~ **çorbası** pea soup
 ~**li pilav** rice with peas
bıldırcın quail
biber pepper
 ~ **dolması** stuffed green peppers
 ~ **turşusu** pickled peppers

bonfile sirloin steak
böbrek kidney
~ **ızgara** grilled kidneys
böğürtlen blackberry
börek various kinds of flaky pastry
Brüksel lahanası Brussels sprouts
buğulama steamed (food)
bulgur boiled and pounded wheat
~ **pilavı** pilaf made of boiled and pounded wheat
buzlu iced
bülbülyuvası pastry filled with pistachios and soaked in syrup
cacık diced cucumbers with a dressing of yoghurt, olive oil and garlic
ceviz walnut
ciğer liver
~ **tavası** fried liver
çavdar ekmeği rye bread, pumpernickel
çerez appetizer
çerkez peyniri a kind of creamy cheese
çerkez tavuğu minced chicken mixed with chopped walnuts, chili pepper and bread
çılbır poached eggs with yoghurt
çiğ raw, underdone
~**köfte** dish made of ground raw meat, pounded wheat and red pepper
çikolata chocolate
çilek strawberry
~ **reçeli** strawberry preserves
çinekop medium-sized bluefish
çiroz sun-dried thin mackerel, cured mackerel
~ **salatası** cured mackerel salad
çoban salatası shepherd's salad; salad of onions, tomatoes, cucumbers and green peppers
çorba soup
çöp kebabı small bits of meat grilled on tiny wooden skewers
dana (eti) veal
~ **budu rosto** roast leg of veal
~ **rozbif** roast veal
deniz ürünleri seafood
dereotu dill
dilbalığı sole
dilberdudağı beauty's lips; lip-shaped pastry soaked in syrup
dilim slice
dolma meat *or* vegetables stuffed with rice and forcemeat
~ **içi** stuffing
domates tomato
~ **çorbası** tomato soup
~ **dolması** stuffed tomatoes
~ **salatası** tomato salad
~ **salçası** tomato paste
dondurma ice cream
çikolatalı ~ chocolate ice cream
kaymaklı ~ milk based ice cream, vanilla ice cream
meyveli ~ sherbet; fruit flavored ice cream
döner (kebap) meat wrapped round and roasted on a vertical rotating spit
döş brisket
dut mulberry
düğün çorbası lamb soup flavored with lemon juice and thickened with beaten eggs
ekmek bread
~ **kadayıfı** dessert made of bread dough baked and soaked in syrup
~ **somunu** loaf of bread
elma apple
~ **kompostosu** apple compote
erik plum
erimiş melted
erişte homemade noodles
et meat
~ **suyu** gravy, consommé, broth
~**li bezelye** green pea stew

~li dolma green peppers, tomatoes, zucchinis, grape leaves *or* cabbages stuffed with ground meat and rice

~li kuru fasulye white beans with chunks of meat

~li nohut chick-peas with chunks of meat

~li patates lamb with potatoes

~li taze fasulye green bean stew

evde yapılmış homemade

ezo gelin çorbası red lentil soup with mint

fasulye bean

~ pilakisi cold white bean stew in olive oil

~ piyazı boiled bean salad with onions, eggs, etc.

fava (kuru bakla ezmesi) mashed broad beans

fındık hazelnut

fırında baked

~ kuzu budu roasted lamb

~ piliç roasted chicken

fırın makarna baked spaghetti, pasta pie

fırın sütlaç baked rice pudding

fıstık pistachio nut

fileto loin, fillet

~ bifteği sirloin steak

frape milk shake

füme smoked

garnitür garnishings, trimmings

gofret wafer

göğüs breast

greyfurt grapefruit

gül rose

~ reçeli rose petal jam

güllaç starch wafers with cream and rose water

gümüşbalığı sand-smelt, atherine

güveç stew, casserole

~ kebabı broiled meat casserole

~te deniz mahsulleri seafood casserole

hamsi (balığı) anchovy, sprat

hamur işi, hamur tatlısı pastry

hanımgöbeği, kadıngöbeği lady's navel; sweet dish made with flour and eggs

hardal mustard

haşlama boiled (meat)

haşlanmış boiled

havuç carrot

~ kızartması sautéed carrots

~ rende salatası shredded carrot salad

havyar caviar, roe

helva a sweet prepared in many varieties with sesame oil, various cereals, and syrup *or* honey; halvah

ıspanak spinach

içliköfte mutton croquettes stuffed with ground meat, onions and walnuts

ilik marrow

~li kemik marrow bone

imambayıldı eggplant in olive oil

incir fig

~ reçeli fig preserves

irmik semolina

~ helvası halvah made of semolina

islim kebabı lamb stew with vegetables

İskender kebabı döner kebab with flat bread and yoghurt

istiridye oyster

işkembe tripe

~ çorbası mutton tripe soup seasoned with vinegar, garlic and red pepper

~ dolması mutton tripe stuffed with rice and liver

İzmir köftesi meat balls in tomato sauce

jambon ham

~**lu yumurta** ham and eggs
jöle jelly
meyveli ~ fruit flavored jelly
kabak squash, vegetable marrow, zucchini
~ **çekirdeği** pumpkin seed
~ **dolması** stuffed squash
~ **mücver** squash croquette
~ **tatlısı** sweet dish prepared with pumpkin, walnuts and sugar
kabuklu deniz hayvanı shellfish
kadayıf name for various types of sweet pastry
kadınbudu köfte meat ball with eggs and rice
kâğıthelvası pastry in thin layers
kâğıt kebabı pieces of meat cooked in paper
kahvaltı breakfast
kalkan (balığı) turbot
kapama lamb and onion stew
kapuska cabbage stew with lamb and hot pepper
karabiber black pepper
karaciğer liver
karışık mixed
~ **hamur tatlıları** assorted pastries
~ **ızgara** mixed grill
~ **turşu** mixed pickles
karides shrimp
~ **güveç** shrimp casserole
~ **şiş** skewered shrimps
~ **tavası** fried shrimps
karnabahar cauliflower
~ **kızartması** fried cauliflower
~ **salatası** cauliflower salad
~ **tavası** fried cauliflower
karnıyarık split eggplant stuffed with chopped meat
karpuz watermelon
kaşarpeyniri firm, yellowish, cheddar-type cheese
kaşık helvası spoon halvah; a sweet made of flour, margarine and sugar
kavun melon, muskmelon
kayısı apricot
~ **kompostosu** apricot compote
~ **reçeli** apricot preserves
kaymak cream, clotted cream
~**lı** made *or* served with cream
kaz goose
~ **kızartması** roast goose
kazandibi slightly burnt milk pudding
kebap roast, broiled meat
Adana ~ spicy ground meat grilled on a spit
çoban ~ı mutton braised with garlic
döner ~ meat roasted on a revolving vertical spit
islim ~ı lamb stew with vegetables
tencere ~ı mutton stew with peas and potatoes
yoğurtlu ~ döner kebap with yoghurt
kefal gray mullet
~ **pilakisi** gray mullet stew
kek cake, tea cake
kekik thyme
keklik partridge
kemik bone
kereviz celery
kestane chestnut
keşkül custard with almonds and pistachios
ketçap ketchup, catsup
kılıç (balığı) swordfish
~ **ızgara** grilled swordfish
~ **şiş** chunks of swordfish skewered and charcoal-grilled with bay leaves, tomatoes and green peppers
kırlangıç (balığı) gurnard
kırmızıbiber chili pepper, red pep-

per, paprika
kırmızı mercimek çorbası red lentil soup
kısır cold dish made with cracked wheat, salad vegetables and olive oil
kış türlüsü stew with winter vegetables
kıyma minced meat, ground beef
~**lı bamya** okra with ground beef
~**lı börek** minced meat pie
~**lı ıspanak** spinach with ground beef
~**lı makarna** macaroni with ground beef
~**lı pide** flat bread with minced meat filling
~**lı suböreği** börek made of layers of noodle-like pastry filled with minced meat
~**lı taze fasulye** green beans with ground meat
~**lı yumurta** eggs with ground meat
kızarmış fried, roasted, grilled
~ **ekmek** toast
~ **patates** French fries, chips
kızartma fried, roasted
kızılcık cornelian cherry
kiraz cherry
kokoreç sheep's chitterlings cooked on a spit
komposto stewed fruit, compote
koyun eti mutton
köfte meat balls
krema cream
~**lı** creamy; served with cream
krem karamel egg pudding with caramel sauce
krik-krak bread sticks
kurabiye cookie, shortbread
kuru dried
~ **bakla ezmesi** mashed broad beans
~ **erik** prune
~ **fasulye** haricot beans, white beans
~ **köfte** fried meat balls
~ **üzüm** raisins
kuşbaşı in small pieces
~ **et** stewing meat
kuşkonmaz asparagus
~ **sapı** asparagus tip
kuşüzümü currant
kuzu (eti) lamb
~ **budu** leg of lamb
~ **dolması** lamb stuffed with savory rice, liver and pistachios
~ **fırında** roast leg of lamb
~ **güveç** lamb casserole
~ **haşlama** lamb stew
~ **kapama** lamb with chard and dill in lemon sauce
~ **pirzolası** lamb chops
~ **tandır** lamb roasted in a cylindrical oven
~ **tas kebabı** lamb kebab in a casserole
kümes hayvanları poultry
kürek eti shoulder; front quarter of an animal
lahana cabbage
~ **dolması** stuffed cabbage
~ **salatası** cabbage salad, coleslaw
~ **turşusu** pickled cabbage
lahmacun type of pizza with ground meat, tomatoes and green peppers
lakerda salted bonito
levrek (balığı) sea bass
~ **buğulama** steamed sea bass
~ **ızgara** grilled sea bass
~ **mayonezli** sea bass with mayonnaise
~ **tavası** fried sea bass
limon lemon
lokum Turkish delight
lor peyniri goat's cheese

lüfer bluefish
 ~ **ızgara** grilled bluefish
makarna macaroni
 ~ **fırında** pasta pie
mandalina tangerine, mandarin
mantar mushroom
 ~**lı omlet** mushroom omelet
mantı dish prepared with paste, ground meat and yoghurt
marmelat marmalade, jam
marul romaine lettuce
maydanoz parsley
mayonez mayonnaise
 ~**li** prepared *or* served with mayonnaise
menemen omelet with green peppers and tomatoes
mercan (balığı) red sea bream
mercimek lentil
 ~ **çorbası** lentil soup
 ~**li köfte** lentil croquettes
mersinbalığı sturgeon
meyve fruit
 ~**li turta** fruit pie, fruit cake
meze appetizer, snack
mezgit (balığı) haddock
mısır corn
 ~ **gevreği** cornflakes
 patlamış ~ popcorn
midye mussel
 ~ **dolması** stuffed mussels
 ~ **pilakisi** mussels braised with vegetables
 ~ **tavası** fried mussels
misket limonu lime
morina (balığı) cod
muhallebi sweet dish of rice flour and milk
musakka mousaka; dish made of one vegetable and ground meat
muska böreği amulet shaped pastry with cheese filling
muz banana
mücver fried patty mostly made with squash, flour and eggs
nane mint, peppermint
nar pomegranate
nemse böreği a kind of meat pasty
nohut chick-pea
 ~ **yahnisi** chick-pea stew
 ~**lu paça** lamb knuckles with chick-peas
omlet omelet
ordövr appetizer, starter
orman kebabı stewed mutton and vegetables
orta pişmiş medium (done)
oturtma minced meat with vegetables
öğle yemeği lunch
ördek duck
 ~ **kızartması** roast duckling
paça dish made from trotters
palamut (balığı) bonito
pancar beet, beetroot
 ~ **salatası** beet salad
 ~ **turşusu** pickled beets
pandispanya sponge cake
papaz yahnisi mutton stewed in wine *or* vinegar
paskalya çöreği Easter braid
pasta sweet cake, pastry, tart
pastırma pressed, cured, spiced meat
patates potato
 ~ **kızartması** French fries, chips
 ~ **köftesi** potato croquettes
 ~ **püresi** mashed potatoes
 ~ **salatası** potato salad
patlıcan eggplant, aubergine
 ~ **ezme** mashed eggplant
 ~ **kebabı** lamb stew with eggplant
 ~ **oturtma** dish of ground meat with eggplants
 ~ **salatası** eggplant salad
 ~ **tava** fried eggplant
 ~ **turşusu** stuffed eggplant pick-

les
peksimet hard biscuit, melba toast
pelte jelly-like pudding made of fruit juice, starch and sugar
peşmelba ice cream with peaches and whipped cream
peynir cheese
~li börek cheese pie
~li omlet cheese omelet
~li pide flat bread with cheese filling
~li suböreği börek made of layers of noodle-like pastry filled with cheese
pırasa leek
pide slightly leavened flat bread
pilaki fish *or* bean stew with olive oil and onions
pilav pilaf; boiled rice prepared with butter
domatesli ~ tomato pilaf
iç ~ pilaf with liver and currants
sade ~ plain rice pilaf
şehriyeli ~ pilaf with vermicelli
tavuklu ~ pilaf with diced chicken
piliç chicken
pirinç rice
pirzola cutlet, chop
pisi (balığı) plaice
poğaça flaky, savory pastry
porsiyon helping, portion
portakal orange
~lı pelte orange dessert
~• reçeli orange marmalade
pufböreği puffy pastry stuffed with meat *or* cheese
reçel jam, fruit preserve
rendelenmiş grated
revani a kind of sweet made with semolina
ringa (balığı) herring
rulo köfte meat loaf
sakatat giblets; liver and kidney
salata salad
~ sosu salad dressing
çoban ~sı cucumber, tomato and onion salad
havuç ~sı carrot salad
karışık ~ tossed salad
kereviz ~sı celery salad
marul ~sı romaine lettuce salad
mevsim ~sı salad of the season
pancar ~sı beet salad
patlıcan ~sı eggplant salad
salatalık cucumber
~ turşusu pickled cucumbers
salça tomato sauce, tomato paste
~lı köfte meat balls in tomato sauce
~lı makarna macaroni with tomato sauce
sandviç sandwich
~ ekmeği roll
saray lokması small, round, fried cakes in syrup
sardalye sardine
sarmısak garlic
sazan (balığı) carp
sebze vegetable
~ çorbası vegetable soup
sığır eti beef
sigara böreği cigarette shaped pastry filled with cheese
simit ring-shaped savory roll covered with sesame seeds
sirke vinegar
soğan onion
som (balığı) salmon
sosis sausage
~li sandviç hot dog
spagetti spaghetti
suböreği pastry of pre-boiled sheets of dough (filled with cheese *or* minced meat)
sucuk sausage flavored with garlic
sufle soufflé; dish made light and fluffy by adding beaten egg whites

before baking
sulu köfte meat balls in broth
suteresi watercress
sülün pheasant
sütlaç rice pudding
süzme strained, filtered
~ **bal** run honey
~ **yoğurt** yoghurt partially dried by hanging in a cloth bag
şalgam turnip
şambaba type of pastry soaked in syrup
şeftali peach
~ **kompostosu** peach compote
şehriye vermicelli
~ **çorbası** vermicelli soup
şekerpare little sweet cakes soaked in syrup
şiş skewer
~**kebabı** shish kebab; meat roasted on a spit *or* skewers
~**köfte** skewered lamb croquettes
tabak dish
tahıl cereals
talaşkebabı meat pie
tarama creamed red caviar
tarator rich sauce made with walnuts, bread, garlic, vinegar and olive oil
tarçın cinnamon
tarhana çorbası soup made with yoghurt, flour, tomatoes, pimentos
tart pie (sweet, usually fruit-filled pastry)
tatarböreği type of ravioli with yoghurt
tatlı dessert; sweet
tatlısu levreği perch
tava frying pan; fried (food)
tavşan rabbit
tavuk chicken
~ **çorbası** chicken soup
~ **dolması** stuffed chicken
~**göğsü** sweet dish of milk and very finely shredded chicken breast
~ **haşlaması** boiled chicken
~ **ızgara** grilled chicken
~ **suyu** chicken consommé
taze fresh
~ **beyaz peynir** fresh white cheese
~ **fasulye** green beans
tepsi böreği pastry made in a baking tray (filled with cheese, meat, etc.)
terbiye sauce made with lemon and eggs
~**li kereviz** celery root with lemon and egg sauce
~**li köfte** rice and meat balls cooked and served with lemon and egg sauce
~**li kuzu eti** lamb with lemon and egg dressing
~**li tavuk çorbası** chicken soup with lemon and egg sauce
tere cress
tereyağı butter
tereyağlı buttered; cooked with butter
~ **kereviz** celery roots cooked with butter
~ **pilav** rice cooked with butter
tonbalığı tuna fish
torik large bonito
tulum peyniri salty goat's milk cheese
tulumba tatlısı sweetmeat of dough soaked in syrup
turnabalığı pike
turp radish
~ **salatası** radish salad
turşu pickled vegetables
turta tart, pie, cake
tuz salt
türlü mixed vegetable stew
un flour
~ **çorbası** flour soup

~ **helvası** sweet dish made with flour, sugar and water
uskumru mackerel
üzüm grape
vanilya vanilla
vişne morello cherry
~ **reçeli** morello cherry jam
~ **tatlısı** baked slices of bread soaked in morello cherry sauce
yabanturpu horseradish
yağ oil, fat
yağsız lean
yaprak dolması stuffed vine leaves
yayınbalığı catfish
yayla çorbası peasant soup with rice and yoghurt
yaz türlüsü stew with summer vegetables
yemek meal
~ **listesi** menu, bill of fare
yerelması Jerusalem artichoke
yerfıstığı peanut
yeşil green
~ **biber** green pepper
~ **fasulye** French beans
~ **salata** lettuce, green salad
yoğurt yoghurt
yufka very thin sheet of dough
yumurta egg
haşlanmış ~ hard-boiled egg
lop ~ hard-boiled egg
rafadan ~ soft-boiled egg
sahanda ~ fried eggs, sunny side up
yürek heart
zencefil ginger
zerdali wild apricot
zerde dish of saffron-flavored sweet rice
zeytin olive
zeytinyağlı cooked with olive oil
~ **bakla** broad beans in olive oil
~ **barbunya** red haricot beans in olive oil
~ **dolma** stuffed vegetables in olive oil
~ **enginar** artichokes in olive oil
~ **fasulye** string beans in olive oil
~ **kereviz** celery roots in olive oil
~ **pırasa** leeks in olive oil
~ **türlü** mixed vegetable stew in olive oil
~ **yerelması** Jerusalem artichokes in olive oil

Drinks

adaçayı sage tea
aperitif aperitif
ayran drink made with yoghurt and water; buttermilk
bira beer
boza beverage made of fermented millet
buzlu iced; on the rocks
cin gin
~ **fiz** gin-fizz; lemon juice, sugar, soda and gin
~ **tonik** gin and tonic
çay tea
buzlu ~ iced tea
limonlu ~ tea with lemon
sütlü ~ tea with milk
domates suyu tomato juice
duble double (shot)
elma suyu apple juice
frape milk shake

greyfurt suyu grapefruit juice
ıhlamur linden tea
kahve coffee
az şekerli ~ slightly sweetened coffee
orta şekerli ~ medium-sweet coffee
sütlü ~ coffee with milk
şekerli ~ sweet coffee
Türk ~si Turkish coffee; very strong black coffee served in small cups
kakao cocoa; chocolate drink
kanyak, konyak brandy, cognac
kokteyl cocktail
likör liqueur
kakao ~ü crème de cacao
muz ~ü banana liqueur
nane ~ü mint flavored liqueur; crème de menthe
portakal ~ü orange liqueur
vişne ~ü sour cherry brandy
limonata lemonade
limon suyu lemon juice
maden suyu mineral water
meyveli gazoz fruit flavored fizzy drink
meyve suyu fruit juice
portakal suyu orange juice
porto port (wine)
rakı raki, arrack
rom rum
salep hot drink made with milk and powdered root of early purple orchid
sek dry; neat, straight
Skoç whiskey
soda soda water
su water
süt milk
çilekli ~ thick drink made of fresh strawberries and milk
muzlu ~ thick drink made of bananas and milk
şarap wine
beyaz ~ white wine
kırmızı ~ red wine
köpüklü ~ sparkling wine
pembe ~ rosé wine
sek ~ dry wine
tatlı ~ sweet wine
şeri sherry; white Spanish wine
şıra slightly fermented grape juice
tek single (shot)
tonik tonic water
üzüm suyu grape juice
vermut vermouth
viski whiskey
~ soda whiskey and soda
vişne suyu sour cherry juice
votka vodka
~ portakal suyu screwdriver

Turkish Abbreviations

AA	*Anadolu Ajansı*	Anatolian News Agency
ABD	*Amerika Birleşik Devletleri*	United States of America
AET	*Avrupa Ekonomik Topluluğu*	European Economic Community
Ank.	*Ankara*	Ankara
Apt.	*apartman*	apartment house
As.	*askeri*	military
Ass.	*asistan*	assistant
AŞ	*Anonim Şirketi*	joint-stock company
B.	*Bay*	Mister
Bkz.	*bakınız*	cf., see
BM	*Birleşmiş Milletler*	United Nations
Bn.	*Bayan*	Miss, Mrs., Ms.
Bşk.	*Başkan; Başkanlık*	president; presidency
Bul.	*Bulvarı*	boulevard
c.	*cilt*	volume
Cad.	*Caddesi*	avenue
d.	*dakika*	minute
DDY	*Devlet Deniz Yolları*	State Maritime Lines
DHMİ	*Devlet Hava Meydanları İşletmesi*	State Airports Administration
doğ.	*doğum*	birth
DMO	*Devlet Malzeme Ofisi*	State Procurement and Supply Office
DPT	*Devlet Planlama Teşkilatı*	State Planning Organization
Dz. Kuv.	*Deniz Kuvvetleri*	navy
Ecz.	*eczacı; eczane*	pharmacist; pharmacy
F.	*fiyat*	price
Fak.	*fakülte*	faculty
Gmr.	*gümrük*	customs
Gön.	*gönderen*	sender
GSMH	*Gayri Safi Milli Hasıla*	Gross National Product
Hst.	*hastane*	hospital
Hv. Kuv.	*Hava Kuvvetleri*	air force
İETT	*İstanbul Elektrik, Tünel, Tramvay İşletmesi*	Istanbul Municipality Services
İng.	*İngiltere; İngiliz*	England; English
İst.	*İstanbul*	Istanbul
İzm.	*İzmir*	Izmir
J.	*Jandarma*	gendarmerie

KDV	*Katma Değer Vergisi*	value added tax
KİT	*Kamu İktisati Teşekkülü*	state economic enterprise
K.Kuv.	*Kara Kuvvetleri*	army
krş.	*kuruş; karşılaştırınız*	kurush; compare
Ltd.	*Limitet (şirketi)*	Limited (Company)
Mah.	*Mahallesi*	quarter, district
Md.	*Müdür; Müdürlük*	director; directorate
Mey.	*Meydan*	(public) square
MİT	*Milli İstihbarat Teşkilatı*	National Intelligence Organization
MÖ	*Milattan Önce*	B.C., before Christ
MS	*Milattan Sonra*	A.D., anno Domini
no.	*numara*	number
p.	*paragraf*	paragraph
PK	*Posta Kutusu*	post office box
PTT	*Posta, Telgraf, Telefon (İdaresi)*	Post, Telegraph, Telephone (office)
s.	*sayfa*	page
sa.	*saat*	hour
Sn.	*Sayın*	esteemed
Sok.	*Sokak*	street
SSK	*Sosyal Sigortalar Kurumu*	Social Security Office
Şb.	*şube*	branch, department
Şrt. / Şti.	*şirket, şirketi*	company
TAŞ	*Türk Anonim Şirketi*	Turkish joint-stock company
TBMM	*Türkiye Büyük Millet Meclisi*	Turkish National Assembly
TC	*Türkiye Cumhuriyeti*	Turkish Republic
TCDD	*Türkiye Cumhuriyeti Devlet Demiryolları*	Turkish State Railways
THY	*Türk Hava Yolları*	Turkish Airlines
TL	*Türk Lirası*	Turkish Lira
TM	*Türk malı*	made in Turkey
TRT	*Türkiye Radyo Televizyon Kurumu*	Turkish Radio and Television Corporation
TSE	*Türk Standartlar Enstitüsü*	Turkish Standards Institute
TÜBİTAK	*Türkiye Bilimsel ve Teknik Araştırmalar Kurumu*	Turkish Scientific and Technical Research Institute
TTOK	*Türk Turing Otomobil Kurumu*	Turkish Touring Club
vb., vs.	*ve benzeri/vesaire*	etc., et cetera
yy.	*yüzyıl*	century
00	*yüznumara, tuvalet*	WC

Numerals

Cardinal numbers		Ordinal numbers	
0	sıfır	1.	birinci
1	bir	2.	ikinci
2	iki	3.	üçüncü
3	üç	4.	dördüncü
4	dört	5.	beşinci
5	beş	6.	altıncı
6	altı	7.	yedinci
7	yedi	8.	sekizinci
8	sekiz	9.	dokuzuncu
9	dokuz	10.	onuncu
10	on	11.	on birinci
11	on bir	12.	on ikinci
12	on iki	13.	on üçüncü
13	on üç	14.	on dördüncü
14	on dört	15.	on beşinci
15	on beş	16.	on altıncı
16	on altı	17.	on yedinci
17	on yedi	18.	on sekizinci
18	on sekiz	19.	on dokuzuncu
19	on dokuz	20.	yirminci
20	yirmi	21.	yirmi birinci
21	yirmi bir	22.	yirmi ikinci
22	yirmi iki	23.	yirmi üçüncü
30	otuz	30.	otuzuncu
40	kırk	40.	kırkıncı
50	elli	50.	ellinci
60	altmış	60.	altmışıncı
70	yetmiş	70.	yetmişinci
80	seksen	80.	sekseninci
90	doksan	90.	doksanıncı
100	yüz	100.	yüzüncü
101	yüz bir	101.	yüz birinci
230	iki yüz otuz	200.	iki yüzüncü
1 000	bin	230.	iki yüz otuzuncu
1 107	bin yüz yedi	1 000.	bininci
2 000	iki bin	1 107.	bin yüz yedinci
1 000 000	bir milyon	2 000.	iki bininci

Time

Although official time in Turkey is based on the 24-hour clock, the 12-hour system is used in conversation.

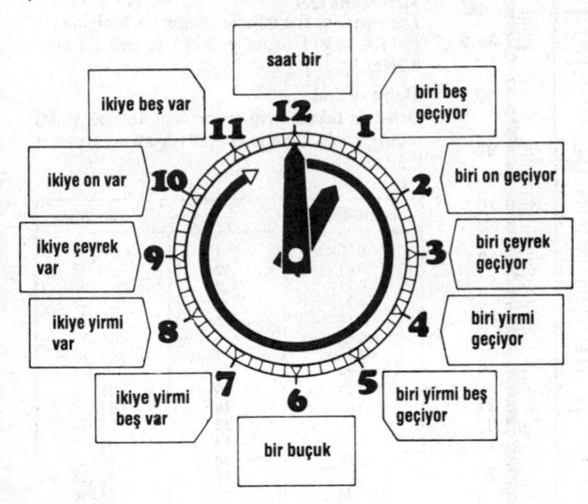

If you have to indicate that it is a.m. or p.m., add *sabah, öğleden sonra* or *akşam.*

Thus:

sabah saat sekiz	8 a.m.
saat öğleden sonra iki	2 p.m.
akşam saat sekiz	8 p.m.

Days of the Week

pazar	Sunday	*perşembe*	Thursday
pazartesi	Monday	*cuma*	Friday
salı	Tuesday	*cumartesi*	Saturday
çarşamba	Wednesday		

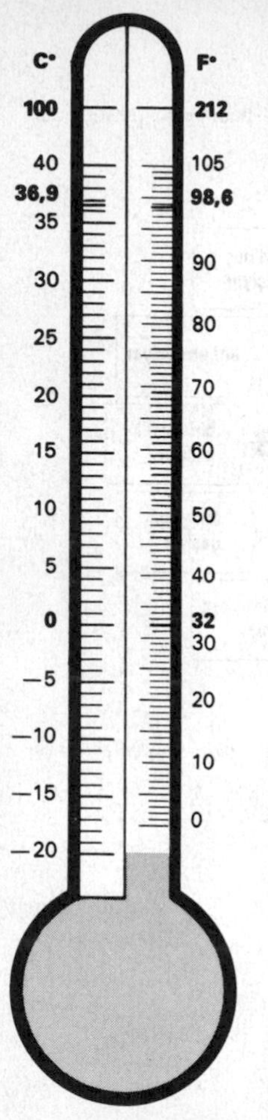

Conversion tables/ Çeviri tabloları

Meters and feet
The figure in the middle stands for both meters and feet, e.g. 1 meter = 3.281 ft. and 1 foot = 0.30 m.

Metre ve ayak
Ortadaki rakam hem metre hem de ayak yerini tutar. Örnek: 1 metre = 3,281 ayak ve 1 ayak = 0,30 m.

Meters/Metre		Feet/Ayak
0.30	**1**	3.281
0.61	**2**	6.563
0.91	**3**	9.843
1.22	**4**	13.124
1.52	**5**	16.403
1.83	**6**	19.686
2.13	**7**	22.967
2.44	**8**	26.248
2.74	**9**	29.529
3.05	**10**	32.810
3.66	**12**	39.372
4.27	**14**	45.934
6.10	**20**	65.620
7.62	**25**	82.023
15.24	**50**	164.046
22.86	**75**	246.069
30.48	**100**	328.092

Temperature
To convert Centigrade to Fahrenheit, multiply by 1.8 and add 32.
To convert Fahrenheit to Centigrade, subtract 32 from Fahrenheit and divide by 1.8.

Isı
Santigrat ısı derecelerini Fahrenhayt'a çevirmek için Santigrat'ı 1,8 ile çarpıp sonuca 32 ekleyin. Fahrenhayt ısı derecelerini Santigrat'a çevirmek için Fahrenhayt'tan 32 çıkarıp sonucu 1,8 rakamına bölün.

Some Basic Phrases	Bazı Temel Kalıplar
Please.	Lütfen.
Thank you very much.	Çok teşekkür ederim.
You're welcome.	Bir şey değil.
Good morning.	Günaydın.
Good afternoon.	İyi günler *(öğleden sonra)*.
Good evening.	İyi akşamlar.
Good night.	İyi geceler.
Good-by.	Allahaısmarladık.
See you later.	Tekrar görüşmek üzere.
Where is / Where are . . . ?	. . . nerede bulunur?
What do you call this?	Bunun adı ne?
What does that mean?	Bu ne demek?
Do you speak English?	İngilizce bilir misiniz?
Do you speak German?	Almanca bilir misiniz?
Do you speak French?	Fransızca bilir misiniz?
Do you speak Spanish?	İspanyolca bilir misiniz?
Do you speak Italian?	İtalyanca bilir misiniz?
Could you speak more slowly, please?	Lütfen daha yavaş konuşur musunuz?
I don't understand.	Anlamıyorum.
Can I have . . . ?	. . . rica ediyorum.
Can you show me . . . ?	Bana . . . gösterebilir misiniz?
Can you tell me . . . ?	Bana . . . söyleyebilir misiniz?
Can you help me, please?	Lütfen bana yardım eder misiniz?
I'd like . . .	. . . rica ediyorum/istiyorum.
We'd like . . .	. . . rica ediyoruz/istiyoruz.
Please give me . . .	Lütfen bana . . . verin.
Please bring me . . .	Lütfen bana . . . getirin.
I'm hungry.	Acıktım.
I'm thirsty.	Susadım.
I'm lost.	Yolumu kaybettim.
Hurry up!	Çabuk olun!

There is/There are . . .	. . . var.
There isn't/There aren't . . .	. . . yok.

Arrival	**Varış**
Your passport, please.	Lütfen pasaportunuzu gösterin.
Do you have anything to declare?	Gümrüğe tabi bir şeyiniz var mı?
No, nothing at all.	Hayır, hiçbir şeyim yok.
Can you help me with my luggage, please?	Lütfen valizlerimi alır mısınız?
Where's the bus to the center of town, please?	Şehrin merkezine giden otobüs nereden kalkıyor?
This way, please.	Bu taraftan lütfen.
Where can I get a taxi?	Nereden taksiye binebilirim?
What's the fare to . . . ?	. . . 'e ücret ne kadardır?
Take me to this address, please.	Lütfen beni bu adrese götürün.
I'm in a hurry.	Acelem var.

Hotel	**Otelde**
My name is . . .	Adım . . . 'dir.
Do you have a reservation?	Rezervasyonunuz var mı?
I'd like a room with a bath.	Banyolu bir oda istiyorum.
What's the price per night?	Bir gecelik ücret ne kadar?
May I see the room?	Odayı görebilir miyim?
What's my room number, please?	Oda numaram kaç acaba?
There's no hot water.	Sıcak su yok.
May I see the manager, please?	Müdürle görüşebilir miyim lütfen?
Did anyone telephone me?	Beni arayan oldu mu?
Is there any mail for me?	Bana mektup var mı?
May I have my bill (check), please?	Hesabı rica edebilir miyim?

Eating out	**Lokantada**
Do you have a fixed-price menu?	Tabldotunuz var mı?

May I see the menu?	Yemek listesini görebilir miyim?
May we have an ashtray, please?	Bir kül tablası rica edebilir miyiz?
Where's the bathroom, please?	Tuvalet nerede acaba?
I'd like an hors d'œuvre (starter).	Ordövr rica ediyorum.
Have you any soup?	Çorbanız var mı?
I'd like some fish.	Balık rica ediyorum.
What kind of fish do you have?	Balık olarak neyiniz var?
I'd like a steak.	Biftek rica ediyorum.
What vegetables do you have?	Sebzelerden ne var?
Nothing more, thanks.	Başka bir şey yok, teşekkürler.
What would you like to drink?	Ne içmek istersiniz?
I'll have a beer, please.	Bir bira istiyorum lütfen.
I'd like a bottle of wine.	Bir şişe şarap rica ediyorum.
May I have the bill (check), please?	Hesabı rica edebilir miyim?
Is service included?	Servis dahil mi?
Thank you, that was a very good meal.	Teşekkür ederim yemekten çok memnun kaldım.

Traveling	**Yolculukta**
Where's the railway station, please?	Gar ne tarafta acaba?
Where's the ticket office, please?	Gişe ne tarafta acaba?
I'd like a ticket to ...	...'e bir bilet istiyorum.
First or second class?	Birinci mevki mi, ikinci mevki mi?
First class, please.	Birinci mevki lütfen.
One-way or roundtrip (single or return)?	Yalnız gidiş mi, yoksa gidiş-dönüş mü?
Do I have to change trains?	Tren değiştirmem gerekir mi? (Aktarma yapmam gerekir mi?)
What platform does the train for ... leave from?	...'e gidecek tren hangi perondan kalkıyor?
Where's the nearest subway (underground) station?	En yakın metro istasyonu nerede acaba?
Where's the bus station, please?	Otobüs terminali nerede acaba?
When's the first bus to ... ?	...'e ilk otobüs ne zaman?
Please let me off at the next stop.	Lütfen beni bir sonraki durakta indirin.

Relaxing	Eğlence
What's on at the movies (cinema)?	Sinemada ne oynuyor?
What time does the film begin?	Film kaçta başlıyor?
Are there any tickets for tonight?	Bu akşam için bilet var mı?
Where can we go dancing?	Dansetmek için nereye gidebiliriz?

Meeting people	Tanışma
How do you do.	Memnun oldum.
How are you?	Nasılsınız?
Very well, thank you. And you?	Çok iyiyim, teşekkür ederim. Ya siz?
May I introduce . . . ?	Size . . .'i takdim edebilir miyim?
My name is . . .	Adım . . .
I'm very pleased to meet you.	Tanıştığımıza çok memnun oldum.
How long have you been here?	Ne kadar zamandır buradasınız?
It was nice meeting you.	Sizi tanımaktan memnunluk duydum.
Do you mind if I smoke?	Sigara içmemden rahatsız olur musunuz?
Do you have a light, please?	Kibritiniz/ateşiniz var mı acaba?
May I get you a drink?	Size bir içki ikram edebilir miyim?
May I invite you for dinner tonight?	Sizi bu akşam yemeğe davet edebilir miyim?
Where shall we meet?	Nerede buluşalım?

Shops, stores and services	Dükkânlar ve hizmetler
Where's the nearest bank, please?	En yakın banka nerede acaba?
Where can I cash some traveler's checks?	Seyahat çeklerini nerede bozdurabilirim?
Can you give me some small change, please?	Bana biraz bozuk para verebilir misiniz lütfen?
Where's the nearest pharmacy (chemist's)?	En yakın eczane nerededir?
How do I get there?	Oraya nasıl gidebilirim?
Is it within walking distance?	Yürüyerek gidilecek uzaklıkta mı?

Can you help me, lease?	Lütfen bana yardım eder misiniz?
How much is this? And that?	Bu ne kadar? Ya şu?
It's not quite what I want.	Bu tam istediğim değil.
I like it.	Bunu beğendim.
Can you recommend me something for sunburn?	Güneş yanığına karşı bir şey tavsiye edebilir misiniz?
I'd like a haircut, please.	Saçlarımı kestirmek istiyorum lütfen.
I'd like a manicure, please.	Manikür istiyorum lütfen.

Street directions	**Yol sorma**
Can you show me on the map where I am?	Bulunduğum yeri haritada gösterebilir misiniz?
You are on the wrong road.	Yanlış yoldasınız.
Go/walk straight ahead.	Dosdoğru gidin/yürüyün.
It's on the left/on the right.	Soldadır/sağdadır.

Emergencies	**Acil durumlar**
Call a doctor quickly.	Hemen bir doktor çağırın.
Call an ambulance.	Bir ambülans çağırın.
Please call the police.	Lütfen polis çağırın.

ingilizce-türkçe

---

english-turkish

Giriş

Bu sözlük pratik ihtiyaçlarınıza cevap vermek amacıyla hazırlanmıştır. Bu bakımdan, gereksiz dilbilimsel açıklamalardan kaçınılmıştır. Madde başlıkları tek kelimeden de, iki veya daha fazla kelimeden de oluşmuş olsa alfabetik sıraya göre verilmiştir. Bu kuralın tek istisnası, birkaç deyimin, deyimdeki en önemli kelime esas alınarak alfabetik sıraya konulmasıdır.

Her ana kelimenin ardından bu kelimenin okunuşu ve vurguları belirtilmiştir (bkz. "İngilizcenin Telaffuzu" bölümü). Bunun ardından da, geçerli olduğu durumlarda, kelimenin dilbilgisi açısından türü (isim, sıfat, fiil vs.) verilmiştir. Bir kelimenin dilde birden fazla türde görev yapabildiği durumlarda, karşılıklar ilgili türleri izleyecek şekilde gruplanmıştır.

İsimlerin çoğul halleri, kurallara uygunluğun söz konusu olmadığı durumlarda verilmiştir.

Tekrarlardan kaçınmak amacıyla, gerektiğinde ana kelimenin yerine tilde (~) işareti kullanılmıştır.

Kelimelerin çoğul hallerini verirken de kelimenin değişmeyen bölümünü göstermek için tire (-) işareti kullanılmıştır.

Bir fiilin önündeki yıldız (*) işareti, o fiilin düzensiz olduğunu belirtmektedir. Bu konuda daha fazla bilgi edinmek için düzensiz fiiller listesine başvurabilirsiniz.

Bu sözlükte, kelimelerin Amerikan İngilizcesindeki yazılış ve okunuşları temel alınmıştır. Ancak, kelimelerin yazılışları arasındaki farklar sözlükte aranıp bulunmalarını güçleştirecek türde ise, hem Amerikan hem de İngiliz İngilizcesindeki yazılışlar verilmiştir. Kelimelerin yazılış değil anlam açısından farklılık gösterdikleri durumlarda ise, anlamlar Amerikan (*Am*) veya İngiliz (*Br*) kullanımı oldukları belirtilerek verilmiştir.

Kısaltmalar

adj	sıfat	*p*	geçmiş zaman
adjAm	sıfat (Amerikan)	*pl*	çoğul
adjBr	sıfat (İngiliz)	*plAm*	çoğul (Amerikan)
adv	zarf	*plBr*	çoğul (İngiliz)
Am	Amerikan	*pp*	geçmiş zaman ortacı
art	tanımlık	*pr*	geniş zaman
Br	İngiliz	*pref*	önek
conj	bağlaç	*prep*	edat
n	isim	*pron*	zamir
nAm	isim (Amerikan)	*v*	fiil
nBr	isim (İngiliz)	*vAm*	fiil (Amerikan)
num	sayı	*vBr*	fiil (İngiliz)

İngilizcenin Telaffuzu

Sözlüğün bu bölümünde, satırbaşındaki her kelimeyi izleyen eğik çizgiler arasında, kelimenin Amerikan İngilizcesindeki en yaygın telaffuzu verilmiştir. Bu amaçla kullanılan sembollerin gösterdiği sesler aşağıda açıklanmıştır. Verilen açıklamalar dikkatle incelenirse, İngilizce kelimeler kolaylıkla ve yanlışsız olarak telaffuz edilebilir. Bu konuda size yardımcı olmak üzere verilen telaffuz ve vurgu işaretleri, dilin ses yapısını en berrak bir şekilde belirtmeyi amaçlamaktadır.

Ünsüzler

N — **n** sesinin ardından **g** sesini çıkarmaya çalışıp ancak henüz çıkarmamışken duyulan ses (si**ng**)

D — dil ucu üst ön dişlerin uçlarına değdirilip yumuşakça üfleyerek çıkarılan peltek **z** sesi (**th**en)

T — dil ucu üst ön dişlerin uçlarına değdirilip sertçe üflenerek çıkarılan peltek **s** sesi (**th**ink)

L — ka**l**mak kelimesindeki gibi kalın olarak çıkarılan **l** sesi (**l**ight)

v — Türkçedekinden daha sert olan ve üst ön dişlerle alt dudağı keserek çıkarılan **v** sesi (**v**ine)

İngilizcedeki diğer ünsüzler aşağı yukarı Türkçedeki gibi söylenir.

Ünlüler ve çiftünlüler

A — Türkçedeki **a** sesinden daha kısa ve kapalı bir ses (h**u**t)

E — **e** sesini ağzı iyice açarak çıkardığımız zaman duyulan, **a** ve **e** arası bir ses (h**a**t)

i — g**i**t kelimesindeki **i** sesinden daha açık bir ses (s**i**t)

O — Türkçedeki **o** ve **a** sesleri arasında bir ses (h**o**t)

u — çab**u**k kelimesindeki **u**'dan daha açık bir ses (b**oo**k)

aa — **a** sesi iki misli uzatılarak çıkarılan ses (c**a**r)

ii — Türkçede **iğ** derken çıkarılan uzun ses (n**ee**dle)

OO — **O** sesinden daha kapalı olan ve dudaklar pek yuvarlaklaşmadan ağız boşluğunun arka kısmından çıkarılan ses (c**au**ght)

uu — Türkçede **uğ** derken çıkarılan uzun ses (t**oo**)

au, ay, ey, iyı, ou, Oy gibi çiftünlüler çabuk ve bir arada çıkarılan iki sesten oluşurlar.

Vurgu düzeni

Bu sözlükte tam vurgulu olarak okunan heceler önlerindeki (ˈ) işareti ile, yarım vurgulu heceler ise önlerindeki (ˌ) işareti ile vurgusuz hecelerden ayrılmaktadır. İngilizcenin vurgu düzeni Türkçeye oranla daha belirgin olduğundan, vurgulu ve vurgusuz heceler arasındaki ayrım çok daha açık ve çarpıcıdır.

A

a /ey, ı/ *art* (an) bir, belirlemeyen tanımlık
abandon /ı'bEndın/ *v* bırakmak, terk etmek
abbey /'Ebii/ *n* manastır
abbreviate /ı'briivi,yeyt/ *v* kısaltmak
abbreviation /ı,briivi'yeyşın/ *n* kısaltma
aberration /,Ebı'reyşın/ *n* sapma, doğru yoldan ayrılma
ability /ı'biLıtii/ *n* iktidar, ehliyet, muktedir olma
able /'eybıL/ *adj* muktedir; hünerli; ***be ~ to*** gücü yetmek, yapabilmek
abnormal /,ıb'nOOrmıL/ *adj* anormal
aboard /ı'bOOrd/ *adv* gemi, tren vb. içine *veya* içinde
abolish /ı'bOLiş/ *v* kaldırmak
abortion /ı'bOOrşın/ *n* çocuk düşürme, kürtaj
about /ı'baut/ *prep* hakkında; *adv* yaklaşık; yakında, civarda
above /ı'bAv/ *prep* üstünde; *adv* üstte, yukarıda
abroad /ı'brOOd/ *adv* yabancı ülkede, yurt dışında
abrupt /ı'brApt/ *adj* beklenmedik, ani
abscess /'Ebses/ *n* apse, çıban
absence /'Ebsıns/ *n* yokluk, bulunmayış
absent /'Ebsınt/ *adj* yok, bulunmayan
absentminded /'Ebsınt'mayndid/ *adj* dalgın
absolutely /'EbsıLuutLii/ *adv* tamamen; kesin olarak
absorb /ıb'sOOrb/ *v* içine çekmek, emmek
abstain from /ıb'steyn/ -den kaçınmak, -den çekinmek
abstract /'EbstrEkt/ *adj* soyut
absurd /ıb'sÖrd/ *adj* anlamsız; gülünç
abundance /ı'bAndıns/ *n* bolluk, bereket
abundant /ı'bAndınt/ *adj* bol, bereketli
abuse /ı'byuus/ *n* kötüye kullanma; sövüp sayma
abyss /ı'bis/ *n* cehennem; uçurum
academy /ı'kEdımii/ *n* akademi
accelerate /ık'seLı,reyt/ *v* hızlanmak; hızlandırmak
accelerator /ık'seLı,reytır/ *n* gaz pedalı
accent /'Eksent/ *n* aksan; vurgu
accept /ık'sept/ *v* kabul etmek
access /Ek'ses/ *n* giriş; geçit; yaklaşma
accessible /ık'sesıbıL/ *adj* erişilebilir
accessory /ık'sesırii/ *n* aksesuar; suç ortağı

accident /'Eksıdınt/ *n* kaza
accidental /ˌEksı'dentıL/ *adj* kaza eseri, tesadüfi
accommodate /ı'kOmıˌdeyt/ *v* yerleştirmek, barındırmak; uydurmak
accomodations /ıˌkOmı'deyşınz/ *pl* yatacak yer
accompany /ı'kAmpınii/ *v* eşlik etmek
accomplish /ı'kAmpLiş/ *v* başarmak, üstesinden gelmek
in accordance with /in ı'kOOrdıns wiT/ -e göre, -e uygun olarak
according to /ı'kOOrdiN tu/ -e göre, -e nazaran
account /ı'kaunt/ *n* hesap; rapor; **~ for** hesap vermek; **on ~ of** için, -den dolayı
accountable /ı'kauntıbıL/ *adj* sorumlu
accumulate /ı'kyuumyıˌLeyt/ *v* toplamak, biriktirmek; birikmek, yığılmak
accurate /'Ekyırıt/ *adj* doğru, tam
accuse /ı'kyuuz/ *v* suçlamak, itham etmek
accused /ı'kyuuzd/ *n* sanık
accustom /ı'kAstım/ *v* alıştırmak; **accustomed** *adj* alışık, alışkın
ace /eys/ *n* iskambilde birli, as
ache /eyk/ *v* ağrımak; *n* acı, ağrı
achieve /ı'çiiv/ *v* başarmak; elde etmek
achievement /ı'çiivmınt/ *n* başarı
acid /'Esid/ *n* asit
acknowledge /ık'nOLic/ *v* onaylamak, kabul etmek
acne /'Eknii/ *n* sivilce, akne
acorn /'eykOOrn/ *n* meşe palamutu
acquaintance /ı'kweyntıns/ *n* tanıdık
acquire /ı'kwayr/ *v* ele geçirmek, kazanmak
acquisition /ˌEkwı'zişın/ *n* kazanılan şey
acquit /ı'kwit/ *v* aklamak, beraat ettirmek
acquittal /ı'kwitıL/ *n* suçsuzluk hükmü, beraat
across /ı'krOOs/ *prep* karşıdan karşıya, çapraz; *adv* ortasından, içinden *veya* üstünden karşıya geçerek
act /Ekt/ *n* yapılan şey, hareket; *v* hareket etmek; rol yapmak
action /'Ekşın/ *n* iş, eylem
active /'Ektiv/ *adj* canlı, hareketli
activity /Ek'tivıtii/ *n* faaliyet, etkinlik
actor /'Ektır/ *n* aktör, tiyatro oyuncusu
actress /'Ektris/ *n* aktris
actual /'EkçuuıL/ *adj* gerçek; şu andaki
actually /'EkçuuıLii/ *adv* gerçekten
acute /ı'kyuut/ *adj* şiddetli, keskin
adapt /ı'dEpt/ *v* uydurmak; uyarlamak
add /Ed/ *v* eklemek; toplamak
addict /'Edikt/ *n* tiryaki, müptela
adding machine /'EdiN mıˌşiin/ hesap makinesi
addition /ı'dişın/ *n* toplama; ek
additional /ı'dişınıL/ *adj* biraz daha; eklenilen
address /ı'dres/ *n* adres; *v* hitap etmek, söylev vermek
addressee /ˌEdre'sii/ *n* (postada) alıcı
adequate /'Edıkwıt/ *adj* uygun; yeterli
adjective /'Eciktiv/ *n* sıfat
adjourn /ı'cÖrn/ *v* ertelemek
adjust /ı'cAst/ *v* düzeltmek, ayar etmek
administer /Ed'ministır/ *v* yönetmek
administration /Edˌminis'treyşın/ *n* yönetim
administrative /Ed'minisˌtreytiv/ *adj* yönetimle ilgili
admiral /'EdmırıL/ *n* amiral
admiration /ˌEdmı'reyşın/ *n* hayranlık
admire /Ed'mayr/ *v* hayran olmak

admission /Ed'mişın/ *n* kabul; giriş; giriş ücreti
admit /Ed'mit/ *v* kabul etmek; izin vermek
admittance /Ed'mitıns/ *n* kabul, giriş; **no ~** girilmez
adolescent /,EdıL'esınt/ *adj, n* delikanlı, genç
adopt /ı'dOpt/ *v* benimsemek; kabul etmek; evlat edinmek
adorable /ı'dOOrıbıL/ *adj* çok güzel; çok iyi
adult /ı'dALt/ *n, adj* büyük, ergin
advance /ıd'vEns/ *n* ilerleme, yükselme; *v* ilerlemek, yükselmek; **in ~** önde, ileride; peşin olarak
advanced /ıd'vEnst/ *adj* ilerlemiş, ileri
advantage /ıd'vEntic/ *n* yarar, üstünlük
advantageous /Edvın'teycıs/ *adj* kârlı, yararlı
adventure /Ed'vençır/ *n* serüven
adverb /'Ed,vÖrb/ *n* zarf
advertisement /,Edvır'tayzmınt/ *n* ilan, reklam
advertising /'Edvır,tayziN/ *n* ilan; reklamcılık
advice /ıd'vays/ *n* öğüt; tavsiye
advise /ıd'vayz/ *v* öğüt vermek; tavsiye etmek
advocate /'Edvıkıt/ *n* avukat; taraftar
Aegean Sea /i'ciyın ,sii/ Ege Denizi
aerial /'eyriyıL/ *nBr* anten
aeroplane /'eyrı,pleyn/ *nBr* uçak
affair /ı'feyr/ *n* iş; olay; gönül macerası
affect /ı'fekt/ *v* etkilemek
affected /ı'fektid/ *adj* sahte tavırlı; yapmacık
affection /ı'fekşın/ *n* sevgi
affectionate /ı'fekşınit/ *adj* seven, sevgi gösteren
affiliated /ı'fili,yeytid/ *adj* yakın ilişki kurulan, birbirine bağlı
affirmative /ı'fÖrmıtiv/ *adj* olumlu
affliction /ı'fLikşın/ *n* keder; bela
afford /ı'fOOrd/ *v* yeterince parası olmak; işine gelmek
afraid /ı'freyd/ *adj* korkan, korkmuş; ***be ~ of** -den korkmak
Africa /'Efrikı/ Afrika
African /'Efrikın/ *adj* Afrika'ya ait; *n* Afrikalı
after /'Eftır/ *prep* -den sonra, arkasından
afternoon /,Eftır'nuun/ *n* öğleden sonra
afterward /'Eftırwırd/ *adv* sonra, sonradan
again /ı'gen/ *adv* tekrar, bir daha; **~ and again** sürekli olarak, tekrar tekrar
against /ı'genst/ *prep* -e karşı; -in aleyhinde
age /eyc/ *n* yaş; **of ~** reşit; **under ~** reşit olmayan
aged /'eycid/ *adj* yaşlı, ihtiyar
agency /'eycınsii/ *n* acente; ajans
agenda /ı'cendı/ *n* gündem, görülecek işler listesi
agent /'eycınt/ *n* temsilci, vekil
aggressive /ı'gresiv/ *adj* saldırgan
agitate /'Eci,teyt/ *v* kışkırtmak, karıştırmak
ago /ı'gou/ *adv* önce, evvel
agony /'Egınii/ *n* acı, ıstırap
agrarian /ı'greyriyın/ *adj* tarımsal
agree /ı'grii/ *v* razı olmak; uyuşmak
agreeable /ı'grii-ıbıL/ *adj* hoş; münasip, iyi
agreement /ı'griimınt/ *n* anlaşma; sözleşme
agriculture /'Egrı,kALçır/ *n* tarım
ahead /ı'hed/ *adv* ileride, ileriye; **~ of** önünde; ***go ~** devam etmek; **straight ~** dosdoğru

aid /eyd/ *n* yardım; *v* yardım etmek
ailment /'eyLmınt/ *n* rahatsızlık, hastalık
aim /eym/ *n* amaç, hedef; ~ **at** nişan almak; amaçlamak
air /eyr/ *n* hava; *v* havalandırmak
air-conditioning /,eyrkın'dişıniN/ *n* klima sistemi; **air-conditioned** *adj* klimalı
aircraft /'eyr,krEft/ *n* (pl ~) uçak
airfield /'eyr,fiiLd) *n* havaalanı
airfilter /'eyr,fiLtır/ *n* hava filtresi
airline /'eyr,Layn/ *n* havayolu
airmail /'eyr,meyL/ *n* uçak postası
airplane /'eyr,pLeyn/ *nAm* uçak
airport /'eyr,pOOrt/ *n* havalimanı
airsickness /'eyr,siknıs/ *n* uçak tutması
airtight /'eyr,tayt/ *adj* hava geçirmez
airy /'eyrii/ *adj* havadar
aisle /ayL/ *n* iki sıra koltuk arasındaki yol
alarm /ı'Laarm/ *n* korku; tehlike işareti; *v* korkutmak; tehlikeyi haber vermek; ~ **clock** çalar saat
Albania /EL'beyniyı/ Arnavutluk
Albanian /EL'beyniyın/ *adj* Arnavutluk'a ait; *n* Arnavut; Arnavutça
album /'ELbım/ *n* albüm
alcohol /'ELkı,hOOL/ *n* alkol
alcoholic /,ELkı'hOOLik/ *adj, n* alkolik
ale /eyL/ *n* bir tür bira
alert /ı'LÖrt/ *adj* tetik, açıkgöz, uyanık
algebra /'ELcıbrı/ *n* cebir
Algeria /EL'ciiriyı/ Cezayir
Algerian /EL'ciiriyın/ *adj* Cezayir'le ilgili; *n* Cezayirli
alien /'eyLiyın/ *n, adj* yabancı
alike /ı'Layk/ *adj* benzer, aynı; *adv* benzer biçimde
alimony /'ELimınii/ *n* nafaka
alive /ı'Layv/ *adj* canlı, hayatta olan, yaşayan
all /OOL/ *adj* bütün, hepsi; **in** ~ her şey dahil; ~ **right!** peki, olur!
all-around /'OOLı'raund/ *adj Am* birçok alanda başarılı
allergy /'ELırcii/ *n* alerji
alley /'ELii/ n dar yol
alliance /ı'Layıns/ *n* birleşme, ittifak
allocate /'ELı,keyt/ *v* ayırmak, tahsis etmek
allot /ı'LOt/ *v* pay dağıtmak, paylaştırmak; tahsis etmek
allow /ı'Lau/ *v* izin vermek; ***be allowed** izin verilmiş olmak
allowance /ı'Lauıns/ *n* ödenek
all-round /'OOL'raund/ *adj Br* çok yönlü
ally /'ELay/ *n* müttefik, dost; **Allies** *pl* Müttefik Devletler
almanac /'OOLmı,nEk/ *n* almanak, yıllık
almond /'aamınd/ *n* badem
almost /'OOLmoust/ *adv* hemen hemen, neredeyse
alone /ı'Loun/ *adv* yalnız
along /ı'LON/ *prep* boyunca
aloud /ı'Laud/ *adv* yüksek sesle
alphabet /'ELfı,bet/ *n* alfabe, abece
already /OOL'redii/ *adv* zaten, şimdiden, halihazırda
also /'OOLsou/ *adv* dahi, de, da
altar /'OOLtır/ *n* minber
alter /'OOLtır/ *v* değiştirmek
alteration /,OOLtı'reyşın/ *n* değişiklik, düzeltme
alternate /OOL'tÖrnıt/ *adj* sıra ile olan, nöbetleşe değişen
alternative /OOL'tÖrnıtiv/ *n* iki şıktan biri, seçenek
although /OOL'Dou/ *conj* her ne kadar, ise de
altitude /'ELtı,tuud/ *n* yükseklik
alto /'ELtou/ *n* (pl ~s) tenordan kalın erkek sesi

altogether /ˌOOLtı'geDır/ *adv* bütünüyle, tamamen
aluminum /ı'Luumınım/ *n* alüminyum
always /'OOLweyz/ *adv* her zaman
am /Em/ *v* (pr be)
amaze /ı'meyz/ *v* şaşırtmak
amazement /ı'meyzmınt/ *n* şaşkınlık
ambassador /Em'bEsıdır/ *n* büyükelçi
amber /'Embır/ *n* kehribar
ambiguous /Em'bigyuuıs/ *adj* belirgin olmayan; iki anlamlı
ambitious /Em'bişıs/ *adj* hırslı
ambulance /'EmbyıLıns/ *n* ambülans
ambush /'Embuş/ *n* pusu
amend /ı'mend/ *v* düzeltmek
America /ı'merikı/ Amerika
American /ı'merikın/ *adj* Amerika'ya ait; *n* Amerikalı
amethyst /'EmiTist/ *n* mor yakut
amiable /'eymiyıbıL/ *adj* cana yakın, hoş, sevimli
amid /ı'mid/ *prep* arasında, ortasında
ammonia /ı'mouniyı/ *n* amonyak
amnesty /'Emnistii/ *n* genel af
among /ı'mAN/ *prep* arasında; ~ **other things** diğerleri arasında
amount /ı'maunt/ *n* miktar; ~ **to** tutarında olmak, tutmak; varmak
amuse /ı'myuuz/ *v* eğlendirmek, hoşça vakit geçirtmek
amusement /ı'myuuzmınt/ *n* eğlence
amusing /ı'myuuziN/ *adj* hoş, eğlendirici
analysis /ı'nELısis/ *n* (pl -ses) analiz, tahlil
analyst /'EnıList/ *n* tahlilci; psikanalist
analyze /'EnıLˌayz/ *v* analiz etmek, tahlil etmek
anarchy /'Enırkii/ *n* anarşi, kargaşa
Anatolia /ˌEnı'touLiyı/ Anadolu
anatomy /ı'nEtımii/ *n* anatomi
ancestor /'Enˌsestır/ *n* ata, cet
anchor /'ENkır/ *n* gemi demiri, çapa
anchovy /'Enˌçouvii/ *n* hamsi; ançüez
ancient /'eynşınt/ *adj* eski dönemlere ait
and /ınd, ın; En/ *conj* ve
anemia /ı'niimiyı/ *n* kansızlık
anesthesia /ˌEnis'Tiijı/ *n* anestezi, duyumsuzlaştırma
anesthetic /ˌEnis'Tetik/ *n* anestetik, uyuşturucu
angel /'eyncıL/ *n* melek
anger /'ENgır/ *n* öfke, kızgınlık
angle /'ENgıL/ *v* olta ile balık avlamak; *n* açı
angry /'ENgrii/ *adj* kızgın, öfkeli
animal /'EnımıL/ *n* hayvan
ankle /'ENkıL/ *n* ayak bileği
annex[1] /'Eneks/ *n* ek
annex[2] /ı'neks/ *v* eklemek
anniversary /ˌEnı'vÖrsırii/ *n* yıldönümü
announce /ı'nauns/ *v* bildirmek, açıklamak, duyurmak
announcement /ı'naunsmınt/ *n* anons, bildiri, duyuru
annoy /ı'nOy/ *v* usandırmak, taciz etmek, sinirlendirmek
annoyance /ı'nOyıns/ *n* can sıkıntısı, öfke
annoying /ı'nOyiN/ *adj* sinirlendirici
annual /'EnyuuıL/ *adj* yıllık
annul /ı'nAL/ *v* iptal etmek, bozmak
per annum /ˌpır 'Enım/ yılda
anonymous /ı'nOnımıs/ *adj* isimsiz, anonim
another /ı'nADır/ *adj* bir diğer
answer /'Ensır/ *v* cevaplamak; *n* cevap
ant /Ent/ *n* karınca
antenna /En'tenı/ *n* anten
anthology /En'TOLıcii/ *n* antoloji
anthropology /ˌEnTrı'pOLıcii/ *n* antropoloji, insanbilim

antibiotic /ˌEntiiba'yOtik/ *n* antibiyotik
anticipate /En'tisıˌpeyt/ *v* önceden görmek, ummak, beklemek
antifreeze /'EntiˌfriiZ/ *n* antifriz
antipathy /En'tipıTii/ *n* antipati, karşıt duygu
antique /En'tiik/ *adj* eski zamanlara ait; *n* antika; ~ **dealer** antikacı
antiquity /En'tikwıtii/ *n* eski çağ; **antiquities** *pl* antikalar, eski zaman kalıntıları
antiseptic /ˌEnti'septik/ *n* antiseptik
anxiety /EN'zayıtii/ *n* endişe
anxious /'ENkşıs/ *adj* endişeli; istekli, sabırsız
any /'enii/ *adj* herhangi bir
anybody /'eniiˌbOdii/ *pron* herhangi biri
anyhow /'eniiˌhau/ *adv* her nasılsa, nasıl olursa olsun
anyone /'eniiˌwAn/ *pron* herhangi biri
anything /'eniiˌTiN/ *pron* herhangi bir şey
anyway /'eniiˌwey/ *adv* nasıl olursa olsun
anywhere /'EniiˌhweyR/ *adv* herhangi bir yere *veya* yerde
apart /ı'paart/ *adv* ayrı; ~ **from** -den başka
apartment /ı'paartmınt/ *nAm* apartman dairesi; ~ **house** *Am* apartman
aperitif /ıˌperı'tiif/ *n* aperitif
apologize /ı'pOLıˌcayz/ *v* özür dilemek
apology /ı'pOLıcii/ *n* özür
apparatus /ˌEpı'reytıs/ *n* aygıt, cihaz
apparent /ı'pErınt/ *adj* açıkça görünen
apparently /ı'pErıntLii/ *adv* görünüşe göre, galiba
apparition /ˌEpı'rişın/ *n* görüntü, hayalet
appeal /ı'piiL/ *n* çekicilik, cazibe
appear /ı'piir/ *v* görünmek; ortaya çıkmak
appearance /ı'piirıns/ *n* görünüş
appendicitis /ıˌpendı'saytis/ *n* apandisit
appendix /ı'pendiks/ *n* (pl -dices, -dixes) ilave, ek
appetite /'EpıˌtayT/ *n* iştah
appetizer /'Epıˌtayzır/ *n* iştah açıcı şey, çerez
appetizing /'EpıˌtayziN/ *adj* iştah kabartan
applaud /ı'pLOOd/ *v* alkışlamak
applause /ı'pLOOz/ *n* alkış, alkışlama
apple /'EpıL/ *n* elma
appliance /ı'pLayıns/ *n* alet
application /ˌEpLı'keyşın/ *n* uygulama; dilekçe, başvuru
apply /ı'pLay/ *v* uygulamak; başvurmak
appoint /ı'pOynt/ *v* tayin etmek, atamak
appointment /ı'pOyntmınt/ *n* tayin, atama
appreciate /ı'priişiˌyeyt/ *v* takdir etmek
appreciation /ıˌpriişi'yeyşın/ *n* takdir
approach /ı'prouç/ *v* yaklaşmak; *n* yanaşma, yaklaşma
appropriate /ı'proupriyit/ *adj* uygun
approval /ı'pruuvıL/ *n* onaylama, tasvip; **on** ~ beğenildiği takdirde
approve /ı'pruuv/ *v* onaylamak; ~ **of** uygun bulmak
approximate /ı'prOksımit/ *adj* yaklaşık
approximately /ı'prOksımitLii/ *adv* yaklaşık olarak
apricot /'eyprıˌkOt/ *n* kayısı
April /'eyprıL/ nisan
apron /'eyprın/ *n* önlük
aquarium /ı'kweyriyım/ *n* akvaryum
Aquarius /ı'kweyriyıs/ Kova burcu
aqueduct /'EkwıˌdAkt/ *n* sukemeri

Arab /'Erıb/ *adj* Araplara ait; *n* Arap
Arabic /'Erıbik/ *n* Arapça
arbitrary /'aarbı,trerii/ *adj* kendince, keyfi
arcade /'aar,keyd/ *n* pasaj, kemer altı, üstü kapalı çarşı
arch /aarç/ *n* kemer, tak
archaeologist /,aarki'yOLıcist/ *n* arkeolog
archaeology /,aarki'yOLıcii/ *n* arkeoloji
archbishop /'aarç'bişıp/ *n* başpiskopos
arched /aarçt/ *adj* kemerli
architect /'aarkı,tekt/ *n* mimar
architecture /'aarkı,tekçır/ *n* mimarlık
archives /'aarkayvz/ *pl* arşiv
are /aar/ *v* (pr be)
area /'eyriyı/ *n* alan, bölge; ~ **code** *Am* telefon yerel kodu
Argentina /,aarcın'tiinı/ Arjantin
Argentinian /,aarcın'tiniyın/ *adj* Arjantin'e ait; *n* Arjantinli
argue /'aargyuu/ *v* tartışmak
argument /'aargyımınt/ *n* tartışma, münakaşa
arid /'Erid/ *adj* kurak, çorak
Aries /'eyriiz/ Koç burcu
***arise** /ı'rayz/ *v* yükselmek, doğmak; kalkmak
arithmetic /ı'riTmı,tik/ *n* aritmetik
arm /aarm/ *n* kol; silah; *v* silahlanmak
armchair /'aarm,çeyr/ *n* koltuk
armed /aarmd/ *adj* silahlı; ~ **forces** silahlı kuvvetler
Armenian /aar,miiniyın/ *adj* Ermenilere ait; *n* Ermeni; Ermenice
armor /'aarmır/ *n* zırh
army /'aarmii/ *n* ordu
aroma /ı'roumı/ *n* hoş koku
around /ı'raund/ *prep* çevresinde
arrange /ı'reync/ *v* düzenlemek
arrangement /ı'reyncmınt/ *n* düzenleme
arrest /ı'rest/ *v* tutuklamak
arrival /ı'rayvıL/ *n* varış
arrive /ı'rayv/ *v* varmak
arrow /'Erou/ *n* ok
art /aart/ *n* sanat; ustalık; ~ **collection** sanat koleksiyonu; ~ **gallery** sanat galerisi; ~ **history** sanat tarihi; ~ **school** güzel sanatlar akademisi
artery /'aartırii/ *n* atardamar
artichoke /'aartı,çouk/ *n* enginar
article /'aartikıL/ *n* makale; madde
artifice /'aartıfis/ *n* hüner
artificial /aartı'fişıL/ *adj* yapay; sahte
artist /'aartist/ *n* sanatçı
artistic /aar'tistik/ *adj* sanat yönü olan
as /Ez/ *conj* gibi, kadar, olarak, iken; ~ **if** sanki, güya
asbestos /Es'bestıs/ *n* amyant
ascend /ı'send/ *v* yükselmek
ascent /ı'sent/ *n* yükselme, yükseliş
ascertain /,Esır'teyn/ *v* doğrusunu anlamak, araştırmak
ash /Eş/ *n* kül
ashamed /ı'şeymd/ *adj* mahcup, utanmış; ***be** ~ utanmak
ashore /ı'şOOr/ *adv* kıyıda, kıyıya
ashtray /'Eş,trey/ *n* kül tablası
Asia /'eyjı/ Asya
Asian /'eyjın/ *adj* Asya'ya ait; *n* Asyalı
aside /ı'sayd/ *adv* bir kenara, kenarda
ask /Esk/ *v* sormak; istemek
asleep /ı'sLiip/ *adj* uykuda
asparagus /ı'spErıgıs/ *n* kuşkonmaz
aspect /'Espekt/ *n* görünüş; cephe
asphalt /'EsfOOLt/ *n* asfalt
aspire /ı'spayr/ *v* arzu etmek, amaç edinmek

aspirin /'Espırin/ *n* aspirin
ass /Es/ *n* eşek
assassination /ı,sesı'neyşın/ *n* suikast
assault /ı'sOOLt/ *v* hücum etmek, saldırmak
assemble /ı'sembıL/ *v* toplanmak
assembly /ı'sembLii/ *n* toplantı, meclis
assignment /ı'saynmınt/ *n* atama; ödev; tahsis
assign to /ı'sayn/ atamak; ayırmak, tahsis etmek
assist /ı'sist/ *v* yardım etmek
assistance /ı'sistıns/ *n* yardım
assistant /ı'sistınt/ *n* asistan, yardımcı
associate[1] /ı'souşiyit/ *n* iş arkadaşı; ~ **professor** doçent
associate[2] /ı'souşi,yeyt/ *v* ortak olmak; birleştirmek; bağlantı kurmak; ~ **with** sık sık birlikte olmak
association /ı,sousi'yeyşın/ *n* kurum, dernek
assort /ı'sOOrt/ *v* sınıflandırmak
assortment /ı'sOOrtmınt/ *n* çeşitler
assume /ı'suum/ *v* üzerine almak; varsaymak
assumption /ı'sAmpşın/ *n* farz, varsayım
assure /ı'şuur/ *v* temin etmek
asthma /'Ezmı/ *n* astım
astonish /ı'stOniş/ *v* şaşırtmak
astonishing /ı'stOnişiN/ *adj* şaşırtıcı
astonishment /ı'stOnişmınt/ *n* hayret, şaşkınlık
astronomy /ı'strOnımii/ *n* astronomi
asylum /ı'sayLım/ *n* sığınak; kimsesiz veya düşkünleri barındıran kurum
at /Et, ıt/ *prep* -de, -da
ate /eyt/ *v* (p eat)
atheist /'eyTii-ist/ *n* Tanrıtanımaz
Athens /'ETınz/ Atina
athlete /'ETLiit/ *n* atlet, sporcu
athletics /ET'Letiks/ *pl* atletizm
Atlantic /ıt'LEntik/ Atlas Okyanusu
atmosphere /'Etmıs,fiir/ *n* atmosfer
atom /'Etım/ *n* atom
atomic /ı'tOmik/ *adj* atomla ilgili, nükleer
atomizer /'Etı,mayzır/ *n* püskürteç
attach /ı'tEç/ *v* bağlamak, iliştirmek
attack /ı'tEk/ *v* saldırmak; *n* saldırı, hücum
attain /ı'teyn/ *v* erişmek, elde etmek
attainable /ı'teynıbıL/ *adj* erişilebilir
attempt /ı'tempt/ *v* teşebbüs etmek; *n* girişim
attend /ı'tend/ *v* gidip hazır bulunmak, katılmak; ~ **on** refakatinde bulunmak; ~ **to** ilgilenmek
attendance /ı'tendıns/ *n* hazır bulunma; devam
attendant /ı'tendınt/ *n* hizmetçi; refakatçi
attention /ı'tenşın/ *n* dikkat; ***pay** ~ dikkat etmek
attentive /ı'tentiv/ *adj* dikkatli
attic /'Etik/ *n* tavan arası
attitude /'Eti,tuud/ *n* tutum, tavır
attorney /ı'tÖrnii/ *n* avukat, vekil
attract /ı'trEkt/ *v* çekmek, cezbetmek
attraction /ı'trEkşın/ *n* cazibe, çekim
attractive /ı'trEktiv/ *adj* cazip
auburn /'OObırn/ *adj* kumral, kestane rengi
auction /'OOkşın/ *n* açık artırma ile satış
audible /'OOdıbıL/ *adj* duyulabilir
audience /'OOdiyıns/ *n* dinleyiciler, seyirciler
auditor /'OOdıtır/ *n* dinleyici; hesap kontrolörü
auditorium /,OOdı'tOOriyım/ *n* konferans salonu
August /'OOgıst/ ağustos
aunt /Ent/ *n* hala, teyze
Australia /OOs'treyLyı/ Avustralya

Australian /OOs'treyLyın/ *adj* Avustralya'ya ait; *n* Avustralyalı
Austria /'OOstriyı/ Avusturya
Austrian /'OOstriyın/ *adj* Avusturya'ya ait; *n* Avusturyalı
authentic /OO'Tentik/ *adj* gerçek, inanılır
author /'OOTır/ *n* yazar
authoritarian /ı,TOOrı'teyriyın/ *adj* otoriter, otorite yanlısı
authority /ı'TOOrıtii/ *n* otorite, yetki; makam
authorization /,OOTırı'zeyşın/ *n* yetki verme; izin
automatic /,OOtı'mEtik/ *adj* otomatik
automation /,OOtı'meyşın/ *n* makineleşme, otomasyon
automobile /'OOtımı,biiL/ *n* otomobil; ~ **club** otomobil kulübü
autonomous /OO'tOnımıs/ *adj* özerk
autopsy /'OO,tOpsii/ *n* otopsi
autumn /'OOtım/ *n* sonbahar
available /ı'veyLıbıL/ *adj* kullanılabilir; geçerli; elde mevcut
avalanche /'Evı,LEnç/ *n* çığ
avaricious /,Evı'rişıs/ *adj* tamahkâr, haris
avenue /'Evı,nuu/ *n* bulvar
average /'Evric/ *adj* ortalama; **on the** ~ ortalama olarak
averse /ı'vÖrs/ *adj* karşı, zıt
aversion /ı'vÖrjın/ *n* hoşlanmayış; nefret
avert /ı'vÖrt/ *v* başka tarafa çevirmek
aviation /,eyvi'yeyşın/ *n* havacılık
avoid /ı'vOyd/ *v* kaçınmak
await /ı'weyt/ *v* beklemek
awake /ı'weyk/ *adj* uyanık, uyanmış
***awake** /ı'weyk/ *v* uyanmak; uyandırmak
award /ı'wOOrd/ *n* ödül; *v* ödül olarak vermek
aware /ı'weyr/ *adj* haberdar, farkında
away /ı'wey/ *adv* uzağa, uzakta; ***go** ~ gitmek, ayrılmak
awful /'OOfıL/ *adj* korkunç, müthiş
awkward /'OOkwırd/ *adj* beceriksiz; hantal
axe /Eks/ *n* balta
axle /'EksıL/ *n* araba mili, dingil

B

baby /'beybii/ *n* bebek; ~ **carriage** *Am* bebek arabası
baby-sitter /'beybii,sitır/ *n* bebek bakıcısı
bachelor /'bEçıLır/ *n* bekâr erkek
back /bEk/ *n* arka; sırt; *adv* geriye, arkaya; ***go** ~ dönmek
backache /'bEk,eyk/ *n* sırt ağrısı
backbone /'bEk,boun/ *n* belkemiği
backgammon /'bEk,gEmın/ *n* tavla
background /'bEk,graund/ *n* arka plan, zemin; formasyon
backward /'bEkwırd/ *adv* geriye doğru
bacon /'beykın/ *n* tuzlanmış domuz eti
bacterium /bEk'tiiriyım/ *n* (pl -ria) bakteri
bad /bEd/ *adj* kötü; zararlı
bag /bEg/ *n* çanta
baggage /'bEgic/ *n* bagaj, yolcu eşyası; ~ **deposit office** *Am* (bagaj) emanet bürosu; **hand** ~ el çantası
Baghdad /'bEgdEd/ Bağdat
bail /beyL/ *n* kefalet
bait /beyt/ *n* olta yemi
bake /beyk/ *v* fırında pişirmek
baker /'beykır/ *n* ekmekçi
bakery /'beykırii/ *n* fırın, ekmekçi dükkânı
balance /'bELıns/ *n* denge; terazi;

bakiye
balcony /'bELkınii/ *n* balkon
bald /bOOLd/ *adj* dazlak
ball /bOOL/ *n* top; balo
ballet /bE'Ley/ *n* bale
balloon /bı'Luun/ *n* balon
ball-point pen /'bOOL,pOynt 'pen/ tükenmez kalem
ballroom /'bOOL,ruum/ *n* balo salonu
bamboo /bEm'buu/ *n* (pl ~s) bambu
ban /bEn/ *v* yasaklamak
banana /bı'nEnı/ *n* muz
band /bEnd/ *n* bağ; kuşak; bando
bandage /'bEndic/ *n* sargı bezi
bandit /'bEndit/ *n* haydut, eşkıya
bangle /'bENgıL/ *n* bilezik
banisters /'bEnistırz/ *pl* tırabzan
bank /bENk/ *n* banka; set, kıyı; ~ **account** banka hesabı; ~ **note** banknot, kâğıt para; ~ **rate** faiz oranı
bankbook /'bENk,buk/ *n* banka cüzdanı
bankrupt /'bENk,rApt/ *adj* müflis, meteliksiz
banner /'bEnır/ *n* bayrak, sancak
banquet /'bENkwit/ *n* şölen, ziyafet; ~ **hall** şölen salonu
baptism /'bEp,tizım/ *n* vaftiz
baptize /bEp'tayz/ *v* vaftiz etmek
bar /bar/ *n* çubuk; engel; bar; baro
barbarian /baar'beyriyın/ *n* vahşi, barbar
barber /'baarbır/ *n* berber, kuaför
bare /beyr/ *adj* çıplak; çorak
barely /'beyrLii/ *adv* ancak, zar zor
bargain /'baargin/ *n* kelepir; *v* pazarlık etmek
baritone /'bErı,toun/ *n* bariton
bark /baark/ *n* ağaç kabuğu; havlama; *v* havlamak
barley /'baarLii/ *n* arpa
barmaid /'baar,meyd/ *n* barda içki servisi yapan kadın
barman /'baarmın/ *n* (pl -men) barmen
barn /baarn/ *n* ahır; samanlık
barometer /bı'rOmıtır/ *n* barometre
baroque /bı'rouk/ *adj* barok
barracks /'bErıks/ *pl* kışla; baraka
barrel /'bErıL/ *n* varil
barricade /'bErı,keyd/ *n* barikat, siper; *v* barikat kurmak, engelle kapatmak
barrier /'bEriyır/ *n* engel
bartender /'baar,tendır/ *n* barmen
base /beys/ *n* esas, temel; *v* dayandırmak
baseball /'beys,bOOL/ *n* beysbol
basement /'beysmınt/ *n* bodrum katı
basic /'beysik/ *adj* esas, temel
basilica /bı'siLikı/ *n* bazilika, kilise
basin /'beysin/ *n* leğen; lavabo
basis /'beysis/ *n* (pl bases) temel, ilke
basket /'bEskit/ *n* sepet
basketball /'bEskit,bOOL/ *n* basketbol
bass[1] /beys/ *n* bas, kalın ses
bass[2] /bEs/ *n* (pl ~) levrek
bastard /'bEstırd/ *n* piç
batch /bEç/ *n* bir defada alınan miktar, bölüm
bath /bET/ *n* banyo; ~ **towel** büyük havlu;
bathe /beyD/ *v* banyo yapmak; banyo yaptırmak
bathing cap /'beyDiN ,kEp/ banyo başlığı, bone
bathing suit /'beyDiN ,suut/ mayo
bathing trunks /'beyDiN ,trANks/ erkek mayosu
bathrobe /'bET,roub/ *n* bornoz
bathroom /'bET,ruum/ *n* banyo; tuvalet
bathtub /'bET,tAb/ *n* banyo küveti
batter /'bEtır/ *n* sulu hamur
battery /'bEtırii/ *n* pil; akü
battle /'bEtıL/ *n* çarpışma; savaş;

v çarpışmak
bay /bey/ *n* körfez; *v* havlamak, ulumak
***be** /bii/ *v* olmak
beach /biiç/ *n* kumsal, plaj; **nudist** ~ çıplaklar kampı
bead /biid/ *n* boncuk; **beads** *pl* kolye
beak /biik/ *n* gaga
beam /biim/ *n* şua, ışın; kiriş
bean /biin/ *n* fasulye
bear /beyr/ *n* ayı
***bear** /beyr/ *v* taşımak; tahammül etmek; doğurmak
beard /biird/ *n* sakal
bearer /'beyrır/ *n* taşıyan kimse, hamil
beast /biist/ *n* hayvan; ~ **of prey** yırtıcı hayvan
***beat** /biit/ *v* dövmek; çırpmak
beautiful /'byuutifıL/ *adj* güzel
beauty /'byuutii/ *n* güzellik; ~ **parlor** güzellik salonu; ~ **treatment** cilt ve vücut bakımı
beaver /'biivır/ *n* kunduz
because /bi'kOOz/ *conj* çünkü; ~ **of** -den dolayı
***become** /bi'kAm/ *v* olmak; yakışmak
bed /bed/ *n* yatak; ~ **and board** tam pansiyon; ~ **and breakfast** yatak ve kahvaltı dahil pansiyon
bedbug /'bed,bAg/ *n* tahtakurusu
bedding /'bediN/ *n* yatak takımı
bedroom /'bed,ruum/ *n* yatak odası
bedspread /'bed,spred/ *n* yatak örtüsü
bee /bii/ *n* arı
beech /biiç/ *n* kayın ağacı
beef /biif/ *n* sığır eti
beehive /'bii,hayv/ *n* arı kovanı
been /bin/ *v* (pp be)
beer /biir/ *n* bira
beeswax /'biiz,wEks/ *n* balmumu
beet /biit/ *n* pancar
beetroot /'biit,ruut/ *n* pancar
before /bi'fOOr/ *prep* -den önce; *adv* önceleri
beg /beg/ *v* dilenmek; yalvarmak
beggar /'begır/ *n* dilenci
***begin** /bi'gin/ *v* başlamak
beginner /bi'ginır/ *n* yeni başlayan kimse, acemi
beginning /bi'giniN/ *n* başlangıç
on behalf of /On bi'hEf ıv/ adına, namına
behave /bi'heyv/ *v* davranmak
behavior /bi'heyvyır/ *n* davranış, hareket, tavır
behind /bi'haynd/ *prep* arkasında, gerisinde; *adv* geride, arkada
beige /beyj/ *adj* bej rengi
being /'bii-iN/ *n* varlık; oluş
Belgian /'beLcın/ *adj* Belçika'ya ait; *n* Belçikalı
Belgium /'beLcım/ Belçika
belief /bi'Liif/ *n* inanç
believe /bi'Liiv/ *v* inanmak
bell /beL/ *n* çan, zil
bellboy /'beL,bOy/ *n* komi
belly /'beLii/ *n* karın, göbek
belong /bi'LOON/ *v* ait olmak
belongings /bi'LOONiNz/ *pl* kişisel eşyalar
beloved /bi'LAvd/ *adj* sevgili
below /bi'Lou/ *prep* aşağısında, altında; *adv* altta, aşağıda
belt /beLt/ *n* kemer, kuşak; **garter** ~ *Am* jartiyer
bench /benç/ *n* sıra, bank
bend /bend/ *n* kıvrım; dönemeç, viraj
***bend** /bend/ *v* bükmek, eğmek; ~ **down** eğilmek
beneath /bi'niiT/ *prep* -in altında; *adv* altta
beneficial /,benı'fişıL/ *adj* yararlı
benefit /'benıfit/ *n* yarar, menfaat; *v* yararlanmak, yarar sağlamak

bent /bent/ *adj* (pp bend) eğri, bükük, eğik
beret /bı'rey/ *n* bere
berry /'berii/ *n* çekirdeksiz, sulu küçük meyve
berth /bÖrT/ *n* taşıt ranzası
beside /bi'sayd/ *prep* yanında, yakınında
besides /bi'saydz/ *adv* bundan başka; üstelik; *prep* yanına, yanında; -den başka, -den fazla
best /best/ *adj* en iyi
bet /bet/ *n* bahis
***bet** /bet/ *v* bahse girmek
betray /bi'trey/ *v* ihanet etmek
better /'betır/ *adj* daha iyi
between /bi'twiin/ *prep* arasında
beverage /'bevıric/ *n* içecek
beware /bi'weyr/ *v* sakınmak, dikkat etmek
bewilder /bi'wiLdır/ *v* şaşırtmak, sersemletmek
bewitch /bi'wiç/ *v* büyülemek
beyond /bi'yOnd/ *prep* ilerisinde, ötesinde; *adv* ötede, öteye
Bible /'baybıL/ *n* Kutsal Kitap
bicycle /'baysıkıL/ *n* bisiklet
bid /bid/ *n* fiyat teklifi
***bid** /bid/ *v* fiyat teklif etmek
biennial /ba'yeniyıl/ *adj* iki yılda bir olan
big /big/ *adj* büyük; önemli
bike /bayk/ *n* bisiklet
bile /bayL/ *n* safra
bilingual /bay'LiNgwıL/ *adj* iki dil konuşan
bill /biL/ *n* hesap; kâğıt para; afiş; *v* fatura etmek
billboard /'biL,bOOrd/ *n* ilan tahtası
billiards /'biLyırdz/ *pl* bilardo
billion /'biLyın/ *num Am* milyar; *Br* trilyon
***bind** /baynd/ *v* bağlamak; ciltlemek
binding /'bayndiN/ *n* bağlama; cilt
binoculars /bı'nOkyıLırz/ *pl* dürbün
biology /ba'yOLıcii/ *n* biyoloji
birch /bÖrç/ *n* huş ağacı
bird /bÖrd/ *n* kuş
Biro /'bayrou/ *nBr* tükenmez kalem
birth /bÖrT/ *n* doğum
birthday /'bÖrT,dey/ *n* doğum günü
birthplace /'bÖrT,pLeys/ *n* doğum yeri
biscuit /'biskit/ *n* bisküvi
bishop /'bişıp/ *n* piskopos
bit /bit/ *n* parça, kırıntı
bitch /biç/ *n* dişi köpek; kötü kadın
bite /bayt/ *n* lokma
***bite** /bayt/ *v* ısırmak
bitter /'bitır/ *adj* acı, keskin
black /bLEk/ *adj* siyah; ~ **market** karaborsa; **Black Sea** Karadeniz
blackberry /'bLEk,berii/ *n* böğürtlen
blackboard /'bLEk,bOOrd/ *n* karatahta
blacken /'bLEkın/ *v* karartmak; karalamak
blackmail /'bLEk,meyL/ *n* şantaj; *v* şantaj yapmak
blacksmith /'bLEk,smiT/ *n* demirci, nalbant
bladder /'bLEdır/ *n* mesane, sidik torbası
blade /bLeyd/ *n* bıçak ağzı
blame /bLeym/ *n* kabahat; *v* suçlamak, sorumlu tutmak
blank /bLENk/ *adj* boş; yazısız
blanket /'bLENkit/ *n* battaniye
blast /bLEst/ *n* patlama
blazer /'bLeyzır/ *n* spor ceket
bleach /bLiiç/ *v* beyazlatmak, rengini açmak
bleak /bLiik/ *adj* çıplak; soğuk
***bleed** /bLiid/ *v* kanamak
bless /bLes/ *v* iyilik dilemek; kutsamak
blessing /'bLesiN/ *n* nimet; hayırdua

blind /bLaynd/ *n* kepenk; *adj* kör; *v* kör etmek; **Venetian ~** jaluzi
blister /'bListır/ *n* kabarcık; *v* su toplamak
blizzard /'bLizırd/ *n* tipi
block /bLOk/ *v* tıkamak; *n* blok; iki sokak arasındaki bina grubu, ada
blockade /bLO'keyd/ *n* abluka; *v* abluka etmek; ***run the ~** ablukayı yarmak
blond /bLOnd/ *adj, n* sarışın
blood /bLAd/ *n* kan;
~ pressure tansiyon;
~ poisoning kan zehirlenmesi,
~ vessel kan damarı
blot /bLOt/ *n* leke; **blotting paper** kurutma kâğıdı
blouse /bLaus/ *n* bluz
blow /bLou/ *n* darbe, vuruş
***blow** /bLou/ *v* üflemek; esmek
blowout /'bLou,aut/ *n* lastik patlaması; sönme
blowup /'bLou,Ap/ *n* infilak, patlama
blue /bLuu/ *adj* mavi; kederli ve ümitsiz
blunt /bLAnt/ *adj* kesmez, kör
blush /bLAş/ *v* yüzü kızarmak, utanmak
board /bOOrd/ *n* tahta; pansiyonda yemek; **~ and lodging** tam pansiyon
boarder /'bOOrdır/ *n* pansiyoner; yatılı öğrenci
boarding house /'bOOrdiN ,haus/ pansiyon
boarding school /'bOOrdiN ,skuuL/ yatılı okul
boast /boust/ *v* övünmek
boat /bout/ *n* kayık, sandal
body /'bOdii/ *n* beden
bodyguard /'bOdii,gaard/ *n* koruma polisi
bog /bOg/ *n* bataklık
boil /bOyL/ *v* kaynatmak; kaynamak; *n* çıban
bold /bouLd/ *adj* cesur, gözüpek; küstah
Bolivia /bı'Liviyı/ Bolivya
Bolivian /bı'Liviyın/ *adj* Bolivya'ya ait; *n* Bolivyalı
bolt /bouLt/ *n* sürme; cıvata; *v* sürmelemek
bomb /bOm/ *n* bomba; *v* bombalamak
bond /bOnd/ *n* bağ, ilişki; bono
bone /boun/ *n* kemik
bonfire /'bOn,fayr/ *n* şenlik ateşi
bonito /bı'niitou/ *n* palamut
bonnet /'bOnit/ *n* başlık; *nBr* motor kapağı, kaporta
bonus /'bounıs/ *n* ikramiye, prim
book /buk/ *n* kitap; *v* yer ayırtmak
booking /'bukiN/ *nBr* yer ayırtma, rezervasyon
booklet /'bukLit/ *n* broşür, kitapçık
bookseller /'buk,seLır/ *n* kitapçı
bookshop /'buk,şOp/ *nBr* kitabevi
bookstand /'buk,stEnd/ *n* kitap tezgâhı
bookstore /'buk,stOOr/ *nAm* kitabevi
boot /buut/ *n* çizme
booth /buuT/ *n* kulübe, kabin
border /'bOOrdır/ *n* sınır
bore[1] /bOOr/ *v* can sıkmak; delmek
bore[2] /bOOr/ *v* (p bear)
boring /'bOOriN/ *adj* can sıkıcı
born /bOOrn/ *adj* doğmuş, doğuştan
borrow /'bOOrou/ *v* ödünç almak
bosom /'buzım/ *n* göğüs
Bosphorus /'bOsfırıs/ , **Bosporus** /'bOspırıs/ İstanbul Boğazı, Boğaziçi
boss /bOOs/ *n* patron
botany /'bOtınii/ *n* botanik
both /bouT/ *adj* ikisi de;
both . . . and . . . hem . . . hem . . .
bother /'bODır/ *v* taciz etmek, sıkıntı vermek; *n* üzüntü, sıkıntı
bottle /'bOtıL/ *n* şişe;

~ **opener** şişe açacağı;
hot-water ~ sıcak su şişesi
bottleneck /'bOtıL,nek/ *n* darboğaz
bottom /'bOtım/ *n* dip, alt; *adj* en alttaki
bough /bau/ *n* dal
bought /bOOt/ *v* (p, pp buy)
boulder /'bouLdır/ *n* büyük kaya parçası
bounce /bauns/ *v* zıplamak, sıçramak
bound[1] /baund/ *adj* (p,pp bind) ciltli
bound[2] /baund/ *n* sınır; ***be** ~ **to** mecbur olmak; ~ **for** -e yönelik
boundary /'baundırii/ *n* sınır
bouquet /bou'key/ *n* buket
bourgeois /'burjwa/ *adj* burjuva
boutique /buu'tiik/ *n* butik
bow[1] /bau/ *v* eğilmek; eğmek
bow[2] /bou/ *n* yay; kavis; ~ **tie** papyon
bowels /'bauıLz/ *pl* kalın bağırsak
bowl /bouL/ *n* kâse, çanak
bowling /'bouLiN/ *n* bovling; ~ **alley** bovling salonu
box[1] /bOks/ *v* boks yapmak; **boxing match** boks maçı
box[2] /bOks/ *n* kutu; ~ **office** gişe
boy /bOy/ *n* erkek çocuk; ~ **scout** izci
bra /braa/ *n* sütyen
bracelet /'breysLit/ *n* bilezik
braces /'breysiz/ *plBr* pantolon askısı
brain /breyn/ *n* beyin; zekâ
brainwash /'breyn,wOOş/ *v* beyin yıkamak
brake /breyk/ *n* fren; ~ **drum** fren kasnağı; ~ **lights** stop lambaları
branch /brEnç/ *n* dal; şube
brand /brEnd/ *n* marka
brand-new /'brEnd'nuu/ *adj* yepyeni
brass /brEs/ *n* pirinç; ~ **band** askeri mızıka
brassiere /brı'ziir/ *n* sütyen
brassware /'brEs,weyr/ *n* pirinç eşya
brave /breyv/ *adj* cesur
Brazil /brı'ziL/ Brezilya
Brazilian /brı'ziLyın/ *adj* Brezilya'ya ait; *n* Brezilyalı
breach /briiç/ *n* bir kuralı bozma
bread /bred/ *n* ekmek; **wholemeal** ~ elenmemiş undan yapılmış ekmek
breadth /bredT/ *n* genişlik, en
break /breyk/ *n* kırma, bozma; ara, fasıla
***break** /breyk/ *v* kırmak, bozmak; ~ **down** arıza yapmak; çökmek
breakdown /'breyk,daun/ *n* arıza
breakfast /'brekfıst/ *n* kahvaltı
breast /brest/ *n* göğüs, meme ; ~ **stroke** kurbağalama yüzüş
breath /breT/ *n* soluk
breathe /briiD/ *v* soluk almak
breathing /'briiDiN/ *n* soluk alma, soluma
breed /briid/ *n* cins, soy
***breed** /briid/ *v* yavrulamak; üretmek
breeze /briiz/ *n* meltem
brew /bruu/ *v* bira yapmak
brewery /'bruuırii/ *n* bira fabrikası
bribe /brayb/ *n* rüşvet
bribery /'braybırii/ *n* rüşvet verme
brick /brik/ *n* tuğla
bricklayer /'brik,Leyır/ *n* duvarcı
bride /brayd/ *n* gelin
bridegroom /'brayd,gruum/ *n* damat
bridge /bric/ *n* köprü; briç
brief /briif/ *adj* kısa
briefcase /'briif,keys/ *n* evrak çantası
briefing /'briifiN/ *n* brifing, özet bilgi verme
briefs /briifs/ *pl* külot
bright /brayt/ *adj* parlak
brill /briL/ *n* pisi balığı
brilliant /'briLyınt/ *adj* çok parlak, çok zeki

brim /brim/ *n* bardak ağzı; kenar
***bring** /briN/ *v* getirmek;
~ **back** geri getirmek;
~ **up** yetiştirmek, büyütmek
brisk /brisk/ *adj* canlı, uyanık
Britain /'britın/ Britanya
British /'britiş/ *adj* Britanyalı, İngiliz
Briton /'britın/ *n* Britanyalı, İngiliz
broad /brOOd/ *adj* geniş
broadcast /'brOOd,kEst/ *n* radyo, TV yayını; *v* yayın yapmak
brochure /brou'şuur/ *n* broşür
broke[1] /brouk/ *v* (p break)
broke[2] /brouk/ *adj* meteliksiz, cebi delik
broken /'broukın/ *adj* (pp break) kırık, bozuk
broker /'broukır/ *n* komisyoncu
bronchitis /brON'kaytis/ *n* bronşit
bronze /brOnz/ *n* bronz madeni
brooch /brouç/ *n* broş
brook /bruk/ *n* dere, ırmak
broom /bruum/ *n* süpürge
brothel /'brOTıL/ *n* genelev
brother /'brADır/ *n* erkek kardeş, birader
brother-in-law /'brADırin,LOO/ *n* (pl brothers-) kayınbirader
brought /brOOt/ *v* (p, pp bring)
brown /braun/ *adj* kahverengi
bruise /bruuz/ *n* yara, bere, çürük
brunette /bruu'net/ *n* esmer kadın
brush /brAş/ *n* fırça; *v* fırçalamak
brutal /'bruutıL/ *adj* zalim, kaba
bubble /'bAbıL/ *n* hava kabarcığı
Bucharest /'buukı,rest/ Bükreş
bucket /'bAkit/ *n* kova
buckle /'bakıL/ *n* toka, kopça
bud /bAd/ *n* tomurcuk
budget /'bAcit/ *n* bütçe
buffet /bı'fey/ *n* büfe
bug /bAg/ *n* böcek
***build** /biLd/ *v* inşa etmek, kurmak
building /'biLdiN/ *n* bina, yapı
bulb /bALb/ *n* ampul; çiçek soğanı;
light ~ ampul
Bulgaria /bAL'geyriyı/ Bulgaristan
Bulgarian /bAL'geyriyın/ *adj* Bulgaristan'a ait; *n* Bulgar
bulk /bALk/ *n* hacim, oylum; çoğunluk
bulky /'bALkii/ *adj* hantal; iri cüsseli
bull /buL/ *n* boğa
bullet /'buLit/ *n* mermi
bullfight /'buL,fayt/ *n* boğa güreşi
bullring /'buL,riN/ *n* arena
bump /bAmp/ *v* vurmak, çarpmak; *n* vuruş, çarpma; şiş, tümsek
bumper /'bAmpır/ *n* tampon
bumpy /'bAmpii/ *adj* tümsekli, engebeli
bun /bAn/ *n* çörek; saç topuzu
bunch /bAnç/ *n* salkım, demet
bundle /'bAndıL/ *n* paket; bohça; *v* toplamak, bohçalamak
bunk /bANk/ *n* ranza
buoy /bOy/ *n* şamandıra
burden /'bÖrdın/ *n* yük
bureau /'byurou/ *n* (pl ~x, ~s) büro; yazı masası
bureaucracy /byu'rOkrısii/ *n* bürokrasi
burglar /'bÖrgLır/ *n* ev soyan hırsız
burgle /'bÖrgıL/ *v* ev soymak
burial /'beriyıL/ *n* gömme, defin
burn /bÖrn/ *n* yanık, yanık yeri
***burn** /bÖrn/ *v* yanmak; yakmak
***burst** /bÖrst/ *v* patlamak, yarılmak
bury /'berii/ *v* gömmek, defnetmek
bus /bAs/ *n* otobüs; ~ **stop** otobüs durağı
bush /buş/ *n* çalı, çalılık
business /'biznis/ *n* iş, ticaret; meslek; ~ **hours** iş saatleri; ~ **trip** iş seyahati; **on** ~ iş ile ilgili, iş için
businessman /'biznis,mEn/ *n* (pl -men) işadamı
bust /bAst/ *n* büst

bustle /'bAsıL/ *n* telaş, koşuşturma
busy /'bizii/ *adj* meşgul; hareketli
but /bAt/ *conj* ama, ancak, halbuki; *prep* -den gayri, -den hariç
butcher /'buçır/ *n* kasap
butter /'bAtır/ *n* tereyağı
butterfly /'bAtır,fLay/ *n* kelebek; ~ **stroke** kelebek stili yüzme
buttock /'bAtık/ *n* kalça
button /'bAtın/ *n* düğme; *v* düğmelemek
buttonhole /'bAtın,houL/ *n* düğme iliği
***buy** /bay/ *v* satın almak
buyer /'bayır/ *n* alıcı, müşteri
buzz /bAz/ *n* vızıltı; *v* vızıldamak
by /bay/ *prep* yanında, yakınında; vasıtasıyla
by-pass /'bay,pEs/ *n* atlama, dolaştırma; baypas; *v* bertaraf etmek, atlatmak
Byzantine /'bizın,tiin/ *adj* Bizans'a ait

C

cab /kEb/ *n* taksi
cabaret /,kEbı'rey/ *n* kabare
cabbage /'kEbic/ *n* lahana
cabdriver /'kEb,drayvır/ *n* taksi şoförü
cabin /'kEbin/ *n* kabin, kulübe
cabinet /'kEbınit/ *n* camlı, raflı dolap; bakanlar kurulu
cable /'keybıL/ *n* kablo; telgraf; *v* telgraf çekmek
café /kE'fey/ *n* kahvehane; pastane
cafeteria /,kEfı'tiiriyı/ *n* kafeterya
caffeine /kE'fiin/ *n* kafein
cage /keyc/ *n* kafes
cake /keyk/ *n* pasta, kek
calamity /kı'LEmıtii/ *n* bela, felaket
calcium /'kELsiyım/ *n* kalsiyum
calculate /'kELkyı,Leyt/ *n* hesaplamak
calculation /,kELkyı'Leyşın/ *n* hesaplama
calendar /'kELındır/ *n* takvim
calf /kEf/ *n* (pl calves) dana, buzağı
calfskin /'kEf,skin/ *n* dana derisi
call /kOOL/ *v* çağırmak; adlandırmak; telefon etmek; *n* ziyaret; telefon; ***be called . . .** adı . . . olmak; ~ **names** aşağılayıcı isimlerle hakaret etmek; ~ **on** ziyaret etmek; ~ **up** *Am* telefon etmek
callus /'kELıs/ *n* nasır
calm /kaam/ *adj* sakin, durgun; ~ **down** yatışmak, yatıştırmak
calorie /'kELırii/ *n* kalori
came /keym/ *v* (p come)
camel /'kEmıL/ *n* deve
cameo /'kEmii,you/ *n* (pl ~s) işlemeli kıymetli taş
camera /'kEmırı/ *n* fotoğraf makinesi
camp /kEmp/ *n* kamp; *v* kamp yapmak; ~ **bed** portatif karyola
campaign /kEm'peyn/ *n* kampanya
camper /'kEmpır/ *n* kamp yapan kimse
camping /'kEmpiN/ *n* kamp yapma; ~ **site** kamp yeri
can /kEn/ *nAm* teneke kutu; ~ **opener** *Am* konserve açacağı; **canned food** *Am* konserve
***can** /kEn/ *v* yapabilmek
Canada /'kEnıdı/ Kanada
Canadian /kı'neydiyın/ *adj* Kanada'ya ait; *n* Kanadalı
canal /kı'nEL/ *n* kanal
canary /kı'neyrii/ *n* kanarya
cancel /'kEnsıL/ *v* silmek; iptal etmek
cancellation /,kEnsı'Leyşın/ *n* iptal etme
cancer /'kEnsır/ *n* kanser; Yengeç burcu
candidate /'kEndi,deyt/ *n* aday
candle /'kEndıL/ *n* mum

candy /'kEndii/ *nAm* şekerleme, bonbon; ~ **store** *Am* şekerci dükkânı
cane /keyn/ *n* baston; kamış
canoe /kı'nuu/ *n* kano
canteen /kEn'tiin/ *n* kantin
canvas /'kEnvıs/ *n* yelken bezi; tuval
cap /kEp/ *n* kasket, başlık
capable /'keypıbıL/ *adj* muktedir
capacity /kı'pEsıtii/ *n* hacim; yetenek, güç
cape /keyp/ *n* burun; pelerin
capital /'kEpitıL/ *n* başkent; sermaye; *adj* önemli, belli başlı; ~ **letter** büyük harf
capitalism /'kEpitı,Lizım/ *n* kapitalizm
Capricorn /'kEpri,kOOrn/ Oğlak burcu
capsule /'kEpsıL/ *n* kapsül
captain /'kEptın/ *n* yüzbaşı; kaptan
captive /'kEptiv/ *n* esir, tutsak; *adj* esir düşmüş
capture /'kEpçır/ *v* zapt etmek, ele geçirmek; *n* zaptetme, ele geçirme
car /kaar/ *n* otomobil; ~ **hire** *Br* otomobil kiralama; ~ **park** *Br* otopark; ~ **rental** *Am* otomobil kiralama
carafe /kı'rEf/ *n* sürahi
caramel /'kErımıL/ *n* karamela
carat /'kErıt/ *n* ayar; kırat
caravan /'kErı,vEn/ *n* karavan; kervan
carburetor /'kaarbı,reytır/ *n* karbüratör
card /kaard/ *n* kart; kartpostal
cardboard /'kaard,bOOrd/ *n* karton; *adj* kartondan
cardigan /'kaardigın/ *n* hırka, ceket
cardinal /'kaardinıL/ *n* kardinal; *adj* belli başlı, önemli
care /keyr/ *n* endişe; bakım, ilgi; ~ **about** ilgi duymak, önem vermek; ~ **for** istemek, ilgilenmek, sevmek; ***take** ~ **of** ilgilenmek, bakmak
career /kı'riir/ *n* meslek, kariyer
carefree /'keyr,frii/ *adj* kaygısız, dertsiz
careful /'keyrfıL/ *adj* dikkatli, tedbirli
careless /'keyrLıs/ *adj* dikkatsiz
caretaker /'keyr,teykır/ *n* kapıcı, bakıcı
cargo /'kaargou/ *n* (pl ~es) kargo, yük
carnival /'kaarnıvıL/ *n* karnaval
carp /kaarp/ *n* (pl ~) sazan balığı
carpenter /'kaarpıntır/ *n* marangoz
carpet /'kaarpit/ *n* halı
carriage /'kEric/ *n* araba; vagon
carrot /'kErıt/ *n* havuç
carry /'kErii/ *v* taşımak, nakletmek; ~ **out** gerçekleştirmek
carry-cot /'kErii,kOt/ *n* port-bebe
cart /kaart/ *n* genellikle atlar tarafından çekilen araba
cartilage /'kaartıLic/ *n* kıkırdak
carton /'kaartın/ *n* karton kutu, mukavva kutu
cartoon /kaar'tuun/ *n* karikatür; çizgi film
cartridge /'kaartric/ *n* fişek; kartuş
carve /kaarv/ *v* eti parçalayıp dağıtmak; oyma yapmak
carving /'kaarviN/ *n* oymacılık
case /keys/ *n* durum, olay; kutu, sandık; kılıf; **attaché** ~ evrak çantası; **in** ~ eğer, şayet; **in** ~ **of** olduğu takdirde
cash /kEş/ *n* para; peşin para; *v* paraya çevirmek
cashier /kE'şiir/ *n* veznedar, kasadar
cashmere /'kEşmiir/ *n* kaşmir yünü; kaşmir kumaş *veya* şal
casino /kı'siinou/ *n* (pl ~s) kumar ve eğlence yeri
cask /kEsk/ *n* varil, fıçı
cast /kEst/ *n* atma, fırlatma
***cast** /kEst/ *v* atmak, fırlatmak;

~ **iron** dökme demir
castle /'kEsıL/ *n* şato; kale
casual /'kEjuuıL/ *adj* tesadüfi, rasgele
casualty /'kEjuuıLtii/ *n* kazada ölü
cat /kEt/ *n* kedi
catacomb /'kEtı,koum/ *n* yeraltı mezarlığı
catalog /'kEtıLOg/ *n* katalog
catastrophe /kı'tEstrıfii/ *n* felaket, afet
***catch** /kEç/ *v* yakalamak, tutmak; kapmak
category /'kEtı,gOOrii/ *n* kategori
cater /'keytır/ *v* yiyecek sağlamak
cathedral /kı'TiidrıL/ *n* katedral, büyük kilise
Catholic /'kETıLik/ *adj* Katolik
cattle /'kEtıL/ *pl* sığır, davar
caught /kOOt/ *v* (p, pp catch)
cauliflower /'kOOLi,fLauır/ *n* karnabahar
cause /kOOz/ *v* sebep olmak; *n* sebep; hedef
caution /'kOOşın/ *n* tedbir; uyarı
cautious /'kOOşıs/ *adj* ihtiyatlı
cave /keyv/ *n* mağara
cavern /'kEvırn/ *n* büyük mağara
caviar /'kEvii,yaar/ *n* havyar
cavity /'kEvıtii/ *n* oyuk, boşluk
cease /siis/ *v* durmak, bitmek
cease-fire /'siis'fayr/ *n* ateşkes
ceiling /'siiLiN/ *n* tavan
celebrate /'seLı,breyt/ *v* kutlamak
celebration /,seLı'breyşın/ *n* kutlama, tören
celebrity /sı'Lebrıtii/ *n* ünlü kimse
celery /'seLırii/ *n* kereviz
celibacy /'seLibısii/ *n* bekârlık
cell /seL/ *n* hücre
cellar /'seLır/ *n* kiler, bodrum
cellophane /'seLı,feyn/ *n* selofan
cement /si'ment/ *n* çimento
cemetery /'semı,terii/ *n* mezarlık
censor /'sensır/ *v* sansür etmek
censorship /'sensır,şip/ *n* sansür
censure /'senşır/ *n* tenkit, kınama; *v* tenkit etmek, kınamak
center /'sentır/ *n* merkez
centigrade /'sentı,greyd/ *adj* santigrat
centimeter /'sentı,miitır/ *n* santimetre
central /'sentrıL/ *adj* merkezi; ~ **heating** merkezi ısıtma; ~ **station** merkez istasyonu
centralize /'sentrı,Layz/ *v* merkezileştirmek
century /'sençırii/ *n* yüzyıl
ceramics /sı'rEmiks/ *pl* seramik; seramik eşya
ceremony /'serı,mounii/ *n* tören
certain /'sÖrtın/ *adj* kesin; emin
certificate /sır'tifikıt/ *n* sertifika, belge
chain /çeyn/ *n* zincir
chair /çeyr/ *n* iskemle
chairman /'çeyrmın/ *n* (pl -men) başkan
chalet /şE'Ley/ *n* dağ evi
chalk /çOOk/ *n* tebeşir
challenge /'çELınc/ *v* meydan okumak; *n* meydan okuma
chamber /'çeymbır/ *n* oda
chambermaid /'çeymbır,meyd/ *n* oda hizmetçisi kadın
champagne /şEm'peyn/ *n* şampanya
champion /'çEmpiyın/ *n* şampiyon; savunucu kimse
chance /çEns/ *n* şans, fırsat; olasılık; **by** ~ tesadüfen
change /çeync/ *v* değişmek; değiştirmek; (para) bozdurmak; *n* değişiklik; bozuk para
channel /'çEnıL/ *n* kanal; **English Channel** Manş Denizi
chaos /'keyOs/ *n* keşmekeş, kaos
chaotic /key'Otik/ *adj* karmakarışık, düzensiz
chap /çEp/ *n* adam
chapel /'çEpıL/ *n* küçük kilise
chaplain /'çEpLın/ *n* papaz

character /'kErıktır/ *n* karakter
characteristic /ˌkErıktı'ristik/ *adj* tipik, kendine özgü
characterize /'kErıktıˌrayz/ *v* nitelendirmek; ayırıcı özelliği olmak
charcoal /'çaarˌkouL/ *n* mangal kömürü
charge /çaarc/ *v* para talep etmek; suçlamak; *n* yük; bedel; suç; **~ plate** *Am* kredi kartı; ***be in ~ of** -den sorumlu olmak; **free of ~** ücretsiz; ***take ~ of** üzerine sorumluluk almak
charity /'çErıtii/ *n* hayırseverlik
charm /çaarm/ *n* cazibe, alım; *v* büyülemek, cezbetmek
charming /'çaarmiN/ *adj* çekici, hoşa giden
chart /çaart/ *n* tablo, çizelge; deniz haritası; **conversion ~** değişim tablosu
charter /'çaartır/ *v* (uçak) kiralamak; **~ plane** kiralanmış ucuz tarifeli uçak
chase /çeys/ *v* kovalamak; avlamak; *n* kovalama; av
chasm /'kEzım/ *n* yarık, uçurum
chassis /'şEsii/ *n* (pl ~) şasi
chaste /çeyst/ *adj* iffetli, temiz
chat /çEt/ *v* çene çalmak; *n* sohbet
chatterbox /'çEtırˌbOks/ *n* çok geveze kimse
cheap /çiip/ *adj* ucuz; değersiz
cheat /çiit/ *v* aldatmak; hile yapmak; kopya çekmek
check /çek/ *v* kontrol etmek; doğruluğunu araştırmak; *nAm* çek; hesap pusulası; **check!** şah!; **~ in** otele giriş kaydı yapmak; **~ out** otelden hesabı ödeyerek çıkmak
checkbook /'çekˌbuk/ *nAm* çek defteri
checkerboard /'çekırˌbOOrd/ *nAm* dama tahtası
checkered /'çekırd/ *adjAm* damalı
checkers /'çekırz/ *nAm* dama oyunu
checkroom /'çekˌruum/ *nAm* vestiyer
checkup /'çekˌAp/ *n* genel sağlık kontrolü
cheek /çiik/ *n* yanak
cheekbone /'çiikˌboun/ *n* yanak kemiği
cheer /çiir/ *v* alkış tutmak; **~ up** moralini düzeltmek; neşelendirmek
cheerful /'çiirfıL/ *adj* neşeli
cheese /çiiz/ *n* peynir
chef /şef/ *n* aşçıbaşı
chemical /'kemikıL/ *adj* kimyasal
chemist /'kemist/ *n* kimyager; **chemist's** *nBr* eczane
chemistry /'kemistrii/ *n* kimya
cheque /çek/ *nBr* çek
cheque-book /'çekˌbuk/ *nBr* çek defteri
chequered /'çekırd/ *adjBr* damalı
cherry /'çerii/ *n* kiraz
chess /çes/ *n* satranç
chest /çest/ *n* göğüs; **~ of drawers** konsol
chestnut /'çesˌnAt/ *n* kestane
chew /çuu/ *v* çiğnemek
chewing gum /'çuuiN 'gAm/ çiklet
chicken /'çikın/ *n* piliç, tavuk
chicken pox /'çikın ˌpOks/ suçiçeği
chick-pea /'çikˌpii/ *n* nohut
chief /çiif/ *n* şef; *adj* belli başlı
chieftain /'çiiftın/ *n* başkan; kabile reisi
child /çayLd/ *n* (pl children) çocuk
childbirth /'çayLdˌbÖrT/ *n* doğum
childhood /'çayLdˌhud/ *n* çocukluk
Chile /'çiLi/ Şili
Chilean /'çiLiyın/ *adj* Şili'ye ait; *n* Şilili
chill /çiL/ *n* soğuk; üşüme

chilly /'çiLii/ *adj* serin
chimes /çaymz/ *pl* ahenkli çan sesi
chimney /'çimnii/ *n* baca
chin /çin/ *n* çene
China /'çaynı/ Çin
china /'çaynı/ *n* porselen, çini
Chinese /çay'niiz/ *adj* Çin'e ait; *n* Çinli
chip /çip/ *n* yonga, çentik; *v* yontmak, çentmek; **chips** kızarmış patates
chisel /'çizıL/ *n* keski
chlorine /'kLOOriin/ *n* klor
chock-a-block /'çOkı,bLOk/ *adj* dopdolu
chock-full /'çOk'fuL/ *adj* dopdolu
chocolate /'çOkLıt/ *n* çikolata
choice /çOys/ *n* seçme; tercih; seçenek
choir /kwayr/ *n* kilise korosu
choke /çouk/ *v* boğmak; boğulmak; *n* jikle
***choose** /çuuz/ *v* seçmek
chop /çOp/ *n* pirzola; *v* kesmek, doğramak
Christ /krayst/ Hz. İsa
christen /'krisın/ *v* vaftiz etmek
christening /'krisıniN/ *n* vaftiz
Christian /'krisçın/ *adj, n* Hıristiyan; ~ **name** ad
Christianity /,krisçi'yEnıtii/ *n* Hıristiyanlık
Christmas /'krismıs/ Noel
chromium /'kroumiyım/ *n* krom
chronic /'krOnik/ *adj* müzmin
chronological /,krOnı'LOcikıL/ *adj* tarih sırasına göre
chuckle /'çAkıL/ *v* kıkırdayarak gülmek
chunk /çANk/ *n* iri parça
church /çÖrç/ *n* kilise
churchyard /'çÖrç,yaard/ *n* mezarlık
cigar /si'gaar/ *n* puro; ~ **shop** puro satan dükkân
cigarette /sigı'ret/ *n* sigara; ~ **case** sigara tabakası; ~ **holder** ağızlık; ~ **lighter** çakmak
cinema /'sinımı/ *n* sinema
cinnamon /'sinımın/ *n* tarçın
circle /'sÖrkıL/ *n* daire, çember; *v* etrafını çevirmek
circuit /'sÖrkıt/ *n* devre; **short** ~ kısa devre
circular /'sÖrkyıLır/ *adj* daire şeklinde, yuvarlak; *n* sirküler
circulation /,sÖrkyı'Leyşın/ *n* devir, dolaşım
circumcise /'sÖrkım,sayz/ *v* sünnet etmek
circumcision /,sÖrkım'sijın/ *n* sünnet
circumstance /'sÖrkım,stEns/ *n* durum; koşul
circus /'sÖrkıs/ *n* sirk
citadel /'sitıdıL/ *n* hisar, kale
citizen /'sitızın/ *n* vatandaş
citizenship /'sitızın,şip/ *n* vatandaşlık
citrus /'sitrıs/ *adj* turunçgillere ait; ~ **fruit** turunçgillerden bir meyve
city /'sitii/ *n* şehir
civic /'sivik/ *adj* şehre ait
civil /'sivıL/ *adj* vatandaşa ait; uygar, kibar; ~ **law** medeni hukuk; ~ **servant** devlet memuru
civilian /si'viLyın/ *n, adj* sivil
civilization /,sivıLi'zeyşın/ *n* uygarlık
civilized /'sivıLayzd/ *adj* uygar
claim /kLeym/ *v* talep etmek; iddia etmek; *n* talep; iddia
clamp /kLEmp/ *n* mengene
clap /kLEp/ *v* alkışlamak
clarify /'kLErifay/ *v* aydınlatmak
clash /kLEş/ *v* çarpışmak; uyuşmamak; *n* çarpışma; uyuşmazlık
class /kLEs/ *n* sınıf
classical /'kLEsikıL/ *adj* klasik
classify /'kLEsifay/ *v* sınıflandırmak
classmate /'kLEs,meyt/ *n* sınıf

arkadaşı
classroom /ˈkLEs,ruum/ *n* dershane, derslik
clause /kLOOz/ *n* madde, hüküm; cümlecik
claustrophobia /ˌkLOOstrıˈfoubiyı/ *n* kapalı yer fobisi, klostrofobi
claw /kLOO/ *n* pençe
clay /kLey/ *n* kil, çamur
clean /kLiin/ *adj* temiz, saf; *v* temizlemek, arıtmak
cleaning /ˈkLiiniN/ *n* temizleme; ~ **fluid** sıvı deterjan
clear /kLiir/ *adj* açık; berrak; *v* açık, berrak hale getirmek
clearing /ˈkLiiriN/ *n* ormanda ağaçsız alan; bankalar arası çek takası
cleft /kLeft/ *n* çatlak, yarık
clergyman /ˈkLÖrciimın/ *n* (pl -men) rahip, papaz
clerk /kLÖrk/ *n* kâtip; küçük memur; *nAm* tezgâhtar
clever /ˈkLevır/ *adj* zeki, akıllı; becerikli
client /ˈkLayınt/ *n* müşteri
cliff /kLif/ *n* uçurum
climate /ˈkLaymit/ *n* iklim
climax /ˈkLaymEks/ *n* doruk, zirve
climb /kLaym/ *v* tırmanmak; *n* tırmanış; tırmanacak yer
***cling** /kLiN/ *v* yapışmak, sıkıca sarılmak, tutunmak
clinic /ˈkLinik/ *n* klinik
cloak /kLouk/ *n* manto; pelerin
cloakroom /ˈkLouk,ruum/ *n* vestiyer
clock /kLOk/ *n* saat; **at . . . o'clock** saat . . .'de
clockwise /ˈkLOk,wayz/ *adv* saat yelkovanı yönünde
cloister /ˈkLOystır/ *n* manastır
close[1] /kLouz/ *v* kapatmak; **closed** *adj* kapalı
close[2] /kLous/ *adj* yakın
closet /ˈkLOzıt/ *n* dolap; küçük oda
cloth /kLOT/ *n* kumaş, bez
clothes /kLouDz/ *pl* elbise; ~ **brush** elbise fırçası
clothing /ˈkLouDiN/ *n* giyim, elbise
cloud /kLaud/ *n* bulut
cloudburst /ˈklaud,bÖrst/ *n* ani sağanak yağış
cloudy /ˈkLaudii/ *adj* bulutlu
clover /ˈkLouvır/ *n* yonca
clown /kLAun/ *n* palyaço
club /kLAb/ *n* kulüp; sopa
clumsy /ˈkLAmzii/ *adj* hantal; beceriksiz
clung /kLAN/ *v* (p, pp cling)
cluster /ˈkLAstır/ *n* salkım; demet; küme
clutch /kLAç/ *n* tutma, kavrama
coach /kouç/ *n* fayton; vagon; otobüs; antrenör
coagulate /kouˈEgyı,Leyt/ *v* pıhtılaşmak; pıhtılaştırmak
coal /kouL/ *n* kömür
coalition /kouıˈLişın/ *n* birleşme; koalisyon
coarse /kOOrs/ *adj* kaba; adi
coast /koust/ *n* sahil
coat /kout/ *n* palto
coathanger /ˈkout,hENır/ *n* elbise askısı
cobweb /ˈkOb,web/ *n* örümcek ağı
cocaine /kouˈkeyn/ *n* kokain
cock /kOk/ *n* horoz
cockroach /ˈkOk,rouç/ *n* hamamböceği
cocktail /ˈkOk,teyL/ *n* kokteyl
coconut /ˈkoukı,nAt/ *n* hindistan cevizi
cod /kOd/ *n* (pl ~) morina balığı
code /koud/ *n* kod, şifre; kanun; ~ **number** *Br* telefon yerel kodu
coeducation /ˌkoueciˈkeyşın/ *n* karma öğretim
coffee /ˈkOOfii/ *n* kahve
coffin /ˈkOOfin/ *n* tabut

cognac /'koun,yEk/ *n* konyak
coherence /kou'hiirıns/ *n* tutarlılık, uygunluk
coin /kOyn/ *n* madeni para
coincide /,kouin'sayd/ *v* tesadüf etmek; uymak
cold /kouLd/ *adj* soğuk; *n* soğuk hava; soğuk algınlığı; ***catch a** ~ soğuk almak, nezle olmak
collapse /kı'LEps/ *v* çökmek, yıkılmak
collar /'kOLır/ *n* yaka; tasma; ~ **stud** yaka düğmesi
collarbone /'kOLır,boun/ *n* köprücük kemiği
colleague /'kOLiig/ *n* meslektaş
collect /kı'Lekt/ *v* toplamak, biriktirmek
collection /kı'Lekşın/ *n* koleksiyon; para toplama
collective /kı'Lektiv/ *adj* toplu; müşterek
collector /kı'Lektır/ *n* koleksiyoncu; tahsildar
college /'kOLic/ *n* yüksek okul; üniversite
collide /kı'Layd/ *v* çarpışmak
collision /kı'Lijın/ *n* çarpışma; fikir ayrılığı
Colombia /kı'LAmbiyı/ Kolombiya
Colombian /kı'LAmbiyın/ *adj* Kolombiya'ya ait; *n* Kolombiyalı
colonel /'kÖrnıL/ *n* albay
colony /'kOLınii/ *n* sömürge
color /'kALır/ *n* renk; *v* boyamak; ~ **film** renkli film
colorant /'kALırınt/ *n* boya
color-blind /'kALır,bLaynd/ *adj* renk körü
colored /'kALırd/ *adj* renkli
colorful /'kALırfıL/ *adj* renkli, canlı
column /'kOLım/ *n* kolon, sütun
coma /'koumı/ *n* koma
comb /koum/ *v* taramak; *n* tarak
combat /'kOmbEt/ *n* dövüş, çarpışma; *v* dövüşmek, mücadele etmek
combination /,kOmbi'neyşın/ *n* bileşim
combine /kım'bayn/ *v* birleşmek; birleştirmek
***come** /kAm/ *v* gelmek; ~ **across** rastlamak
comedian /kı'miidiyın/ *n* komedyen
comedy /'kOmıdii/ *n* komedi; **musical** ~ müzikal komedi
comfort /'kAmfırt/ *n* konfor, rahatlık; *v* teselli etmek
comfortable /'kAmfırtıbıL/ *adj* rahat
comic /'kOmik/ *adj* gülünç, komik
comics /'kOmiks/ *pl* karikatür dizisi
coming /'kAmiN/ *adj* gelecek
comma /'kOmı/ *n* virgül
command /kı'mEnd/ *v* emretmek; *n* emir
commander /kı'mEndır/ *n* komutan
commemoration /kı,memı'reyşın/ *n* anma
commence /kı'mens/ *v* başlamak
comment /'kOment/ *n* yorum; eleştiri; *v* eleştirmek; yorum yapmak
commerce /'kOmırs/ *n* ticaret
commercial /kı'mÖrşıL/ *adj* ticari; *n* reklam; ~ **law** ticaret hukuku
commission /kı'mişın/ *n* görev; komisyon
commit /kı'mit/ *v* işlemek, yapmak; söz vererek bağlamak
commitment /kı'mitmınt/ *n* söz, taahhüt; kesin karar
committee /kı'mitii/ *n* komite, komisyon, kurul
common /'kOmın/ *adj* ortak; yaygın; sıradan; **Common Market** Ortak Pazar, Avrupa Ekonomik Topluluğu
commune /'kOmyuun/ *n* komün; en

küçük idari bölge
communicate /kı'myuuni,keyt/ *v* bildirmek, nakletmek; iletişim kurmak
communication /kı,myuuni'keyşın/ *n* iletişim; haberleşme
communism /'kOmyı,nizım/ *n* komünizm
communist /'kOmyınist/ *n* komünist
community /kı'myuunıtii/ *n* topluluk, toplum
commuter /kı'myuutır/ *n* evden işe gidip gelen kimse
compact /,kım'pEkt/ *adj* sıkı; yoğun; kısa, öz
companion /kım'pEnyın/ *n* arkadaş, yoldaş
company /'kAmpınii/ *n* şirket; grup; eşlik, arkadaşlık
comparative /kım'pErıtiv/ *adj* karşılaştırmalı
compare /kım'peyr/ *v* kıyaslamak
comparison /kım'pErisın/ *n* kıyaslama
compartment /kım'paartmınt/ *n* kompartıman
compass /'kAmpıs/ *n* pusula; pergel
compel /kım'peL/ *v* zorlamak
compensate /'kOmpın,seyt/ *v* tazmin etmek, karşılamak
compensation /,kOmpın'seyşın/ *n* tazmin, telafi
compete /kım'piit/ *v* rekabet etmek, yarışmak
competition /,kOmpı'tişın/ *n* rekabet, yarışma
competitor /kım'petitır/ *n* rakip, yarışmacı
compile /kım'payL/ *v* derlemek
complain /kım'pLeyn/ *v* şikâyet etmek
complaint /kım'pLeynt/ *n* şikayet
complementary /,kOmpLı'mentırii/ *adj* tamamlayıcı
complete /kım'pLiit/ *adj* tam, eksiksiz; *v* tamamlamak
completely /kım'pLiitLii/ *adv* tamamen, bütünüyle
complex /'kOmpLeks/ *n* bileşik *veya* karmaşık şey; kompleks; *adj* karmaşık, çapraşık
complexion /kım'pLekşın/ *n* ten
complicated /'kOmpLi,keytid/ *adj* karmaşık, çapraşık
compliment[1] /'kOmpLımınt/ *n* iltifat; **compliments** *pl* selamlar, iyi dilekler
compliment[2] /'kOmpLı,ment/ *v* iltifat etmek
complimentary /,kOmpLı'mentırii/ *adj* hediye olarak, parasız
comply with /kım'pLay/ uymak, itaat etmek
compose /kım'pouz/ *v* meydana getirmek; bestelemek
composer /kım'pouzır/ *n* besteci
composition /,kOmpı'zişın/ *n* belli bir düzen içinde derleme; bileşim; kompozisyon
comprehensive /,kOmpri'hensiv/ *adj* geniş, etraflı
comprise /kım'prayz/ *v* kapsamak, içermek
compromise /'kOmprı,mayz/ *n* uzlaşma; *v* uzlaştırmak, aralarını bulmak
compulsory /kım'pALsırii/ *adj* zorunlu
computer /kım'pyuutır/ *n* bilgisayar
comrade /'kOmrEd/ *n* arkadaş, yoldaş
conceal /kın'siiL/ *v* gizlemek
conceited /kın'siitid/ *adj* kibirli
conceive /kın'siiv/ *v* gebe kalmak; kavramak
concentrate /'kOnsın,treyt/ *v* yoğunlaştırmak; dikkati bir noktaya toplamak
concentration /,kOnsın'treyşın/ *n* dikkatini toplama; yoğunluk

conception /kın'sepşın/ *n* fikir; kavram
concern /kın'sÖrn/ *v* ilgilendirmek; etkilemek; *n* kaygı; ilgi; iş
concerned /kın'sÖrnd/ *adj* ilgili; kaygılı
concerning /kın'sÖrniN/ *prep* hakkında, konusunda
concert /'kOnsırt/ *n* konser; ~ **hall** konser salonu
concession /kın'seşın/ *n* kabul; ödün, taviz
concierge /kOnsi'yerj/ *n* kapıcı
concise /kın'says/ *adj* öz, kısa
conclusion /kıN'kLuujın/ *n* sonuç
concrete /'kONkriit/ *adj* somut; *n* beton
concurrence /kıN'kÖrıns/ *n* uygun görme; rastlantı
concussion /kıN'kAşın/ *n* sarsma; darbe
condition /kın'dişın/ *n* hal, durum; koşul
conditional /kın'dişınıL/ *adj* şarta bağlı
conduct[1] /'kOndAkt/ *n* davranış, tavır
conduct[2] /kın'dAkt/ *v* yol göstermek; önderlik etmek; yönetmek
conductor /kın'dAktır/ *n* biletçi; orkestra şefi
confectioner /kın'fekşınır/ *n* şekerci
conference /'kOnfırıns/ *n* konferans
confess /kın'fes/ *v* itiraf etmek; doğrulamak
confession /kın'feşın/ *n* itiraf; doğrulama
confidence /'kOnfıdıns/ *n* güven; gizlilik
confident /'kOnfıdınt/ *adj* emin, güvenli
confidential /ˌkOnfı'denşıl/ *adj* gizli, mahrem; güvenilir
confine /kın'fayn/ *v* sınırlamak; kuşatmak; hapsetmek
confirm /kın'fÖrm/ *v* doğrulamak, onaylamak
confirmation /ˌkOnfır'meyşın/ *n* tasdik, doğrulama
confiscate /'kOnfis,keyt/ *v* el koymak; kamulaştırmak
conflict /'kOnfLikt/ *n* çatışma, anlaşmazlık
confuse /kın'fyuuz/ *v* karıştırmak, ayırt edememek; **confused** *adj* karışık, anlaşılmaz, belirsiz
confusion /kın'fyuujın/ *n* karışıklık; şaşkınlık
congratulate /kın'grEçı,Leyt/ *v* kutlamak, tebrik etmek
congratulation /kın,grEçı'Leyşın/ *n* tebrik, kutlama
congregation /ˌkOngrı'geyşın/ *n* cemaat, topluluk
congress /'kOngrıs/ *n* kongre; toplantı
connect /kı'nekt/ *v* birleştirmek, bağlamak
connection /kı'nekşın/ *n* bağlantı, ilgi, ilişki
connoisseur /ˌkOnı'sÖr/ *n* erbab, ehil
connotation /ˌkOnı'teyşın/ *n* çağrışım, diğer anlam
conquer /'kONkır/ *v* fethetmek, żapt etmek
conqueror /'kONkırır/ *n* fatih, galip
conquest /'kOnkwest/ *n* fetih, zafer
conscience /'kOnşıns/ *n* vicdan
conscious /'kOnşıs/ *adj* bilinçli
consciousness /'kOnşısnıs/ *n* bilinç; kendine malik olma
conscript /'kOnskript/ *n* askere alınmış genç
consent /kın'sent/ *v* muvafakat etmek, razı olmak; *n* rıza, muvafakat
consequence /'kOnsikwıns/ *n* sonuç, netice
consequently /'kOnsikwıntLii/ *adv*

sonuç olarak
conservative /kın'sÖrvıtiv/ *adj* tutucu, tedbirli
consider /kın'sidır/ *v* düşünmek, hesaba katmak
considerable /kın'sidırıbıL/ *adj* önemli; hatırı sayılır; çok, epey
considerate /kın'sidırıt/ *adj* anlayışlı; hassas
consideration /kın,sidı'reyşın/ *n* düşünme, göz önüne alma
considering /kın'sidıriN/ *prep* -e göre, -e nazaran
consignment /kın'saynmınt/ *n* sevkıyat; gönderilen mal
consistent /kın'sistınt/ *adj* tutarlı
consist of /kın'sist/ -den oluşmak, -den meydana gelmek
consolation /kOnsı'Leyşın/ *n* teselli
console /kın'souL/ *v* teselli etmek, avutmak
conspire /kın'spayr/ *v* kötülük amacıyla gizlice anlaşmak
constant /'kOnstınt/ *adj* devamlı; değişmez
constipated /'kOnstı,peytid/ *adj* kabız olmuş
constipation /,kOnstı'peyşın/ *n* kabızlık, peklik
constituency /kın'stiçuuınsii/ *n* bir seçim bölgesindeki seçmenler
constitution /,kOnstı'tuuşın/ *n* anayasa
construct /kın'strAkt/ *v* inşa etmek
construction /kın'strAkşın/ *n* yapı, inşaat
consul /'kOnsıL/ *n* konsolos
consulate /'kOnsıLıt/ *n* konsolosluk
consult /kın'sALt/ *v* danışmak, başvurmak
consultation /,kOnsıL'teyşın/ *n* istişare, danışma; ~ **hours** danışma saatleri
consumer /kın'suumır/ *n* tüketici
consumption /kın'sAmpşın/ *n* tüketim
contact /'kOntEkt/ *n* temas; ~ **lenses** kontakt lensler
contagious /kın'teycıs/ *adj* bulaşıcı; yayılan
contain /kın'teyn/ *v* kapsamak, ihtiva etmek
container /kın'teynır/ *n* kap; konteyner
contemporary /kın'tempı,rerii/ *adj* çağdaş
contempt /kın'tempt/ *n* hor görme; saygısızlık
content /kın'tent/ *adj* memnun, hoşnut
contents /'kOntents/ *pl* içindekiler
contest /'kOntest/ *n* yarışma
continent /'kOntınınt/ *n* kıta
continental /,kOntı'nentıL/ *adj* kıtasal, karasal; ~ breakfast (Avrupa kıtasına özgü) hafif kahvaltı
continual /kın'tinyuuıL/ *adj* sürekli
continue /kın'tinyuu/ *v* devam etmek, sürdürmek
continuous /kın'tinyuuıs/ *adj* sürekli, aralıksız
contour /'kOntuur/ *n* dış hatlar, şekil
contraceptive /,kOntrı'septiv/ *n* gebeliği önleyici hap *veya* alet
contract[1] /'kOntrEkt/ *n* kontrat, sözleşme
contract[2] /kın'trEkt/ *v* kasmak, daraltmak; tutulmak
contractor /kın'trEktır/ *n* müteahhit
contradict /,kOntrı'dikt/ *v* yalanlamak; aksini söylemek
contradictory /,kOntrı'diktırii/ *adj* çelişik, karşıt
contrary /'kOntrerii/ *adj* karşıt, zıt; aykırı; **on the** ~ aksine
contrast /'kOntrEst/ *n* zıtlık, fark
contribute /kın'tribyuut/ *v* bağışlamak; katkıda bulunmak; yardım etmek
contribution /,kOntrı'byuuşın/ *n*

yardım, katkı; bağış
control /kın'trouL/ *n* yönetim; kontrol; *v* yönetmek; kontrol etmek
controversial /ˌkOntrı'vÖrşıL/ *adj* çekişmeli, ihtilaflı
convenience /kın'viinyıns/ *n* uygunluk; rahatlık
convenient /kın'viinyınt/ *adj* uygun, elverişli; pratik
convent /'kOnvınt/ *n* manastır
conversation /ˌkOnvır'seyşın/ *n* konuşma, sohbet
convert /kın'vÖrt/ *v* değiştirmek, döndürmek, çevirmek
convict[1] /kın'vikt/ *v* mahkûm etmek
convict[2] /'kOnvikt/ *n* mahkûm, suçlu
conviction /kın'vikşın/ *n* kanaat, inanç; mahkûmiyet
convince /kın'vins/ *v* inandırmak, ikna etmek
convulsion /kın'vALşın/ *n* kıvranma; sarsılma, çırpınma
cook /kuk/ *n* aşçı; *v* pişirmek
cookbook /'kukˌbuk/ *n* yemek kitabı
cooker /'kukır/ *nAm* ocak; **gas ~** gaz ocağı
cookie /'kukii/ *n* bisküvi, kurabiye
cool /kuuL/ *adj* serin; soğukkanlı; **cooling system** soğutma sistemi
cooperation /kouˌOpı'reyşın/ *n* işbirliği
cooperative /kou'Opıritiv/ *adj* işbirliğine ait; birlikte çalışmaya hazır, istekli; *n* kooperatif
coordinate /kou'OOrdıˌneyt/ *v* düzenlemek, birbirine göre ayarlamak
coordination /kouˌOOrdı'neyşın/ *n* koordinasyon; düzenleme
cop /kOp/ *n* polis
Copenhagen /ˌkoupın'heygın/ Kopenhag
copper /'kOpır/ *n* bakır
copy /'kOpii/ *n* kopya, nüsha; *v* kopyasını çıkarmak; taklit etmek; **carbon ~** karbon kâğıdı ile çıkarılan suret
coral /'kOOrıL/ *n* mercan
cord /kOOrd/ *n* ip, sicim
cordial /'kOOrcıL/ *adj* samimi, candan
corduroy /'kOOrdırOy/ *n* fitilli kadife
core /kOOr/ *n* iç, öz, esas
cork /kOOrk/ *n* mantar, tıpa
corkscrew /'kOOrkˌskruu/ *n* tirbuşon
corn /kOOrn/ *nBr* hububat, tahıl; *nAm* mısır; nasır
corner /'kOOrnır/ *n* köşe
cornfield /'kOOrnˌfiiLd/ *nBr* buğday tarlası; *nAm* mısır tarlası
corpse /kOOrps/ *n* ceset
corpulent /'kOOrpyıLınt/ *adj* şişman, etli
correct /kı'rekt/ *adj* doğru, yanlışsız; *v* düzeltmek
correction /kı'rekşın/ *n* düzeltme; cezalandırma
correctness /kı'rektnıs/ *n* doğruluk, dürüstlük
correspond /ˌkOOrı'spOnd/ *v* uygun gelmek; haberleşmek, mektuplaşmak
correspondence /ˌkOOrı'spOndıns/ *n* uygunluk; mektuplaşma
correspondent /ˌkOOrı'spOndınt/ *n* muhabir; mektup arkadaşı
corridor /'kOOridOOr/ *n* koridor
corrupt /kı'rApt/ *adj* ahlakı bozuk; *v* ahlakını bozmak, kötü yola sevk etmek
corruption /kı'rApşın/ *n* ahlak bozulması
corset /'kOOrsit/ *n* korse
cosmetics /kOz'metiks/ *pl* makyaj malzemeleri
cost /kOst/ *n* bedel; maliyet

***cost** /kOst/ *v* mal olmak
costume /'kOstuum/ *n* kıyafet, kostüm
cosy /'kouzii/ *adj* rahat, kuytu
cot /kOt/ *n* portatif karyola
cottage /'kOtic/ *n* küçük ev, kulübe
cotton /'kOtın/ *n* pamuk; pamuklu kumaş; ~ **wool** ham pamuk
couch /kauç/ *n* kanepe
cough /kOOf/ *n* öksürük; *v* öksürmek
could /kud/ *v* (p can)
council /'kaunsıL/ *n* meclis, konsey
councilor /'kaunsıLır/ *n* meclis üyesi
counsel /'kaunsıL/ *n* danışma; öğüt
counselor /'kaunsıLır/ *n* danışman
count /kaunt/ *v* saymak; hesaplamak; *n* sayma; hesap; kont
counter /'kauntır/ *n* tezgâh; sayaç
counterclockwise /ˌkauntır'kLOkwayz/ *adv* saat yelkovanının ters yönünde
counterfeit /'kauntırˌfit/ *v* taklit etmek; sahte para basmak
countess /'kauntıs/ *n* kontes
country /'kAntrii/ *n* ülke; kır, taşra; ~ **house** sayfiye evi
countryman /'kAntriimın/ *n* (pl -men) yurttaş; taşralı
countryside /'kAntriiˌsayd/ *n* kırsal alan
county /'kauntii/ *n* idari bölge
couple /'kApıL/ *n* çift; karıkoca
coupon /'kuupOn/ *n* kupon
courage /'kÖric/ *n* cesaret, mertlik
courageous /kı'reycıs/ *adj* cesur, mert
course /kOOrs/ *n* yol; gidiş; yön; kurs; ders; **intensive** ~ yoğunlaştırılmış kurs; **of** ~ şüphesiz, elbette
court /kOOrt/ *n* avlu; oyun alanı; mahkeme
courteous /'kÖrtiyıs/ *adj* nazik, saygılı
cousin /'kAzın/ *n* kuzen
cover /'kAvır/ *v* örtmek; kaplamak; *n* kap; örtü; kılıf; siper
cow /kau/ *n* inek
coward /'kauırd/ *n* korkak kimse
cowardly /'kauırdLii/ *adj* korkak; alçak
crab /krEb/ *n* yengeç
crack /krEk/ *n* çatlak
cracker /'krEkır/ *n* bisküvi, kraker
cradle /'kreydıL/ *n* beşik
cramp /krEmp/ *n* kramp
crane /kreyn/ *n* turna kuşu; vinç
crash /krEş/ *n* çarpışma, kaza; *v* çarpmak; gürültüyle çarpmak, parçalanmak; ~ **barrier** güvenlik engeli
crate /kreyt/ *n* sandık
crater /'kreytır/ *n* krater
crawl /krOOL/ *v* sürünmek; emeklemek; *n* sürünme; emekleme; krol yüzme
craze /kreyz/ *n* geçici moda; çılgınlık
crazy /'kreyzii/ *adj* çılgın
creak /kriik/ *v* gıcırdamak
cream /kriim/ *n* krema; cilt kremi; *adj* krem rengi, açık bej
creamy /'kriimii/ *adj* krema gibi, krema kıvamında
crease /kriis/ *v* kırıştırmak; buruşturmak; *n* pli, kat çizgisi
create /kri'yeyt/ *v* yaratmak
creation /kri'yeyşın/ *n* yaradılış; yaratılan şey; dünya kâinat
creature /'kriiçır/ *n* yaratık
credible /'kredıbıL/ *adj* inanılır, güvenilir
credit /'kredit/ *n* itibar, kredi; *v* inanmak; alacaklandırmak; ~ **card** kredi kartı
creditor /'kreditır/ *n* alacaklı
credulous /'krecılıs/ *adj* saf, çabucak inanan

creek /kriik/ *n* çay, dere; *nBr* koy
***creep** /kriip/ *v* sürünmek; emeklemek
creepy /'kriipii/ *adj* tüyler ürpertici; sürünen
cremate /krii'meyt/ *v* ölü yakmak
cremation /krii'meyşın/ *n* ölüyü yakma
crescent /'kresınt/ *n* hilal, yarımay; **Red Crescent** Kızılay
crew /kruu/ *n* mürettebat; grup, kitle
cricket /'krikit/ *n* cırcırböceği; kriket oyunu
crime /kraym/ *n* suç
criminal /'krimınıL/ *n* suç işlemiş kimse; *adj* suça ait; cezai; ~ **law** ceza hukuku
criminality /,krimı'nELıtii/ *n* suçluluk
crimson /'krimzın/ *adj* koyu kırmızı
crippled /'kripıLd/ *adj* sakat
crisis /'kraysis/ *n* (pl crises) kriz, buhran
crisp /krisp/ *adj* gevrek
criterion /kray'tiiriyın/ (pl criteria) *n* ölçüt, kıstas
critic /'kritik/ *n* eleştirmen
critical /'kritikıL/ *adj* eleştirel; tehlikeli, nazik
criticism /'kriti,sizım/ *n* eleştiri
criticize /'kritisayz/ *v* eleştirmek
crochet/krou'şey/ *v* tığla işlemek
crockery /'krOkırii/ *n* çanak çömlek
crocodile /'krOkı,dayL/ *n* timsah
crooked /'krukid/ *adj* eğri, çarpık; dolandırıcı
crop /krOp/ *n* ürün, ekin
cross /krOOs/ *v* karşıdan karşıya geçmek; *adj* dargın, huysuz; *n* haç; çapraz işareti
cross-eyed /'krOOs,ayd/ *adj* şaşı
crossing /'krOOsiN/ *n* geçit; geçiş yeri
crossroads /'krOOs,roudz/ *n* kavşak
crosswalk /'krOOs,wOOk/ *nAm* yaya geçidi
crow /krou/ *n* karga
crowbar /'krou,baar/ *n* manivela
crowd /kraud/ *n* kalabalık
crowded /'kraudid/ *adj* kalabalık
crown /kraun/ *n* taç; *v* taç giydirmek
crucifix /'kruusı,fiks/ *n* çarmıha gerilmiş İsa resmi veya heykeli
crucifixion /,kruusı'fikşın/ *n* çarmıha gerilme
crucify /'kruusı,fay/ *v* çarmıha germek
cruel /'kruuıL/ *adj* zalim, insafsız
cruise/kruuz/ *n* deniz seyahati
crumb /krAm/ *n* ekmek kırıntısı; kırıntı
crusade /kruu'seyd/ *n* haçlı seferi; hararetli mücadele
crust /krAst/ *n* ekmek kabuğu; kabuk
crutch /krAç/ *n* koltuk değneği
cry /kray/ *v* ağlamak; bağırmak; *n* ağlama; feryat
crystal /'kristıL/ *n* kristal, billur; *adj* şeffaf, berrak
Cuba /'kyuubı/ Küba
Cuban /'kyuubın/ *adj* Küba'ya ait; *n* Kübalı
cube /kyuub/ *n* küp
cuckoo /'kuukuu/ *n* guguk kuşu
cucumber /'kyuu,kambır/ *n* salatalık
cuddle /'kAdıL/ *v* kucaklamak; sokulup yatmak
cuff /kAf/ *n* kol ağzı, manşet; ~ **links** *pl* kol düğmesi
cultivate /'kALtı,veyt/ *v* toprağı sürüp ekmek
culture /'kALçır/ *n* kültür
cultured /'kALçırd/ *adj* kültürlü
cunning /'kAniN/ *adj* kurnaz, hilekâr; marifetli
cup /kAp/ *n* fincan; kâse
cupboard /'kAbırd/ *n* dolap
curb /kÖrb/ *n* fren, engel; kaldırım kenarı; *v* frenlemek, zapt etmek

cure /kyuur/ *v* tedavi etmek; *n* tedavi
curiosity /ˌkyuuri'yOsıtii/ *n* merak
curious /'kyuuriyıs/ *adj* meraklı; tuhaf
curl /kÖrL/ *v* kıvırmak; kıvrılmak; bükülmek; *n* bukle, kıvrım
curler /'kÖrLır/ *n* bigudi
curling tongs /'kÖrLiN,tONz/ *pl* saç maşası
curly /'kÖrLii/ *adj* kıvırcık, bukleli
currant /'kArınt/ *n* frenküzümü, kuşüzümü
currency /'kÖrınsii/ *n* nakit para; geçerlik; **foreign** ~ döviz
current /'kÖrınt/ *n* cereyan, akım; *adj* geçerli; şimdiki zamana ait; **alternating** ~ dalgalı akım; **direct** ~ doğru akım
curry /'kÖrii/ *n* bir Hint baharatı ile pişirilen yemek; köri
curse /'kÖrs/ *v* lanetlemek
curtain /'kÖrtın/ *n* perde; tiyatro perdesi
curve /kÖrv/ *n* dönemeç
curved /kÖrvd/ *adj* kavisli
cushion /'kuşın/ *n* yastık, minder
custard /'kAstırd/ *n* yumurtalı, sütlü krema
custodian /ˌkıs'toudiyın/ *n* gardiyan, muhafız
custody /'kAstıdii/ *n* muhafaza; hapsetme
custom /'kAstım/ *n* gelenek; alışkanlık
customary /'kAstıˌmerii/ *adj* alışılmış
customer /'kAstımır/ *n* müşteri
customs /'kAstımz/ *pl* gümrük; ~ **duty** gümrük resmi; ~ **officer** gümrük memuru
cut /kAt/ *n* kesilmiş parça; kesim
***cut** /kAt/ *v* kesmek; kısaltmak; ~ **off** kesip koparmak; yolunu kesmek
cutlery /'kAtLırii/ *n* çatal bıçak takımı
cutlet /'kAtLıt/ *n* pirzola
cycle /'saykıL/ *n* dönme, devir; bisiklet, motosiklet
cyclist /'saykList/ *n* bisikletçi
cylinder /'siLındır/ *n* silindir
Cypriot /'sipriyıt/ *n* Kıbrıslı
Cyprus /'sayprıs/ Kıbrıs
cystitis /sis'taytıs/ *n* mesane iltihabı
Czech /çek/ *adj* Çekoslovakya'ya ait; *n* Çek
Czechoslovakia /ˌçekısLı'vEkiyı/ Çekoslovakya

D

dad /dEd/ *n* baba
daddy /'dEdii/ *n* babacığım
daffodil /'dEfıdiL/ *n* zerrin, nergis
dagger /'dEgır/ *n* kama, hançer
daily /'deyLii/ *adj* günlük; *n* günlük gazete
dairy /'deyrii/ *n* mandıra; sütçü dükkânı
dam /dEm/ *n* baraj, set
damage /'dEmic/ *n* zarar, ziyan; *v* zarar vermek
damp /dEmp/ *adj* nemli, yaş; *n* nem; *v* nemlendirmek
dance /dEns/ *v* dans etmek; *n* dans
dandelion /'dEndıLˌayın/ *n* kara hindiba
dandruff /'dEndrıf/ *n* saç kepeği
Dane /deyn/ *n* Danimarkalı
danger /'deyncır/ *n* tehlike
dangerous /'deyncırıs/ *adj* tehlikeli
Danish /'deyniş/ *adj* Danimarka'ya ait; *n* Danimarka dili
Danube /'dEnyuub/ Tuna nehri
Dardanelles /ˌdaardı'neLz/ Çanakkale Boğazı
dare /'deyr/ *v* cesaret etmek; meydan okumak
daring /'deyriN/ *adj* cesur

dark /daark/ *adj* karanlık, koyu; esmer; *n* karanlık; akşam
darling /'daarLiN/ *n* sevgili
darn /daarn/ *v* örerek tamir etmek
dash /dEş/ *v* şiddetle atmak; atılmak; *n* tire işareti
dashboard /'dEş,bOOrd/ *n* kontrol paneli
data /'deytı/ *pl* veri, bilgi; ~ **processing** bilgiişlem
date[1] /deyt/ *n* tarih; randevu; flört; *v* tarih atmak; flört etmek; **out of** ~ modası geçmiş; up to ~ çağdaş, modaya uygun
date[2] /deyt/ *n* hurma
daughter /'dOOtır/ *n* kız evlat
dawn /dOOn/ *n* şafak
day /dey/ *n* gün; **by** ~ gündüzün; ~ **trip** günlük gezinti; **per** ~ günde; **the** ~ **before yesterday** önceki gün
daybreak /'dey,breyk/ *n* tan, gün ağarması
daylight /'dey,Layt/ *n* gün ışığı
dead /ded/ *adj* ölmüş
deaf /def/ *adj* sağır
deal /diiL/ *n* ticari işlem; pazarlık
***deal** /diiL/ *v* dağıtmak; ilgilenmek; ~ **with** meşgul olmak; ticaret yapmak
dealer /'diiLır/ *n* satıcı, tüccar
dear /diir/ *adj* sevgili; pahalı
death /deT/ *n* ölüm; ~ **penalty** ölüm cezası
debate /di'beyt/ *n* tartışma
debit /'debit/ *n* borç, zimmet
debtor /'detır/ *n* borçlu
debt /det/ *n* borç
decaffeinated /dii'kEfiineytid/ *adj* kafeini alınmış
deceit /di'siit/ *n* hile
deceive /di'siiv/ *v* aldatmak
December /di'sembır/ aralık ayı
decency /'diisınsii/ *n* terbiye, nezaket
decent /'diisınt/ *adj* nezih, terbiyeli
deception /di'sepşın/ *n* aldatma; aldanma; hile
decide /di'sayd/ *v* karar vermek
decision /di'sijın/ *n* karar
deck /dek/ *n* güverte; ~ **cabin** güverte kabini; ~ **chair** şezlong
declaration /,dekLı'reyşın/ *n* açıklama, bildiri
declare /di'kLeyr/ *v* açıkça söylemek; bildirmek
decoration /,dekı'reyşın/ *n* süsleme; dekorasyon
decrease /di'kriis/ *v* azalmak; azaltmak; *n* azalma
dedicate /'dedi,keyt/ *v* adamak, ithaf etmek
deduce /di'duus/ *v* sonuç çıkarmak
deduct /di'dAkt/ *v* çıkarmak; hesaptan düşmek
deed /diid/ *n* iş; eylem
deep /diip/ *adj* derin
deepfreeze /,diip'friiz/ *n* buzluk, dipfriz
deer /diir/ *n* (pl ~) geyik
defeat /di'fiit/ *v* yenmek; *n* yenilgi
defective /di'fektiv/ *adj* kusurlu, sakat; eksik, noksan
defend /di'fend/ *v* savunmak
defense /di'fens/ / *n* savunma
deficiency /di'fişınsii/ *n* eksiklik
deficit /'defisit/ *n* hesap açığı
define /di'fayn/ *v* tanımlamak
definite /'defınit/ *adj* kesin; belirli
definition /defi'nişın/ *n* tanımlama
deformed /di'fOOrmd/ *adj* biçimi bozulmuş
defrost /di'frOOst/ *v* buzlarını eritmek
defy /di'fay/ *v* meydan okumak
degree /di'grii/ *n* derece; rütbe; diploma
delay /di'Ley/ *v* ertelemek, geciktirmek; gecikmek; *n* gecikme
delegate[1] /'deLigıt/ *n* delege, temsilci

delegate[2] /'delı,geyt/ *v* havale etmek
delegation /,deLı'geyşın/ *n* temsilci heyet, delegasyon
deliberate[1] /di'Libı,reyt/ *v* uzun uzun düşünmek; müzakere etmek
deliberate[2] /di'Libırıt/ *adj* kasti
deliberation /di,Libı'reyşın/ *n* üzerinde düşünme; tartışma
delicacy /'deLikısii/ *n* incelik, naziklik
delicate /'deLikıt/ *adj* nazik, hassas
delicatessen /,deLikı'tesın/ *n* mezeler; mezeci dükkânı
delicious /di'Lişıs/ *adj* lezzetli
delight /di'Layt/ *n* zevk, sevinç; *v* zevk vermek, sevindirmek
delightful /di'Laytfıl/ *adj* zevk verici, hoş; lezzetli
deliver /di'Livır/ *v* teslim etmek
delivery /di'Livırii/ *n* teslim; dağıtım; doğum:; ~ **van** dağıtım aracı
deluxe /di'LAks/ *adj* lüks, ihtişamlı
demand /di'mEnd/ *v* istekte bulunmak; *n* talep
democracy /di'mOkrısii/ *n* demokrasi
democratic /,demı'krEtik/ *adj* demokratik
demolish /di'mOLiş/ *v* yıkmak, tahrip etmek
demolition /,demı'Lişın/ *n* yıkma, tahribat
demon /'diimın/ *n* kötü ruh, şeytan
demonstrate /'demın,streyt/ *v* uygulamalı açıklama yapmak
demonstration /,demın'streyşın/ *n* gösteri; uygulamalı açıklama
demoralize /di'mOOrı,Layz/ *v* cesaretini kırmak, moralini bozmak
den /den/ *n* in; küçük oda
Denmark /'denmaark/ Danimarka
denomination /di,nOmi'neyşın/ *n* adlandırma; sınıf, mezhep
dense /dens/ *adj* yoğun
dent /dent/ *n* çentik
dentist /'dentist/ *n* diş hekimi
denture /'dençır/ *n* takma diş
deny /di'nay/ *v* inkâr etmek
deodorant /di'oudırınt/ *n* koku giderici madde, deodoran
depart /di'paart/ *v* ayrılmak; kalkmak (otobüs, uçak vs.)
department /di'paartmınt/ *n* bölüm, şube; ~ **store** büyük mağaza
departure /di'paarçır/ *n* kalkış
dependent /di'pendınt/ *adj* bağımlı
depend on /di'pend/ bağlı olmak, tabi olmak
deposit /di'pOzit/ *n* emanet; mevduat; tortu
depository /di'pOzi,tOOrii/ *n* emanetçi; depo
depress /di'pres/ *v* bastırmak; kasvet vermek
depression /di'preşın/ *n* sıkıntı, bunalım
deprive of /di'prayv/ mahrum etmek
depth /depT/ *n* derinlik
deputy /'depyıtii/ *n* vekil
dermatology /,dÖrmı'tOLıcii/ *n* cildiye, dermatoloji
descend /di'send/ *v* inmek
descendant /di'sendınt/ *n* torun; sonraki kuşak
descent /di'sent/ *n* iniş; soy
describe /di'skrayb/ *v* tanımlamak
description /di'skripşin/ *n* tarif, tasvir, niteleme
desert[1] /'dezırt/ *n* çöl; *adj* ıssız, çorak
desert[2] /di'zÖrt/ *v* terk etmek, kaçmak
deserve /di'zÖrv/ *v* hak etmek, layık olmak
design /di'zayn/ *v* çizmek, tasarlamak; *n* plan, taslak
designate /'dezigneyt/ *v* tayin etmek, belirlemek
desirable /di'zayrıbıL/ *adj* arzu edilen

desire /di'zayr/ *n* istek, arzu; *v* arzu etmek
desk /desk/ *n* okul sırası; çalışma masası
despair /di'speyr/ *n* yeis, ümitsizlik; *v* ümitsizliğe kapılmak
despatch /di'spEç/ *vBr* göndermek, sevk etmek
desperate /'despırıt/ *adj* ümitsiz; çaresiz, vahim
despise /di'spayz/ *v* küçük görmek
despite /di'spayt/ *prep* -e rağmen
dessert /di'zÖrt/ *n* yemek sonunda yenen meyve, tatlı
destination /,desti'neyşın/ *n* gidilecek yer; varış noktası
destine /'destin/ *v* nasip etmek; önceden belirlemek
destiny /'destinii/ *n* kader
destroy /di'strOy/ *v* tahrip etmek
destruction /di'strAkşın/ *n* tahrip, yıkma
detach /di'tEç/ *v* ayırmak, koparmak; **detached house** *Br* müstakil ev
detail /'diiteyL/ *n* ayrıntı
detailed /'diiteyLd/ *adj* ayrıntılı
detect /di'tekt/ *v* keşfetmek; sezmek
detective /di'tektiv/ *n* dedektif; ~ **story** polisiye roman
detergent /di'tÖrcınt/ *n* deterjan
deteriorate /di'tiiriyı,reyt/ *v* fenalaşmak, bozulmak, gerilemek
determine /di'tÖrmin/ *v* karar vermek; belirlemek
determined /di'tÖrmind/ *adj* azimli, kararlı
detour /'diituur/ *n* geçici yol, dolambaçlı yol
devaluation /dii,vELyuu'eyşın/ *n* devalüasyon
devalue /dii'vELyuu/ *v* değerini düşürmek
develop /di'veLıp/ *v* geliştirmek; gelişmek
development /di'veLıpmınt/ *n* gelişme; kalkınma
deviate /'diivi,yeyt/ *v* sapmak
device /di'vays/ *n* aygıt, alet
devil /'devıL/ *n* şeytan
devise /di'vayz/ *v* icat etmek; tasarlamak
devote /di'vout/ *v* adamak, vakfetmek
dew /duu/ *n* çiy, şebnem
diabetes /dayı'biitis/ *n* şeker hastalığı
diabetic /dayı'betik/ *n* şeker hastası
diagnose /'dayıg,nouz/ *v* teşhis etmek
diagnosis /,dayıg'nousis/ *n* (pl -ses) teşhis
diagonal /day'EgınıL/ *n* köşegen
diagram /'dayı,grEm/ *n* şekil, şema
dial /'dayıL/ *n* kadran; *v* telefon numarasını çevirmek
dialect /'dayı,Lekt/ *n* lehçe
diamond /'day,mınd/ *n* elmas
diaper /'dayıpır/ *nAm* çocuk bezi
diaphragm /'dayı,frEm/ *n* diyafram kası; zar
diarrhea /,dayı'riiyı/ *n* ishal, sürgün
diary /'dayırii/ *n* günlük, hatıra defteri
dice /days/ *pl* oyun zarları
dictate /dik'teyt/ *v* söyleyip yazdırmak; emretmek
dictation /dik'teyşın/ *n* yazdırma, dikte; emretme
dictator /,dik'teytır/ *n* diktatör
dictionary /'dikşı,nerii/ *n* sözlük
did /did/ *v* (p do)
die /day/ *v* ölmek
diet /'dayıt/ *n* rejim, perhiz
differ /'difır/ *v* farklı olmak
difference /'difırıns/ *n* ayrılık, fark
different /'difırınt/ *adj* farklı
difficult /'difikıLt/ *adj* güç, zor; titiz, huysuz
difficulty /'difi,kıltii/ *n* güçlük
***dig** /dig/ *v* kazmak

digest /day'cest/ *v* sindirmek
digestible /day'cestıbıL/ *adj* sindirimi kolay
digestion /day'cesçın/ *n* sindirim
digit /'dicit/ *n* rakam
dignified /'digni,fayd/ *adj* ağırbaşlı
dike /dayk/ *n* suyolu, hendek; su seddi
dilapidated /di'LEpı,deytid/ *adj* bakımsız, harap
dilemma /di'lemı/ *n* ikilem; çıkmaz
diligence /'diLıcıns/ *n* gayret, çalışkanlık
diligent /'diLıcınt/ *adj* gayretli, çalışkan
dilute /day'Luut/ *v* sulandırmak
dim /dim/ *adj* loş; donuk
dime /daym/ *n* 10 cent'lik ABD parası
dine /dayn/ *v* akşam yemeği yemek
dinghy /'diNgii/ *n* küçük sandal
diningcar /'dayniN,kar/ *n* vagon restoran
dining room /'dayniN,ruum/ yemek odası
dinner /'dinır/ *n* akşam yemeği
dip /dip/ *v* batırmak, daldırmak; batmak, dalmak
diphtheria /dif'Tiiriyı/ *n* difteri
diploma /di'pLoumı/ *n* diploma
diplomat /'dipLı,mEt/ *n* diplomat
direct /di'rekt/ *adj* dolaysız; duraksız; *v* yönetmek
direction /di'rekşın/ *n* yön; **directions** izahat, tarif; **directions for use** kullanma talimatı
directive /di'rektiv/ *n* emir
director /di'rektır/ *n* yönetici
directory /di'rektırii/ *n* rehber
dirt /dÖrt/ *n* kir
dirty /'dÖrtii/ *adj* kirli
disabled /di'seybıLd/ *adj* sakat
disadvantage /,disıd'vEntic/ *n* aleyhte olan durum, mahzur
disagree /,disı'grii/ *v* uyuşmamak
disagreeable /,disı'griyıbıL/ *adj* hoş olmayan, kötü
disappear /,disı'piir/ *v* gözden kaybolmak
disappoint /,disı'pOynt/ *v* hayal kırıklığına uğratmak
disappointment /,disı'pOyntmınt/ *n* hayal kırıklığı
disapproval /,disı'pruuvıL/ *n* beğenmeyiş, hoşnutsuzluk
disapprove /,disı'pruuv/ *v* uygun bulmamak, beğenmemek
disarmament /di'saarmımınt/ *n* silahsızlanma
disaster /di'zEstır/ *n* felaket, bela
disastrous /di'zEstrıs/ *adj* felaket getiren, feci
disc /disk/ *nBr* disk; plak
discard /di'skaard/ *v* ıskartaya çıkarmak, atmak
discharge /dis'çaarc/ *v* boşaltmak
disciple /di'saypıL/ *n* mürit; havari
discipline /'disıpLın/ *n* disiplin
disclose /dis'kLouz/ *v* ifşa etmek, açığa vurmak
discolor /dis'kALır/ *v* rengini bozmak, soldurmak
disconnect /,diskı'nekt/ *v* bağlantısını kesmek
discontented /,diskın'tentid/ *adj* hoşnutsuz
discontinue /,diskın'tinyuu/ *v* kesmek, devam etmemek
discount /'dis,kaunt/ *n* indirim
discourage /dis'kÖric/ *v* hevesini kırmak, cesaretini kırmak
discover /dis'kAvır/ *v* keşfetmek
discovery /dis'kAvırii/ *n* keşif
discuss /dis'kAs/ *v* görüşmek, tartışmak
discussion /dis'kAşın/ *n* görüşme, tartışma

disease /di'ziiz/ / *n* hastalık
disembark /ˌdisim'baark/ *v* karaya çıkmak *veya* çıkarmak
disgrace /dis'greys/ *n* gözden düşme, rezalet
disguise /dis'gayz/ *v* kılık değiştirmek
disgusting /dis'gAstiN/ *adj* iğrenç
dish /diş/ *n* tabak; yemek
dishwasher /'diş,wOOşır/ *n* bulaşıkçı; bulaşık makinesi
dishonest /dis'Onist/ *adj* dürüst olmayan, namussuz
disinfect /ˌdisin'fekt/ *v* dezenfekte etmek
disinfectant /ˌdisin'fektınt/ *n* mikrop öldürücü ilaç
disk /disk/ *nAm* disk; plak
dislike /dis'Layk/ *v* hoşlanmamak
dislocated /'disLouˌkeytid/ *adj* yerinden çıkmış
dismiss /dis'mis/ *v* işinden çıkarmak; gitmesine izin vermek
disorder /dis'OOrdır/ *n* düzensizlik, karışıklık
dispatch /dis'pEç/ *vAm* göndermek, sevk etmek
display /dis'pLey/ *v* göstermek, sergilemek; *n* gösteri, sergi
displease /dis'pLiiz/ *v* canını sıkmak, gücendirmek
disposable /dis'pOuzıbıL/ *adj* atılabilir;
disposal /dis'pouzıL/ *n* elden çıkarma
dispose of /dis'pouz/ satmak, elden çıkarmak
dispute /dis'pyuut/ *n* tartışma, anlaşmazlık
disrespect /ˌdisri'spekt/ *n* saygısızlık
dissatisfied /dis'sEtis,fayd/ *adj* hoşnutsuz, tatmin olmamış
dissertation /disır'teyşın/ *n* tez
dissolve /di'zOLv/ *v* eritmek; erimek
dissuade from /di'sweyd/ -den vazgeçirmek
distance /'distıns/ *n* uzaklık; ~ **in kilometers** km cinsinden uzaklık
distant /'distınt/ *adj* uzak
distill /dis,tiL/ *v* damıtmak
distinct /dis'tiNkt/ *adj* ayrı; açık, kesin
distinction /dis'tiNkşın/ *n* ayırt etme; fark; üstünlük
distinguish /dis'tiNgwiş/ *v* ayırt etmek; kendini göstermek
distinguished /dis'tiNgwişt/ *adj* seçkin, üstün
distress /dis'tres/ *n* üzüntü; sıkıntı; ~ **signal** imdat işareti
distribute /dis'tribyuut/ *v* dağıtmak
distributor /dis'tribyuutır/ *n* dağıtıcı
district /'distrikt/ *n* bölge, semt
disturb /dis'tÖrb/ *v* rahatsız etmek
disturbance /dis'tÖrbıns/ *n* karışıklık, rahatsızlık
ditch /diç/ *n* hendek
dive /dayv/ *v* suya dalmak
diversion /dı'vÖrjın/ *n* başka tarafa çevirme; eğlence
divide /di'vayd/ *v* bölmek, ayırmak
divine /di'vayn/ *adj* tanrısal
division /di'vijın/ *n* bölme; bölüm
divorce /di'vOOrs/ *n* boşanma; *v* boşanmak, boşamak
dizziness /'diziinıs/ *n* baş dönmesi
dizzy /'dizii/ *adj* başı dönen; baş döndürücü
***do** /duu/ *v* yapmak, etmek
dock /dOk/ *n* rıhtım; *v* rıhtıma yanaşmak
docker /'dOkır/ *n* tersane işçisi
doctor /'dOktır/ *n* doktor
document /'dOkyımınt/ *n* belge
dog /dOOg/ *n* köpek
dogged /'dOOgid/ *adj* inatçı
doll /dOL/ *n* oyuncak bebek
dolphin /'dOLfin/ *n* yunus balığı
dome /doum/ *n* kubbe

domestic /dı'mestik/ *adj* eve ait; evcil; yerli; *n* hizmetçi
domicile /'dOmisiL/ *n* konut, ev
dominant /'dOminınt/ *adj* hakim, galip, nüfuzlu
domination /,dOmi'neyşın/ *n* hâkimiyet
dominion /dı'minyın/ *n* hâkimiyet; sömürge
donate /'douneyt/ *v* bağışta bulunmak
donation /dou'neyşın/ *n* bağış
done /dAn/ *v* (pp do)
donkey /'dOnkii/ *n* eşek
door /dOOr/ *n* kapı;
revolving ~ döner kapı;
sliding ~ kayar kapı
doorbell /'dOOr,beL/ *n* kapı zili
doorkeeper /'dOOr,kiipır/ *n* kapıcı
doorman /'dOOrmın/ *n* (pl -men) kapıcı
dormitory /'dOOrmı,tOOrii/ *n* yatakhane
dose /dous/ *n* doz, bir defalık miktar
dot /dOt/ *n* nokta
double /'dAbıL/ *adj* çift; *n* dublör
doubt /daut/ *v* kuşkulanmak; *n* kuşku, tereddüt;
without ~ kuşkusuz
doubtful /'dautfıL/ *adj* kuşkulu
dough /dou/ *n* hamur
down[1] /daun/ *adv* aşağı, aşağıya; *adj* keyifsiz, hüzünlü; *prep* boyunca; ~ **payment** peşinat
down[2] /daun/ *n* ince kuş tüyü
downpour /'daun,pOOr/ *n* sağanak
downstairs /'daun'steyrz/ *adv* aşağıda, alt katta
downstream /'daun'striim/ *adv* akıntı yönünde
down-to-earth /,dauntu'ÖrT/ *adj* gerçekçi; uygulanabilir
downtown /'daun,taun/ *nAm* şehrin iş merkezi
downward /'daunwırd/ *adv* aşağıya doğru
dozen /dAzın/ *n* (pl ~ s) düzine
draft /drEft/ *nAm* çekme; taslak; hava akımı
drag /drEg/ *v* sürüklemek
dragon /'drEgın/ *n* ejderha
drain /dreyn/ *v* suyunu akıtmak, boşaltmak
drama /'draamı/ *n* oyun; tiyatro sanatı
dramatic /drı'mEtik/ tiyatroya ait; etkileyici; dramatik
dramatist /'drEmıtist/ *n* oyun yazarı
drank /drENk/ *v* (p drink)
draper /'dreypır/ *nBr* kumaşçı, tuhafiyeci
drapery /'dreypırii/ *nBr* tuhafiye mağazası
draught /drEft/ *nBr* hava akımı, cereyan; **draughts** *Br* dama oyunu
draught-board /'drEft,bOOrd/ *nBr* dama tahtası
draw /drOO/ *n* çekme, çekiliş; çekilen şey
***draw** /drOO/ *v* çizmek, resim yapmak; çekmek; ~ **up** yazmak, düzenlemek
drawbridge /'drOO,bric/ *n* açılır kapanır köprü
drawer /'drOOır/ *n* çekmece
drawing /'drOOiN/ *n* çizim, resim taslağı; plan
drawing pin /'drOOiN,pin/ raptiye
drawing room /'drOOiN,ruum/ salon, misafir odası
dread /dred/ *v* korkmak; *n* korku
dreadful /'dredfıL/ *adj* korkunç
dream /driim/ *n* rüya
***dream** /driim/ *v* rüya görmek
dress /dres/ *v* giyinmek; *n* elbise
dressing gown /'dresiN,gaun/ sabahlık
dressing table /'dresıN,teybıL/ tuvalet

masası
dressmaker /'dres,meykır/ *n* kadın terzisi
drift /drift/ *v* rüzgâr *veya u* akıntıyla sürüklenmek
drill /driL/ *v* matkapla delmek; talim yaptırmak; *n* matkap; talim; alıştırma
drink /driNk/ *n* içki, içecek şey
***drink** /driNk/ *v* içmek
drinking water /'driNkiN,wOOtır/ içme suyu
drip-dry /'drip,dray/ *adj* sıkmadan askıya asılarak kurutulan ve buruşmayan
drive /drayv/ *n* araba yolu; araba gezintisi; itki; hamle, enerji
***drive** /drayv/ *v* araba kullanmak
driver /'drayvır/ *n* sürücü
drizzle /'drizıL/ *n* çiseleme
drop /drOp/ *v* damlatmak; damlamak; düşürmek; *n* damla
drought /draut/ *n* kuraklık
drown /draun/ *v* suda boğmak; boğulmak; ***be drowned** boğulmak
drug /drAg/ *n* ilaç; uyuşturucu madde
drugstore /'drAg,stOOr/ *nAm* eczane; ilaç, yiyecek, kırtasiye, vs. satan dükkân
drum /drAm/ *n* davul
drunk /drANk/ *adj* (pp drink) sarhoş
dry /dray/ *adj* kuru; *v* kurumak; kurutmak
dry-clean /'dray,kLiin/ *v* kuru temizleme yapmak
dry cleaner's /'dray'kLiinırz/ kuru temizleyici
dryer /drayır/ *n* kurutucu
duchess /'dAçıs/ *n* düşes
duck /dAk/ *n* ördek
due /duu/ *adj* uygun; ödeme zamanı gelmiş
dues /duuz/ *pl* aidat, vergi
dug /dAg/ *v* (p, pp dig)
duke /duuk/ *n* dük
dull /dAL/ *adj* aptal; sıkıcı; donuk
dumb /dAm/ *adj* dilsiz; aptal
dummy /'dAmii/ *n* kukla; manken; taklit
dump /dAmp/ *v* boşaltmak, atmak
dung /dAN/ *n* gübre
duplicate[1] /'duuplikit/ *n* eş, kopya
duplicate[2] /'duupli,keyt/ *v* kopyasını çıkarmak
durable /'duurıbıL/ *adj* dayanıklı, sağlam
duration /duu'reyşın/ *n* süre
during /'duuriN/ *prep* sırasında, süresince
dusk /dAsk/ *n* akşam karanlığı
dust /dAst/ *n* toz
dustbin /'dAst,bin/ *nBr* çöp tenekesi
dusty /'dAstii/ *adj* tozlu
Dutch /dAç/ *adj* Hollanda'ya ait; *n* Hollanda dili
Dutchman /'dAçmın/ *n* (pl -men) Hollandalı
dutiable /'duutiyıbıL/ *adj* gümrüğe tabi
duty /'duutii/ *n* görev; resim, vergi; **Customs** ~ gümrük resmi
duty-free /'duutii,frii/ *adj* gümrük resminden muaf
dwarf /dwOOrf/ *n* cüce
dwelling /'dweLiN/ *n* konut, ev
dye /day/ *v* boyamak; *n* boya
dynamo /'daynı,mou/ *n* (pl ~s) dinamo
dysentery /'disın,terii/ *n* dizanteri

E

each /iiç/ *adj* her bir; ~ **other** birbirini
eager /'iigır/ *adj* istekli
eagle /'iigıL/ *n* kartal

ear /iir/ *n* kulak
earache /'iir,eyk/ *n* kulak ağrısı
eardrum /'iir,drAm/ *n* kulak zarı
earl /ÖrL/ *n* kont
early /'ÖrLii/ *adj* erken
earn /Örn/ *v* kazanmak
earnest /'Örnist/ *adj* ciddi
earnings /'ÖrniNz/ *pl* kazanç
earring /'iir,riN/ *n* küpe
earth /ÖrT/ *n* dünya; toprak
earthenware /'ÖrTın,weyr/ *n* çanak çömlek
earthquake /'ÖrT,kweyk/ *n* deprem
ease /iiz/ *n* kolaylık
east /iist/ *n* doğu
Easter /'iistır/ Paskalya
easterly /'iistırLii/ *adj* doğuya ait
eastern /'iistırn/ *adj* doğuya ait
easy /'iizii/ *adj* kolay, rahat; ~ **chair** koltuk
easygoing /'iizii,gouiN/ *adj* sakin, uysal; kayıtsız
***eat** /iit/ *v* yemek
eavesdrop /'iivz,drOp/ *v* kulak misafiri olmak
ebony /'ebınii/ *n* abanoz
eccentric /ik'sentrik/ *adj* acayip, alışılmışın dışında
echo /'ekou/ *n* (pl ~es) yankı
eclipse /i'kLips/ *n* güneş *veya* ay tutulması
economic /,ekı'nOmik/ *adj* iktisadi, ekonomik
economical /,ekı'nOmikıL/ *adj* az masraflı, tutumlu
economist /i'kOnımist/ *n* iktisatçı
economize /i'kOnımayz/ *v* tutumlu kullanmak
economy /i'kOnımii/ *n* iktisat; tutum
ecstasy /'ekstısii/ *n* yoğun coşku
Ecuador /'ekwı,dOOr/ Ekvator
Ecuadorian /,ekwı'dOOriyın/ *n* Ekvatorlu
eczema /'eksimı/ *n* egzema
edge /ec/ *n* kenar
edible /'edibıL/ *adj* yenebilir
edition /i'dişın/ *n* baskı; **morning** ~ sabah baskısı
editor /'editır/ *n* editör; bir eseri yayına hazırlayan kimse
editorial /,edı'tOOriyıl/ *n* başyazı
educate /'ecı,keyt/ *v* eğitip öğretmek
education /,ecı'keyşın/ *n* eğitim; öğrenim
eel /iiL/ *n* yılan balığı
effect /i'fekt/ *n* etki; *v* etkilemek; **in** ~ aslında
effective /i'fektiv/ *adj* etkili
efficient /i'fişınt/ *adj* işbilir, ehliyetli; verimli
effort /'efırt/ *n* çaba
egg /eg/ *n* yumurta
egg cup /'eg,kAp/ yumurtalık
eggplant /'eg,pLEnt/ *n* patlıcan
egg yolk /'eg,youk/ yumurta sarısı
egoistic /,iigou'istik/ *adj* bencil
Egypt /'iicipt/ Mısır
Egyptian /i'cipşın/ *adj* Mısır'a ait; *n* Mısırlı
eiderdown /'aydır,daun/ *n* kuştüyü yorgan
eight /eyt/ *num* sekiz
eighteen /,ey'tiin/ *num* on sekiz
eighteenth /,ey'tiinT/ *num* on sekizinci
eighth /eyT/ *num* sekizinci
eighty /'eytii/ *num* seksen
either /'iiDır/ *adj* ikisinden biri, her biri; **either . . . or** ya . . . ya da
elaborate /i'LEbı,reyt/ *v* özenle hazırlamak; üzerinde işlemek
elastic /i'LEstik/ *adj* elastiki, esnek
elasticity /i,LEs'tisıtii/ *n* elastikiyet, esneklik
elbow /'eLbou/ *n* dirsek
elder /'eLdır/ *adj* daha yaşlı
elderly /'eLdırLii/ *adj* oldukça yaşlı
eldest /'eLdist/ *adj* en yaşlı

elect /i'Lekt/ *v* seçmek
election /i'Lekşın/ *n* seçim
electric /i'Lektrik/ *adj* elektrikli; ~ **razor** elektrikli tıraş makinesi; ~ **cable** elektrik kablosu
electrician /i,Lek'trişın/ *n* elektrikçi
electricity /i,Lek'trisıtii/ *n* elektrik
electronic /i,Lek'trOnik/ *adj* elektronik
elegance /'eLigıns/ *n* zariflik, şıklık
elegant /'eLigınt/ *adj* zarif, şık
element /'eLimınt/ *n* öğe, unsur
elementary /,eLı'mentırii/ *adj* basit; temel; ilk; ~ **education** ilköğretim; ~ **school** ilkokul
elephant /'eLifınt/ *n* fil
elevator /'eLı,veytır/ *n* asansör
eleven /i'Levın/ *num* on bir
eleventh /i'LevınT/ *num* on birinci
elf /eLf/ *n* (pl elves) peri
eligible /'eLicıbıL/ *adj* uygun; seçilebilir
eliminate /i'Limı,neyt/ *v* elemek, çıkarmak
elm /eLm/ *n* karaağaç
else /eLs/ *adv* başka; yoksa
elsewhere /'eLs,hweyr/ *adv* başka yerde
elucidate /i'Luusı,deyt/ *v* açıklamak, aydınlatmak
emancipation /i,mEnsı'peyşın/ *n* serbest bırakma, özgür kılma
embankment /im'bENkmınt/ *n* toprak set; bent
embargo /im'baargou/ *n* (pl ~s) ambargo
embark /im'baark/ *v* gemiye binmek *veya* bindirmek
embarkation /,imbaar'keyşın/ *n* gemiye binme *veya* bindirme
embarrass /im'bErıs/ *v* sıkıntıya sokup utandırmak; **embarrassed** *adj* utanmış, sıkılmış
embassy /'embısii/ *n* sefaret, elçilik
emblem /'embLım/ *n* amblem, simge
embrace /im'breys/ *v* kucaklamak; *n* kucaklama
embroider /im'brOydır/ *v* nakış işlemek
embroidery /im'brOydırii/ *n* nakış
embryo /'embriyou/ *n* oğulcuk, embriyon
emerald /'emırıLd/ *n* zümrüt
emergency /i'mÖrcınsii/ *n* acil durum; ~ **exit** tehlike çıkışı
emigrant /'emigrınt/ *n* göçmen
emigrate /'emi,greyt/ *v* göç etmek
emigration /,emi'greyşın/ *n* göç
emotion /i'mouşın/ *n* heyecan; duygu
emperor /'empırır/ *n* imparator
emphasize /'emfı,sayz/ *v* önemini belirtmek, vurgulamak
empire /'empayr/ *n* imparatorluk
employ /em'pLOy/ *v* işe almak
employee /em'pLOyii/ *n* işçi, memur
employer /em'pLOyır/ *n* işveren
employment /em'pLOymınt/ iş; istihdam; ~ **exchange** iş bulma kurumu
empress /'empris/ *n* imparatoriçe
empty /'emptii/ *adj* boş; *v* boşaltmak
enable /i'neybıL/ *v* mümkün kılmak; muktedir kılmak
enamel /i'nEmıL/ *n* mine
enamelled /i'nEmıLd/ *adj* mineli
enchanting /in'çEntiN/ *adj* büyüleyici
encircle /in'sÖrkıL/ *v* çevrelemek, kuşatmak
enclose /in'kLouz/ *v* sarmak, kuşatmak; zarf içine koymak
enclosure /in'kLoujır/ *n* kuşatma; çevrilmiş arsa; ilişikte gönderilen şey
encounter /in'kauntır/ *v* karşılaşmak; *n* rastlaşma
encourage /in'kÖric/ *v* cesaretlendirmek
encyclopedia /in,saykLı'piidiyı/ *n* ansiklopedi

end /end/ *n* son; amaç; *v* bitirmek; bitmek
ending /'endiN/ *n* bitiş
endless /'endLıs/ *adj* sonsuz
endorse /in'dOOrs/ *v* ciro etmek
endure /in'duur/ *v* dayanmak
enemy /'enımii/ *n* düşman
energetic /,enır'cetik/ *adj* enerjik
energy /'enırcii/ *n* enerji, güç
engage /in'geyc/ *v* işe almak; işgal etmek; **engaged** *adj* nişanlı; meşgul
engagement /in'geycmınt/ *n* nişanlanma; meşguliyet; ~ **ring** nişan yüzüğü
engine /'encin/ *n* makine; motor; lokomotif
engineer /,enci'niir/ *n* mühendis
England /'iNgLınd/ İngiltere
English /'iNgLiş/ *adj* İngiliz; *n* İngilizce
Englishman /'iNglişmın/ *n* (pl -men) İngiliz
engrave /in'greyv/ *v* oymak, işlemek
engraver /in'greyvır/ *n* oymacı
engraving /in'greyviN/ *n* oymacılık; gravür; klişe
enigma /i'nigmı/ *n* muamma
enjoy /in'cOy/ *v* zevk almak; hoşlanmak
enjoyable /in'cOyıbıL/ *adj* zevk verici, hoş
enjoyment /in'cOymınt/ *n* zevk, hoşlanma
enlarge /in'Laarc/ *v* büyütmek
enlargement /in'Laarcmınt/ *n* büyütme
enlighten /en'Laytın/ *v* bilgi vermek, aydınlatmak
enormous /i'nOOrmıs/ *adj* pek büyük
enough /i'nAf/ *adv* yeteri kadar; *adj* yeterli
enquire /in'kwayr/ *v* soruşturmak
enquiry /in'kwayrii/ *n* soruşturma
enter /'entır/ *v* girmek; kaydetmek
enterprise /'entırprayz/ *n* girişim, teşebbüs
entertain /,entır'teyn/ *v* ağırlamak; eğlendirmek
entertainer /,entır'teynır/ *n* profesyonel eğlendirici, animatör
entertaining /,entır'teyniN/ *adj* eğlendirici
entertainment /,entır'teynmınt/ *n* eğlence
enthusiasm /in'Tuuzii,yEzım/ *n* şevk, heves
enthusiastic /in,Tuuzii'yEstik/ *adj* hevesli, coşkulu
entire /in'tayır/ *adj* tam, bütün
entirely /in'tayırLii/ *adv* tamamen
entrance /'entrıns/ *n* giriş; ~ **fee** giriş ücreti
entry /'entrii/ *n* giriş; kayıt; **no** ~ girilmez
envelope /'envıLoup/ *n* mektup zarfı
envious /'enviyıs/ *adj* kıskanç
environment /in'vayrınmınt/ *n* çevre
envoy /'envOy/ *n* elçi
envy /'envii/ *n* kıskançlık; *v* kıskanmak
epic /'epik/ *n* destan; *adj* destansı
epidemic /epı'demik/ *n* salgın hastalık
epilepsy /'epı,Lepsii/ *n* sara hastalığı
epilogue /epı,LOOg/ *n* sonsöz
equal /'iikwıL/ *adj* eşit
equality /i'kwOLıtii/ eşitlik
equalize /'iikwı,Layz/ *v* eşitlemek
equally /'iikwıLii/ *adv* eşit olarak
equation /i'kweyjın/ *n* denklem
equator /i'kweytır/ *n* ekvator
equilibrium /,iikwı'Libriyım/ *n* denge
equip /i'kwip/ *v* donatmak
equipment /i'kwipmınt/ *n* donatım, teçhizat
equivalent /i'kwivıLınt/ *adj* eşit; eşdeğerli
era /'iirı/ *n* devir, çağ

eraser /i'reysır/ *n* lastik silgi
erect /i'rekt/ *v* dikmek; *adj* dimdik
erosion /i'roujın/ *n* aşındırma, aşınma, erozyon
err /Ör/ *v* yanılmak, hata yapmak
errand /'erınd/ *n* bir haber *veya* iş için gönderme
error /'erır/ *n* yanlışlık
escalator /'eskı,Leytır/ *n* yürüyen merdiven
escape /is'keyp/ *v* kaçmak, kurtulmak; *n* kaçış
escort[1] /'eskOOrt/ *n* kavalye; muhafız
escort[2] /is'kOOrt/ *v* refakat etmek
especially /is'peşıLii/ *adv* özellikle
esplanade /,espLı'neyd/ *n* gezinti alanı
essence /'esıns/ *n* öz, esas
essential /i'senşıl/ *adj* gerekli, temel
essentially /i'senşıLii/ *adv* esas olarak
establish /is'tEbLiş/ *v* kurmak
estate /is'teyt// *n* arazi, mülk
esteem /is'tiim/ *n* saygı, itibar; *v* saygı göstermek
estimate[1] /'esti,meyt/ *v* tahmin etmek; değer biçmek
estimate[2] /'estımıt/ *n* tahmin
estuary /'esçuu,erii/ *n* nehir ağzı
et cetera /et 'setırı/ vesaire
etching /'eçiN/ *n* kezzapla kazılmış resim, ofort
eternal /i'tÖrnıL/ *adj* başı ve sonu olmayan; daimi
eternity /i'tÖrnıtii/ *n* sonsuzluk, ebediyet
ether /'iiTır/ *n* eter
ethical /'eTikıL/ *adj* ahlaki, törel
Ethiopia /,iiTii'youpiyı/ Etiyopya
Ethiopian /iiTii'youpiyın/ *adj* Etiyopya'ya ait; *n* Etiyopyalı
Europe /'yuurıp/ Avrupa
European /,yuurı'piyın/ *adj* Avrupa'ya özgü; *n* Avrupalı
evacuate /i'vEkyu,eyt/ *v* boşaltmak
evaluate /i'vELyueyt/ *v* değerlendirmek, değer biçmek
evaporate /i'vEpı,reyt/ *v* buharlaşmak
eve /iiv/ *n* arife gecesi, arife
even /'iivın/ *adj* düz; eşit; çift; *adv* hatta, bile
evening /'iivniN/ *n* akşam; **~ dress** gece elbisesi
event /i'vent/ *n* olay
eventual /i'vençuuıL/ *adj* sonuçta olan, en sonraki
ever /'evır/ *adv* herhangi bir zamanda; her zaman
every /'evrii/ *adj* her
everybody /'evrii,bOdii/ *pron* herkes
everyday /'evri,dey/ *adj* her günkü, olağan
everyone /'evrii,wAn/ *pron* herkes
everything /'evrii,Tin/ *pron* her şey
everywhere /'evrii,hweyr/ *adv* her yerde
evidence /'evıdıns/ *n* kanıt
evident /'evıdınt/ *adj* açık, belli
evil /'iivıL/ *n* kötülük; *adj* kötü
evolution /,evı'Luuşın/ *n* evrim
exact /ig'zEkt/ *adj* kesin
exactly /ig'zEktLii/ *adv* kesinlikle, tamamen
exaggerate /ig'zEcı,reyt/ *v* abartmak
examination /ig,zEmi'neyşın/ *n* sınav; muayene
examine /ig'zEmin/ *v* incelemek; muayene etmek
example /ig'zEmpıL/ *n* örnek; **for ~** mesela, örneğin
excavation /,ekskı'veyşın/ *n* kazı
exceed /ik'siid/ *v* aşmak, geçmek
excel /ik'seL/ *v* üstün olmak
excellent /'eksıLınt/ *adj* mükemmel
except /ik'sept/ *prep* hariç, dışında
exception /ik'sepşın/ *n* istisna
exceptional /ik'sepşınıL/ *adj* müstesna, bulunmaz

excerpt /'eksÖrpt/ *n* alıntı, seçme parça
excess /ik'ses/ *n* aşırılık
excessive /ik'sesiv/ *adj* aşırı
exchange /iks'çeync/ *v* değiş tokuş etmek; döviz bozdurmak; *n* değiş tokuş; borsa; ~ **office** döviz bozdurma büfesi; ~ **rate** döviz kuru
excite /ik'sayt/ *v* heyecanlandırmak
excitement /ik'saytmınt/ *n* heyecan, telaş
exciting /ik'saytiN/ *adj* heyecan verici
exclaim /iks'kLeym/ *v* sevinç *veya* hayretten bağırmak
exclamation /,ekskLı'meyşın/ *n* nida, ünlem
exclude /iks'kLuud/ *v* istisna etmek, dışlamak
exclusive /iks'kLuusiv/ *adj* münhasır, tek, özel; seçkin
exclusively /iks'kLuusivLii/ *adv* münhasıran, yalnız, sırf
excursion /iks'kÖrjın/ *n* gezi
excuse[1] /iks'kyuus/ *n* bahane, özür
excuse[2] /iks'kyuuz/ *v* affetmek, mazur görmek
execute /'eksı,kyuut/ *v* yapmak, yerine getirmek
execution /,eksı'kyuuşın/ *n* yerine getirme; idam
executioner /,eksi'kyuuşınır/ *n* cellat
executive /ig'zekyıtiv/ *adj* yetki sahibi; *n* yönetici, yetkili kişi
exempt /ig'zempt/ *v* muaf tutmak; *adj* muaf
exemption /ig'zempşın/ *n* muafiyet
exercise /'eksır,sayz/ *n* alıştırma; *v* alıştırma yapmak
exhale /eks'heyL/ *v* nefesi dışarı vermek
exhaust /ig'zOOst/ *n* egzoz; *v* tüketmek; çok yormak; ~ **gases** egzoz gazı
exhibit /ig'zibit/ *v* sergilemek
exhibition /,eksi'bişın/ *n* sergi
exile /'egzayL/ *n* sürgün
exist /ig'zist/ *v* var olmak
existence /ig'zistıns/ *n* varlık, varoluş
exit /'egzit/ *n* çıkış
exotic /ig'zOtik/ *adj* başka iklime ait; yabancı
expand /iks'pEnd/ *v* genişlemek; genişletmek
expect /iks'pekt/ *v* ümit etmek, beklemek
expectation /,ekspek'teyşın/ *n* beklenti
expedition /,ekspı'dişın/ *n* sefer; sevkıyat
expel /iks'peL/ *v* kovmak, çıkarmak
expenditure /iks'pendiçır/ *n* harcama, masraf
expense /iks'pens/ *n* harcama
expensive /iks'pensiv/ *adj* pahalı
experience /iks'spiiriyıns/ *n* tecrübe; **experienced** *adj* tecrübeli
experiment /iks'perıment/ *n* deney; *v* deney yapmak
expert /'ekspÖrt/ *n* usta, uzman; *adj* becerikli, usta
expire /iks'payr/ *v* sona ermek; nefes vermek; ölmek; **expired** *adj* süresi bitmiş
expiry /iks'payrii/ *n* süre bitimi
explain /iks'pLeyn/ *v* açıklamak
explanation /,ekspLı'neyşın/ *v* açıklama
explicit /eks'pLisit/ *adj* açık, belirgin
explode /iks'pLoud/ *v* patlamak
exploit /iks'pLOyt/ *v* sömürmek; işletmek
explore /iks'pLOOr/ *v* keşfetmek; incelemek, araştırmak
explosion /iks'pLoujın/ *n* patlama
explosive /iks'pLousiv/ *adj* patlayıcı; *n* patlayıcı madde
export[1] /iks'pOOrt/ *v* ihraç etmek

export[2] /'eks,pOOrt/ *n* ihraç; ihraç malı
exportation /,ekspOOr'teyşın/ *n* ihracat
exports /'eks,pOOrts/ *pl* ihraç malları
exposition /,ekspı'zişın/ *n* sergi, teşhir
exposure /iks'poujır/ *n* ortaya koyma, teşhir
express /iks'pres/ *v* ifade etmek, söylemek; *adj* açık, kesin; ~ **train** sürat katarı, ekspres
expression /iks'preşın/ *n* ifade
exquisite /eks'kwizit/ *adj* enfes, pek güzel
extend /iks'tend/ *v* uzanmak; uzatmak; sunmak
extension /iks'tenşın/ *n* uzatma; büyütme; ilave; ~ **cord** uzatma kablosu
extensive /iks'tensiv/ *adj* geniş, büyük çapta
extent /iks'tent/ *n* derece, ölçü, miktar
exterior /eks'tiiriyır/ *adj* harici, dış; *n* dış, dış taraf
external /eks'tÖrnıL/ *adj* harici
extinct /iks'tiNkt/ *adj* nesli tükenmiş
extinguish /iks'tiNgwiş/ *v* söndürmek
extort /iks'tOOrt/ *v* zorla almak; gaspetmek
extortion /iks'tOOrşın/ *n* zorla, tehditle alma; gasp
extra /'ekstrı/ *adj* fazla; üstün, fevkalade
extract[1] /iks'trEkt/ *v* çıkarmak, elde etmek
extract[2] /'ekstrEkt/ *n* öz; parça, alıntı
extradite /'ekstrı,dayt/ *v* suçluyu ülkesine iade etmek
extraordinary /iks'trOOrdı,nerii/ *adj* olağanüstü
extravagant /iks'trEvıgınt/ *adj* savurgan; fazla, aşırı
extreme /iks'triim/ *adj* aşırı
exuberant /ig'zuubırınt/ *adj* coşkun, taşkın
eye /ay/ *n* göz ~ **pencil** göz kalemi ~ **shadow** far
eyebrow /'ay,brau/ *n* kaş
eyelash /'ay,LEş/ *n* kirpik
eyelid /'ay,Lid/ *n* göz kapağı
eyewitness /'ay,witnıs/ *n* görgü tanığı

F

fable /'feybıL/ *n* masal
fabric /'fEbrik/ *n* yapı; kumaş
fabulous /'fEbyıLıs/ *adj* inanılmaz, hayret verici; efsanevi
façade /fı'saad/ *n* binanın ön cephesi
face /feys/ *n* yüz; *v* karşısında durmak; ~ **cream** yüz kremi; ~ **massage** yüz masajı; ~ **pack** güzellik maskesi; ~ **powder** yüz pudrası; **facing** karşısında
facility /fı'siLıtii/ *n* kolaylık, rahatlık; tesis
fact /fEkt/ *n* gerçek; **in** ~ aslında
factor /'fEktır/ *n* etken
factory /'fEktırii/ *n* fabrika
factual /'fEkçuuıL/ *adj* gerçek
faculty /'fEkıLtii/ *n* yetenek; iktidar; fakülte; üniversitenin öğretim üyeleri
fad /fEd/ *n* geçici moda
fade /feyd/ *v* solmak
faience /fay'aans/ *n* çini
fail /feyL/ *v* başarısızlığa uğramak; yetmemek, tükenmek; zayıflamak; **without** ~ mutlaka
failure /'feyLyır/ *n* başarısızlık; başarısız kişi
faint /feynt/ *v* bayılmak; *adj* zayıf, hafif
fair[1] /feyr/ *n* pazar, panayır; sergi, fuar
fair[2] /feyr/ *adj* güzel; sarışın; dürüst, adil

fairly /'feyrLii/ *adv* haklı olarak; oldukça
fairy /'feyrii/ *n* peri; ~ **tale** peri masalı
faith /feyT/ *n* inanç; güven
faithful /'feyTfıL/ *adj* sadık
fake /feyk/ *n* sahte şey, taklit
falcon /'fELkın/ *n* şahin, doğan
fall[1] /fOOL/ *n* düşüş; *nAm* sonbahar
***fall**[2] /fOOL/ *v* düşmek
false /fOOLs/ *adj* sahte; yanlış; asılsız; ~ **teeth** takma diş
falter /'fOOLtır/ *v* bocalamak; kekelemek
fame /feym/ *n* ün, şöhret
familiar /fı'miLyır/ *adj* bildik, aşina
family /'fEmıLii/ *n* aile; ~ **name** soyadı
famine /'fEmin/ *n* kıtlık, açlık
famous /'feymıs/ *adj* ünlü
fan /fEn/ *n* yelpaze; vantilatör; hayran *veya* meraklı kimse; ~ **belt** vantilatör kayışı
fanatical /fı'nEtikıL/ *adj* aşırı tutucu, fanatik
fancy /'fEnsii/ *v* hayal etmek; beğenmek, sevmek; *n* hayal; kapris; *adj* süslü, tuhaf, fantezi
fantastic /fEn'tEstik/ *adj* garip, acayip; harika, şahane
fantasy /'fEntısii/ *n* hayal, garip fikir
far /faar/ *adj* uzak, uzun; ilerlemiş; *adv* epeyce, çok; **by** ~ hatırı sayılır derecede, büyük farkla; **so** ~ şu ana kadar
faraway /'faarı,wey/ *adj* uzak
farce /faars/ *n* komedi, güldürü
fare /feyr/ *n* seyahat ücreti
farewell /'feyr,weL/ uğurlar olsun! güle güle!; *n* veda
farm /faarm/ *n* çiftlik
farmer /'faarmır/ *n* çiftçi
farmhouse /'faarm,haus/ *n* çiftlik evi
farsighted /'faar,saytid/ *adj* hipermetrop; uzak görüşlü
far-off /'faar'OOf/ *adj* uzak
fascinate /'fEsı,neyt/ *v* büyülemek
fascism /'fEşizım/ *n* faşizm
fascist /'fEşist/ *adj* faşist
fashion /'fEşın/ *n* moda
fashionable /'fEşınıbıL/ *adj* modaya uygun
fast[1] /fEst/ *adj* hızlı
fast[2] /fEst/ *v* oruç tutmak; *n* oruç, perhiz
fasten /'fEsın/ *v* raptetmek, bağlamak
fastener /'fEsınır/ *n* bağ; toka; raptiye
fat /fEt/ *adj* şişman; *n* yağ
fatal /'feytıL/ *adj* öldürücü
fatalist /'feytıList/ *n* kaderci
fate /feyt/ *n* kader
father /'faaDır/ *n* baba
father-in-law /'faaDırin,LOO/ *n* (pl fathers-) kayınpeder
fatherland /'faaDır,LEnd/ *n* vatan
fatigue /fı'tiig/ *n* bitkinlik
fatness /'fEtnıs/ *n* şişmanlık
fatty /'fEtii/ *adj* yağlı, şişko
faucet /'fOOsıt/ *nAm* musluk
fault /fOOLt/ *n* kusur; kabahat; eksiklik
faultless /'fOOLtLıs/ *adj* kusursuz, mükemmel
faulty /'fOOLtii/ *adj* kusurlu
favor /'feyvır/ *n* lütuf; *v* lehinde olmak; iltimas etmek
favorable /'feyvırıbıL/ *adj* uygun; olumlu
favorite /'feyvırıt/ *n* çok sevilen kimse *veya* şey; *adj* en çok beğenilen, gözde
fear /fiir/ *n* korku; *v* korkmak
feasible /'fiizıbıL/ *adj* yapılabilen
feast /fiist/ *n* ziyafet; bayram
feat /fiit/ *n* cesaret *veya* *U* ustalık gerektiren iş
feather /'feDır/ *n* tüy, kuştüyü
feature /'fiiçır/ *n* özellik; röportaj,

inceleme yazısı
February /'februu,erii/ şubat
federal /'fedırıL/ *adj* federal, birleşik
federation /,fedı'reyşın/ *n* federasyon, birlik
fee /fii/ *n* ücret, giriş ücreti
feeble /'fiibıL/ *adj* zayıf
***feed** /fiid/ *v* beslemek; beslenmek; **fed up with** bıkmış, usanmış
feedback /'fiid,bEk/ *n* geribildirim, besleyici yankı
***feel** /fiiL/ *v* hissetmek; dokunmak; ~ **like** canı istemek
feeling /'fiiLiN/ *n* duygu
fell /feL/ *v* (p fall)
fellow /'feLou/ *n* adam; yoldaş
felt[1] /feLt/ *n* keçe
felt[2] /feLt/ *v* (p, pp feel)
female /'fiimeyL/ *adj* dişi; dişil
feminine /'feminin/ *adj* dişi
fence /fens/ *n* çit, parmaklık; *v* çitle çevirmek; eskrim yapmak
fender /'fendır/ *n* tampon; ocak siperi
ferment /fÖr'ment/ *v* mayalanmak
ferryboat /'ferii,bout/ *n* feribot
fertile /'fÖrtıL/ *adj* verimli
fertilization /,fÖrtıLı'zeyşın/ *n* döllenme; gübreleme
fertilize /'fÖrtıL,ayz/ *v* gübrelemek, verimini artırmak
fertilizer /'fÖrtıL,ayzır/ *n* gübre
festival /'festıvıL/ *n* festival
festive /'festiv/ *adj* bayramla ilgili, şenlikli, neşeli
fetch /feç/ *v* gidip getirmek
feudal /'fyuudıL/ *adj* derebeyliğe ait
fever /'fiivır/ *n* vücut harareti, ateş
feverish /'fiivıriş/ *adj* ateşli
few /fyuu/ *adj* az
fiancé /fiyan'sey/ *n* erkek nişanlı
fiancée /fiyan'sey/ *n* kız nişanlı
fiasco /fii'yEskou/ *n* başarısızlık, bozgun, fiyasko
fiber /'faybır/ *n* lif, tel
fiction /'fikşın/ *n* hayal ürünü; roman ve öykü türü
fidelity /fi'deLıtii/ *n* sadakat, vefa
field /fiiLd/ *n* tarla; alan; ~ **glasses** çifte dürbün
fierce /fiirs/ *adj* azgın, şiddetli
fifteen /fif'tiin/ *num* on beş
fifteenth /fif'tiinT/ *num* on beşinci
fifth /fifT/ *num* beşinci
fifty /'fiftii/ *num* elli
fig /fig/ *n* incir
fight /fayt/ *n* kavga, dövüş
***fight** /fayt/ *v* dövüşmek, savaşmak
figure /'figyır/ *n* şekil; rakam; vücut yapısı
file /fayL/ *n* eğe; dosya
Filipino /,fiLı'piinou/ *n* Filipinli
fill /fiL/ *v* doldurmak; ~ **in** doldurmak; **filling station** petrol istasyonu; ~ **out** *Am* doldurmak; ~ **up** tamamen doldurmak
filling /'fiLiN/ *n* doldurma; dolgu
film /fiLm/ *n* film; ince tabaka; *v* film çekmek
filter /'fiLtır/ *n* filtre, süzgeç
filthy /'fiLTii/ *adj* pis; müstehcen
final /'faynıL/ *adj* son
finance /fay'nEns/ *v* masraflarını karşılamak; *n* mali durum, para durumu
finances /fay'nEnsiz/ *pl* maliye, finans
financial /fay'nEnşıL/ *adj* mali
***find** /faynd/ *v* bulmak
fine /fayn/ *n* para cezası; *adj* güzel, ince; hassas; mükemmel; ~ **arts** güzel sanatlar
finger /'fiNgır/ *n* parmak; **little** ~ serçeparmak
fingerprint /'fiNgır,print/ *n* parmak izi
finish /'finiş/ *v* bitirmek; *n* son, bitiş; bitirme çizgisi
Finland /'finLınd/ Finlandiya
Finn /fin/ *n* Finlandiyalı
Finnish /'finiş/ *adj* Finlandiya'ya ait;

n Fin dili
fir /fÖr/ *n* köknar
fire /fayr/ *n* ateş; yangın; *v* tutuşturmak; ateş etmek; ~ **alarm** yangın alarmı; ~ **brigade** itfaiye; ~ **escape** yangın çıkışı; ~ **extinguisher** yangın söndürücü
fireman /'fayrmın/ (pl -men) *n* itfaiyeci; ateşçi
fireplace /'fayr,pLeys/ *n* şömine
fireproof /'fayr,pruuf/ *adj* yanmaz, ateş geçirmez
firm /fÖrm/ *adj* sağlam, katı; sabit; *n* firma
first /fÖrst/ *num* ilk, birinci; **at** ~ ilk önce; ~ **name** ad
first aid /'fÖrst ,eyd/ ilkyardım; ~ **kit** ilkyardım çantası; ~ **post** ilkyardım ekibi
first-class /'fÖrst'kLEs/ *adj* birinci sınıf, mükemmel
firsthand /'fÖrst 'hEnd/ *adv* doğrudan doğruya; *adj* kaynağından aracısız gelen
first-rate /'fÖrst'reyt/ *adj* en iyi kaliteden
fish /fiş/ *n* (pl ~, ~es) balık; ~ **shop** balıkçı dükkânı; *v* balık avlamak; **fishing gear** balık avlama takımı; **fishing hook** olta iğnesi; **fishing industry** balıkçılık endüstrisi; **fishing license** balıkçılık ruhsatı; **fishing net** balık ağı; **fishing rod** olta kamışı; **fishing tackle** balık avlama takımı
fishbone /'fiş,boun/ *n* kılçık
fisherman /'fişırmın/ *n* (pl -men) balıkçı
fishy /'fişii/ *adj* şüpheli, inanılmaz
fist /fist/ *n* yumruk
fit /fit/ *adj* uygun, elverişli; *n* sara, hastalık vs. nöbeti; *v* uymak; uydurmak; takmak; **fitting room** prova kabini
five /fayv/ *num* beş
fix /fix/ *v* sabitleştirmek; kararlaştırmak; tamir etmek
fixed /fikst/ *adj* sabit; belirli
fizz /fiz/ *n* fışırdama
fizzy /'fizii/ *adj* gazoz gibi, gazlı
fjord /fyOOrd/ *n* fiyort
flag /fLEg/ *n* bayrak
flame /fLeym/ *n* alev
flamingo /fLı'miNgou/ *n* (pl ~s, ~es) flamingo
flannel /'fLEnıL/ *n* fanila; yumuşak tüylü kumaş
flash /fLEş/ *n* ani ışık, parıltı
flashbulb /'fLEş,bALb/ *n* flaş ampulü
flashlight /'fLEş,Layt/ *n* el feneri
flask /fLEsk/ *n* küçük şişe; **thermos** ~ termos
flat /fLEt/ *adj* düz, yassı; *nBr* apartman dairesi; ~ **tire** patlak araba lastiği
flatter /'fLEtır/ *v* yaltaklanmak; fazla övmek
flavor /'fLeyvır/ *n* tat, lezzet; *v* tat vermek, lezzetlendirmek
flaw /fLOO/ *n* kusur, hata; yarık, çatlak
flea /fLii/ *n* pire; ~ **market** bit pazarı
fleet /fLiit/ *n* filo, donanma
flesh /fLeş/ *n* et; vücut; ten
flew /fLuu/ *v* (p fly)
flexible /'fLeksibıL/ *adj* esnek
flight /fLayt/ *n* uçuş; **charter** ~ uçak dolmuş seferi
flint /fLint/ *n* çakmaktaşı
flirt /fLÖrt/ *v* flört etmek, kur yapmak
float /fLout/ *v* yüzmek; yüzdürmek; havada durmak
flock /fLOk/ *n* sürü; küme
flood /fLAd/ *n* sel, su taşması
floodlight /'fLAd,Layt/ *n* ışıldak, projektör
floor /fLOOr/ *n* döşeme, yer, zemin;

~ **show** gece kulübü programı
florist /'fLOOrist/ *n* çiçekçi
flour /fLaur/ *n* un
flow /fLou/ *v* akmak
flower /'fLauır/ *n* çiçek;
~ **bed** çiçek tarhı
flowerpot /'fLAur,pOt/ *n* saksı
flower-shop /'fLaur,şOp/ *nBr* çiçek satılan dükkân
flown /fLoun/ *v* (pp fly)
flu /fLuu/ *n* grip
fluctuate /'fLAkçuu,eyt/ *v* düzensizce değişmek, kararsız olmak
fluent /'fLuuınt/ *adj* akıcı
fluid /'fLuuid/ *adj* akışkan, sulu; *n* sıvı madde
flute /fLuut/ *n* flüt
fly /fLay/ *n* sinek; uçuş
***fly** /fLay/ *v* uçmak
foam /foum/ *n* köpük; *v* köpürmek;
~ **rubber** yapay sünger
focus /'foukıs/ *n* odak
fog /fOOg/ *n* sis, duman
foggy /'fOOgii/ *adj* sisli, dumanlı
foglamp /'fOOg,LEmp/ *n* sis lambası
fold /fouLd/ *v* katlamak, bükmek; *n* kat, kıvrım
folder /'fouLdır/ *n* dosya
folk /fouk/ *n* halk; ~ **dance** halk oyunu; ~ **song** halk şarkısı
folklore /'fouk,LOOr/ *n* folklor
follow /'fOLou/ *v* izlemek;
following bir sonraki, izleyen
***be fond of** /bii 'fOnd ıv/ sevmek
food /fuud/ *n* yiyecek, besin;
~ **poisoning** gıda zehirlenmesi
foodstuffs /'fuud,stAfs/ *pl* gıda maddeleri
fool /fuuL/ *n* budala, ahmak; *v* aldatmak
foolish /'fuuLiş/ *adj* akılsız; saçma
foot /fut/ *n* (pl feet) ayak; taban, dip; ~ **brake** ayak freni;
~ **powder** ayak pudrası;
on ~ yürüyerek, yaya

football /'fut,bOOL/ *n* futbol
footnote /'fut,nout/ *n* dipnot
footpath /'fut,pET/ *n* patika, keçiyolu
footprint /'fut,print/ *n* ayak izi
footstep /'fut,step/ *n* adım; ayak izi
footwear /'fut,weyr/ *n* ayakkabı
for /fır, fOOr/ *prep* için; -den dolayı; *conj* çünkü
***forbid** /fır'bid/ *v* yasaklamak
force /fOOrs/ *v* zorlamak, mecbur etmek; *n* güç, kuvvet; **by** ~ zor kullanarak; **driving** ~ itici güç
forecast /'fOOr,kEst/ *n* tahmin; *v* önceden tahmin etmek
foreground /'fOOr,graund/ *n* ön plan
forehead /'fOOrid/ *n* alın
foreign /'fOOrın/ *adj* yabancı; dış; ecnebi
foreigner /'fOOrınır/ *n* yabancı
foreman /'fOOrmın/ *n* (pl -men) ustabaşı
foremost /'fOOr,moust/ *adj* en başta gelen
foresail /'fOOr,seyL/ *n* trinketa yelkeni
forest /'fOOrist/ *n* orman
forester /'fOOristır/ *n* orman memuru
***foretell** /fOOr'teL/ *v* önceden haber vermek, kehanette bulunmak
forever /fOOr'evır/ *adv* ebediyen, daima
foreword /'fOOr,wÖrd/ *n* önsöz
forge /fOOrc/ *v* uydurmak, sahtesini yapmak
***forget** /fır'get/ *v* unutmak
forgetful /fır'getfıL/ *adj* unutkan
***forgive** /fır'giv/ *v* bağışlamak, affetmek
fork /fOOrk/ *n* çatal; *v* çatallaşmak
form /fOOrm/ *n* biçim; yöntem; bilgi formu; *v* biçimlendirmek; oluşturmak
formal /'fOOrmıL/ *adj* resmi
formality /fOOr'mELıtii/ *n* resmiyet; usul, işlem

former /'fOOrmır/ *adj* önceki, eski; **formerly** eskiden, vaktiyle
formula /'fOOrmyıLı/ *n* (pl ~e, ~s) formül
fort /fOOrt/ *n* kale
fortnight /'fOOrt,nayt/ *n* on beş gün
fortress /'fOOrtris/ *n* kale, hisar
fortunate /'fOOrçınıt/ *adj* mutlu, talihli
fortune /'fOOrçın/ *n* talih, şans, baht, kader
fortuneteller /'fOOrçın,teLır/ *n* falcı
forty /'fOOrtii/ *num* kırk
forward /'fOOrwırd/ *adv* ileri, ileri doğru, ilerde; *v* ilerletmek; göndermek, sevk etmek
foster parents /'fOOstır ,peyrınts/ *üvey anne baba*
fought /fOOt/ *v* (p, pp fight)
foul /fauL/ *adj* pis; iğrenç
found[1] /faund/ *v* (p, pp find)
found[2] /faund/ *v* kurmak, tesis etmek
foundation /faun'deyşın/ *n* vakıf; kurum; temel; ~ **cream** fondöten
fountain /'fauntın/ *n* çeşme; fıskıye; pınar; ~ **pen** dolmakalem
four /fOOr/ *num* dört
fourteen /'fOOr'tiin/ *num* on dört
fourteenth /'fOOr'tiinT/ *num* on dördüncü
fourth /fOOrT/ *num* dördüncü
fowl /fauL/ *n* (pl ~s) kuş; kümes hayvanı
fox /fOks/ *n* tilki
fraction /'frEkşın/ *n* parça; kesir
fracture /'frEkçır/ *v* kırmak; kırılmak; *n* kırık
fragile /'frEcıL/ *adj* kolay kırılır, nazik
fragment /'frEgmınt/ *n* kısım, kırılmış parça
frame /freym/ *n* çerçeve; yapı; çatı
France /frEns/ Fransa
franchise /'frEnçayz/ *n* oy verme hakkı; özel pazarlama hakkı, acentelik
fraternity /frı'tÖrnıtii/ *n* kardeşlik; kardeşlik cemiyeti
fraud /frOOd/ *n* hile, sahtekârlık
free /frii/ *adj* serbest; özgür; ücretsiz; ~ **of charge** bedava; ~ **ticket** bedava bilet
freedom /'friidım/ *n* özgürlük
free-lance /'frii,LEns/ *adj* bağımsız, kendi hesabına çalışan
freeway /'frii,wey/ *n* ekspres otomobil yolu
***freeze** /friiz/ *v* donmak; dondurmak
freezing /'friiziN/ *adj* dondurucu; ~ **point** donma noktası
freight /freyt/ *n* navlun, nakliye ücreti; yük; ~ **train** yük treni
French /frenç/ *adj* Fransa'ya ait; *n* Fransızca
Frenchman /'frençmın/ *n* (pl -men) Fransız
frequency /'friikwınsii/ *n* sık sık olma; tekrar oranı
frequent /'friikwınt/ *adj* sık sık olan; **frequently** *adv* sık sık
fresh /freş/ *adj* taze, yeni; ~ **water** tatlı su
friction /'frikşın/ *n* sürtünme
Friday /'fraydii/ cuma
fridge /fric/ *nBr* buzdolabı
friend /frend/ *n* arkadaş, dost
friendly /'frendLii/ *adj* dostça; dosta yakışır
friendship /'frend,şip/ *n* arkadaşlık
fright /frayt/ *n* korku, dehşet
frighten /'fraytın/ *v* korkutmak
frightened /'fraytınd/ *adj* korkmuş, ürkmüş; ***be** ~ korkmak
frightful /'fraytfıL/ *adj* korkunç, müthiş
fringe /frinc/ *n* saçak; kenar; ~ **benefit** ücret ve maaş dışındaki yan imkân
frock /frOk/ *n* kadın elbisesi; cüppe;

iş gömleği
frog /frOOg/ *n* kurbağa
from /frOm/ *prep* -den, -dan
front /frAnt/ *n* ön, ön taraf;
in ~ of önünde
frontier /frAn'tiir/ *n* sınır
frost /frOOst/ *n* ayaz, don
froth /frOOT/ *n* köpük
frown /fraun/ *v* kaşlarını çatmak, hiddetle bakmak; *n* kaş çatma
frozen /'frouzın/ *adj* donmuş;
~ food donmuş yiyecek
fruit /fruut/ *n* meyve, yemiş; mahsul
frustration /frAs'treyşın/ *n* engellenme; boşuna uğraşma; hayal kırıklığı
fry /fray/ *v* kızartmak
frying pan /'frayiN ,pEn/ tava
fuel /'fyuuıL/ *n* yakıt;
~ pump yakıt pompası
fulfill /fuL'fiL/ *v* yerine getirmek; yapmak; tamamlamak
full /fuL/ *adj* dolu; dolgun; tam;
~ board tam pansiyon;
~ stop nokta;
~ up dopdolu
fun /fAn/ *n* eğlence, zevk
function /'fANkşın/ *n* iş, görev; işlev
fund /fAnd/ *n* fon; bir iş için ayrılmış para
fundamental /fAndı'mentıL/ *adj* temel; önemli
fundamentalist /,fAndı'mentıList/ *n* dinci
funeral /'fyuunırıL/ *n* cenaze
funnel /'fAnıL/ *n* huni, boru
funny /'fAnii/ *adj* eğlenceli; acayip, gülünç
fur /fÖr/ *n* kürk; **~ coat** kürk manto
furious /'fyuuriyıs/ *adj* kudurmuş, öfkeli
furnace /'fÖrnıs/ *n* ocak, fırın
furnish /'fÖrniş/ *v* donatmak; döşemek; **~ with** sağlamak, tedarik etmek
furniture /'fÖrniçır/ *n* mobilya, mefruşat
furrier /'fÖriyır/ *n* kürkçü
further /'fÖrDır/ *adj* daha ileri; daha ötedeki; *adv* ayrıca
furthermore /'fÖrDır,mOOr/ *adv* bundan başka, ayrıca
furthest /'fÖrDist/ *adj* en uzak
fuse /fyuuz/ *n* sigorta; fitil
fuss /fAs/ *n* telaş, yaygara
future /'fyuuçır/ *n* gelecek; *adj* gelecekteki

G

gable /'geybıL/ *n* damın üçgen biçimindeki yanı
gadget /'gEcit/ *n* hünerli küçük alet
gaiety /'geyıtii/ *n* şenlik, neşe
gain /geyn/ *v* kazanmak; *n* kazanç
gait /geyt/ *n* yürüyüş, gidiş
gale /geyL/ *n* kuvvetli rüzgâr
gall /gOOL/ *n* safra, öd;
~ bladder safra kesesi
gallery /'gELırii/ *n* koridor, dehliz; galeri
gallon /'gELın/ *n* galon; *Am* 3,785 litre, *Br* 4,546 litre
gallop /'gELıp/ *n* dörtnala gidiş
gallows /'gELouz/ *n* darağacı
gallstone /'gOOL,stoun/ *n* safra taşı
gamble /'gEmbıL/ *v* kumar oynamak; *n* kumar; riskli iş
game /geym/ *n* oyun, eğlence; av; av eti; **~ reserve** av koruma bölgesi
gang /gEN/ *n* çete; takım; sürü
gangway /'gEN,wey/ *n* geçit, yol
gaol /ceyL/ *nBr* hapishane
gap /gEp/ *n* aralık, yarık; geçit
garage /gı'raaj/ *n* garaj; *v* garaja çekmek
garbage /'gaarbic/ *nAm* çöp,

süprüntü; ~ **can** *Am* çöp kutusu; ~ **man** *Am* çöpçü
garden /'gaardın/ *n* bahçe; **public** ~ umumi park; **zoological** ~ hayvanat bahçesi
gardener /'gaardnır/ *n* bahçıvan
gargle /'gaargıL/ *v* gargara etmek
garlic /'gaarLik/ *n* sarmısak
gas /gEs/ *n* gaz; *nAm* benzin; ~ **cooker** havagazı ocağı; ~ **station** *Am* benzin istasyonu; ~ **stove** gaz sobası
gasoline /gesı'Liin/ *n* benzin
gastric /'gEstrik/ *adj* mideye ait; ~ **ulcer** mide ülseri
gasworks /'gEs,wÖrks/ *n* havagazı üretilen yer; gazhane
gate /geyt/ *n* kapı; giriş
gather /'gEDır/ *v* toplamak; toplanmak
gauge /geyc/ *n* ölçü; ölçme aleti
gauze /gOOz/ *n* tül
gave /geyv/ *v* (p give)
gay /gey/ *adj* neşeli, şen; parlak; homoseksüel
gaze /geyz/ *v* sabit gözlerle bakmak
gear /giir/ *n* vites; dişli; **change** ~ vites değiştirmek; ~ **lever** vites kolu
gearbox /'giir,bOks/ *n* vites kutusu
gem /cem/ *n* kıymetli taş, mücevher
Gemini /'cemı,nii/ İkizler burcu
gendarme /'jaandaarm/ *n* jandarma
gender /'cendır/ *n* ismin cinsi
general /'cenırıL/ *adj* genel; ~ **practitioner** pratisyen hekim; **in** ~ genellikle
generate /'cenı,reyt/ *v* üretmek; meydana getirmek
generation /,cenı'reyşın/ *n* kuşak, nesil
generator /'cenı,reytır/ *n* jeneratör
generosity /,cenı'rOsıtii/ *n* cömertlik
generous /'cenırıs/ *adj* cömert
genital /'cenitıl/ *adj* üremeye ait
genius /'ciinyıs/ *n* deha; dâhi
gentle /'centıL/ *adj* kibar, nazik; ılımlı, yumuşak
gentleman /'centıLmın/ *n* (pl -men) beyefendi
genuine /'cenyuuin/ *adj* gerçek; içten
geography /ci'yOgrıfii/ *n* coğrafya
geology /ci'yOLıcii/ *n* yerbilim, jeoloji
geometry /ci'yOmıtrii/ *n* geometri
germ /cÖrm/ *n* mikrop; tohum, öz
German /'cÖrmın/ *adj* Almanya'ya ait; *n* Alman; Almanca
Germany /'cÖrmınii/ Almanya
gesticulate /ces'tikyı,Leyt/ *v* konuşurken el hareketleri yapmak
gesture /'cesçır/ *n* hareket, jest; *v* el kol hareketleri yapmak
***get** /get/ *v* almak, elde etmek; olmak; tutmak; ~ **back** geri gelmek; geri almak; ~ **off** inmek; ~ **on** binmek; ilerlemek; ~ **up** kalkmak
ghetto /'getou/ *n* azınlığın oturduğu yoksul semt
ghost /goust/ *n* hayalet, hortlak
giant /'cayınt/ *n* dev
giddiness /'gidiinıs/ *n* baş dönmesi
giddy /'gidii/ *adj* başı dönmüş; baş döndürücü
gift /gift/ *n* armağan; yetenek
gifted /'giftid/ *adj* yetenekli
gigantic /cay'gEntik/ *adj* kocaman, dev gibi
giggle /'gigıL/ *v* kıkır kıkır gülmek
gill /giL/ *n* solungaç
gilt /giLt/ *adj* yaldızlı
ginger /'cincır/ *n* zencefil
gipsy /'cipsii/ *n* çingene
girdle /'gÖrdıL/ *n* kuşak, kemer
girl /gÖrL/ *n* kız; ~ **scout** kız izci
***give** /giv/ *v* vermek; ~ **away** ele vermek; ifşa etmek; ~ **in** teslim olmak; ~ **up** vazgeçmek
glacier /'gLeyşır/ *n* buzul
glad /gLEd/ *adj* memnun;

gladly *adv* memnuniyetle
gladness /'gLEdnıs/ *n* sevinç, memnunluk
glamor /'gLEmır/ *n* büyü; parlaklık
glamorous /'gLEmırıs/ *adj* göz alıcı; parlak
glance /gLEns/ *n* kısa bakış; *v* göz atmak
gland /gLEnd/ *n* bez, gudde
glare /gLeyr/ *n* öfkeli bakış
glaring /'gLeyriN/ *adj* göz kamaştıran; göze batan
glass /gLEs/ *n* cam; bardak, kadeh; **glasses** *pl* gözlük; **magnifying** ~ büyüteç
glaze /gLeyz/ *v* sırlamak, cilalamak
glide /gLayd/ *v* kaymak
glider /'gLaydır/ *n* planör
glimpse /gLimps/ *n* kısa bakış; gözüne ilişme; *v* bir an için görmek
glitter /'gLitır/ *v* parıldamak, ışıldamak; *n* parıltı; gösteriş
global /'gLoubıL/ *adj* küresel; bütün dünyayı kapsayan
globe /gLoub/ *n* küre; dünya
gloom /gLuum/ *n* karanlık; sıkıntı
gloomy /'gLuumii/ *adj* karanlık; sıkıntılı
glorious /'gLOOriyıs/ *adj* şanlı, parlak
glory /'gLOOrii/ *n* şan, şeref; debdebe; parlaklık
gloss /gLOOs/ *n* cila; parlaklık
glossy /'gLOOsii/ *adj* parlak, cilalı
glove /gLAv/ *n* eldiven
glow /gLou/ *v* parlamak; yanmak; *n* parlaklık
glue /gLuu/ *n* yapıştırıcı
*__go__ /gou/ *v* gitmek; olmak; işlemek; çalışmak; ~ **ahead** başlamak; devam etmek; ~ **away** ayrılıp gitmek, uzaklaşmak; ~ **back** dönmek; ~ **home** eve gitmek; ~ **in** girmek; ~ **on** devam etmek; ~ **out** çıkmak; ~ **through** gözden geçirmek; içinden geçmek
goal /gouL/ *n* amaç, hedef; gol
goalkeeper /'gouL,kiipır/ *n* kaleci
goat /gout/ *n* keçi
God /gOd/ *n* Tanrı
goddess /'gOdis/ *n* dişi tanrı, ilahe
godfather /'gOd,faaDır/ *n* vaftiz babası
goggles /'gOgıLz/ *pl* sualtı gözlüğü; pilot gözlüğü
gold /gouLd/ *n* altın; ~ **leaf** altın varak; ~ **mine** altın madeni
golden /'gouLdın/ *adj* altın işi, altından; **Golden Horn** Haliç
goldsmith /'gouLd,smiT/ *n* kuyumcu
golf /gOLf/ *n* golf; ~ **club** golf sopası; ~ **course,** ~ **links** golf sahası
gondola /'gOndıLı/ *n* gondol
gone /gOn/ *adv* (pp go) geçmiş; kaybolmuş
good /gud/ *adj* iyi; güzel; uygun; yararlı
good-by /gud'bay/ hoşça kal, allahaısmarladık, güle güle
good-humored /'gud'hyuumırd/ *adj* hoş mizaçlı, şakacı
good-looking /'gud'LukiN/ *adj* yakışıklı, güzel
good-natured /'gud'neyçırd/ *adj* iyi huylu, uslu
goods /gudz/ *pl* eşya, mal; ~ **train** *Br* marşandiz, yük katarı
good-tempered /'gud'tempırd/ *adj* iyi huylu
goodwill /'gud'wiL/ *n* iyi niyet
goose /guus/ *n* (pl geese) kaz; ~ **flesh** soğuktan *veya* korkudan tüyleri ürpermiş deri
gorge /gOOrc/ *n* boğaz; vadi
gorgeous /'gOOrcıs/ *adj* pek parlak, görkemli
Gospel /'gOspıL/ *n* İncil
gossip /'gOsip/ *n* dedikodu; dedikoducu; *v* dedikodu yapmak

got /gOt/ *v* (p get); *vBr* (pp get)
gotten /'gOtın/ *vAm* (pp get)
gout /gaut/ *n* damla hastalığı
govern /'gAvırn/ *v* hâkim olmak; yönetmek
governess /'gAvırnıs/ *n* mürebbiye, dadı
government /'gAvırnmınt/ *n* hükümet; yönetim
governor /'gAvırnır/ *n* vali
gown /gaun/ *n* kadın elbisesi; hukukçu *veya* profesör cüppesi
grace /greys/ *n* zarafet; çekicilik; lütuf
graceful /'greysfıL/ *adj* ince, hoş, endamlı
grade /greyd/ *n* rütbe; derece; not; *v* sınıflandırmak, derecelere ayırmak
gradient /'greydiyınt/ *n* eğim; rampa
gradual /'grEcuuıL/ *adj* tedrici; derece derece olan
graduate[1] /'grEcuu,eyt/ *v* mezun olmak
graduate[2] /'grEcuuıt/ *n* mezun, diplomalı kimse
graduation /,grEcuu'eyşın/ *n* mezun olma
grain /greyn/ *n* tane, tohum; hububat
gram /grEm/ *n* gram
grammar /'grEmır/ *n* gramer, dilbilgisi
grammatical /grı'mEtikıL/ *adj* dilbilgisi ile ilgili
gramophone /'grEmı,foun/ *n* pikap
grand /grEnd/ *adj* büyük ve görkemli; en önemli, baş
granddad /'grEn,dEd/ *n* büyükbaba, dede
granddaughter /'grEn,dOOtır/ *n* kız torun
grandfather /'grEn,faaDır/ *n* büyükbaba, dede
grandmother /'grEn,mADır/ *n* büyükanne, nine
grandparents /'grEn,peyrınts/ *pl* dede ve nine
grandson /'grEn,sAn/ *n* erkek torun
granite /'grEnit/ *n* granit taşı
grant /grEnt/ *v* ihsan etmek, imtiyaz vermek; bağışlamak; *n* bağış; ödenek
grape /greyp/ *n* üzüm
grapefruit /'greyp,fruut/ *n* greyfurt
graph /grEf/ *n* grafik, çizge
graphic /'grEfik/ *adj* resim *veya* yazıya ait; grafikle gösterilen
grasp /grEsp/ *v* kavramak, sımsıkı tutmak; *n* kavrama
grass /grEs/ *n* çimen, ot
grasshopper /'grEs,hOpır/ *n* çayır çekirgesi
grate /greyt/ *n* demir parmaklık, ızgara; *v* rendelemek
grateful /'greytfıl / *adj* minnettar, müteşekkir
grater /'greytır/ *n* rende
gratis /'grEtis/ *adj* bedava
gratitude /'grEtı,tuud/ *n* minnet, şükran
gratuity /grı'tuuıtii/ *n* bahşiş
grave /greyv/ *n* mezar; *adj* önemli, ciddi; ağırbaşlı
gravel /'grEvıL/ *n* çakıllı kum
gravestone /'greyv,stoun/ *n* mezartaşı
graveyard /'greyv,yaard/ *n* mezarlık
gravity /'grEvıtii/ *n* çekim gücü; ciddiyet
gravy /'greyvii/ *n* et suyundan yapılan sos
gray /grey/ *adj* gri
graze /greyz/ *v* otlamak; sıyırmak; *n* sıyrık, bere
grease /griis/ *n* yağ; *v* yağlamak
greasy /'griisii/ *adj* yağlı
great /greyt/ *adj* büyük;
Great Britain Büyük Britanya
Greece /griis/ Yunanistan
greed /griid/ *n* açgözlülük
greedy /'griidii/ *adj* obur, doymaz,

açgözlü
Greek /griik/ *adj* Yunanistan'a ait; *n* Yunanlı; Yunanca
green /griin/ *adj* yeşil, yeşermiş; ~ **card** *Am* Amerika'da oturma ve çalışma izin belgesi
greengrocer /'griin,grousır/ *n* manav
greenhouse /'griin,haus/ *n* limonluk, sera
greens /griinz/ *pl* yaprak sebze
greet /griit/ *v* selamlamak; karşılamak
greeting /'griitiN/ *n* selam; ~ **card** tebrik kartı
grey /grey/ *adj* gri
greyhound /'grey,haund/ *n* tazı
grief /griif/ *n* keder, üzüntü, tasa
grieve /griiv/ *v* kederlenmek; keder vermek; dertlendirmek
grill /griL/ *n* ızgara; *v* ızgarada pişirmek
grillroom /'griL,ruum/ *n* et *veya* balık lokantası
grin /grin/ *n* sırıtma; zorla gülme
***grind** /graynd/ *v* ezmek, öğütmek
grip /grip/ *v* sıkı tutmak; kavramak; *n* kavrama; *nAm* valiz
groan /groun/ *v* inlemek, sızlanmak
grocer /'grousır/ *n* bakkal; **grocer's** *nBr* bakkal (dükkânı)
groceries /'grousıriiz/ *pl* bakkalda satılan şeyler
grocery /'grousırii/ *nAm* bakkal (dükkânı)
groin /grOyn/ *n* kasık; iki kavsin kesiştiği yer
groove /gruuv/ *n* yiv, oluk
gross[1] /grous/ *n* (pl ~) on iki düzine
gross[2] /grous/ *adj* brüt, daralı; kaba
grotto /'grOtou/ *n* (pl ~es, ~s) ufak ve güzel mağara
ground[1] /graund/ *n* yer, toprak; arsa; ~ **floor** zemin kat; **grounds** *pl* özel arazi; oyun sahası; sebep
ground[2] /graund/ *v* (p, pp grind)
group /gruup/ *n* grup, küme, öbek
grove /grouv/ *n* koru; ağaçlık
***grow** /grou/ *v* büyümek; yetişmek; artmak
growl /grauL/ *v* hırlamak, homurdanmak
grown-up /'groun'Ap/ *adj* büyümüş; *n* yetişkin kimse
growth /grouT/ *n* büyüme; yetişme; tümör
grudge /grAc/ *v* esirgemek, çok görmek
grumble /'grAmbıL/ *v* dırdır etmek, yakınmak
guarantee /,gErın'tii/ *n* teminat, garanti; *v* garanti etmek, kefil olmak
guarantor /'gErın,tOOr/ *n* garanti eden kimse *veya* firma
guard /gaard/ *n* koruma, muhafaza; *v* korumak, muhafaza etmek
guardian /'gaardiyın/ *n* vasi; bekçi, gardiyan
guess /ges/ *v* tahmin etmek; zannetmek; keşfetmek; *n* tahmin
guest /gest/ *n* konuk, davetli; otel müşterisi; pansiyoner; ~ **house** konukevi; ~ **room** konuk yatak odası
guide /gayd/ *n* rehber, kılavuz; yönetmelik; *v* yol göstermek
guidebook /'gayd,buk/ *n* rehber kitap
guilt /giLt/ *n* suçluluk
guilty /'giLtii/ *adj* suçlu, günahkâr
guinea pig /'gini ,pig/ kobay
guitar /gi'taar/ *n* gitar
gulf /gALf/ *n* körfez; uçurum
gull /gAL/ *n* martı
gum /gAm/ *n* dişeti; zamk
gun /gAn/ *n* top, tüfek; tabanca
gunpowder /'gAn,paudır/ *n* barut
gust /gAst/ *n* ani rüzgâr, bora
gusty /'gAstii/ *adj* boralı, ara sıra şiddetle esen

gut /gAt/ *n* bağırsak; **guts** *pl* cesaret
gutter /'gAtır/ *n* oluk, suyolu
guy /gay/ *n* adam
gymnasium /cim'neyziyım/ *n* (pl ~s, -sia) spor salonu
gymnast /'cimnEst/ *n* beden eğitimi uzmanı
gymnastics /cim'nEstiks/ *pl* jimnastik, idman, beden eğitimi
gynecologist /gaynı'kOLıcist/ *n* kadın hastalıkları uzmanı
gypsy /'cipsii/ *n* çingene

H

haberdashery /'hEbır,dEşırii/ *nAm* erkek giyimi satan mağaza; *nBr* tuhafiyeci
habit /'hEbit/ *n* alışkanlık
habitable /'hEbıtıbıL/ *adj* oturulabilir, yaşanabilir
habitual /hı'biçuuıL/ *adj* alışılagelmiş
had /hEd/ *v* (p, pp have)
haddock /'hEdık/ *n* (pl ~) mezgit balığı
hail /heyL/ *n* dolu
hair /heyr/ *n* saç; ~ **cream** saç kremi; ~ **dryer** saç kurutma makinesi; ~ **net** saç filesi; ~ **oil** saç yağı; ~ **piece** takma saç; ~ **rollers** bigudi; ~ **spray** saç spreyi; ~ **tonic** saç toniği
hairbrush /'heyr,brAş/ *n* saç fırçası
haircut /'heyr,kAt/ *n* saç tıraşı, saç kesimi
hairdo /'heyr,duu/ *n* saç tuvaleti
hairdresser /'heyr,dresır/ *n* kuaför, berber
hairpin /'heyr,pin/ *n* saç tokası
hairy /'heyrii/ *adj* kıllı, tüylü
half[1] /hEf/ *adj* yarım, yarı; buçuk; *adv* yarı yarıya; ~ **time** haftaym, devre
half[2] /hEf/ *n* (*pl* halves) yarım, yarı
halfway /'hEf'wey/ *adv* yarı yolda
hall /hOOL/ *n* büyük salon; hol
hallucination /hı,Luusı'neyşın/ *n* sanrı, vehim, kuruntu
halt /hOOLt/ *v* durmak
halve /hEv/ *v* iki eşit parçaya bölmek
ham /hEm/ *n* jambon
hammer /'hEmır/ *n* çekiç
hammock /'hEmık/ *n* hamak; branda yatak
hamper /'hEmpır/ *v* zorluk çıkarmak, engel olmak
hand /hEnd/ *n* el; *v* elle uzatmak; vermek; ~ **brake** el freni; ~ **cream** el kremi
handbag /'hEnd,bEg/ *n* el çantası
handbook /'hEnd,buk/ *n* elkitabı, rehber
handcuffs /'hEnd,kAfs/ *pl* kelepçe
handful /'hEnd,fuL/ *n* avuç dolusu
handicraft /'hEndii,krEft/ *n* el sanatı
handkerchief /'hENkırçif/ *n* mendil
handle /'hEndıL/ *n* sap, kulp
handmade /'hEnd'meyd/ *adj* elişi, el yapısı
handshake /'hEnd,şeyk/ *n* el sıkma
handsome /'hEnsım/ *adj* yakışıklı
handwork /'hEnd,wÖrk/ *n* elişi
handwriting /'hEnd,raytiN/ *n* el yazısı
handy /'hEndii/ *adj* kullanışlı, yararlı; becerikli, hünerli
***hang** /hEN/ *v* asmak
hang /hEN/ *v* idam etmek
hanger /'hENır/ *n* askı, çengel
hangover /'hEN,ouvır/ *n* içki sonrası rahatsızlığı
haphazard /,hEp'hEzırd/ *adj* rasgele, gelişigüzel
happen /'hEpın/ *v* olmak, olup bitmek
happening /'hEpıniN/ *n* olay
happiness /'hEpiinis/ *n* mutluluk
happy /'hEpii/ *adj* mutlu
harbor /'haarbır/ *n* liman; barınak
hard /haard/ *adj* katı, sert; çetin,

güç; **hardly** *adv* güçlükle; ancak
hardware /'haard,weyr/ *n* madeni eşya, hırdavat; bilgisayar aksamı; ~ **store** nalbur dükkânı
hare /heyr/ *n* tavşan
harm /haarm/ *n* zarar, hasar; *v* zarar vermek
harmful /'haarmfıL/ *adj* zararlı
harmless /'haarmLıs/ *adj* zararsız
harmony /'haarmınii/ *n* ahenk, uyum
harp /haarp/ *n* harp (çalgı)
harpoon /haar'puun/ *n* zıpkın; *v* zıpkınlamak
harpsichord /'haarpsi,kOOrd/ *n* klavsen, çembalo,
harsh /haarş/ *adj* sert; haşin
harvest /'haarvist/ *n* hasat; ürün
has /hEz/ *v* (pr have)
hashish /'hEşiiş/ *n* haşiş, esrar
haste /heyst/ *n* acele
hasten /'heysın/ *v* acele etmek
hasty /'heystii/ *adj* acele, çabuk; aceleci
hat /hEt/ *n* şapka; ~ **rack** şapka askısı
hatch /hEç/ *n* ambar ağzı
hate /heyt/ *v* nefret etmek; *n* nefret, kin
hatred /'heytrid/ *n* nefret, kin
haughty /'hOOtii/ *adj* mağrur, kibirli
haul /hOOL/ *v* kuvvetle çekmek; çekerek taşımak
***have** /hEv/ *v* sahip olmak; ~ **to** mecbur olmak
hawk /hOOk/ *n* atmaca, şahin
hay /hey/ *n* kuru ot, saman; ~ **fever** saman nezlesi
hazard /'hEzırd/ *n* tehlike; risk
haze /heyz/ *n* hafif sis, pus
hazelnut /'heyzıL,nAt/ *n* fındık
hazy /'heyzii/ *adj* sisli, puslu
he /hii/ *pron* o (eril)
head /hed/ *n* baş; *v* başta gelmek, önde gelmek; ~ **of state** devlet başkanı; ~ **teacher** okul müdürü, başöğretmen
headache /'hed,eyk/ *n* baş ağrısı
heading /'hediN/ *n* başlık
headlamp /'hed,LEmp/ *nBr* far, projektör
headland /'hedLınd/ *n* karanın denize çıkıntısı, burun
headlight /'hed,Layt/ *n* araba farı
headline /'hed,Layn/ *n* başlık, manşet
headmaster /'hed'mEstır/ *n* başöğretmen
headquarters /'hed,kwOOrtırz/ *pl* karargâh; merkez
headstrong /'hed,strOON/ *adj* inatçı, dikkafalı
headwaiter /'hed'weytır/ *n* başgarson
healthy /'heLTii/ *adj* sağlıklı; sağlığa yararlı
heap /hiip/ *n* yığın, küme
***hear** /hiir/ *v* işitmek
hearing /'hiiriN/ *n* celse, duruşma
heart /haart/ *n* kalp; iskambilde kupa; **by** ~ ezberden; ~ **attack** kalp krizi
heartbeat /'haart,biit/ *n* kalp atışı
heartbreak /'haart,breyk/ *n* kalp kırıklığı
heartburn /'haart,bÖrn/ *n* mide ekşimesi
hearth /haarT/ *n* ocak, şömine
heartless /'haartLıs/ *adj* kalpsiz, duygusuz
hearty /'haartii/ *adj* candan, samimi
heat /hiit/ *n* ısı, sıcaklık; *v* ısıtmak; **heating pad** ısıtıcı yastık
heater /'hiitır/ *n* ısıtıcı şey; ocak, soba
heath /hiiT/ *n* fundalık; çorak arazi
heathen /'hiiDın/ *n* putperest, kâfir
heating /'hiitiN/ *n* ısıtma
heaven /'hevın/ *n* gök; cennet
heavy /'hevii/ *adj* ağır; şiddetli; iri
Hebrew /'hiibruu/ *n* Yahudi; İbranice

hedge /'hec/ *n* çit; engel
hedgehog /'hec,hOg/ *n* kirpi
heel /hiiL/ *n* topuk; ökçe
height /hayt/ *n* yükseklik
hell /heL/ *n* cehennem
hello /he'Lou/ merhaba
helm /heLm/ *n* dümen
helmet /'heLmit/ *n* miğfer
helmsman /'heLmzmın/ *n* dümenci
help /heLp/ *v* yardım etmek; *n* yardım
helper /'heLpır/ *n* yardımcı
helpful /'heLpfıL/ *adj* yardım eden, işe yarar
helping /'heLpiN/ *n* porsiyon, bir tabak yemek
hem /hem/ *n* dikilmiş kenar
hemorrhage /'hemıric/ *n* kanama, kan kaybı
hemorrhoids /'hemı,rOydz/ *pl* basur, hemoroid
hemp /hemp/ *n* kendir, kenevir
hen /hen/ *n* tavuk
henceforth /'hens'fOOrT/ *adv* bundan sonra, bundan böyle
henna /'henı/ *n* kına
henpecked /'hen,pekt/ *adj* kılıbık
hepatitis /,hepı'taytis/ *n* karaciğer iltihabı
her /hÖr/ *pron* onu, ona (dişil); *adj* onun (dişil)
herb /hÖrb/ *n* ot; baharat; şifalı bitki
herd /hÖrd/ *n* hayvan sürüsü
here /hiir/ *adv* burada; ~ **you are** buyurun, işte
hereditary /hı'redı,terii/ *adj* miras olarak kalan; kalıtsal
hernia /'hÖrniyı/ *n* fıtık
hero /'hiirou/ *n* (pl ~es) kahraman
heroin /'herouin/ *n* eroin
heron /'herın/ *n* balıkçıl kuşu
herring /'heriN/ *n* ringa balığı
herself /hÖr'seLf/ *pron* kendisi (dişil)
hesitate /'hezi,teyt/ *v* tereddüt etmek, duraksamak
heterosexual /,hetırı'sekşuuıL/ *adj* karşı cinse ilgi duyan
hibernation /,haybır'neyşın/ *n* kış uykusu
hiccup /'hikAp/ *n* hıçkırık
hide /hayd/ *n* deri, post
***hide** /hayd/ *v* saklanmak; saklamak
hide-and-seek /'haydın'siik/ *n* saklambaç
hideous /'hidiyıs/ *adj* son derece çirkin, biçimsiz
hierarchy /'hayı,raarkii/ *n* hiyerarşi
high /hay/ *adj* yüksek
highway /'hay,wey/ *n* anayol; *nAm* otoyol
hijack /'hay,cEk/ *v* uçak kaçırmak
hijacker /'hay,cEkır/ *n* hava korsanı
hike /hayk/ *v* uzun yürüyüş yapmak
hill /hiL/ *n* tepe
hillock /'hiLık/ *n* tepecik, tümsek
hillside /'hiL,sayd/ *n* yamaç
hilltop /'hiL,tOp/ *n* doruk
hilly /'hiLii/ *adj* engebeli
him /him/ *pron* onu, ona (eril)
himself /him'seLf/ *pron* kendisi (eril)
hinder /'hindır/ *v* engellemek
hinge /hinc/ *n* menteşe; dayanak noktası
hint /hint/ *n* ima, üstü kapalı söz; *v* ima etmek, çıtlatmak
hip /hip/ *n* kalça
hire /hayr/ *v* kiralamak; **for** ~ kiralık
hire-purchase /'hayr'pÖrçıs/ *nBr* taksitle satın alma
his /hiz/ *adj* onun (eril)
historian /his'tOOriyın/ *n* tarihçi
historic /his'tOOrik/ *adj* tarihsel
historical /his'tOOrikıL/ *adj* tarihi, tarihsel
history /'histırii/ *n* tarih
hit /hit/ *n* vurma; isabet; başarı
***hit** /hit/ *v* vurmak; isabet etmek

hitchhike /'hiç,hayk/ *v* otostop yapmak
hitchhiker /'hiç,haykır/ *n* otostopçu
hoarse /hOOrs/ *adj* kısık, boğuk
hobby /'hObii/ *n* hobi, merak
hockey /'hOkii/ *n* hokey
hoist /hOyst/ *n* yukarı kaldırmak, yükseltmek
hold /houLd/ *n* tutunacak yer; gemi ambarı
***hold** /houLd/ *v* tutmak, alıkoymak; ~ **on** tutunmak; durup beklemek; ~ **up** durdurmak; geciktirmek
holdup /'houLd,Ap/ *n* durdurma; gecikme; yol kesip soyma
hole /houL/ *n* delik
holiday /'hOLı,dey/ *v* tatil; ~ **camp** tatil kampı; ~ **resort** tatil köyü; **on** ~ tatilde
Holland /'hOLınd/ Hollanda
hollow /'hOLou/ *adj* içi boş, oyuk
holy /'houLii/ *adj* kutsal
homage /'hOmic/ *n* sadakat yemini; saygı
home /houm/ *n* ev, yuva; *adv* evine; ülkesine; **at** ~ evde, yuvada
homemade /'houm'meyd/ *adj* evde yapılmış
homesickness /'houm,siknıs/ *n* vatan özlemi
homework /'houm,wÖrk/ *n* ev ödevi
homosexual /,houmı'sekşuuıL/ *adj* eşcinsel
honest /'Onıst/ *adj* dürüst, doğru
honesty /'Onıstii/ *n* dürüstlük, doğruluk
honey /'hAnii/ *n* bal
honeymoon /'hAnii,muun/ *n* balayı
honk /hOnk/ *vAm* korna çalmak
honor /'Onır/ *n* şeref, onur; *v* saygı göstermek, şeref vermek
honorable /'OnırıbıL/ *adj* onurlu; saygıdeğer
hood /hud/ *n* kukuleta; *nAm* motor kapağı, kaporta
hoof /huuf/ *n* toynak; at, sığır vs. tırnağı
hook /huk/ *n* çengel, kanca
hooter /'huutır/ *n* klakson, korna
hop[1] /hOp/ *v* sıçramak, zıplamak; *n* sıçrama, zıplama
hop[2] /hOp/ *n* şerbetçi otu
hope /houp/ *n* ümit; *v* ümit etmek
hopeful /'houpfıL/ *adj* ümit verici; ümitli
hopeless /'houpLıs/ *adj* ümitsiz
horizon /hı'rayzın/ *n* ufuk
horizontal /,hOOrı'zOntıL/ *adj* ufki, yatay
horn /hOOrn/ *n* boynuz; korna, boru
horrible /'hOOrıbıL/ *adj* korkunç, iğrenç, berbat
horrid /'hOOrid/ *adj* korkunç, iğrenç
horrify /'hOOrıfay/ *v* korkutmak, dehşet vermek
horror /'hOOrır/ *n* dehşet, korku; nefret
hors d'oeuvre /OOr'dÖvr/ ordövr, meze
horse /hOOrs/ *n* at
horseman /'hOOrsmın/ *n* (pl -men) atlı, binici
horsepower /'hOOrs,pauır/ *n* beygirgücü
horserace /'hOOrs,reys/ *n* at yarışı
horseradish /'hOOrs,rEdiş/ *n* yabanturpu
horseshoe /'hOOrs,şuu/ *n* at nalı
horticulture /'hOOrtı,kALçır/ *n* bahçıvanlık
hosiery /'houjırii/ *nBr* çorap ve iç çamaşırı gibi giyim eşyası
hospitable /'hOspitıbıL/ *adj* konuksever
hospital /'hOspitıL/ *n* hastane
hospitality /,hOspı'tELıtii/ *n* konukseverlik
host /houst/ *n* konuklarını ağırlayan

ev sahibi
hostage /'hOstic/ *n* rehine
hostel /'hOstıL/ *n* han, öğrenci yurdu
hostess /'houstis/ *n* ev sahibesi; hostes
hostile /'hOstıL/ *adj* düşmanca, saldırgan
hostility /hOs'tiLıtii/ *n* düşmanlık
hot /hOt/ *adj* sıcak, kızgın
hotel /hou'teL/ *n* otel
hot-tempered /'hOt'tempırd/ *adj* çabuk öfkelenen
hour /aur/ *n* saat
hourly /'aurLii/ *adj* saatte bir olan
house /haus/ *n* ev; ~ **agent** emlakçı; **public** ~ *Br* birahane
household /'haus,houLd/ *n* ev halkı; *adj* eve ait
housekeeper /'haus,kiipır/ *n* evde kâhya kadın
housekeeping /'haus,kiipiN/ *n* ev idaresi
housemaid /'haus,meyd/ *n* ortalık hizmetçisi
housewife /'haus,wayf/ *n* ev hanımı
housework /'haus,wÖrk/ *n* ev işi
how /hau/ *adv* nasıl; ~ **many** kaç tane, ne kadar; ~ **much** ne kadar
however /hau'evır/ *conj* bununla birlikte
hug /hAg/ *v* kucaklamak, sarılmak; *n* sıkıca kucaklama, sarılma
huge /hyuuc/ *adj* çok iri, kocaman
hum /hAm/ *v* vızıldamak, mırıldanmak
human /'hyuumın/ *adj* insana ait, insani; ~ **being** insanoğlu, insan
humane /hyuu'meyn/ *adj* insancı, merhametli
humanitarian /hyuu,mEnı'teyriyın/ *adj* iyiliksever, insancı
humanity /hyuu'mEnıtii/ *n* insanlık
humble /'hAmbıL/ *adj* alçakgönüllü
humid /'hyuumid/ *adj* nemli
humidity /hyuu'midıtii/ *n* nem
humiliate /hyuu'mili,yeyt/ *v* kibrini kırmak, küçük düşürmek
humiliation /hyuu,mili'yeyşın/ *n* kibrini kırma, utandırma
humor /'hyuumır/ *n* mizah
humorous /'hyuumırıs/ *adj* mizahi, gülünç
hundred /'hAndrıd/ *num* yüz
hunchback /'hAnç,bEk/ *n* kambur
Hungarian /hAn'geyriyın/ *adj* Macaristan'a ait; *n* Macarca; Macar
Hungary /'hANgırii/ Macaristan
hunger /'hANgır/ *n* açlık
hungry /'hANgrii/ *adj* aç, acıkmış
hunt /hAnt/ *v* avlanmak; avlamak; *n* av; ~ **for** aramak
hunter /'hAntır/ *n* avcı
hurricane /'hÖrı,keyn/ *n* şiddetli fırtına, kasırga; ~ **lamp** rüzgârda sönmeyen fener
hurry /'hÖrii/ *v* acele etmek; acele ettirmek; **in a** ~ aceleyle
***hurt** /hÖrt/ *v* incitmek, acıtmak; gücendirmek
hurtful /'hÖrtfıL/ *adj* zararlı
husband /'hAzbınd/ *n* koca
hut /hAt/ *n* kulübe, baraka
hydrogen /'haydrıcın/ *n* hidrojen
hygiene /'hayciin/ *n* sağlık bilgisi
hygienic /,hayci'yenik/ *adj* sağlıkla ilgili, sağlığa yararlı
hymn /him/ *n* ilahi
hypertension /,haypır'tenşın/ *n* yüksek tansiyon
hyphen /'hayfın/ *n* tire
hypocrisy /hay'pOkrısii/ *n* ikiyüzlülük
hypocrite /'hipı,krit/ *n* ikiyüzlü kimse
hypocritical /,hipı'kritikıL/ *adj* ikiyüzlü
hysterical /hi'sterikıL/ *adj* isterik, isteriye ait

I

I /ay/ *pron* ben
ice /ays/ *n* buz; ~ **bag** buz kesesi; ~ **cream** dondurma
Iceland /'aysLınd/ İzlanda
Icelander /'aysLındır/ *n* İzlandalı
Icelandic /ays'LEndik/ *adj* İzlanda'ya ait
icon /'aykOn/ *n* resim, heykel; ikon
idea /ay'diyı/ *n* fikir, düşünce; inanç; tahmin
ideal /ay'diyıL/ *adj* ideal; mükemmel; *n* ülkü
identical /ay'dentikıL/ *adj* tıpatıp aynı
identification /ay,dentıfi'keyşın/ *n* kimlik saptama; kimlik
identify /ay'dentıfay/ *v* kimliğini saptamak; özdeşlemek
identity /ay'dentitii/ *n* kimlik; özdeşlik; ~ **card** kimlik kartı
idiom /'idiyım/ *n* deyim
idiomatic /,idyi'mEtik/ *adj* deyimsel, özel deyimlere ait
idiot /'idiyıt/ *n* geri zekâlı kimse
idiotic /,idi'yOtik/ *adj* aptalca, ahmakça
idle /'aydıL/ *adj* işsiz, aylak; yararsız, boş
idol /'aydıL/ *n* put; çok sevilen kişi
if /if/ *conj* eğer
ignition /ig'nişın/ *n* ateşleme; ~ **coil** ateşleme bobini
ignorant /'ignırınt/ *adj* cahil, bilgisiz
ignore /ig'nOOr/ *v* aldırmamak; hesaba katmamak, yok saymak
ill /iL/ *adj* hasta; kötü
illegal /i'LiigıL/ *adj* yasadışı
illegible /i'LecıbıL/ *adj* okunaksız
illiterate /i'Litırıt/ *n* okuma yazma bilmeyen kişi
illness /'iLnıs/ *n* hastalık
illuminate /i'Luumı,neyt/ *v* aydınlatmak
illumination /i,Luumı'neyşın/ *n* aydınlatma
illusion /i'Luujın/ *n* hayal; aldatıcı görüş
illustrate /'iLıs,treyt/ *v* resimlemek; örnekle açıklamak
illustration /,iLıs'treyşın/ *n* resim; açıklama
image /'imic/ *n* resim; görüntü, hayal
imaginary /i'mEcı,nerii/ *adj* hayali, düşsel
imagination /i,mEcı'neyşın/ *n* hayal gücü
imagine /i'mEcin/ *v* hayal etmek, hayalde canlandırmak; sanmak, farz etmek
imitate /'imı,teyt/ *v* taklit etmek
imitation /,imı'teyşın/ *n* taklit
immediate /i'miidiyıt/ *adj* derhal olan; hemen ardından gelen; yakın
immediately /i'miidiyıtLii/ *adv* hemen, derhal
immense /i'mens/ *adj* çok geniş, engin
immigrant /'imıgrınt/ *n* göçmen
immigrate /'imı,greyt/ *v* göç etmek
immigration /,imı'greyşın/ *n* göç
immodest /i'mOdist/ *adj* utanmaz, arsız, haddini bilmez
immunity /i'myuunitii/ *n* bağışıklık; dokunulmazlık
immunize /'imyınayz/ *v* bağışıklık kazandırmak
impartial /im'paarşıL/ *adj* tarafsız
impassable /im'pEsıbıL/ *adj* geçilmez, geçit vermez
impatient /im'peyşınt/ *adj* sabırsız
impede /im'piid/ *v* engellemek
impediment /im'pedımınt/ *n* engel
imperfect /im'pÖrfikt/ *adj* kusurlu
imperial /im'piiriyıL/ *adj* imparatora ait; şahane

impersonal /im'pÖrsınıL/ *adj* kişisel olmayan
impertinence /im'pÖrtınıns/ *n* küstahlık; münasebetsizlik
impertinent /im'pÖrtınınt/ *adj* küstah; münasebetsiz
implement[1] /'impLımınt/ *n* alet, araç
implement[2] /'impLı,ment/ *v* uygulamaya koymak
imply /im'pLay/ *v* dolaylı belirtmek; ima etmek
impolite /,impı'Layt/ *adj* kaba, terbiyesiz
import[1] /im'pOOrt/ *v* ithal etmek
import[2] /'im,pOOrt/ *n* ithal; ~ **duty** ithal vergisi
importance /im'pOOrtıns/ *n* önem
important /im'pOOrtınt/ *adj* önemli
importer /im'pOOrtır/ *n* ithalatçı
imposing /im'pouziN/ *adj* heybetli; güçlü ve etkileyici
impossible /im'pOsıbıL/ *adj* imkânsız, olanaksız
impotence /'impıtıns/ *n* güçsüzlük; iktidarsızlık
impotent /'impıtınt/ *adj* güçsüz; iktidarsız
impound /im'paund/ *v* el koymak
impress /im'pres/ *v* etkilemek; izlenim bırakmak
impression /im'preşın/ *n* izlenim; baskı
impressive /im'presiv/ *adj* etkileyici, hayranlık uyandırıcı
imprison /im'prizın/ *v* hapsetmek
imprisonment /im'prizınmınt/ *n* hapsetme
improbable /im'prObıbıL/ *adj* olası olmayan, umulmayan
improper /im'prOpır/ *adj* münasebetsiz, yersiz
improve /im'pruuv/ *v* iyileştirmek, düzeltmek, geliştirmek
improvement /im'pruuvmınt/ *n* iyileştirme, düzeltme, geliştirme
improvise /'imprı,vayz/ *v* irticalen söylemek
impudent /'impyıdınt/ *adj* yüzsüz, küstah; saygısız
impulse /'impALs/ *n* itici güç, dürtü
impulsive /im'pALsiv/ *adj* düşüncesizce hareket eden
in /in/ *prep* içinde, içine; *adv* içeride, içeriye
inaccessible /,inık'sesıbıL/ *adj* erişilemez, ulaşılamaz
inaccurate /in'Ekyırıt/ *adj* yanlış, kusurlu
inadequate /in'Edikwıt/ *adj* yetersiz
incapable /in'keypıbıL/ *adj* yeteneksiz, güçsüz
incense /'in,sens/ *n* tütsü, buhur
incident /'insıdınt/ *n* olay, vaka
incidental /,insı'dentıL/ *adj* rastlantısal
incidentally /,insı'dentıLii/ *adv* tesadüfen, arızi olarak; aklıma gelmişken
incite /in'sayt/ *v* kışkırtmak; teşvik etmek
inclination /,inkLı'neyşın/ *n* eğim; eğilim, istek
incline /in'kLayn/ *v* eğmek, yatırmak, meylettirmek
inclined /in'kLaynd/ *adj* istekli, eğilimli; ***be ~ to** yatkın olmak; canı istemek
include /in'kLuud/ *v* kapsamak, içine almak
inclusive /in'kLuusiv/ *adj* dahil, içeren
income /'in,kAm/ *n* gelir; ~ **tax** gelir vergisi
incompetent /in'kOmpıtınt/ *adj* yetersiz, ehliyetsiz
incomplete /,inkım'pLiit/ *adj* eksik, tam olmayan
inconceivable /,inkın'siivıbıL/ *adj* hayal edilemez; inanılmaz; kavranamaz
inconspicuous /,inkın'spikyuuıs/ *adj*

göze çarpmayan, önemsiz
inconvenience /ˌinkın'viinyıns/ *n* zahmet, rahatsızlık
inconvenient /ˌinkın'viinyınt/ *adj* rahatsızlık veren, uygun düşmeyen
incorrect /ˌinkı'rekt/ *adj* yanlış
increase[1] /in'kriis/ *v* artmak, çoğalmak; artırmak, çoğaltmak
increase[2] /'inkriis/ *n* artış, artan miktar
incredible /in'kredıbıl/ *adj* inanılmaz
incurable /in'kyuurıbıL/ *adj* iyileşmez, tedavi edilemez
indecent /in'diisınt/ *adj* açık saçık; yakışıksız
indeed /in'diid/ *adv* gerçekten, doğrusu
indefinite /in'defınıt/ *adj* belirsiz
indemnify /in'demnıˌfay/ *v* tazmin etmek
indemnity /in'demnıtii/ *n* tazminat
independence /ˌindi'pendıns/ *n* bağımsızlık
independent /ˌindi'pendınt/ *adj* bağımsız
index /'indeks/ *n* fihrist, dizin; ~ **finger** işaret parmağı
India /'indiyı/ Hindistan
Indian /'indiyın/ *adj* Hindistan'a ait; *n* Hintli; Kızılderili
indicate /'indiˌkeyt/ *v* göstermek, belirtmek, işaret etmek
indication /ˌindi'keyşın/ *n* işaret, belirti
indicator /'indiˌkeytır/ *n* gösterge
indifferent /in'difırınt/ *adj* kayıtsız, kaygısız; ilgisiz
indigestion /ˌindi'cesçın/ *n* hazımsızlık
indignation /ˌindig'neyşın/ *n* haksızlığa karşı duyulan öfke
indirect /ˌindı'rekt/ *adj* dolaylı, dolambaçlı
individual /ˌindı'vicuuıL/ *adj* bireysel, bir kişiye ait; *n* birey
Indonesia /ˌindı'niijı/ Endonezya
Indonesian /ˌindı'niijın/ *adj* Endonezya'ya ait; *n* Endonezyalı
indoor /'inˌdOOr/ *adj* bina içinde olan
indoors /'in'dOOrz/ *adv* bina içine *veya* içinde
indulge /in'dALc/ *v* kendisinin *veya* bir başkasının isteklerine sınır tanımadan boyun eğmek; aşırı hoşgörü göstermek
industrial /in'dAstriyıL/ *adj* sanayiye ait, sınai; ~ **area** sanayi bölgesi
industrious /in'dAstriyıs/ *adj* çalışkan
industry /'indıstrii/ *n* sanayi
inedible /in'edıbıL/ *adj* yenmez
inefficient /ˌini'fişınt/ *adj* etkisiz; yetersiz
inevitable /in'evıtıbıl/ *adj* kaçınılmaz
inexpensive /ˌiniks'pensiv/ *adj* ucuz
inexperienced /ˌiniks'piiriyınst/ *adj* tecrübesiz, acemi
infant /'infınt/ *n* bebek, küçük çocuk
infantry /'infıntrii/ *n* piyade sınıfı
infect /in'fekt/ *v* mikrop bulaştırmak
infection /in'fekşın/ *n* bulaşma, mikrop kapma; mikroplu hastalık
infectious /in'fekşıs/ *adj* bulaşıcı
infer /in'fÖr/ *v* sonuç çıkarmak; anlam çıkarmak
inferior /in'fiiriyır/ *adj* aşağı, adi; ikinci derecede
infinite /'infınit/ *adj* sonsuz, sınırsız
infinitive /in'finıtiv/ *n* fiilin mastar biçimi
infirmary /in'fÖrmırii/ *n* revir
inflammable /in'fLEmıbıL/ *adj* kolayca tutuşabilir
inflammation /ˌinfLı'meyşın/ *n* iltihap, yangı
inflatable /in'fLeytıbıL/ *adj* şişirilebilir
inflate /in'fLeyt/ *v* şişirmek
inflation /in'fLeyşın/ *n* enflasyon
influence /'infLuuıns/ *n* nüfuz, etki;

v etkilemek
influential /ˌinfLuu'enşıL/ *adj* etkili, sözü geçen
influenza /ˌinfLuu'enzı/ *n* grip
inform /in'fOOrm/ *v* bilgi vermek, haber vermek
informal /in'fOOrmıL/ *adj* gayri resmi; teklifsiz, samimi
information /ˌinfır'meyşın/ *n* bilgi, danışma; ~ **bureau** danışma bürosu
infrared /ˌinfrı'red/ *adj* kızılötesi
infrequent /in'friikwınt/ *adj* seyrek
ingredient /in'griidiyınt/ *n* bir karışımdaki maddelerden her biri
inhabit /in'hEbit/ *v* içinde oturmak
inhabitable /in'hEbitıbıL/ *adj* içinde yaşanabilir
inhabitant /in'hEbitınt/ *n* yaşayan kişi, sakin
inhale /in'heyL/ *v* solukla içeriye çekmek
inherit /in'herit/ *v* miras olarak almak
inheritance /in'heritıns/ *n* miras
initial /i'nişıL/ *adj* ilk baştaki; *n* adın ilk harfi; *v* adın baş harfleriyle imza atmak, parafe etmek
initiative /i'nişıtiv/ *n* başlama yetkisi; kişisel girişim, inisiyatif
inject /in'cekt/ *v* iğne, şırınga yapmak
injection /in'cekşın/ *n* iğne, enjeksiyon
injure /'incır/ *v* zarar vermek, zedelemek; sakatlamak; incitmek
injury /'incırii/ *n* yara; zarar
injustice /in'cAstis/ *n* haksızlık
ink /iNk/ *n* mürekkep
in-laws /'inˌLOOz/ *pl* evlilik vasıtasıyla yakın akrabalar
inlet /'inˌLet/ *n* koy, küçük körfez; giriş
inn /in/ *n* han
inner /'inır/ *adj* iç; ~ **tube** iç lastik
innkeeper /'inˌkiipır/ *n* hancı
innocence /'inısıns/ *n* masumiyet, suçsuzluk
innocent /'inısınt/ *adj* masum, suçsuz
inoculate /i'nOkyıˌLeyt/ *v* aşılamak
inoculation /iˌnOkyı'Leyşın/ *n* aşı, aşılama
input /'inˌput/ *n* girdi
inquire /in'kwayr/ *v* sormak; soruşturmak, araştırmak
inquiry /in'kwayrii/ *n* sorgu, soruşturma; ~ **office** danışma bürosu
inquisitive /in'kwizıtiv/ *adj* meraklı
insane /in'seyn/ *adj* deli
inscription /in'skripşın/ *n* yazıt, kitabe
insect /'insekt/ *n* böcek; ~ **repellent** böcek kovucu
insecticide /in'sektıˌsayd/ *n* böcek öldürücü
insensitive /in'sensıtiv/ *adj* duyarsız, hassas olmayan
insert /in'sÖrt/ *v* içine sokmak
inside /in'sayd/ *n* iç taraf; *adj* içteki; *adv* içeride; *prep* içerisinde; ~ **out** tersyüz; **insides** *pl* bağırsaklar
insight /'inˌsayt/ *n* bir şeyin içyüzünü kavrama
insignificant /ˌinsig'nifikınt/ *adj* önemsiz
insist /in'sist/ *v* ısrar etmek
insolence /'insıLıns/ *n* küstahlık
insolent /'insıLınt/ *adj* küstah, terbiyesiz
insomnia /in'sOmniyı/ *n* uykusuzluk
inspect /in'spekt/ *v* denetlemek, teftiş etmek
inspection /in'spekşın/ *n* denetleme
inspector /in'spektır/ *n* müfettiş, denetçi
inspire /in'spayr/ *v* ilham vermek, esindirmek
install /in'stOOL/ *v* kurmak,

yerleştirmek
installation /ˌinstı'Leyşın/ *n* yerleştirme; tesisat
installment /in'stOOLmınt/ *n* taksit
instance /'instıns/ *n* örnek, misal; olay; **for ~** örneğin
instant /'instınt/ *n* an, çok kısa süre
instantly /'instıntLii/ *adv* hemen, derhal
instead of /in'sted ıv/ yerine
instinct /'instiNkt/ *n* içgüdü
institute /'insti,tuut/ *n* kuruluş, enstitü; *v* kurmak
institution /ˌinsti'tuuşın/ *n* kuruluş; yerleşmiş gelenek
instruct /in'strAkt/ *v* öğretmek, ders vermek; talimat vermek
instruction /in'strAkşın/ *n* öğretim; talimat
instructive /in'strAktiv/ *adj* öğretici; ders verici
instructor /in'strAktır/ *n* öğretmen, eğitmen
instrument /'instrımınt/ *n* alet; araç; **musical ~** müzik aleti, çalgı
insufficient /ˌinsı'fişınt/ *adj* yetersiz
insulate /'insı,Leyt/ *v* izole etmek, yalıtmak
insulation /ˌinsı'Leyşın/ *n* tecrit, yalıtım
insulator /'insı,Leytır/ *n* izolatör, yalıtkan
insult[1] /in'sALt/ *v* hakaret etmek
insult[2] /'insALt/ *n* hakaret
insurance /in'şuurıns/ *n* sigorta; **~ policy** sigorta poliçesi
insure /in'şuur/ *v* sigorta etmek; sağlamak
intact /in'tEkt/ *adj* dokunulmamış, zedelenmemiş
intellect /'intıL,ekt/ *n* akıl, zekâ
intellectual /ˌintıL'ekçuuıL/ *n* aydın kimse; *adj* akıllı, bilgili
intelligence /in'teLıcıns/ *n* zekâ; istihbarat
intelligent /in'teLıcınt/ *adj* zeki
intend /in'tend/ *v* niyet etmek
intense /in'tens/ *adj* şiddetli, yoğun
intention /in'tenşın/ *n* niyet
intentional /in'tenşınıL/ *adj* kasti
intercourse /'intır,kOOrs/ *n* ilişki; cinsel birleşme
interest /'intrist/ *n* ilgi; faiz; *v* ilgilendirmek, ilgi çekmek
interesting /'intristiN/ *adj* ilginç
interfere /ˌintır'fiir/ *v* karışmak, müdahale etmek; **~ with** karışmak, burnunu sokmak
interference /ˌintır'fiirıns/ *n* müdahale, karışma; parazit
interim /'intırim/ *n* aralık, fasıla
interior /in'tiiriyır/ *n* iç
interlude /'intır,Luud/ *n* ara, aralık
intermediary /ˌintır'miidiyerii/ *n, adj* aracı
intermission /ˌintır'mişın/ *n* fasıla; ara verme
internal /in'tÖrnıl/ *adj* iç, dahili
international /ˌintır'nEşınıL/ *adj* uluslararası
interpret /in'tÖrprit/ *v* tercüme etmek; yorumlamak
interpreter /in'tÖrpritır/ *n* tercüman; yorumcu
interrogate /in'terı,geyt/ *v* sorguya çekmek
interrogation /in,terı'geyşın/ *n* soru; sorgu
interrogative /ˌintı'rOgıtiv/ *adj* soru ifade eden, sorulu
interrupt /ˌintı'rApt/ *v* kesmek; sözünü kesmek
interruption /ˌintı'rApşın/ *n* kesilme, ara
intersection /ˌintır'sekşın/ *n* kesişme; yolağzı, kavşak
interval /'intırvıL/ *n* ara
intervene /ˌintır'viin/ *v* araya girmek,

müdahale etmek
intervention /,intır'venşın/ *n* araya girme, müdahale
interview /'intır,vyuu/ *n* mülakat, görüşme
intestine /in'testin/ *n* bağırsak
intimate /'intimıt/ *adj* yakın; mahrem
into /'intu/ *prep* içine
intolerable /in'tOLırıbıL/ *adj* çekilmez, dayanılmaz
intoxicated /in'tOksı,keytid/ *adj* sarhoş
intrigue /in'triig/ *n* entrika, dolap; *v* merakını uyandırmak
introduce /,intrı'duus/ *v* tanıtmak, takdim etmek
introduction /,intrı'dAkşın/ *n* takdim, tanıtma; başlangıç, giriş
invade /in'veyd/ *v* istila etmek
invalid[1] /'invıLid/ *n* sakat, hasta
invalid[2] /in'vELid/ *adj* hükümsüz, geçersiz
invasion /in'veyjın/ *n* istila
invent /in'vent/ *v* icat etmek
invention /in'venşın/ *n* icat, buluş
inventive /in'ventiv/ *adj* yaratıcı, buluşları olan
inventor /in'ventır/ *n* mucit
inventory /'invın,tOOrii/ *n* envanter
invert /in'vÖrt/ *v* ters çevirmek
invest /in'vest/ *v* yatırım yapmak
investigate /in'vestı,geyt/ *v* incelemek, araştırmak
investigation /in,vestı'geyşın/ *n* araştırma, soruşturma
investment /in'vestmınt/ *n* para yatırma, yatırım
investor /in'vestır/ *n* yatırımcı
invisible /in'vizıbıL/ *adj* gözle görülemez
invitation /,invı'teyşın/ *n* davet
invite /in'vayt/ *v* davet etmek, çağırmak
invoice /'in,vOys/ *n* fatura
involve /in'vOLv/ *v* karıştırmak; gerektirmek; ***be involved in** -e karışmak, bulaşmak
inward /'inwırd/ *adv* içe doğru
iodine /'ayı,dayn/ *n* iyot
Iran /i'rEn/ İran
Iranian /i'reyniyın/ *adj* İran'a ait; *n* İranlı
Iraq /i'raak/ Irak
Iraqi /i'raakii/ *adj* Irak'a ait; *n* Iraklı
irascible /i'rEsıbıL/ *adj* çabuk öfkelenir
Ireland /'ayrLınd/ İrlanda
Irish /'ayriş/ *adj* İrlanda'ya ait
Irishman /'ayrişmın/ *n* (pl -men) İrlandalı
iron /'ayırn/ *n* demir; ütü; *v* ütülemek
ironical /ay'rOnikıL/ *adj* ince alaylı; kaderin bir cilvesi gibi olan
ironworks /'ayırn,wÖrks/ *n* demirhane, dökümhane
irony /'ayrınii/ *n* kinaye
irregular /i'regyıLır/ *adj* düzensiz, kuralsız
irreparable /i'repırıbıL/ *adj* tamir edilemez, giderilmesi mümkün olmayan
irrevocable /i'revıkıbıL/ *adj* değiştirilemez, geri alınamaz
irritable /'iritıbıL/ *adj* çabuk kızan; çabuk tahriş olan
irritate /'iri,teyt/ *v* sinirlendirmek; tahriş etmek
is /iz/ *v* (pr be)
Islam /'isLEm/ *n* Müslümanlık; İslam dünyası
island /'ayLınd/ *n* ada
isolate /'aysı,Leyt/ *v* tecrit etmek, ayırmak
isolation /,aysı'Leyşın/ *n* tecrit, yalnızlık
Israel /'izriyıL/ İsrail
Israeli /iz'reyLii/ *adj* İsrail'e ait; *n* İsrailli

issue /'işuu/ *v* çıkarmak; yayımlamak; *n* çıkış; konu, sorun; yayımlanmış sayı
isthmus /'ismıs/ *n* berzah, kıstak
it /it/ *pron* o, onu, ona
Italian /i'tELyın/ *adj* İtalya'ya ait; *n* İtalyan; İtalyanca
italics /i'tELiks/ *pl* italik harfler
Italy /'itıLii/ İtalya
itch /iç/ *n* kaşıntı; *v* kaşınmak
item /'aytım/ *n* madde, kalem
itinerant /ay'tinırınt/ *adj* gezgin
itinerary /ay'tinı,rerii/ *n* yolculuk programı; yolculukta izlenecek yol
ivory /'ayvırii/ *n* fildişi; *adj* krem rengi
ivy /'ayvii/ *n* sarmaşık

J

jack /cEk/ *n* kriko
jacket /'cEkit/ *n* ceket; kitap kabı
jacknife /'cEk,nayf/ *n* iri çakı
jade /ceyd/ *n* yeşim taşı
jail /ceyL/ *nAm* hapishane
jailer /'ceyLır/ *nAm* gardiyan
jam /cEm/ *n* reçel; sıkışıklık, tıkanıklık
janitor /'cEnıtır/ *n* kapıcı
January /'cEnyuu,erii/ ocak ayı
Japan /cı'pEn/ Japonya
Japanese /cEpı'niiz/ *adj* Japonya'ya ait; *n* Japon; Japonca
jar /caar/ *n* kavanoz
jargon /'caargın/ *n* bir mesleğe özgü dil
jaundice /'cOOndis/ *n* sarılık hastalığı
jaw /cOO/ *n* çene
jazz /cEz/ *n* caz müziği
jealous /'ceLıs/ *adj* kıskanç
jealousy /'ceLısii/ *n* kıskançlık
jeans /ciinz/ *pl* blucin
jelly /'ceLii/ *n* pelte, jöle
jellyfish /'ceLii,fiş/ *n* denizanası
jersey /'cÖrzii/ *n* jarse; kazak, süveter
jet /cet/ *n* fıskıye; jet uçağı; ~ **lag** yolculuklarda zaman farklarından dolayı vücuttaki doğal dengenin bozulması
jetty /'cetii/ *n* dalgakıran; iskele
Jew /cuu/ *n* Musevi
jewel /'cuuıL/ *n* mücevher
jeweler /'cuuıLır/ *n* kuyumcu
jewelry /'cuuıLrii/ *n* mücevherat
Jewish /'cuuiş/ *adj* Musevi, Musevilere ait
job /cOb/ *n* iş, görev; götürü iş
jockey /'cOkii/ *n* cokey, binici
jog /cOg/ *v* sarsmak, dürtmek; yavaş bir tempoda koşmak
jogging /'cOgiN/ *n* idman için yavaş koşma
join /cOyn/ *v* birleştirmek; birleşmek; katılmak
joint /cOynt/ *n* birleşme yeri; eklem; *adj* birleşik; ortak
jointly /'cOyntLii/ *adv* birlikte, ortaklaşa
joke /couk/ *n* şaka; fıkra
jolly /'cOLii/ *adj* neşeli, şen
Jordan /'cOOrdın/ Ürdün
Jordanian /cOOr'deyniyın/ *adj* Ürdün'e ait; *n* Ürdünlü
journal /'cÖrnıL/ *n* dergi
journalism /'cÖrnıL,izım/ *n* gazetecilik
journalist /'cÖrnıList/ *n* gazeteci
journey /'cÖrnii/ *n* yolculuk
joy /cOy/ *n* sevinç, neşe, zevk
joyful /'cOyfıL/ *adj* sevindirici; sevinçli
jubilee /'cuubı,Lii/ *n* ellinci yıldönümü, jübile
judge /cAc/ *n* yargıç; *v* yargılamak
judgment /'cAcmınt/ *n* yargı
judicial /,cuu'dişıL/ *adj* adli, hukuki
jug /cAg/ *n* testi

Jugoslav /'yuugou,sLaav/ *adj* Yugoslavya'ya ait; *n* Yugoslav
Jugoslavia /,yuugou'sLEviyı/ Yugoslavya
juice /cuus/ *n* meyve *veya* sebze suyu
juicy /'cuusii/ *adj* sulu
July /cu'Lay/ temmuz
jump /cAmp/ *v* atlamak, sıçramak; *n* atlayış, sıçrayış
jumper /'cAmpır/ *n* bol gömlek *veya* ceket; *nAm* bluz *veya* kazak üstüne giyilen kolsuz elbise
junction /'cANkşın/ *n* kavşak, birleşme yeri
June /cuuń/ haziran
jungle /'cANgıL/ *n* çok sık ağaçlı orman, cengel
junior /'cuunyır/ *adj* daha genç, ufak
junk /cANk/ *n* hurda; kalitesiz, değersiz şey
jury /'cuurii/ *n* jüri
just /cAst/ *adj* doğru, haklı; tam; *adv* tam tamına; şimdi, biraz önce; ancak
justice /'cAstis/ *n* adalet
justify /'cAstı,fay/ *v* doğrulamak, haklı çıkarmak; mazur göstermek
juvenile /'cuuvınıL/ *adj* gençliğe özgü

K

kangaroo /,kEngı'ruu/ *n* kanguru
keen /kiin/ *adj* keskin; hevesli
***keep** /kiip/ *v* tutmak, alıkoymak; saklamak; ~ **away from** -den uzak durmak; ~ **off** dokunmamak; ~ **on** devam etmek; ~ **quiet** susmak; ~ **up** sürdürmek; ~ **up with** -den geri kalmamak
kennel /'kenıL/ *n* köpek kulübesi
Kenya /'kenyı/ Kenya
kerosene /'kerı,siin/ *n* gazyağı
kettle /'ketıL/ *n* çaydanlık
key /kii/ *n* anahtar
keyboard /'kii,bOOrd/ *n* klavye
keyhole /'kii,houL/ *n* anahtar deliği
khaki /'kEkii/ *n* haki renkte kumaş
kick /kik/ *v* tekme atmak; *n* tekme, çifte, vuruş
kickoff /'kik,OOf/ *n* futbolda başlama vuruşu; başlangıç
kid /kid/ *n* çocuk; oğlak; *v* takılmak, şakadan aldatmak
kidnap /'kid,nEp/ *v* zorla *veya* hile ile kaçırmak
kidney /'kidnii/ *n* böbrek
kill /kiL/ *v* öldürmek
kilogram /'kiLı,grEm/ *n* kilo
kilometer /ki'LOmıtır/ *n* kilometre
kind /kaynd/ *adj* iyi kalpli, nazik, müşfik; *n* çeşit, cins
kindergarten /'kindır,gaartın/ *n* anaokulu
king /kiN/ *n* kral; iskambilde papaz
kingdom /'kiNdım/ *n* krallık
kiosk /'kiiyOsk/ *n* gazete satılan kulübe
kiss /kis/ *n* öpücük; v öpmek
kit /kit/ *n* takım; alet takımı
kite /kayt/ *n* uçurtma
kitchen /'kiçın/ *n* mutfak; ~ **garden** sebze bahçesi
Kleenex /'kLiineks/ *n* kâğıt mendil
knapsack /'nEp,sEk/ *n* sırt çantası
knave /neyv/ *n* hilekâr kimse; iskambilde bacak, vale
knee /nii/ *n* diz
kneecap /'nii,kEp/ *n* dizkapağı
***kneel** /niiL/ *v* diz çökmek
knew /nuu/ *v* (p know)
knickers /'nikırz/ *pl* kısa pantolon
knife /nayf/ *n* (pl knives) bıçak
knight /nayt/ *n* silahşor
***knit** /nit/ *v* örmek

knob /nOb/ *n* tokmak, topuz
knock /nOk/ *v* vurmak; *n* darbe; ~ **against** çarpmak, çarpışmak; ~ **down** yere sermek
knot /nOt/ *n* düğüm; *v* düğüm atmak
***know** /nou/ *v* bilmek; tanımak
knowledge /'nOLic/ *n* bilgi
knuckle /'nAkıL/ *n* parmak eklemi
Koran /kou'raan/ *n* Kuran

L

label /'LeybıL/ *n* etiket, marka; *v* etiketlemek
labor /'Leybır/ *n* emek, çalışma; doğum sancısı; *v* çabalamak, uğraşmak; ~ **permit** çalışma izni
laboratory /'LEbrı,tOOrii/ *n* laboratuvar
laborer /'Leybırır/ *n* işçi
laborsaving /'Leybır,seyviN/ *adj* işten tasarruf sağlayan
labyrinth /'LEbı,rinT/ *n* labirent, dolambaçlı yer
lace /Leys/ *n* dantel
lack /LEk/ *n* eksiklik; ihtiyaç; *v* eksiği olmak; ihtiyacı olmak
lad /LEd/ *n* delikanlı
ladder /'LEdır/ *n* merdiven
lady /'Leydii/ *n* hanımefendi; **ladies' room** bayanlar tuvaleti
lag /LEg/ *v* geri kalmak, oyalanmak; *n* gecikme, geri kalma
lagoon /Lı'guun/ *n* sığ göl
lake /Leyk/ *n* göl
lamb /LEm/ *n* kuzu; kuzu eti
lame /Leym/ *adj* topal, sakat
lamentable /'LEmıntıbıL/ *adj* ağlanacak, acınacak
lamp /LEmp/ *n* lamba
lamppost /'LEmp,poust/ *n* elektrik direği
lampshade /'LEmp,şeyd/ *n* abajur
land /LEnd/ *n* kara; toprak; ülke; *v* karaya çıkmak; (uçak) inmek
landlady /'LEnd,Leydii/ *n* ev sahibesi
landlord /'LEnd,LOOrd/ *n* ev sahibi
landmark /'LEnd,maark/ *n* sınır işareti; dönüm noktası
landscape /'LEnd,skeyp/ *n* manzara; manzara resmi
landslide /'LEnd,sLayd/ *n* heyelan, toprak kayması
lane /Leyn/ *n* dar yol *veya* sokak
language /'LENgwic/ *n* dil; ~ **laboratory** dil laboratuvarı
lantern /'LEntırn/ *n* fener
lap /LEp/ *n* kucak
lapel /Lı'peL/ *n* yaka devriği, klapa
larder /'Laardır/ *n* kiler
large /Laarc/ *adj* geniş
lark /Laark/ *n* tarlakuşu
laryngitis /,LErin'caytis/ *n* gırtlak iltihabı
last /LEst/ *adj* son, sonuncu; geçen; *v* sürmek; dayanmak; **at** ~ sonunda, nihayet
lasting /'LEstiN/ *adj* dayanıklı; kalıcı
latch /LEç/ *n* mandal, ispanyolet
late /Leyt/ *adj* geç
lately /'LeytLii/ *adv* son zamanlarda
lather /'LEDır/ *n* sabun köpüğü
Latin America /'LEtin ı'merikı/ Güney Amerika
Latin-American /'LEtin ı'merikın/ *adj* Güney Amerika'ya ait
latitude /'LEtı,tuud/ *n* enlem
laugh /LEf/ *v* gülmek; *n* gülüş
laughter /'LEftır/ *n* kahkaha
launch /LOOnç/ *v* harekete geçirmek; başlatmak
launching /'LOOnçiN/ *n* atma, fırlatma; hareket ettirme
launderette /,LOOndı'ret/ *n*

çamaşırhane
laundry /'LOOndrii/ *n* çamaşırhane
lavatory /'LEvı,tOOrii/ *n* tuvalet
lavish /'LEviş/ *adj* savurgan
law /LOO/ *n* yasa; hukuk; ~ **court** mahkeme
lawful /'LOOfıL/ *adj* yasal
lawn /LOOn/ *n* çimenlik
lawsuit /'LOO,suut/ *n* dava
lawyer /'LOOyır/ *n* avukat
laxative /'LEksıtiv/ *n* müshil
***lay** /Ley/ *v* koymak, yerleştirmek; ~ **bricks** duvar örmek; ~ **eggs** yumurtlamak; ~ **the table** sofrayı kurmak
layer /'Leyır/ *n* kat, tabaka
layman /'Leymın/ *n* bir meslek *veya* bilimin yabancısı
lazy /'Leyzii/ *adj* tembel
lead[1] /Liid/ *n* rehberlik, öncülük
lead[2] /Led/ *n* kurşun
***lead** /Liid/ *v* yol göstermek; götürmek; yönetmek
leader /'Liidır/ *n* önder, lider, yönetici; başyazı
leadership /'Liidır,şip/ *n* önderlik, liderlik
leading /'LiidiN/ *adj* önde giden, en önemli
leaf /Liif/ *n* (pl leaves) yaprak
league /Liig/ *n* birleşme; birlik; lig
leak /Liik/ *v* sızdırmak; sızmak; *n* sızıntı
leaky /'Liikii/ *adj* sızdıran, sızıntılı
lean /Liin/ *adj* zayıf; yağsız
***lean** /Liin/ *v* yaslanmak, dayanmak
leap /Liip/ *n* atlama; ~ **year** artık yıl
***leap** /Liip/ *v* atlamak, sıçramak; ~ **year** artık yıl
***learn** /LÖrn/ *v* öğrenmek
learner /'LÖrnır/ *n* öğrenen kimse, acemi
lease /Liis/ *n* kiralama; kira sözleşmesi; *v* kiralamak
leash /Liiş/ *n* tasma kayışı
least /Liist/ *adj* en az; **at** ~ hiç değilse
leather /'LeDır/ *n* deri, kösele, meşin
leave /Liiv/ *n* izin
***leave** /Liiv/ *v* bırakmak, terk etmek, gitmek, ayrılmak; ~ **out** atlamak, dışarıda bırakmak; üstünde durmamak
Lebanese /,Lebı'niiz/ *adj* Lübnan'a ait; *n* Lübnanlı
Lebanon /'Lebının/ Lübnan
lecture /'Lekçır/ *n* genel ders; konferans
left[1] /Left/ *adj* sol
left[2] /Left/ *v* (p, pp leave)
left-hand /'Left'hEnd/ *adj* sol taraftaki
left-handed /'Left'hEndid/ *adj* solak
leg /Leg/ *n* bacak
legacy /'Legısii/ *n* miras, kalıt
legal /'LiigıL/ *adj* yasal; meşru; hukuki
legalization /,LiigıLı'zeyşın/ *n* yasallaştırma
legend /'Lecınd/ *n* efsane, hikâye
legendary /'Lecın,derii/ *adj* efsanevi
legible /'LecibıL/ *adj* okunaklı
legitimate /Li'citımıt/ *adj* meşru, yasal
leisure /'Liijır/ *n* boş vakit
lemon /'Lemın/ *n* limon
lemonade /,Lemı'neyd/ *n* limonata; *nBr* gazoz
***lend** /Lend/ *v* ödünç vermek
length /LeNT/ *n* uzunluk
lengthen /'LeNTın/ *v* uzatmak
lengthwise /'LeNT,wayz/ *adv* uzunlamasına
lens /Lenz/ *n* mercek; **telephoto** ~ teleobjektif; **zoom** ~ mesafeyi ayarlayan mercek
lentil /'LentiL/ *n* mercimek
Leo /'Liiyou/ Aslan burcu
leprosy /'Leprısii/ *n* cüzam

lesbian /'Lezbiyın/ *n* homoseksüel kadın, sevici
less /Les/ *adj* daha az
lessen /'Lesın/ *v* azalmak; azaltmak
lesson /'Lesın/ *n* ders
***let** /Let/ *v* izin vermek; ~ **down** hayal kırıklığına uğratmak
letter /'Letır/ *n* mektup; harf; ~ **box** mektup kutusu; ~ **of credit** akreditif; ~ **of recommendation** tavsiye mektubu
lettuce /'Letıs/ *n* salata, marul
leukemia /Luu'kiimiyı/ *n* lösemi, kan kanseri
level /'LevıL/ *adj* düz, yatay; *n* düzey, hiza, derece; *v* düzlemek, tesviye etmek; ~ **crossing** *Br* hemzemin geçit
lever /'Levır/ *n* manivela, kaldıraç
Levi's /'Liivayz/ *pl* blucin
liability /,Layı'biLıtii/ *n* sorumluluk; yükümlülük
liable /'LayıbıL/ *adj* sorumlu; yükümlü; ~ **to** maruz, tabi
liberal /'LibırıL/ *adj* cömert, eli açık; serbest düşünceli
liberate /'Libı,reyt/ *v* serbest bırakmak; kurtarmak
liberation /,Libı'reyşın/ *n* kurtuluş; serbest bırakma
Liberia /Lay'biiriyı/ Liberya
Liberian /Lay'biiriyın/ *adj* Liberya'ya ait; *n* Liberyalı
liberty /'Libırtii/ *n* özgürlük
Libra /'Liibrı/ Terazi burcu
library /'Lay,brerii/ *n* kütüphane
license /'Laysıns/ *n* izin; lisans; ehliyet; *v* ruhsat *veya* yetki vermek; **driving** ~ sürücü ehliyeti; ~ **number** *Am* plaka numarası; ~ **plate** *Am* araba plakası
lick /lik/ *v* yalamak
licorice /'Likıriş/ *nAm* meyankökü
lid /Lid/ *n* kapak
lie /Lay/ *v* yalan söylemek; *n* yalan
***lie** /Lay/ *v* yatmak, uzanmak; ~ **down** yatmak
lieutenant /Luu'tenınt/ *n* teğmen; deniz yüzbaşısı
life /Layf/ *n* (pl lives) hayat, yaşam; ~ **belt** cankurtaran kemeri; ~ **insurance** yaşam sigortası
lifetime /'Layf,taym/ *n* yaşam süresi
lift /Lift/ *v* kaldırmak, yükseltmek; *n* kaldırış, yükseltme; *nBr* asansör
light /Layt/ *n* ışık, aydınlık; *adj* hafif; açık (renk); ~ **bulb** ampul
***light** /Layt/ *v* yakmak; aydınlatmak
lighter /'Laytır/ *n* çakmak
lighthouse /'Layt,haus/ *n* fener kulesi
lighting /'LaytiN/ *n* aydınlatma
lightning /'LaytniN/ *n* şimşek, yıldırım
like /Layk/ *v* hoşlanmak, sevmek; *adj* benzer; *conj* gibi
likely /'LaykLii/ *adj* muhtemel, olası
like-minded /'Layk'mayndid/ *adj* aynı görüşte, hemfikir
likewise /'Layk,wayz/ *adv* aynı şekilde
lilac /'Laylık/ *n* leylak; *adj* leylak rengi, açık mor
lily /'LiLii/ *n* zambak
limb /Lim/ *n* uzuv; dal
lime /Laym/ *n* misket limonu; kireç; ıhlamur
limetree /'Laym,trii/ *n* ıhlamur ağacı
limit /'Limit/ *n* had; sınır; *v* sınırlamak
limitation /,Limı'teyşın/ *n* sınırlama; sınırlayıcı şey
limp /Limp/ *v* topallamak, aksamak; *adj* gevşek, yumuşak
line /Layn/ *n* çizgi; yol; satır; kuyruk; ***stand in** ~ *Am* sıraya girmek
linen /'Linın/ *n* keten bezi; keten

çamaşır
liner /'Laynır/ *n* yolcu vapuru *veya* uçağı
lining /'LayniN/ *n* astar
link /LiNk/ *v* bağlamak, birleştirmek; *n* bağ; zincir halkası
lion /'Layın/ *n* aslan
lip /lip/ *n* dudak
lipstick /'Lip,stik/ *n* ruj
liqueur /Li'kÖr/ *n* likör
liquid /'Likwid/ *adj, n* sıvı
liquor /'Likır/ *n* içki
liquorice /'Likıris/ *nBr* meyankökü
list /List/ *n* liste; *v* listeye yazmak; liste halinde yazmak
listen /'Lisın/ *v* dinlemek
listener /'Lisınır/ *n* dinleyici
liter /'Liitır/ *n* litre
literacy /'Litırısii/ *n* okuryazarlık
literary /'Litı,rerii/ *adj* edebi
literature /'Litırıçır/ *n* edebiyat
litter /'Litır/ *n* çöp, döküntü
little /'LitıL/ *adj* küçük; az
live[1] /Liv/ *v* yaşamak; **living room** oturma odası
live[2] /Layv/ *adj* canlı
livelihood /'LayvLii,hud/ *n* geçim, geçinme
lively /'LayvLii/ *adj* canlı, neşeli; parlak
liver /'Livır/ *n* karaciğer
lizard /'Lizırd/ *n* kertenkele
load /Loud/ *n* yük; *v* yüklemek
loaf /Louf/ *n* (pl loaves) somun (ekmek)
loan /Loun/ *n* ödünç verilen şey; *v* ödünç vermek
lobby /'LObii/ *n* koridor; antre; lobi
lobster /'LObstır/ *n* ıstakoz
local /'LoukıL/ *adj* yerel; ~ **call** şehir içi telefon görüşmesi; ~ **train** banliyö treni
locality /Lou'kELıtii/ *n* yer, yöre
locate /'Loukeyt/ *v* yerleştirmek; yerini bulmak
location /Lou'keyşın/ *n* yer, mahal
lock /LOk/ *v* kilitlemek; *n* lüle, bukle; kilit; ~ **up** kilit altında saklamak
locker /'LOkır/ *n* kilitli çekmece *veya* dolap
lockout /'LOk,aut/ *n* lokavt, iş kapatma
locomotive /,Loukı'moutiv/ *n* lokomotif
locust /'Loukıst/ *n* çekirge
lodge /LOc/ *v* geçici olarak yer vermek; *n* kapıcı *veya* bahçıvan evi
lodger /'LOcır/ *n* pansiyoner
lodgings /'LOciNz/ *pl* pansiyon
log /LOg/ *n* kütük
logic /'LOcik/ *n* mantık
logical /'LOcikıL/ *adj* mantıki
lonely /'LounLii/ *adj* yalnız
long /LOON/ *adj* uzun; ~ **for** özlemek, arzulamak; **no longer** artık değil
long-distance /'LOON'distıns/ *adj* uzun mesafeli; şehirlerarası
longing /'LOONiN/ *n* arzu
longitude /'LONci,tuud/ *n* boylam
look /Luk/ *v* bakmak; görünmek; *n* bakış, görünüş; ~ **after** ilgilenmek, bakmak; ~ **at** bakmak; ~ **for** aramak; ~ **like** benzemek; ~ **out** dikkat etmek; ~ **up** aramak; **looking glass** ayna
loop /Luup/ *n* ilmik
loose /Luus/ *adj* gevşek
loosen /'Luusın/ *v* gevşetmek
lord /LOOrd/ *n* efendi; **Lord** Tanrı
lorry /'LOOrii/ *nBr* kamyon
***lose** /Luuz/ *v* kaybetmek
loss /LOs/ *n* kayıp
lost /LOst/ *adj* kayıp; ~ **and found**

kayıp eşya; ~ **property office** kayıp eşya bürosu
lot /LOt/ *n* kura, piyango; kısmet; arsa
lotion /'Louşın/ *n* losyon; **aftershave** ~ tıraş losyonu
lottery /'LOtırii/ *n* piyango
loud /Laud/ *adj* yüksek (ses)
loudspeaker /'Laud,spiikır/ *n* hoparlör
lounge /Launc/ *n* hol, salon
louse /Laus/ *n* (pl lice) bit
love /LAv/ *v* sevmek; *n* sevgi, aşk; **in** ~ aşık
lovely /'LAvLii/ *adj* güzel, hoş
lover /'LAvır/ *n* sevgili
low /Lou/ *adj* alçak; karamsar, üzgün; ~ **tide** denizin alçalması
lower /'Louır/ *v* indirmek; *adj* aşağı, alt
loyal /'LOyıL/ *adj* sadık
lubricate /'Luubri,keyt/ *v* yağlamak
lubrication /,Luubri'keyşın/ *n* yağlama; ~ **oil** araba yağı; ~ **system** yağlama sistemi
luck /LAk/ *n* şans, talih; **bad** ~ kötü şans
lucky /'LAkii/ *adj* şanslı; ~ **charm** nazarlık, uğur
ludicrous /'Luudıkrıs/ *adj* gülünç
luggage /'LAgic/ *n* yolcu eşyası, bagaj; **hand** ~ el bagajı; **left** ~ **office** *Br* (bagaj) emanet bürosu; ~ **rack** bagaj rafı; ~ **van** *Br* eşya vagonu
lukewarm /'Luuk,wOOrm/ *adj* ılık; kayıtsız, ilgisiz
lullaby /'LALı,bay/ *n* ninni
lumbago /LAm'beygou/ *n* bel ağrısı
luminous /'Luumınıs/ *adj* parlak, aydınlık
lump /LAmp/ *n* parça; topak; ~ **of sugar** şeker parçası
lumpy /'LAmpii/ *adj* pıhtılı, topaklı
lunacy /'Luunısii/ *n* cinnet, delilik
lunatic /'Luunıtik/ *adj* deli; *n* deli kimse, akıl hastası
lunch /LAnç/ *n* öğle yemeği
luncheon /'LAnçın/ *n* hafif öğle yemeği
lung /LAN/ *n* akciğer
lust /LAst/ *n* şehvet
luxurious /LAg'juuriyıs/ *adj* lüks, konforlu
luxury /'LAkşırii/ *n* lüks; çok zevk veren şey

M

ma'am /mEm/ *n* madam, hanımefendi
machine /mı'şiin/ *n* makine, alet
machinery /mı'şiinırii/ *n* makineler; mekanizma
mackerel /'mEkırıL/ *n* (pl ~) uskumru
mad /mEd/ *adj* deli
madam /'mEdım/ *n* bayan
madness /'mEdnıs/ *n* delilik
magazine /,mEgı'ziin/ *n* dergi
magic /'mEcik/ *n* büyü; *adj* büyülü
magician /mı'cişın/ *n* sihirbaz, büyücü
magistrate /'mEcis,treyt/ *n* sulh hâkimi
magnet /'mEgnit/ *n* mıknatıs
magnetic /mEg'netik/ *adj* mıknatıslı; çekici
magnificent /mEg'nifısınt/ *adj* görkemli, muhteşem
magnolia /mEg'nouLyı/ *n* manolya
magpie /'mEgpay/ *n* saksağan
maid /meyd/ *n* kız; kadın hizmetçi
maiden name /'meydın ,neym/ kızlık soyadı
mail /meyL/ *n* posta; v posta ile göndermek; ~ **order** *Am* posta ile gönderilen sipariş
mailbox /'meyL,bOks/ *nAm* posta

kutusu
main /meyn/ *adj* ana, belli başlı, önemli; ~ **deck** ana güverte; ~ **line** ana hat; ~ **road** anayol; ~ **street** ana cadde
mainland /'meyn,LEnd/ *n* anakara
mainly /'meynLii/ *adv* başlıca
mains /meynz/ *pl* şebeke, ana hat (su, gaz, elektrik)
maintain /meyn'teyn/ *v* sürdürmek; korumak
maintenance /'meyntınıns/ *n* bakım; nafaka
maize /meyz/ *n* mısır
major /'meycır/ *adj* büyük; *n* binbaşı
majority /mı'cOrıtii/ *n* çoğunluk
***make** /meyk/ *v* yapmak, etmek, kılmak; kazanmak, başarmak; ~ **do with** ile yetinmek, idare etmek; ~ **good** telafi etmek; ~ **up** uydurmak; telafi etmek
make-up /'meyk,Ap/ *n* makyaj
malaria /mı'Leyriyı/ *n* sıtma
Malay /mı'Ley/ *n* Malezyalı
Malaysia /mı'Leyjı/ Malezya
Malaysian /mı'Leyjın/ *adj* Malezya'ya ait
male /meyL/ *adj* erkek
malicious /mı'Lişıs/ *adj* kötü, hain; kindar
malignant /mı'Lignınt/ *adj* kötü; habis (tümör); vahim, öldürücü
mall /mOOL/ *n* alışveriş merkezi
mallet /'mELit/ *n* tokmak, tokaç
malnutrition /,mELnuu'trişın/ *n* gıdasızlık; fena beslenme
malpractice /mEL'prEktis/ *n* yolsuzluk; doktorun yanlış tedavisi *veya* ihmali
mammal /'mEmıL/ *n* memeli hayvan
mammoth /'mEmıT/ *n* mamut; *adj* dev gibi, kocaman
man /mEn/ *n* (pl men) adam, insan, erkek; **men's room** erkek tuvaleti
manage /'mEnic/ *v* yönetmek; çekip çevirmek; becermek
manageable /'mEnicıbıL/ *adj* yönetilebilir; kullanışlı
management /'mEnicmınt/ *n* yönetim; müdürlük
manager /'mEnicır/ *n* müdür, yönetici
mandarin /'mEndırin/ *n* mandalina
mandate /'mEndeyt/ *n* emir; vekillik; manda
maneuver /mı'nuuvır/ *n* manevra; *v* manevra yapmak
manger /'meyncır/ *n* yemlik
mania /'meyniyı/ *n* tutku; cinnet
manicure /'mEni,kyuur/ *n* manikür; *v* manikür yapmak
mankind /'mEn,kaynd/ *n* insanlık, insanoğlu
mannequin /'mEnikin/ *n* manken
manner /'mEnır/ *n* tavır; yöntem, yol; **manners** *pl* görgü, terbiye
man-of-war /,mEnıv'wOOr/ *n* harp gemisi
manor house /'mEnır ,haus/ malikâne sahibinin köşkü
mansion /'mEnşın/ *n* büyük konak
manual /'mEnyuuıL/ *adj* elle yapılan *veya* idare edilen; *n* elkitabı
manufacture /,mEnyı'fEkçır/ *v* yapmak, imal etmek
manufacturer /,mEnyı'fEkçırır/ *n* fabrikatör, imalatçı
manure /mı'nuur/ *n* gübre
manuscript /'mEnyı,skript/ *n* yazma; el yazması; müsvedde
many /'menii/ *adj* çok
map /mEp/ *n* harita
maple /'meypıL/ *n* akçaağaç
marble /'maarbıL/ *n* mermer; bilye
March /maarç/ mart
march /maarç/ *v* yürümek; *n* askeri yürüyüş
mare /meyr/ *n* kısrak

margarine /'maarcırin/ *n* margarin
margin /'maarcin/ *n* kenar; sayfa kenarındaki boşluk; pay
marijuana /ˌmErı'waanı/ *n* haşiş, esrar
marine /mı'riin/ *adj* denizsel; deniz kuvvetlerine ait; *n* deniz kuvvetleri mensubu
maritime /'mErıˌtaym/ *adj* denizciliğe ait
mark /maark/ *v* işaret koymak, belirtmek; *n* işaret, belirti; marka
market /'maarkit/ *n* çarşı, pazar
marketplace /'maarkitˌpLeys/ *n* pazar yeri
marmalade /'maarmıˌLeyd/ *n* marmelat
maroon /mı'ruun/ *adj* kestane rengi
marriage /'mEric/ *n* evlilik
marrow /'mErou/ *n* ilik; öz
marry /'mErii/ *v* evlenmek;
married couple evli çift
marsh /maarş/ *n* bataklık
marshy /'maarşii/ *adj* bataklık gibi, bataklı
martyr /'maartır/ *n* şehit
marvel /'maarvıL/ *n* şaşılacak şey; mucize; *v* şaşmak
marvelous /'maarvıLıs/ *adj* olağanüstü, şaşırtıcı
mascara /mEs'kErı/ *n* kirpik boyası, rimel
masculine /'mEskyıLin/ *adj* erkek cinsine ait; erkeksi; eril
mash /mEş/ *v* ezmek
mask /mEsk/ *n* maske
Mass /mEs/ *n* dini ayin
mass /mEs/ *n* kütle, yığın;
~ **production** seri üretim
massage /mı'saaj/ *n* masaj; *v* masaj yapmak
masseur /mı'sÖr/ *n* masör, masajcı
massive /'mEsiv/ *adj* ağır ve kalın
mast /mEst/ *n* gemi direği
master /'mEstır/ *n* sahip; efendi; üstat; öğretmen; *v* zapt etmek, yenmek; iyice öğrenmek, hâkim olmak
masterpiece /'mEstırˌpiis/ *n* başyapıt
mat /mEt/ *n* paspas; *adj* donuk, mat
match /mEç/ *n* kibrit; maç; *v* birbirine uydurmak; uymak
matchbox /'mEçˌbOks/ *n* kibrit kutusu
material /mı'tiiriyıL/ *n* madde; kumaş; *adj* maddi, fiziksel
mathematical /ˌmETı'mEtikıL/ *adj* matematiksel
mathematics /ˌmETı'mEtiks/ *n* matematik
matrimonial /ˌmEtri'mouniyıL/ *adj* evliliğe ait
matrimony /'mEtriˌmounii/ *n* evlilik
matter /'mEtır/ *n* madde, sorun, konu; *v* önemi olmak;
as a ~ of fact doğrusu, zaten
mattress /'mEtrıs/ *n* yatak
mature /mı'çuur/ *adj* olgun
maturity /mı'çuurıtii/ *n* olgunluk
mausoleum /ˌmOOsı'Liiyım/ *n* türbe, anıtkabir
mauve /mouv/ *adj* açık mor
maximum /'mEksımım/ *n* en yüksek derece, en büyük miktar
May /mey/ mayıs
***may** /mey/ *v* yapabilmek
maybe /'meybii/ *adv* belki
mayor /'meyır/ *n* belediye başkanı
maze /meyz/ *n* labirent
me /mii/ *pron* beni, bana
meadow /'medou/ *n* çayır, otlak
meal /miiL/ *n* yemek, öğün
mean /miin/ *n* orta; *adj* cimri
***mean** /miin/ *v* demek istemek; anlamı olmak
meaning /'miiniN/ *n* anlam
meaningless /'miiniNLıs/ *adj* anlamsız
means /miinz/ *n* vasıta;

by no ~ katiyen, hiçbir surette
in the meantime /in Dı 'miintaym/ bu arada, bu zaman zarfında
meanwhile /'miin,hwayL/ *adv* bu arada
measles /'miizıLz/ *n* kızamık
measure /'mejır/ *v* ölçmek; *n* ölçü; önlem
meat /miit/ *n* et
mechanic /mı'kEnik/ *n* makine ustası *veya* tamircisi
mechanical /mı'kEnikıL/ *adj* mekanik
mechanism /'mekı,nizım/ *n* mekanizma
medal /'medıL/ *n* madalya
media /'miidiyı/ *pl* vasıtalar, araçlar; **mass ~** yayın araçları, medya
mediate /'miidi,yeyt/ *v* aracı olmak, araya girmek
mediator /'miidi,yeytır/ *n* aracı
medical /'medikıL/ *adj* tıbbi
medicine /'medısin/ *n* ilaç; tıp
medieval /,miidi'iivıL/ *adj* orta çağlara ait
meditate /'medı,teyt/ *v* düşünceye dalmak
meditation /,medı'teyşın/ *n* düşünceye dalma
Mediterranean /,medití'reyniyın/ Akdeniz
medium /'miidiyım/ *adj* orta; *n* araç; ortam
meerschaum /'miirşım/ *n* eskişehirtaşı, lületaşı
***meet** /miit/ *v* rastlamak; buluşmak, bir araya gelmek
meeting /'miitiN/ *n* toplantı; **~ place** buluşma yeri
melancholy /'meLıN,kOLii/ *n* karasevda, hüzün, gam
mellow /'meLou/ *adj* olgun, yumuşak
melodrama /'meLı,draamı/ *n* heyecanlı, acıklı tiyatro oyunu
melody /'meLıdii/ *n* ezgi, nağme
melon /'meLın/ *n* kavun
melt /meLt/ *v* eritmek; erimek
member /'membır/ *n* üye; **Member of Parliament** milletvekili
membership /'membır,şip/ *n* üyelik
memo /'memou/ *n* (pl ~s) hatırlatıcı not
memorable /'memırıbıL/ *adj* unutulmaz
memorial /mı'mOOriyıL/ *n* anıt
memorize /'memı,rayz/ *v* ezberlemek
memory /'memırii/ *n* anı; bellek
mend /mend/ *v* onarmak
meningitis /,menin'caytis/ *n* menenjit
menstruation /,menstru'eyşın/ *n* aybaşı kanaması
mental /'mentıL/ *adj* zihni, akla ait
mentality /men'tELıtii/ *n* zihniyet, düşünüş
mention /'menşın/ *v* sözünü etmek; *n* anma, konu etme
menu /'menyuu/ *n* yemek listesi
merchandise /'mÖrçın,dayz/ *n* mal, ticaret eşyası
merchant /'mÖrçınt/ *n* tüccar
merciful /'mÖrsifıL/ *adj* merhametli
mercury /'mÖrkyırii/ *n* cıva
mercy /'mÖrsii/ *n* merhamet, acıma
mere /miir/ *adj* saf, sırf
merely /'miirLii/ *adv* yalnızca, sadece
merger /'mÖrcır/ *n* birleşme
merit /'merit/ *v* hak etmek; değmek; *n* değer
mermaid /'mÖr,meyd/ *n* denizkızı
merry /'merii/ *adj* şen, neşeli
merry-go-round /'meriigou,raund/ *n* atlıkarınca
mess /mes/ *n* karışıklık, dağınıklık; **~ up** karmakarışık etmek
message /'mesic/ *n* haber, mesaj
messenger /'mesıncır/ *n* haberci
metal /'metıL/ *n* maden, metal; *adj* madeni
meter /'miitır/ *n* sayaç; metre
method /'meTıd/ *n* yöntem; düzen

methodical /mı'TOdikıL/ *adj* düzenli, usule uygun
metric /'metrik/ *adj* metre birimine göre
Mexican /'meksikın/ *adj* Meksika'ya ait; *n* Meksikalı
Mexico /'meksi,kou/ Meksika
mezzanine /'mezı,niin/ *n* asmakat, ara kat
microphone /'maykrı,foun/ *n* mikrofon
midday /'mid,dey/ *n* öğle üzeri
middle /'midıL/ *adj* orta, ortadaki; **Middle Ages** Orta Çağ; ~ **class** orta sınıf
midnight /'mid,nayt/ *n* gece yarısı
midst /midst/ *n* orta
midsummer /'mid,sAmır/ *n* yaz ortası
midwife /'mid,wayf/ *n* ebe
might /mayt/ *n* güç, kudret
***might** /mayt/ *v* yapabilmek
mighty /'maytii/ *adj* güçlü
mild /mayLd/ *adj* yumuşak; ılımlı
mildew /'miL,dyuu/ *n* bitki küfü
mile /mayL/ *n* mil
mileage /'mayLic/ *n* mil hesabıyla uzaklık
milepost /'mayL,poust/ *n* mil işaret direği
milestone /'mayL,stoun/ *n* mil taşı; dönüm noktası
milieu /miiL'yuu/ *n* çevre, ortam
military /'miLı,terii/ *adj* askeri; ~ **force** silahlı kuvvetler
milk /miLk/ *n* süt; ~ **shake** dondurma ve şurupla karıştırılıp çalkalanmış süt
milkman /'miLk,mEn/ *n* sütçü
milky /'miLkii/ *adj* sütlü; **Milky Way** Samanyolu
mill /miL/ *n* değirmen; fabrika
miller /'miLır/ *n* değirmenci
million /'miLyın/ *n* milyon
millionaire /,miLyı'neyr/ *n* milyoner
minaret /,minı'ret/ *n* minare
mince /mins/ *v* kıymak
mind /maynd/ *n* akıl, zihin; *v* dikkat etmek, bakmak; aldırış etmek
mine[1] /mayn/ *n* maden ocağı
mine[2] /mayn/ *pron* benim, benimki
miner /'maynır/ *n* madenci
mineral /'minırıL/ *n* maden, mineral; ~ **water** maden suyu
miniature /'minyıçır/ *n* minyatür; *adj* küçücük
minimum /'minımım/ *n* en küçük miktar, en düşük derece
mining /'mayniN/ *n* madencilik
minister /'ministır/ *n* bakan; papaz; **Prime Minister** başbakan
ministry /'ministrii/ *n* bakanlık
mink /miNk/ *n* vizon
minor /'maynır/ *adj* nispeten küçük *veya* önemsiz; *n* ergin olmayan çocuk
minority /mı'nOOrıtii/ *n* azınlık
mint /mint/ *n* nane; darphane
minus /'maynıs/ *prep* eksi
minute[1] /'minit/ *n* dakika; **minutes** *pl* tutanak
minute[2] /may'nuut/ *adj* çok ufak; çok ince
miracle /'mirıkıL/ *n* mucize, harika
miraculous /mi'rEkyıLıs/ *adj* harikulade
mirror /'mirır/ *n* ayna
misbehave /,misbi'heyv/ *v* yaramazlık etmek; fena hareket etmek
miscarriage /mis'kEric/ *n* çocuk düşürme
miscellaneous /,misı'Leyniyıs/ *adj* çeşitli, türlü türlü
mischief /'mis,çif/ *n* yaramazlık; kötülük; zarar
mischievous /'misçıvıs/ *adj* yaramaz, arabozucu; zararlı
miser /'mayzır/ *n* cimri kimse
miserable /'mizırıbıL/ *adj* dertli; sefil;

berbat
miserly /'mayzırLii/ *adj* cimri, hasis
misery /'mizırii/ *n* sefalet; acı
misfortune /mis'fOOrçın/ *n* talihsizlik
***mislay** /mis'Ley/ *v* hatırlanmayan bir yere koymak; kaybetmek
***mislead** /mis'Liid/ *v* yanlış yola yöneltmek
misplaced /mis'pLeyst/ *adj* yanlış bir yere konmuş
mispronounce /ˌmisprı'nauns/ *v* yanlış telaffuz etmek
miss[1] /mis/ bayan (evlenmemiş hanımlar için)
miss[2] /mis/ *v* isabet ettirememek; kaçırmak; özlemek
missile /'misıL/ *n* mermi; füze, roket
missing /'misiN/ *adj* eksik; ~ **person** kayıp kişi
mission /'mişın/ *n* memuriyet, görev; *nAm* elçilik
mist /mist/ *n* sis; buğu
mistake /mis'teyk/ *n* yanlışlık, hata
***mistake** /mis'teyk/ *v* yanlış anlamak, yanlış görmek
mistaken /mis'teykın/ *adj* hatalı, yanlış; ***be** ~ yanılmak
mister /'mistır/ bay, beyefendi
mistress /'mistrıs/ *n* evin hanımı; öğretmen; metres
mistrust /mis'trAst/ *v* güvenmemek
misty /'mistii/ *adj* sisli
***misunderstand** /ˌmisAndır'stEnd/ *v* yanlış anlamak
misunderstanding /ˌmisAndır'stEndiN/ *n* yanlış anlama
misuse /mis'yuus/ *n* yanlış kullanma, hor kullanma
mittens /'mitınz/ *pl* parmaksız eldiven
mix /miks/ *v* karıştırmak; ~ **with** ilişki kurmak, arasına karışmak
mixed /mikst/ *adj* karışık
mixer /'miksır/ *n* mikser, karıştırıcı
mixture /'miksçır/ *n* karışım
moan /moun/ *v* inlemek
mob /mOb/ *n* kalabalık; ayaktakımı
mobile /'moubıL/ *adj* hareketli
mobilization /ˌmoubıLi'zeyşın/ *n* seferberlik
mock /mOk/ *v* alay etmek
mockery /'mOkırii/ *n* alay
model /'mOdıL/ *n* model, örnek; manken; *v* örneğe göre yapmak
moderate /'mOdırıt/ *adj* ılımlı, orta
modern /'mOdırn/ *adj* modern, çağdaş
modest /'mOdist/ *adj* alçakgönüllü
modesty /'mOdistii/ *n* alçakgönüllülük
modify /'mOdiiˌfay/ *v* biraz değiştirmek
mohair /'mouˌheyr/ *n* tiftik, moher
moist /mOyst/ *adj* yaş, nemli
moisten /'mOysın/ *v* hafifçe ıslatmak; nemlenmek
moisture /'mOysçır/ *n* nem, ıslaklık; **moisturizing cream** nemlendirici krem
molar /'mouLır/ *n* azıdişi
mold /mouLd/ *n* küf; kalıp; *v* küflenmek; biçimlendirmek; kalıba dökmek
moldy /'mouLdii/ *adj* küflü
mole /mouL/ *n* köstebek; ben
mom /mOm/ *n* anne, anneciğim
moment /'moumınt/ *n* an
momentary /'moumınˌterii/ *adj* bir anlık; geçici
monarch /'mOnırk/ *n* hükümdar, kral
monarchy /'mOnırkii/ *n* krallık, monarşi
monastery /'mOnısˌterii/ *n* manastır
Monday /'mAndii/ pazartesi
monetary /'mOnıˌterii/ *adj* paraya ait, nakdi; ~ **unit** para birimi
money /'mAnii/ *n* para; ~ **exchange** döviz büfesi; ~ **order** para havalesi

monk /mANk/ *n* keşiş, rahip
monkey /'mANkii/ *n* maymun
monologue /'mOnı,LOOg/ *n* monolog
monopoly /mı'nOpıLii/ *n* tekel
monotonous /mı'nOtınıs/ *adj* yeknesak, tekdüze
monster /'mOnstır/ *n* canavar
monstrous /'mOnstrıs/ *adj* korkunç; kocaman
month /mAnT/ *n* ay
monthly /'mAnTLii/ *adj* aylık; ~ **magazine** aylık dergi
monument /'mOnyımınt/ *n* anıt
mood /muud/ *n* ruh durumu, keyif
moon /muun/ *n* ay
moonlight /'muun,Layt/ *n* ay ışığı, mehtap
moose /muus/ *n* (pl ~, ~s) çok iri ve yassı boynuzlu bir geyik
moped /'mouped/ *n* motorlu bisiklet
moral /'mOOrıL/ *n* ahlak dersi; *adj* ahlaki, doğru; **morals** *pl* ahlak
morale /mı'rEL/ *n* moral, maneviyat
morality /mı'rELıtii/ *n* ahlak ilmi
more /mOOr/ *adj* daha çok; **once** ~ bir kez daha
moreover /mOOr'ouvır/ *adv* ayrıca, bundan başka, üstelik
morning /'mOOrniN/ *n* sabah; ~ **paper** sabah gazetesi
Moroccan /mı'rOkın/ *adj* Fas'a ait; *n* Faslı
Morocco /mı'rOkou/ Fas
morphine /'mOOrfiin/ *n* morfin
morsel /'mOOrsıL/ *n* parça, lokma
mortal /'mOOrtıL/ *adj* öldürücü; ölümlü
mortgage /'mOOrgic/ *n* ipotek
mosaic /mou'zeyik/ *n* mozaik
Moscow /'mOskau/ Moskova
Moslem /'mOzLım/ *n* Müslüman; *adj* Müslüman
mosque /mOsk/ *n* cami
mosquito /mıs'kiitou/ *n* (pl ~es) sivrisinek; ~ **net** cibinlik
moss /mOs/ *n* yosun
most /moust/ *adj* en çok; **at** ~ en fazla, olsa olsa; ~ **of all** özellikle
mostly /'moustLii/ *adv* genellikle, çok defa
motel /mou'teL/ *n* motel
moth /mOT/ *n* pervane; güve
mother /'mADır/ *n* anne; ~ **tongue** anadili
mother-in-law /'mADırin,LOO/ *n* (pl mothers-) kayınvalide
mother-of-pearl /,mADırıv'pÖrL/ *n* sedef
motion /'mouşın/ *n* hareket; teklif
motivate /'moutı,veyt/ *v* harekete getirmek; motive etmek
motive /'moutiv/ *n* güdü, gerekçe
motor /'moutır/ *n* motor; *v* otomobille gitmek; ~ **body** *Am* karoser; ~ **starter** motoru çalıştırmaya yarayan aygıt
motorbike /'moutır,bayk/ *n* motosiklet
motorboat /'moutır,bout/ *n* deniz motoru
motorcar /'moutır,kaar/ *nBr* otomobil
motorcycle /'moutır,saykıL/ *n* motosiklet
motoring /'moutıriN/ *n* otomobilcilik; araba sürme
motorist /'moutırist/ *n* sürücü; otomobil kullanan kimse
motorway /'moutır,wey/ *nBr* ekspres yol, otoyol
motto /'mOtou/ *n* (pl ~es, ~s) parola; düstur
mound /maund/ *n* küme; tepecik
mount /maunt/ *v* binmek; takmak; *n* dağ, tepe
mountain /'mauntın/ *n* dağ; ~ **pass** dağ geçidi; ~ **range** dağ silsilesi
mountaineering /,mauntı'niiriN/ *n* dağcılık

mountainous /'mauntınıs/ *adj* dağlık
mourning /'mOOrniN/ *n* yas
mouse /maus/ *n* (pl mice) fındık faresi
mouth /mauT/ *n* ağız
mouthwash /'mauT,wOOş/ *n* gargara
movable /'muuvıbıL/ *adj* hareket edebilen
move /muuv/ *v* kımıldatmak, yerinden oynatmak; kımıldamak; etkilemek; *n* hareket; tedbir; taşınma
movement /'muuvmınt/ *n* hareket, kımıldanış
movie /'muuvii/ *nAm* film; **movies** *pl* sinema; ~ **theater** sinema binası
much /mAç/ *adj* çok; *adv* fazla; **as** ~ kadar fazla
muck /mAk/ *n* gübre; pislik
mud /mAd/ *n* çamur
muddle /'mAdıL/ *n* karışıklık; şaşkınlık; *v* karıştırmak, yüzüne gözüne bulaştırmak
muddy /'mAdii/ *adj* çamurlu
mudguard /'mAd,gaard/ *n* çamurluk
muffler /'mAfLır/ *nAm* susturucu
mug /mAg/ *n* maşrapa, büyük bardak
mulberry /'mAL,berii/ *n* dut
mule /myuuL/ *n* katır; inatçı adam
mullet /'mALit/ *n* bir tür kefal
multiplication /,mALtıpLi'keyşın/ *n* çoğaltma; çarpma; ~ **table** çarpım tablosu
multiply /'mALtı,pLay/ *v* çarpmak; çoğaltmak
mumps /mAmps/ *n* kabakulak
municipal /myuu'nisıpıL/ *adj* belediyeye ait
municipality /myuu,nisı'pELıtii/ *n* belediye
murder /'mÖrdır/ *n* cinayet, *v* katletmek
murderer /'mÖrdırır/ *n* katil
muscle /'mAsıL/ *n* kas
muscular /'mAskyıLır/ *adj* kaslı
museum /myuu'ziyım/ *n* müze
mushroom /'mAş,ruum/ *n* mantar
music /'myuuzik/ *n* müzik; ~ **academy** konservatuvar; ~ **hall** konser salonu
musical /'myuuzikıL/ *adj* müzikli; *n* müzikli oyun
musician /myuu'zişın/ *n* müzisyen
muslin /'mAzLin/ *n* ince dokunmuş pamuklu kumaş, muslin
mussel /'mAsıL/ *n* midye
***must** /mAst/ *v* gerekmek; mecbur olmak
mustache /'mAs,tEş/ *n* bıyık
mustard /'mAstırd/ *n* hardal
mute /myuut/ *adj* dilsiz; sessiz
mutiny /'myuutınii/ *n* isyan, ayaklanma
mutton /'mAtın/ *n* koyun eti
mutual /'myuuçuuıL/ *adj* karşılıklı; ortak
my /may/ *adj* benim
myself /may'seLf/ *pron* ben, kendim, bizzat
mysterious /mis'tiiriyıs/ *adj* esrarengiz, gizemli
mystery /'mistırii/ *n* gizem, sır
myth /miT/ *n* efsane, mit; hayali kimse *veya* şey

N

nail /neyL/ *n* tırnak; çivi; ~ **brush** tırnak fırçası; ~ **file** tırnak törpüsü; ~ **polish** tırnak cilası; ~ **scissors** tırnak makası
naive /naa'iiv/ *adj* saf
naked /'neykid/ *adj* çıplak
name /neym/ *n* ad; *v* ad vermek;

in the ~ of adına
namely /'neymLii/ *adv* yani, şöyle ki
nap /nEp/ *n* kısa uyku, şekerleme
napkin /'nEpkin/ *n* peçete
Naples /'neypıLz/ Napoli
nappy /'nEpii/ *nBr* çocuk bezi
narcosis /naar'kousis/ *n* (pl -ses) narkoz
narcotic /naar'kOtik/ *n* narkotik, uyuşturucu
narrow /'nErou/ *adj* dar; sınırlı
narrow-minded /'nErou'mayndid/ *adj* dar görüşlü
nasty /'nEstii/ *adj* pis, hoşa gitmeyen, iğrenç
nation /'neyşın/ *n* ulus, millet
national /'nEşınıL/ *adj* ulusal, milli; **~ anthem** milli marş; **~ dress** milli kıyafet; **~ park** milli park
nationality /,nEşı'nELıtii/ *n* milliyet; uyrukluk
nationalize /'nEşını,Layz/ *v* millileştirmek
native /'neytiv/ *n* yerli; *adj* yerli, doğal; **~ country** anavatan; **~ language** anadil
natural /'nEçırıL/ *adj* doğal; doğuştan
naturally /'nEçırıLii/ *adv* doğal olarak
nature /'neyçır/ *n* doğa, tabiat
naughty /'nOOtii/ *adj* yaramaz, huysuz
nausea /'nOOziyı/ *n* bulantı; iğrenme
naval /'neyvıL/ *adj* savaş gemilerine *veya* denize ait
navel /'neyvıL/ *n* göbek
navigable /'nEvigıbıL/ *adj* deniz trafiğine elverişli
navigate /'nEvi,geyt/ *v* gemi yolculuğu yapmak
navigation /,nEvi'geyşın/ *n* deniz seferi
navy /'neyvii/ *n* deniz kuvvetleri
near /niir/ *prep* yakınında; *adj* yakın
nearby /'niir'bay/ *adj* yakın, yakındaki
nearly /'niirLii/ *adv* hemen hemen
neat /niit/ *adj* temiz, düzenli, zarif
necessary /'nesı,serii/ *adj* gerekli
necessity /nı'sesıtii/ *n* ihtiyaç, zorunluluk
neck /nek/ *n* boyun; **nape of the ~** ense
necklace /'nekLıs/ *n* kolye
necktie /'nek,tay/ *n* kravat
need /niid/ *v* muhtaç olmak, gereksinmek; *n* ihtiyaç, lüzum; **~ to** gerekmek
needle /'niidıL/ *n* iğne
needlework /'niidıL,wÖrk/ *n* iğne işi
negative /'negıtiv/ *adj* olumsuz
neglect /nig'Lekt/ *v* ihmal etmek; *n* ihmal
neglectful /nig'LektfıL/ *adj* ihmalkâr
negotiate /ni'gouşi,yeyt/ *v* müzakere etmek
negotiation /ni,gouşi'yeyşın/ *n* müzakere, görüşme
negro /'niigrou/ *n* (pl ~es) zenci
neighbor /'neybır/ *n* komşu
neighborhood /'neybır,hud/ *n* komşu; yakın, bitişik
neighboring /'neybıriN/ *adj* çevre, mahalle; komşular
neither /'niiDır/ *pron* ne bu, ne öteki; **neither . . . nor** ne . . . ne de
neon /'niiyOn/ *n* neon
nephew /'nefyuu/ *n* erkek yeğen
nerve /nÖrv/ *n* sinir
nervous /'nÖrvıs/ *adj* sinirli, tedirgin
nest /nest/ *n* yuva
net /net/ *n* ağ; *adj* net, safi
the Netherlands /'neDırLındz/ Hollanda
network /'netwÖrk/ *n* şebeke, ağ
neuralgia /nuu'rELcı/ *n* nevralji
neurosis /nuu'rousis/ *n* nevroz
neuter /'nuutır/ *adj* cinsiyetsiz, nötr
neutral /'nuutrıL/ *adj* tarafsız
never /'nevır/ *adv* asla, hiçbir zaman

nevertheless /ˌnevırDı'Les/ *adv* bununla beraber
new /nuu/ *adj* yeni; **New Year** yeni yıl
news /nuuz/ *n* haber; ~ **agency** haber ajansı
newsagent /'nuuzˌeycınt/ *nBr* bayi, gazeteci dükkânı
newspaper /'nuuzˌpeypır/ *n* gazete
newsreel /'nuuzˌriiL/ *n* aktüalite filmi
newsstand /'nuuzˌstEnd/ *n* gazete tezgâhı
New Zealand /ˌnuu 'ziiLınd/ Yeni Zelanda
next /nekst/ *adj* en yakın, sonraki; gelecek; ~ **door** bitişik; ~ **to** bitişik, hemen sonra
nice /nays/ *adj* hoş, sevimli; nazik
nickel /'nikıL/ *n* nikel; 5 cent'lik ABD parası
nickname /'nikˌneym/ *n* takma ad, lakap
nicotine /'nikıˌtiin/ *n* nikotin
niece /niis/ *n* kız yeğen
Nigeria /nay'ciiriyı/ Nijerya
Nigerian /nay'ciiriyın/ *adj* Nijerya'ya ait; *n* Nijeryalı
night /nayt/ *n* gece; **by** ~ geceleyin; ~ **cream** gece kremi; ~ **flight** gece uçuşu; ~ **rate** gece tarifesi; ~ **train** gece treni
nightclub /'naytˌkLAb/ *n* gece kulübü
nightdress /'naytˌdres/ *n* gecelik
nightingale /'naytiNˌgeyL/ *n* bülbül
nil /niL/ *n* sıfır, hiç
Nile /nayL/ Nil nehri
nine /nayn/ *num* dokuz
nineteen /ˌnayn'tiin/ *num* on dokuz
nineteenth /ˌnayn'tiinT/ *num* on dokuzuncu
ninety /'nayntii/ *num* doksan
ninth /naynT/ *num* dokuzuncu
nitrogen /'naytrıcın/ *n* azot
no /nou/ hayır; *adj* hiç; ~ **one** hiç kimse
nobility /nou'biLıtii/ *n* soyluluk, asalet
noble /'noubıL/ *adj* soylu
nobody /'nouˌbOdii/ *pron* hiç kimse
nod /nOd/ *n* baş sallama; *v* baş sallamak; başla onaylamak *veya* selam vermek
noise /nOyz/ *n* gürültü, patırtı; ses, şamata; parazit
noisy /'nOyzii/ *adj* gürültülü; gürültücü
nomad /'noumEd/ *n* göçebe; *adj* göçebe; göçebeye ait
nominal /'nOmınıL/ *adj* itibari, nominal; adlara ait
nominate /'nOmıˌneyt/ *v* atamak; adaylığa seçmek
nomination /ˌnOmı'neyşın/ *n* aday gösterme; atama
none /nAn/ *pron* hiçbiri, hiç kimse
nonprofit /nOn'prOfit/ *adj* kâr gayesi gütmeyen
nonsense /'nOnsens/ *n* saçma
nonstop /'nOn'stop/ *adj* aralıksız yapılan; *adv* duraklamadan
noon /nuun/ *n* öğle vakti
normal /'nOOrmıL/ *adj* normal
north /nOOrT/ *n* kuzey; **North Pole** Kuzey Kutbu
northeast /ˌnOOrT'iist/ *n* kuzeydoğu
northerly /'nOrDırLii/ *adj* kuzeye ait
northern /'nOOrDırn/ *adj* kuzeye ait
northwest /ˌnOOrT'west/ *n* kuzeybatı
Norway /'nOOrwey/ Norveç
Norwegian /nOOr'wiicın/ *adj* Norveç'e ait; *n* Norveçli; Norveç dili
nose /nouz/ *n* burun
nosebleed /'nouzˌbLiid/ *n* burun kanaması
nostalgia /nOs'tELcı/ *n* geçmişe duyulan özlem; vatan özlemi
nostril /'nOstrıL/ *n* burun deliği
not /nOt/ *adv* değil
notary /'noutırii/ *n* noter

note /nout/ *n* not; nota; *v* kaydetmek; dikkat etmek
notebook /'nout,buk/ *n* defter
noted /'noutid/ *adj* ünlü, seçkin
nothing /'nATiN/ *n* hiçbir şey
notice /'noutis/ *v* farkına varmak; dikkat etmek; *n* duyuru, ilan
noticeable /'noutisıbıL/ *adj* dikkate değer; göze çarpan
notify /'noutı,fay/ *v* haberdar etmek, bildirmek
notion /'nouşın/ *n* fikir; kavram; inanç
notorious /nou'tOOriyıs/ *adj* adı çıkmış, dile düşmüş
nougat /'nuugıt/ *n* kozhelva
nought /nOOt/ *n* sıfır
noun /naun/ *n* isim, ad
nourishing /'nÖrişiN/ *adj* besleyici
novel /'nOvıL/ *n* roman
novelist /'nOvıList/ *n* romancı
November /nou'vembır/ kasım
now /nau/ *adv* şimdi, şu anda; ~ **and then** ara sıra, bazen
nowadays /'nauı,deyz/ *adv* bugünlerde
nowhere /'nou,hweyr/ *adv* hiçbir yerde
nozzle /'nOzıL/ *n* ağızlık; hortum başı
nuance /'nuuaans/ *n* nüans, ince fark
nuclear /'nuukLiyır/ *adj* nükleer; ~ **energy** nükleer enerji
nucleus /'nuukliyıs/ *n* çekirdek, öz
nude /nuud/ *adj, n* çıplak
nuisance /'nuusıns/ *n* sıkıcı kimse *veya* şey, sıkıntı, baş belası
numb /nAm/ *adj* uyuşuk
number /'nAmbır/ *n* sayı, numara
numeral /'nuumırıL/ *n* sayı, rakam
numerous /'nuumırıs/ *adj* birçok, çok sayıda
nun /nAn/ *n* rahibe
nunnery /'nAnırii/ *n* rahibe manastırı
nurse /nÖrs/ *n* hastabakıcı; dadı; *v* hastabakıcılık yapmak; emzirmek
nursery /'nÖrsırii/ *n* çocuk odası; kreş
nut /nAt/ *n* fındık, ceviz; cıvata somunu
nutcrackers /'nAt,krEkırz/ *pl* fındık *veya* ceviz kıracağı
nutmeg /'nAt,meg/ *n* baharat olarak kullanılan kokulu bir tohum
nutritious /nuu'trişıs/ *adj* besleyici
nutshell /'nAt,şeL/ *n* fındık kabuğu
nylon /'nayLOn/ *n* naylon

O

oak /ouk/ *n* meşe ağacı
oar /OOr/ *n* kürek
oasis /ou'eysis/ *n* (pl oases) vaha
oath /ouT/ *n* yemin, ant
oats /outs/ *pl* yulaf
obedience /ou'biidiyıns/ *n* itaat, uysallık
obedient /ou'biidiyınt/ *adj* uysal, söz dinler
obey /ou'bey/ *v* söz dinlemek; uymak
object[1] /'Obcikt/ *n* şey, nesne
object[2] /ıb'cekt/ *v* itiraz etmek; ~ **to** uygun görmemek, karşı çıkmak
objection /ıb'cekşın/ *n* itiraz
objective /ıb'cektiv/ *adj* tarafsız, nesnel; *n* amaç, gaye
obligatory /ı'bLigı,tOOrii/ *adj* zorunlu
oblige /ıb'Layc/ *v* zorunlu kılmak; minnettar bırakmak; ***be obliged to** minnettar olmak; zorunlu olmak
obliging /ıb'LayciN/ *adj* nazik, yardımsever
oblong /Ob'LOON/ *adj* dikdörtgen şeklinde; *n* dikdörtgen

obscene /ıb'siin/ *adj* açık saçık, müstehcen
obscure /ıb'skyuur/ *adj* çapraşık; belirsiz; karanlık
observation /,Obzır'veyşın/ *n* gözetleme; inceleme; gözlem
observatory /ıb'zÖrvı,tOOrii/ *n* gözlem evi
observe /ıb'zÖrv/ *v* gözlemek; incelemek; uymak
obsession /ıb'seşın/ *n* saplantı; sabit fikir
obsolete /,Obsı'Liit/ *adj* kullanılmayan, modası geçmiş
obstacle /'ObstıkıL/ *n* engel, mânia
obstinate /'Obstınıt/ *adj* inatçı, dik kafalı
obtain /ıb'teyn/ *v* elde etmek, sağlamak; kazanmak
obtainable /ıb'teynıbıL/ *adj* bulunabilir, elde edilebilir
obvious /'Obviyıs/ *adj* besbelli, apaçık
occasion /ı'keyjın/ *n* fırsat; vesile; özel olay
occasionally /ı'keyjınıLii/ *adv* ara sıra, bazen
occupant /'Okyı,pınt/ *n* işgal eden kimse
occupation /,Okyı'peyşın/ *n* meslek, iş, sanat
occupy /'Okyıpay/ *v* işgal etmek
occur /ı'kÖr/ *v* olmak, meydana gelmek
occurrence /ı'kÖrıns/ *n* olay
ocean /'ouşın/ *n* okyanus
October /Ok'toubır/ ekim ayı
octopus /'Oktıpıs/ *n* ahtapot
oculist /'OkyıList/ *n* göz doktoru
odd /Od/ *adj* tuhaf; ikiye bölünmeyen, tek
odor /'oudır/ *n* koku
of /ıv, Ov/ *prep* -nın, -lı, -den
off /OOf/ *prep* -den uzak
offend /ı'fend/ *v* gücendirmek
offense /ı'fens/ *n* kabahat: gücendirme; saldırı
offensive /ı'fensiv/ *adj* çirkin, iğrenç; hatır kırıcı; *n* saldırı
offer /'OOfır/ *v* teklif etmek; sunmak; *n* teklif; sunma
office /'OOfis/ *n* büro; ~ **hours** çalışma saatleri
officer /'OOfisır/ *n* subay; memur
official /ı'fişıL/ *adj* resmi
off-licence *nBr* içki satılan dükkân
often /'OOfın/ *adv* çoğu kez, sık sık
oil /OyL/ *n* yağ, sıvı yağ; petrol; **fuel** ~ mazot; ~ **filter** yağ filtresi; ~ **painting** yağlıboya; ~ **refinery** petrol rafinerisi; ~ **well** petrol kuyusu
oily /'OyLii/ *adj* yağlı
ointment /'Oyntmınt/ *n* merhem
OK, okay, okey /,ou'key/ peki, olur, tamam
old /ouLd/ *adj* yaşlı; eski; ~ **age** yaşlılık
old-fashioned /'ouLd'fEşınd/ *adj* modası geçmiş; eski kafalı
olive /'OLiv/ *n* zeytin; ~ **oil** zeytinyağı
omelet /'OmLıt/ *n* omlet
ominous /'Omınıs/ *adj* uğursuz; tehditkâr
omission /ou'mişın/ *n* ihmal, atlama; atlanan şey
omit /ı'mit/ *v* yanlışlıkla unutmak; atlamak
omnipotent /Om'nipıtınt/ *adj* her şeye gücü yeten
on /On/ *prep* üzerinde, üstünde
once /wAns/ *adv* bir kez; bir zamanlar; **at** ~ hemen, derhal; ~ **more** bir kez daha
oncoming /'On,kAmiN/ *adj* yaklaşan, ilerleyen
one /wAn/ *num* bir, tek; *pron* biri,

herhangi biri
oneself /wAn'seLf/ *pron* kendisi
one-way /'wAn'wey/ *adj* tek yönlü
onion /'Anyın/ *n* soğan
only /'ounLii/ *adj* tek, biricik; *adv* yalnız, ancak
onward /'Onwırd/ *adv* ileri, ileriye doğru
onyx /'Oniks/ *n* damarlı akik, oniks
opal /'oupıL/ *n* opal, panzehirtaşı
open /'oupın/ *v* açmak; *adj* açık; serbest; açık sözlü
opening /'oupıniN/ *n* açılış, başlangıç; açıklık; delik
open-minded /ˌoupın'mayndid/ *adj* açık fikirli
opera /'Opırı/ *n* opera; ~ **house** opera binası
operate /'Opıˌreyt/ *v* işletmek, çalıştırmak; ameliyat etmek
operation /ˌOpı'reyşın/ *n* işletme; çalışma; işlem; ameliyat
operator /'Opıˌreytır/ *n* santral memuru; operatör
operetta /ˌOpı'retı/ *n* operet
opinion /ı'pinyın/ *n* fikir, düşünce, kanı
opium /'oupiyım/ *n* afyon
opponent /ı'pounınt/ *n* muhalif; rakip
opportunity /ˌOpır'çuunıtii/ *n* fırsat, elverişli durum
oppose /ı'pouz/ *v* direnmek, karşı çıkmak; engel olmak
opposite /'Opızit/ *prep* karşısında; *adj* karşı; zıt
opposition /ˌOpı'zişın/ *n* zıtlık; karşı koyma; muhalefet
oppress /ı'pres/ *v* sıkıştırmak, baskı yapmak; zulmetmek
optician /Op'tişın/ *n* gözlükçü
optimism /'Optıˌmizım/ *n* iyimserlik
optimist /'Optımist/ *n* iyimser kimse
optimistic /ˌOptı'mistik/ *adj* iyimser
optional /'OpşınıL/ *adj* isteğe bağlı, seçmeli
or /OOr/ *conj* veya; yoksa
oral /'OOrıL/ *adj* sözlü
orange /'OOrinc/ *n* portakal; *adj* portakal rengi
orbit /'OOrbit/ *n* yörünge
orchard /'OOrçırd/ *n* meyve bahçesi
orchestra /'OOrkistrı/ *n* orkestra; ~ **seat** *Am* sahnede orkestra yeri
orchid /'OOrkid/ *n* orkide
order /'OOrdır/ *v* emretmek; düzenlemek; sipariş etmek; *n* sipariş; sıra, düzen; emir; **in** ~ düzenli; usule uygun; **in** ~ **to** -mek için; **made to** ~ siparişe, emre göre yapılmış; **out of** ~ bozuk; **postal** ~ posta havalesi; ~ **form** sipariş formu
ordinary /'OOrdınˌerii/ *adj* alışılmış; sıradan
ore /OOr/ *n* maden filizi
organ /'OOrgın/ *n* organ, uzuv; org
organic /OOr'gEnik/ *adj* uzvi; organik
organization /ˌOOrgını'zeyşın/ *n* örgütlenme; düzenleme; örgüt
organize /'OOrgıˌnayz/ *v* düzenlemek, örgütlemek
Orient /'OOriyınt/ *n* doğu
oriental /ˌOOri'yentıL/ *adj* doğuya ait
orientate /'OOriyınˌteyt/ *v* yönelmek; yöneltmek
origin /'Orıcin/ *n* kaynak; kök; soy
original /ı'ricınıL/ *adj* asıl, ilk, orijinal
originally /ı'ricınıLii/ *adv* başlangıçta
ornament /'OOrnımınt/ *n* süs; *v* süslemek
ornamental /ˌOOrnı'mentıL/ *adj* süslü, gösterişli; süs kabilinden
orphan/'OOrfın/ *n* öksüz, yetim
orthodox /'OOrTıˌdOks/ *adj* genellikle kabul edilen fikre *veya* inanca uygun; **Orthodox** ortodoks
ostrich /'OOstriç/ *n* devekuşu
other /'ADır/ *adj* diğer, öteki

otherwise /'ADır,wayz/ *conj* aksi takdirde; *adv* başka şekilde; başka bakımdan
Ottoman /'Otımın/ *adj, n* Osmanlı
***ought to** /OOt/ zorunda olmak
ounce /auns/ *n* ons; 28,3 gram
our /aur/ *adj* bizim
ourselves /aur'seLvz/ *pron* kendimiz
out /aut/ *adv* dışarı, dışarıda; ~ **of** dışında
outbreak /'aut,breyk/ *n* vuku bulma; patlak verme
outcome /'aut,kAm/ *n* sonuç
***outdo** /,aut'duu/ *v* üstün gelmek; geçmek
outdoor /'aut,dOOr/ *adj* açık havada yapılan
outdoors /,aut'dOOrz/ *adv* dışarıda, açık havada
outer /'autır/ *adj* dış
outfit /'aut,fit/ *n* donatım; gereçler; elbise
outline /'aut,Layn/ *n* taslak; ana hatlar; *v* taslağını çizmek
outlook /'aut,Luk/ *n* görünüş
output /'aut,put/ *n* verim; üretim; çıktı
outrage /'aut,reyc/ *n* zorbalık, tecavüz
outset /'aut,set/ *n* başlangıç
outside /'aut'sayd/ *adv* dışarıda, dışarıya; *prep* dışında; *n* dış taraf
outsize /'aut,sayz/ *n* çok büyük boy
outskirts /'aut,skÖrts/ *pl* kenar, civar; dış mahalleler
outstanding /,aut'stEndiN/ *adj* göze çarpan, önemli
outward /'autwırd/ *adj* dış, harici; *adv* dışarıya doğru
oval /'ouvıl/ *adj* oval, beyzi
oven /'Avın/ *n* fırın
over /'ouvır/ *adv* öbür tarafa; yukarıya; son bulmuş; *prep* ötesinde; üzerinde; ~ **there** orada, ötede
overall /,ouvır'OOL/ *adj* kapsamlı; tam, toplam
overalls /'ouvır,OOLz/ *pl* iş tulumu
overcast /'ouvır,kEst/ *adj* bulutlu
overcharge /,ouvır'çaarc/ *v* fazla fiyat istemek; fazla yüklemek
overcoat /'ouvır,kout/ *n* palto
***overcome** /,ouvır'kAm/ *v* yenmek, alt etmek
overdue /,ouvır'duu/ *adj* gecikmiş; vadesi geçmiş
***overeat** /,ouvır'iit/ *v* fazla yemek, oburluk etmek
overgrown /,ouvır'groun/ *adj* otlarla kaplanmış
overhaul /,ouvır'hOOL/ *v* elden geçirmek, onarmak
overhead /,ouvır'hed/ *adv* yukarıda
overheads /'ouvır,hedz/ *pl* genel masraflar
overlook /,ouvır'Luk/ *v* gözden kaçırmak; görmezlikten gelmek
overnight /,ouvır'nayt/ *adv* geceleyin
overseas /,ouvır'siiz/ *adj* denizaşırı
oversight /'ouvır,sayt/ *n* dikkatsizlik, yanlışlık
***oversleep** /,ouvır'sliip/ *v* uyuyakalıp gecikmek
overstrung /,ouvır'strAN/ *adj* çok gergin, çok sinirli
***overtake** /,ouvır'teyk/ *v* yetişip geçmek; sollamak; **no overtaking** sollamak yasaktır
overtired /,ouvır'tayrd/ *adj* aşırı yorgun
overture /'ouvırçır/ *n* uvertür; görüşme önerisi
overweight /'ouvır,weyt/ *n* fazla ağırlık
overwhelm /,ouvır'hweLm/ *v* baştan başa kaplamak; ezmek, yok etmek
overwork /,ouvır'wÖrk/ *v* aşırı çalıştırmak

owe /ou/ *v* borçlu olmak;
owing to nedeniyle, -den dolayı
owl /auL/ *n* baykuş
own /oun/ *v* sahip olmak; *adj* kendi, kendisinin
owner /'ounır/ *n* sahip
ox /Oks/ *n* (pl oxen) öküz
oxygen /'Oksicın/ *n* oksijen
oyster /'Oystır/ *n* istiridye

P

pace /peys/ *n* adım; yürüyüş; hız
Pacific Ocean /pı'sifik 'ouşın/ Büyük Okyanus, Pasifik Okyanusu
pacifism /'pEsı,fizım/ *n* barışseverlik
pacifist /'pEsı,fist/ *n* barışçı kimse
pack /pEk/ *v* paketlemek, ambalaj yapmak; ~ **up** ambalajlamak
package /'pEkic/ *n* paket, koli
packet /'pEkit/ *n* paket
packing /'pEkiN/ *n* ambalaj; paketleme
pad /pEd/ *n* küçük yastık; bloknot
paddle /'pEdıL/ *n* kısa kürek, pala
padlock /'pEd,LOk/ *n* asma kilit
pagan /'peygın/ *adj* putlara tapan; *n* putperest
page /peyc/ *n* sayfa; ~ **boy** komi
pail /peyL/ *n* kova
pain /peyn/ *n* ağrı, acı;
pains *pl* zahmet
painful /'peynfıL/ *adj* acı veren; zahmetli, güç
painkiller /'peyn,kiLır/ *n* ağrı dindirici ilaç
painless /'peynLıs/ *adj* acısız, ağrısız
paint /peynt/ *n* boya; *v* boyamak; ~ **box** boya kutusu
paintbrush /'peynt,brAş/ *n* boya fırçası
painter /'peyntır/ *n* ressam
painting /'peyntiN/ *n* boyalı resim, tablo; ressamlık
pair /peyr/ *n* çift
Pakistan /,pEkis'tEn/ Pakistan
Pakistani /,pEkis'tEnii/ *adj* Pakistan'a ait; *n* Pakistanlı
palace /'pELıs/ *n* saray
pale /peyL/ *adj* soluk
Palestine /'pELıstayn/ Filistin
Palestinian /,pELıs'tiiniyın/ *adj* Filistin'e ait; *n* Filistinli
palm /paam/ *n* avuç içi; palmiye
palpable /'pELpıbıL/ *adj* hissedilebilir, dokunulabilir; somut
palpitation /,pELpı'teyşın/ *n* çarpıntı
pan /pEn/ *n* tava; çanak
pane /peyn/ *n* pencere camı
panel /'pEnıL/ *n* pano; panel
paneling /'pEnıLiN/ *n* tahta kaplama
panic /'pEnik/ *n* panik
pant /pEnt/ *v* solumak, soluk soluğa kalmak
panties /'pEntiiz/ *pl* kadın külotu
pants /pEnts/ *pl* pantolon; külot
pantyhose /'pEntii,houz/ *n* külotlu çorap
paper /'peypır/ *n* kâğıt; gazete; **carbon** ~ karbon kâğıdı; ~ **bag** kesekâğıdı; ~ **knife** zarf açacağı; ~ **napkin** kâğıt peçete; **typing** ~ daktilo kâğıdı; **wrapping** ~ ambalaj kâğıdı
paperback /'peypır,bEk/ *n* kâğıt kapaklı, ciltlenmemiş kitap
paprika /pı'priikı/ *n* kırmızı biber
parade /pı'reyd/ *n* geçit, gösteri
paradise /'pErı,days/ *n* cennet
paraffin /'pErıfin/ *n* parafin
paragraph /'pErı,grEf/ *n* paragraf
parakeet /'pErı,kiit/ *n* ufak papağan
parallel /'pErı,LeL/ *adj* paralel, koşut; *n* paralel çizgi
paralyze /'pErı,Layz/ *v* felce

uğratmak; etkisiz bırakmak
parcel /'paarsıL/ *n* paket, koli
pardon /'paardın/ *n* af, bağışlama
parents /'peyrınts/ *pl* ana baba, ebeveyn
parish /'pEriş/ *n* bir papazın dinsel bölgesi
park /paark/ *n* park; *v* park etmek
parking /'paarkiN/ *n* park etme; **no ~** park etmek yasaktır; **~ fee** park ücreti; **~ light** park lambası; **~ lot** *Am* araba park yeri; **~ meter** otopark sayacı; **~ zone** park bölgesi
parliament /'paarLımınt/ *n* parlamento
parliamentary /ˌpaarLı'mentırii/ *adj* parlamentoya ait
parlor /'paarlır/ *n* oturma odası, salon
parrot /'pErıt/ *n* papağan
parsley /'paarsLii/ *n* maydanoz
parson /'paarsın/ *n* papaz
parsonage /'paarsınic/ *n* papaz evi
part /paart/ *n* parça; bölüm; *v* ayrılmak; ayırmak; **spare ~** yedek parça
partial /'paarşıL/ *adj* kısmi; taraf tutan
participant /paar'tisıˌpınt/ *n* katılan kimse
participate /paar'tisıˌpeyt/ *v* katılmak
particular /pır'tikyıLır/ *adj* özel, belirli; titiz, güç beğenir; **in ~** özellikle
parting /'paartiN/ *n* ayrılma, veda
partition /paar'tişın/ *n* bölme duvarı; bölme
partly /'paartLii/ *adv* kısmen
partner /'paartnır/ *n* ortak
partridge /'paartric/ *n* keklik
part-time /'paart'taym/ *adj* yarım günlük
party /'paartii/ *n* grup; parti; toplantı, eğlence
pass /pEs/ *v* geçmek; başarmak; *v Am* sollamak; **no passing** *Am* sollamak yasaktır; **~ by** yanından *veya* önünden geçmek; **~ through** içinden geçmek
passage /'pEsic/ *n* geçme; geçit; koridor; pasaj
passenger /'pEsıncır/ *n* yolcu; **~ car** *Am* vagon; **~ train** yolcu treni
passerby /'pEsır'bay/ *n* gelip geçen kimse
passion /'pEşın/ *n* ihtiras, tutku; öfke
passionate /'pEşınıt/ *adj* heyecanlı, ateşli, tutkulu
passive /'pEsiv/ *adj* pasif, eylemsiz
passport /'pEsˌpOOrt/ *n* pasaport; **~ control** pasaport kontrolu; **~ photograph** vesikalık fotoğraf
password /'pEsˌwÖrd/ *n* parola
past /pEst/ *n* geçmiş ; geçmiş zaman; *adj* geçen; *prep* -den sonra
paste /peyst/ *n* hamur; kola; macun; *v* yapıştırmak
pastry /'peystrii/ *n* hamur işi; pasta; **~ shop** pastane
pasture /'pEsçır/ *n* çayır, otlak
pat /pEt/ *v* okşamak, hafifçe vurmak; *n* okşama, hafif vuruş
patch /pEç/ *v* yama vurmak, yamalamak
patent /'pEtınt/ *n* buluş belgesi, patent
path /pET/ *n* keçiyolu, patika
patience /'peyşıns/ *n* sabır
patient /'peyşınt/ *adj* sabırlı; *n* hasta
patriot /'peytriyıt/ *n* yurtsever
patrol /pı'trouL/ *n* devriye, kol; *v* devriye gezmek
pattern /'pEtırn/ *n* model; örnek; desen
pause /pOOz/ *n* ara; duraklama; *v* duraklamak

pave /peyv/ *v* kaldırım döşemek
pavement /'peyvmınt/ *n* yolu kaplayan döşeme; *nBr* kaldırım
pavilion /pı'viLyın/ *n* büyük çadır; pavyon
paw /pOO/ *n* pençe
pawn /pOOn/ *v* rehine koymak; tehlikeye atmak; *n* rehin
pawnbroker /'pOOn,brouker/ *n* rehinci, tefeci
pay /pey/ *n* maaş, ücret
***pay** /pey/ *v* ödemek; ~ **attention** dikkat etmek; ~ **desk** vezne; **paying** kârlı, kazançlı; ~ **off** karşılığını vermek, işe yaramak
payday /'pey,dey/ *n* maaş günü
payee /,pey'ii/ *n* alacaklı kimse
payment /'peymınt/ *n* ödeme; ücret, maaş
payroll /'pey,roul/ *n* maaş bordrosu; maaşların toplamı
pea /pii/ *n* bezelye
peace /piis/ *n* barış
peaceful /'piisfıL/ *adj* sakin, rahat, barışsever
peach /piiç/ *n* şeftali
peacock /'pii,kOk/ *n* tavus
peak /piik/ *n* zirve; doruk; ~ **hour** sıkışık saat; ~ **season** işlerin yoğun olduğu mevsim
peanut /'pii,nAt/ *n* yerfıstığı
pear /'peyr/ *n* armut
pearl /pÖrL/ *n* inci
peasant /'pezınt/ *n* köylü
pebble /'pebıL/ *n* çakıl taşı
peculiar /pi'kyuuLyır/ *adj* özel; acayip
peculiarity /pi,kyuuL'yErıtii/ *n* özellik; gariplik
pedal /'pedıL/ *n* pedal
pedestrian /pi'destriyın/ *n* yaya; **no pedestrians** yayalar giremez; ~ **crossing** yaya geçidi
pediatrician /,piidiyı'trişın/ *n* çocuk doktoru
pedicure /'pedi,kyuur/ *n* pedikür
peel /piiL/ *v* kabuğunu soymak; *n* kabuk
peep /piip/ *v* gizlice bakmak
peg /peg/ *n* ağaç çivi; mandal
pelican /'peLikın/ *n* pelikan
pelvis /'peLvis/ *n* alt karın, leğen
pen /pen/ *n* mürekkepli kalem; ~ **pal** mektup arkadaşı
penalty /'penıLtii/ *n* ceza; ~ **kick** penaltı vuruşu
pencil /'pensıL/ *n* kurşunkalem; ~ **sharpener** kalemtıraş
pendant /'pendınt/ *n* asılı şey; avize; kolye
pending /'pendiN/ *adj* muallakta olan, henüz kararlaştırılmamış
penetrate /'penı,treyt/ *v* delip girmek; içine işlemek
penguin /'pengwin/ *n* penguen
penicillin /,penı'siLin/ *n* penisilin
peninsula /pı'ninsıLı/ *n* yarımada
penknife /'pen,nayf/ *n* (pl -knives) çakı
pension[1] /'penşın/ *n* emekli aylığı
pension[2] /paaN'syouN/ *n* pansiyon
people /'piipıL/ *pl* halk, ahali
pepper /'pepır/ *n* biber
peppermint /'pepır,mint/ *n* nane
perceive /pır'siiv/ *v* görmek, anlamak, idrak etmek
percent /pır'sent/ *n* yüzde
percentage /pır'sentic/ *n* yüzdelik, oran, nispet
perceptible /pır'septibıL/ *adj* anlaşılabilir, idrak edilebilir
perception /pır'sepşın/ *n* idrak, algı, anlayış, seziş
perch /pÖrç/ (pl ~) *n* tatlı su levreği
percolator /'pÖrkı,Leytır/ *n* perkolatör
perfect /'pÖrfikt/ *adj* tam, kusursuz, mükemmel, fevkalade

perfection /pır'fekşın/ *n* kusursuzluk
perform /pır'fOOrm/ *v* yapmak, yerine getirmek
performance /pır'fOOrmıns/ *n* temsil, oyun, gösteri; iş, icra
perfume /'pÖr,fyuum/ *n* parfüm
perhaps /pır'hEps/ *adv* belki
peril /'periL/ *n* tehlike, risk
perilous /'perı,Lıs/ *adj* tehlikeli, riskli
period /'piiriyıd/ *n* süre, devre; çağ
periodical /,piiri'yOdikıL/ *n* dergi; *adj* periyodik
perish /'periş/ *v* ölmek, yok olmak
perishable /'perişıbıl/ *adj* kolay bozulan
perjury /'pÖrcırii/ *n* yalan yere yemin
permanent /'pÖrmınınt/ *adj* sürekli; ~ **press** ütü istemez; ~ **wave** perma, bozulmayan ondüle
permission /pÖr'mişın/ *n* izin
permit[1] /pır'mit/ *v* izin vermek
permit[2] /'pÖrmit/ *n* permi, ruhsat
peroxide /pı'rOksayd/ *n* oksijenli su
perpendicular /,pÖrpın'dikyıLır/ *adj* düşey, dikey
perpetual /pır'peçuuıL/ *adj* daimi, sürekli
Persia /'pÖrjı/ İran'ın eski adı
Persian /'pÖrjın/ *adj* İran'a ait; *n* İranlı; Farsça
person /'pÖrsın/ *n* kimse, adam, şahıs; **per** ~ kişi başına
personal /'pÖrsınıL/ *adj* özel, hususi
personality /,pÖrsı'nELıtii/ *n* şahsiyet, kişilik
personnel /,pörsı'neL/ *n* kadro, personel
perspective /pır'spektiv/ *n* görüş açısı
perspiration /,pÖrspı'reyşın/ *n* ter, terleme
perspire /pır'spayr/ *v* terlemek
persuade /pır'sweyd/ *v* ikna etmek, razı etmek
persuasion /pır'sweyjın/ *n* inanç; inandırma
perversion /pır'vÖrjın/ *n* sapıklık; sapkınlık
pessimism /'pesı,mizım/ *n* kötümserlik
pessimist /'pesımist/ *n* kötümser kişi
pessimistic /,pesı'mistik/ *adj* kötümser, karamsar
pest /pest/ *n* baş belası; veba
pet /pet/ *n* evde beslenen hayvan; çok sevilen kimse
petal /'petıL/ *n* çiçek yaprağı
petition /pı'tişın/ *n* dilekçe
petrol /'petrıL/ *nBr* benzin; ~ **pump** *Br* benzin pompası; ~ **station** *Br* benzin istasyonu; ~ **tank** *Br* benzin deposu
petroleum /pi'trouLiyım/ *n* petrol
petty /'petii/ *adj* küçük, önemsiz, adi, ufak tefek; ~ **cash** bozuk para
pewter /'pyuutır/ *n* kurşun ve kalay alaşımı
phantom /'fEntım/ *n* hayal, hayalet
pharmacology /,faarmı'kOLıcii/ *n* eczacılık
pharmacy /'faarmısii/ *n* eczane
phase /feyz/ *n* safha, aşama; faz
pheasant /'fezınt/ *n* sülün
phenomenon /fı'nOmı,nOn/ *n* (pl -na) olay; olağanüstü şey, harika
Philippine /'fiLıpiin/ *adj* Filipinlere ait
Philippines /'fiLı,piinz/ *pl* Filipinler
philosopher /fi'LOsıfır/ *n* filozof
philosophy /fı'LOsıfii/ *n* felsefe
phone /foun/ *n* telefon; *v* telefon etmek
phonetic /fı'netik/ *adj* fonetik
phosphorus /'fOsfırıs/ *n* fosfor
photo /'foutou/ *n* (pl ~s) fotoğraf
photograph /'foutı,grEf/ *n* fotoğraf; *v* fotoğraf çekmek

photographer /fı'tOgrıfır/ *n* fotoğrafçı
photography /fı'tOgrıfii/ *n* fotoğrafçılık
photostat /'foutı,stEt/ *n* fotokopi
phrase /freyz/ *n* ibare, deyim; ~ **book** konuşma kılavuzu
physical /'fizikıL/ *adj* fiziksel
physician /fi'zişın/ *n* doktor
physicist /'fizısist/ *n* fizikçi
physics /'fiziks/ *n* fizik
physiology /fizi'yOLıcii/ *n* fizyoloji
pianist /pii'yEnist/ *n* piyanist
piano /pii'yEnou/ *n* piyano; **grand** ~ kuyruklu piyano
pick /pik/ *v* seçmek, toplamak; *n* seçme; ~ **up** kaldırmak, toplamak
pickup truck /'pik,Ap 'trAk/ kamyonet
pickles /'pikıLz/ *pl* turşu
picnic /'piknik/ *n* piknik; *v* piknik yapmak
picture /'pikçır/ *n* resim, tablo, tasvir; ~ **postcard** kartpostal
picturesque /,pikçı'resk/ *adj* resim konusu olmaya elverişli, canlı, etkili
piece /piis/ *n* parça
pier /piir/ *n* iskele, rıhtım
pierce /piirs/ *v* delmek, delip geçmek
pig /pig/ *n* domuz
pigeon /'picın/ *n* güvercin
pig-headed /'pig,hedid/ *adj* aksi, inatçı
piglet /'pigLıt/ *n* domuz yavrusu
pigskin /'pig,skin/ *n* domuz derisi
pike /payk/ *n* kargı, mızrak
pile /payL/ *n* yığın, küme; *v* yığmak, kümelemek; **piles** *pl* basur memesi, hemoroid
pilgrim /'piLgrım/ *n* hacı, yolcu, seyyah
pilgrimage /'piLgrımic/ *n* hac
pill /pil/ *n* hap
pillar /'piLır/ *n* direk, sütun
pillar-box /'piLır,bOks/ *nBr* posta kutusu
pillow /'piLou/ *n* yastık
pillowcase /'piLou,keys/ *n* yastık kılıfı
pilot /'payLıt/ *n* pilot
pimple /'pimpıL/ *n* sivilce
pin /pin/ *n* toplu iğne; *v* iğnelemek; iliştirmek; **bobby** ~ *Am* madeni saç tokası
pincers /'pinsırz/ *pl* kerpeten, kıskaç
pinch /pinç/ *v* çimdiklemek
pine /payn/ *n* çam
pineapple /'payn,EpıL/ *n* ananas
ping-pong /'piN,pON/ *n* masa tenisi, ping pong
pink /piNk/ *adj* pembe
pint /paynt/ *n* yaklaşık yarım litrelik sıvı ölçü birimi
pioneer /,payı'niir/ *n* öncü
pious /'payıs/ *adj* dindar
pip /pip/ *n* elma, portakal vs. çekirdeği
pipe /payp/ *n* boru; pipo; ~ **cleaner** pipo temizleyicisi; ~ **tobacco** pipo tütünü
pipeline /'payp,Layn/ *n* boruyolu; petrol vs. nakil borusu
pirate /'payrıt/ *n* korsan
Pisces /'pay,siiz/ Balık burcu
pistol /'pistıL/ *n* tabanca
piston /'pistın/ *n* piston; segman
pit /pit/ *n* çukur; koltuk altı
pitcher /'piçır/ *n* testi, sürahi, maşrapa
pity /'pitii/ *n* merhamet, acıma, şefkat; *v* acımak; **what a pity!** ne yazık!
placard /'pLEkaard/ *n* afiş, poster
place /pLeys/ *n* yer; *v* koymak, yerleştirmek; ~ **of birth** doğum yeri; ***take** ~ olmak, vuku bulmak
plague /pLeyg/ *n* veba; bela, musibet

plaice /pLeys/ *n* (pl ~) pisi balığı
plain /pLeyn/ *adj* düz, sade, basit; apaçık; *n* ova, düzlük
plan /pLEn/ *n* plan; *v* planlamak, tasarlamak
plane /pLeyn/ *adj* düz, dümdüz; *n* uçak; ~ **crash** uçak kazası
planet /'pLEnit/ *n* gezegen
planetarium /,pLEnı'teyriyım/ *n* planetaryum, gökevi
plank /pLENk/ *n* uzun tahta, kalas
plant /pLEnt/ *n* bitki; fabrika; *v* dikmek, ekmek; kurmak
plantation /pLEn'teyşın/ *n* koru, fidanlık; büyük çiftlik, geniş tarla
plaster /'pLEstır/ *n* alçı, sıva, yakı
plastic /'pLEstik/ *adj* plastik
plate /pLeyt/ *n* tabak; levha
plateau /pLE'tou/ *n* (pl ~x, ~s) plato, yayla
platform /'pLEt,fOOrm/ *n* platform, sahanlık; peron; ~ **ticket** peron bileti
platinum /'pLEtınım/ *n* platin
play /pLey/ *v* oynamak; *n* oyun; piyes; **one-act** ~ bir perdelik oyun; ~ **truant** dersi asmak, okulu kırmak
player /'pLeyır/ *n* oyuncu
playground /'pLey,graund/ *n* oyun sahası
playing card /'pLeyiN kaard/ iskambil kâğıdı
playwright /'pLey,rayt/ n oyun yazarı
plea /pLii/ *n* müdafaa, savunma
plead /pLiid/ *v* yalvarmak, rica etmek
pleasant /'pLezınt/ *adj* hoş, güzel, cana yakın
please /pLiiz/ lütfen; *v* memnun etmek, hoşa gitmek; **pleased** memnun; **pleasing** hoş
pleasure /'pLejır/ *n* zevk
plentiful /'pLentifıL/ *adj* bol, bereketli
plenty /'pLentii/ *n* bolluk, bereket; ~ **of** çok miktarda
pliers /'pLAyırz/ *pl* kerpeten
plimsolls /'pLimsıLz/ *plBr* lastik spor ayakkabısı
plot /pLOt/ *n* entrika, gizli plan; romanın konusu
plough /pLau/ *n* saban, pulluk; *v* sabanla işlemek
plug /pLAg/ *n* fiş; ~ **in** prize sokmak
plum /pLAm/ *n* erik
plumber /'pLAmır/ *n* su tesisatçısı, muslukçu
plump /pLAmp/ *adj* dolgun, tombul
plural /'pLuurıL/ *n* çoğul
plus /pLAs/ *prep* artı
pneumatic /nuu'mEtik/ *adj* hava basıncı ile çalışan
pneumonia /nuu'mounyı/ *n* zatürree; akciğer iltihabı
poach /pouç/ *v* kaçak avlanmak
pocket /'pOkit/ *n* cep
pocketbook /'pOkit,buk/ *n* cüzdan; cep kitabı
pocketknife /'pOkit,nayf/ *n* (pl -knives) çakı
poem /'pouim/ *n* şiir
poet /'pouit/ *n* şair
poetry /'pouitrii/ *n* şiir sanatı, şiirler
point /pOynt/ *n* nokta; *v* göstermek; ~ **of view** görüş; ~ **out** göstermek, işaret etmek
pointed /'pOyntid/ *adj* sivri uçlu
poison /'pOyzın/ *n* zehir; *v* zehirlemek
poisonous /'pOyzınıs/ *adj* zehirli
poker /'poukır/ *n* poker
Poland /'pouLınd/ Polonya
Pole /pouL/ *n* Polonyalı
pole /pouL/ *n* direk, sırık; kutup
police /pı'Liis/ *pl* polis; ~ **station** karakol
policeman /pı'Liismın/ *n* (pl -men) polis memuru

policy /'pOLısii/ *n* poliçe; politika
polio /'pouLi,you/ *n* çocuk felci
Polish /'pouLiş/ *adj* Polonya'ya ait
polish /'pOLiş/ *v* cilalamak
polite /pı'Layt/ *adj* terbiyeli, kibar, nazik
political /pı'LitikıL/ *adj* siyasi
politician /,pOLı'tişın/ *n* politikacı
politics /'pOLıtiks/ *n* siyaset, politika
pollution /pı'Luuşın/ *n* pisletme, kirletme, kirlilik
pomegranate /'pOm,grEnit/ *n* nar
pond /pOnd/ *n* havuz, gölcük
pony /'pounii/ *n* midilli
poor /puur/ *adj* fakir, yoksul, muhtaç
pope /poup/ *n* papa
poplar /'pOpLır/ *n* kavak
poplin /'pOplin/ *n* poplin
pop music /'pOp ,myuuzik/ popüler hafif müzik
poppy /'pOpii/ *n* gelincik, haşhaş, afyon
popular /'pOpyıLır/ *adj* halka ait, popüler
population /,pOpyı'Leyşın/ *n* nüfus
populous /'pOpyıLıs/ *adj* kalabalık, nüfusu çok
porcelain /'pOOrsıLin/ *n* porselen
pork /pOOrk/ *n* domuz eti
port /pOOrt/ *n* liman, liman şehri
portable /'pOOrtıbıL/ *adj* taşınabilir, portatif
porter /'pOOrtır/ *n* kapıcı; hamal
porthole /'pOOrt,houL/ *n* lombar (kapağı)
portion /'pOOrşın/ *n* hisse, kısım
portrait /'pOOrtrit/ *n* portre
Portugal /'pOOrçugıL/ Portekiz
Portuguese /,pOOrçu'giiz/ adj, n Portekizli
position /pı'zişın/ *n* durum, vaziyet, mevki
positive /'pOzıtiv/ *adj* kesin; olumlu
possess /pı'zes/ *v* sahip olmak, elinde bulundurmak; **possessed** *adj* deli, çılgın, düşkün
possession /pı'zeşın/ *n* sahiplik; **possessions** *pl* mal, mülk, servet
possibility /,pOsı'biLıtii/ *n* imkân, olanak
possible /'pOsıbıL/ *adj* mümkün, olası, makul, akla yatkın
post /poust/ *n* direk, kazık, destek; ~ **card** kartpostal, görev; posta; *v* postalamak; ~ **office** postane
postage /'poustic/ *n* posta ücreti; ~ **paid** posta ücreti ödenmiş; ~ **stamp** posta pulu
poster /'poustır/ *n* afiş, poster
postman /'poustmın/ *n* (pl -men) postacı
postpaid /'poust,peyd/ *adj* posta ücreti ödenmiş
postpone /poust'poun/ *v* ertelemek, tehir etmek
pot /pOt/ *n* çömlek, kap
potato /pı'teytou/ *n* (pl ~es) patates
potential /pı'tenşıL/ *adj* muhtemel; gerçekleşebilecek olan; potansiyel
pottery /'pOtırii/ *n* çanak çömlek
pouch /pauç/ *n* torba, kese
poultry /'pouLtrii/ *n* kümes hayvanları
pound /paund/ *n* libre, 454 gr
pour /pOOr/ *v* dökmek
poverty /'pOvırtii/ *n* fakirlik
powder /'paudır/ *n* pudra; ~ **compact** pudralık; pudra kutusu; ~ **puff** pudra ponponu; ~ **room** bayan tuvaleti; **talcum** ~ talk pudrası
power /,pauır/ *n* güç, kuvvet, kudret; ~ **station** elektrik santralı
powerful /'pauırfıL/ *adj* kuvvetli, güçlü
powerless /'pauırLıs/ *adj* güçsüz
practical /'prEktikıL/ *adj* pratik
practically /'prEktikıLii/ *adv* pratik

olarak; hemen hemen; gerçekte
practice /'prEktis/ *n* uygulama
practise /'prEktis/ *v* yapmak, uygulamak
praise /preyz/ *v* övmek, methetmek
pram /prEm/ *nBr* çocuk arabası; bebek arabası
prawn /prOOn/ *n* büyük karides
pray /prey/ *v* dua etmek
prayer /'preyır/ *n* dua
preach /priiç/ *v* vaaz vermek
precarious /pri'keyriyıs/ *adj* kararsız, şüpheli; tehlikeli
precaution /pri'kOOşın/ *n* tedbir, önlem, ihtiyat
precede /pri'siid/ *v* önce gelmek, önce olmak
preceding /pri'siidiN/ *adj* önceki
precious /'preşıs/ *adj* kıymetli
precipice /'presıpis/ *n* uçurum, sarp kayalık
precipitation /pri,sipı'teyşın/ *n* yağış; yağış miktarı
precise /pri'says/ *adj* tam, kesin; titiz, kusursuz
predecessor /'predı,sesır/ *n* öncel, selef; ata, cet
predict /pri'dikt/ *v* önceden bildirmek, kehanette bulunmak
preface /'prefis/ *n* önsöz, başlangıç
prefer /pri'fÖr/ *v* tercih etmek, yeğlemek
preferable /'prefırıbıL/ *adj* daha iyi, tercih edilir
preference /'prefırıns/ *n* yeğleme, tercih
prefix /'prii,fiks/ *n* önek
pregnant /'pregnınt/ *adj* gebe, hamile
prehistoric /,priihis'tOOrik/ *adj* tarihöncesi
prejudice /'precıdis/ *n* önyargı, peşin hüküm
preliminary /pri'Limı,nerii/ *adj* hazırlayıcı, ön, başlangıç niteliğinde
premature /'priimıçuur/ *adj* zamanından evvel olan, erken doğan
premier /'priimiyır/ *n* başbakan
premises /'premisiz/ *pl* bina ve arazisi
premium /'priimiyım/ *n* prim, hediye; sigorta ücreti
prepaid /'prii,peyd/ *adj* ücreti önceden ödenmiş
preparation /prepı'reyşın/ *n* hazırlık
prepare /pri'peyr/ *v* hazırlamak
prepared /pri'peyrd/ *adj* hazır
preposition /,prepı'zişın/ *n* edat, ilgeç
prescribe /pris'krayb/ *v* emretmek; salık vermek; reçete yazmak
prescription /pri'skripşın/ *n* emir, talimat; reçete
presence /'prezıns/ *n* varlık; hazır bulunma
present[1] /'prezınt/ *n* hediye; şimdiki zaman; *adj* şimdiki
present[2] /pri'zent/ *v* sunmak; tanıştırmak
presently /'prezıntLii/ *adv* şu anda; birazdan
preservation /,prezır'veyşın/ *n* saklama, koruma
preserve /pri'zÖrv/ *v* korumak, saklamak
president /'prezıdınt/ *n* başkan
press /pres/ *n* basın; baskı, sıkıştırma; *v* sıkıştırmak; ~ **conference** basın konferansı
pressing /'presiN/ *adj* acele, acil; sıkboğaz eden
pressure /'preşır/ *n* basınç, tazyik; baskı; **atmospheric** ~ atmosfer basıncı; ~ **cooker** düdüklü tencere
prestige /pres'tiij/ *n* saygınlık, itibar
presumable /pri'zuumıbıL/ *adj* tahmin edilir
presumptuous /pri'zAmpçuuıs/ *adj*

kibirli, küstah
pretend /pri'tend/ *v* yalandan yapmak; taslamak
pretense /pri'tens/ *n* bahane; yapmacık; hile
pretext /'prii,tekst/ *n* bahane, sudan sebep
pretty /'pritii/ *adj* güzel, sevimli; *adv* oldukça, hayli, epeyce
prevail /pri'veyL/ *v* yenmek; hâkim olmak; yaygın olmak
prevent /pri'vent/ *v* önlemek, engellemek, durdurmak
preventive /pri'ventiv/ *adj* önleyici
previous /'priiviyıs/ *adj* önceki, evvelki, eski
price /prays/ *n* fiyat; *v* fiyat koymak, paha biçmek; ~ **list** fiyat listesi
priceless /'praysLıs/ *adj* çok değerli, paha biçilmez
prick /prik/ *v* sokmak, delmek
pride /prayd/ *n* kibir, gurur
priest /priist/ *n* papaz, rahip
primary /'pray,merii/ *adj* ilk, başlangıç, temel
primitive /'primıtiv/ *adj* ilkel
prince /prins/ *n* prens
princess /'prinses/ *n* prenses
principal /'prinsıpıL/ *adj* en önemli, ana, büyük, asıl; *n* okul müdürü
principle /'prinsıpıL/ *n* prensip, ilke
print /print/ *v* basmak, yayımlamak; **printed matter** basılı yazı, matbua
prior /prayır/ *adj* önceki, evvelki
priority /pra'yOOrıtii/ *n* öncelik
prison /'prizın/ *n* hapishane
prisoner /'prizınır/ *n* tutuklu, hükümlü, mahkûm; ~ **of war** savaş esiri
privacy /'prayvısii/ *n* özellik, gizlilik, mahremiyet
private /'prayvit/ *adj* özel, kişisel
privilege /'privıLic/ *n* ayrıcalık, imtiyaz
prize /prayz/ *n* ödül
probable /'prObıbıL/ *adj* muhtemel, olası
probably /'prObıbLii/ *adv* muhtemelen
problem /'prObLım/ *n* sorun, mesele
procedure /prı'siicır/ *n* işlem, muamele
proceed /prı'siid/ *v* ilerlemek
process /'prOses/ *n* yöntem, metot, işlem
procession /prı'seşın/ *n* alay, geçit töreni
proclaim /prı'kLeym/ *v* ilan etmek, beyan etmek
produce[1] /prı'duus/ *v* üretmek
produce[2] /'prOduus/ *n* ürün
producer /prı'duusır/ *n* üretici
product /'prOdıkt/ *n* ürün, mahsul
production /prı'dAkşın/ *n* üretim
productive /prı'dAktiv/ *adj* verimli; kazançlı
productivity /,proudAk'tivıtii/ *n* verimlilik
profession /prı'feşın/ *n* uğraş, iş, meslek, sanat
professional /prı'feşınıL/ *adj* mesleki; profesyonel
professor /prı'fesır/ *n* profesör
profit /'prOfit/ *n* kâr, kazanç, menfaat; *v* kâr etmek
profitable /'prOfitıbıL/ *adj* kazançlı, kârlı, faydalı
profound /prı'faund/ *adj* derin, engin
program /'prougrEm/ *n* program
progress[1] /'prOgres/ *n* gelişme
progress[2] /prı'gress/ *v* gelişmek
progressive /prı'gresiv/ *adj* ilerleyen, ilerici
prohibit /prou'hibit/ *v* yasaklamak
prohibition /,proui'bişın/ *n* yasaklama
prohibitive /prou'hibıtiv/ *adj* yasaklayıcı, engelleyici
project /'prOcekt/ *n* plan, proje

promenade /ˌprOmı'neyd/ *n* gezinti, gezme
promise /'prOmis/ *n* söz, vaat; taahhüt; *v* söz vermek
promote /prı'mout/ *v* ilerletmek; terfi ettirmek; kıymetini arttırmak
promotion /prı'mouşın/ *n* terfi; promosyon
prompt /prOmpt/ *adj* hemen, çabuk olan; tez davranan
pronoun /'prouˌnaun/ *n* zamir
pronounce /prı'nauns/ *v* telaffuz etmek
pronunciation /prıˌnAnsi'yeyşın/ *n* telaffuz
proof /pruuf/ *n* delil, kanıt
propaganda /prOpı'gEndı/ *n* propaganda
propel /prı'peL/ *v* sevk etmek, itmek
propeller /prı'peLır/ *n* pervane
proper /'prOpır/ *adj* uygun, yakışır, layık
property /'prOpırtii/ *n* mal, mülk, emlak
prophet /'prOfit/ *n* peygamber
proportion /prı'pOOrşın/ *n* oran, nispet
proportional /prı'pOOrşınıL/ *adj* orantılı
proposal /prı'pouzıL/ *n* önerme, teklif
propose /prı'pouz/ *v* önermek
proposition /ˌprOpı'zişın/ *n* teklif, öneri
proprietor /prı'prayıtır/ *n* mal sahibi, mülk sahibi
prosecute /'prOsıˌkyuut/ *v* aleyhine dava açmak
prospect /'prOspekt/ *n* görünüş; umut; muhtemel müşteri
prospectus /prı'spektıs/ *n* broşür
prosperity /prOs'perıtii/ *n* başarı, refah, saadet
prosperous /'prOspırıs/ *adj* başarılı, bayındır; uygun, elverişli
prostitute /'prOstiˌtuut/ *n* fahişe
protect /prı'tekt/ *v* korumak
protection /prı'tekşın/ *n* koruma
protein /'proutiin/ *n* protein
protest[1] /'proutest/ *n* itiraz, protesto
protest[2] /prı'test/ *v* itiraz etmek, protesto etmek
Protestant /'prOtistınt/ *adj* Protestan
proud /praud/ *adj* gururlu, mağrur
prove /pruuv/ *v* kanıtlamak, ispat etmek
proverb /'prOvÖrb/ *n* atasözü
provide /prı'vayd/ *v* sağlamak; **provided that** -mek şartıyla; yeter ki
province /'prOvins/ *n* il, vilayet; taşra
provincial /prı'vinşıL/ *adj* taşralı, darkafalı
provisional /prı'vijınıL/ *adj* geçici, muvakkat
provisions /prı'vijınz/ *pl* erzak, zahire
provoke /prı'vouk/ *v* kışkırtmak, dürtmek; kızdırmak
prune /pruun/ *n* kuru erik
psychiatrist /say'kayıtrist/ *n* ruh doktoru, psikiyatr
psychic /'saykik/ *adj* ruhsal, ruhi
psychoanalyst /ˌsaykou'EnıList/ *n* psikanalist
psychological /ˌsaykı'LOcikıL/ *adj* psikolojik
psychologist /say'kOLıcist/ *n* psikolog
psychology /say'kOLıcii/ *n* psikoloji
pub /pAb/ *nBr* birahane, meyhane
public /'pAbLik/ *adj* halka ait, umuma ait; *n* halk, kitle; ~ **garden** umumi park; ~ **house** *Am* han, otel; *Br* birahane, meyhane
publication /ˌpAbLi'keyşın/ *n* yayınlama; yayın
publicity /pA'bLisıtii/ *n* reklam

publicize /'pAbLı,sayz/ *v* reklamını yapmak
publish /'pAbLiş/ *v* yayınlamak
publisher /'pAbLişır/ *n* yayıncı
puddle /'pAdıL/ *n* kirli su birikintisi, gölcük
pull /puL/ *v* çekmek; ~ **out** çekip çıkarmak; ayrılmak; ~ **up** durmak
pulley /'puLii/ *n* (pl ~s) makara; kasnak
Pullman /'puLmın/ *n* pulmanlı vagon
pullover /'puL,ouvır/ *n* kazak, süveter
pulp /pALp/ *n* sebze *veya* meyvelerin etli kısmı; kâğıt hamuru
pulpit /'puLpit/ *n* minber, kürsü
pulse /pALs/ *n* nabız
pump /pAmp/ *n* pompa; *v* tulumba ile çekmek; pompa ile şişirmek
pumpkin /'pAmpkin/ *n* balkabağı
punch /pAnç/ *v* yumruk atmak; *n* yumruk
punctual /'pANkçuuıL/ *adj* dakik
puncture /'pANkçır/ *n* lastik patlaması; delik
punctured /'pANkçırd/ *adj* patlak, patlamış
punish /'pAniş/ *v* cezalandırmak
punishment /'pAnişmınt/ *n* ceza
pupil /'pyuupıL/ *n* öğrenci
puppet /'pApit/ *n* kukla; ~ **show** kukla oyunu
purchase /'pÖrçıs/ *v* satın almak; ~ **price** satış fiyatı
purchaser /'pÖrçısır/ *n* alıcı, müşteri
pure /pyuur/ *adj* saf
purple /'pÖrpıL/ *adj* mor
purpose /'pÖrpıs/ *n* maksat, niyet; **on** ~ isteyerek, kasten, bile bile
purse /pÖrs/ *n* para çantası
pursue /pır'suu/ *v* takip etmek, izlemek
pus /pAs/ *n* irin, cerahat
push /puş/ *n* itiş, kakış, dürtüş; *v* itmek; ~ **button** elektrik düğmesi
***put** /put/ *v* koymak, yerleştirmek, sokmak; ~ **away** kaldırmak, bir kenara ayırmak; ~ **off** ertelemek; ~ **out** söndürmek
puzzle /'pAzıl/ *n* bulmaca; *v* şaşırtmak, hayrete düşürmek; **crossword** ~ çapraz bulmaca; **jigsaw** ~ boz-yap
puzzling /'pAzLiN/ *adj* şaşırtıcı, üzücü
pyjamas /pı'cEmız/ *pl* pijama

Q

quack /kwEk/ *n* yalancı doktor, şarlatan
quail /kweyL/ *n* (pl ~, ~s) bıldırcın
quaint /kweynt/ *adj* tuhaf, acayip; antika
qualification /,kwOLıfi'keyşın/ *n* nitelik, vasıf, meziyet
qualified /'kwOLı,fayd/ *adj* ehliyetli, uzman
qualify /'kwOLı,fay/ *v* hak kazanmak
quality /'kwOLıtii/ *n* kalite, nitelik, vasıf
quantity /'kwOntıtii/ *n* kemiyet, nicelik
quarantine /'kwOrın,tiin/ *n* karantina
quarrel /'kwOrıL/ *v* kavga etmek, münakaşa etmek, çekişmek; *n* kavga, münakaşa, çekişme
quart /kwOOrt/ *n* galonun dörtte biri; 1,04 litre
quarter /'kwOOrtır/ *n* dörtte bir, çeyrek; ~ **of an hour** çeyrek saat
quarterly /'kwOOrtırLii/ *adj* üç aylık, üç ayda bir (olan); *n* üç ayda bir çıkan dergi
quay /kii/ *n* rıhtım, iskele

queen /kwiin/ *n* kraliçe; iskambilde dam, kız
queer /kwiir/ *adj* acayip, tuhaf, alışılmamış, şüpheli
query /'kwiirii/ *n* sorgu; *v* sormak, araştırmak
question /'kwesçın/ *n* soru; sorun; *v* soru sormak, sorguya çekmek; ~ **mark** soru işareti
questionnaire /,kwesçı'neyr/ *n* anket; soru formu
queue /kyuu/ *n* kuyruk, sıra; ~ **up** kuyruğa girmek, kuyruk olmak
quick /kwik/ *adj* çabuk
quick-tempered /'kwik'tempırd/ *adj* kolay ve çabuk öfkelenen
quiet /'kwayıt/ *adj* sessiz, sakin, durgun; *n* sessizlik, sükûnet, hareketsizlik
quilt /kwiLt/ *n* yorgan
quince /kwins/ *n* ayva
quinine /'kwiiniin/ *n* kinin
quit /kwit/ *v* bırakmak, terk etmek
quite /kwayt/ *adv* tamamen, pek, gayet, oldukça
quiz /kwiz/ *n* (pl ~zes) küçük sınav; yarışma
quota /'kwoutı/ *n* hisse, pay, kota
quotation /kwou'teyşın/ *n* aktarma, aktarılan söz; ~ **marks** tırnak işareti
quote /kwout/ *v* aktarmak, birinin sözünü tekrarlamak

R

rabbit /'rEbit/ *n* tavşan
rabies /'reybiiz/ *n* kuduz hastalığı
race /reys/ *n* yarış
racecourse /'reys,kOOrs/ *n* yarış pisti, koşu yolu, parkur, hipodrom
racehorse /'reys,hOOrs/ *n* yarış atı
racetrack /'reys,trEk/ *n* yarış pisti, koşu yolu, parkur
racial /'reyşıL/ *adj* ırka ait, ırksal
racism /'rey,sizım/ *n* ırkçılık
racket /'rEkit/ *n* gürültü, patırtı, şamata
racquet /'rEkit/ *n* raket
radiator /'reydi,yeytır/ *n* radyatör
radical /'rEdikıL/ *adj* temel, köklü; radikal
radio /'reydi,you/ *n* radyo
radish /'rEdiş/ *n* turp
radius /'reydiyıs/ *n* (pl radii) yarıçap
raft /rEft/ *n* sal
rag /rEg/ *n* paçavra, bez parçası
rage /reyc/ *n* öfke, hiddet, gazap; *v* hiddetlenmek
raid /reyd/ *n* akın, baskın
rail /reyL/ *n* parmaklık, tırabzan
railing /'reyLiN/ *n* parmaklık, korkuluk
railroad /'reyL,roud/ *n* demiryolu
railway /'reyL,wey/ *n* demiryolu
rain /reyn/ *n* yağmur; *v* yağmur yağmak
rainbow /'reyn,bou/ *n* gökkuşağı
raincoat /'reyn,kout/ *n* yağmurluk
rainfall /'reyn,fOOL/ *n* yağış miktarı
rainproof /'reyn,pruuf/ *adj* su geçirmez
rainy /'reynii/ *adj* yağmurlu
raise /reyz/ *v* yükseltmek; inşa etmek; yetiştirmek; *nAm* ücret artışı
raisin /'reyzın/ *n* kuru üzüm
rake /reyk/ *n* tırmık
rally /'rELii/ *n* toplanma; ralli
ramp /rEmp/ *n* rampa, meyilli yol
rancid /'rEnsid/ *adj* kokmuş, ekşimiş
random /'rEndım/ *adj* tesadüfi, rasgele; **at** ~ rasgele, tesadüfen
rang /rEN/ *v* (p ring)
range /reync/ *n* sıra, dizi; menzil; ~ **finder** telemetre
rank /rENk/ *n* rütbe, derece; sıra

ransom /'rEnsım/ *n* fidye
rape /reyp/ *v* ırza geçmek
rapid /'rEpid/ *adj* hızlı, seri
rare /reyr/ *adj* az bulunur, nadir
rarely /'reyrLii/ *adv* nadiren
rascal /'rEskıL/ *n* çapkın, serseri, alçak kimse
rash /rEş/ *adj* aceleci, ihtiyatsız; *n* deride ufak kızıl lekeler, isilik
raspberry /'rEz,berii/ *n* ahududu
rat /rEt/ *n* sıçan, iri fare
rate /reyt/ *n* oran; fiyat; hız; **at any** ~ her halde, her nasılsa; **exchange** ~ döviz kuru
rather /'rEDır/ *adv* oldukça, bir hayli; tercihan
ratio /'reyşou/ *n* nispet, oran
ration /'rEşın/ *n* pay, hisse
rational /'rEşınıL/ *adj* akıl sahibi; mantıklı, makul
raven /'reyvın/ *n* kuzgun
raw /rOO/ *adj* çiğ; ham; ~ **material** hammadde
ray /rey/ *n* şua, ışın
rayon /'reyOn/ *n* suni ipekli kumaş
razor /'reyzır/ *n* ustura; ~ **blade** jilet; ustura ağzı
reach /riiç/ *v* uzanmak; varmak; *n* uzanma; erişilebilen uzaklık
reaction /ri'yEkşın/ *n* tepki, reaksiyon
***read** /riid/ *v* okumak
reading /'riidiN/ *n* okuma; ~ **lamp** masa lambası; ~ **room** okuma odası
ready /'redii/ *adj* hazır
ready-made /'redii'meyd/ *adj* hazır; ~ **clothes** hazır giyim
real /riiL/ *adj* gerçek
reality /ri'yELıtii/ *n* gerçeklik, hakikat
realizable /'riyı,LayzıbıL/ *adj* gerçekleştirilebilir
realize /'riyı,Layz/ *v* anlamak; gerçekleştirmek
really /'riilii/ *adv* gerçekten, aslında
rear /riir/ *n* arka, geri; *v* yetiştirmek, büyütmek; ~ **light** arka lambası
reason /'riizın/ *n* sebep; akıl; *v* muhakeme etmek; sonuç çıkartmak
reasonable /'riizınıbıL/ *adj* makul
reassure /,riyı'şuur/ *v* güvenini tazelemek; temin etmek
rebate /'riibeyt/ *n* iskonto, indirim
rebellion /ri'beLyın/ *n* isyan, ayaklanma
recall /ri'kOOL/ *v* geri çağırmak; anımsamak
receipt /ri'siit/ *n* makbuz; satış fişi
receive /ri'siiv/ *v* almak; kabul etmek
receiver /ri'siivır/ *n* alıcı; almaç, ahize
recent /'riisınt/ *adj* yeni; son zamanda olan
recently /'riisıntLii/ *adv* geçenlerde, son zamanlarda
reception /ri'sepşın/ *n* kabul; kabul töreni; resepsiyon; ~ **office** kabul bürosu
receptionist /ri'sepşınist/ *n* resepsiyon memuru
recession /ri'seşın/ *n* geri çekilme; ekonomik durgunluk
recipe /'resıpii/ *n* reçete; yemek tarifi
recital /ri'saytıL/ *n* ifade; resital
reckless /'rekLıs/ *adj* dünyayı umursamayan; pervasız; kayıtsız
reckon /'rekın/ *v* hesap etmek; tahmin etmek
recognition /,rekıg'nişın/ *n* tanıma, tanınma; kabul
recognize /'rekıg,nayz/ *v* tanımak; onaylamak
recollect /,rekı'Lekt/ *v* hatırlamak
recommence /,rekı'mens/ *v* yeniden başlamak
recommend /,rekı'mend/ *v* tavsiye

etmek
recommendation /ˌrekımen'deyşın/ *n* tavsiye
reconciliation /ˌrekınsiLi'yeyşın/ *n* uzlaşma, barışma
record[1] /'rekırd/ *n* plak; kayıt; rekor; **long-playing ~** uzunçalar; **~ player** pikap
record[2] /ri'kOOrd/ *v* kaydetmek
recorder /ri'kOOrdır/ *n* kayıt cihazı, teyp
recording /ri'kOOrdiN/ *n* plak, bant
recover /ri'kAvır/ *v* iyileşmek; tekrar ele geçirmek, geri almak
recovery /ri'kAvırii/ *n* geri alma; iyileşme
recreation /ˌrekri'yeyşın/ *n* dinlenme, eğlence; **~ center** dinlenme ve eğlence merkezi; **~ ground** spor sahası, oyun sahası
recruit /ri'kruut/ *n* acemi er; yeni üye
rectangle /'rekˌtEngıL/ *n* dikdörtgen
rectangular /rek'tENgyıLır/ *adj* dikdörtgen şeklinde
rector /'rektır/ *n* papaz; rektör
rectory /'rektırii/ *n* papaz konutu
rectum /'rektım/ *n* kalın bağırsağın son kısmı
red /red/ *adj* kırmızı
redeem /ri'diim/ *v* rehinden kurtarmak
red-handed /'red'hEndid/ *adj* suçüstü
reduce /ri'duus/ *v* azaltmak, küçültmek
reduction /ri'dAkşın/ *n* azaltma, küçültme
redundant /ri'dAndınt/ *adj* gereken-den fazla
reed /riid/ *n* saz, kamış
reef /riif/ *n* resif, kayalık
referee /ˌrefı'rii/ *n* hakem
reference /'refırıns/ *n* başvuru; referans; **with ~ to** münasebetiyle
refer to /ri'fÖr/ göndermek, havale etmek
refill /'riiˌfiL/ *n* boşalan maddenin yedeği
refinery /ri'faynırii/ *n* rafineri
reflect /ri'fLekt/ *v* aksettirmek, yansıtmak
reflection /ri'fLekşın/ *n* yansıma, aksetme
reflector /ri'fLektır/ *n* reflektör, yansıtıcı
reformation /ˌrefır'meyşın/ *n* düzeltme, düzelme
refrain from /ri'freyn/ kendini tutmak, sakınmak, kaçınmak
refresh /ri'freş/ *v* canlandırmak; tazelemek
refreshment /ri'freşmınt/ *n* canlan-dırıcı şey; yiyecek içecek
refrigerator /ri'fricıˌreytır/ *n* buzdolabı
refuge /'refyuuc/ *n* sığınak; barınak
refugee /ˌrefyuu'cii/ *n* mülteci
refund[1] /ri'fAnd/ *v* (parayı) geri vermek
refund[2] /'riifAnd/ *n* geri ödeme; geri ödenen meblağ
refusal /ri'fyuuzıL/ *n* ret, kabul etmeyiş
refuse[1] /ri'fyuuz/ *v* reddetmek, vazgeçmek
refuse[2] /'refyuus/ *n* süprüntü, döküntü
regard /ri'gaard/ *v* itibar etmek, dikkat etmek; **regards** *pl* saygılar, selamlar; **as regards** hakkında, hususunda
regarding /ri'gaardiN/ *prep* hakkında, hususunda
regime /rı'jiim/ *n* rejim, idare
region /'riicın/ *n* memleket; mıntıka, bölge
regional /'riicınıL/ *adj* bölgesel
register /'recistır/ *v* deftere geçirmek, kaydetmek; **registered letter**

taahhütlü mektup
registration /ˌrecis'treyşın/ *n* kayıt, tescil; ~ **form** kayıt formu; ~ **number** kayıt numarası; ~ **plate** plaka
regret /ri'gret/ *v* kederlenmek; pişman olmak; *n* keder, pişmanlık
regular /'regyıLır/ *adj* muntazam, düzenli
regulate /'regyıˌLeyt/ *v* düzenlemek, ayar etmek
regulation /ˌregyı'Leyşın/ *n* nizam, düzen; talimat
rehabilitation /ˌriihıˌbiLı'teyşın/ *n* eski haline kavuşma
rehearsal /ri'hÖrsıL/ *n* piyes *veya* müzik provası
rehearse /ri'hÖrs/ *v* tekrarlamak, prova etmek
reign /reyn/ *n* saltanat; *v* saltanat sürmek
reimburse /ˌrii-im'bÖrs/ *v* harcanan parayı ödemek, parasını geri vermek
reindeer /'reynˌdiir/ *n* (pl ~) ren geyiği
reject /ri'cekt/ *v* reddetmek
rejoice /ri'cOys/ *v* sevinmek, memnun olmak
relate /ri'Leyt/ *v* anlatmak; ilgili olmak
related /ri'Leytid/ *adj* anlatılmış; ilgili
relation /ri'Leyşın/ *n* ilişki, alaka; akrabalık
relative /'reLıtiv/ *n* akraba
relax /ri'LEks/ *v* gevşemek, dinlenmek
relaxation /riLEk'seyşın/ *n* gevşeyerek dinlenme
release /ri'Liis/ *v* serbest bırakmak; *n* kurtarma; tahliye
reliable /ri'LayıbıL/ *adj* güvenilir
relic /'reLik/ *n* kalıntı; hatıra; kutsal emanet
relief /ri'Liif/ *n* iç rahatlaması, imdat, çare; kabartma resim
relieve /ri'Liiv/ *v* gönlünü ferahlatmak
religion /ri'Licın/ *n* din
religious /ri'Licıs/ *adj* dindar; dine ait
reluctant /ri'LAktınt/ *adj* isteksiz, gönülsüz
rely on /ri'Lay/ güvenmek, itimat etmek
remain /ri'meyn/ *v* kalmak, olduğu gibi kalmak
remainder /ri'meyndır/ *n* bakiye, artan şey
remaining /ri'meyniN/ *adj* geri kalan
remark /ri'maark/ *n* işaret, söz; *v* söylemek; dikkat edip görmek
remarkable /ri'maarkıbıL/ *adj* dikkate değer
remedy /'remıdii/ *n* çare; ilaç
remember /ri'membır/ *v* hatırlamak, anmak
remembrance /ri'membrıns/ *n* hatıra
remind /ri'maynd/ *v* hatırlatmak
remit /ri'mit/ *v* havale etmek
remittance /ri'mitıns/ *n* para havalesi
remnant /'remnınt/ *n* bakiye, fazla miktar
remote /ri'mout/ *adj* uzak, yabancı
removal /ri'muuvıL/ *n* yerini değiştirme, kaldırma
remove /ri'muuv/ *v* kaldırmak, yerini değiştirmek
remunerate /ri'myuunıˌreyt/ *v* hakkını vermek; mükâfatlandırmak
remuneration /riˌmyuunı'reyşın/ *n* karşılık, mükâfat
renew /ri'nuu/ *v* yenilemek; müddeti uzatmak
rent /rent/ *v* kiralamak; *n* kira
repair /ri'peyr/ *v* onarmak; *n* onarım
reparation /repı'reyşın/ *n* tamirat, onarım
***repay** /ri'pey/ *v* geri vermek; karşılığını ödemek

repeat /ri'piit/ *v* tekrarlamak
repellent /ri'peLınt/ *adj* def edici, uzaklaştırıcı
repentance /ri'pentıns/ *n* pişmanlık, tövbe
repertory /'repır,tOOrii/ *n* hazırlanmış piyesler listesi, repertuar
repetition /repı'tişın/ *n* tekrarlama
replace /ri'pLeys/ *v* yerine başka bir şey koymak
reply /ri'pLay/ *v* yanıtlamak; *n* yanıt; **in ~** yanıt olarak
report /ri'pOOrt/ *v* söylemek; rapor vermek, haber yaymak; *n* söylenti; rapor
reporter /ri'pOOrtır/ *n* gazete muhabiri
represent /,repri'zent/ *v* göstermek, ifade etmek, temsil etmek
representation /,reprizen'teyşın/ *n* temsil etme *veya* edilme
representative /,repri'zentıtiv/ *adj* temsil eden; tipik; *n* temsilci
reprimand /'reprı,mEnd/ *v* azarlamak
reproach /ri'prouç/ *n* azar, sitem; *v* kınamak, sitem etmek
reproduce /,riiprı'duus/ *v* kopya etmek, çoğaltmak
reproduction /,riiprı'dAkşın/ *n* üreme; tekrar elde etme
reptile /'reptiL/ *n* sürüngen
republic /ri'pAbLik/ *n* cumhuriyet
republican /ri'pAbLikın/ *adj* cumhuriyetçi
repulsive /ri'pALsiv/ *adj* iğrenç, tiksindirici
reputation /,repyı'teyşın/ *n* şöhret, ün
request /ri'kwest/ *n* dilek, temenni; *v* rica etmek, istemek
require /ri'kwayr/ *v* gerektirmek; istemek, talep etmek
requirement /ri'kwayrmınt/ *n* gerek, icap, ihtiyaç
requisite /'rekwızit/ *adj* lazım, gerekli, zaruri
rescue /'reskyuu/ *v* kurtarmak; *n* kurtarma; imdada yetişme
research /ri'sÖrç/ *n* dikkatle arama, araştırma; *v* araştırmak
resemblance /ri'zembLıns/ *n* benzeyiş
resemble /ri'zembıL/ *v* benzemek
resent /ri'zent/ *v* gücenmek; içerlemek
reservation /,rezır'veyşın/ *n* yer ayırtma
reserve /ri'zÖrv/ *v* ilerisi için saklamak; *n* ihtiyaten saklanan şey
reserved /ri'zÖrvd/ *adj* saklı; ketum; çekingen
reservoir /'rezır,vuar/ *n* su haznesi
reside /ri'zayd/ *v* ikamet etmek, oturmak
residence /'rezıdıns/ *n* oturma, ikamet; **~ permit** ikamet belgesi
resident /'rezıdınt/ *n* bir yerde yerleşmiş kimse, sakin; *adj* yerleşmiş, oturan
resign /ri'zayn/ *v* istifa etmek
resignation /,rezig'neyşın/ *n* istifa
resin /'rezin/ *n* reçine, çamsakızı
resist /ri'zist/ *v* dayanmak, karşı gelmek
resistance /ri'zistıns/ *n* dayanma, dayanıklılık, direnç
resolute /'rezı,Luut/ *adj* azimkâr, kararlı
resource /'rii,sOOrs/ *n* kaynak; çare
respect /ri'spekt/ *n* saygı, hürmet; *v* hürmet etmek, saygı göstermek
respectable /ri'spektıbıL/ *adj* saygıya layık
respectful /ri'spektfıL/ *adj* saygılı
respective /ri'spektiv/ *adj* sıraya göre olan
respiration /,respı'reyşın/ *n* teneffüs, soluk alma, solunum
respite /'respit/ *n* mühlet; geçici olarak erteleme

responsibility /ri,spOnsı'biLıtii/ *n* sorumluluk
responsible /ri'spOnsıbıL/ *adj* sorumlu
rest /rest/ *n* dinlenme; *v* dinlenmek; ~ **home** dinlenme evi; *Am* sanatoryum
restaurant /'restırınt/ *n* lokanta
restful /'restfıL/ *adj* rahatlatıcı, dinlendirici
restless /'restLıs/ *adj* hiç durmayan; huzursuz
restrain /ri'streyn/ *v* zapt etmek, frenlemek; sınırlamak
restriction /ri'strikşın/ *n* sınırlama
result /ri'zALt/ *n* sonuç; *v* meydana gelmek, sonuçlanmak
resume /ri'zuum/ *v* yeniden başlamak *veya* devam etmek
résumé /'rezu,mey/ *n* özet; *nAm* özgeçmiş
retail /'riiteyL/ *n* perakende satış
retailer /'rii,teyLır/ *n* perakendeci
retina /'retını/ *n* retina, ağtabaka
retired /ri'tayrd/ *adj* emekli
return /ri'tÖrn/ *v* geri dönmek; *n* dönüş; iade; ~ **flight** dönüş uçuşu; ~ **journey** dönüş yolculuğu; ~ **ticket** *Br* gidiş dönüş bileti
reunite /,riiyuu'nayt/ *v* yeniden birleştirmek
reveal /ri'viiL/ *v* açığa vurmak
revelation /,revı'Leyşın/ *n* açığa vurma; vahiy
revenge /ri'venc/ *n* intikam
revenue /'revı,nyuu/ *n* gelir
reverse /ri'vÖrs/ *n* ters taraf; *adj* karşıt; geri; *v* geri vitese almak
review /ri'vyuu/ *n* yeniden gözden geçirme; eleştiri; edebiyat ve fikir dergisi
revise /ri'vayz/ *v* tekrar gözden geçirmek; düzeltmek
revision /ri'vijın/ *n* düzeltme; yeniden gözden geçirme
revival /ri'vayvıL/ *n* yeniden canlanma; kendine gelme
revolt /ri'vouLt/ *v* isyan etmek; *n* ayaklanma
revolting /ri'vouLtiN/ *adj* tiksindirici
revolution /,revı'Luuşın/ devrim; *n* dönme, devir
revolutionary /,revı'Luuşı,nerii/ *adj* devrimci
revolver /ri'vOLvır/ *n* altıpatlar, revolver
revue /ri'vyuu/ *n* revü, sahne gösterisi
reward /ri'wOOrd/ *n* ödül; *v* ödül vermek
rheumatism /'ruumı,tizım/ *n* romatizma
rhinoceros /ray'nOsırıs/ *n* (pl ~, ~es) gergedan
rhubarb /'ruubaarb/ *n* ravent bitkisi
rhyme /raym/ *n* kafiye, uyak
rhythm /'riDım/ *n* vezin; uyum, ritim
rib /rib/ *n* kaburga kemiği
ribbon /'ribın/ *n* kurdele
rice /rays/ *n* pirinç
rich /riç/ *adj* zengin
riches /'riçiz/ *pl* zenginlik, servet
riddle /'ridıL/ *n* bilmece
ride /rayd/ *n* ata binme; bir taşıtla yolculuk
***ride** /rayd/ *v* arabaya, ata, bisiklete binmek
rider /'raydır/ *n* binici
ridge /ric/ *n* sırt, bayır
ridicule /'ridı,kyuuL/ *v* alay etmek
ridiculous /ri'dikyıLıs/ *adj* gülünç
riding /'raydiN/ *n* binicilik; ~ **school** binicilik okulu
rifle /'rayfıL/ *v* yivli silah, tüfek
right /rayt/ *n* hakikat; hak; adalet; doğruluk; *adj* doğru; haklı; uygun; gerçek; **all right!** pekâlâ!; ***be** ~ haklı olmak; ~ **away**

hemen, derhal; ~ **of way** geçiş hakkı
righteous /'rayçıs/ *adj* dürüst, adil, erdemli
right-hand /'rayt'hEnd/ *adj* sağdaki
rightly /'raytLii/ *adv* haklı olarak, doğru olarak
rigid /'ricid/ *adj* eğilmez, bükülmez; sert
rim /rim/ *n* jant; kenar
ring /riN/ *n* yüzük, halka
***ring** /riN/ *v* tınlamak, çınlamak, çalmak; ~ **up** telefon etmek
rinse /rins/ *v* çalkalamak, durulamak; *n* durulama
riot /'rayıt/ *n* ayaklanma
rip /rip/ *v* yarmak, yırtmak
ripe /rayp/ *adj* olgun
rise /rayz/ *n* yükseliş; doğuş; *nBr* ücret artışı
***rise** /rayz/ *v* kalkmak; doğmak (güneş); yükselmek
rising /'rayziN/ *n* yükseliş; isyan
risk /risk/ *n* risk; tehlike; *v* tehlikeye atmak
risky /'riskii/ *adj* tehlikeli, riskli
rival /'rayvıL/ *n* rakip; *v* rakip olmak
rivalry /'rayvıLrii/ *n* rekabet
river /'rivır/ *n* ırmak, nehir; ~ **bank** ırmak kenarı
riverside /'rivır,sayd/ *n* ırmak kenarı
road /roud/ *n* yol; ~ **fork** yol ayrımı; ~ **map** yol haritası; ~ **system** yol şebekesi; ~ **up** yol onarımda
roadhouse /'roud,haus/ *n* şehir dışında yol kenarındaki lokanta *veya* gece kulübü
roadside /'roud,sayd/ *n* yol kenarı; ~ **restaurant** şehir dışındaki konaklama yerlerindeki lokanta
roadway /'roud,wey/ *nAm* yolun taşıt geçen kısmı
roam /roum/ *v* dolaşmak, gezmek
roar /rOOr/ *v* gürlemek, kükremek; *n* gürleme, kükreme
roast /roust/ *v* fırında kızartmak
rob /rOb/ *v* soymak
robber /'rObır/ *n* hırsız, haydut
robbery /'rObırii/ *n* soygun
robe /roub/ *n* cüppe; uzun elbise
robust /rou'bAst/ *adj* sağlam, dinç
rock /rOk/ *n* kaya
rocket /'rOkit/ *n* roket; füze
rocky /'rOkii/ *adj* kayalık
rod /rOd/ *n* çubuk, değnek
roe /rou/ *n* balık yumurtası
roll /rouL/ *v* yuvarlamak; yuvarlanmak; *n* rulo; küçük ekmek
roller-skating /'rouLır,skeytiN/ *n* tekerlekli patenle kayma
Roman Catholic /'roumın 'kETıLik/ Katolik
romance /rou'mEns/ *n* öykü, masal; aşk macerası
romantic /rou'mEntik/ *adj* romantik
Rome /roum/ Roma
roof /ruuf/ *n* çatı; **thatched** ~ saz *veya* samanla örtülmüş çatı
room /ruum/ *n* oda; yer; ~ **and board** tam pansiyon; ~ **service** oda servisi; ~ **temperature** oda ısısı
roomy /'ruumii/ *adj* geniş
rooster /'ruustır/ *n* horoz
root /ruut/ *n* kök; kaynak
rope /roup/ *n* ip, halat
rosary /'rouzırii/ *n* tespih
rose /rouz/ *n* gül; *adj* pembe
rotate /'rou,teyt/ *v* eksen üzerinde dönmek; döndürmek; sıra ile çalıştırmak
rotten /'rOtın/ *adj* çürümüş
rouge /ruuj/ *n* ruj; allık
rough /rAf/ *adj* pürüzlü, kaba
roulette /ruu'Let/ *n* rulet
round /raund/ *adj* yuvarlak; *prep*

etrafında; *n* daire; devir; ~ **trip** *Am* gidiş dönüş, tur
roundabout /ˌraundı'baut/ *adj* dolambaçlı; dolaylı; *nBr* atlıkarınca
rounded /'raundid/ *adj* yuvarlak
route /ruut/ *n* yol, rota
routine /ruu'tiin/ *n* alışılmış iş *veya* hareket yöntemi
row[1] /rou/ *n* sıra, dizi; *v* kürek çekmek
row[2] /rau/ *n* kavga, kargaşa
rowboat /'rou,bout/ *n* kayık, sandal
royal /'rOyıL/ *adj* krala ait; görkemli
rub /rAb/ *v* ovmak
rubber /'rAbır/ *n* kauçuk; lastik; *nBr* silgi; ~ **band** ambalaj lastiği
rubbish /'rAbiş/ *n* çerçöp, süprüntü; **talk** ~ saçmalamak
rubbish-bin /'rAbiş,bin/ *nBr* çöp kutusu
ruby /'ruubii/ *n* yakut
rucksack /'rAk,sEk/ *n* sırt çantası
rudder /'rAdır/ *n* dümen
rude /ruud/ *adj* kaba, nezaketsiz
rug /rAg/ *n* halı, kilim
ruin /'ruuin/ *v* harap etmek; *n* harabe, enkaz
ruination /ˌruui'neyşın/ *n* mahvetme; yıkılma
rule /ruuL/ *n* kural; rejim, yönetim; *v* hüküm sürmek, idare etmek; **as a** ~ çoğunlukla, genellikle
ruler /'ruuLır/ *n* hükümdar, yönetici; cetvel
Rumania /ruu'meyniyı/ Romanya
Rumanian /ruu'meyniyın/ *adj* Romanya'ya ait; *n* Romen; Romence
rumor /'ruumır/ *n* söylenti, rivayet
***run** /rAn/ *v* koşmak; yönetmek; akmak; işletmek; ~ **into** rastlamak
runaway /'ranı,wey/ *n* kaçak
rung /rAN/ *v* (pp ring)
runway /'rAn,wey/ *n* uçak pisti
rural /'ruurıL/ *adj* kırsal
ruse /ruuz/ *n* hile, düzen
rush /rAş/ *v* koşmak, acele etmek; *n* koşma, acele etme; ~ **hour** işin *veya* trafiğin en yoğun olduğu zaman
Russia /'rAşı/ Rusya
Russian /'rAşın/ *adj* Rusya'ya ait; *n* Rus; Rusça
rust /rAst/ *n* pas
rustic /'rAstik/ *adj* kırlara, köye ait
rusty /'rastii/ *adj* paslı

S

saccharin /'sEkırin/ *n* sakarin
sack /sEk/ *n* torba, çuval
sacred /'seykrid/ *adj* kutsal
sacrifice /'sEkri,fays/ *n* kurban; fedakârlık; *v* kurban etmek; feda etmek
sacrilege /'sEkrıLic/ *n* kutsal bir şeye karşı hürmetsizlik
sad /sEd/ *adj* üzgün; hazin
saddle /'sEdıL/ *n* eyer, semer
sadness /'sEdnıs/ *n* keder, hüzün
safe /seyf/ *adj* emniyette; emniyetli, güvenilir; *n* kasa
safety /'seyftii/ *n* güvenlik, selamet; ~ **belt** emniyet kemeri; ~ **pin** çengelli iğne; ~ **razor** tıraş makinesi
Sagittarius /ˌsEcı'teyriyıs/ Yay burcu
sail /seyL/ *v* yelkenli *veya* gemi ile gitmek; *n* yelken
sailboat /'seyL,bout/ *n* yelkenli gemi
sailor /'seyLır/ *n* gemici
saint /seynt/ *n* aziz, evliya
sake /seyk/ *n* hatır, uğur; **for heaven's** ~ Allah aşkına; **for my** ~ hatırım için

salad /'sELıd/ *n* salata; ~ **oil** sofrada kullanılan sıvı yağ
salami /sı'Laami/ *n* salam
salary /'sELırii/ *n* maaş, aylık ücret
sale /seyL/ *n* satış; **clearance** ~ indirimli satışlar; **for** ~ satılık; **sales** indirimli satışlar
saleable /'seyLıbıL/ *adj* satılabilir
salesgirl /'seyLz,gÖrL/ *n* satıcı kız
salesman /'seyLzmın/ *n* (pl -men) satıcı erkek
saliva /sı'Layvı/ *n* salya, tükürük
salmon /'sEmın/ *n* (pl ~) som balığı
salon /sı'LOn/ *nAm* salon, misafir odası
Salonika /sı'LOnikı/ Selanik
saloon /sı'Luun/ *nAm* meyhane, bar
salt /sOOLt/ *n* tuz
saltcellar /'sOOLt,seLır/ *n* tuzluk
salty /'sOOLtii/ *adj* tuzlu
salute /sı'Luut/ *v* selamlamak
salvation /sEL'veyşın/ *n* kurtarış; kurtuluş
salve /sEv/ *n* merhem
same /seym/ *adj* aynı; eşit
sample /'sEmpıL/ *n* örnek, model
sanatorium /,sEnı'tOOriyım/ *n* (pl ~s, -ria) sanatoryum
sand /sEnd/ *n* kum
sandal /'sEndıL/ *n* çarık; sandal
sandpaper /'sEnd,peypır/ *n* zımpara kâğıdı
sandwich /'sEndwiç/ *n* sandviç
sandy /'sEndii/ *adj* kumlu, kumsal
sanitary /'sEnı,terii/ *adj* sağlıkla ilgili, sıhhi; ~ **towel** adet bezi
sapphire /'sEfayr/ *n* safir
sarcastic /saar'kEstik/ *adj* iğneleyici, alaylı
sardine /saar'diin/ *n* sardalye
sat /sEt/ *v* (p, pp sit)
satchel /'sEçıL/ *n* el çantası
satellite /'sEtı,Layt/ *n* uydu
satin /'sEtin/ *n* saten, atlas
satire /'sEtayr/ *n* hiciv, taşlama
satisfaction /,sEtis'fEkşın/ *n* memnuniyet, hoşnutluk; tatmin
satisfy /'sEtis,fay/ *v* memnun etmek; tatmin etmek
Saturday /'sEtırdii/ cumartesi
sauce /sOOs/ *n* sos, salça
saucepan /'sOOs,pEn/ *n* kulplu tencere
saucer /'sOOsır/ *n* fincan tabağı; **flying** ~ uçan daire
Saudi /saa'uudii/ *n* Suudi Arabistanlı
Saudi Arabia /saa'uudii ı'reybiyı/ Suudi Arabistan
Saudi Arabian /saa'uudii ı'reybiyın/ *adj* Suudi Arabistan'a ait
sauna /'saunı/ *n* sauna
sausage /'sOOsic/ *n* sucuk, sosis
savage /'sEvic/ *adj* vahşi, yabani
save /seyv/ *v* kurtarmak; korumak; biriktirmek
savings /'seyviNz/ *pl* tasarruf; ~ **bank** tasarruf bankası *veya* sandığı
savior /'seyvyır/ *n* kurtarıcı
savory /'seyvırii/ *adj* lezzetli, iştah açıcı; hoş kokulu
saw[1] /sOO/ *v* (p see)
saw[2] /sOO/ *n* testere
sawdust /'sOO,dAst/ *n* bıçkı tozu, talaş
sawmill /'sOO,miL/ *n* bıçkıhane
***say** /sey/ *v* demek, söylemek
scaffold /'skEfıLd/ *n* yapı iskelesi; darağacı platformu
scale /skeyL/ *n* terazi gözü, kefe; balık pulu; **scales** *pl* terazi
scandal /'skEndıL/ *n* skandal, rezalet
Scandinavia /,skEndi'neyviyı/ İskandinavya
Scandinavian /,skEndi'neyviyın/ *adj* İskandinavya'ya ait; *n* İskandinav; İskandinav dilleri
scapegoat /'skeyp,gout/ *n* günah

keçisi; başkalarının ceza ve sorumluluğunu yüklenen kimse
scar /skaar/ *n* yara izi
scarce /skeyrs/ *adj* nadir; eksik, kıt
scarcely /'skeyrsLii/ *adv* ancak, güçbela
scarcity /'skeyrsıtii/ *n* kıtlık, nadir oluş
scare /skeyr/ *v* ürkütmek; *n* korku, panik
scarf /skaarf/ *n* (pl ~s, scarves) eşarp
scarlet /'skaarLıt/ *adj* al, kırmızı; ~ **fever** kızıl hastalığı
scary /'skeyrii/ *adj* korku veren; korkak
scatter /'skEtır/ *v* dağıtmak, saçmak
scene /siin/ *n* manzara; sahne
scenery /'siinırii/ *n* manzara
scenic /'siinik/ *adj* sahneye ait; manzaraya ait
scent /sent/ *n* koku, güzel koku
schedule /'skecuuL/ *n* tarife, program
scheme /'skiim/ *n* plan, proje
schizophrenia /,skitsı'friiniyı/ *n* şizofreni
scholar /'skOLır/ *n* alim, bilgin
scholarship /'skOLır,şip/ *n* alimlik, ilim; burs
school /skuuL/ *n* okul
schoolboy /'skuuL,bOy/ *n* erkek öğrenci
schoolgirl /'skuuL,gÖrL/ *n* kız öğrenci
science /'sayıns/ *n* fen, ilim
scientific /,sayın'tifik/ *adj* bilimsel, fenni
scientist /'sayıntist/ *n* bilim adamı
scissors /'sizırz/ *pl* makas
sclerosis /skLı'rousis/ *n* doku sertleşmesi, skleroz
scold /skouLd/ *v* azarlamak
scooter /'skuutır/ *n* küçük motosiklet; tekerlekli çocuk kızağı
score /skOOr/ *n* skor; *v* sayı kaydetmek, puan yazmak
scorn /skOOrn/ *n* küçük görme; *v* hor görmek, küçümsemek
Scorpio /'skOOrpi,you/ Akrep burcu
scorpion /'skOOrpiyın/ *n* akrep; ~ **fish** iskorpit
Scot /skOt/ *n* İskoçyalı
Scotch /skOç/ *adj* İskoçya'ya ait; **scotch tape** seloteyp
Scotland /'skOtLınd/ İskoçya
Scottish /'skOtiş/ *adj* İskoçyalı
scout /'skaut/ *n* izci, gözcü
scrap /skrEp/ *n* parça, kırıntı; ~ **iron** hurda demir
scrapbook /'skrEp,buk/ *n* kesilen resimlerin yapıştırıldığı albüm
scrape /skreyp/ *v* kazımak
scratch /skrEç/ *v* çizmek, tırmalamak; kaşımak; *n* sıyrık, çizik
scream /skriim/ *v* bağırmak, feryat etmek; *n* çığlık
screen /skriin/ *n* ekran
screw /skruu/ *n* vida; *v* vidalamak
screwdriver /'skruu,drayvır/ *n* tornavida
scrub /skrAb/ *v* ovmak, fırçalamak; *n* çalılık, fundalık
sculptor /'skALptır/ *n* heykeltıraş
sculpture /'skALpçır/ *n* heykel
sea /sii/ *n* deniz; ~ **bird** deniz kuşu; ~ **gull** martı; ~ **urchin** deniz kestanesi; ~ **water** deniz suyu
seacoast /'sii,koust/ *n* deniz kıyısı
seal /siiL/ *n* mühür; ayıbalığı, fok
seam /siim/ *n* dikiş, dikiş yeri
seaman /'siimın/ *n* (pl -men) denizci, gemici
seamless /'siimLıs/ *adj* dikişsiz
seaport /'sii,pOOrt/ *n* liman
search /sÖrç/ *v* araştırmak; *n* arama, araştırma
searchlight /'sÖrç,Layt/ *n* projektör,

ışıldak
seascape /'sii,skeyp/ *n* deniz manzarası
seashell /'sii,şeL/ *n* deniz kabuğu
seashore /'sii,şOOr/ *n* deniz kıyısı
seasick /'sii,sik/ *adj* deniz tutmasından muztarip
seasickness /'sii,siknis/ *n* deniz tutması
seaside /'sii,sayd/ *n* deniz kıyısı; ~ **resort** deniz kıyısındaki yazlık
season /'siizın/ *n* mevsim; **high** ~ canlı mevsim; **low** ~ ölü mevsim; **off** ~ sezon dışı; ~ **ticket** abonman kartı *veya* bileti
seat /siit/ *n* oturulacak yer; ~ **belt** emniyet kemeri
second /'sekınd/ *num* ikinci
secondary /'sekın,derii/ *adj* ikincil, ikinci derecede; ~ **school** orta ve lise düzeyindeki okul
secondhand /'sekınd'hEnd/ *adj* kullanılmış, elden düşme
secret /'siikrit/ *n* sır; *adj* gizli
secretary /'sekrı,terii/ *n* sekreter
secrete /si'kriit/ *v* salgılamak
section /'sekşın/ *n* bölüm; parça
secular /'sekyıLır/ *adj* dünyevi; laik
secure /si'kyuur/ *adj* korkudan, kuşkudan uzak; güvenli, emin
securities /si'kyuurıtiiz/ *pl* menkul kıymetler
security /si'kyuurıtii/ *n* güvenlik; teminat
sedate /si'deyt/ *adj* temkinli; sakin
sedative /'sedıtiv/ *n* teskin edici, yatıştırıcı
seduce /si'duus/ *v* baştan çıkarmak, ayartmak
***see** /sii/ *v* görmek; anlamak; ~ **to** icabına bakmak
seed /siid/ *n* tohum; çekirdek
***seek** /siik/ *v* aramak, araştırmak
seem /siim/ *v* görünmek; gibi gelmek
seen /siin/ *v* (pp see)
seesaw /'sii,sOO/ *n* tahterevalli
seize /siiz/ *v* kapmak; yakalamak; zapt etmek
seldom /'seLdım/ *adv* nadiren, seyrek
select /si'Lekt/ *v* seçmek, ayırmak; *adj* seçilmiş, seçkin
selection /si'Lekşın/ *n* seçme; seçme parçalar
self-centered /'seLf'sentırd/ *adj* hep kendini düşünen
self-employed /'selfim'pLOyd/ *adj* serbest çalışan
self-evident /,self'evıdınt/ *adj* aşikâr, açık
self-government /'seLf'gAvırnmınt/ *n* özerklik, muhtariyet
selfish /'sELfiş/ *adj* bencil, egoist
selfishness /'seLfişnıs/ *n* bencillik, egoizm
self-respect /,selfri'spekt/ *n* özsaygı, onur
self-service /'seLf'sÖrvis/ *n* selfservis
***sell** /seL/ *v* satmak
semblance /'sembLıns/ *n* dış görünüş, yalancı görünüş
semi- /'semi/ *pref* yarım
semiannual /,semiy'EnyuuıL/ *adj* altı ayda bir olan
semicircle /'semi,sÖrkıL/ *n* yarım daire
semicolon /'semi,kouLın/ *n* noktalı virgül
semi-detached house /'semidi,tEçt ,haus/ *Br* bir yandan bitişik müstakil ev
senate /'senıt/ *n* senato
senator /'senıtır/ *n* senatör
***send** /send/ *v* göndermek, yollamak; ~ **back** geri göndermek; ~ **for** aratmak, çağırtmak; istetmek

senile /'siinayL/ *adj* ihtiyarlığa mahsus
sensation /sen'seyşın/ *n* duygu; heyecan
sensational /sen'seyşınıL/ *adj* heyecan yaratan, sansasyonel
sense /sens/ *n* duyu; his; akıl; anlam; *v* hissetmek; sezmek; **common** ~ sağduyu
senseless /'sensLıs/ *adj* anlamsız; akılsız
sensible /'sensıbıL/ *adj* makul, akla yatkın
sensitive /'sensıtiv/ *adj* duyarlı; alıngan
sentence /'sentıns/ *n* cümle; *v* mahkûm etmek
sentimental /,sentı'mentıL/ *adj* duygusal
separate[1] /'sepı,reyt/ *v* ayırmak, bölmek
separate[2] /'sepırıt/ *adj* ayrı, ayrılmış, müstakil
separately /'sepırıtLii/ *adv* ayrı ayrı; bağlantısız olarak
September /sep'tembır/ eylül
septic /'septik/ *adj* çürütücü, mikroplu; ***become** ~ bulaşıcı olmak
sequel /'siikwıL/ *n* bir şeyin devamı; sonuç
sequence /'siikwıns/ *n* ardışıklık, sıra
serene /sı'riin/ *adj* sakin; açık, durgun
sergeant /'saarcınt/ *n* çavuş
serial /'siiriyıL/ *n* tefrika, dizi
series /'siiriiz/ *n* (pl ~) sıra; seri, dizi
serious /'siiriyıs/ *adj* ciddi; önemli
seriousness /'siiriyısnıs/ *n* ciddiyet
sermon /'sÖrmın/ *n* vaaz, dinsel öğüt
serum /'siirım/ *n* serum
servant /'sÖrvınt/ *n* hizmetçi, uşak
serve /sÖrv/ *v* hizmet etmek
service /'sÖrvis/ *n* hizmet; servis; ~ **charge** servis ücreti; ~ **station** benzin istasyonu; servis istasyonu
serviette /sÖrvi'yet/ *nBr* sofra peçetesi
session /'seşın/ *n* oturum, toplantı
set /set/ *n* takım, grup
***set** /set/ *v* koymak, yerleştirmek; ~ **menu** fiks mönü; ~ **out** yola çıkmak
setting /'setiN/ *n* ortam; durum; ~ **lotion** saçın biçimini koruyan losyon
settle /'setıL/ *v* yerleştirmek; kararlaştırmak, halletmek; ~ **down** yerleşmek, oturmak
settlement /'setıLmınt/ *n* halletme; yerleşme; yerleşim yeri
seven /'sevın/ *num* yedi
seventeen /,sevın'tiin/ *num* on yedi
seventeenth /,sevın'tiinT/ *num* on yedinci
seventh /'sevınT/ *num* yedinci
seventy /'sevıntii/ *num* yetmiş
several /'sevırıL/ *adj* birkaç; birçok
severe /sı'viir/ *adj* sert; şiddetli; vahim
sew /sou/ *v* dikmek; ~ **up** dikip kapamak
sewer /'suuır/ *n* lağım
sewing machine /'souiN mı,şiin/ dikiş makinesi
sex /seks/ *n* seks, cinsiyet
sexual /'sekşuuıL/ *adj* cinsel
sexuality /,sekşuu'ELıtii/ *n* cinsiyet, cinsellik
shade /şeyd/ *n* gölge; ince fark
shadow /'şEdou/ *n* gölge
shady /'şeydii/ *adj* gölgeli
***shake** /şeyk/ *v* sallamak; sarsmak; çalkalamak
shaky /'şeykii/ *adj* zayıf; titrek
***shall** /şEL/ *v* -ecek; -meli
shallow /'şELou/ *adj* sığ; yüzeysel

shame /şeym/ *n* utanç; ayıp; **shame!** ayıp!, utan!, yazıklar olsun!
shampoo /şEm'puu/ *n* şampuan; *v* (başı) şampuanla yıkamak
shamrock /'şEm,rOk/ *n* yonca
shape /şeyp/ *n* biçim; *v* biçimlendirmek
share /şeyr/ *v* paylaşmak; *n* pay, hisse
shark /şaark/ *n* köpekbalığı
sharp /şaarp/ *n* keskin; açıkgöz
sharpen /'şaarpın/ *v* bilemek, sivriltmek
shave /şeyv/ *v* sakal tıraşı olmak; **shaving brush** tıraş fırçası; **shaving cream** tıraş kremi; **shaving soap** tıraş sabunu
shaver /'şeyvır/ *n* elektrikli tıraş makinesi
shawl /şOOL/ *n* şal
she /şii/ *pron* o (dişil)
shed /şed/ *n* sundurma; baraka
***shed** /şed/ *v* dökmek, akıtmak
sheep /şiip/ *n* (pl ~) koyun
sheer /şiir/ *adj* tam; halis, saf; çok ince ve şeffaf
sheet /şiit/ *n* çarşaf; levha, tabaka
shelf /şeLf/ *n* (pl shelves) raf
shell /şeL/ *n* kabuk
shellfish /'şeL,fiş/ *n* kabuklu deniz hayvanı
shelter /'şeLtır/ *n* sığınak; *v* barındırmak; korumak
shepherd /'şepırd/ *n* çoban
shift /şift/ *n* değiştirme; vardiya
***shine** /şayn/ *v* parlamak; üstün olmak
ship /şip/ *n* gemi, vapur; *v* sevk etmek, yollamak; **shipping line** denizcilik şirketi
shipowner /'şip,ounır/ *n* armatör, gemi sahibi
shipyard /'şip,yaard/ *n* tersane
shirt /şÖrt/ *n* gömlek
shiver /'şivır/ *v* titremek; *n* titreme, üşüme
shivery /'şivırii/ *adj* titrek; tüyler ürpertici
shock /şOk/ *n* şok; *v* sarsmak; çok şaşırtmak; ~ **absorber** amortisör
shocking /'şOkiN/ *adj* şaşırtıcı, şok tesiri yapan
shoe /şuu/ *n* ayakkabı; **gym shoes** jimnastik ayakkabısı; ~ **polish** ayakkabı boyası
shoelace /'şuu,Leys/ *n* ayakkabı bağı
shoemaker /'şuu,meykır/ *n* kunduracı
shoe-shop /'şuu,şOp/ *nBr* ayakkabı dükkânı
shook /şuk/ *v* (p shake)
***shoot** /şuut/ *v* atmak, fırlatmak; ateş etmek
shop /şOp/ *n* dükkân, mağaza; *v* çarşıya gitmek, alışverişe çıkmak; ~ **assistant** *Br* tezgâhtar; **shopping bag** alışveriş çantası; **shopping center** alışveriş merkezi
shopkeeper /'şOp,kiipır/ *n* dükkâncı
shopwindow /'şOp,windou/ *n* vitrin
shore /şOOr/ *n* sahil, kıyı
short /şOOrt/ *adj* kısa; bodur; ~ **circuit** kısa devre
shortage /'şOOrtic/ *n* eksiklik, açık
shortcoming /'şOOrt,kAmiN/ *n* kusur, eksiklik
shorten /'şOOrtın/ *v* kısaltmak; kısalmak
shorthand /'şOOrt,hEnd/ *n* stenografi
shortly /'şOOrtLii/ *adv* yakında; kısaca
shorts /şOOrts/ *pl* kısa pantolon; *plAm* iç donu
shortsighted /'şOOrt'saytid/ *adj* miyop; ileriyi göremeyen, basiretsiz
shot[1] /şOt/ *v* (p, pp shoot)
shot[2] /şOt/ *n* atış; şırınga, aşı

***should** /şud/ *v* -meli
shoulder /'şouLdır/ *n* omuz
shout /şaut/ *v* bağırmak; *n* bağırma, feryat
shovel /'şAvıL/ *n* kürek
show /şou/ *n* gösteri; sergi
***show** /şou/ *v* göstermek
showcase /'şou,keys/ *n* vitrin, dükkân camekânı
shower /şauır/ *n* duş; sağanak
showroom /'şou,ruum/ *n* sergi salonu
shriek /şriik/ *v* çığlık atmak; *n* çığlık
shrimp /şrimp/ *n* karides
shrine /şrayn/ *n* türbe
***shrink** /şriNk/ *v* çekmek, küçülmek; büzülmek
shrinkproof /'şriNk,pruuf/ *adj* çekmez, küçülmez
shrub /şrAb/ *n* çalı, bodur ağaç
shudder /'şAdır/ *n* titreme, ürperti
shuffle /'şAfıL/ *v* karıştırmak
***shut** /şAt/ *v* kapamak; **shut** *adj* kapalı; ~ **in** içeri kapatmak
shutter /'şAtır/ *n* kepenk, panjur
shy /şay/ *adj* ürkek, utangaç
shyness /'şaynıs/ *n* çekingenlik, utangaçlık
Siam /sa'yEm/ Siyam, Tayland
Siamese /,sayı'miiz/ *adj* Siyam'a ait; *n* Siyamlı, Taylandlı; Siyamca
sick /sik/ *adj* hasta, keyifsiz; bulantılı; ***be** ~ **of** bıkmak, usanmak
sickness /'siknıs/ *n* hastalık; mide bulantısı
side /sayd/ *n* yan; taraf; kenar; **one sided** *adj* tek taraflı; ~ **street** yan sokak, tali yol
sideburns /'sayd,bÖrnz/ *pl* kısa favori
sidelight /'sayd,Layt/ *n* borda feneri
sidewalk /'sayd,wOOk/ *n* yaya kaldırımı
sideways /'sayd,weyz/ *adv* yandan, yan taraftan
siege /siic/ *n* kuşatma, muhasara
sieve /siiv/ *n* elek, kalbur; *v* elemek
sift /sift/ *v* kalburdan geçirmek
sight /sayt/ *n* görme; gözlem; manzara
sightseeing /'sayt,sii-iN/ *n* gezme, ilginç yerleri ziyaret
sign /sayn/ *n* işaret, alamet; *v* imzalamak; işaret etmek
signal /'signıL/ *n* işaret; *v* işaret vermek
signature /'signıçır/ *n* imza
significant /sig'nifikınt/ *adj* anlamlı; önemli
signpost /'sayn,poust/ *n* işaret direği
silence /'sayLıns/ *n* sessizlik; *v* susturmak, sesini kesmek
silencer /'sayLınsır/ *n* susturucu
silent /'sayLınt/ *adj* sessiz, suskun; ***be** ~ susmak, ses çıkarmamak
silk /siLk/ *n* ipek
silken /'siLkın/ *adj* ipek gibi, ipekli
silly /'siLii/ *adj* sersem, şaşkın
silver /'siLvır/ *n* gümüş; gümüş para; gümüş eşya
silversmith /'siLvır,smiT/ *n* gümüş işleyen kuyumcu
silverware /'siLvır,weyr/ *n* gümüş eşya
similar /'simıLır/ *adj* benzer, birbirine yakın
similarity /,simı'LErıtii/ *n* benzeyiş, benzerlik
simple /'simpıL/ *adj* basit; sade
simply /'simpLii/ *adv* ancak; basit olarak
simulate /'simyı,Leyt/ *v* taklit etmek
simultaneous /,saymıL'teyniyıs/ *adj* aynı zamanda olan, eşzamanlı
sin /sin/ *n* günah, suç
since /sins/ *prep* -den beri; -den; sonra; *adv* o zamandan beri; ondan sonra; *conj* -den beri, -den dolayı; çünkü
sincere /sin'siir/ *adj* samimi

sinew /'sinyuu/ *n* kiriş, kas teli
***sing** /siN/ *v* şarkı söylemek
singer /'siNır/ *n* şarkıcı
single /'siNgıL/ *adj* tek, yalnız; evlenmemiş, bekâr
singular /'siNgyıLır/ *n* tekil; tek şey; *adj* acayip; eşsiz, tek
sinister /'sinistır/ *adj* uğursuz
sink /siNk/ *n* lavabo
***sink** /siNk/ *v* batmak; dalmak; düşmek
sip /sip/ *n* yudum
siphon /'sayfın/ *n* sifon
sir /sÖr/ efendim; beyefendi
siren /'sayrın/ *n* siren, canavar düdüğü
sister /'sistır/ *n* kız kardeş
sister-in-law /'sistırin,LOO/ *n* (pl sisters-) görümce, yenge, baldız
***sit** /sit/ *v* oturmak; ~ **down** oturmak; **sitting room** salon, oturma odası
site /sayt/ *n* yer, mevki
situated /'siçuu,eytid/ *adj* bulunan, olan, yerleşmiş
situation /,siçuu'eyşın/ *n* yer, mevki; hal, durum
six /siks/ *num* altı
sixteen /'siks'tiin/ *num* on altı
sixteenth /'siks'tiinT/ *num* on altıncı
sixth /sikT/ *num* altıncı
sixty /'sikstii/ *num* altmış
size /sayz/ *n* büyüklük, beden; boy
skate /skeyt/ *v* paten yapmak; *n* paten
skating /'skeytiN/ *n* paten yapma; ~ **rink** suni patinaj sahası
skeleton /'skeLıtın/ *n* iskelet
sketch /skeç/ *n* resim, kroki; *v* taslak yapmak
sketchbook /'skeç,buk/ *n* resim müsvedde defteri
skewer /'skyuuır/ *n* kebap şişi
ski[1] /skii/ *v* kayak yapmak
ski[2] /skii/ *n* (pl ~, ~s) kayak; ~ **boots** kayak ayakkabısı; ~ **jump** kayakçının yaptığı atlama; ~ **lift** teleksi; kayakçı teleferiği; ~ **pants** kayak pantolonu; ~ **poles**, ~ **sticks** kayak sopaları
skid /skid/ *v* yana doğru kaymak, yana savrulmak
skier /'ski-ır/ *n* kayakçı
skiing /'skii-iN/ *n* kayak yapma, kayma
skill /skiL/ *n* hüner, ustalık
skilled /skiLd/ *adj* mahir, usta
skillful /'skiLfıL/ *adj* hünerli, becerikli
skin /skin/ *n* deri; ~ **cream** cilt kremi
skip /skip/ *v* sıçramak, sekmek
skirt /skÖrt/ *n* etek
skull /skAL/ *n* kafatası
skunk /skANk/ *n* kokarca
sky /skay/ *n* gökyüzü
skyline /'skay,Layn/ *n* ufuk çizgisi
skyscraper /'skay,skreypır/ *n* gökdelen
slack /sLEk/ *adj* gevşek; ağır; dikkatsiz
slacks /sLEks/ *pl* pantolon
slam /sLEm/ *v* çarpıp kapamak, vurmak
slander /'sLEndır/ *n* sözle iftira, çamur atma
slang /sLEN/ *n* argo
slant /sLEnt/ *v* eğim vermek, yana yatmak; gerçeği çarpıtmak
slanting /'sLEntiN/ *adj* meyilli, verev
slap /sLEp/ *v* tokat atmak; *n* tokat, şamar
slate /sLeyt/ *n* yazboz tahtası
slave /sLeyv/ *n* köle
sledge /sLec/ *n* büyük kızak
sleep /sLiip/ *n* uyku
***sleep** /sLiip/ *v* uyumak; **sleeping bag** uyku tulumu; **sleeping car**

yataklı vagon; **sleeping pill** uyku hapı
sleepless /'sLiipLıs/ *adj* uykusuz
sleepy /'sLiipii/ *adj* uykulu
sleeve /sLiiv/ *n* elbise kolu
sleigh /sLey/ *n* yolcu taşıyan büyük kızak
slender /'sLendır/ *adj* ince; narin
slice /sLays/ *n* dilim
slide /sLayd/ *n* kayma; kaydırak; slayt
***slide** /sLayd/ *v* kaymak; kızak yapmak
slight /sLayt/ *adj* önemsiz; cüzi; hafif
slim /sLim/ *adj* ince, uzun yapılı
slip /sLip/ *v* kaymak; kaydırmak; *n* kayma; yanlışlık; iç eteklik, kombinezon
slipper /'slipır/ *n* terlik
slippery /'sLipırii/ *adj* kaypak, kaygan; güvenilmez
slogan /'sLougın/ *n* slogan, parola
slope /sLoup/ *n* eğimli yüzey; *v* eğimli olmak
sloping /'sLoupiN/ *adj* eğimli
sloppy /'sLOpii/ *adj* dikkatsizce yapılmış; dikkatsiz; şapşal, çapaçul
slot /sLOt/ *n* dar ve uzun yiv, delik; ~ **machine** içine para atılan satış makinesi
slovenly /'sLAvınLii/ *adj* intizamsız, gevşek
slow /sLou/ *adj* yavaş, ağır; ~ **down** hızını azaltmak
sluice /sLuus/ *n* savak; savaktan akan su
slum /sLAm/ *n* yoksul semt, gecekondu bölgesi
slump /sLAmp/ *n* fiyat düşüşü; çökme
slush /sLAş/ *n* sulu çamur; yarı erimiş kar
sly /sLay/ *adj* sinsi; kurnaz
smack /smEk/ *v* şapırtı ile öpmek *veya* tokat atmak; *n* tokat, şamar
small /smOOL/ *adj* küçük; önemsiz
smallpox /'smOOL,pOks/ *n* çiçek hastalığı
smart /smaart/ *adj* şık, zarif; akıllı; açıkgöz
smell /smeL/ *n* koku
***smell** /smeL/ *v* kokmak; koklamak
smelly /'smeLii/ *adj* kötü kokulu, kokmuş
smile /smayL/ *v* gülümsemek; *n* tebessüm, gülümseme
smith /smiT/ *n* demirci
smoke /smouk/ *v* sigara içmek; tütmek; *n* duman; **no smoking** sigara içilmez; **smoking compartment** sigara içilen kompartıman; **smoking room** sigara içilen salon
smoker /'smoukır/ *n* sigara içen kimse
smooth /smuuD/ *adj* düz, pürüzsüz, kaygan; hoş
smuggle /'smAgıL/ *v* kaçakçılık yapmak
snack /snEk/ *n* hafif yemek, çerez; ~ **bar** hafif yemeklerin yendiği lokanta
snail /sneyL/ *n* salyangoz, sümüklüböcek
snake /sneyk/ *n* yılan
snapshot /'snEp,şOt/ *n* enstantane fotoğraf
sneakers /'sniikırz/ *plAm* lastik spor ayakkabısı
sneeze /sniiz/ *v* aksırmak, hapşırmak
sniper /'snaypır/ *n* pusuya yatan nişancı
snob /snOb/ *n* züppe
snooty /'snuutii/ *adj* züppe, kendini beğenmiş
snore /snOOr/ *v* horlamak

snorkel /'snOOrkıL/ *n* şnorkel; dalgıç tüpü
snout /snaut/ *n* uzun hayvan burnu
snow /snou/ *n* kar; *v* kar yağmak
snowstorm /'snou,stOOrm/ *n* kar fırtınası
snowy /'snouii/ *adj* karlı
so /sou/ *conj* öyle ise, şu halde, bunun için; *adv* öyle, böyle; o kadar ki; çok; **and ~ on** vesaire, ve diğerleri; **~ far** şimdiye kadar; **~ that** öyle ki
soak /souk/ *v* iyice ıslatmak, sırılsıklam etmek
soap /soup/ *n* sabun; **~ powder** toz sabun
sober /'soubır/ *adj* kendine hâkim, ayık; ciddi, ağırbaşlı
so-called /'sou'kOOLd/ *adj* güya, sözde
soccer /'sOkır/ *n* futbol; **~ team** futbol takımı
social /'souşıL/ *adj* sosyal, toplumsal
socialism /'souşı,Lizım/ *n* sosyalizm
socialist /'souşıList/ *adj* sosyalist; *n* sosyalist kimse
society /sı'sayıtii/ *n* toplum; dernek; şirket
sock /sOk/ *n* kısa çorap
socket /'sOkit/ *n* duy; priz
soda water /'soudı 'wOOtır/ gazoz, maden sodası
sofa /'soufı/ *n* sedir, kanepe
soft /sOOft/ *adj* yumuşak; **~ drink** alkolsüz içki
soften /'sOOfın/ *v* yumuşatmak
soil /sOyL/ *n* toprak
soiled /sOyLd/ *adj* kirli, lekeli
sold /souLd/ *v* (p, pp sell); **~ out** bitmiş, hepsi satılmış
solder /'sOdır/ *v* lehimlemek
soldier /'souLcır/ *n* asker, er
sole[1] /souL/ *adj* tek, yegâne
sole[2] /souL/ *n* taban; dilbalığı
solely /'souLLii/ *adv* yalnız, sadece
solemn /'sOLım/ *adj* ağırbaşlı, vakur
solicitor /sı'Lisıtır/ *nAm* aracı, hukuk müşaviri; *nBr* avukat, dava vekili
solid /'sOLid/ *adj* katı; sağlam; bütün; *n* katı madde
solitude /'sOLı,tuud/ *n* yalnızlık, tek başına olma
soluble /'sOLyıbıL/ *adj* eritilebilir, çözülebilir
solution /sı'Luuşın/ *n* çözüm; çözelti
solve /sOLv/ *v* halletmek, çözmek
somber /'sOmbır/ *adj* loş, karanlık
some /sAm/ *adj* birkaç; bazı; biraz; *pron* bazısı, kimisi; **~ day** bir gün, günün birinde; **~ more** biraz daha
somebody /'sAm,bOdii/ *pron* birisi
somehow /'sAm,hau/ *adv* bir yolunu bulup, her nasılsa
someone /'sAm,wAn/ *pron* birisi
something /'sAmTiN/ *pron* bir şey
sometime /'sam,taym/ *adv* bir zaman, bir ara
sometimes /'sAm,taymz/ *adv* bazen, ara sıra
somewhat /'sAm,hwaat/ *adv* biraz, bir dereceye kadar
somewhere /'sAm,hweyr/ *adv* bir yere, bir yerde
son /sAn/ *n* erkek evlat, oğul
song /sON/ *n* şarkı
son-in-law /'sAnin,LOO/ *n* (pl sons-) damat
soon /suun/ *adv* yakında, birazdan; hemen; **as ~ as** olur olmaz
sooner /'suunır/ *adv* tercihan, daha ziyade; **~ or later** er geç
sophisticated /sı'fistı,keytid/ *adj* bilgiç, görmüş geçirmiş; incelikli
sore /sOOr/ *adj* dokununca acıyan; kırgın, küskün; *n* yara, acıyan yer; **~ throat** boğaz ağrısı
sorrow /'sOrou/ *n* keder, elem.

hüzün
sorry /'sOrii/ *adj* üzgün; **sorry!** özür dilerim!, pardon!
sort /sOOrt/ *v* ayırmak, ayıklamak, sınıflandırmak; *n* çeşit, tür; **all sorts of** her çeşit
sought /sOOt/ *v* (p, pp seek)
soul /souL/ *n* ruh, can
sound /saund/ *n* ses; gürültü; *v* ses çıkarmak; *adj* sağlam, mükemmel
soundproof /'saund,pruuf/ *adj* ses geçirmez
soup /suup/ *n* çorba
soupplate /'suup,pLeyt/ *n* çorba tabağı
soupspoon /'suup,spuun/ *n* çorba kaşığı
sour /'saur/ *adj* ekşi; huysuz
source /sOOrs/ *n* kaynak, köken
south /sauT/ *n* güney; **South Pole** Güney Kutbu
South Africa /,sauT 'Efrikı/ Güney Afrika
southeast /,sauT'iist/ *n* güneydoğu
southerly /'sADırLii/ *adj* güneye ait
southern /'sADırn/ *adj* güneye ait
southwest /,sauT'west/ *n* güneybatı
souvenir /,suuvıniir/ *n* hatıra, andaç
sovereign /,sOvırın/ *n* hükümdar, kral
Soviet /'souvi,yet/ *adj* Sovyet
Soviet Union /'souvi,yet 'yuunyın/ Sovyetler Birliği
***sow** /sou/ *v* (tohum) ekmek
spa /spaa/ *n* kaplıca
space /speys/ *n* yer, alan; uzay; uzaklık; aralık; *v* aralık koymak
spaceship /'speys,şip/ *n* uzay gemisi
spacious /'speyşıs/ *adj* geniş, açık, ferah
spade /speyd/ *n* bahçıvan beli; iskambilde maça
Spain /speyn/ İspanya
Spaniard /'spEnyırd/ *n* İspanyol
Spanish /'spEniş/ *adj* İspanya'ya ait; *n* İspanyolca
spanking /'spENkiN/ *n* dayak; şaplak
spanner /'spEnır/ *n* somun anahtarı
spare /speyr/ *adj* yedek; az, kıt; *v* esirgemek, kıymamak; idareli kullanmak; ~ **part** yedek parça; ~ **room** misafir yatak odası; ~ **time** boş zaman; ~ **tire** yedek lastik; ~ **wheel** yedek tekerlek, stepne
spark /spaark/ *n* kıvılcım; ~ **plug** buji
sparkling /'spaarkLiN/ *adj* parlayan, canlı; köpüklü
sparrow /'spErou/ *n* serçe
spat /spEt/ *v* (p, pp spit)
***speak** /spiik/ *v* konuşmak; söylev vermek
spear /spiir/ *n* mızrak; zıpkın
special /'speşıL/ *adj* özel; ~ **delivery** özel ulak
specialist /'speşıList/ *n* mütehassıs, uzman
speciality /speşi'yELıtii/ *nBr* özellik; ihtisas, uzmanlık; spesiyalite
specially /'speşıLii/ *adv* özellikle
specialty /'speşıLtii/ *n* ihtisas, uzmanlık; özellik
species /'spiişiiz/ *n* (pl ~) tür, çeşit
specific /spi'sifik/ *adj* kendine has, özel
specify /'spesı,fay/ *v* ayrıntılı olarak belirtmek, belirlemek
specimen /'spesımın/ *n* örnek, numune
speck /spek/ *n* leke, benek
spectacle /'spektıkıL/ *n* gösteri; manzara; **spectacles** *pl* gözlük
spectator /'spek,teytır/ *n* seyirci
speculate /'spekyı,Leyt/ *v* düşünmek, zihinde tartmak; spekülasyon yapmak
speech /spiiç/ *n* konuşma yeteneği;

konuşma; söz; dil; söylev
speechless /'spiiçLıs/ *adj* dili tutulmuş
speed /spiid/ *n* hız, çabuk gitme; **cruising ~** seyir sürati; **~ limit** hız sınırı
***speed** /spiid/ *v* çabuk gitmek; hız vermek
speeding /'spiidiN/ *n* hız yapma
speedometer /spii'dOmıtır/ *n* hız göstergesi
spell /speL/ *n* büyü
***spell** /speL/ *v* harflerini bir bir söylemek
spelling /'speLiN/ *n* imla, yazım
***spend** /spend/ *v* harcamak
sphere /sfiir/ *n* küre
spice /spays/ *n* baharat
spicy /'spaysii/ *adj* baharatlı, hoş kokulu
spider /'spaydır/ *n* örümcek; **spider's web** örümcek ağı
***spill** /spiL/ *v* dökmek
***spin** /spin/ *v* eğirmek, bükmek; döndürmek
spinach /'spiniç/ *n* ıspanak
spine /spayn/ *n* belkemiği, omurga
spinster /'spinstır/ *n* evde kalmış kız
spire /spayr/ *n* kulenin sivri tepesi
spirit /'spirit/ *n* ruh; şevk, cesaret; **spirits** *pl* alkollü içki; keyif, moral; **~ stove** ispirto ocağı
spiritual /'spiriçuuıL/ *adj* ruhsal
spit /spit/ *n* tükürük, salya; şiş
***spit** /spit/ *v* tükürmek
in spite of /in 'spayt ıv/ rağmen, hiçe sayarak
spiteful /'spaytfıL/ *adj* garezkâr, kinci
splash /spLEş/ *v* çamur *veya* su sıçratmak
spleen /spLiin/ *n* dalak; terslik, huysuzluk
splendid /'spLendid/ *adj* şahane, mükemmel
splendor /'spLendır/ *n* parlaklık, şaşaa
splinter /'spLintır/ *n* kıymık, ince tahta parçası
***split** /spLit/ *v* yarmak; bölmek
***spoil** /spOyL/ *v* bozmak; şımartmak
spoke /spouk/ *v* (p speak)
sponge /spAnc/ *n* sünger
spook /spuuk/ *n* hayalet; hortlak
spool /spuuL/ *n* makara, bobin
spoon /spuun/ *n* kaşık
spoonful /'spuun,fuL/ *n* kaşık dolusu
spontaneous /spOn'teyniyıs/ *adj* kendi kendine olan, içten doğan
sport /spOOrt/ *n* spor
sports car /'spOOrts ,kaar/ spor otomobil
sports jacket /'spOOrts ,cEkit/ spor ceket
sportsman /'spOOrtsmın/ *n* (pl -men) sporcu
sportswear /'spOOrts,weyr/ *n* spor giysi
spot /spOt/ *n* benek, nokta
spotless /'spOtLıs/ *adj* lekesiz, tertemiz; kusursuz
spotlight /'spOt,Layt/ *n* projektör ışığı
spotted /'spOtid/ *adj* noktalı, benekli
spouse /spaus/ *n* eş; koca *veya* karı
spout /spaut/ *n* fışkırma; içinden sıvı çıkan ağız *veya* uç
sprain /spreyn/ *v* burkmak; *n* burkulma, incinme
***spread** /spred/ *v* yaymak, sermek
spring /spriN/ *n* ilkbahar; yay, zemberek; kaynak
springtime /'spriN,taym/ *n* bahar mevsimi
sprout /spraut/ *n* filiz, tomurcuk; **Brussels ~** Brüksel lahanası
spun /spAn/ *v* (p, pp spin)
spy /spay/ *n* casus, ajan
squadron /'skwOdrın/ *n* süvari bölüğü; ufak donanma, filo

square /skweyr/ *adj* kare şeklinde; *n* kare; meydan
squash /skwOş/ *n* kabak; *nBr* meyve suyu ile yapılan içecek; bir çeşit top oyunu
squirrel /'skwırıL/ *n* sincap
stable /'steybıL/ *adj* sabit; dengeli; yıkılmaz; *n* ahır
stack /stEk/ *n* büyük yığın
stadium /'steydiyım/ *n* stadyum
staff /stEf/ *n* memurlar, personel; kadro
stage /steyc/ *n* sahne; safha; derece
stain /steyn/ *v* lekelemek; **stained glass** vitray; ~ **remover** leke çıkarıcı
stainless /'steynLıs/ *adj* lekesiz, kusursuz; ~ **steel** paslanmaz çelik
staircase /'steyr,keys/ *n* binanın merdiven kısmı
stairs /steyrz/ *pl* merdiven
stale /steyL/ *adj* bayat
stall /stOOL/ *n* ahır bölmesi; küçük dükkân
stamina /'stEmını/ *n* dayanıklılık
stamp /stEmp/ *n* pul; ıstampa; damga; *v* damgalamak; pul yapıştırmak; ~ **machine** otomatik pul makinesi
stand /stEnd/ *n* duruş; sehpa; tribün
***stand** /stEnd/ *v* ayakta durmak; tahammül etmek
standard /'stEndırd/ *n* standart, ölçü birimi; ~ **of living** yaşam düzeyi
stanza /'stEnzı/ *n* şiir kıtası, dörtlük
staple /'steypıL/ *n* zımba teli
stapler /'steypLır/ *n* zımba
star /staar/ *n* yıldız; **the Stars and Stripes** ABD bayrağı
starboard /'staarbırd/ *n* geminin sancak tarafı
starch /staarç/ *n* nişasta; kola; *v* kolalamak
stare /steyr/ *v* gözünü dikip bakmak
starling /'staarLiN/ *n* sığırcık kuşu
start /staart/ *v* başlamak; başlatmak; harekete geçirmek; *n* başlangıç; **starter motor** marş motoru; **starting point** başlangıç noktası
starve /staarv/ *v* açlıktan ölecek hale gelmek; yiyeceksiz bırakmak
state /steyt/ *n* devlet; eyalet; durum; *v* ifade etmek, belirtmek; **the States** Amerika Birleşik Devletleri
statement /'steytmınt/ *n* ifade, demeç
statesman /'steytsmın/ *n* (pl -men) devlet adamı
station /'steyşın/ *n* gar, istasyon; mevki; ~ **master** istasyon şefi
stationary /'steyşı,nerii/ *adj* sabit, durağan
stationer's /'steyşınırz/ *n* kırtasiye dükkânı
stationery /'steyşı,nerii/ *n* kırtasiye
statistics /stı'tistiks/ *pl* istatistik
statue /'stEçuu/ *n* heykel
stay /stey/ *v* durmak; kalmak; *n* kalma; oturma, ikamet
steadfast /'sted,fEst/ *adj* sabit, değişmez
steady /'stedii/ *adj* sabit; sağlam; düzenli
steak /steyk/ *n* biftek
***steal** /stiiL/ *v* çalmak, aşırmak
steam /stiim/ *n* buhar
steamer /'stiimır/ *n* buharlı gemi
steel /stiiL/ *n* çelik
steep /stiip/ *adj* dik, sarp
steeple /'stiipıL/ *n* kilise kulesi
steering wheel /'stiiriN ,hwiiL/ direksiyon
steersman /'stiirzmın/ *n* (pl -men) dümenci
stem /stem/ *n* sap, gövde
stenographer /stı'nOgrıfır/ *n*

stenograf
step /step/ *n* adım; basamak; *v* adım atmak; yürümek
stepchild /'step,çayLd/ *n* (pl -children) üvey çocuk
stepfather /'step,faaDır/ *n* üvey baba
stepmother /'step,mADır/ *n* üvey ana
sterile /'sterıL/ *adj* kısır, ürün vermeyen; mikropsuz
sterilize /'sterı,Layz/ *v* mikroplarını öldürmek, kısırlaştırmak
steward /'stuuwırd/ *n* kamarot; kâhya; erkek hostes
stewardess /'stuuwırdıs/ *n* hostes; kadın kamarot
stick /stik/ *n* değnek, sopa, baston
***stick** /stik/ *v* yapıştırmak; yapışmak
sticker /'stikır/ *n* etiket
sticky /'stikii/ *adj* yapışkan
stiff /stif/ *adj* katı; inatçı; dik; gergin
still /stiL/ *adv* hâlâ; daha, yine; *adj* sessiz; durgun
stillness /'stiLnıs/ *n* sessizlik
stimulant /'stimyıLınt/ *n* uyarıcı
stimulate /'stimyı,Leyt/ *v* uyarmak, kamçılamak, tahrik etmek
sting /stiN/ *n* arı iğnesi, zehirli iğne
***sting** /stiN/ *v* arı gibi sokmak, batmak
stingy /'stincii/ *adj* pinti, cimri
***stink** /stiNk/ *v* pis kokmak
stipulate /'stipyı,Leyt/ *v* şart koşmak
stipulation /,stipyı'Leyşın/ *n* şart, taahhüt
stir /stÖr/ *v* karıştırmak; harekete geçirmek; kımıldanmak
stirrup /'stÖrıp/ *n* üzengi
stitch /stiç/ *n* dikiş; ilmik
stock /stOk/ *n* stok; mevcut mal; hisse senedi; *v* stok yapmak; ~ **exchange** borsa; ~ **market** borsa; **stocks and shares** hisse senetleri
stocking /'stOkiN/ *n* çorap
stole[1] /stouL/ *v* (p steal)
stole[2] /stouL/ *n* etol, şal
stomach /'stAmık/ *n* mide
stomachache /'stAmık,eyk/ *n* mide sancısı, karın ağrısı
stone /stoun/ *n* taş; değerli taş; meyve çekirdeği; **pumice** ~ süngertaşı
stood /stud/ *v* (p, pp stand)
stop /stOp/ *v* durmak; durdurmak; *n* durma
stoplight /'stOp,Layt/ *n* otomobilin stop lambası
stopper /'stOpır/ *n* tapa, tıkaç
storage /'stOOric/ *n* depolama; depo
store /stOOr/ *nAm* mağaza, dükkân; ambar; *v* saklamak, biriktirmek
storehouse /'stOOr,haus/ *n* ambar, ardiye, depo
stork /stOOrk/ *n* leylek
storey 'stOOrii/ *nBr* kat
storm /stOOrm/ *n* fırtına
stormy /'stOOrmii/ *adj* fırtınalı
story /'stOOrii/ *n* hikâye; *nAm* kat
stout /staut/ *adj* kalın; sağlam; şişman
stove /stouv/ *n* soba; fırın; ocak
straight /streyt/ *adj* doğru, düz; *adv* doğrudan doğruya; ~ **ahead** doğruca; ~ **away** hemen, derhal; ~ **on**
strain /streyn/ *n* gerginlik; baskı; *v* zorlamak; süzmek
strainer /'streynır/ *n* süzgeç
the Straits /streyts/ İstanbul ve Çanakkale Boğazları
strange /streync/ *adj* tuhaf, acayip; yabancı
stranger /'streyncır/ *n* yabancı
strangle /'strENgıL/ *v* boğazlamak
strap /strEp/ *n* kayış; şerit
straw /strOO/ *n* saman
strawberry /'strOO,berii/ *n* çilek

stream /striim/ *n* akarsu; akıntı; *v* akmak
street /striit/ *n* sokak, cadde; ~ **organ** laterna
streetcar /'striit,kaar/ *n* tramway
strength /streNT/ *n* kuvvet, güç
stress /stres/ *n* baskı; gerilim; vurgu; *v* vurgulamak; önemini belirtmek
stretch /streç/ *v* uzatmak, germek
strict /strikt/ *adj* sıkı; çok titiz
strife /strayf/ *n* didişme, çekişme
strike /strayk/ *n* vurma; grev
***strike** /strayk/ *v* vurmak, çarpmak; grev yapmak
striking /'straykiN/ *adj* dikkati çeken, göze çarpan
string /striN/ *n* ip, sicim, kordon
strip /strip/ *n* uzun ve dar parça, şerit
stripe /strayp/ *n* çubuk, yol, çizgi
striped /straypt/ *adj* çizgili, yollu
stroke /strouk/ *n* vuruş, darbe
stroll /strouL/ *v* gezinmek
strong /strOON/ *adj* kuvvetli, sağlam; metin, iradeli
stronghold /'strOON,houLd/ *n* müstahkem yer, kale
struck /strAk/ *v* (p, pp strike)
structure /'strAkçır/ *n* yapı, bina
struggle /'strAgıL/ *n* mücadele, uğraş; *v* çabalamak, mücadele etmek
stub /stAb/ *n* kütük; izmarit
stubborn /'stAbırn/ *adj* inatçı
student /'stuudınt/ *n* öğrenci
study /'stAdii/ *v* okumak, çalışmak; araştırmak; *n* çalışma, araştırma; çalışma odası
stuff /stAf/ *n* madde; asıl, esas; kumaş
stuffed /stAft/ *adj* doldurulmuş; dolma
stuffing /'stAfiN/ *n* doldurma; dolma içi
stuffy /'stAfii/ *adj* havasız, boğucu
stumble /'stAmbıL/ *v* sendelemek; dili sürçmek
stung /stAN/ *v* (p, pp sting)
stupid /'stuupid/ *adj* akılsız, budala; saçma
stutter /'stAtır/ *v* kekelemek; *n* kekemelik
style /stayL/ *n* tarz, üslup
subject[1] /'sAbcikt/ *n* konu; uyruk; kul; *adj* bağımlı; maruz; ***be** ~ **to** maruz kalmak; bağlı olmak
subject[2] /sıb'cekt/ *v* boyun eğdirmek; maruz bırakmak
submarine /'sAbmı,riin/ *n* denizaltı
submit /sıb'mit/ *v* teslim etmek, onayına sunmak; boyun eğmek
subordinate /sı'bOOrdınıt/ *adj* alt, aşağı; ikincil
subscriber /sıb'skraybır/ *n* abone
subscription /sıb'skripşın/ *n* abone olma
subsequent /'sAbsıkwınt/ *adj* sonra gelen; sonuç olarak izleyen
subsidy /'sAbsıdii/ *n* bağış, iane
substance /'sAbstıns/ *n* madde, cisim; öz
substantial /sıb'stEnşıL/ *adj* cismani; sağlam; önemli; esaslı
substitute /'sAbstı,tuut/ *v* başka bir şeyin *veya* kişinin yerine koymak; *n* vekil; ikame
subtitle /'sAb,taytıL/ *n* filmlerde altyazı
subtle /'sAtıL/ *adj* kurnaz; ince; mahir; gizli
subtract /sıb'trEkt/ *v* çıkartmak, hesaptan düşmek
suburb /'sAbÖrb/ *n* banliyö, dış mahalle
suburban /sı'bÖrbın/ *adj* banliyöye ait
subway /'sAb,wey/ *nAm* metro; *nBr* altgeçit

succeed /sık'siid/ *v* başarmak; becermek
success /sık'ses/ *n* başarı
successful /sık'sesfıL/ *adj* başarılı
succumb /sı'kAm/ *v* yenilmek; ölmek
such /sAç/ *adj* öyle, bu gibi, o kadar; *adv* o kadar ki, o derecede; ~ **as** gibi, örneğin
suck /sAk/ *v* emmek
sudden /'sAdın/ *adj* apansız, ani
suddenly /'sAdınLii/ *adv* birdenbire, ansızın
sue /suu/ *v* dava açmak
suede /sweyd/ *n* süet
Suez /suu'ez/ Süveyş
suffer /'sAfır/ *v* ıstırap çekmek; müptela olmak
suffering /'sAfıriN/ *n* ıstırap, acı
suffice /sı'fays/ *v* kâfi gelmek, yetişmek
sufficient /sı'fişınt/ *adj* yeterli; uygun
suffrage /'sAfric/ *n* oy kullanma hakkı
sugar /'şugır/ *n* şeker
suggest /sıg'cest/ *v* öne sürmek; teklif etmek
suggestion /sıg'cesçın/ *n* öneri; ima; telkin
suicide /'suuı,sayd/ *n* intihar
suit /suut/ *v* uymak; uygun gelmek; yakışmak; *n* takım elbise, tayyör, kostüm
suitable /'suutıbıL/ *adj* uygun, yerinde
suitcase /'suut,keys/ *n* valiz, bavul
suite /swiit/ *n* maiyet; daire; takım
sulfur /'sALfır/ *n* kükürt
sulk /sALk/ *v* somurtmak
sum /sAm/ *n* toplam; tutar
summary /'sAmırii/ *n* özet
summer /'sAmır/ *n* yaz; ~ **time** yaz saati
summit /'sAmit/ *n* doruk, zirve
summons /'sAmınz/ *n* (pl ~es) resmi davet, celp; celp kâğıdı
sun /sAn/ *n* güneş
sunbathe /'sAn,beyD/ *v* güneş banyosu yapmak
sunburn /'sAn,bÖrn/ *n* güneş yanığı
Sunday /'sAndii/ pazar günü
sunflower /'sAn,fLauır/ *n* ayçiçeği
sunglasses /'sAn,gLEsız/ *pl* güneş gözlüğü
sunlight /'sAn,Layt/ *n* güneş ışığı
sunny /'sAnii/ *adj* güneşli
sunrise /'sAn,rayz/ *n* gün doğuşu
sunset /'sAn,set/ *n* gün batımı, gurup
sunshade /'sAn,şeyd/ *n* güneş şemsiyesi; tente
sunshine /'sAn,şayn/ *n* güneş ışığı
sunstroke /'sAn,strouk/ *n* güneş çarpması
suntan oil /'sAn,tEn 'OyL/ güneş yağı
superb /su'pÖrb/ *adj* muhteşem, görkemli
superficial /,suupır'fişıL/ *adj* yüzeysel
superfluous /su'pÖrfLuuıs/ *adj* fazla, lüzumsuz, gereksiz
superior /sı'piiriyır/ *adj* üstün, daha iyi
superlative /sı'pÖrLıtiv/ *adj* en yüksek; eşsiz; *n* en yüksek derece *veya* miktar
supermarket /'suupır,maarkit/ *n* süpermarket
supersonic /,suupır'sOnik/ *adj* süpersonik, sesten hızlı
superstition /,suupır'stişın/ *n* batıl, itikat, boş inanç
supervise /'suupır,vayz/ *v* gözetmek, denetlemek; idare etmek
supervision /,suupır'vijın/ *n* denetleme, gözetim; idare
supervisor /'suupır,vayzır/ *n* müfettiş, denetçi; amir
supper /'sApır/ *n* hafif akşam yemeği
supple /'sApıL/ *adj* yumuşak, esnek

supplement /'sApLımınt/ *n* ilave, ek
supply /sı'pLay/ *n* tedarik; stok; *v* sağlamak, temin etmek
support /sı'pOOrt/ *v* desteklemek; yardım etmek, geçindirmek; *n* destekleme, destek; ~ **hose** elastiki çorap
supporter /sı'pOOrtır/ *n* taraftar; yardımcı; jartiyer
suppose /sı'pouz/ *v* zannetmek, farz etmek; **supposing that** farz edelim ki
suppository /sı'pOzı,tOOrii/ *n* fitil
suppress /sı'pres/ *v* bastırmak, sindirmek
surcharge /'sÖr,çaarc/ *n* çok fazla yükleme
sure /şuur/ *adj* kesin; emin, güvenilir; ***make** ~ sağlama bağlamak
surely /'şuurLii/ *adv* elbette, muhakkak
surface /'sÖrfıs/ *n* yüzey; dış görünüş
surgeon /'sÖrcın/ *n* cerrah; **veterinary** ~ *Br* veteriner
surgery /'sÖrcırii/ *n* operatörlük, cerrahlık; ameliyathane; *nBr* muayenehane
surname /'sÖr,neym/ *n* soyadı
surpass /sır'pEs/ *v* baskın çıkmak, üstün olmak, geçmek
surplus /'sÖrpLıs/ *n* artan miktar
surprise /sır'prayz/ *n* sürpriz; hayret; *v* şaşırtmak
surrender /sı'rendır/ *v* teslim etmek; teslim olmak; *n* teslim, feragat
surround /sı'raund/ *v* kuşatmak, çevirmek
surrounding /sı'raundiN/ *adj* çevresinde bulunan, çevreleyen
surroundings /sı'raundiNz/ *pl* çevre, muhit
survey /'sÖrvey/ *n* inceleme, yoklama; denetleme
survival /sır'vayvıL/ *n* hayatta kalma
survive /sır'vayv/ *v* hayatta kalmak
suspect[1] /sıs'pekt/ *v* şüphelenmek, kuşkulanmak
suspect[2] /'sAs,pekt/ *n* zan altında olan kimse, sanık
suspend /sıs'pend/ *v* geçici olarak durdurmak, ertelemek; asmak
suspenders /sıs'pendırz/ *plAm* pantolon askısı; *plBr* çorap jartiyeri
suspension /sı'spenşın/ *n* asma, asılma; ~ **bridge** asma köprü
suspicion /sı'spişın/ *n* şüphe, kuşku
suspicious /sı'spişıs/ *adj* şüpheli; şüphe eden; şüphe edilir
sustain /sıs'teyn/ *v* destek olmak; beslemek; katlanmak
swallow /'swOLou/ *v* yutmak; *n* kırlangıç
swam /swEm/ *v* (p swim)
swamp /swOmp/ *n* batak, bataklık
swan /swOn/ *n* kuğu
swap /swOp/ *v* değiş tokuş etmek
***swear** /sweyr/ *v* yemin etmek; küfretmek
sweat /swet/ *n* ter; *v* terlemek
sweater /'swetır/ *n* kazak
Swede /swiid/ *n* İsveçli
Sweden /'swiidın/ İsveç
Swedish /'swiidiş/ *adj* İsveç'e ait; *n* İsveççe
***sweep** /swiip/ *v* süpürmek; sürüklemek
sweet /swiit/ *adj* tatlı, şekerli; nazik, yumuşak; *nBr* tatlı yiyecek; **sweets** *pl* bonbon, şekerleme
sweeten /'swiitın/ *v* tatlılaştırmak
sweetheart /'swiit,haart/ *n* sevgili
sweetshop /'swiit,şOp/ *nBr* şekerci dükkânı
swell /sweL/ *adj* şık, modaya uygun
***swell** /sweL/ *v* şişmek, kabarmak

swelling /'sweLiN/ *n* şişlik
swept /swept/ *v* (p, pp sweep)
swift /swift/ *adj* çabuk, süratli
***swim** /swim/ *v* yüzmek; ~ **overarm** kulaç yüzmek
swimmer /'swimır/ *n* yüzücü
swimming /'swimiN/ *n* yüzme; ~ **pool** yüzme havuzu
swimming-trunks /'swimiN,trANks/ *nBr* erkek mayosu
swimsuit /'swim,suut/ *n* mayo
swindle /'swindıL/ *v* dolandırmak; *n* dolandırıcılık
swindler /'swindLır/ *n* dolandırıcı
swing /swiN/ *n* salıncak
***swing** /swiN/ *v* sallanmak
Swiss /swis/ *adj* İsviçre'ye ait; *n* İsviçreli
switch /swiç/ *n* devre anahtarı, şalter; *v* değiştirmek, değiş tokuş etmek; ~ **off** elektriği kapatmak, söndürmek; ~ **on** elektriği açmak, yakmak
switchboard /'swiç,bOOrd/ *n* dağıtım tablosu
Switzerland /'switsırLınd/ İsviçre
sword /sOOrd/ *n* kılıç
swordfish /'sOOrd,fiş/ *n* (pl ~, ~es) kılıçbalığı
swum /swAm/ *v* (pp swim)
syllable /'siLıbıL/ *n* hece
symbol /'simbıL/ *n* sembol, simge
sympathetic /,simpı'Tetik/ *adj* başkasının duygularına katılan
sympathy /'simpıTii/ *n* halden anlama, duygudaşlık, sempati
symphony /'simfınii/ *n* senfoni
symptom /'simptım/ *n* belirti, araz
synagogue /'sinı,gOg/ *n* sinagog, havra
synonym /'sinınim/ *n* eşanlamlı sözcük
synthetic /sin'Tetik/ *adj* sentetik, suni
syphon /'sayfın/ *n* sifon
Syria /'siriyı/ Suriye
Syrian /'siriyın/ *adj* Suriye'ye ait; *n* Suriyeli
syringe /sı'rinc/ *n* şırınga
syrup /'sirıp/ *n* şurup
system /'sistım/ *n* sistem; **decimal** ~ ondalık sistem
systematic /,sistı'mEtik/ *adj* usul ve kurala uygun, sistematik

T

table /'teybıL/ *n* masa; çizelge, tablo; ~ **of contents** içindekiler; ~ **tennis** masa tenisi
tablecloth /'teybıL,kLOT/ *n* masa örtüsü
tablespoon /'teybıL,spuun/ *n* çorba kaşığı
tablet /'tEbLit/ *n* levha, kitabe; tablet
taboo /tı'buu/ *n* tabu, yasak
tactics /'tEktiks/ *pl* muharebe usulü, manevra; taktik
tag /tEg/ *n* etiket
tail /teyL/ *n* kuyruk
taiilight /'teyL,Layt/ *n* arka lamba
tailor /'teyLır/ *n* terzi
tailor-made /'teyLır'meyd/ *adj* terzi elinden çıkmış
***take** /teyk/ *v* almak; yakalamak; el koymak; ~ **away** alıp götürmek; ~ **for granted** doğru kabul etmek; değerinin bilincine varmadan doğal kabul etmek; ~ **off** havalanmak; ~ **out** çıkartmak; götürmek; ~ **over** teslim almak; ~ **place** vuku bulmak; ~ **up** ele almak
takeoff /'teyk,OOf/ *n* kalkış, havalanma
tale /teyL/ *n* hikâye, masal

talent /'tELınt/ *n* yetenek
talented /'tELıntid/ *adj* yetenekli
talk /tOOk/ *v* konuşmak; *n* konuşma; söz; müzakere
talkative /'tOOkıtiv/ *adj* konuşkan
tall /tOOL/ *adj* uzun boylu; yüksek
tame /teym/ *adj* evcilleştirilmiş; uysal; *v* ehlileştirmek; uslandırmak
tampon /'tEmpOn/ *n* tampon
tangerine /,tEncı'riin/ *n* mandalina
tangible /'tEncıbıl/ *adj* elle tutulur; maddi
tank /tENk/ *n* sarnıç; depo
tanker /'tENkır/ *n* tanker
tanned /tEnd/ *adj* güneşte kararmış
tap /tEp/ *n* musluk; tıkaç; hafif darbe; *v* hafifçe vurmak
tape /teyp/ *n* bant, şerit; **adhesive ~** yapıştırıcı bant, seloteyp; **~ measure** şerit metre; **~ recorder** teyp, ses alma cihazı
tapestry /'tEpistrii/ *n* resim dokumalı kalın perde, örtü
tar /taar/ *n* katran, zift
target /'taargit/ *n* hedef; amaç
tariff /'tErif/ *n* tarife; ithalat *veya* ihracat vergisi
tarpaulin /taar'pOOLin/ *n* katranlı muşamba
task /tEsk/ *n* iş, görev
taste /teyst/ *n* lezzet, tat; zevk; *v* tatmak; tat almak; tadı olmak
tasteless /'teystLıs/ *adj* tatsız, yavan
tasty /'teystii/ *adj* lezzetli
tattoo /tE'tuu/ *v* vücuda dövme yapmak; *n* dövme
taught /tOOt/ *v* (p, pp teach)
Taurus /'TOOrıs/ Boğa burcu
tavern /'tEvırn/ *n* taverna, meyhane
tax /tEks/ *n* vergi; *v* vergilendirmek
taxation /tEk'seyşın/ *n* vergilendirme; vergi
tax-free /'tEks,frii/ *adj* vergiden muaf
taxi /'tEksii/ *n* taksi; **~ driver** taksi şoförü; **~ rank** *Br* taksi durağı; **~ stand** *Am* taksi durağı
taximeter /'tEksii,miitır/ *n* taksimetre
tea /tii/ *n* çay; **~ set** çay takımı
***teach** /tiiç/ *v* öğretmek
teacher /'tiiçır/ *n* öğretmen
teachings /'tiiçiNz/ *pl* öğretiler
teacup /'tii,kAp/ *n* çay fincanı
teahouse /'tii,haus/ *nAm* çay salonu, çayhane
team /tiim/ *n* ekip, takım
teapot /'tii,pOt/ *n* çaydanlık
tear[1] /tiir/ *n* gözyaşı
tear[2] /teyr/ *n* yırtık
***tear** /teyr/ *v* yırtmak; kopartmak
tear-jerker /'tiir,cÖrkır/ *n* acıklı film *veya* roman
tease /tiiz/ *v* kızdırmak, tedirgin etmek; takılmak
tea-shop /'tii,şOp/ *nBr* çay salonu, çayhane
teaspoon /'tii,spuun/ *n* çay kaşığı
teaspoonful /'tiispuun,fuL/ *n* çay kaşığı dolusu
technical /'teknikıL/ *adj* bilimsel, fenni; teknik
technician /tek'nişın/ *n* teknisyen
technique /tek'niik/ *n* teknik; yöntem
technology /tek'nOLıcii/ *n* teknoloji
tedious /'tiidiyıs/ *adj* sıkıcı, usandırıcı
teenager /'tiin,eycır/ *n* on üç on dokuz yaşları arasındaki kimse
teetotaller /'tii'toutıLır/ *n* ağzına içki almayan kimse
Tehran /,tehı'rEn/ Tahran
telegram /'teLı,grEm/ *n* telgraf
telegraph /'teLı,grEf/ *v* telgraf çekmek
telepathy /tı'LepıTii/ *n* telepati
telephone /'teLı,foun/ *n* telefon; **~ book** *Am* telefon rehberi; **~ booth** telefon kulübesi; **~ call** telefon konuşması; **~ directory** *Br* telefon rehberi;

~ **exchange** telefon santralı; ~ **operator** telefon memuru
telephonist /tı'Lefınist/ *nBr* santral memuru
television /'teLı,vijın/ *n* televizyon; ~ **set** televizyon cihazı
telex /'teLeks/ *n* teleks
***tell** /teL/ *v* söylemek; anlatmak
teller /'teLır/ *n* veznedar, kasa memuru
temper /'tempır/ *n* huysuzluk; mizaç
temperature /'temprıçır/ *n* ısı derecesi; sıcaklık
tempest /'tempist/ *n* fırtına, bora
temple /'tempıL/ *n* tapınak; şakak
temporary /'tempı,rerii/ *adj* geçici
tempt /tempt/ *v* baştan çıkartmak; kandırmak
temptation /temp'teyşın/ *n* günaha teşvik etme, kışkırtma
ten /ten/ *num* on
tenant /'tenınt/ *n* kiracı
tend /tend/ *v* bakmak, gözetmek; meyletmek; ~ **to** bakmak, dikkat etmek
tendency /'tendınsii/ *n* eğilim
tender /'tendır/ *adj* nazik; hassas; müşfik; *n* teklif mektubu
tendon /'tendın/ *n* veter, kiriş
tennis /'tenis/ *n* tenis; ~ **court** tenis kortu; ~ **shoes** tenis ayakkabısı
tense /tens/ *adj* gergin, sinirli; *n* fiil kipi, zaman
tension /'tenşın/ *n* gerilim; gerginlik
tent /tent/ *n* çadır
tentative /'tentıtiv/ *adj* nihai olmayan, geçici
tenth /tenT/ *num* onuncu
tepid /'tepid/ *adj* ılık, sıcakça
term /tÖrm/ *n* terim; süre; dönem
terminal /'tÖrmınıL/ *n* son istasyon
terrace /'terıs/ *n* taraça, teras; **terrace(d) house** *Br* bitişik nizam evlerin biri
terrain /tı'reyn/ *n* yer, arazi
terrible /'terıbıL/ *adj* dehşetli, korkunç
terrific /tı'rifik/ *adj* korkunç; fevkalade, çok güzel
terrify /'terı,fay/ *v* dehşete düşürmek
territory /'terı,tOOrii/ *n* ülke; toprak; bölge
terror /'terır/ *n* dehşet; terör
terrorism /'terı,rizım/ *n* terörizm, tedhişçilik
terrorist /'terırist/ *n* terörist, tedhişçi
terylene /'terıLiin/ *n* terilen
test /test/ *n* sınav, test; tecrübe, muayene; *v* sınamak; denemek
testify /'testı,fay/ *v* tanıklık etmek
text /tekst/ *n* metin, parça
textbook /'tekst,buk/ *n* ders kitabı
textile /'teks,tayL/ *n* tekstil, dokuma
texture /'teksçır/ *n* dokunuş; doku, yapı
Thai /tay/ *adj* Tayland'a ait; *n* Taylandlı; Tay dili
Thailand /'tay,LEnd/ Tayland
than /DEn/ *conj* -den
thank /TENk/ *v* teşekkür etmek; ~ **you** teşekkür ederim; **thanks** *pl* teşekkürler; **thanks to** sayesinde
thankful /'TENkfıL/ *adj* müteşekkir
that /DEt/ *adj, pron* o, şu; *conj* ki; diye
thaw /TOO/ *v* erimek, buzları çözülmek; *n* erime, çözülme
the /Dı, Di/ *art* belirleyen tanımlık; **the . . . the** ne kadar . . . o kadar
theater /'Tiyıtır/ *n* tiyatro; tiyatro binası
theft /Teft/ *n* hırsızlık
their /Deyr/ *adj* onların
them /Dem/ *pron* onları, onlara
theme /Tiim/ *n* konu, tema
themselves /Dem'seLvz/ *pron*

kendileri, kendilerini, kendilerine
then /Den/ *adv* o zaman; ondan sonra
theology /Ti'yOLıcii/ *n* ilahiyat, teoloji
theoretical /,Tiyı'retikıL/ *adj* teorik, kuramsal
theory /'Tiyırii/ *n* kuram, teori
therapy /'Terıpii/ *n* tedavi, terapi
there /Deyr/ *adv* orada, oraya
therefore /'Deyr,fOOr/ *conj* bu yüzden, bundan dolayı
thermometer /Tır'mOmıtır/ *n* termometre
thermostat /'TÖrmı,stEt/ *n* termostat
these /Diiz/ *adj* bu; *pron* bunlar
thesis /'Tiisis/ *n* (pl theses) sav, dava, tez
they /Dey/ *pron* onlar
thick /Tik/ *adj* kalın; koyu; sık
thicken /'Tikın/ *v* kalınlaştırmak; koyulaştırmak; sıklaştırmak; kalınlaşmak; koyulaşmak; sıklaşmak
thickness /'Tiknıs/ *n* kalınlık; sıklık
thief /Tiif/ *n* (pl thieves) hırsız
thigh /Tay/ *n* uyluk, but
thimble /'TimbıL/ *n* yüksük
thin /Tin/ *adj* ince; zayıf; seyrek
thing /TiN/ *n* şey, nesne
***think** /TiNk/ *v* düşünmek; zannetmek; ~ **of** hatırlamak; düşünmek; ~ **over** düşünüp taşınmak
thinker /'TiNkır/ *n* düşünen kimse, düşünür
third /TÖrd/ *num* üçüncü
thirst /TÖrst/ *n* susuzluk
thirsty /'TÖrstii/ *adj* susamış
thirteen /'TÖr'tiin/ *num* on üç
thirteenth /'TÖr'tiinT/ *num* on üçüncü
thirtieth /'TÖrtiyıT/ *num* otuzuncu
thirty /'TÖrtii/ *num* otuz
this /Dis/ *adj, pron* bu
thistle /'TisıL/ *n* devedikeni
thorn /TOOrn/ *n* diken
thorough /'TÖrou/ *adj* tam, mükemmel
thouroughbred /'TÖrı,bred/ *adj* saf; soylu
thoroughfare /'TÖrı,feyr/ *n* anayol; genel geçit
thoroughly /'TÖrouLii/ *adv* tamamen, adamakıllı
those /Douz/ *adj* şu; *pron* şunlar
though /Dou/ *conj* her ne kadar, ise de; *adv* bununla beraber, buna rağmen
thought[1] /TOOt/ *v* (p, pp think)
thought[2] /TOOt/ *n* düşünce, fikir
thoughtful /'TOOtfıL/ *adj* düşünceli; dikkatli; saygılı
thousand /'Tauzınd/ *num* bin
Thrace /Treys/ Trakya
thread /Tred/ *n* iplik; *v* ipliğe dizmek, iplik geçirmek
threadbare /'Tred,beyr/ *adj* havı dökülmüş; yıpranmış
threat /Tret/ *n* tehdit, gözdağı
threaten /'Tretın/ *v* tehdit etmek;
threatening *adj* tehdit edici
three /Trii/ *num* üç
three-quarter /,Trii'kwOOrtır/ *adj* üç çeyrek
threshold /'TreşouLd/ *n* eşik
threw /Truu/ *v* (p throw)
thrifty /'Triftii/ *adj* idareli, tutumlu
throat /Trout/ *n* boğaz, gırtlak
throne /Troun/ *n* taht
through /Truu/ *prep* arasından
throughout /Truu'aut/ *adv* baştan başa; *prep* her yerinde
throw /Trou/ *n* atış, atma
***throw** /Trou/ *v* atmak, fırlatmak
thrush /TrAş/ *n* ardıçkuşu
thumb /TAm/ *n* başparmak
thumbtack /'TAm,tEk/ *n* raptiye
thump /TAmp/ *v* güm güm vurmak; dövmek

thunder /'TAndır/ *n* gök gürlemesi; *v* gümbürdemek, gürlemek
thunderstorm /'TAndır,stOOrm/ *n* şimşekli, yıldırımlı fırtına
thundery /'TAndırii/ *adj* fırtınalı
Thursday /'TÖrzdii/ perşembe
thus /DAs/ *adv* böylece; nitekim
thyme /taym/ *n* kekik
tick /tik/ *n* ritmik tıkırtı
ticket /'tikit/ *n* bilet; etiket; trafik cezası; ~ **collector** bilet kontrol eden memur; ~ **machine** bilet satan makine
tickle /'tikıL/ *v* gıdıklamak
tide /tayd/ *n* gelgit; **high** ~ denizin yükselmesi; **low** ~ denizin çekilmesi
tidings /'taydiNz/ *pl* haber, havadis
tidy /'taydii/ *adj* temiz ve düzenli; ~ **up** derleyip toplamak
tie /tay/ *v* bağlamak; birleştirmek; *n* kravat
tiger /'taygır/ *n* kaplan
tight /tayt/ *adj* sıkı, gergin; dar; *adv* sımsıkı
tighten /'taytın/ *v* sıkıştırmak; kasmak; gerginleşmek
tights /tayts/ *pl* külotlu çorap
tile /tayL/ *n* kiremit; duvar çinisi
till /tiL/ *prep, conj* -e kadar
timber /'timbır/ *n* kereste
time /taym/ *n* zaman;
all the ~ sürekli, aralıksız;
in ~ zamanında;
~ **of arrival** varış zamanı;
~ **of departure** hareket zamanı
timesaving /'taym,seyviN/ *adj* zaman kazandıran
timetable /'taym,teybıL/ *n* taşıtların kalkış ve varış saatlerini gösteren tarife
timid /'timid/ *adj* ürkek, çekingen
timidity /ti'midıtii/ *n* utangaçlık
tin /tin/ *n* kalay; teneke; *nBr* teneke kutu; **tinned food** *Br* konserve
tinfoil /'tin,fOyL/ *n* kalay yaprağı
tin-opener /'tin,oupınır/ *nBr* konserve açacağı
tiny /'taynii/ *adj* minicik, küçücük
tip /tip/ *n* bahşiş; uç
tire[1] /tayr/ *nAm* lastik, tekerlek çemberi; ~ **pressure** lastik basıncı
tire[2] /tayr/ *v* yormak; usandırmak
tired /tayrd/ *adj* yorgun; ***be** ~ **of** bıkmak, usanmak
tiresome /'tayrsım/ *adj* yorucu, sıkıcı
tiring /'tayriN/ *adj* yorucu
tissue /'tişuu/ *n* doku; ince kumaş; kâğıt mendil
title /'taytıL/ *n* başlık; ünvan; kitap
to /tu/ *prep* -e; için; -e kadar
toad /toud/ *n* karakurbağa
toadstool /'toud,stuuL/ *n* şapkalı mantar
toast /toust/ *n* kızarmış ekmek
tobacco /tı'bEkou/ *n* (pl ~s) tütün; ~ **pouch** tütün torbası
tobacconist /tı'bEkınist/ *n* tütüncü, tütün satıcısı; **tobacconist's** tütüncü dükkânı
today /tı'dey/ *adv* bugün
toddler /'tOdLır/ *n* yeni yürümeye başlayan çocuk
toe /tou/ *n* ayak parmağı
toffee /'tOOfii/ *n* karamela
together /tı'geDır/ *adv* beraber, birlikte
toilet /'tOyLit/ *n* tuvalet; ~ **case** tuvalet çantası; ~ **paper** tuvalet kâğıdı
toiletry /'tOyLitrii/ *n* sabun ve tarak gibi tuvalet eşyası
token /'toukın/ *n* belirti, nişan; jeton
told /touLd/ *v* (p, pp tell)
tolerable /'tOLırıbıL/ *adj* dayanılabilir, çekilebilir
tolerance /'tOLırıns/ *n* hoşgörü;

katlanma
tolerant /'tOLınınt/ *adj* hoşgörülü
toll /touL/ *n* köprü *veya* yol parası
tomato /tı'meytou/ *n* (pl ~es) domates
tomb /tuum/ *n* mezar; türbe
tombstone /'tuum,stoun/ *n* mezar taşı
tomorrow /tı'mOrou/ *adv* yarın
ton /tAn/ *n* ton, 1000 kg
tone /toun/ *n* ses rengi; perde, ton
tongs /tONz/ *pl* maşa
tongue /tAN/ *n* dil; lisan
tonic /'tOnik/ *n* tonik, kuvvet ilacı
tonight /tı'nayt/ *adv* bu gece
tonsilitis /,tOnsı'Laytis/ *n* bademcik iltihabı
tonsils /'tOnsıLz/ *pl* bademcikler
too /tuu/ *adv* lüzumundan fazla; de, dahi
took /tuk/ *v* (p take)
tool /tuuL/ *n* alet; ~ **kit** alet çantası
toot /tuut/ *vAm* boru, klakson çalmak
tooth /tuuT/ *n* (pl teeth) diş; ~ **powder** diş tozu
toothache /'tuuT,eyk/ *n* diş ağrısı
toothbrush /'tuuT,brAş/ *n* diş fırçası
toothpaste /'tuuT,peyst/ *n* diş macunu
toothpick /'tuuT,pik/ *n* kürdan
top /tOp/ *n* üst, tepe, zirve; **on** ~ **of** üstünde; ilaveten; ~ **side** üst kısım
topcoat /'tOp,kout/ *n* palto, pardösü
topic /'tOpik/ *n* konu
topical /'tOpikıL/ *adj* konuya ait; güncel
torch /tOOrç/ *n* meşale
torment[1] /tOOr'ment/ *v* eziyet etmek; canını sıkmak
torment[2] /'tOOrment/ *n* eziyet, cefa
torpedo /tOOr'piidou/ *n* torpil, torpido
torture /'tOOrçır/ *n* işkence; *v* işkence etmek
toss /tOOs/ *v* atmak; havaya fırlatmak; çalkalamak; karıştırmak
tot /tOt/ *n* ufak çocuk, yeni yürüyen çocuk
total /'toutıL/ *adj* bütün, tam; *n* toplam, tutar
totalitarian /tou,tELı'teyriyın/ *adj* totaliter, bütüncül
totalizator /'toutıLı,zeytır/ *n* at yarışlarında müşterek bahisleri toplayıp kaydeden makine
touch /tAç/ *v* dokunmak; tesir etmek; *n* dokunma, temas
touching /'tAçiN/ *adj* dokunaklı, etkili
touchy /'tAçii/ *adj* alıngan; titiz, huysuz
tough /tAf/ *adj* sert, dayanıklı
tour /tuur/ *n* gezi, tur
tourism /'tuu,rizım/ *n* turizm
tourist /'tuurist/ *n* turist; ~ **class** turistik mevki; ~ **office** turist bürosu
tournament /'tuurnımınt/ *n* yarışma, turnuva
tow /tou/ *v* yedeğe alıp çekmek
toward /tOOrd/ *prep* -e doğru, doğrultusunda
towel /'tauıL/ *n* havlu
tower /'tauır/ *n* kule; burç
town /taun/ *n* kasaba, şehir; ~ **center** şehir merkezi; ~ **hall** belediye binası
townspeople /'taunz,piipıL/ *pl* şehir halkı
toxic /'tOksik/ *adj* zehirli
toy /tOy/ *n* oyuncak; ~ **shop** oyuncak mağazası
trace /treys/ *n* iz, işaret; *v* izlemek; izini araştırıp bulmak
track /trEk/ *n* iz; yol, koşu yolu
tractor /'trEktır/ *n* traktör

trade /treyd/ *n* ticaret; *v* ticaret yapmak; ~ **union** sendika
trademark /'treyd,maark/ *n* marka, alameti farika
trader /'treydır/ *n* tüccar
tradesman /'treydzmın/ *n* (pl -men) dükkâncı, esnaf
tradition /trı'dişın/ *n* gelenek
traditional /trı'dişınıL/ *adj* geleneksel
traffic /'trEfik/ *n* trafik; ~ **jam** trafik sıkışıklığı; ~ **light** trafik lambası
trafficator /'trEfi,keytır/ *nBr* oto sinyal lambası
tragedy /'trEcıdii/ *n* trajedi, facia
tragic /'trEcik/ *adj* trajik, korkunç
trail /treyL/ *n* patika; iz
trailer /'treyLır/ *n* römork; *nAm* karavan
train /treyn/ *n* tren; *v* alıştırmak, eğitmek; **stopping** ~ posta treni; **through** ~ ekspres tren; ~ **ferry** tren feribotu
training /'treyniN/ *n* talim, terbiye; antrenman
trait /treyt/ *n* özellik
traitor /'treytır/ *n* vatan haini
tram /trEm/ *n* tramvay
tramp /trEmp/ *n* serseri; *v* serserice dolaşmak
tranquil /'trENkwıL/ *adj* sakin, rahat; durgun
tranquilizer /'trENkwı,Layzır/ *n* yatıştırıcı şey; müsekkin
transaction /trEn'sEkşın/ *n* muamele, işlem
transatlantic /,trEnsıt'LEntik/ *n* transatlantik; *adj* Atlantik'i geçen
transfer[1] /'trEns,fır/ *n* devretme, transfer
transfer[2] /trEns'fÖr/ *v* nakletmek; aktarmak; devretmek
transform /trEns'fOOrm/ *v* biçimini değiştirmek
transformer /trEns'fOOrmır/ *n* transformatör
transition /trEn'zişın/ *n* geçiş, intikal
translate /trEns'Leyt/ *v* tercüme etmek
translation /trEns'Leyşın/ *n* çeviri, tercüme
translator /trEns'Leytır/ *n* çevirmen, mütercim
transmission /trEns'mişın/ *n* nakil, gönderme
transmit /trEns'mit/ *v* göndermek, nakletmek
transmitter /trEns'mitır/ *n* verici istasyon
transparent /trEns'peyrınt/ *adj* şeffaf, saydam
transport[1] /'trEns,pOOrt/ *n* nakil; taşıtlar; taşıma işi
transport[2] /trEns'pOOrt/ *v* nakletmek, taşımak
transportation /,trEnspır'teyşın/ *n* ulaşım; taşıma işi
trap /trEp/ *n* tuzak, kapan
trash /trEş/ *n* çerçöp, süprüntü; ~ **can** *Am* çöp tenekesi
travel /'trEvıL/ *v* seyahat etmek; ~ **agency** seyahat bürosu; ~ **agent** seyahat acentesi; ~ **expenses** seyahat masrafları; ~ **insurance** seyahat sigortası
traveler /'trEvıLır/ *n* yolcu; **traveler's check** seyahat çeki
tray /trey/ *n* tepsi
treason /'triizın/ *n* hıyanet, hainlik
treasure /'trejır/ *n* hazine
treasurer /'trejırır/ *n* hazinedar; veznedar
treasury /'trejırii/ *n* hazine; devlet hazinesi
treat /triit/ *v* davranmak, muamele etmek; işlemden geçirmek
treatment /'triitmınt/ *n* muamele, davranış; işlem
treaty /'triitii/ *n* antlaşma

tree /trii/ *n* ağaç
tremble /'trembıL/ *v* titremek, ürpermek
tremendous /tri'mendıs/ *adj* heybetli, çok büyük
trend /trend/ *n* eğilim; yön
trespass /'trespıs/ *v* tecavüz etmek; yasak bir yere ayak basmak
trespasser /'trespısır/ *n* başkasının arazisine izinsiz giren kimse
trial /'trayıL/ *n* yargılama, duruşma; deneme
triangle /'tray,ENgıL/ *n* üçgen
triangular /tray'ENgyıLır/ *adj* üçgen şeklinde
tribe /trayb/ *n* kabile, aşiret
tribunal /tray'byuunıL/ *n* mahkeme
tributary /'tribyı,terii/ *n* ırmak ayağı
tribute /'tribyuut/ *n* haraç
trick /trik/ *n* hile, oyun
trifle /'trayfıL/ *n* önemsiz şey; az miktar
trigger /'trigır/ *n* tetik
trim /trim/ *v* budamak; kesip düzeltmek
trip /trip/ *n* kısa seyahat, tur
triumph /'trayAmf/ *n* zafer; *v* zafer kazanmak
triumphant /tray'Amfınt/ *adj* muzaffer
trivial /'triviyıL/ *adj* önemsiz; abes
Trojan /'troucın/ *n* Truvalı; *adj* Truva'ya ait
trolleybus /'trOLii,bAs/ *n* troleybüs
troops /truups/ *pl* askerler; süvari bölüğü
tropical /'trOpikıL/ *adj* tropikal
tropics /'trOpiks/ *pl* tropikal kuşak
trouble /'trAbıL/ *n* zahmet, sıkıntı, dert; *v* rahatsız etmek, canını sıkmak
troublesome /'trAbıLsım/ *adj* zahmetli, sıkıntılı
trousers /'trauzırz/ *pl* pantolon
trout /traut/ *n* (pl ~) alabalık
truck /trAk/ *n* kamyon
true /truu/ *adj* gerçek; doğru; sadık
trumpet /'trAmpit/ *n* boru, borazan
trunk /trANk/ *n* gövde, beden; *nAm* sandık; ~ **call** şehirlerarası telefon görüşmesi; **trunks** *pl* erkek mayosu
trust /trAst/ *v* güvenmek, itimat etmek; *n* itimat, güven
trustworthy /'trAst,wÖrDii/ *adj* güvenilir, itimada layık
truth /truuT/ *n* hakikat, gerçeklik
truthful /'truuTfıL/ *adj* doğru sözlü, samimi
try /tray/ *v* uğraşmak; denemek; ~ **on** prova etmek, giyip denemek
T-shirt /'tii,şÖrt/ *n* tişört
tube /tuub/ *n* tüp, boru
tuberculosis /tu,bÖrkyı'Lousis/ *n* tüberküloz, verem
Tuesday /'tuuzdii/ salı
tug /tAg/ *v* kuvvetle çekmek; *n* kuvvetli çekiş; römorkör
tuition /tuu'işın/ *n* okul taksiti; öğretim
tulip /'tuuLip/ *n* lale
tumble /'tAmbıL/ *v* düşmek, devrilmek; yuvarlanmak
tumbler /'tAmbLır/ *n* su bardağı
tumor /'tuumır/ *n* şiş, ur, tümör
tuna /'tuunı/ *n* (pl ~, ~s) ton balığı
tune /tuun/ *n* melodi, ezgi; uyum; akort; ~ **in** ayarlamak
tuneful /'tuunfıL/ *adj* uyumlu, ahenkli
tunic /'tuunik/ *n* gömlek; tünik
Tunisia /tuu'niijı/ Tunus
Tunisian /tuu'niijın/ *adj* Tunus'a ait; *n* Tunuslu
tunnel /'tAnıL/ *n* tünel; yeraltı yolu
turbine /'tÖrbin/ *n* türbin
turbojet /'tÖrbou,cet/ *n* türbinli jet motoruyla işleyen uçak
Turk /tÖrk/ *n* Türk
Turkey /'tÖrkii/ Türkiye

turkey /'tÖrkii/ *n* hindi
Turkish /'tÖrkiş/ *adj* Türklere ait; *n* Türkçe; ~ **bath** Türk hamamı; ~ **delight** lokum
turn /tÖrn/ *v* döndürmek, çevirmek; dönmek; *n* dönüş, devir; viraj; sıra; ~ **back** geri dönmek; ~ **down** reddetmek; ~ **into** olmak, haline gelmek; ~ **off** kapamak; kesmek; ~ **on** açmak; canlandırmak; ~ **over** çevirmek, devirmek; ~ **round** çevirmek, dönmek
turning /'tÖrniN/ *n* dönüş, viraj; ~ **point** dönüm noktası
turnip /'tÖrnip/ *n* şalgam
turnover /'tÖrn,ouvır/ *n* ciro; devir, dönüşüm; ~ **tax** işletme vergisi
turnpike /'tÖrn,payk/ *nAm* geçiş parası alınan yol
turpentine /'tÖrpın,tayn/ *n* neftyağı, terebentin
turtle /'tÖrtıL/ *n* kaplumbağa
tusk /tAsk/ *n* fil, yabandomuzu gibi hayvanların uzun sivri dişi
tutor /'tuutır/ *n* özel öğretmen
tuxedo /tAk'siidou/ *nAm* (pl ~s, ~es) smokin
tweed /twiid/ *n* yünlü kumaş
tweezers /'twiizırz/ *pl* cımbız
twelfth /tweLfT/ *num* on ikinci
twelve /tweLv/ *num* on iki
twentieth /'twentiyıT/ *num* yirminci
twenty /'twentii/ *num* yirmi
twice /tways/ *adv* iki kez
twig /twig/ *n* ince dal
twilight /'tway,Layt/ *n* alacakaranlık
twine /twayn/ *n* sicim
twins /twinz/ *pl* ikizler; **twin beds** çift yatak
twist /twist/ *v* bükmek; bükülmek; burmak; *n* bükülme, burma
two /tuu/ *num* iki
two-piece /'tuu,piis/ *adj* iki parçalı
type /tayp/ *v* daktilo etmek; *n* tip, çeşit
typewriter /'tayp,raytır/ *n* daktilo makinesi
typewritten /'tayp,ritın/ *adj* daktiloda yazılmış
typhoid /'tayfOyd/ *n* tifo
typhoon /tay'fuun/ *n* kasırga, tayfun
typical /'tipikıL/ *adj* karakteristik, tipik
typist /'taypist/ *n* daktilo yazan kimse
tyrant /'tayrınt/ *n* müstebit hükümdar, zorba
tyre /tayr/ *nBr* lastik, tekerlek çemberi; ~ **pressure** lastik basıncı

U

ugly /'AgLii/ *adj* çirkin
ulcer /'ALsır/ *n* ülser, yara
ultimate /'ALtımit/ *adj* son, nihai
ultraviolet /,ALtrı'vayıLit/ *adj* ültraviyole, morötesi
umbrella /Am'breLı/ *n* şemsiye
umpire /'Ampayr/ *n* hakem
unable /An'eybıL/ *adj* elinden gelmez, iktidarsız
unacceptable /,Anık'septıbıL/ *adj* kabul edilemez
unaccountable /,Anı'kauntıbıL/ *adj* anlatılamaz, garip; sorumlu değil
unaccustomed /,Anı'kAstımd/ *adj* alışılmamış
unanimous /yuu'nEnımıs/ *adj* aynı fikirde
unanimously /yuu'nEnımıslii/ *adv* oybirliğiyle
unanswered /,An'Ensırd/ *adj* cevaplanmamış
unauthorized /An'OOTı,rayzd/ *adj* yetkisiz; izinsiz
unavoidable /,Anı'vOydıbıL/ *adj*

kaçınılmaz
unaware /ˌAnı'weyr/ *adj* farkında olmayan, habersiz
unbearable /An'beyrıbıL/ *adj* çekilmez, dayanılmaz
unbelievable /ˌAnbi'LiivıbıL/ *adj* inanılmaz
unbreakable /An'breykıbıL/ *adj* kırılmaz
unbroken /An'broukın/ *adj* kırılmamış, bütün
unbutton /An'bAtın/ *v* düğmelerini açmak
uncertain /An'sÖrtın/ *adj* tahmin olunamaz; kararsız
uncle /'ANkıL/ *n* amca, dayı, enişte
unclean /An'kLiin/ *adj* kirli, pis
uncomfortable /An'kAmfırtıbıL/ *adj* rahatsız; huzursuz
uncommon /An'kOmın/ *adj* nadir; olağanüstü
unconditional /ˌAnkın'dişınıL/ *adj* kayıtsız şartsız
unconscious /An'kOnşıs/ *adj* şuursuz, bilinçsiz; baygın
uncontrolled /ˌAnkın'trouLd/ *adj* kontrolsüz; baskısız
uncork /An'kOOrk/ *v* tapasını çıkarmak
uncover /An'kAvır/ *v* örtüsünü kaldırmak; açığa çıkarmak
uncultivated /An'kALtıˌveytid/ *adj* işlenmemiş
undeniable /Anˌdi'nayıbıL/ *adj* yadsınamaz, inkâr edilemez
under /'Andır/ *prep* altına, altında
undercurrent /'andırˌkÖrınt/ *n* alt cereyan *veya* akıntı; gizli cereyan
underestimate /ˌAndır'estimeyt/ *v* değerinin altında paha biçmek
undergraduate /ˌAndır'grEcuuit/ *n* üniversite öğrencisi
underground /'Andırˌgraund/ *adj* yeraltında olan; gizli; *nBr* metro
underline /ˌAndır'Layn/ *v* altını çizmek; önemini belirtmek
underneath /ˌAndır'niiT/ *prep* altına, altında; *adv* alta, altta
underpants /'AndırˌpEnts/ *plAm* don, külot
undershirt /'Andırˌşört/ *n* iç gömleği, fanila
undersigned /'Andır'saynd/ *n* altta imzası bulunan kişi
***understand** /ˌAndır'stEnd/ *v* anlamak, kavramak
understanding /ˌAndır'stEndiN/ *n* anlayış, zekâ
***undertake** /ˌAndır'teyk/ *v* üzerine almak, yüklenmek
undertaking /ˌAndır'teykiN/ *n* el atma; teşebbüs, girişim
underwater /'Andır'wOOtır/ *adj* sualtında olan *veya* kullanılan
underwear /'Andırˌweyr/ *n* iç çamaşırı
undesirable /ˌAndi'zayrıbıL/ *adj* istenilmeyen; sakıncalı
***undo** /An'duu/ *v* bozmak; çözmek
undoubtedly /An'dautıdLii/ *adv* şüphesiz olarak
undress /An'dres/ *v* elbiselerini çıkartmak, soyunmak
undulating /'AncıˌLeytiN/ *adj* dalgalı
unearned /An'Örnd/ *adj* çalışarak hak edilmemiş
uneasy /An'iizii/ *adj* huzursuz, rahatsız
uneducated /An'ecıˌkeytid/ *adj* cahil, eğitimsiz
unemployed /ˌAnem'pLOyd/ *adj* işsiz
unemployment /ˌAnem'pLOymınt/ *n* işsizlik
unequal /An'iikwıL/ *adj* eşit olmayan
uneven /An'iivın/ *adj* düz olmayan, pürüzlü; eşit olmayan
unexpected /ˌAniks'pektid/ *adj* beklenmedik
unfair /An'feyr/ *adj* haksız, adaletsiz

unfaithful /An'feyTfıL/ *adj* sadakatsiz; güvenilmez
unfamiliar /,Anfı'miLyır/ *adj* alışılmamış; yabancı
unfasten /An'fEsın/ *v* çözmek, gevşetmek
unfavorable /An'feyvırıbıL/ *adj* elverişsiz; mahzurlu
unfit /An'fit/ *adj* uygunsuz
unfold /An'fouLd/ *v* kıvrımlarını açmak, yaymak
unforgettable /,Anfır'getıbıL/ *adj* unutulmaz
unfortunate /An'fOOrçınit/ *adj* talihsiz, bedbaht
unfortunately /An'fOOrçınitLii/ *adv* yazık ki, maalesef
unfriendly /An'frendLii/ *adj* dostça olmayan
unfurnished /An'fÖrniştl/ *adj* mobilyasız, döşenmemiş
ungrateful /An'greytfıL/ *adj* nankör; değerbilmez
unhappy /An'hEpii/ *adj* mutsuz; talihsiz
unhealthy /An'heLTii/ *adj* sağlıksız; sağlığa zararlı
unhurt /An'hÖrt/ *adj* zarar görmemiş, acımamış
uniform /'yuunı,fOOrm/ *n* üniforma; resmi elbise; *adj* yeknesak; değişmeyen
unimportant /,Anim'pOOrtınt/ *adj* önemsiz
uninhabitable /,Anin'hEbitıbıL/ *adj* yerleşilmez, ikamete müsait olmayan
uninhabited /,Anin'hEbitid/ *adj* meskûn olmayan, boş
unintentional /,Anin'tenşınıL/ *adj* istemeyerek yapılan, kasıtsız
union /'yuunyın/ *n* birleşme; birlik; sendika
unique /yuu'niik/ *adj* tek, eşsiz
unit /'yuunit/ *n* birim, ünite
unite /yuu'nayt/ *v* birleşmek; birleştirmek
United States /yuu'naytid ,steyts/ Amerika Birleşik Devletleri
unity /'yuunıtii/ *n* birlik, ittifak
universal /,yuunı'vÖrsıL/ *adj* evrensel; genel
universe /'yuunı,vÖrs/ *n* evren, kâinat
university /,yuunı'vÖrsıtii/ *n* üniversite
unjust /An'cAst/ *adj* haksız, adaletsiz
unkind /An'kaynd/ *adj* şefkatsiz; zalim; hatır kıran
unknown /An'noun/ *adj* bilinmeyen, meçhul
unlawful /An'LOOfıL/ *adj* yasadışı
unlearn /An'LÖrn/ *v* öğrendiğini unutmak, alıştığından vazgeçmek
unless /An'Les/ *conj* -medikçe, meğer ki
unlike /An'Layk/ *adj* birbirine benzemeyen, farklı
unlikely /An'LaykLii/ *adj* olası olmayan, umulmaz
unlimited /An'Limıtid/ *adj* sınırsız, sonsuz
unload /An'Loud/ *v* yükünü boşaltmak
unlock /An'LOk/ *v* kilidi açmak
unlucky /An'LAkii/ *adj* talihsiz; meşum
unnecessary /An'nesı,serii/ *adj* gereksiz
unoccupied /An'Okyı,payd/ *adj* boş, işgal edilmemiş
unofficial /,Anı'fişıL/ *adj* resmi olmayan
unpack /An'pEk/ *v* bavul vs. açıp boşaltmak
unpleasant /An'pLezınt/ *adj* nahoş, tatsız
unpopular /An'pOpyıLır/ *adj* rağbet görmeyen, tutulmayan
unprotected /,Anprı'tektid/ *adj*

korunmasız, açık
unqualified /An'kwOLı,fayd/ *adj* ehliyetsiz, uygun nitelikleri olmayan
unreal /An'riiL/ *adj* gerçek olmayan, hayali
unreasonable /An'riizınıbıL/ *adj* mantıksız, makul olmayan
unreliable /ˌAnri'LayıbıL/ *adj* güvenilmez
unrest /An'rest/ *n* huzursuzluk, kargaşa
unsafe /An'seyf/ *adj* emniyetsiz, güvenilmez
unsatisfactory /ˌAnsEtis'fEktırii/ *adj* memnuniyet vermeyen, tatminkâr olmayan
unscrew /An'skruu/ *v* vidasını çıkarmak
unselfish /ˌAn'seLfiş/ *adj* kendi çıkarını düşünmeyen
unskilled /An'skiLd/ *adj* maharetsiz, hünersiz
unsound /An'saund/ *adj* sağlıksız, geçersiz, sağlam olmayan
unstable /An'steybıL/ *adj* sabit *veya* sağlam olmayan; kararsız
unsteady /An'stedii/ *adj* sabit olmayan, değişken
unsuccessful /ˌAnsık'sesfıL/ *adj* başarısız
unsuitable /An'suutıbıL/ *adj* uygunsuz, yakışıksız
unsurpassed /ˌAnsır'pEst/ *adj* geçilmez, üstün
untidy /An'taydii/ *adj* düzensiz, dağınık
untie /An'tay/ *v* çözmek, açmak
until /ın'tiL/ *prep* -e kadar, -e değin
untrue /An'truu/ *adj* yalan, uydurma; sadakatsiz
untrustworthy /An'trAst,wÖrDii/ *adj* güvenilmez, itimada layık olmayan
unusual /An'yuujuuıL/ *adj* alışılmamış, olağandışı
unwelcome /An'weLkım/ *adj* hoş karşılanmayan, istenilmeyen
unwell /An'weL/ *adj* rahatsız, keyifsiz
unwilling /An'wiLiN/ *adj* isteksiz, gönülsüz
unwise /An'wayz/ *adj* akılsız, makul olmayan
unwrap /An'rEp/ *v* açmak, ambalajını çıkarmak
up /Ap/ *adv* yukarıya, yukarıda
update /Ap'deyt/ *v* güncelleştirmek
upholster /Ap'houLstır/ *v* döşemek, doldurup kumaşla kaplamak
upkeep /'Ap,kiip/ *n* bakım; bakım masrafı
upland /'ApLınd/ *n* yüksek arazi, yayla
upon /ı'pOOn/ *prep* üstüne, üstünde
upper /'Apır/ *adj* üstteki, yukarıdaki
upright /'Ap,rayt/ *adj* dik, dikey; *adv* dik, dimdik
***upset** /Ap'set/ *v* devirmek; canını sıkmak, sinirlendirmek; *adj* altüst olmuş, keyfi kaçmış
upside-down /ˌıpsayd'daun/ *adv* tepetaklak, altüst
upstairs /'Ap'steyrz/ *adv* üst kata, üst katta
upstream /'Ap'striim/ *adv* akıntıya karşı
upward /'Apwırd/ *adv* yukarıya doğru
urban /'Örbın/ *adj* şehre ait, şehirde bulunan
urge /Örc/ *v* sevk etmek; ısrar etmek; *n* dürtü; zorlama
urgency /'Örcınsii/ *n* ivedilik; önem
urgent /'Örcınt/ *adj* acil; çok önemli
urine /'yurin/ *n* idrar
Uruguay /'yurı,gwey/ Uruguay
Uruguayan /ˌyurı'gweyın/ *adj* Uruguay'a ait; *n* Uruguaylı
us /As/ *pron* bize, bizi
usable /'yuuzıbıL/ *adj* kullanılabilir

usage /'yuusic/ *n* kullanış
use[1] /yuuz/ *v* kullanmak; ***be used to** alışkın olmak; ~ **up** tüketmek, kullanıp bitirmek
use[2] /yuus/ *n* kullanma; yarar; ***be of** ~ işe yaramak
useful /'yuusfıL/ *adj* yararlı
useless /'yuusLıs/ *adj* yararsız
user /'yuuzır/ *n* kullanıcı
usher /'Aşır/ *n* teşrifatçı; yer gösterici
usherette /ˌAşı'ret/ *n* yer gösteren kız *veya* kadın
usual /'yuujuuıL/ *adj* alışılmış, olağan
usually /'yuujuuıLii/ *adv* çoğunlukla
utensil /yuu'tensıL/ *n* kap; alet
utility /yuu'tiLıtii/ *n* fayda, yarar
utilize /'yuutıˌLayz/ *v* kullanmak; yararlanmak
utmost /'AtˌmousT/ *adj* en uzak, en son, en fazla
utter /'Atır/ *adj* bütün, tam, mutlak; *v* söylemek; dile getirmek

V

vacancy /'veykınsii/ *n* boşluk, münhal yer
vacant /'veykınt/ *adj* boş, münhal
vacate /'veykeyt/ *v* terk etmek, boşaltmak
vacation /vey'keyşın/ *n* tatil
vaccinate /'vEksıˌneyt/ *v* aşılamak
vaccination /ˌvEksı'neyşın/ *n* aşı; çiçek aşısı yapma
vacuum /'vEkyuuım/ *n* boşluk; *vAm* elektrik süpürgesi kullanmak; ~ **cleaner** elektrik süpürgesi; ~ **bottle** *Am* termos, ~ **flask** *Br* termos
vagrancy /'veygrınsii/ *n* serserilik
vague /veyg/ *adj* belirsiz, müphem
vain /veyn/ *adj* kibirli, kendini beğenmiş; **in** ~ boşuna
valet /'vELit/ *n* uşak, erkek oda hizmetçisi
valid /'vELid/ *adj* geçerli
valley /'vELii/ *n* vadi
valuable /'vELyuuıbıL/ *adj* değerli; **valuables** *pl* kıymetli şeyler, mücevherat
value /'vELyuu/ *n* değer, kıymet; *v* değerini takdir etmek
valve /vELv/ *n* supap, valf
van /vEn/ *n* üstü kapalı yük arabası, kamyonet; *nBr* yük vagonu
vanilla /vı'niLı/ *n* vanilya
vanish /'vEniş/ *v* gözden kaybolmak
vapor /'veypır/ *n* buhar
variable /'veyriyıbıL/ *adj* değişir, değişken
variation /ˌveyri'yeyşın/ *n* değişme, değişim; çeşitleme
varied /'veyriid/ *adj* çeşitli, türlü türlü
variety /vı'rayıtii/ *n* değişiklik, çeşitlilik; ~ **show** varyete; ~ **theater** varyete tiyatrosu
various /'veyriyıs/ *adj* farklı, çeşitli
varnish /'vaarniş/ *n* vernik, cila; *v* cilalamak, verniklemek
vary /'veyrii/ *v* değişmek; değiştirmek
vase /veys/ *n* vazo
vaseline /'vEsıˌLiin/ *n* vazelin
vast /vEst/ *adj* geniş, engin
vault /vOOLt/ *n* çatı kemeri, kemer; kasa odası
veal /viiL/ *n* dana eti, buzağı eti
vegetable /'vecıtıbıL/ *n* sebze; ~ **merchant** manav
vegetarian /ˌvecı'teyriyın/ *n* etyemez kimse
vegetation /ˌvecı'teyşın/ *n* bitkiler; bitki gibi büyüme
vehicle /'viyıkıL/ *n* vasıta, taşıt
veil /veyL/ *n* peçe, yaşmak
vein /veyn/ *n* damar, toplardamar;

varicose ~ varis
velocity /vi'LOsıtii/ *n* hız, sürat
velvet /'veLvit/ *n* kadife
velveteen /ˌveLvı'tiin/ *n* pamuklu kadife
venerable /'venırıbıL/ *adj* muhterem, saygıdeğer
venereal disease /vı'niiriyıL di'ziiz/ zühreví hastalık
Venezuela /ˌvenı'zweyLı/ Venezüella
Venezuelan /ˌvenı'zweyLın/ *adj* Venezüella'ya ait; *n* Venezüellalı
vengeance /'vencıns/ *n* öç, intikam
Venice /'venis/ Venedik
ventilate /'ventıˌLeyt/ *v* havalandırmak
ventilation /ˌventı'Leyşın/ *n* havalandırma
ventilator /'ventıˌLeytır/ *n* vantilatör
venture /'vençır/ *v* tehlikeye atmak; cüret etmek
veranda /vı'rEndı/ *n* veranda, taraça
verb /vÖrb/ *n* fiil
verbal /'vÖrbıL/ *adj* söze ait; sözlü
verdict /'vÖrdikt/ *n* jüri kararı; hüküm
verge /vÖrc/ *n* sınır, kenar
verify /'verıˌfay/ *v* gerçeklemek, doğrulamak
verse /vÖrs/ *n* mısra; şiir; beyit
version /'vÖrjın/ *n* aynı konunun, yazının *veya* çevirinin değişik ifadelerinin her biri
versus /'vÖrsıs/ *prep* karşı
vertebra /'vÖrtıbrı/ *n* omur
vertical /'vÖrtikıL/ *adj* düşey, dikey
vertigo /'vÖrtiˌgou/ *n* baş dönmesi
very /'verii/ *adj* pek, çok, ziyadesiyle
vessel /'vesıL/ *n* tekne, gemi; kap; damar
vest /vest/ *nAm* yelek; *nBr* iç gömleği
veterinarian /ˌvetırı'neyriyın/ *nAm* veteriner, baytar
veterinary surgeon /'vetırıˌnerii 'sÖrcın/ *Br* veteriner, baytar
via /'vayı/ *prep* yolu ile, -den geçerek
viaduct /'vayıˌdAkt/ *n* sıra kemerli köprü, viyadük
vibrate /'vaybreyt/ *v* titremek; sallanmak
vibration /vay'breyşın/ *n* titreme, titreşim
vicar /'vikır/ *n* papaz
vicarage /'vikıric/ *n* papaz evi *veya* papazın görevi
vice-president /'vays 'prezıdınt/ *n* başkan yardımcısı; ikinci başkan
vice versa /'vaysı 'vÖrsı/ karşılıklı olarak; aksi
vicinity /vi'sinıtii/ *n* civardaki yerler; havali, semt
vicious /'vişıs/ *adj* kötü; kusurlu; hırçın; ~ **circle** kısırdöngü
victim /'viktim/ *n* kurban, mağdur kimse
victory /'viktırii/ *n* zafer, başarı
Vienna /vi'yenı/ Viyana
view /vyuu/ *n* görüş; manzara; *v* görmek, bakmak
viewfinder /'vyuuˌfayndır/ *n* vizör, gözleme merceği
vigilant /'viciLınt/ *adj* uyanık, tetikte olan
vigor /'vigır/ *n* kuvvet, dinçlik, enerji
vigorous /'vigırıs/ *adj* kuvvetli, dinç
villa /'viLı/ *n* villa, köşk
village /'viLic/ *n* köy
villain /'viLın/ *n* aşağılık, kötü adam
vine /vayn/ *n* asma, bağ kütüğü
vinegar /'vinıgır/ *n* sirke
vineyard /'vinyırd/ *n* üzüm bağı
vintage /'vintic/ *n* bağbozumu
violation /ˌvayı'Leyşın/ *n* ihlal; tecavüz
violence /'vayıLıns/ *n* zorbalık, şiddet
violent /'vayıLınt/ *adj* sert, şiddetli
violet /'vayıLit/ *n* menekşe;

adj menekşe renkli
violin /ˌvayı'Lin/ *n* keman
virgin /'vÖrcin/ *n* bakire
Virgo /'vÖrgou/ Başak burcu
virtue /'vÖrçuu/ *n* erdem; haslet
virus /'vayrıs/ *n* virüs
visa /'viizı/ *n* vize
visibility /ˌvizı'biLıtii/ *n* görme imkânı; görünürlük
visible /'vizıbıL/ *adj* görülebilir
vision /'vijın/ *n* görüş; görme kuvveti; hayal
visit /'vizit/ *v* ziyaret etmek; *n* ziyaret; **visiting card** kartvizit; **visiting hours** ziyaret saatleri
visitor /'vizitır/ *n* misafir, ziyaretçi
visualize /'vijuuıˌLayz/ *v* gözünde canlandırmak
vital /'vaytıL/ *adj* hayati; çok önemli
vitamin /'vaytımin/ *n* vitamin
vivid /'vivid/ *adj* çok parlak, canlı
vocabulary /vou'kEbyıˌLerii/ *n* kelime bilgisi; kelime listesi, kısa sözlük
vocal /'voukıL/ *adj* sese ait; sesli
vocalist /'voukıList/ *n* şarkıcı
voice /vOys/ *n* ses
void /vOyd/ *adj* hükümsüz; boş; faydasız
volcano /vOL'keynou/ *n* (pl ~es, ~s) volkan
volleyball /'vOLiiˌbOOL/ *n* voleybol
volt /vouLt/ *n* volt
voltage /'vouLtic/ *n* voltaj
volume /'vOLyuum/ *n* hacim; cilt, kitap; sesin kuvveti
voluntary /'vOLınˌterii/ *adj* isteyerek yapılan; gönüllü
volunteer /ˌvOLın'tiir/ *n* gönüllü kimse
vomit /'vOmit/ *v* kusmak
vote /vout/ *v* oy vermek; *n* oy
voucher /'vauçır/ *n* kefil; senet; makbuz
vow /vau/ *n* ant, yemin; *v* ant içmek; adamak
vowel /'vauıL/ *n* sesli harf
voyage /'vOyic/ *n* yolculuk; deniz yolculuğu
vulgar /'vALgır/ *adj* kaba, aşağılık, bayağı
vulnerable /'vALnırıbıL/ *adj* kolayca yaralanır; savunmasız
vulture /'vALçır/ *n* akbaba; haris kimse

W

wade /weyd/ *v* suda *veya* çamurda yürümek
wafer /'weyfır/ *n* çok ince bisküvi, kâğıt helvası
waffle /'wOfıL/ *n* kalıpla yapılan bir çeşit gözleme
wages /'weyciz/ *pl* ücret
wagon /'wEgın/ *n* dört tekerlekli yük arabası; yük vagonu
waist /weyst/ *n* bel
waistcoat /'weysˌkout/ *nBr* yelek
wait /weyt/ *v* beklemek; ~ **on** hizmet etmek, bakmak
waiter /'weytır/ *n* garson
waiting /'weytiN/ *n* bekleme; ~ **list** bekleme listesi; yedek liste; ~ **room** bekleme odası
waitress /'weytris/ *n* bayan garson
***wake** /weyk/ *v* uyanmak; uyandırmak; ~ **up** uyanmak; uyandırmak
Wales /weyLz/ Galler ülkesi
walk /wOOk/ *v* yürümek, dolaşmak; *n* yürüyüş, gezinti; **walking** yayan; **walking stick** baston
wall /wOOL/ *n* duvar; sur
wallet /'wOLit/ *n* para cüzdanı
wallpaper /'wOOLˌpeypır/ *n* duvar kâğıdı
walnut /'wOOLˌnAt/ *n* ceviz; ceviz ağacı

waltz /wOOLts/ *n* vals
wander /'wOndır/ *v* başıboş dolaşmak, gezinmek
want /wOnt/ *v* istemek, arzulamak; *n* yokluk; eksiklik; ihtiyaç
war /wOOr/ *n* savaş, harp
warden /'wOOrdın/ *n* bekçi; muhafız
wardrobe /'wOOrd,roub/ *n* gardırop
warehouse /'weyr,haus/ *n* depo, ambar
wares /weyrz/ *pl* satılacak mallar
warm /wOOrm/ *adj* ılık; ısıtan; *v* ısıtmak
warmth /wOOrmT/ *n* sıcaklık; samimiyet
warn /wOOrn/ *v* ikaz etmek, uyarmak
warning /'wOOrniN/ *n* ihtar, uyarı
Warsaw /'wOOrsOO/ Varşova
wary /'weyrii/ *adj* ihtiyatlı, uyanık
was /wOz/ *v* (p be)
wash /wOOş/ *v* yıkamak; ~ **and wear** ütü istemeyen; ~ **up** elini yüzünü yıkamak; *Br* bulaşıkları yıkamak
washable /'wOOşıbıL/ *adj* yıkanabilir
wash-basin /'wOOş,beysın/ *nBr* lavabo
washbowl /'wOOş,bouL/ *nAm* lavabo
washing /'wOOşiN/ *n* yıkama; yıkanma; ~ **machine** çamaşır makinesi; ~ **powder** çamaşır tozu
washroom /'wOOş,ruum/ *nAm* tuvalet
washstand /'wOOş,stEnd/ *n* lavabo
wasp /wOsp/ *n* yabanarısı
waste /weyst/ *v* boş yere harcamak; *n* israf; *adj* işe yaramaz, artık
wasteful /'weystfıL/ *adj* müsrif, savurgan
wastebasket /'weyst,bEskit/ *n* çöp sepeti
watch /wOç/ *v* seyretmek; gözlemek; *n* kol saati; ~ **for** kollamak; ~ **out** dikkat etmek; ~ **strap** kol saati kayışı
watchmaker /'wOç,meykır/ *n* saatçi
water /'wOOtır/ *n* su; **iced** ~ buzlu su; **running** ~ akar su, musluk suyu; ~ **color** suluboya; ~ **pump** su pompası; ~ **ski** su kayağı; ~ **softener** soda, su yumuşatıcısı
watercress /'wOOtır,kres/ *n* suteresi
waterfall /'wOOtır,fOOL/ *n* çağlayan, şelale
watermelon /'wOOtır,meLın/ *n* karpuz
waterproof /'wOOtır,pruuf/ *adj* su geçirmez
waterway /'wOOtır,wey/ *n* suyolu
watt /wOt/ *n* vat
wave /'weyv/ *n* dalga; el sallama; *v* sallamak; dalgalanmak
wavelength /'weyv,LenT/ *n* dalga boyu
wavy /'weyvii/ *adj* dalgalı
wax /wEks/ *n* balmumu
waxworks /'wEks,wÖrks/ *pl* balmumundan yapılmış insan heykelleri sergisi *veya* müzesi
way /wey/ *n* yol; usul; yön; mesafe; **by the** ~ aklıma gelmişken; **one-way traffic** tek yönlü trafik; **out of the** ~ sapa; **the other** ~ **round** söylenilenin tam tersi; ~ **back** dönüş yolu; ~ **in** giriş yolu; ~ **out** çıkış yolu
wayside /'wey,sayd/ *n* yol kenarı
we /wii/ *pron* biz
weak /wiik/ *adj* zayıf, kuvvetsiz; hafif
weakness /'wiiknıs/ *n* kuvvetsizlik; zaaf
wealth /weLT/ *n* zenginlik, servet
wealthy /'weLTii/ *adj* zengin, varlıklı
weapon /'wepın/ *n* silah
***wear** /weyr/ *v* giymek; ~ **out** iyice eskitmek

weary /'wiirii/ *adj* yorgun, bitkin
weather /'weDır/ *n* hava (durumu); ~ **forecast** hava raporu
***weave** /wiiv/ *v* dokumak, örmek
weaver /'wiivır/ *n* dokumacı
wedding /'wediN/ *n* nikâh, evlenme töreni; ~ **ring** alyans, nikâh yüzüğü
wedge /wec/ *n* takoz, kama
Wednesday /'wenzdii/ çarşamba
weed /wiid/ *n* yabani ot
week /wiik/ *n* hafta
weekday /'wiik,dey/ *n* işgünü, sair gün
weekend /'wiik,end/ *n* hafta sonu
weekly /'wiikLii/ *adj* haftalık; *n* haftalık dergi
***weep** /wiip/ *v* ağlamak
weigh /wey/ *v* tartmak; ağırlığında olmak; **weighing machine** kantar, baskül
weight /weyt/ *n* ağırlık
welcome /'weLkım/ *adj* sevindirici, hoşa giden; *n* karşılama; *v* hoş karşılamak, hoş geldiniz demek
weld /weLd/ *v* kaynak yapmak; sıkıca birleştirmek
welfare /'weL,feyr/ *n* refah, rahatlık, huzur
well[1] /weL/ *adv* iyi; *adj* iyi; sağlıklı; **as** ~ dahi, de; **as** ~ **as** kadar, hem ... hem de; **well!** pekala!, ya!, hayret!; **well** ... şey ...
well[2] /weL/ *n* kuyu; kaynak
well-founded /'weL'faundid/ *adj* sağlam mantık, bilgi, zemin vs. üzerine kurulmuş
well-known /'weL'noun/ *adj* meşhur, ünlü
well-to-do /'weLtı'duu/ *adj* zengin, hali vakti yerinde
went /went/ *v* (p go)
wept /wept/ *v* (p. pp weep)
were /wÖr/ *v* (p be)
west /west/ *n* batı
westerly /'westırLii/ *adj* batıya ait
western /'westırn/ *adj* batıya ait; *n* kovboy filmi
wet /wet/ *adj* yaş, ıslak
whale /hweyL/ *n* balina
wharf /hwOrf/ *n* (pl ~s, wharves) rıhtım, iskele
what /hwAt/ *pron* ne, hangi; ~ **for** niçin
whatever /hwAt'evır/ *pron* her ne, -in hepsi
wheat /hwiit/ *n* buğday
wheel /hwiiL/ *n* tekerlek
wheelbarrow /'hwiiL,bErou/ *n* tekerlekli el arabası
wheelchair /'hwiiL,çeyr/ *n* tekerlekli sandalye
when /hwen/ *adv* ne zaman; *conj* -dığı zaman
whenever /hwen'evır/ *conj* her ne zaman
where /hweyr/ *adv* nerede, nereye; *conj* -dığı yerde, ki orada
wherever /hweyr'evır/ *conj* her nereye, her nerede
whether /'hweDır/ *conj* olup olmadığını; olursa; ise de; **whether . . . or not** . . . olsa da olmasa da
which /hwiç/ *pron* hangi, hangisi
whichever /hwiç'evır/ *adj* hangisi olursa
while /hwayL/ *conj* iken, süresince; *n* zaman, süre
whilst /hwayLst/ *conj* iken
whim /hwim/ *n* saçma arzu, kapris
whip /hwip/ *n* kırbaç; *v* çırpmak; kamçılamak
whirlpool /'hwÖrl,puuL/ *n* girdap
whiskers /'hwiskırz/ *pl* favori; hayvan bıyığı
whiskey /'hwiskii/ *n* viski
whisper /'hwispır/ *v* fısıldamak;

n fısıltı
whistle /'hwisıL/ *v* ıslık çalmak; *n* ıslık
white /hwayt/ *adj* beyaz
Whitsun /'hwitsın/ Paskalya'dan sonraki yedinci pazar
who /huu/ *pron* kim
whoever /huu'evır/ *pron* her kim
whole /houL/ *adj* tam, bütün; sağlam; *n* tam, bütün şey
wholesale /'houL,seyL/ *n* toptan satış
wholesaler /'houL,seyLır/ *n* toptancı
wholesome /'houLsım/ *adj* sağlığa yararlı; sıhhatli
wholly /'houLii/ *adv* büsbütün, tamamen
whom /huum/ *pron* kimi
whooping cough /'huupiN ,kOOf/ boğmaca
whore /hOOr/ *n* fahişe
whose /huuz/ *pron* kimin, ki onun
why /hway/ *adv* niçin, neden
wicked /'wikid/ *adj* günahkâr; kötü
wide /wayd/ *adj* geniş, enli
widen /'waydın/ *v* genişletmek
widow /'widou/ *n* dul kadın
widower /'widouır/ *n* dul erkek
width /widT/ *n* en, genişlik
wife /wayf/ *n* (pl wives) karı, zevce
wig /wig/ *n* peruka, takma saç
wild /wayLd/ *adj* yabani, vahşi
wilderness /'wiLdırnis/ *n* kır, sahra; el değmemiş, ıssız bölge
wildlife /'wayLd,Layf/ *n* yabani hayat; yabani hayvanlar
will /wiL/ *n* arzu; irade
***will** /wiL/ *v* istemek; azmetmek
willing /'wiLiN/ *adj* istekli, gönüllü
willingly /'wiLiNLii/ *adv* isteyerek, seve seve
willpower /'wiL,pauır/ *n* irade
***win** /win/ *v* kazanmak; galip gelmek
wind /wind/ *n* rüzgâr
***wind** /waynd/ *v* dolamak; dolaşmak; kurmak
winding /'wayndiN/ *adj* sarmal; dolambaçlı
windmill /'wind,miL/ *n* yel değirmeni
window /'windou/ *n* pencere
windowsill /'windou,siL/ *n* pencere eşiği
windscreen /'wind,skriin/ *nBr* oto ön camı; ~ **wiper** *Br* oto cam sileceği
windshield /'wind,şiiLd/ *nAm* oto ön camı; ~ **wiper** *Am* oto cam sileceği
windy /'windii/ *adj* rüzgârlı, fırtınalı
wine /wayn/ *n* şarap; ~ **cellar** şarap mahzeni; ~ **list** şarap listesi; ~ **merchant** şarap tüccarı
wing /wiN/ *n* kanat
winner /'winır/ *n* galip kişi
winning /'winiN/ *adj* kazanan, galip; **winnings** *pl* kazanç
winter /'wintır/ *n* kış; ~ **sports** kış sporları
wipe /wayp/ *v* silmek, silip kurulamak
wire /'wayr/ *n* tel; telgraf
wireless /'wayrLıs/ *n* telsiz
wisdom /'wizdım/ *n* akıl; irfan; bilgelik
wise /wayz/ *adj* akıllı, tedbirli; bilge
wish /wiş/ *v* arzu etmek, dilemek; *n* dilek
wishbone /'wiş,boun/ *n* lades kemiği
wit /wit/ *n* akıl, zekâ; nüktecilik
witch /wiç/ *n* büyücü kadın
with /wiD/ *prep* ile
***withdraw** /wiD'drOO/ *v* geri çekmek; çekilmek
within /wiD'in/ *prep* içinde, içine; *adv* içeride, içeriye
without /wiD'aut/ *prep* -sız, -meyerek, -meden
witness /'witnıs/ *n* şahit, tanık
wits /wits/ *pl* akıl, fikir

witty /'witii/ *adj* esprili, hazırcevap
wolf /wuLf/ *n* (pl wolves) kurt
woman /'wumın/ *n* (pl women) kadın
women's lib kadın özgürlüğü hareketi
womb /wuum/ *n* rahim, dölyatağı
won /wOn/ *v* (p, pp win)
wonder /'wAndır/ *n* mucize, harika; şaşkınlık; *v* şaşmak; merak etmek
wonderful /'wAndırfıl/ *adj* harikulade, fevkalade
wood /wud/ *n* tahta, odun; koru; ~ **carving** tahta oymacılığı
wooded /'wudid/ *adj* ağaçlı, ormanlık
wooden /'wudın/ *adj* tahtadan yapılmış
woodland /'wudLınd/ *n* ormanlık yer
wool/wuL/ *n* yün; **darning** ~ örgü yünü
woolen /'wuLın/ *adj* yünden yapılmış
word /wÖrd/ *n* söz; kelime
wore /wOOr/ *v* (p wear)
work /wÖrk/ *n* iş, çalışma; *v* çalışmak, iş yapmak; ~ **of art** sanat eseri; ~ **permit** çalışma izni
workday /'wÖrk,dey/ *n* işgünü, adi gün
worker /'wÖrkır/ *n* işçi
working /'wÖrkiN/ *n* çalışma
workman /'wÖrkmın/ *n* (pl -men) işçi
works /wÖrks/ *pl* fabrika, tesis
workshop /'wÖrk,şOp/ *n* atölye
world /wÖrLd/ *n* dünya; ~ **war** dünya savaşı
world-famous /'wÖrLd'feymıs/ *adj* dünyaca ünlü
worldwide /'wÖrLd'wayd/ *adj* evrensel
worm /wÖrm/ *n* kurt, solucan
worn /wOOrn/ *adj* (pp wear) aşınmış
worn-out /'wOOrn'aut/ *adj* yıpranmış
worried /'wÖriid/ *adj* kaygılı, tasalı
worry /'wÖrii/ *v* kaygılanmak; *n* kaygı, endişe
worse /wÖrs/ *adj* daha fena, daha kötü; *adv* daha fena, daha kötü
worship /'wÖrşip/ *v* tapmak; tapınmak; *n* tapınma, ibadet
worst /wÖrst/ *adj* en fena, en kötü
worsted /'wustid/ *n* bükme yün
worth /wÖrT/ *n* değer; ***be** ~ değerinde olmak; ***be worthwhile** zahmetine değmek
worthless /'wÖrTLıs/ *adj* değersiz
worthy of /'wÖrDii ıv/ uygun, yaraşır, layık
would /wud/ *v* (p will)
wound[1] /wuund/ *n* yara; *v* yaralamak
wound[2] /waund/ *v* (p, pp wind)
wrap /rEp/ *v* sarmalamak; paket yapmak
wreath /riiT/ *n* çelenk
wreck /rek/ *n* gemi enkazı; *v* kazaya uğratmak; yıkmak
wrench /renç/ *n* somun anahtarı, İngiliz anahtarı
wrestle /'resıL/ *v* güreşmek; uğraşmak
wrestler /'resLır/ *n* güreşçi, pehlivan
wrinkle /'riNkıL/ *n* buruşuk, kırışık
wrist /rist/ *n* bilek
wristwatch /'rist,wOç/ *n* kol saati
***write** /rayt/ *v* yazmak; **in writing** yazı ile; ~ **down** yazmak, not etmek; **writing pad** bloknot **writing paper** yazı kâğıdı
writer /'raytır/ *n* yazar
written /'ritın/ *adj* (pp write) yazılı
wrong /rOON/ *adj* yanlış; hatalı; *n* hata, kusur; *v* hakkını yemek, zarar vermek; ***be** ~ yanılmak; haksız olmak
wrote /rout/ *v* (p write)

Xmas /'krismıs/ Noel
X-ray /'eks,rey/ *n* röntgen ışını; röntgen filmi; *v* röntgen çekmek

Y

yacht /yOt/ *n* yat; ~ **club** yat kulübü
yachting /'yOtiN/ *n* yatçılık
Yankee /'yENkii/ *n* Amerikalı; *adj* Amerikan
yard /yaard/ *n* yarda; 0,9144m; avlu
yarn /yaarn/ *n* pamuk *veya* yün ipliği
yawn /yOOn/ *v* esnemek
year /yiir/ *n* yıl
yearly /'yiirLii/ *adj* yılda bir olan
yeast /yiist/ *n* maya
yell /yeL/ *v* avazı çıktığı kadar bağırmak
yellow /'yeLou/ *adj* sarı
yes /yes/ evet
yesterday /'yestır,dey/ *adv* dün
yet /yet/ *adv* henüz, daha, hâlâ
yield /yiiLd/ *v* (ürün) vermek; teslim olmak
yoke /youk/ *n* boyunduruk
yolk /youk/ *n* yumurta sarısı
you /yuu/ *pron* sen, seni, sana; siz, sizi, size
young /yAN/ *adj* genç
your /yır/ *adj* senin, sizin
yourself /yır'seLf/ *pron* kendin, kendiniz
yourselves /yır'seLvz/ *pron* sizler, kendiniz
youth /yuuT/ *n* delikanlı, genç adam; ~ **hostel** öğrenci yurdu
Yugoslav /,Yuugou'sLaav/ *n* Yugoslav
Yugoslavia /,Yuugou'sLaavyı/ Yugoslavya
Yugoslavian /,yuugou'sLaaviyın/ *adj* Yugoslavya'ya ait

Z

zeal /ziiL/ *n* gayret, şevk
zealous /'zeLıs/ *adj* gayretli, ateşli
zebra /'ziibrı/ *n* zebra
zenith /'ziiniT/ *n* en yüksek nokta
zero/'ziirou/ *n* (pl ~s) sıfır
zest /zest/ *n* tat, şevk; hoşlanma
zinc /ziNk/ *n* çinko
zip /zip/ *nBr* fermuar; ~ **code** *Am* posta kodu
zipper /'zipır/ *n* fermuar
zodiac /'zoudi,yEk/ *n* burçlar kuşağı
zone /zoun/ *n* kuşak, bölge
zoo /zuu/ *n* (pl ~s) hayvanat bahçesi
zoology /zou'OLıcii/ *n* hayvanlar bilimi, zooloji

Yemek Listesi Kılavuzu

Yiyecekler

almond badem
anchovy hamsi balığı, ançüez
angel food cake beyaz ve hafif bir çeşit pasta
angels on horseback domuz yağına bulanıp ızgarada pişirilen ve kızarmış ekmek üzerinde yenen istiridye
appetizer çerez, meze, aperitif
apple elma
~ **dumpling** bir çeşit elmalı hamur tatlısı
~ **sauce** haşlanmış elma püresi
~ **pie** elmalı pay
Arbroath smoky füme morina balığı
artichoke enginar
asparagus kuşkonmaz
~ **tip** kuşkonmaz sapı
assorted çeşitli
avocado (pear) Amerikan armudu, avokado
bacon domuz pastırması
~ **and eggs** domuz pastırmalı yumurta
bagel bir cins tatlı küçük ekmek
baked fırında pişmiş
~ **Alaska** dondurma, kek ve yumurta akından yapılan bir tatlı
~ **beans** fırında salçalı kuru fasulye
~ **potato** fırında kabuğuyla pişirilmiş patates
Bakewell tart bademezmeli ve reçelli bir turta çeşidi
baloney bir çeşit İtalyan salamı
banana muz
~ **split** muz, dondurma ve cevizle hazırlanıp üzerine çikolatalı *veya* meyveli sos dökülen bir tatlı
barbecue 1) küçük bir ekmek içine konarak yenen baharatlı ve salçalı bir et yemeği 2) açık havada yenen yemek, mangal partisi
~ **sauce** baharatlı ve salçalı sos
barbecued odun kömüründe pişmiş
basil fesleğen
bass levrek
bean fasulye
beef sığır eti
~ **olive** sarılmış ve içi doldurulmuş sığır eti dilimi
beefburger kıyılmış biftekten yapılan ve ızgarada pişirilip küçük bir ekmeğin arasında yenen köfte
beet, beetroot pancar
bilberry yabanmersini
bill hesap
~ **of fare** yemek listesi, mönü
biscuit 1) kuru pasta, bisküvi (İng.)

2) küçük ekmek (ABD)
black pudding kıyma, yulaf unu ve kan ile yapılan domuz sucuğu
blackberry böğürtlen
black currant siyah frenküzümü
bloater tuzlanmış ve tütsülenmiş ringa balığı
blood sausage kıyma, yulaf unu ve kan ile yapılan domuz sosisi
blueberry yabanmersini
boiled haşlanmış, kaynatılmış
Bologna (sausage) içinde çeşitli etler bulunan iri cins bir salam
bone kemik
boned kemikleri, kılçıkları çıkarılmış
Boston baked beans fırında yağlı ve salçalı kuru fasulye
Boston cream pie üstü genellikle çikolata kaplı kremalı pasta
brains beyin
braised ağır ateşte pişmiş
bramble pudding böğürtlenli puding (genellikle elma ile yenir)
braunschweiger füme karaciğer sucuğu
bread ekmek
breaded peksimet ununa bulanıp kızartılmış *veya* pişirilmiş
breakfast sabah kahvaltısı
bream çipura, karagöz, mercan gibi balıklar
breast göğüs, tavuk göğsü
brisket (kasaplık hayvanın) göğüs eti, döş
broad bean bakla
broth et, balık *veya* sebze suyu
brown Betty elma, ekmek içi, şeker ve baharatla yapılan bir tatlı
brunch sabah ile öğle arasında yenen, hem kahvaltı hem de öğle yemeği yerine geçen öğün
Brussels sprout Brüksel lahanası
bubble and squeak patates ve lahanadan yapılan ve bazen etle birlikte yenen bir çeşit yemek
bun 1) bir çeşit küçük ekmek (ABD) 2) kuru meyveli, sütlü çörek (İng.)
butter tereyağı
buttered tereyağlı
cabbage lahana
Caesar salad içine sarmısak, ançüez, kızarmış ekmek ve rendelenmiş peynir konulan yeşil salata
cake kek, pasta
cakes bisküviler, kekler
calf dana eti
Canadian bacon ince dilimler halinde kesilmiş domuz pastırması
caper gebreotunun meyvesi, kapari
capercaillie, capercailzie çalıhorozu, yabankuşu
carp sazan balığı
carrot havuç
cashew mahun cevizi
casserole güveçte pişmiş
catfish yayınbalığı
catsup ketçap, baharatlı domates sosu
cauliflower karnabahar
celery kereviz
cereal tahıl; herhangi bir tahıl ile hazırlanmış ve kahvaltıda yenen bir yiyecek
hot ~ sıcak yulaf lapası (İng.)
check hesap, hesap pusulası
Cheddar (cheese) tadı keskince olan ve kaşara benzer bir çeşit peynir
cheese peynir
~ board peynir tahtası; seçme peynirler
~ cake krem peynir, yumurta, süt ve şekerle yapılmış bir çeşit pasta
cheeseburger peynirli hamburger
chef's salad içinde jambon, piliç eti,

lop yumurta, domates, marul ve peynir bulunan salata
cherry kiraz
chestnut kestane
chicken piliç, tavuk
chicory hindiba
chili con carne kıyma, kırmızıbiber ve kuru fasulyeden yapılmış bir yemek
chili pepper kırmızıbiber
chips 1) patates kızartması (İng.) 2) patates cips (ABD)
chitt(er)lings domuz bağırsağından yapılan bir yemek
chive bir tür sarmısak
chocolate çikolata
choice seçme, üstün kalite
chop pirzola, kotlet
~ **suey** etli ve sebzeli bir Çin yemeği
chopped doğranmış, kıyılmış
chowder balıklı sebze çorbası
Christmas pudding Noel'de yenilen bir cins kuruyemişli İngiliz keki
chutney bir çeşit Hint turşusu
cinnamon tarçın
clam bir tür istiridye, tarak
club sandwich içine jambon, tavuk eti, domates, marul ve mayonez konarak yapılan iki katlı sandviç
cobbler yalnızca üstü hamurla örtülmüş meyveli tart
cock-a-leekie soup pırasalı tavuk çorbası
coconut hindistan cevizi
cod morina balığı
Colchester oyster pek meşhur İngiliz istiridyesi
cold cuts/meat (salam, sosis, sucuk gibi) yenmeye hazır soğuk et, söğüş
coleslaw lahana salatası
cooked pişmiş
cookie kurabiye, çörek, bisküvi
corn 1) buğday (İng.) 2) mısır (ABD)
~ **on the cob** koçan üstünde mısır
cornflakes mısır gevreği
cottage cheese süzme peynir, taze peynir
cottage pie soğanlı kıymalı patates yemeği
course tabak, yemek
cover charge (restoranlarda) kuver (ücreti)
crab yengeç, pavurya
cracker tuzlu bisküvi, kraker
cranberry kızılcığa benzer bir meyve; kırmızı yabanmersini
~ **sauce** bu meyveden yapılan tatlı sos
crawfish, crayfish kerevit, suböceği; tatlısu ıstakozu
cream 1) krema 2) kremalı (çorba) 3) kaymak
~ **cheese** krem peynir
~ **puff** içi kremalı pasta
creamed potatoes kremalı beyaz salça içinde küp şeklinde kesilmiş patatesler
creole biber, domates ve soğanlı sosla pişirilip, pilavla yenen baharatlı yemek
cress tere
crisps kızarmış patates, cips
crumpet yassı kadayıfa benzer kızarmış bir hamur tatlısı
cucumber salatalık, hıyar
Cumberland ham ünlü bir cins füme jambon
Cumberland sauce mayhoş sos; şarap, portakal suyu, limon kabuğu, baharat ve frenküzümü jölesiyle hazırlanmış sos
cupcake ufak kek
cured tuzlanmış ve bazen de dumanla tütsülenmiş

currant frenküzümü, kuşüzümü
curried bir Hint baharatıyla hazırlanmış, körili
custard yumurtalı ve sütlü krema
cutlet pirzola, külbastı, kotlet
dab pisibalığı
Danish pastry bir cins mayalı çörek
date hurma
Derby cheese açık sarı renkte, yumuşak ve keskin lezzetli peynir
devilled çok baharatlı
devil's food cake çikolatalı pasta
devils on horseback kırmızı şarap içinde pişirilmiş ve içi badem ve ançüezle doldurulmuş erik kurusu
Devonshire cream çok yağlı yumuşak kaymak
diced küp şeklinde kesilmiş
diet food perhiz yemeği
dill dereotu
dinner akşam yemeği
dish tabak, çanak, yemek
donut, doughnut yağda kızarmış şekerli yuvarlak çörek
double cream tam yağlı kaymak
Dover sole ünlü bir cins dilbalığı
dressing 1) salata sosu 2) tavuk dolması içi (ABD)
Dublin Bay prawn bir cins küçük ıstakoz
duck ördek
duckling ördek yavrusu
dumpling meyveli hamur tatlısı
Dutch apple pie üzerine şurup dökülmüş *veya* kahverengi şeker serpilmiş elmalı tart
eel yılanbalığı
egg yumurta
  boiled ~ haşlanmış yumurta
  fried ~ sahanda yumurta
  hard-boiled ~ lop yumurta
  poached ~ sıcak suya kırılıp pişirilmiş yumurta, çılbır
  scrambled ~ beyazları ve sarıları karıştırılarak yağda pişirilmiş yumurta
  soft-boiled ~ rafadan yumurta
eggplant patlıcan
endive 1) bostan hindibası (İng.) 2) hindiba (ABD)
entrée 1) sofraya ilk getirilen yemek (İng.) 2) esas yemek (ABD)
fennel rezene
fig incir
fillet et *veya* balık filetosu
finnan haddock füme mezgit balığı
fish balık
  ~ **and chips** kızartılmış balık filetosu ve patates kızartması
  ~ **cake** patatesli balık köftesi
flan börek, tart
flapjack kalın krep
flounder dere pisisi
forcemeat dolma içine konan baharatlı kıyma
fowl kümes hayvanı
frankfurter bir çeşit baharatlı sosis
French bean yeşil fasulye
French bread uzun francala
French dressing 1) sirkeli salata sosu (İng.) 2) ketçaplı ve kremalı salata sosu (ABD)
French fries kızarmış patates
French toast süt ve yumurtaya batırılıp kızartılmış ekmek
fresh taze
fried tavada kızartılmış
fritter yağda kızartılmış börek
frogs' legs kurbağa bacağı
frosting keklerin üzerine konan şekerli krema
fry kızartılmış yemek
game av eti
gammon füme jambon
garfish zargana
garlic sarmısak
garnish garnitür

gherkin ufak salatalık
giblets tavuk vb. hayvanların yürek, ciğer gibi yenebilir iç kısımları
ginger zencefil
goose kaz
~**berry** bektaşi üzümü
grape üzüm
~**fruit** greyfurt
grated rendelenmiş
gravy et suyundan yapılan koyu sos
grayling tatlısu som balığı
green bean taze fasulye
green pepper yeşil biber
green salad marul, yeşil salata
greens yaprak sebze
grilled ızgarada pişmiş
grilse sombalığı yavrusu
grouse ormantavuğu
gumbo 1) bamya 2) et, balık *veya* **diğer deniz ürünleri ile pişirilen sulu bamya yemeği**
haddock mezgit balığı
haggis koyun *veya* dana ciğeri ve yüreği ile yapılan soğanlı yahni
hake barlam balığı
half yarım
halibut kalkana benzeyen yassı bir balık
ham jambon
~ **and eggs** jambonlu yumurta
hare yabani tavşan
haricot bean kuru fasulye
hash 1) kıyılmış et 2) kıymalı patates
hazelnut fındık
heart yürek
herb yemeklere tat vermek için kullanılan bitki
herring ringa balığı
homemade evde yapılmış
hominy grits mısır lapası
honey bal
~**dew melon** bir çeşit tatlı kavun
horse radish yabanturpu, bayırturpu
hot 1) sıcak 2) baharatlı, acı
~ **cross bun** üzümlü çörek (Hıristiyanlıkta büyük perhiz döneminde yenir)
~ **dog** sosisli sandviç
huckleberry yabanmersinine benzer bir cins ufak ve siyah meyve
hush puppy mısır unundan yapılmış börek
ice cream dondurma
iced buzlu
icing pasta ve kek üzerine sürülen şekerli krema
Idaho baked patato fırında kabuğuyla pişirilmiş patates
Irish stew soğanlı, patatesli, koyun etli yahni
Italian dressing sirkeli salata sosu
jam reçel
jellied jöleli
Jell-O jöleli tatlı
jelly meyveli jöle
Jerusalem artichoke yerelması
John Dory dülgerbalığı
jugged hare tavşan yahnisi
juice meyve, sebze *veya* **et suyu**
juniper berry ardıç meyvesi
junket bir çeşit şekerli kaymak
kale kıvırcık lahana
kedgeree balıklı, yumurtalı pilav
kidney böbrek
kipper tütsülenmiş ringa balığı
lamb kuzu, kuzu eti
Lanchashire hot pot soğan, patates, kuzu böbreği ve pirzola ile yapılan yahni
larded domuz yağına bulanmış
lean yağsız
leek pırasa
leg but
lemon limon
~ **curd** limonlu krema
~ **sole** kızıl dilbalığı

lentil mercimek
lettuce marul, yeşil salata, kıvırcık salata
lima bean lima fasulyesi, bir tür bakla
lime misket limonu
liver karaciğer
loaf ekmek, somun
lobster ıstakoz
loin fileto
Long Island duck ünlü Long Island ördeği
low-calorie düşük kalorili
lox füme sombalığı
lunch öğle yemeği
macaroni makarna
macaroon acıbadem kurabiyesi
mackerel uskumru balığı
maize mısır
mandarin mandalina
maple syrup akçaağaç şurubu
marinated zeytinyağlı salamuraya yatırılmış
marjoram mercanköşk adlı bitki
marmalade marmelat
marrow ilik
~ **bone** ilikli kemik
marshmallow hatmi çiçeğinden yapılan bir çeşit hafif, yumuşak şekerleme
marzipan bademezmesi
mashed potatoes patates püresi
meal yemek, öğün
meat et
~ **ball** köfte
~ **loaf** rulo köfte
medium (done) orta pişmiş
melted erimiş
Melton Mowbray pie etli börek
milk süt
mince kıyma (İng.)
~ **pie** üzümlü ve baharlı elma ile yapılmış tart
minced kıyılmış, doğranmış
~ **meat** kıyma
mint nane
mixed karışık
~ **grill** karışık ızgara
molasses melas, şeker tortusu
morel kuzumantarı
mulberry dut
mullet kefal balığı
mulligatawny soup tavuk etli ve baharatlı Hint çorbası
mushroom mantar
muskmelon bir cins kokulu kavun
mussel midye
mustard hardal
mutton koyun eti
noodle erişte, şehriye
nut ceviz, fındık
oatmeal (porridge) yulaf lapası, yulaf ezmesi
oil sıvı yağ
okra bamya
omelet omlet
onion soğan
ox tongue sığır dili
oyster istiridye
pancake süt, yumurta, un ve şekerden yapılıp genellikle tavada pişirilen bir hamur işi
parsley maydanoz
parsnip yabanhavucu
partridge keklik
pastry hamur işi, pasta
pasty kıymalı börek, etli börek, mantı
pea bezelye
peach şeftali
peanut yerfıstığı
~ **butter** çekilmiş fıstıktan yapılmış tuzlu ezme, krem-fıstık
pear armut
pearl barley kabuğu soyulmuş ve yuvarlak hale getirilmiş arpa
pepper biber
~**mint** nane, nane şekeri

perch tatlısu levreği
persimmon Trabzon hurması
pheasant sülün
pickerel küçük turnabalığı
pickle 1) turşu, salamura 2) salatalık turşusu (ABD)
pickled salamura yapılmış, turşu yapılmış
pie tart, börek, pay
pig domuz, domuz eti
pike turnabalığı
pineapple ananas
plaice pisibalığı
plain baharatsız, sade
plum 1) erik 2) erik kurusu 3) kuru üzüm
~ **pudding** üzümlü ve baharatlı Noel yortusu keki
poached haşlanmış
popcorn patlamış mısır
popover sütlü, yumurtalı, hafif bir ekmek
pork domuz eti
porterhouse steak kalın ve yumuşak biftek
pot roast ağır ateşte pişmiş sebzeli et, kapama
potato patates
~ **chips** 1) patates kızartması (İng.) 2) patates cips (ABD)
~ **in its jacket** kabuğuyla pişirilmiş patates
potted shrimps çömlekte pişirilen baharatlı karides
poultry kümes hayvanları
prawn pembe renkli iri karides
prune kuru erik
ptarmigan kartavuğu
pudding 1) puding, muhallebi 2) et, balık, sebze *veya* meyve karıştırılmış börek
pumpernickel elenmemiş çavdar unundan yapılan siyah ekmek
pumpkin balkabağı, helvacı kabağı
quail bıldırcın
quince ayva
rabbit tavşan, adatavşanı
radish turp
rainbow trout çelikbaş alabalık
raisin kuru üzüm
rare az pişmiş
raspberry ağaççileği, ahududu
raw çiğ, pişmemiş
red mullet barbunya balığı
red (sweet) pepper (tatlı) kırmızıbiber
redcurrant kırmızı frenküzümü, kırmızı kuşüzümü
relish salça *veya* hardal gibi lezzet veren şey
rhubarb ravent
rib (of beef) etin kaburgadan olan kısmı, sığır pirzolası
rice pirinç, pilav
rissole bir çeşit et *veya* balık köftesi
river trout nehir alabalığı
roast(ed) kızarmış, kızartılmış
Rock Cornish hen yemle beslenmiş bir cins kaliteli tavuk
roe balık yumurtası
roll küçük ekmek
rollmop herring beyaz şaraba yatırılmış ve salatalık turşusu üzerine sarılmış ringa balığı filetosu
round steak dana ya da sığır budunun üst kısmı
Rubens sandwich kızarmış ekmek üzerine konmuş lahana turşusu, peynir ve konserve sığır etinden oluşan sandviç
rump steak sığır budunun en üst kısmı, biftek
rusk peksimet, fırında kurutulmuş ekmek dilimi
rye bread çavdar ekmeği
saddle sırtın alt ucundan kesilmiş et (koyun vb.)

saffron safran
sage adaçayı
salad salata
~ **bar** salata çeşitlerinin sunulduğu açık büfe
~ **cream** az şekerli, kremalı salata sosu
~ **dressing** salata sosu
salmon som balığı
~ **trout** kırmızı etli alabalık
salt tuz
salted tuzlu, tuzlanmış
sauerkraut lahana turşusu, lahana turşusundan yapılan yemek
sausage sucuk, sosis
sauté(ed) tavada hafif kızartılmış, sote
scallop 1) tarak denilen deniz böceği
2) ince et dilimi
scone arpa *veya* buğday unundan yapılmış bir çeşit yumuşak, küçük ekmek
Scotch broth etli ve sebzeli çorba
Scotch woodcock yumurtalı ve ançüezli kızarmış ekmek
sea bass levrek balığı
sea kale yabani lahana, deniz lahanası
seafood denüz ürünleri
(in) season zamanında, mevsiminde
seasoning yemeklere lezzet veren baharat vb. şeyler
service charge servis (ücreti)
service (not) included servis (ücreti) dahil (hariç)
set menu fiks mönü
shad tirsi balığı (bir cins sardalye)
shallot yabani sarmısak
shellfish kabuklu deniz hayvanı (yengeç, ıstakoz, karides gibi)
sherbet 1) meyveli dondurma (ABD) 2) şerbet (İng.)
shoulder kürek eti
shredded wheat gevrek buğday köftesi (kahvaltıda yenir)
shrimp karides
silverside (of beef) sığır budunun dış parçası
sirloin steak bonfile
skewer kebap şişi
slice dilim
sliced dilimlenmiş
sloppy Joe içine baharat katılmış domates soslu kıyma yemeği
smelt çamuka balığı
sand ~ gümüşbalığı
smoked füme
snack hafif yemek
soup çorba, et suyu
sour ekşi
soused herring sirkeli ve baharatlı ringa balığı
spare rib domuz pirzolası
spice baharat
spinach ıspanak
spiny lobster langust, makassız ıstakoz
(on a) spit şişte kızartılmış (şişe takılmış)
sponge cake pandispanya
sprat çaçabalığı
squash kabak
starter ordövr (birinci yemekten önce yenen soğuk yiyecekler)
steak and kidney pie etli ve böbrekli börek
steamed buğulama
stew türlü, güveç
Stilton (cheese) beyaz *veya* küflü İngiliz peyniri
strawberry çilek
string bean çalı fasulyesi
stuffed içi doldurulmuş, dolma; ~ ...... dolması
stuffing dolma içi, dolmalık iç
suck(l)ing pig süt domuzu

sugar şeker
sugarless şekersiz
sundae üstüne ceviz, meyve, krem şanti ve bazen de şurup konulan dondurma; kup
supper hafif olarak yenen akşam yemeği
swede sarı şalgam, şalgam lahanası
sweet 1) şekerli 2) tatlı şey, tatlı
~ **corn** tatlı mısır
~ **potato** tatlı patates
sweetbread dana *veya* kuzu uykuluğu
Swiss cheese İsviçre'de yapılan iri delikli sarı bir peynir
Swiss roll reçelli rulo pasta
Swiss steak ağır ateşte, sebze ve baharatla pişirilen biftek
T-bone steak T şeklinde kemikli biftek
table d'hôte tabldot, fiks mönü
tangerine mandalina
tarragon tarhun otu
tart tart (genellikle meyveli)
tenderloin sığır filetosu
Thousand Island dressing içine kırmızı biber *veya* ketçap, zeytin ve lop yumurta konarak hazırlanan mayonez
thyme kekik
toad-in-the-hole hamur içinde pişirilmiş sosis *veya* biftek
toasted ızgarada pişirilmiş
~ **cheese** kızartılmış peynir
tomato domates
tongue dil
treacle şeker pekmezi
trifle pandispanya, şarap ve meyvelerden yapılan bir tür tatlı
trout alabalık
tuna, tunny tonbalığı, orkinos
turkey hindi
turnip şalgam
turnover meyveli tatlı
turtle kaplumbağa
underdone az pişmiş
vanilla vanilya
veal dana eti
~ **bird** sarılmış ve içi doldurulmuş dana eti dilimi
vegetable sebze
~ **marrow** kabak
venison geyik eti, karaca eti
vichyssoise kremalı, patatesli ve pırasalı soğuk çorba
vinegar sirke
Virginia baked ham karanfil, ananas, kiraz ve meyve suyu ilave edilerek fırında pişirilen jambon
wafer gofret, çok ince bisküvi
waffle kalıpla yapılan bir çeşit hamur işi
walnut ceviz
water ice meyve suyundan yapılan dondurma
watercress suteresi
watermelon karpuz
well-done iyi pişmiş
Welsh rabbit/rarebit kızarmış ekmeğe sürülen birada eritilmiş peynir
whelk bir çeşit deniz salyangozu
whipped cream krem şanti
whitebait ringa familyasından bir çeşit küçük beyaz balık
Wiener Schnitzel şnitzel
wine list şarap listesi
woodcock çulluk
Worcestershire sauce karışık baharatlı et sosu
yoghurt yoğurt
York ham füme jambon
Yorkshire pudding rosto ile beraber pişirilen bir çeşit hamur işi
zucchini bir çeşit dolmalık kabak
zwieback önce pişirilip sonra dilim dilim kızartılan bir çeşit peksimet

ale yüksek sıcakta mayalanmış, hafif tatlı bir çeşit siyah bira
bitter ~ acı ve oldukça sert siyah bira
brown ~ şişe içinde hafif tatlı siyah bira
light ~ şişe içinde açık sarı bira
mild ~ hafif, siyah fıçı birası
pale ~ şişe içinde açık sarı bira
angostura kokteyllere katılan acı, aromalı sıvı
applejack elma rakısı, elma şarabı
Athol Brose viski, bal, su ve bazen yulaf ezmesinden yapılan İskoç içkisi
Bacardi cocktail ekşi limon, nar suyu, cin ve romdan yapılan kokteyl
barley water arpa suyu ve limondan yapılan serinletici bir içki
barley wine alkol derecesi yüksek siyah bira
beer bira
bottled ~ şişe(lenmiş) bira
draft, draught ~ fıçı birası
bitters içine bitki kökü, kabuğu *veya* otlar karıştırılan iştah açıcı ve sindirimi kolaylaştırıcı içkiler
black velvet genellikle istiridye yenirken içilen siyah biralı şampanya
bloody Mary votka, domates suyu ve baharattan yapılan içki
bourbon mısırdan yapılan Amerikan viskisi
brandy konyak, brandi
~ Alexander kakao likörü, konyak ve taze kremadan yapılan içki
British wines ithal üzüm *veya* üzüm suyundan yapılan İngiliz şarapları
cherry brandy kiraz likörü
chocolate çikolata; sütlü kakao
cider elma suyu, elma şarabı
~ cup baharat, şeker, elma suyu ve buzla yapılan içecek
claret kırmızı Bordeaux şarabı
cobbler buzlu meyve suyuna şarap *veya* likör katılarak hazırlanan bir içki
coffee kahve
~ with cream sütlü kahve
black ~ içine süt *veya* krema karıştırılmamış kahve
caffeine-free ~ kafeini alınmış kahve
white ~ sütlü, kremalı kahve
cordial likör
cream krema
cup buzlu şarap, soda ve alkollü içkiden yapılan, portakal, limon *veya* salatalık dilimleriyle süslenen serinletici bir içki
daiquiri rom, misket limonu ve ananas suyundan yapılan içki
double duble
Drambuie viski ve baldan yapılan likör
dry martini 1) sek vermut (İng.) 2) sek vermut ve cin ile yapılan kokteyl (ABD)
eggnog çırpılmış yumurta sarısı, şeker, rom *veya* başka bir sert içki karıştırılarak yapılan içecek
gin and it cin ve İtalyan vermutundan yapılmış içki
gin-fizz limon suyu, şeker ve soda karıştırılmış cin
ginger ale zencefilli gazoz
ginger beer zencefil ve şeker katılarak yapılmış hafif alkollü içki
grasshopper kakao ve nane likörleri ile taze kremadan yapılmış içki

Guinness (stout) malt ve şerbetçiotundan yapılmış hafif şekerli, sert siyah bira
half pint bir bardaklık ölçü
highball su, soda *veya* gazoz karıştırılmış buzlu viski
iced buzlu
Irish coffee İrlanda viskisi ve krem şanti eklenmiş şekerli kahve
Irish Mist viski ve baldan yapılmış İrlanda likörü
Irish whiskey içinde arpanın yanı sıra çavdar, yulaf ve buğday bulunan İrlanda viskisi (İskoç viskisinden daha az sert)
juice meyve *veya* sebze suyu
lager bir çeşit hafif bira
lemon squash limonata; gazoz
lemonade limonata
lime juice misket limonunun suyu
liquor alkollü içki
long drink buzlu ve gazozlu hafif içki
madeira Madeira şarabı
Manhattan viski ve vermutla yapılmış aromalı Amerikan içkisi
milk süt
~ **shake** sütü, şeker, meyve esansı ve bazen de dondurma ile çalkalayarak yapılan serinletici içecek
mineral water maden suyu
mulled wine baharatlı sıcak şarap
neat susuz ve buzsuz (içki), sek
old-fashioned viski, aroma, kiraz likörü ve şekerden yapılmış içki
on the rocks buzlu
Ovaltine malt özünden yapılmış içecek
Pimm's cup(s) soda *veya* meyve suyu katılmış alkollü içki
~ **No. 1** cin ilave edilmiş
~ **No. 2** viski ilave edilmiş
~ **No. 3** rom ilave edilmiş
~ **No. 4** konyak ilave edilmiş
pink champagne pembe şampanya
pink lady yumurta akı, elma rakısı, limon ve nar suyu ile cin karıştırılarak yapılmış içki
pint yaklaşık yarım litre
port (wine) Portekiz'in ünlü tatlı şarabı, porto
porter acı siyah bira
quart 1,14 litre (İng.); 0,95 litre (ABD)
root beer bitki kökü ve ottan yapılmış tatlı, gazozlu içecek
rum rom
rye (whiskey) çavdar viskisi
scotch (whiskey) İskoç viskisi
screwdriver votka ve portakal suyu
shandy zencefilli gazoz karıştırılmış acı siyah bira
sherry beyaz İspanyol şarabı
short drink su katılmamış alkollü içki
shot bir kadeh içki
sloe gin-fizz soda ve limon suyu karıştırılmış erik likörü
soda water soda
soft drink alkolsüz içki
spirits alkollü içki
stinger konyak ve nane likörü karıştırılarak yapılmış içki
stout sert siyah bira
straight sek, saf
tea çay
toddy viski *veya* konyak ile şeker ve sıcak sudan yapılmış içki
Tom Collins cin, limon suyu, şeker ve sodadan yapılmış içki
tonic (water) tonik
water su
whiskey sour viski, limon suyu, şeker ve sodadan yapılmış içki
wine şarap
dry ~ sek şarap
red ~ kırmızı şarap
sparkling ~ köpüklü şarap
sweet ~ tatlı şarap
white ~ beyaz şarap

İngilizcedeki Düzensiz Fiiller

Aşağıdaki listede İngilizcedeki düzensiz fiiller verilmiştir. Birleşik fiiller veya bir önek taşıyan fiiller, esas kökü oluşturan fiil gibi çekilirler. Örneğin, *withdraw* fiili *draw* gibi, *mistake* fiili de *take* gibi çekilir.

Mastar	*Di'li geçmiş zaman*	*Geçmiş zaman ortacı*	
arise	arose	arisen	*kalkmak*
awake	awoke	awoken	*uyanmak*
be	was	been	*olmak*
bear	bore	borne	*taşımak*
beat	beat	beaten	*dövmek*
become	became	become	*olmak*
begin	began	begun	*başlamak*
bend	bent	bent	*bükmek*
bet	bet	bet	*bahse girmek*
bid	bade/bid	bidden/bid	*fiyat önermek*
bind	bound	bound	*bağlamak*
bite	bit	bitten	*ısırmak*
bleed	bled	bled	*kanamak*
blow	blew	blown	*üflemek*
break	broke	broken	*kırmak*
breed	bred	bred	*yavrulamak*
bring	brought	brought	*getirmek*
build	built	built	*inşa etmek*
burn	burnt/burned	burnt/burned	*yakmak*
burst	burst	burst	*patlamak*
buy	bought	bought	*satın almak*
can*	could	—	*yapabilmek*
cast	cast	cast	*atmak*
catch	caught	caught	*yakalamak*
choose	chose	chosen	*seçmek*
cling	clung	clung	*yapışmak*
clothe	clothed/clad	clothed/clad	*giydirmek*
come	came	come	*gelmek*
cost	cost	cost	*mal olmak*
creep	crept	crept	*sürünmek*
cut	cut	cut	*kesmek*
deal	dealt	dealt	*dağıtmak*
dig	dug	dug	*kazmak*
do* (he does)	did	done	*yapmak*
draw	drew	drawn	*çizmek*
dream	dreamt/dreamed	dreamt/dreamed	*rüya görmek*
drink	drank	drunk	*içmek*
drive	drove	driven	*(araba) kullanmak*
dwell	dwelt	dwelt	*ikamet etmek*
eat	ate	eaten	*yemek*
fall	fell	fallen	*düşmek*

* Yardımcı fiil

feed	fed	fed	*beslemek*
feel	felt	felt	*hissetmek*
fight	fought	fought	*savaşmak*
find	found	found	*bulmak*
flee	fled	fled	*kaçmak*
fling	flung	flung	*fırlatmak*
fly	flew	flown	*uçmak*
forsake	forsook	forsaken	*terk etmek*
freeze	froze	frozen	*donmak*
get	got	got/gotten	*almak*
give	gave	given	*vermek*
go	went	gone	*gitmek*
grind	ground	ground	*öğütmek*
grow	grew	grown	*büyümek*
hang	hung	hung	*asmak*
have	had	had	*sahip olmak*
hear	heard	heard	*işitmek*
hew	hewed	hewed/hewn	*(balta vb. ile) kesmek*
hide	hid	hidden	*sakla(n)mak*
hit	hit	hit	*vurmak*
hold	held	held	*tutmak*
hurt	hurt	hurt	*incitmek*
keep	kept	kept	*muhafaza etmek*
kneel	knelt	knelt	*diz çökmek*
knit	knitted/knit	knitted/knit	*örmek*
know	knew	known	*bilmek*
lay	laid	laid	*koymak, sermek*
lead	led	led	*yol göstermek*
lean	leant/leaned	leant/leaned	*dayanmak*
leap	leapt/leaped	leapt/leaped	*sıçramak*
learn	learnt/learned	learnt/learned	*öğrenmek*
leave	left	left	*bırakmak*
lend	lent	lent	*ödünç vermek*
let	let	let	*izin vermek*
lie	lay	lain	*yatmak*
light	lit/lighted	lit/lighted	*yakmak*
lose	lost	lost	*kaybetmek*
make	made	made	*yapmak*
may*	might	—	*yapabilmek*
mean	meant	meant	*anlamına gelmek*
meet	met	met	*rastlamak*
mow	mowed	mowed/mown	*biçmek*
must*	—	—	*zorunda olmak*
ought (to)*	—	—	*-meli, -malı*
pay	paid	paid	*ödemek*
put	put	put	*koymak*
read	read	read	*okumak*
rid	rid	rid	*kurtarmak*
ride	rode	ridden	*(ata) binmek*

* Yardımcı fiil

ring	rang	rung	*çınlamak, çalmak*
rise	rose	risen	*kalkmak, yükselmek*
run	ran	run	*koşmak*
saw	sawed	sawn	*testere ile kesmek*
say	said	said	*söylemek*
see	saw	seen	*görmek*
seek	sought	sought	*aramak*
sell	sold	sold	*satmak*
send	sent	sent	*göndermek*
set	set	set	*koymak*
sew	sewed	sewed/sewn	*dikmek*
shake	shook	shaken	*sarsmak*
shall*	should	—	*-ecek*
shed	shed	shed	*dökmek*
shine	shone	shone	*parlamak*
shoot	shot	shot	*atmak, ateş etmek*
show	showed	shown	*göstermek*
shrink	shrank	shrunk	*çekmek, küçülmek*
shut	shut	shut	*kapamak*
sing	sang	sung	*şarkı söylemek*
sink	sank	sunk	*batmak*
sit	sat	sat	*oturmak*
sleep	slept	slept	*uyumak*
slide	slid	slid	*kaymak*
sling	slung	slung	*sapanla atmak*
slink	slunk	slunk	*sıvışmak*
slit	slit	slit	*yarmak*
smell	smelled/smelt	smelled/smelt	*koklamak*
sow	sowed	sown/sowed	*(tohum) ekmek*
speak	spoke	spoken	*konuşmak*
speed	sped/speeded	sped/speeded	*çabuk gitmek*
spell	spelt/spelled	spelt/spelled	*hecelemek*
spend	spent	spent	*harcamak*
spill	spilt/spilled	spilt/spilled	*dökmek*
spin	spun	spun	*eğirmek*
spit	spat	spat	*tükürmek*
split	split	split	*yarmak*
spoil	spoilt/spoiled	spoilt/spoiled	*bozmak*
spread	spread	spread	*yaymak*
spring	sprang	sprung	*fırlamak*
stand	stood	stood	*ayakta durmak*
steal	stole	stolen	*çalmak, aşırmak*
stick	stuck	stuck	*yapıştırmak*
sting	stung	stung	*sokmak, batmak*
stink	stank/stunk	stunk	*pis kokmak*
strew	strewed	strewed/strewn	*saçmak*
stride	strode	stridden	*uzun adımlarla yürümek*
strike	struck	struck/stricken	*vurmak*
string	strung	strung	*ipliğe dizmek*

* Yardımcı fiil

strive	strove	striven	*çabalamak*
swear	swore	sworn	*yemin etmek*
sweep	swept	swept	*süpürmek*
swell	swelled	swollen	*şişmek*
swim	swam	swum	*yüzmek*
swing	swung	swung	*sallanmak*
take	took	taken	*almak*
teach	taught	taught	*öğretmek*
tear	tore	torn	*yırtmak*
tell	told	told	*söylemek, anlatmak*
think	thought	thought	*düşünmek*
throw	threw	thrown	*fırlatmak*
thrust	thrust	thrust	*itmek*
tread	trod	trodden	*basmak*
wake	woke/waked	woken/waked	*uyandırmak*
wear	wore	worn	*giymek*
weave	wove	woven	*dokumak*
weep	wept	wept	*ağlamak*
will*	would	—	*-ecek*
win	won	won	*kazanmak*
wind	wound	wound	*sarmak*
wring	wrung	wrung	*burmak*
write	wrote	written	*yazmak*

* Yardımcı fiil

İngilizce Kısaltmalar

AA	*Automobile Association*	İngiliz Otomobil Derneği
AAA	*American Automobile Association*	Amerikan Otomobil Derneği
ABC	*American Broadcasting Company*	özel bir Amerikan radyo-TV kuruluşu
A.D.	*anno Domini*	MS, milattan sonra
Am.	*America; American*	Amerika; Amerikalı
a.m.	*ante meridiem (before noon)*	öğleden önce
Amtrak	*American Railroad Corporation*	Amerikan Demiryolları Kurumu
AT & T	*American Telephone and Telegraph Company*	Amerikan Telefon ve Telgraf Şirketi
Ave.	*avenue*	cadde
BBC	*British Broadcasting Corporation*	İngiliz Radyo Televizyon Kurumu
B.C.	*before Christ*	MÖ, Milattan önce
bldg.	*building*	bina
Blvd.	*boulevard*	bulvar
B.R.	*British Rail*	İngiliz Demiryolları
Brit.	*Britain; British*	Britanya; Britanyalı
Bros.	*brothers*	kardeşler
¢	*cent*	1/100 dolar
Can.	*Canada; Canadian*	Kanada; Kanadalı
CBS	*Columbia Broadcasting System*	özel bir Amerikan radyo-TV kuruluşu
CID	*Criminal Investigation Department*	Cinayet Araştırma Dairesi
CNR	*Canadian National Railway*	Kanada Devlet Demiryolları
c/o	*in (care of)*	eliyle
Co.	*company*	şirket
Corp.	*corporation*	kurum
CPR	*Canadian Pacific Railways*	özel bir Kanada demiryolu şirketi
D.C.	*District of Columbia*	Columbia Bölgesi (Washington, D.C.)
DDS	*Doctor of Dental Science*	diş doktoru
dept.	*department*	bölüm, şube, daire
EEC	*European Economic Community*	AET, Avrupa Ekonomik Topluluğu
e.g.	*for instance*	örneğin

Eng.	*England; English*	İngiltere; İngiliz
excl.	*excluding; exclusive*	hariç; özel
ft.	*foot/feet*	ayak (30,5 cm)
GB	*Great Britain*	Büyük Britanya
H.E.	*His/Her Excellency*	Ekselans
	His Eminence	kardinallere mahsus şeref unvanı
H.H.	*His Holiness*	Papaya verilen unvan
H.M.	*His/Her Majesty*	zatı şahane
H.M.S.	*Her Majesty's Ship*	İngiliz kraliyet filosuna ait gemi
hp	*horsepower*	beygirgücü
Hwy	*highway*	anayol, otoyol
i.e.	*that is to say*	yani, demek ki
in.	*inch*	inç (2,54 cm)
Inc.	*incorporated*	anonim şirket
incl.	*including, inclusive*	dahil
£	*pound sterling*	İngiliz Lirası, sterlin
L.A.	*Los Angeles*	Los Angeles
Ltd.	*limited*	limitet (şirket)
M.D.	*Doctor of Medicine*	hekim, doktor
M.P.	*Member of Parliament*	milletvekili
mph	*miles per hour*	saatte . . . mil
Mr.	*Mister*	Bay
Mrs.	*Missis*	Bayan (evli)
Ms.	*Missis/Miss*	Bayan (evli) / (bekâr)
nat.	*national*	ulusal
NBC	*National Broadcasting Company*	özel bir Amerikan radyo-TV kuruluşu
No.	*number*	numara
N.Y.C.	*New York City*	New York şehri
O.B.E.	*Officer (of the Order) of the British Empire*	İngiliz kraliyet ordusuna mensup subay
p.	*page; penny/pence*	sayfa; 1/100 sterlin
p.a.	*per annum*	yıllık, yılda
Ph. D.	*Doctor of Philosophy*	doktora derecesi
p.m.	*post meridiem (after noon)*	öğleden sonra
PO	*Post Office*	PTT, postane
POO	*post office order*	posta havalesi
P.T.O.	*please turn over*	lütfen sayfayı çeviriniz
RAC	*Royal Automobile Club*	İngiliz Kraliyet Otomobil Kulübü
RCMP	*Royal Canadian Mounted Police*	Kanada kraliyet atlı polisi

Rd.	*road*	yol, sokak
ref.	*reference*	referans, bkz.
Rev.	*reverend*	değerli, sayın (rahipler için)
RFD	*rural free delivery*	şehir dışı posta örgütü
RR	*railroad*	demiryolu
RSVP	*please reply*	lütfen cevap veriniz
$	*dollar*	dolar
Soc.	*society*	dernek
St.	*saint; street*	aziz; sokak
STD	*Subscriber Trunk Dialling*	otomatik telefon
UN	*United Nations*	Birleşmiş Milletler
UPS	*United Parcel Service*	Paket Yollama Servisi (ABD)
US	*United States*	Amerika Birleşik Devletleri
USS	*United States Ship*	Amerikan savaş filosuna ait gemi
VAT	*value added tax*	KDV, katma değer vergisi
VIP	*very important person*	çok önemli kişi, özel ayrıcalıklara sahip kişi
Xmas	*Christmas*	Noel
yd.	*yard*	yarda (91,44 cm)
YMCA	*Young Men's Christian Association*	Genç Hıristiyan Erkekler Birliği
YWCA	*Young Women's Christian Association*	Genç Hıristiyan Kadınlar Birliği
ZIP	*ZIP code*	posta kodu

Sayılar

Esas sayılar		Sıra sayıları	
0	zero	1st	first
1	one	2nd	second
2	two	3rd	third
3	three	4th	fourth
4	four	5th	fifth
5	five	6th	sixth
6	six	7th	seventh
7	seven	8th	eighth
8	eight	9th	ninth
9	nine	10th	tenth
10	ten	11th	eleventh
11	eleven	12th	twelfth
12	twelve	13th	thirteenth
13	thirteen	14th	fourteenth
14	fourteen	15th	fifteenth
15	fifteen	16th	sixteenth
16	sixteen	17th	seventeenth
17	seventeen	18th	eighteenth
18	eighteen	19th	nineteenth
19	nineteen	20th	twentieth
20	twenty	21st	twenty-first
21	twenty-one	22nd	twenty-second
22	twenty-two	23rd	twenty-third
23	twenty-three	24th	twenty-fourth
24	twenty-four	25th	twenty-fifth
25	twenty-five	26th	twenty-sixth
30	thirty	27th	twenty-seventh
40	forty	28th	twenty-eighth
50	fifty	29th	twenty-ninth
60	sixty	30th	thirtieth
70	seventy	40th	fortieth
80	eighty	50th	fiftieth
90	ninety	60th	sixtieth
100	a/one hundred	70th	seventieth
230	two hundred and thirty	80th	eightieth
1,000	a/one thousand	90th	ninetieth
10,000	ten thousand	100th	hundredth
100,000	a/one hundred thousand	230th	two hundred and thirtieth
1,000,000	a/one million	1,000th	thousandth

Saat

Amerikalılar ve İngilizler gündelik hayatlarında on iki saat sistemini kullanırlar. Öğleden önceki saatleri *a.m. (ante meridiem)* ifadesiyle, öğleden gece yarısına kadar olan saatleri ise *p.m. (post meridiem)* ifadesiyle belirtirler. Resmi kullanımlarda ise yirmi dört saat sistemi yaygındır.

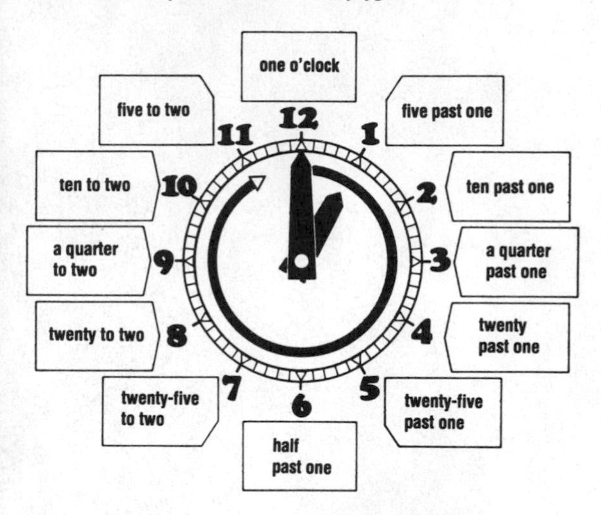

I'll come at seven a.m.	Sabah yedide geleceğim.
I'll come at one p.m.	Öğleden sonra birde geleceğim.
I'll come at eight p.m.	Akşam sekizde geleceğim.

Haftanın Günleri

Sunday	pazar	*Thursday*	perşembe
Monday	pazartesi	*Friday*	cuma
Tuesday	salı	*Saturday*	cumartesi
Wednesday	çarşamba		

Notes

Notes

Notes

Notes

Notes